Edward Miller, Frederick Henry Ambrose Scrivener

A Plain Introduction to the Criticism of the New Testament for the Use of Biblical Students

Vol. 1

Edward Miller, Frederick Henry Ambrose Scrivener

A Plain Introduction to the Criticism of the New Testament for the Use of Biblical Students
Vol. 1

ISBN/EAN: 9783337214401

Printed in Europe, USA, Canada, Australia, Japan

Cover: Foto ©Lupo / pixelio.de

More available books at **www.hansebooks.com**

A

PLAIN INTRODUCTION

TO THE

CRITICISM OF THE NEW TESTAMENT

FOR THE USE OF BIBLICAL STUDENTS

BY THE LATE

FREDERICK HENRY AMBROSE SCRIVENER

M.A., D.C.L., LL.D.

PREBENDARY OF EXETER, VICAR OF HENDON

FOURTH EDITION, EDITED BY

THE REV. EDWARD MILLER, M.A.

FORMERLY FELLOW AND TUTOR OF NEW COLLEGE, OXFORD

VOL. I

London

GEORGE BELL & SONS, York Street, Covent Garden

AND NEW YORK: 66 Fifth Avenue

CAMBRIDGE: Deighton Bell & Co.

1894

In templo Dei offert unusquisque quod potest: alii aurum, argentum, et lapides pretiosos: alii byssum et purpuram et coccum offerunt et hyacinthum. Nobiscum bene agitur, si obtulerimus pelles et caprarum pilos. Et tamen Apostolus contemtibiliora nostra magis necessaria judicat.

HIERONYMI *Prologus Galeatus.*

DEDICATION

[IN THE THIRD EDITION]

TO HIS GRACE

EDWARD, LORD ARCHBISHOP OF CANTERBURY.

MY LORD ARCHBISHOP,

Nearly forty years ago, under encouragement from your venerated predecessor Archbishop Howley, and with the friendly help of his Librarian Dr. Maitland, I entered upon the work of collating manuscripts of the Greek New Testament by examining the copies brought from the East by Professor Carlyle, and purchased for the Lambeth Library in 1805. I was soon called away from this employment—ἑκὼν ἀέκοντί γε θυμῷ—to less congenial duties in that remote county, wherein long after it was your Grace's happy privilege to refresh the spirits of Churchmen and Churchwomen, by giving them pious work to do, and an example in the doing of it. What I have since been able to accomplish in the pursuits of sacred criticism, although very much less than I once anticipated, has proved, I would fain hope, not without its use to those who love Holy Scripture, and the studies which help to the understanding of the same.

Among the scholars whose sympathy cheered and aided my Biblical labours from time to time, I have had the honour of including your Grace; yet it would be at once unseemly and fallacious to assume from that circumstance, that the principles of textual criticism which I have consistently advocated have approved themselves to your judgement. All that I can look for or desire in this respect is that I may seem to you to have stated my case fairly and temperately, in earnest controversy with opponents far my superiors in learning and dialectic power, and for whom, in spite of literary differences, I entertain deep respect and true regard.

My Lord, you have been called by Divine Providence to the first place in our Communion, and have entered upon your great office attended by the applauses, the hopeful wishes, and the hearty prayers of the whole Church. May it please God to endow you richly with the Christian gifts as well of wisdom as of courage: for indeed the highest minister of the Church of England, no less than the humblest, will need courage in the coming time, now that faith is waxing cold and adversaries are many.

I am, my Lord Archbishop,

Your obliged and faithful servant,

F. H. A. SCRIVENER.

Hendon Vicarage,
   Whitsuntide, 1883.

PREFACE TO FOURTH EDITION.

At the time of the lamented death of Dr. Scrivener a new edition of his standard work was called for, and it was supposed that the great Master of Textual Criticism had himself made sufficient corrections and additions for the purpose in the margin of his copy. When the publishers committed to me the task of preparation, I was fully aware of the absolute necessity of going far beyond the materials placed at my disposal, if the book were to be really useful as being abreast of the very great progress accomplished in the last ten years. But it was not till I had laboured with absolute loyalty for some months that I discovered from my own observation, and from the advice of some of the first textual critics, how much alteration must at once be made.

Dr. Scrivener evidently prepared the Third Edition under great disadvantage. He had a parish of more than 5,500 inhabitants upon his hands, with the necessity of making provision for increase in the population. The result was that after adding 125 pages to his book he had an attack of paralysis, and so it is not surprising that his work was not wholly conducted upon the high level of his previous publications. The book has also laboured under another and greater disadvantage of too rapid, though unavoidable, growth. The 506 pages of the First Edition have been successively expanded into 626 pages in the Second, 751 in the Third, and 874 in the Fourth; while the framework originally adopted, consisting only of nine chapters, was manifestly inadequate to the mass of material ultimately gathered. It has therefore been found necessary, as the work proceeded, to do violence, amidst much delicate embarrassment, to feelings of loyalty to the author forbidding alteration. The chief changes that have been made are as follows :—

The first intention of keeping the materials within the compass of one volume has been abandoned, and it has been divided into two volumes, with an increase of chapters in each.

Instead of 2,094 manuscripts, as reckoned in the third edition under the six classes, no less than 3,791 have been recorded in this edition, being an increase of 236 beyond the 3,555 of Dr. Gregory, without counting the numerous vacant places which have been filled up.

Most of the accounts of ancient versions have been rewritten by distinguished scholars, who are leaders in their several departments.

The early part of Volume I has been enriched from the admirable book on 'Greek and Latin Palaeography,' by Mr. E. Maunde Thompson, who with great kindness placed the proof-sheets at my disposal before publication.

Changes have been made in the headlines, the indexes, and in the printing, and sometimes in the arrangement, which will, I trust, enable the reader to find his way more easily about the treatise.

And many corrections suggested by eminent scholars have been introduced in different places all through the work.

A most pleasing duty now is to tender my best thanks to the Right Reverend the Lord Bishop of Salisbury and the Rev. H. J. White, M.A., for the rewriting of the chapter on Latin Versions by the latter under Dr. John Wordsworth's supervision, with help from M. Samuel Berger; to the Rev. G. H. Gwilliam, B.D., Fellow of Hertford College, now editing the Peshitto for the University of Oxford, for the improvement of the passages upon the Peshitto and the Curetonian; the Rev. H. Deane, B.D., for additions to the treatment of the Harkleian; and the Rev. Dr. Walker, Principal of St. John's Hall, Highbury, for the results of a collation of the Peshitto and Curetonian; to the Rev. A. C. Headlam, M.A., Fellow of All Souls College, for a revision of the long chapter upon Egyptian Versions; to F. C. Conybeare, Esq., M.A., late Fellow of University College, for rewriting the sections on the Armenian and Georgian Versions; to Professor Margoliouth, M.A., Fellow of New College, for rewriting the sections on the Arabic and Ethiopic Versions; to the Rev. Ll. J. M. Bebb, M.A., Fellow of Brasenose College, for rewriting the section upon the Slavonic Version; to Dr. James W. Bright, Assistant-Professor in the Johns Hopkins University, for rewriting the section on the Anglo-Saxon Version, through Mr. White's kind offices; to E. Maunde Thompson, Esq., D.C.L., LL.D., F.S.A., &c., for kindness already mentioned, and other help, and to G. F. Warner, Esq., M.A., of the Manuscript Department of the British Museum, for correction of some of the notices of cursive MSS. belonging to the Museum, and for other assistance; to J. Rendel Harris, Esq., M.A., Fellow of Clare College and Reader in Palaeology in the University of Cambridge, for much help of a varied nature; to Professor Isaac H. Hall, Ph.D., of New York City, for sending and placing at my disposal many of his publications; to the lamented Professor Bensly, for writing me a letter upon the Syriac Versions; to the Rev. Nicholas Pocock, M.A., of Clifton, for some results of a collation of F and G of St. Paul; to Professor Bernard, D.D., Trinity College, Dublin, for a paper of suggestions; to the Rev. Walter Slater, M.A., for preparing Index II in Vol. I; and to several other kind friends, for assistance of various kinds freely given. The generosity of scholars in communicating out of their stores of learning is a most pleasing feature in the study of the present day. Whatever may be my own shortcomings—and I fear that they have been enhanced by limitations of time and space, and through the effects of ill-health and sorrow—the contributions enumerated cannot but render the present edition of Dr. Scrivener's great work eminently useful to students.

EDWARD MILLER.

9, Bradmore Road, Oxford,
  January 17, 1894.

CONTENTS.

CHAPTER I.

PRELIMINARY CONSIDERATIONS 1

    Various readings antecedently probable, §§ 1-3 ; actually existent, 4 ; sources of information, 5 ; textual criticism, 6-9 ; classes and extent of various readings, 10-12 ; divisions of the work, 12.

CHAPTER II.

GENERAL CHARACTER OF THE GREEK MSS. OF THE NEW TESTAMENT 21

    Authorities, § 1 ; materials for writing, 2-7 ; form and style, 8-9 ; character of early Uncial writing, 10 ; of Cursive, 11 ; ascript or subscript, 12 ; breathings and accents, 13 ; punctuation, 14 ; abbreviations, 15 ; capitals, 16 ; stichometry, 17 ; correction or revision of MSS., 18.

CHAPTER III.

DIVISIONS OF THE TEXT, AND OTHER PARTICULARS . . . 56

    Earliest Sections, §§ 1-2 ; 'Ammonian' Sections and 'Eusebian' Canons, 3 ; Euthalian Sections and Lessons, 4, 5 ; Subscriptions, 6 ; foreign matter, 7, 8 ; tabular view, 9 ; chapters and verses, 10 ; contents and order, 11, 12 ; Lectionaries, 13, 14.

APPENDIX TO CHAPTER III 80

    Synaxarion and Eclogadion of the Gospels and Apostolic writings daily throughout the year ; Menology.

CHAPTER IV.

THE LARGER UNCIALS OF THE GREEK TESTAMENT . . . 90

    Codex Sinaiticus ; Cod. Alexandrinus ; Cod. Vaticanus ; Cod. Ephraemi ; Cod. Bezae.

CHAPTER V.

UNCIAL MANUSCRIPTS OF THE GOSPELS 131

    From E (Codex Basiliensis) to Ⅎ of St. Andrew of Athos.

CHAPTER VI.

UNCIAL MANUSCRIPTS OF THE ACTS AND CATHOLIC EPISTLES, OF ST. PAUL'S EPISTLES, AND OF THE APOCALYPSE . . . 169

(1) Acts, א–ב; (2) Paul, א–ב; (3) Apocalypse, א–P.

CHAPTER VII.

CURSIVE MANUSCRIPTS OF THE GOSPELS. PART I. 1—449 . . 189

CHAPTER VIII.

CURSIVE MANUSCRIPTS OF THE GOSPELS. PART II. 450—774 . . 241

CHAPTER IX.

CURSIVE MANUSCRIPTS OF THE GOSPELS. PART III. 775—1321 . . 272

CHAPTER X.

CURSIVE MANUSCRIPTS OF THE ACTS AND CATHOLIC EPISTLES, 1—420 . 284

CHAPTER XI.

CURSIVE MANUSCRIPTS OF ST. PAUL'S EPISTLES, 1—491 . . 307

CHAPTER XII.

CURSIVE MANUSCRIPTS OF THE APOCALYPSE, 1—184 320

CHAPTER XIII.

EVANGELISTARIES, OR MANUSCRIPT SERVICE-BOOKS OF THE GOSPELS, 1—963 327

CHAPTER XIV.

LECTIONARIES CONTAINING THE APOSTOLOS OR PRAXAPOSTOLOS, 1—288 368

ADDITIONAL UNCIALS 377
APPENDIX A. CHIEF AUTHORITIES . . 378
,, B. ON FACSIMILES 379
,, C. ON DATING BY INDICTION . . 380
,, D. ON THE 'Ρήματα 381
,, E. TABLE OF DIFFERENCES 384

INDEX I. OF GREEK MANUSCRIPTS . . 391

INDEX II. OF SCRIBES, PAST OWNERS, AND COLLATORS . . 411

DESCRIPTION OF THE CONTENTS OF THE LITHOGRAPHED PLATES[1].

PLATE I . . . . *opposite page* 29
   1. (1) Alphabet from the Rosetta Stone [B.C. 196], a specimen of capitals.
   2. (2) Alphabet from Cod. Sinaiticus ⎫ specimens of uncials.
   3. (3) Alphabet from Cod. Alexandrinus ⎭

PLATE II 32
   1. (4) Alphabet from the Cotton Fragment (Evan. N) and Titus C. xv [vi],
   2. (5) And from Cod. Nitriensis (Evan. R, Brit. Mus. Add. 17,211).

PLATE III 34
   1. (6) Alphabet from Cod. Dublinensis (Evan. Z).
   2. (7) From Brit. Mus. Harl. 5598 (Evst. 150), [A. D. 995].
   3. (8) From Brit. Mus. Burney 19 (Evan. 569).
      Note that above *psi* in 2 stands the cross-like form of that letter as found in Apoc. B [viii].

PLATE IV 90
   1. (9) Extract from Hyperides' Oration for Lycophron, col. 15, 1. 23, &c. ('Ὑπερίδου Λόγοι, ed. Babington, 1853). Dating between B.C. 100 to A.D. 100, on Egyptian papyrus, in a cursive or running hand. λυντασ τινα των πο|λιτων αδικως δεο|μαι υμων και ετωι | και αντιβολωι κε|λευσαι καμε καλεσαι|τους συνερουντασ >. *See* pp. 44, 51.
   2. (10) Extract from Philodemus περὶ κακιῶν (*Herculanensium voluminum quae supersunt*, fol., Tom. 3, Col. xx. ll. 6-15). *See* pp. 30, 33. οντωσ πολυμαθεστατον προσ|αγορευομενον οιεται παντα | δυνασθαι γινω-σκειν και ποι|ειν ουχ οιον εαυτον οσ ενιοισ|ουδεν τι φωραται κατεχων | και ου συνορων οτι πολλα δει|ται τριβης αν και απο τησ αυ|τησ γινηται μεθοδου καθα|περ τα τησ ποιητικησ μερη και | διοτι περι τουσ πολυμαθεισ|.

---

[1] Unfortunately, it did not occur to us till after the work was nearly all in type to transfer the Lithographed Plates to places opposite the pages which they chiefly illustrate, and that in consequence a few expressions in the text ought to be altered. The advantage of this arrangement appears to be so great as to overbalance the slight inaccuracies alluded to, which cannot now be removed. The plates and their references will, it is hoped, be found easily from the explanations here given.

xiv   DESCRIPTION OF THE LITHOGRAPHED PLATES.

3. (11ª) Cod. Friderico-August. [iv], 2 Sam. vii. 10, 11, Septuagint:
σεαυτον καθωσ αρ|χησ και αφ ημερῶ | ων εταξα κριτασ | επι τον λαον μου | ισλ και εταπινω|σα απαντασ τουσ | εχθρουσ σου και | αυξησω σε και οι |.

4. (11ᵇ) Cod. Sinaiticus, א [iv], Luke xxiv. 33–4 : τη ωρα ὑπεστρε|ψαν εισ Ἱερουσα|λημ¹ και ευρον η|θροισμενουσ τουσ | ενδεκα και τουσ | συν αυτοισ λεγο|.

5. (11ᶜ) Cod. Sin., 1 Tim. iii. 16, το τησ ευσεβειασ | μυστηριον οσ ϵ with a recent correction. See II. 391. There are no capital letters in this Plate.

PLATE V 98

1. (12) Cod. Alexandrinus, A [v], Gen. i. 1–2, Septuagint. These four lines are in bright red, with breathings and accents². Henceforth capital letters begin to appear. Ἐν ἀρχῇ ἐπόιησεν ὁ θσ̄ τὸν ὀυ|ρανὸν και τὴν γῆν ἡ δὲ γῆ ἦν ἀ'ό|ρατοσ καὶ ἀκατασκεύαστοσ· | και σκότοσ ἐπάνω τῆσ ἀβύσσου. |

2. (13) Cod. Alex., Acts xx. 28, in common ink. See II. 37. Προσεχετε εαυτοισ και παντι τω | ποιμνιω· εν ω ὑμασ το π̄να το | αγιον εθετο επισκοπουσ· | ποιμαινειν την εκκλησιαν | του κ̄υ ην περιεποιησατο δια | του αιματος του ιδιου· |

3. (14) Cod. Cotton., Titus C. xv, Evan. N, with Ammonian section and Eusebian canon in the margin. John xv. 20: του λογου ου | εγω ειπον ὑ|μιν· ουκ εστιν | δουλοσ μιζῶ | του κ̄υ αυτου.

PLATE VI 145

1. (15) Cod. Burney 21 [A.D. 1292], Evan. 571. See p. 257. John xxi. 17–18 : πρόβατά μου· ἀμὴν ἀμὴν λέγω σοι· | ὅτε ἦσ νεώτεροσ, ἐζώννῡεσ ἐ|αυτὸν· καὶ περιεπάτησ ὅπου ἤθε|λεσ· ὅταν δε γηράσησ, ἐκτενεῖσ|

2. (16) Cod. Arundel 547, Evst. 257 [ix or x]. See p. 345. The open work indicates stops and musical notes in red. John viii. 13–14 : Αυτω ὁι φαρισᾶι | οι+σὺ περὶ σἑαυτῦν | μαρτυρεῖσ ἡ μαρ|τυρία σου ὀυκ ἔσ|τιν ἀληθήσ+ἀπε|

3. (17) Cod. Nitriensis, R of the Gospels, a palimpsest [vi]. Luke v. 26 : ξαζον τον θν | και επλησθη|σαν φοβου λε|γοντεσ οτι|.

PLATE VII 153

1. (18) Cod. Dublin., Z of the Gospels, a palimpsest [vi] from Barrett. Matt. xx. 33–4 : ανοιγωσιν οι οφθαλ|μοι ημων | Cπλαγχνισθεισ δε ο ισ̄ | ηψατο των ομματῶ | αυτων και ευθεωσ|.

2. (19) Cod. Cyprius, K of the Gospels [ix], John vi. 52–3 : 'Εμάχοντο ὀῦν προσ ἀλλήλουσ ὁι Ἰουδαῖοι λε|γοντεσ· πῶσ δύναται ὁῦτοσ ἡμῖν τὴν σάρ|κα δοῦναι φαγεῖν· ἔῖπεν ὀῦν ἀντοῖσ ὁ ἰσ̄· d|. It has the Ammonian section in the margin (ξϛ′=66), and a flourish in the place of the Eusebian canon. See p. 137.

¹ In later manuscripts Proper Names are often distinguished by a horizontal line placed over them, but no such examples occur in these Plates.

² The reader will observe throughout these specimens that the breathings and accents are usually attached to the *first* vowel of a diphthong.

DESCRIPTION OF THE LITHOGRAPHED PLATES. XV

PLATE VIII 105

(20) Cod. Vaticanus, B of the Gospels, Acts and Epistles [iv], taken from Burgon's photograph of the whole page. Mark xvi. 3-8 : μῖν τὸν λίθον ἐκ τῆσ | θύρασ τοῦ μνημείου | κὰι ἀναβλέψασαι θεω|ροῦσιν ὅτι ἀνακεκύ|λισται ὁ λίθοσ ἦν γὰρ | μέγασ σφόδρα κὰι ἐλ|θοῦσαι εἰσ τὸ μνημεῖ|ον εἶδον νεανίσκον | καθήμενον ἐν τοῖσ | δεξιοῖσ περιβεβλημέ|νον στολὴν λευκὴν | κὰι ἐξεθαμβήθησαν | ὁ δὲ λέγει ἀυτᾶισ μὴ | ἐκθαμβεῖσθε ἴν̄ ζητει|τε τὸν ναζαρηνὸν τὸ | ἐσταυρωμένον ἠγέρ|θη ὐυκ ἔ'στιν ὧδε ἴδε | ὁ τύποσ ὅπου ἔθηκᾶ | ἀντὸν ἀλλα ὑπάγετε | ἐἴπατε τοῖσ μαθηταῖσ | ἀυτοῦ κὰι τῶ πέτρω | ὅτι προάγει ὑμᾶς ἐισ | τὴν γαλιλάιαν ἐκε̂ι ἀυ|τὸν ὄψεσθε καθῶσ ἔἶ|πεν ὑμῖν κὰι ἐξελθοῦσαι ἔφυγον ἀπὸ τοῦ | μνημεῖου εἶχεν γὰρ | ἀυτᾶσ τρόμοσ κὰι ἐκ|στασισ κὰι οὐδενὶ ὀυ|δὲν εἶπον ἐφοβοῦνν|το γάρ : Here again, as in Plate IV, no capital letters appear. What follows on the Plate is by a later hand.

PLATE IX 137

1. (21) Cod. Par. Nat. Gr. 62, Evan. L of the Gospels [viii], as also 3 (23) below, are from photographs given by Dean Burgon : see pp. 133-4. In the first column stands Mark xvi. 8 with its Ammonian section (σλγ 233) and Eusebian canon (β=2) : Καὶ ἐξελθοῦσαι ἔ|φυγον ἀπο τοῦ | μνημειον + ἐι|χεν δὲ αὐτας τρο|μοσ καὶ εκστασεισ· | καὶ ουδενι οὐδεν | ειπον + ἐφοβουν|το γάρ' + In the second column, after the strange note transcribed by us (II. 388), εστην δε και | ταῦτα φερο|μενα μετα το | ἐφοβουντο | γαρ + | 'Αναστὰσ δὲ πρωΐ | πρωτη σαββατϛ + (ver. 9)   Χί much resembles that in Plate XI, No. 27.

2. (22) Cod. Nanianus, Evan. U, retraced after Tregelles. Burgon (*Guardian*, Oct. 29, 1873) considers this facsimile unworthy of the original writing, which is 'even, precise, and beautiful.' Mark v. 18 : Βάντοσ αυτου | ἐισ τὸ πλοῖο | παρεκάλει ἀυ|τὸν ὁ δαιμο|νισθεισ ἵνα. The Ammonian section (μη̄=48) is in the margin with the Eusebian canon (B, in error for H) underneath. The ν on the other side is by a much later hand. See p. 149.

3. (23) Cod. Basil. of the Gospels, Evan. 1 [x?]. See p. 190. Luke i. 1, 2 (the title : ἐυαγγέ[λιον] κατὰ λουκᾶν : being under an elegant arcade) : Επειδήπερ πολλοὶ ἐπεχείρησαν ἀνατάξασθαι | διήγησιν περὶ τῶν πεπληροφορημένων | ἐν ἡμῖν πραγματων . καθὼς παρέδοσαν ἡμῖ | δι ἀπαρχῆσ ἀυτόπται καὶ ὑπηρεται γενόμενοι |. The numeral in the margin must indicate the Ammonian section, not the larger κεφάλαιον (see p. 57).

PLATE X 121

1. (24) Cod. Ephraemi, C, a palimpsest [v], from Tischendorf's facsimile. The upper writing [xii ?] is τοῦ τὴν πληθῦν τῶν | ἐμῶν ἀμαρτημά|| σομαι· οἶδα ὅτι μετὰ | τὴν γνῶσιν ἥμαρτον. Translated from St. Ephraem the Syrian. The earlier text is 1 Tim. iii. 15-16 : ωμα τησ αληθειασ· | Και ομολογουμενωσ μέγα ἐστιν το τησ ἐυσεβειασ μυ|'στηριον· ῷᾳ ἐφανερωθη εν σαρκι· ἐδικαιωθη ἐν πνί. For the accents, &c., see p. 123.

xvi   DESCRIPTION OF THE LITHOGRAPHED PLATES.

2. (25) Cod. Laud. 35, E of the Acts [vi], Latin and Greek, in a sort of stichometry. Acts xx. 28 : regere | ecclesiam | domini || ποιμενειν | την εκκλησιαν | του κῡ. Below are specimens of six letters taken from other parts of the manuscript. See p. 169.

3. (26) Matt. i. 1-3, Greek and Latin, from the Complutensian Polyglott, A.D. 1514. See II. 176.

PLATE XI 131

1. (27) Cod. Basil., Evan. E [vii], from a photograph given by Dean Burgon, Mark i. 5-6 : Προσ αυτὸν. πᾶσα ἡ ἰουδαία | χωρα. και οἱ ἱεροσολυμῖται· | και ἐβαπτιζοντο παντεσ, | ἐν τῷ ἰορδάνῃ ποταμῷ ὑ|π' αυτοῦ . ἐξομολογούμε|νοι τὰσ ἁμαρτίασ αυτῶν· | Ηῦ δὲ ὁ Ἰωάννησ ἐνδεδυμένοσ. The harmonizing references will be found underneath, and some stops in the text (see p. 48). The next two specimens are retraced after Tregelles.

2. (28) Cod. Boreeli, Evan. F [viii-x], Mark x. 13 (Ammonian section only, ρ̄ς = 106) : Καὶ προσέφερον | αὐτῷ παιδία | ἵν' ἅψηται αὐ|τῶν· οἱ δὲ μαθη|ταὶ ἐπετίμων |.

3. (29) Cod. Harleian. 5684, Evan. G [x], Matt. v. 30-1 : βληθῇ· εισ γεεν|ναν· τε τῆσ λ̄ε. | 'Ερρηθη δέ· "Οτι ὁσ | ἀν' ἀπολυσῃ την | γυναῖκα αὐτοῦ· | ἀρ (ἀρχή) stands in the margin of the new Lesson.

4. (30) Cod. Bodleian., Λ of the Gospels [x or ix], in sloping uncials, Luke xviii. 26, 27, and 30 : σαντεσ· καὶ Τίσ, | δύναται σωθῆναι· | ὁ δὲ ἰσ. εἶπεν· || τούτω· καὶ ἐν | τῷ αἰῶνι τῷ ἐρ|χομένῳ ζωὴν |. See p. 160.

PLATE XII 134

1. (31) Cod. Wolfii B, Evan. H [ix], John i. 38-40 : τουσ ἀκολουθοῦντασ λέγει αὐτοῖσ + τί ζη|τεῖτε + οἱ δε . εἶπον αὐτῷ + ραββεί· ὅ λέγε|ται ἑρμηνευόμενον διδάσκαλε ποῦ μέ|νεισ + λέγει αὐτοῖσ + ἔρχεσθε και ἴδετε + ἦλ|. Retraced after Tregelles : in the original the dark marks seen in our facsimile are no doubt red musical notes.

2. (32) Cod. Campianus, Evan. M [ix], from a photograph of Burgon's. John vii. 53-viii. 2 : Καὶ ἐπορεύθησαν ἕκα|στοσ : εἰς τὸν οἶκον | αὐτοῦ· ισ δὲ ἐπορεύ|θη εισ τὸ ὄροσ τῶν ἐ|λαιῶν · ὄρθρου δὲ πά|. Observe the asterisk set against the passage.

3. (33) Cod. Emman. Coll. Cantab., Act. 53, Paul. 30 [xii]. See p. 288. This minute and elegant specimen, beginning Rom. v. 21, χ̄υ τοῦ κ̄υ ἡμων· and ending vi. 7, δεδικαίωται ἀ, is left to exercise the reader's skill.

4. (34) Cod. Ruber., Paul. M [x]. See p. 184. 2 Cor. i. 3-5 : παρακλήσεωσ· ὁ παρακαλῶν | ἡμᾶσ ἐπὶ πάσῃ Τῇι θλίψει· εισ τὸ | δύνασθαι ἡμᾶσ παρακαλεῖν | τοὺς ἐν πάσῃ θλίψει διὰ τῆς πα|ρακλήσεωσ ἧσ παρε-καλούμε|θα αὐτοὶ ὑπὸ τοῦ θῦ. ὅτι καθὼσ |.

5. (35) Cod. Bodleian., Evan. Γ of the Gospels [ix]. See p. 155. Mark viii. 33 : πιστραφεὶσ καὶ ἰδὼν τουσ μα|θητὰσ αὐτοῦ. ἐπετίμησεν τῷ | πέτρω λέγων. ὕπαγε ὀπίσω μτ |.

DESCRIPTION OF THE LITHOGRAPHED PLATES.   xvii

PLATE XIII 343
1. (36) Parham. 18, Evst. 234 [A.D. 980], Luke ix. 34: γοντοσ ἐγένετο νε|φέλη καὶ ἐπεσκίασεν | ἀντοὺσ ἐφοβήθησά|. Annexed are six letters taken from other parts of the manuscript.
2. (37) Cod. Burney 22, Evst. 259 [A.D. 1319]. The Scripture text is Mark vii. 30: βεβλημέν ον ἐ|πὶ τὴν κλίνην ἢ | τὸ δαιμόνιον ἐξ ε|λήλυθῶσ:—The subscription which follows is given at length in p. 43, note 3.
3. (38) Cod. Monacensis, Evan. X [ix], retraced after Tregelles. See p. 152. Luke vii. 25-6: τίοισ ἠμφιεσμένον· ἴδου οἱ | ἐν ἱματισμῷ ἐνδόξῳ και τρυ|φῇ ὑπάρχοντεσ ἐν τοισ βασιλεί | οισ εἰσὶν· ἀλλα τί ἐξελήλυθα |.
4. (39) Cod. Par. Nat. Gr. 14, or Evan. 33: from a photograph of Burgon's. See p. 195. Luke i. 8-11: ξει τῆς ἐφημερίασ ἀντοῦ ἔναντι τοῦ κυ κατὰ τὸ ἔθοσ τῆς ἱερατείασ. ἔλαχεν τοῦ θυμιᾶ|σαι εἰσελθὼν εἰς τὸν ναὸν τοῦ κυ . καὶ πᾶν τὸ πλῆθοσ ἦν περ λαῶν προσευχόμενον ἔξω τῇ | ὥρα τοῦ θυμιάματοσ . ὤφθη δὲ ἀντῷ ἄγγελοσ κυ ἐστὼσ ἐκδεξιῶν τοῦ θυσιαστηρίου, τοῦ θυ|.
5. (40) Cod. Leicestrensis, Evan. 69, Paul. 37 [xiv]. See p. 202. 1 Tim. iii. 16: τῆς εὐσεβε(?)ίας μυστήριον· ὁ θθ ἐφανερώθη ἐν σαρ|κί· ἐδικαιώθη ἐν πνεύματι· ὤφθη ἀγγέλοις· | ἐκηρύχθη ἐν ἔθνεσιν· ἐπιστεύθη ἐν κόσμω· ἀνελή—.

PLATE XIV. Contains specimens of open leaves of the two chief bilingual manuscripts 124
1. (41) Cod. Claromontanus or Paul. D (1 Cor. xiii. 5-8), p. 173.
2. (42) Cod. Bezae or Evan. and Act. D (John xxi. 19-23), p. 124. Observe the stichometry, the breathings, &c., of the Pauline facsimile (which we owe to Dean Burgon's kindness). These codices, so remarkably akin as well in their literary history as in their style of writing and date (vi or v), will easily be deciphered by the student.
3. (43) Cod. Rossanensis or Evan. Σ (p. 163), is one of the most interesting, as it is amongst the latest of our discoveries. Our passage is Matt. vi. 13, 14: πονηρον οτι | σου εστιν η βα|σιλεια και η δυ|ναμισ και η δο|ξα εισ τουσ αιω|νασ αμην. | Εαν γαρ αφητε | τοισ ανοισ τα | παραπτωματα |. In the margin below the capital Є is the Ammonian section μδ (44) and the Eusebian canon ϛ (66): ανοισ is an abbreviation for ἀνθρώποις. All is written in silver on fine purple vellum.

PLATE XV 166
Cod. Beratinus or Evan. Φ, Matt. xxvi. 19-20: ως συνεταξεν | αυτοις ισ και ητοιμασαν το | πασχα· | Οψιας δε γενομενης ανε|κειτο μετα των | δωδεκα μαθη|των· και αισθι|. Observe the reference given for the paragraph to the Ammonian section and Eusebian canon on the left: σοθ = 279, δ = 4. The MS. is written in two columns, and the initial letters of each line are exhibited on the right, with Am. and Eus., σπα = 279, and β = 2; which as in the other case are in a different hand.

VOL. I.   b

ADDENDA ET CORRIGENDA.

Pages 1-224, *passim*, for reasons given in Vol. II. 96 note, *for* Memphitic *read* Bohairic ; *for* Thebaic *read* Sahidic.

P. 7, l. 25, *for* Chapter XI *read* Chapter XII.

P. 14, l. 20, *for* Chapter X *read* Chapter XI.

P. 87, l. 19, *for* Synaxaria *read* Menologies.

P. 119, ll. 11 and 12 from bottom, *for* 93 *read* 94 ; *for* Memoranda in our Addenda *read* ingenious argument in n. 1.

P. 149, T^r Horner, *add* now in the Bodleian at Oxford.

P. 214, l. 3 from bottom, *for* 464 *read* iv. 64.

P. 224, Evan. 250, l. 3, *for* p. 144 *read* p. 150.

P. 226, Evan. 274, l. 2 from end, *for* Chapter IX *read* Chapter XII.

P. 255, l. 6 from bottom, *for* Bibl. Gr. L. *read* Bibl. Gr. d.

P. 335, l. 1, *for* 41 *read* 4.

P. 343, l. 12, *for* Ev. 1 (2) *read* Ev. 1 (1).

INTRODUCTION

TO

THE CRITICISM OF THE TEXT OF THE NEW TESTAMENT.

CHAPTER I.

PRELIMINARY CONSIDERATIONS.

1. WHEN God was pleased to make known to man His purpose of redeeming us through the death of His Son, He employed for this end the general laws, and worked according to the ordinary course of His Providential government, so far as they were available for the furtherance of His merciful design. A revelation from heaven, in its very notion, implies supernatural interposition; yet neither in the first promulgation nor in the subsequent propagation of Christ's religion, can we mark any *waste* of miracles. So far as they were needed for the assurance of honest seekers after truth, they were freely resorted to: whensoever the principles which move mankind in the affairs of common life were adequate to the exigences of the case, more unusual and (as we might have thought) more powerful means of producing conviction were withheld, as at once superfluous and ineffectual. Those who heard not Moses and the prophets would scarcely be persuaded, though one rose from the dead.

2. As it was with respect to the *evidences* of our faith, so also with regard to the volume of Scripture. God willed that His Church should enjoy the benefit of His written word, at once as a rule of doctrine and as a guide unto holy living. For

this cause He so enlightened the minds of the Apostles and Evangelists by His Spirit, that they recorded what He had imprinted on their hearts or brought to their remembrance, without the risk of error in anything essential to the verity of the Gospel. But this main point once secured, the rest was left, in a great measure, to themselves. The style, the tone, the language, perhaps the special occasion of writing, seem to have depended much on the taste and judgement of the several penmen. Thus in St. Paul's Epistles we note the profound thinker, the great scholar, the consummate orator: St. John pours forth the simple utterings of his gentle, untutored, affectionate soul: in St. Peter's speeches and letters may be traced the impetuous earnestness of his noble yet not faultless character. Their individual tempers and faculties and intellectual habits are clearly discernible, even while they are speaking to us in the power and by the inspiration of the Holy Ghost.

3. Now this self-same parsimony in the employment of miracles which we observe with reference to Christian evidences and to the inspiration of Scripture, we might look for beforehand, from the analogy of divine things, when we proceed to consider the methods by which Scripture has been preserved and handed down to us. God *might*, if He would, have stamped His revealed will visibly on the heavens, that all should read it there: He *might* have so completely filled the minds of His servants the Prophets and Evangelists, that they should have become mere passive instruments in the promulgation of His counsel, and the writings they have delivered to us have borne no traces whatever of their individual characters: but for certain causes which we can perceive, and doubtless for others beyond the reach of our capacities, He has chosen to do neither the one nor the other. And so again with the subject we propose to discuss in the present work, namely, the relation our existing text of the New Testament bears to that which originally came from the hands of the sacred penmen. Their autographs *might* have been preserved in the Church as the perfect standards by which all accidental variations of the numberless copies scattered throughout the world should be corrected to the end of time: but we know that these autographs perished utterly in the very infancy of Christian history. Or if it be too much to expect that the autographs of the inspired writers should escape the fate which has over-

taken that of every other known relique of ancient literature, God *might* have so guided the hand or fixed the devout attention both of copyists during the long space of fourteen hundred years before the invention of printing, and of compositors and printers of the Bible for the last four centuries, that no jot or tittle should have been changed of all that was written therein. Such a course of Providential arrangement we must confess to be quite possible, but it could have been brought about and maintained by nothing short of a continuous, unceasing miracle;—by making fallible men (nay, many such in every generation) for one purpose absolutely infallible. If the complete identity of all copies of Holy Scripture prove to be a fact, we must of course receive it as such, and refer it to its sole Author: yet we may confidently pronounce beforehand, that such a fact could not have been reasonably anticipated, and is not at all agreeable to the general tenour of God's dealings with us.

4. No one who has taken the trouble to examine any two editions of the Greek New Testament needs be told that this supposed complete resemblance in various copies of the holy books is not founded on fact. Even several impressions derived from the same standard edition, and professing to exhibit a text positively the same, differ from their archetype and from each other, in errors of the press which no amount of care or diligence has yet been able to get rid of. If we extend our researches to the manuscript copies of Scripture or of its versions which abound in every great library in Christendom, we see in the very best of them variations which we must at once impute to the fault of the scribe, together with many others of a graver and more perplexing nature, regarding which we can form no probable judgement, without calling to our aid the resources of critical learning. The more numerous and venerable the documents within our reach, the more extensive is the view we obtain of the variations (or VARIOUS READINGS as they are called) that prevail in manuscripts. If the number of these variations was rightly computed at thirty thousand in Mill's time, a century and a half ago, they must at present amount to at least fourfold that quantity.

5. As the New Testament far surpasses all other remains of antiquity in value and interest, so are the copies of it yet existing in manuscript and dating from the fourth century of our

era downwards, far more numerous than those of the most celebrated writers of Greece or Rome. Such as have been already discovered and set down in catalogues are hardly fewer than three thousand six hundred, and more must still linger unknown in the monastic libraries of the East. On the other hand, manuscripts of the most illustrious classic poets and philosophers are far rarer and comparatively modern. We have no complete copy of Homer himself prior to the thirteenth century, though some considerable fragments have been recently brought to light which may plausibly be assigned to the fifth century; while more than one work of high and deserved repute has been preserved to our times only in a single copy. Now the experience we gain from a critical examination of the few classical manuscripts that survive should make us thankful for the quality and abundance of those of the New Testament. These last present us with a vast and almost inexhaustible supply of materials for tracing the history, and upholding (at least within certain limits) the purity of the sacred text: every copy, if used diligently and with judgement, will contribute somewhat to these ends. So far is the copiousness of our stores from causing doubt or perplexity to the genuine student of Holy Scripture, that it leads him to recognize the more fully its general integrity in the midst of partial variation. What would the thoughtful reader of Aeschylus give for the like guidance through the obscurities which vex his patience, and mar his enjoyment of that sublime poet?

6. In regard to modern works, it is fortunate that the art of printing has wellnigh superseded the use of *verbal* or (as it has been termed) *Textual* criticism. When a book once issues from the press, its author's words are for the most part fixed, beyond all danger of change; graven as with an iron pen upon the rock for ever. Yet even in modern times, as in the case of Barrow's posthumous works and Pepys's Diary and Lord Clarendon's History of the Rebellion, it has been occasionally found necessary to correct or enlarge the early editions, from the original autographs, where they have been preserved. The text of some of our older English writers (Beaumont and Fletcher's plays are a notable instance) would doubtless have been much improved by the same process, had it been possible; but the criticism of Shakespeare's dramas is perhaps the most delicate and difficult problem in the whole history of literature

since that great genius was so strangely contemptuous of the praise of posterity, that even of the few plays that were published in his lifetime the text seems but a gathering from the scraps of their respective parts which had been negligently copied out for the use of the actors.

7. The design of the science of TEXTUAL CRITICISM, as applied to the Greek New Testament, will now be readily understood. By collecting and comparing and weighing the variations of the text to which we have access, it aims at bringing back that text, so far as may be, to the condition in which it stood in the sacred autographs; at removing all spurious additions, if such be found in our present printed copies; at restoring whatsoever may have been lost or corrupted or accidentally changed in the lapse of eighteen hundred years. We need spend no time in proving the value of such a science, if it affords us a fair prospect of appreciable results, resting on grounds of satisfactory evidence. Those who believe the study of the Scriptures to be alike their duty and privilege, will surely grudge no pains when called upon to separate the pure gold of God's word from the dross which has mingled with it through the accretions of so many centuries. Though the criticism of the sacred volume is inferior to its right interpretation in point of dignity and practical results, yet it must take precedence in order of time: for how can we reasonably proceed to investigate the sense of holy writ, till we have done our utmost to ascertain its precise language?

8. The importance of the study of Textual criticism is sometimes freely admitted by those who deem its successful cultivation difficult, or its conclusions precarious; the rather as Biblical scholars of deserved repute are constantly putting forth their several recensions of the text, differing not a little from each other. Now on this point it is right to speak clearly and decidedly. There is certainly nothing in the nature of critical science which ought to be thought hard or abstruse, or even remarkably dry and repulsive. It is conversant with varied, curious, and interesting researches, which have given a certain serious pleasure to many intelligent minds; it patiently gathers and arranges those facts of *external* evidence on which alone it ventures to construct a revised text, and applies them according to rules or canons of *internal* evidence, whether suggested by

experience, or resting for their proof on the plain dictates of common sense. The more industry is brought to these studies, the greater the store of materials accumulated, so much the more fruitful and trustworthy the results have usually proved; although beyond question the true application even of the simplest principles calls for discretion, keenness of intellect, innate tact ripened by constant use, a sound and impartial judgement. No man ever attained eminence in this, or in any other worthy accomplishment, without much labour and some natural aptitude for the pursuit; but the criticism of the Greek Testament is a field in whose culture the humblest student may contribute a little that shall be really serviceable; few branches of theology are able to promise, even to those who seek but a moderate acquaintance with it, so early and abundant reward for their pains.

9. Nor can Textual criticism be reasonably disparaged as tending to precarious conclusions, or helping to unsettle the text of Scripture. Even putting the matter on the lowest ground, critics have not *created* the variations they have discovered in manuscripts or versions. They have only taught us how to look ascertained phaenomena in the face, and try to account for them; they would fain lead us to estimate the relative value of various readings, to decide upon their respective worth, and thus at length to eliminate them. While we confess that much remains to be done in this department of Biblical learning, we are yet bound to say that, chiefly by the exertions of scholars of the last and present generations, the debateable ground is gradually becoming narrower, not a few strong controversies have been decided beyond the possibility of reversal, and while new facts are daily coming to light, critics of very opposite sympathies are learning to agree better as to the right mode of classifying and applying them. But even were the progress of the science less hopeful than we believe it to be, one great truth is admitted on all hands;—the almost complete freedom of Holy Scripture from the bare suspicion of wilful corruption; the absolute identity of the testimony of every known copy in respect to doctrine, and spirit, and the main drift of every argument and every narrative through the entire volume of Inspiration. On a point of such vital moment I am glad to cite the well-known and powerful statement of the great

Bentley, at once the profoundest and the most daring of English critics: 'The real text of the sacred writers does not now (since the originals have been so long lost) lie in any MS. or edition, but is dispersed in them all. 'Tis competently exact indeed in the worst MS. now extant; nor is one article of faith or moral precept either perverted or lost in them; choose as awkwardly as you will, choose the worst by design, out of the whole lump of readings.' And again: 'Make your 30,000 [variations] as many more, if numbers of copies can ever reach that sum: all the better to a knowing and a serious reader, who is thereby more richly furnished to select what he sees genuine. But even put them into the hands of a knave or a fool, and yet with the most sinistrous and absurd choice, he shall not extinguish the light of any one chapter, nor so disguise Christianity, but that every feature of it will still be the same[1].' Thus hath God's Providence kept from harm the treasure of His written word, so far as is needful for the quiet assurance of His church and people.

10. It is now time for us to afford to the uninitiated reader some general notion of the nature and extent of the various readings met with in manuscripts and versions of the Greek Testament. We shall try to reduce them under a few distinct heads, reserving all formal discussion of their respective characters and of the authenticity of the texts we cite for the next volume (Chapter XI).

(1) To begin with variations of the gravest kind. In two, though happily in only two instances, the genuineness of whole passages of considerable extent, which are read in our printed copies of the New Testament, has been brought into question. These are the weighty and characteristic paragraphs Mark xvi. 9-20 and John vii. 53—viii. 11. We shall hereafter defend these passages, the first without the slightest misgiving, the second with certain reservations, as entitled to be regarded authentic portions of the Gospels in which they stand.

(2) Akin to these omissions are several considerable interpolations, which, though they have never obtained a place in the printed text, nor been approved by any critical editor, are

---

[1] 'Remarks upon a late Discourse of Free Thinking by Phileleutherus Lipsiensis,' Part i, Section 32.

supported by authority too respectable to be set aside without some inquiry. One of the longest and best attested of these paragraphs has been appended to Matt. xx. 28, and has been largely borrowed from other passages in the Gospels (see below, class 9). It appears in several forms, slightly varying from each other, and is represented as follows in a document as old as the fifth century:

'But you, seek ye that from little things ye may become great, and not from great things may become little. Whenever ye are invited to the house of a supper, be not sitting down in the honoured place, lest should come he that is more honoured than thou, and to thee the Lord of the supper should say, Come near below, and thou be ashamed in the eyes of the guests. But if thou sit down in the little place, and he that is less than thee should come, and to thee the Lord of the supper shall say, Come near, and come up and sit down, thou also shalt have more glory in the eyes of the guests [1].'

We subjoin another paragraph, inserted after Luke vi. 4 in only a single copy, the celebrated Codex Bezae, now at Cambridge: 'On the same day he beheld a certain man working on the sabbath, and said unto him, Man, blessed art thou if thou knowest what thou doest; but if thou knowest not, thou art cursed and a transgressor of the law.'

(3) A shorter passage or mere clause, whether inserted or not in our printed books, may have appeared originally in the form of a marginal note, and from the margin have crept into the text, through the wrong judgement or mere oversight of the scribe. Such we have reason to think is the history of 1 John v. 7, the verse relating to the Three Heavenly Witnesses, once so earnestly maintained, but now generally given up as spurious. Thus too Acts viii. 37 may have been derived from some Church Ordinal: the last clause of Rom. viii. 1 ($\mu\grave{\eta}$ κατὰ σάρκα περιπατοῦσιν, ἀλλὰ κατὰ πνεῦμα) is perhaps like a gloss on τοῖς ἐν Χριστῷ Ἰησοῦ: εἰκῇ in Matt. v. 22 [2] and ἀναξίως in 1 Cor. xi. 29 might have been inserted to modify statements that seemed too strong: τῇ ἀληθείᾳ

---

[1] I cite from the late Canon Cureton's over-literal translation in his 'Remains of a very antient recension of the four Gospels in Syriac,' in the Preface to which (pp. xxxv–xxxviii) is an elaborate discussion of the evidence for this passage.

[2] But see Dean Burgon's 'The Revision Revised,' pp. 358–361.

μὴ πείθεσθαι Gal. iii. 1 is precisely such an addition as would help to round an abrupt sentence (compare Gal. v. 7). Some critics would account in this way for the adoption of the doxology Matt. vi. 13; of the section relating to the bloody sweat Luke xxii. 43, 44; and of that remarkable verse, John v. 4: but we may well hesitate before we assent to their views.

(4) Or a genuine clause is lost by means of what is technically called Homoeoteleuton (ὁμοιοτέλευτον), when the clause ends in the same word as closed the preceding sentence, and the transcriber's eye has wandered from the one to the other, to the entire omission of the whole passage lying between them. This source of error (though too freely appealed to by Meyer and some other commentators hardly less eminent than he) is familiar to all who are engaged in copying writing, and is far more serious than might be supposed prior to experience. In 1 John ii. 23 ὁ ὁμολογῶν τὸν υἱὸν καὶ τὸν πατέρα ἔχει is omitted in many manuscripts, because τὸν πατέρα ἔχει had ended the preceding clause: it is not found in our commonly received Greek text, and even in the Authorized English version is printed in italics. The whole verse Luke xvii. 36, were it less slenderly supported, might possibly have been early lost through the same cause, since vv. 34, 35, 36 all end in ἀφεθήσεται. A safer example is Luke xviii. 39, which a few copies omit for this reason only. Thus perhaps we might defend in Matt. x. 23 the addition after φεύγετε εἰς τὴν ἄλλην of κἂν ἐν τῇ ἑτέρᾳ διώκωσιν ὑμᾶς, φεύγετε εἰς τὴν ἄλλην (ἑτέραν being substituted for the first ἄλλην), the eye having passed from the first φεύγετε εἰς τήν to the second. The same effect is produced, though less frequently, when two or more sentences *begin* with the same words, as in Matt. xxiii. 14, 15, 16 (each of which commences with οὐαὶ ὑμῖν), one of the verses being left out in some manuscripts.

(5) Numerous variations occur in the order of words, the sense being slightly or not at all affected; on which account this species of various readings was at first much neglected by collators. Examples abound everywhere: e.g. τὶ μέρος or μέρος τι Luke xi. 36; ὀνόματι Ἀνανίαν or Ἀνανίαν ὀνόματι Acts ix. 12; ψυχρὸς οὔτε ζεστός or ζεστὸς οὔτε ψυχρός Apoc. iii. 16. The order of the sacred names Ἰησοῦς Χριστός is perpetually changed, especially in St. Paul's Epistles.

(6) Sometimes the scribe has mistaken one word for another, which differs from it only in one or two letters. This happens chiefly in cases when the *uncial* or capital letters in which the oldest manuscripts are written resemble each other, except in some fine stroke which may have decayed through age. Hence in Mark v. 14 we find ΑΝΗΓΓΕΙΛΑΝ or ΑΠΗΓΓΕΙΛΑΝ; in Luke xvi. 20 ΗΛΚΩΜΕΝΟC or ΕΙΛΚΩΜΕΝΟC; so we read Δαυίδ or Δαβίδ indifferently, as, in the later or *cursive* character, β and υ have nearly the same shape. Akin to these errors of the eye are such transpositions as ΕΛΑΒΟΝ for ΕΒΑΛΟΝ or ΕΒΑΛΛΟΝ, Mark xiv. 65: omissions or insertions of the same or similar letters, as ΕΜΑCCΩΝΤΟ or ΕΜΑCΩΝΤΟ Apoc. xvi. 10: ΑΓΑΛ-ΛΙΑCΘΗΝΑΙ or ΑΓΑΛΛΙΑΘΗΝΑΙ John v. 35: and the dropping or repetition of the same or a similar syllable, as ΕΚΒΑΛΛΟΝΤΑ-ΔΑΙΜΟΝΙΑ or ΕΚΒΑΛΛΟΝΤΑΤΑΔΑΙΜΟΝΙΑ Luke ix. 49; ΟΥΔΕΔΕΔΟΞΑCΤΑΙ or ΟΥΔΕΔΟΞΑCΤΑΙ 2 Cor. iii. 10; ΑΠΑ-ΞΕΞΕΔΕΧΕΤΟ or ΑΠΕΞΕΔΕΧΕΤΟ 1 Pet. iii. 20. It is easy to see how the ancient practice of writing uncial letters without leaving a space between the words must have increased the risk of such variations as the foregoing.

(7) Another source of error is described by some critics as proceeding *ex ore dictantis*, in consequence of the scribe writing from dictation, without having a copy before him. One is not, however, very willing to believe that manuscripts of the better class were executed on so slovenly and careless a plan. It seems more simple to account for the *itacisms* [1] or confusion of certain vowels and diphthongs having nearly the same sound, which exist more or less in manuscripts of every age, by assuming that a vicious pronunciation gradually led to a loose mode of orthography adapted to it. Certain it is that itacisms are much more plentiful in the original subscriptions and marginal notes of the writers of mediaeval books, than in the text which they copied from older documents. Itacisms prevailed the most extensively from the eighth to the twelfth century, but not by any means during that period exclusively:—indeed, they are found frequently in the oldest existing manuscripts. In the most ancient manuscripts the principal changes are between ι and ει, αι and ε,

---

[1] The word ἠτακισμός or ἰτακισμός is said to have been first used by Cassiodorus (A. D. 468-560?). See Migne, Patr. Lat. t. 70, col. 1128.

though others occur: in later times η ι and ει, η οι and υ, even ο and ω, η and ε, are used almost promiscuously. Hence it arises that a very large portion of the various readings brought together by collators are of this description, and although in the vast majority of instances they serve but to illustrate the character of the manuscripts which exhibit them, or the fashion of the age in which they were written, they sometimes affect the grammatical form (e.g. ἔγειρε or ἔγειραι Mark iii. 3; Acts iii. 6; *passim*: ἴδετε or εἴδετε Phil. i. 30), or the construction (e.g. ἰάσωμαι or ἰάσομαι Matt. xiii. 15: οὐ μὴ τιμήσῃ or οὐ μὴ τιμήσει Matt. xv. 5: ἵνα καυθήσωμαι or ἵνα καυθήσομαι 1 Cor. xiii. 3, compare 1 Pet. iii. 1), or even the sense (e.g. ἑταίροις or ἑτέροις Matt. xi. 16: μετὰ διωγμῶν or, as in a few copies, μετὰ διωγμόν Mark x. 30: καυχᾶσθαι δὴ οὐ συμφέρει or καυχᾶσθαι δεῖ· οὐ συμφέρει 2 Cor. xii. 1: ὅτι χρηστὸς ὁ Κύριος or ὅτι χριστὸς ὁ Κύριος 1 Pet. ii. 3). To this cause we may refer the perpetual interchange of ἡμεῖς and ὑμεῖς, with their oblique cases, throughout the whole Greek Testament: e.g. in the single epistle of 1 Peter, ch. i. 3; 12; ii. 21 *bis*; iii. 18; 21; v. 10. Hence we must pay the less regard to the reading ἡμέτερον Luke xvi. 12, though found in two or three of our chief authorities: in Acts xvii. 28 τῶν καθ' ἡμᾶς, the reading of the great Codex Vaticanus and a few late copies, is plainly absurd. On the other hand, a few cases occur wherein that which at first sight seems a mere *itacism*, when once understood, affords an excellent sense, e.g. καθαρίζων Mark iii. 19, and may be really the true form.

(8) Introductory clauses or Proper Names are frequently interpolated at the commencement of Church-lessons (περικοπαί), whether from the margin of ordinary manuscripts of the Greek Testament (where they are usually placed for the convenience of the reader), or from the Lectionaries or proper Service Books, especially those of the Gospels (Evangelistaria). Thus in our English Book of Common Prayer the name of Jesus is introduced into the Gospels for the 14th, 16th, 17th, and 18th Sundays after Trinity; and whole clauses into those for the 3rd and 4th Sundays after Easter, and the 6th and 24th after Trinity[1]. To this cause may be due the prefix εἶπε δὲ ὁ Κύριος Luke

---

[1] To this list of examples from the Book of Common Prayer, Dean Burgon ('The last twelve verses of St. Mark's Gospel Vindicated' p. 215) adds the Gospels

vii. 31; καὶ στραφεὶς πρὸς τοὺς μαθητὰς εἶπε Luke x. 22; and such appellations as ἀδελφοί or τέκνον Τιμόθεε (after σὺ δέ in 2 Tim. iv. 5) in some copies of the Epistles. The inserted prefix in Greek Lectionaries is sometimes rather long, as in the lesson for the Liturgy on Sept. 14 (John xix. 6–35). Hence the frequent interpolation (e.g. Matt. iv. 18; viii. 5; xiv. 22) or changed position (John i. 44) of Ἰησοῦς. A peculiarity of style in 1, 2 Thess. is kept out of sight by the addition of Χριστός in the common text of 1 Thess. ii. 19; iii. 13: 2 Thess. i. 8, 12.

(9) A more extensive and perplexing species of various readings arises from bringing into the text of one of the three earlier Evangelists expressions or whole sentences which of right belong not to him, but to one or both the others[1]. This natural tendency to assimilate the several Gospels must have been aggravated by the laudable efforts of Biblical scholars (beginning with Tatian's Διὰ τεσσάρων in the second century) to construct a satisfactory Harmony of them all. Some of these variations also may possibly have been mere marginal notes in the first instance. As examples of this class we will name εἰς μετάνοιαν interpolated from Luke v. 32 into Mark ii. 17: the prophetic citation Matt. xxvii. 35 ἵνα πληρωθῇ κ. τ. λ. to the end of the verse, unquestionably borrowed from John xix. 24, although the fourth Gospel seldom lends itself to corruptions of this kind. Mark xiii. 14 τὸ ῥηθὲν ὑπὸ Δανιὴλ τοῦ προφήτου, is probably taken from Matt. xxiv. 15: Luke v. 38 καὶ ἀμφότεροι συντηροῦνται from Matt. ix. 17 (where ἀμφότεροι is the true reading): the whole verse Mark xv. 28 seems spurious, being received from Luke xxii. 37. Even in the same book we observe an anxiety to harmonize two separate narratives of the same event, as in Acts ix. 5, 6 compared with xxvi. 14, 15.

(10) In like manner transcribers sometimes quote passages from the Old Testament more fully than the writers of the New Testament had judged necessary for their purpose. Thus ἐγγίζει

---

for Quinquagesima, 2nd Sunday after Easter, 9th, 12th, and 22nd after Trinity, Whitsunday, Ascension Day, SS. Philip and James, All Saints.

[1] Dean Alford (see his critical notes on Luke ix. 56; xxiii. 17) is reasonably unwilling to admit this source of corruption, where the language of the several Evangelists bears no close resemblance throughout the whole of the parallel passages.

μοι...τῷ στόματι αὐτῶν καί Matt. xv. 8 : ἰάσασθαι τοὺς συντετριμμένους τὴν καρδίαν Luke iv. 18: αὐτοῦ ἀκούσεσθε Acts vii. 37 : οὐ ψευδομαρτυρήσεις Rom. xiii. 9 : ἢ βολίδι κατατοξευθήσεται Heb. xii. 20, and (less certainly) καὶ κατέστησας αὐτὸν ἐπὶ τὰ ἔργα τῶν χειρῶν σου Heb. ii. 7, are all open to suspicion as being genuine portions of the Old Testament text, but not also of the New. In Acts xiii. 33, the Codex Bezae at Cambridge stands almost alone in adding Ps. ii. 8 to that portion of the previous verse which was unquestionably cited by St. Paul.

(11) Synonymous words are often interchanged, and so form various readings, the sense undergoing some slight and refined modification, or else being quite unaltered. Thus ἔφη should be preferred to εἶπεν Matt. xxii. 37, where εἶπεν of the common text is supported only by two known manuscripts, that at Leicester, and one used by Erasmus. So also ὀμμάτων is put for ὀφθαλμῶν Matt. ix. 29 by the Codex Bezae. In Matt. xxv. 16 the evidence is almost evenly balanced between ἐποίησεν and ἐκέρδησεν (cf. ver. 17). Where simple verbs are interchanged with their compounds (e. g. μετρηθήσεται with ἀντιμετρηθήσεται Matt. vii. 2 ; ἐτέλεσεν with συνετέλεσεν *ibid.* ver. 28 ; καίεται with κατακαίεται xiii. 40), or different tenses of the same verb (e.g. εἰληφώς with λαβών Acts xiv. 24 ; ἀνθέστηκε with ἀντέστη 2 Tim. iv. 15), there is usually some *internal* reason why one should be chosen rather than the other, if the *external* evidence on the other side does not greatly preponderate. When one of two terms is employed in a sense peculiar to the New Testament dialect, the easier synonym may be suspected of having originated in a gloss or marginal interpretation. Hence *caeteris paribus* we should adopt δικαιοσύνην rather than ἐλεημοσύνην in Matt. vi. 1 ; ἐσκυλμένοι rather than ἐκλελυμένοι ix. 36 ; ἀθῷον rather than δίκαιον xxvii. 4.

(12) An irregular, obscure, or incomplete construction will often be *explained* or *supplied* in the margin by words that are subsequently brought into the text. Of this character is ἐμέμψαντο Mark vii. 2 ; δέξασθαι ἡμᾶς 2 Cor. viii. 4 ; γράφω xiii. 2 ; προσλαβοῦ Philem. 12 (compare ver. 17), and perhaps δῆλον 1 Tim. vi. 7. More considerable is the change in Acts viii. 7, where the true reading πολλοὶ...φωνῇ μεγάλῃ ἐξήρχοντο, if translated with grammatical rigour, affords an almost impossible sense. Or an elegant Greek idiom may be transformed into simpler language,

as in Acts xvi. 3 ᾔδεισαν γὰρ πάντες ὅτι Ἕλλην ὁ πατὴρ αὐτοῦ ὑπῆρχεν for ᾔδεισαν γὰρ ἅπαντες τὸν πατέρα αὐτοῦ ὅτι Ἕλλην ὑπῆρχεν: similarly, τυγχάνοντα is omitted by many in Luke x. 30; compare also Acts xviii. 26 *fin.*; xix. 8, 34 *init*. The classical μέν has often been inserted against the best evidence: e. g. Acts v. 23: xix. 4, 15; 1 Cor. xii. 20; 2 Cor. iv. 12; Heb. vi. 16. On the other hand a Hebraism may be softened by transcribers, as in Matt. xxi. 23, where for ἐλθόντι αὐτῷ many copies prefer the easier ἐλθόντος αὐτοῦ before προσῆλθεν αὐτῷ διδάσκοντι, and in Matt. xv. 5; Mark vii. 12 (to which perhaps we may add Luke v. 35), where καί is dropped in some copies to facilitate the sense. Hence καὶ οἱ ἄνθρωποι may be upheld before οἱ ποιμένες in Luke ii. 15. This perpetual correction of harsh, ungrammatical, or Oriental constructions characterizes the printed text of the Apocalypse and the recent manuscripts on which it is founded (e. g. τὴν γυναῖκα Ἰεζαβὴλ τὴν λέγουσαν ii. 20, for ἡ λέγουσα).

(13) Hence too arises the habit of changing ancient dialectic forms into those in vogue in the transcriber's age. The whole subject will be more fitly discussed at length hereafter (vol. ii. c. x.); we will here merely note a few peculiarities of this kind adopted by some recent critics from the oldest manuscripts, but which have gradually though not entirely disappeared in copies of lower date. Thus in recent critical editions Καφαρναούμ, Μαθθαῖος, τέσσερες, ἔνατος are substituted for Καπερναούμ, Ματθαῖος, τέσσαρες, ἔννατος of the common text; οὕτως (not οὕτω) is used even before a consonant; ἤλθαμεν, ἤλθατε, ἤλθαν, γενάμενος are preferred to ἤλθομεν, ἤλθετε, ἤλθον, γενόμενος: ἐκαθερίσθη, συνζητεῖν, λήμψομαι to ἐκαθαρίσθη, συζητεῖν, λήψομαι: and ν ἐφελκυστικόν (as it is called) is appended to the usual third persons of verbs, even though a consonant follow. On the other hand the more Attic περιπεπατήκει ought not to be converted into περιεπεπατήκει in Acts xiv. 8.

(14) Trifling variations in spelling, though very proper to be noted by a faithful collator, are obviously of little consequence. Such is the choice between καὶ ἐγώ and κἀγώ, ἐάν and ἄν, εὐθέως and εὐθύς, Μωυσῆς and Μωσῆς, or even between πράττουσι and πράσσουσι, between εὐδόκησα, εὐκαίρουν and ηὐδόκησα, ηὐκαίρουν. To this head may be referred the question whether ἀλλά[1], γε, δέ,

---

[1] The oldest manuscripts seem to elide the final syllable of ἀλλά before nouns, but not before verbs: e. g. John vi. 32, 39. The common text, therefore, seems

τε, μετά, παρά &c. should have their final vowel elided or not when the next word begins with a vowel.

(15) A large portion of our various readings arises from the omission or insertion of such words as cause little appreciable difference in the sense. To this class belong the pronouns αὐτοῦ, αὐτῷ, αὐτῶν, αὐτοῖς, the particles οὖν, δέ, τε, and the interchange of οὐδέ and οὔτε, as also of καί and δέ at the opening of a sentence.

(16) Manuscripts greatly fluctuate in adding and rejecting the Greek article, and the sense is often seriously influenced by these variations, though they seem so minute. In Mark ii. 26 ἐπὶ ᾿Αβιάθαρ ἀρχιερέως 'in the time that Abiathar was high priest' would be historically incorrect, while ἐπὶ ᾿Αβιάθαρ τοῦ ἀρχιερέως 'in the days of Abiathar the high priest' is suitable enough. The article will often impart vividness and reality to an expression, where its presence is not indispensable : e. g. Luke xii. 54 τὴν νεφέλην (if τήν be authentic, as looks probable) is the peculiar cloud spoken of in 1 Kings xviii. 44 as portending rain. Bishop Middleton's monograph ('Doctrine of the Greek Article applied to the Criticism and Illustration of the New Testament'), though apparently little known to certain of our most highly esteemed Biblical scholars, even if its philological groundwork be thought a little precarious, must always be regarded as the text-book on this interesting subject, and is a lasting monument of intellectual acuteness and exact learning.

(17) Not a few various readings may be imputed to the peculiarities of the style of writing adopted in the oldest manuscripts. Thus ΠΡΟϹΤΕΤΑΓΜΕΝΟΥϹΚΑΙΡΟΥϹ Acts xvii. 26 may be divided into two words or three; ΚΑΙΠΑΝΤΑ ibid. ver. 25, by a slight change, has degenerated into κατὰ πάντα. The habitual abridgement of such words as Θεός or Κύριος sometimes leads to a corruption of the text. Hence possibly comes the grave variation ΟϹ for Θ͞Ϲ 1 Tim. iii. 16, and the singular reading τῷ καιρῷ δουλεύοντες Rom. xii. 11, where the true word Κυρίῳ was first shortened into Κ͞Ρ͞Ω [1], and then read as Κ͞Ρ͞Ѡ,

wrong in Rom. i. 21; iv. 20; v. 14; viii. 15; 1 Cor. i. 17; vi. 11; ix. 27; xiv. 34; 1 Pet. ii. 25; Jude 9. Yet to this rule there are many exceptions, e. g. Gal. iv. 7 ἀλλὰ υἱός is found in nearly all good authorities.

[1] Tischendorf indeed (Nov. Test. 1871), from a suggestion of Granville Penn

Κ̄ being employed to indicate ΚΑΙ in very early times [1]. Or a large initial letter, which the scribe usually reserved for a subsequent review, may have been altogether neglected: whence we have τι for Ὅτι before στενή Matt. vii. 14. Or —, placed over a letter (especially at the end of a line and word) to denote ν, may have been lost sight of; e.g. λίθον μέγα Matt. xxvii. 60 in several copies, for ΜΕΓΑ. The use of the symbol ⳟ, which in the Herculanean rolls and now and then in Codex Sinaiticus stands for προ and προσ indifferently, may have produced that remarkable confusion of the two prepositions when compounded with verbs which we notice in Matt. xxvi. 39; Mark xiv. 35; Acts xii. 6; xvii. 5, 26; xx. 5, 13; xxii. 25. It will be seen hereafter that as the earliest manuscripts have few marks of punctuation, breathing or accent, these points (often far from indifferent) must be left in a great measure to an editor's taste and judgement.

(18) Slips of the pen, whereby words are manifestly lost or repeated, mis-spelt or half-finished, though of no interest to the critic, must yet be noted by a faithful collator, as they will occasionally throw light on the history of some particular copy in connexion with others, and always indicate the degree of care or skill employed by the scribe, and consequently the weight due to his general testimony.

The great mass of various readings we have hitherto attempted to classify (to our *first* and *second* heads we will recur presently) are manifestly due to mere inadvertence or human frailty, and certainly cannot be imputed to any deliberate intention of transcribers to tamper with the text of Scripture. We must give a different account of a few passages (we are glad they are only a few) which yet remain to be noticed.

(19) The copyist may be tempted to forsake his proper

in loc., says, 'ΚΥΡΙΩ omnino scribi solet κ̄ω̄,' and this no doubt is the usual form, even in manuscripts which have χρω̄ ιη̄ν, as well as χω̄ ιν, for χριστῷ ἰησοῦ. Yet the Codex Augiensis (Paul. F) has κρ̄ν in 1 Cor. ix. 1.

[1] Especially, yet not always, at the end of a line. Και in καιρός is actually thus written in Cod. Sinaiticus (א), 1 Macc. ix. 7; xv. 33; Matt. xxi. 34; Rom. iii. 26; Heb. xi. 11; Apoc. xi. 18. So Cod. Sarravianus of the fourth century in Deut. ix. 20, Cod. Rossanensis of the sixth (but only twice in the text), the Zurich Psalter of the seventh century is Ps. xcvii. 11; cvi. 3; cxvi. 5, and the Bodleian Genesis (ch. vi. 13) of about a century later. Similarly, καινήν is written κνην in Cod. B. 2 John 5.

function for that of a reviser, or critical corrector. He may simply omit what he does not understand (e. g. δευτεροπρώτῳ Luke vi. 1; τὸ μαρτύριον 1 Tim. ii. 6), or may attempt to get over a difficulty by inversions and other changes. Thus the μυστήριον spoken of by St. Paul 1 Cor. xv. 51, which rightly stands in the received text πάντες μὲν οὐ κοιμηθησόμεθα, πάντες δὲ ἀλλαγησόμεθα, was easily varied into πάντες κοιμηθησόμεθα, οὐ π. δὲ ἀλ., as if in mere perplexity. From this source must arise the omission in a few manuscripts of υἱοῦ Βαραχίου in Matt. xxiii. 35; of Ἰερεμίου in Matt. xxvii. 9; the insertion of ἄλλου ἐκ before θυσιαστηρίου in Apoc. xvi. 7; perhaps the substitution of τοῖς προφήταις for Ἡσαΐᾳ τῷ προφήτῃ in Mark i. 2, of οὔπω ἀναβαίνω for οὐκ ἀναβαίνω in John vii. 8, and certainly of τρίτη for ἕκτη in John xix. 14. The variations between Γεργεσηνῶν and Γαδαρηνῶν Matt. viii. 28, and between Βηθαβαρᾶ and Βηθανίᾳ John i. 28, have been attributed, we hope and believe unjustly, to the misplaced conjectures of Origen.

Some would impute such readings as ἔχωμεν for ἔχομεν Rom. v. 1; φορέσωμεν for φορέσομεν 1 Cor. xv. 49, to a desire on the part of copyists to *improve* an assertion into an ethical exhortation, especially in the Apostolical Epistles; but it is at once safer and more simple to regard them with Bishop Chr. Wordsworth (N.T. 1 Cor. xv. 49) as instances of *itacism*: see class (7) above.

(20) Finally, whatever conclusion we arrive at respecting the true reading in the following passages, the discrepancy could hardly have arisen except from doctrinal preconceptions. Matt. xix. 17 Τί με λέγεις ἀγαθόν; οὐδεὶς ἀγαθὸς εἰ μὴ εἷς, ὁ Θεός· or Τί με ἐρωτᾷς περὶ τοῦ ἀγαθοῦ; εἷς ἐστὶν ὁ ἀγαθός : John i. 18 ὁ μονογενὴς υἱός or μονογενὴς Θεός: Acts xvi. 7 τὸ πνεῦμα with or without the addition of Ἰησοῦ: Acts xx. 28 τὴν ἐκκλησίαν τοῦ Θεοῦ or τὴν ἐκκλησίαν τοῦ Κυρίου: perhaps also Jude ver. 4 δεσπότην with or without Θεόν. I do not mention Mark xiii. 32 οὐδὲ ὁ υἱός, as there is hardly any authority for its rejection now extant; nor Luke ii. 22, where τοῦ καθαρισμοῦ αὐτῆς of the Complutensian Polyglott and most of our common editions is supported by almost no evidence whatever.

11. It is very possible that some scattered readings cannot be reduced to any of the above-named classes, but enough has

been said to afford the student a general notion of the nature and extent of the subject[1]. It may be reasonably thought that a portion of these variations, and those among the most considerable, had their origin in a cause which must have operated at least as much in ancient as in modern times, the changes gradually introduced after publication by the authors themselves into the various copies yet within their reach. Such revised copies would circulate independently of those issued previously, and now beyond the writer's control; and thus becoming the parents of a new family of copies, would originate and keep up diversities from the first edition, without any fault on the part of transcribers[2]. It is thus perhaps we may best account for the omission or insertion of whole paragraphs or verses in manuscripts of a certain class [see above (1), (2), (3)]; or, in cases where the work was in much request, for those minute touches and trifling improvements in words, in construction, in tone, or in the mere colouring of the style [(5), (11), (12)], which few authors can help attempting, when engaged on revising their favourite compositions. Even in the Old Testa-

---

[1] My departed friend, Dr. Tregelles, to whose persevering labours in sacred criticism I am anxious, once for all, to express my deepest obligations, ranged various readings under three general heads:—*substitutions; additions; omissions.* Mr. C. E. Hammond, in his scholarlike little work, 'Outlines of Textual Criticism applied to the N. T., 1876, 2nd edition,' divides their possible sources into Unconscious or unintentional errors, (1) of *sight;* (2) of *hearing;* (3) of *memory:* and those that are Conscious or intentional, viz. (4) incorporation of marginal glosses; (5) corrections of harsh or unusual forms of words, or expressions; (6) alterations in the text to produce supposed harmony with another passage, to complete a quotation, or to clear up a presumed difficulty; (7) Liturgical insertions. While he enumerates (8) alterations for dogmatic reasons, he adds that 'there appears to be no strong ground for the suggestion' that any such exist (Hammond, p. 17). Professor Roberts ('Words of the New Testament' by Drs. Milligan and Roberts, 1873) comprehends several of the foregoing divisions under one head: 'Again and again has a word or phrase been slipped in by the transcriber which had no existence in his copy, but which was due to the working of his own mind on the subject before him.' His examples are ἔρχεται inserted in Matt. xxv. 6; ἰδοῦσα in Luke i. 29; ὑπὲρ ἡμῶν in Rom. viii. 26 (Part I. Chap. I. pp. 5, 6).

[2] This source of variations, though not easily discriminated from others, must have suggested itself to many minds, and is well touched upon by the late Isaac Taylor in his 'History of the Transmission of Antient Books to modern times,' 1827, p. 24. So Dr. Hort, when perplexed by some of the textual problems which he fails to solve, throws out as an hypothesis not in itself without plausibility, the notion of 'a first and a second edition of the Gospels, both conceivably apostolic' (Gr. Test. Introduction, p. 177).

ment, the song of David in 2 Sam. xxii is evidently an early draft of the more finished composition, Ps. xviii. Traces of the writer's *curae secundae* may possibly be found in John v. 3, 4; vii. 53—viii. 11; xiii. 26; Acts xx. 4, 15; xxiv. 6-8. To this list some critics feel disposed to add portions of Luke xxi—xxiv.

12. The fullest critical edition of the Greek Testament hitherto published contains but a comparatively small portion of the whole mass of variations already known; as a rule, the editors neglect, and rightly neglect, mere errors of transcription. Such things must be recorded for several reasons, but neither they, nor real various readings that are slenderly supported, can produce any effect in the task of amending or restoring the sacred text. Those who wish to see for themselves how far the common printed editions of what is called the 'textus receptus' differ from the judgement of the most recent critics, may refer if they please to the small Greek Testament published in the series of 'Cambridge Greek and Latin Texts [1],' which exhibits in a thicker type all words and clauses wherein Robert Stephen's edition of 1550 (which is taken as a convenient standard) differs from the other chief modifications of the *textus receptus* (viz. Beza's 1565 and Elzevir's 1624), as also from the revised texts of Lachmann 1842-50, of Tischendorf 1865-72, of Tregelles 1857-72, of the Revisers of the English New Testament (1881), and of Westcott and Hort (1881). The student will thus be enabled to estimate for himself the limits within which the text of the Greek Testament may be regarded as still open to discussion, and to take a general survey of the questions on which the theologian is bound to form an intelligent opinion.

13. The work that lies before us naturally divides itself into three distinct parts.

I. A description of the sources from which various readings are derived (or of their EXTERNAL EVIDENCE), comprising

    (*a*) Manuscripts of the Greek New Testament or of portions thereof.

    (*b*) Ancient versions of the New Testament in various languages.

---

[1] 'Novum Testamentum Textûs Stephanici A.D. 1550 ... curante F. H. A. Scrivener.' Cantabr. 1877 (Editio Major, 1887).

(c) Citations from the Greek Testament or its versions made by early ecclesiastical writers, especially by the Fathers of the Christian Church.

(d) Early printed or later critical editions of the Greek Testament.

II. A discussion of the principles on which external evidence should be applied to the recension of the sacred volume, embracing

(a) The laws of INTERNAL EVIDENCE, and the limits of their legitimate use.

(b) The history of the text and of the principal schemes which have been proposed for restoring it to its primitive state, including recent views of Comparative Criticism.

(c) Considerations derived from the peculiar character and grammatical form of the dialect of the Greek Testament.

III. The application of the foregoing materials and principles to the investigation of the true reading in the chief passages of the New Testament, on which authorities are at variance.

In this edition, as has already been explained in the preface, it has been found necessary to divide the treatise into two volumes, which will contain respectively—

I. First Volume :—Ancient Manuscripts.

II. Second Volume:—Versions, Citations, Editions, Principles, and Selected Passages.

It will be found desirable to read the following pages in the order wherein they stand, although the chief part of Chapters VII-XIV of the first volume and some portions elsewhere (indicated by being printed like them in smaller type) are obviously intended chiefly for reference, or for less searching examination.

CHAPTER II.

GENERAL CHARACTER OF THE GREEK MANUSCRIPTS OF THE NEW TESTAMENT.

AS the extant Greek manuscripts of the New Testament supply both the most copious and the purest sources of Textual Criticism, we propose to present to the reader some account of their peculiarities in regard to material, form, style of writing, date and contents, before we enter into details respecting individual copies, under the several subdivisions to which it is usual to refer them.

1. The subject of the present section has been systematically discussed in the 'Palaeographia Graeca' (Paris, 1708, folio) of Bernard de Montfaucon [1655–1741[1]], the most illustrious member of the learned Society of the Benedictines of St. Maur. This truly great work, although its materials are rather too exclusively drawn from manuscripts deposited in French libraries, and its many illustrative facsimiles are somewhat rudely engraved, still maintains a high authority on all points relating to Greek manuscripts, even after more recent discoveries, especially among the papyri of Egypt and Herculaneum, have necessarily modified not a few of its statements. The four splendid volumes of M. J. B. Silvestre's 'Paléographie Universelle' (Paris, 1839–41, &c. folio) afford us no less than 300 plates of the Greek writing of various ages, sumptuously executed; though the accompanying letter-press descriptions, by F. and A. Champollion Fils, seem in this branch of the subject a little disappointing; nor are the valuable notes appended to his translation of their work by Sir Frederick Madden (London, 2 vols. 1850, 8vo) sufficiently numerous or elaborate to supply the Champollions' defects. Much, however, may also be learnt from the 'Hercu-

---

[1] In this manner we propose to indicate the dates of the birth and death of the person whose name immediately precedes.

lanensium voluminum quae supersunt' (Naples, 10 tom. 1793-1850, fol.); from Mr. Babington's three volumes of papyrus fragments of Hyperides, respectively published in 1850, 1853 and 1858; and especially from the Prolegomena to Tischendorf's editions of the Codices Ephraemi (1843), Friderico-Augustanus (1846), Claromontanus (1852), Sinaiticus (1862), Vaticanus (1867), and those other like publications (c. g. Monumenta sacra inedita 1846-1870, and Anecdota sacra et profana 1855) which have rendered his name perhaps the very highest among scholars in this department of sacred literature. What I have been able to add from my own observation, has been gathered from the study of Biblical manuscripts now in England. To these sources of information may now be added Professor Wattenbach's 'Anleitung zur griechischen Palaeographie' second edition, Leipsic, 1877, Gardthausen's 'Griechische Palaeographie,' Leipsic, 1879; Dr. C. R. Gregory's 'Prolegomena' to the eighth edition of Tischendorf, and especially the publication of 'The Palaeographical Society Greek Testament, Parts I and II, Leipsic, 1884, 1891, 'Facsimiles of Manuscripts and Inscriptions' edited by E. A. Bond and E. M. Thompson, Parts I-XII, London, 1873-82, and a Manual on 'Greek and Latin Palaeography' from the hands of Mr. E. Maunde Thompson, of which the proof-sheets have been most kindly placed by the accomplished author at the disposal of the editor of this work, and have furnished to this chapter many elements of enrichment. It may be added, that since manuscripts have been photographed, all other facsimiles have been put in the shade: and in this edition references as a rule will be given only to photographed copies.

2. The *materials* on which writing has been impressed at different periods and stages of civilization are the following:—Leaves, bark, especially of the lime (*liber*), linen, clay and pottery, wall-spaces, metals, lead, bronze, wood, waxen and other tablets, papyrus, skins, parchment and vellum, and from an early date amongst the Chinese, and in the West after the capture of Samarcand by the Arabs in A.D. 704, paper manufactured from fibrous substances[1]. The most ancient manuscripts of the New Testament now existing are composed of vellum or parchment (*membrana*), the term vellum being

---

[1] 'Greek and Latin Palaeography,' Chaps. II, III.

strictly applied to the delicate skins of very young calves, and parchment to the integuments of sheep and goats, though the terms are as a rule employed convertibly. The word parchment seems to be a corruption of *charta pergamena*, a name first given to skins prepared by some improved process for Eumenes, king of Pergamum, about B.C. 150. In judging of the date of a manuscript on skins, attention must be paid to the quality of the material, the oldest being almost invariably written on the thinnest and whitest vellum that could be procured; while manuscripts of later ages, being usually composed of parchment, are thick, discoloured, and coarsely grained. Thus the Codex Sinaiticus of the fourth century is made of the finest skins of antelopes, the leaves being so large, that a single animal would furnish only two (Tischendorf, Cod. Frid.-August. Prolegomena, § 1). Its contemporary, the far-famed Codex Vaticanus, challenges universal admiration for the beauty of its vellum: every visitor at the British Museum can observe the excellence of that of the Codex Alexandrinus of the fifth century: that of the Codex Claromontanus of the sixth century is even more remarkable: the material of those purple-dyed fragments of the Gospels which Tischendorf denominates N, also of the sixth century, is so subtle and delicate, that some persons have mistaken the leaves preserved in England (Brit. Mus. Cotton, Titus C xv) for Egyptian papyrus. Paper made of cotton[1] (*charta bombycina*, called also *charta Damascena* from its place of manufacture) may have been fabricated in the ninth[2] or tenth century, and linen paper (*charta* proper) as early as 1242 A.D.; but they were seldom used for Biblical manuscripts sooner than the thirteenth, and had not entirely displaced parchment at the era of the invention of printing, about A.D. 1450. Lost portions of parchment or vellum manuscripts are often supplied in paper by some later hand;

---

[1] 'Recent investigations have thrown doubts on the accuracy of this view; and a careful analysis of many samples has proved that, although cotton was occasionally used, no paper that has been examined is entirely made of that substance, hemp or flax being the more usual material.' Maunde Thompson, p. 44.

[2] Tischendorf (Notitia Codicis Sinaitici, p. 54) carried to St. Petersburg a fragment of a Lectionary which cannot well be assigned to a later date than the ninth century, among whose parchment leaves are inserted two of cotton paper, manifestly written on by the original scribe.

but the Codex Leicestrensis of the fourteenth century is composed of a mixture of inferior vellum and worse paper, regularly arranged in the proportion of two parchment to three paper leaves, recurring alternately throughout the whole volume. Like it, in the mixture of parchment and paper, are codd. 233 and Brit. Mus. Harl. 3,161—the latter however not being a New Testament MS.

3. Although parchment was in occasional, if not familiar, use at the period when the New Testament was written (τὰ βιβλία, μάλιστα τὰς μεμβράνας 2 Tim. iv. 13), yet the more perishable papyrus of Egypt was chiefly employed for ordinary purposes. This vegetable production had been used for literary purposes from the earliest times. 'Papyrus rolls are represented on the sculptured walls of Egyptian temples.' The oldest roll now extant is the papyrus Prisse at Paris, which dates from 2500 B.C., or even earlier, unless those which have been lately discovered by Mr. Flinders Petrie reach as far, or even farther, back [1]. The ordinary name applied in Greek to this material was χάρτης (2 John 12), though Herodotus terms it βύβλος (ii. 100, v. 58), and in Latin *charta* (2 Esdr. xv. 2; Tobit vii. 14—Old Latin Version). Papyrus was in those days esteemed more highly than skins: for Herodotus expressly states that the Ionians had been compelled to have recourse to goats and sheep for lack of byblus or papyrus; and Eumenes was driven to prepare parchment because the Alexandrians were too jealous to supply him with the material which he coveted [2]. Indeed, papyrus was used far beyond the borders of Egypt, and was plentiful in Rome under the Empire, being in fact the common material among the Romans during that period: and as many of the manuscripts of the New Testament must have been written upon so perishable a substance in the earliest centuries since the Christian era, this probably is one of the reasons why we possess no considerable copies from before the second quarter of the fourth century. Only a few fragments of the New Testament on papyrus remain. We find a minute, if not a very clear description of the mode of preparing the papyrus for the scribe in the works of the elder Pliny (Hist. Nat. xiii. 11, 12). The plant grew in Egypt, also

---

[1] 'Ten Years Digging in Egypt,' pp. 120, &c.
[2] 'Greek and Latin Palaeography,' p. 35; Pliny, Nat. Hist. xiii. 11.

in Syria, and on the Niger and the Euphrates. Mainly under Christian influence it was supplanted by parchment and vellum, which had superior claims to durability, and its manufacture ceased altogether on the conquest of Egypt by the Mohammedans (A.D. 638).

4. Parchment is said to have been introduced at Rome not long after its employment by Attalus. Nevertheless, if it had been in constant and ordinary use under the first Emperors, we can hardly suppose that specimens of secular writing would have failed to come down to us. Its increased growth and prevalence about synchronize with the rise of Constantinopolitan influence. It may readily be imagined that vellum (especially that fine sort by praiseworthy custom required for copies of Holy Scripture) could never have been otherwise than scarce and dear. Hence arose, at a very early period of the Christian era, the practice and almost the necessity of erasing ancient writing from skins, in order to make room for works in which the living generation felt more interest, especially when clean vellum failed the scribe towards the end of his task. This process of destruction, however, was seldom so fully carried out, but that the strokes of the elder hand might still be traced, more or less completely, under the more modern writing. Such manuscripts are called *codices rescripti* or palimpsests (παλίμψηστα [1]), and several of the most precious monuments of sacred learning are of this description. The Codex Ephraemi at Paris contains large fragments both of the Old and New Testament under the later Greek works of St. Ephraem the Syrian: and the Codex Nitriensis, more recently disinterred from a monastery in the Egyptian desert and brought to the British Museum, comprises a portion of St. Luke's Gospel, nearly obliterated, and covered over by a Syriac treatise of Severus of Antioch against Grammaticus, comparatively of no value whatever. It will be easily believed that the collating or transcribing of palimpsests has cost much toil and patience to those whose loving zeal has led them to the attempt: and after all the true readings will be sometimes (not often) rather uncertain,

---

[1] 'Nam, quod in palimpsesto, laudo equidem parcimoniam.' Cicero, Ad Diversos, vii. 18, though of a waxen tablet. Maunde Thompson, p. 75.

even though chemical mixtures (of which 'the most harmless is probably hydrosulphuret of ammonia') have recently been applied with much success to restore the faded lines and letters of these venerable records.

5. We need say but little of a practice which St. Jerome[1] and others speak of as prevalent towards the end of the fourth century, that of dyeing the vellum purple, and of stamping rather than writing the letters in silver and gold. The Cotton fragment of the Gospels, mentioned above (p. 23), is one of the few remaining copies of this kind, as are the newly discovered Codex Rossanensis and the Codex Beratinus, and it is not unlikely that the great Dublin palimpsest of St. Matthew owes its present wretched discoloration to some such dye. But, as Davidson sensibly observes, 'the value of a manuscript does not depend on such things' (Biblical Criticism, vol. ii. p. 264). We care for them only as they serve to indicate the reverence paid to the Scriptures by men of old. The style, however, of the pictures, illustrations, arabesques and initial ornaments that prevail in later copies from the eighth century downwards, whose colours and gilding are sometimes as fresh and bright as if laid on but yesterday[2], will not only interest the student by tending to throw light on mediaeval art and habits and modes of thought, but will often fix the date of the books which contain them with a precision otherwise quite beyond our reach.

6. The ink found upon ancient manuscripts is of various colours[3]. Black ink, the ordinary writing fluid of centuries (μέλαν, *atramentum*, &c.) differs in tint at various periods and in different countries. In early MSS. it is either pure black or slightly brown; in the Middle Ages it varies a good deal according to age and locality. In Italy and Southern Europe it is generally blacker than in the North, in France and Flanders

---

[1] 'Habeant qui volunt veteres libros, vel in membranis purpureis auro argentoque descriptos.' Praef. in Job. 'Inficiuntur membranae colore purpureo, aurum liquescit in litteras.' Epist. ad Eustochium.

[2] Miniatures are found even as early as in the Cod. Rossanensis (Σ) at the beginning of the sixth century.

[3] This paragraph which has been rewritten, has been abridged from Mr. Maunde Thompson's 'Greek and Latin Palaeography,' pp. 50-52, to which readers are referred for verification and amplification.

it is generally darker than in England; a Spanish MS. of the fourteenth or fifteenth century may usually be recognized by the peculiar blackness of the ink. Deterioration is observable in the course of time. The ink of the fifteenth century particularly is often of a faded grey colour. Inks of green, yellow, and other colours, are also found, but generally only for ornamental purposes. Red, either in the form of a pigment or fluid ink, is of very ancient and common use, being seen even in early Egyptian papyri. Gold was also used as a writing fluid at a very early period. Purple-stained vellum MSS. were usually written upon in gold or silver letters, and ordinary white vellum MSS. were also written in gold, particularly in the ninth and tenth centuries, in the reigns of the Carlovingian kings. Gold writing *as a practice* died out in the thirteenth century: and writing in silver appears to have ceased contemporaneously with the disuse of stained vellum. The ancients used the liquid of cuttle-fish. Pliny mentions soot and gum as the ingredients of writing-ink. Other later authors add gall-apples: metallic infusions at an early period, and vitriol in the Middle Ages were also employed.

7. While papyrus remained in common use, the chief instrument employed was a reed (κάλαμος 3 John ver. 13, *canna*), such as are common in the East at present: a few existing manuscripts (e.g. the Codd. Leicestrensis and Lambeth 1350) appear to have been thus written. Yet the firmness and regularity of the strokes, which often remain impressed on the vellum or paper after the ink has utterly gone, seem to prove that in the great majority of cases the *stilus* made of iron, bronze, or other metal, or ivory or bone, sharp at one end to scratch the letters, and furnished with a knob or flat head at the other for purposes of erasure, had not gone wholly out of use. We must add to our list of writing materials a bodkin or needle (*acus*), by means of which and a ruler the blank leaf was carefully divided, generally on the outer side of the skin, into columns and lines, whose regularity much enhances the beauty of our best copies. The vestiges of such points and marks may yet be seen deeply indented on the surface of nearly all manuscripts, those on one side of each leaf being usually sufficiently visible to guide the scribe when he came to write on the reverse. The quill pen

probably came into use with vellum, for which it is obviously suited. The first notices of it occur in a story respecting Theodoric the Ostrogoth, and in a passage of Isidore's 'Origines'[1] (vi. 13).

8. Little need be said respecting the *form* of manuscripts, which in this particular (*codices*) much resemble printed books. A few are in large folio; the greater part in small folio or quarto, the prevailing shape being a quarto (*quaternio* or quire) whose height but little exceeds its breadth; some are in octavo, a not inconsiderable number smaller still: and quires of three sheets or six leaves, and five sheets or ten leaves (Cod. Vaticanus), are to be met with. In some copies the sheets have marks in the lower margin of their first or last pages, like the *signatures* of a modern volume, the folio at intervals of two, the quarto at intervals of four leaves, as in the Codex Bezae of the Gospels and Acts (D), and the Codex Augiensis of St. Paul's Epistles (F). Not to speak at present of those manuscripts which have a Latin translation in a column parallel to the Greek, as the Codex Bezae, the Codex Laudianus of the Acts, and the Codices Claromontanus and Augiensis of St. Paul, many copies of every age have two Greek columns on each page; of these the Codex Alexandrinus is the oldest: the Codex Vaticanus has three columns on a page, the Codex Sinaiticus four. The unique arrangement[2] of these last two has been urged as an argument

---

[1] 'Greek and Latin Palaeography,' p. 49.

[2] Besides the Cod. Sinaiticus, the beautiful Psalter purchased by the National Library from the Didot sale at Paris has four columns Mr. J. Rendel Harris', and besides the Cod. Vaticanus, the Vatican Dio Cassius, the Milan fragment of Genesis, two copies of the Samaritan Pentateuch at Nablous described by Tischendorf (Cod. Frid.-Aug. Proleg. § 11), the last part of Cod. Monacensis 208 (Evan. 429), and two Hebrew MSS. Cod. Mon. Heb. 422, and Cod. Reg. Heb. 17, are arranged in *three* columns. Tischendorf has more recently discovered a similar arrangement in two palimpsest leaves of Wisdom and Ecclesiasticus from which he gives extracts (Not. Cod. Sinait. p. 49); in a Latin fragment of the Pentateuch, the same as the Ashburnham manuscript below, seen by him at Lyons in 1843; in a Greek Evangelistarium of the eighth century, and a Patristic manuscript at Patmos of the ninth (ibid. p. 10); so that the argument drawn from the *triple* columns must not be pressed too far. He adds also a Turin copy of the Minor Prophets in Greek (Pasinus, Catalogue, 1749), and a Nitrian Syriac codex in the British Museum 'quem circa finem quarti saeculi scriptum esse subscriptio testatur' (Monum. sacra inedita, vol. i, Proleg. p. xxxi). To this not slender list Mr. E. Maunde Thompson enables us to annex B. M. Addit. 24142, a Flemish Latin Bible of the eleventh century. The late Lord Ashburnham in 1868

Plate 1

(1) ΑΒΓΔΕΙΗΘ·ΙΚΛΜΝΞΟΠΡΕΤΥΦΧΨΩ.

(2) ΑΒΓΔΕΖΗΘΙΚΛΜΝΙΟΠΡΟΤΥΦΧΨΩ

(3) ΑΒΓΔϵΖΗΘΙΚΛΜΝΖΟΠΡΟΤΥΦΧΨΩ

for their higher antiquity, as if they were designed to imitate *rolled* books, whose several skins or leaves were fastened together lengthwise, so that their contents always appeared in parallel columns; they were kept in scrolls which were unrolled at one end for reading, and when read rolled up at the other. This fashion prevails in the papyrus fragments yet remaining, and in the most venerated copies of the Old Testament preserved in Jewish synagogues.

9. We now approach a more important question, the *style* of writing adopted in manuscripts, and the shapes of the several letters. These varied widely in different ages, and form the simplest and surest criteria for approximating to the date of the documents themselves. Greek characters are properly divided into 'majuscules' and 'minuscules,' or by a subdivision of the former, into Capitals, which are generally of a square kind, fitted for inscriptions on stones like E; Uncials, or large letters [1], and a modification of Capitals, with a free introduction of curves, and better suited for writing, like Є; and Cursives, or small letters, adapted for the running hand. *Uncial* manuscripts were written in what have frequently been regarded as capital letters, formed separately, having no connexion with each other, and (in the earlier specimens) without any space between the words, the marks of punctuation being few: the *cursive* or running hand comprising letters more easily and rapidly made, those in the same word being usually joined together, with a complete system of punctuation not widely removed from that of printed books. Speaking generally, and limiting our statement to Greek manuscripts of the New Testament, Uncial letters or the Literary or Book-hand prevailed from the fourth to the tenth, or (in the case of liturgical books) as late as the eleventh century; Cursive letters were employed as early as the ninth or tenth century, and continued in use until the invention of

printed his Old Latin fragments of Leviticus and Numbers, also in three columns, with a facsimile page; and the famous Utrecht Psalter, assigned by some to the sixth century, by others to the ninth or tenth, is written with three columns on a page.

[1] 'Uncialibus, ut vulgo aiunt, literis, onera magis exarata, quam codices,' Hieronymi Praef. in Job. From this passage the term *uncial* seems to be derived, *uncia* an inch) referring to the size of the characters. Yet the conjectural reading '*initialibus*' will most approve itself to those who are familiar with the small Latin writing of the Middle Ages, in which *i* is undotted, and *c* much like *t*.

printing superseded the humble labours of the scribe. But cursive writing existed before the Christian era: and it seems impossible to suppose that so very convenient a form of penmanship could have fallen into abeyance in ordinary life, although few documents have come down to us to demonstrate the truth of this supposition.

Besides the broad and palpable distinction between uncial and cursive letters, persons who have had much experience in the study of manuscripts are able to distinguish those of either class from one another in respect of style and character; so that the period at which each was written can be determined within certain inconsiderable limits. After the tenth century many manuscripts bear dates, and such become standards to which we can refer others resembling them which are undated. But since the earliest dated Biblical manuscript yet discovered (Cursive Evan. 481, see below Chap. VII) bears the date May 7, A.D. 835, we must resort to other means for estimating the age of more venerable, and therefore more important, copies. By studying the style and shape of the letters on Greek inscriptions, Montfaucon was led to conclude that the more simple, upright, and regular the form of uncial letters; the less flourish or ornament they exhibit; the nearer their breadth is equal to their height; so much the more ancient they ought to be considered. These results have been signally confirmed by the subsequent discovery of Greek papyri in Egyptian tombs especially in the third century before the Christian era; and yet further from numerous fragments of Philodemus, of Epicurus, and other philosophers, which were buried in the ruins of Herculaneum in A.D. 79 ('Fragmenta Herculanensia,' Walter Scott). The evidence of these papyri, indeed, is even more weighty than that of inscriptions, inasmuch as workers in stone, as has been remarked, were often compelled to prefer straight lines, as better adapted to the hardness of their material, where writings on papyrus or vellum would naturally flow into curves.

10. While we freely grant that a certain tact, the fruit of study and minute observation, can alone make us capable of forming a trustworthy opinion on the age of manuscripts; it is worth while to point out the *principles* on which a true

judgement must be grounded, and to submit to the reader a few leading facts, which his own research may hereafter enable him to apply and to extend.

The first three plates at the beginning of this volume represent the Greek alphabet, as found in the seven following monuments:

(1) The celebrated Rosetta stone, discovered near that place during the French occupation of Egypt in 1799, and now in the British Museum. This most important inscription, which in the hands of Young and Champollion has proved the key to the mysteries of Egyptian hieroglyphics, records events of no intrinsic consequence that occurred B.C. 196, in the reign of Ptolemy V Epiphanes. It is written in the three several forms of hieroglyphics, of the demotic or common characters of the country, and of Greek Capitals, which last may represent the *lapidary* style of the second century before our era. The words are undivided, without breathings, accents, or marks of punctuation, and the uncial letters (excepting ⌶ for *zeta*) approach very nearly to our modern capital type. In shape they are simple, perhaps a little rude; rather square than oblong: and as the carver on this hard black stone was obliged to avoid curve lines whenever he could, the forms of E, Ξ and Σ differ considerably from the specimens we shall produce from documents described on soft materials. Plate I. No. (1).

(2) The Codex Friderico-Augustanus of the fourth century, published in lithographed facsimile in 1846, contains on forty-three leaves fragments of the Septuagint version, chiefly from 1 Chronicles and Jeremiah, with Nehemiah and Esther complete, in oblong folio, with four columns on each page. The plates are so carefully executed that the very form of the ancient letters and the colour of the ink are represented to us by Tischendorf, who discovered it in the East. In 1859 the same indefatigable scholar brought to Europe the remainder of this manuscript, which seems as old as the fourth century, anterior (as he thinks) to the Codex Vaticanus itself, and published it in 1862, in facsimile type cast for the purpose, 4 tom., with twenty pages lithographed or photographed, at the expense of the Emperor Alexander II of Russia, to whom the original had been presented. This book, which Tischendorf calls Codex Sinaiticus, contains, besides much more of the Septuagint, *the whole New Testament*

with Barnabas' Epistle and a part of Hermas' Shepherd annexed. As a kind of *avant-courier* to his great work he had previously put forth a tract entitled 'Notitia Editionis Codicis Bibliorum Sinaitici Auspiciis Imperatoris Alexandri II susceptae' (Leipsic, 1860). Of this most valuable manuscript a complete account will be given in the opening of the fourth chapter, under the appellation of *Aleph* (א), assigned to it by Tischendorf, in the exercise of his right as its discoverer. Plate I. No. 2.

(3) Codex Alexandrinus of the fifth century (A). Plate I.

Plate II. { (4) Codex Purpureus Cotton.: N of the Gospels
(5) Codex Nitriensis Rescriptus, R of the Gospels } of the sixth century

Plate III. { (6) Codex Dublinensis Rescriptus, Z of the Gospels
(7) Evangelistarium Harleian. 5598, *dated* A.D. 995.

The leading features of these manuscripts will be described in the fourth and fifth chapters. At present we wish to compare them with each other for the purpose of tracing, as closely as we may, the different styles and fashions of uncial letters which prevailed from the fourth to the tenth or eleventh century of the Christian era. The varying appearance of cursive manuscripts cannot so well be seen by exhibiting their alphabets, for since each letter is for the most part joined to the others in the same word, *connected* passages alone will afford us a correct notion of their character and general features. For the moment we are considering the uncials only.

If the Rosetta stone, by its necessary avoiding of curve lines, gives only a notion of the manner adopted on stone and not in common writing, it resembles our earliest uncials at least in one respect, that the letters, being as broad as they are high, are all capable of being included within circumscribed squares. Indeed, yet earlier inscriptions are found almost totally destitute of curves, even O and Θ being represented by simple squares, with or without a bisecting horizontal line (see *theta*, p. 35)[1].

[1] The Cotton fragment of the book of Genesis of the fifth century, whose poor shrivelled remains from the fire of 1731 are still preserved in the British Museum, while in common with all other *manuscripts* it exhibits the round shapes of O and Θ, substitutes a lozenge ◊ for the circle in *phi*, after the older fashion (ϕ). *Phi* often has much the same shape in Codex Bezae; e.g. Matt. xiii. 26, Fol. 42 *b*, l. 13, and once in Codex Z (Matt. xxi. 26, Plate xlviii).

(4) ΑΒΓΔΕΖΗΘΙΚΛΜΝΞΟΠΡΣΤΥΦΧΨΩ

(5) ΑΒΓΔΕΖΗΘΙΚΛΜΝΞΟΠΡΣΤΥΦΧΨΩ

The Herculanean papyri, however (a specimen of which we have given in Plate iv. No. 10), are much better suited than inscriptions can be for comparison with our earliest copies of Scripture[1]. Nothing can well be conceived more elegant than these simply-formed graceful little letters (somewhat diminished in size perhaps by the effects of heat) running across the volume, thirty-nine lines in a column, without capitals or breaks between the words. There are scarcely any stops, no breathings, accents, or marks of any kind; only that >, < or ▷ are now and then found at the end of a line, to fill up the space, or to join a word or syllable with what follows. A very few abbreviations occur, such as ῆ in the first line of our specimen, taken from Philodemus περὶ κακιῶν (Hercul. Volum. Tom. iii. Col. xx. ll. 6-15), the very manuscript to which Tischendorf compared his Cod. Friderico-Augustanus (Proleg. § 11). The papyri, buried for so many ages from A. D. 79 downwards, may probably be a century older still, since Philodemus the Epicurean was the contemporary and almost the friend of Cicero[2]. Hence from three to four hundred years must have elapsed betwixt the date of the Herculanean rolls and that of our earliest Biblical manuscripts. Yet the fashion of writing changed but little during the interval, far less in every respect than in the four centuries which next followed, wherein the plain, firm, upright and square uncials were giving place to the compressed, oblong, ornamented, or even sloping forms which predominate from the seventh or eighth century downwards. While advising the reader to exercise his skill on facsimiles of *entire passages*, especially in contrasting the lines from Philodemus (No. 10) with those from the oldest uncials of the New Testament (Nos. 11-14; 17; 18; 20; 24); we purpose to examine the several alphabets (Nos. 1-7) letter by letter, pointing out to the student those variations in shape which palaeographers have judged the safest criteria of their relative ages. *Alpha, delta, theta, xi, pi, omega*, are among the best tests for this purpose.

Alpha is not often found in its present familiar shape, except in

---

[1] Our facsimile is borrowed from the Neapolitan volumes, but Plate 57 in the Paléographie Universelle φιλοδημου περι μουσικη has the advantage of *colours* for giving a lively idea of the present charred appearance of these papyri.

[2] Cicero de Finibus, Lib. ii. c. 35. The same person is apparently meant in Orat. in Pisonem, cc. 28, 29.

inscriptions, where the cross line is sometimes broken into an angle with the vertex downwards (A). Even on the Rosetta stone the left limb leans against the upper part of the right limb, but does not form an angle with its extremity, while the cross line, springing not far from the bottom of the left limb, *ascends* to meet the right about half way down. Modifications of this form may be seen in the Herculanean rolls, only that the cross line more nearly approaches the horizontal, and sometimes is almost entirely so. The Cod. Frid.-August.[1] does not vary much from this form, but the three generating lines are often somewhat curved. In other books, while the right limb is quite straight, the left and cross line form a kind of loop or curve, as is very observable in the Nitrian fragment R, and often in Codd. Alex., Ephraemi, Bezae, the newly discovered Rossanensis, and in the Vatican more frequently still, in all which *alpha* often approximates to the shape of our English *a*. And this curve may be regarded as a proof of antiquity; indeed Tischendorf (Proleg. Cod. Sin. p. xxx, 1863) considers it almost peculiar to the papyri and the Coptic character. Cod. N (which is more recent than those named above) makes the two lines on the left form a sharp angle, as do the Cotton fragment of Genesis (see p. 32, note 1) and Cod. Claromontanus, Plate xiv. No. 41, only that the lines which contain the angle in this last are very fine. In later times, as the letters grew tall and narrow, the modern type of A became more marked, as in the first letter of Arundel 547 (No. 16), of about the tenth century, though the form and thickness seen in the Cod. Claromontanus continued much in vogue to the last. Yet *alpha* even in Cod. Claromontanus and Cotton Genesis occasionally passes from the angle into the loop, though not so often as in Cod. A and its companions. Cod. Borgianus (T), early in the fifth century, exaggerated this loop into a large ellipse, if Giorgi's facsimile may be trusted. In Cod. Laudianus E of the Acts and Cureton's palimpsest Homer too the loop is very decided, the Greek and Latin *a* in Laud. (No. 25) being alike. Mark also its form in the papyrus scrawl No. 9 (from one of the orations of Hyperides edited by Mr. Babington), which *may* be as old as the Rosetta stone. The angular shape adopted in Cod. Z (Nos. 6, 18) is unsightly enough, and (I believe) unique.

Beta varies less than *Alpha*. Originally it consisted of a tall perpendicular line, on the right side of which four straight lines are so placed as to form two triangles, whereof the vertical line comprises the bases, while a small portion of that vertical line entirely separates the triangles (β). This ungraceful figure was modified very early even in inscriptions. On the Rosetta stone (No. 1) the triangles are rounded off into semicircles, and the lower end of the vertical curved. Yet the shape in manuscripts is not quite so elegant. The lower curve is usually the larger, and the curves rarely touch each other.

---

[1] We prefer citing Cod. Frid.-August., because our examples have been actually taken from its exquisitely lithographed pages; but the facsimile of part of a page from Luke xxiv represented in Tischendorf's Cod. Sinaiticus, from which we have borrowed six lines (No. 11 b), will be seen to resemble exactly the portion published in 1846.

(6)

αβγΔϵZHΘIKΛμNΞOΠPCTϒΦΧΨω.

(7)

ΑΒΓΔΕΖΗΘΙΚΛΜΝΞΟΠΡϹΤΥΦΧΨω

(8)

αβγΔεϛZηθїκλμΝξοπρστυφχψω.

Such are Codd. ANRZ, Rossanensis (sometimes), and the Cotton Genesis. In the Herculanean rolls the letter comes near the common cursive β; in some others (as Cod. Rossanensis at times) its shape is quite like the modern B. When oblong letters became common, the top (e.g. in Cod. Bezae) and bottom extremities of the curve ran into straight lines, by way of return into the primitive shape (see No. 36, dated A.D. 980). In the very early papyrus fragment of Hyperides it looks like the English R standing on a base (No. 9, l. 4). But this specimen rather belongs to the semi-cursive hand of common life, than to that of books.

Gamma in its simplest form consists of two lines of equal thickness, the shorter so placed upon the longer, which is vertical, as to make one right angle with it on the right side. Thus we find it in the Rosetta stone, the papyrus of Hyperides, the Herculanean rolls, and very often in Cod. A. The next step was to make the horizontal line very thin, and to strengthen its extremity by a point, or knob, as in Codd. Ephraemi (No. 24), RZ: or the point was thus strengthened without thinning the line, e.g. Codd. Vatican., Rossanensis, N and most later copies, such as Harl. 5598 (No. 7) or its contemporary Parham 18 (No. 36). In Cod. Bezae (No. 42) *gamma* much resembles the Latin r.

Delta should be closely scrutinized. Its most ancient shape is an equilateral triangle, the sides being all of the same thickness (Δ). Cod. Claromontanus, though of the sixth century, is in this instance as simple as any: the Herculanean rolls, Codd. Vatican., Sinait., and the very old copy of the Pentateuch at Paris (Colbert) or 'Cod. Sarravianus' and Leyden, much resemble it, only that sometimes the Herculanean sides are slightly curved, and the right descending stroke of Cod. Vatican. is thickened. In Cod. A begins a tendency to prolong the base on one or both sides, and to strengthen one or both ends by points. We see a little more of this in Cod. Rossanensis and in the palimpsest Homer of the fifth century, published by Cureton. The habit increases and gradually becomes confirmed in Codd. Ephraemi (No. 24), the Vatican Dio Cassius of the fifth or sixth century, in Cod. R, and particularly in N and E of the Acts (Nos. 4, 14, 25). In the oblong later uncials it becomes quite elaborate, e.g. Cod. B of the Apocalypse, or Nos. 7, 21, 36. On the Rosetta stone and in the Cod. Bezae the right side is produced beyond the triangle, and is produced and slightly curved in Hyperides, curved and strongly pointed in Cod. Z.

Epsilon has its angular form on the Rosetta marble and other inscriptions in stone; in the oldest manuscripts it consists as an uncial of a semicircle, from whose centre to the right of it a horizontal radius is drawn to the concave circumference. Thus it appears in the Herculanean rolls (only that here the radius is usually broken off before it meets the circle), in Codd. Frid.-August., Vatican., the two Paris Pentateuchs (Colbert-Leyden fifth century, Coislin. sixth) and the Cotton Genesis. In Cod. Alex. a slight trace is found of the more recent practice of strengthening each of the three extremities with knobs, but only the radius at times in Cod. Rossanensis. The custom increases in Codd. Ephraemi, Bezae, and still more in Codd. NRZ, wherein the curve becomes greater than a semicircle. In Hyperides (and in a slighter degree in Cod. Claromon. No. 41) the shape almost resembles the Latin *e*. The form of this and the other round letters was afterwards much affected in the narrow oblong uncials: see Nos. 7, 16, 36.

Zeta on the Rosetta stone maintains its old form (⊐), which is indeed but the next letter reversed. In manuscripts it receives its usual modern shape (Z), the ends being pointed decidedly, slightly, or not at all, much after the manner described for *epsilon*. In old copies the lower horizontal line is a trifle curved (Cod. R, No. 5), or even both the extreme lines (Cod. Z, No. 6, and Cod. Augiensis of St. Paul). In such late books as Parham 18 (A.D. 980, facsim. No. 36) *Zeta* is so large as to run far below the line, ending in a kind of tail.

Eta does not depart from its normal shape (H) except that in Cod. Ephraemi (No. 24) and some narrow and late uncials (e.g. Nos. 7, 36) the cross line is often more than half way up the letter. In a few later uncials the cross line passes *outside* the two perpendiculars, as in the Cod. Augiensis, twenty-six times on the photographed page of Scrivener's edition.

Theta deserves close attention. In some early inscriptions it is found as a square, bisected horizontally (⊟). On the Rosetta stone and most others (but only in such monuments) it is a circle, with a strong central *point*. On the Herculanean rolls the central point is spread into a short horizontal line, yet not reaching the circumference (No. 10, l. 8). Thence in our uncials from the fourth to the sixth century the line becomes a horizontal diameter to a true circle (Codd. Vatican., Sinait., Codd. ANRZ, Ephraemi, Claromont., Rossanensis, and Cureton's Homer). In the seventh century the diameter began to pass out of the circle on both sides: thence the circle came to be compressed into an ellipse (sometimes very narrow), and the ends of the minor axis to be ornamented with knobs, as in Cod. B of the Apocalypse (eighth century), Cod. Augiensis (ninth century), LX of the Gospels, after the manner of the tenth century (Nos. 7, 16, 21, 36, 38).

Iota would need no remark but for the custom of placing over it and *upsilon*, when they commence a syllable, either a very short straight line, or one or two dots. After the papyrus rolls no copy is quite without them, from the Codex Alexandrinus, the Cotton Genesis and Paris-Leyden Pentateuch, Cod. Z and the Isaiah included in it, to the more recent cursives; although in some manuscripts they are much rarer than in others. By far the most usual practice is to put two points, but Cod. Ephraemi, in its *New* Testament portion, stands nearly alone with the Cotton Genesis (ch. xviii. 9) in exhibiting the straight line; Cod. Alexandrinus in the Old Testament, but not in the New, frequently resembles Codd. Ephraemi and the Cotton

Genesis in placing a straight line over *iota*, and more rarely over *upsilon*, instead of the single or double dots; Cod. Sinaiticus employs two points or a straight line (as in Z's Isaiah) promiscuously over both vowels, and in Wake 12, a cursive of the eleventh century, the former frequently pass into the latter in writing. Codd. Borgianus (T) and Claromont. have but one point; Codd. N and Rossanensis have two for *iota*, one for *upsilon*.

Kappa deserves notice chiefly because the vertex of the angle formed by the two inclined lines very frequently does not meet the perpendicular line, but falls short of it a little to the right: we observe this in Codd. ANR, Ephraemi, Rossanensis, and later books. The copies that have strong points at the end of *epsilon* &c. (e.g. Codd. NR and AZ partly) have the same at the extremity of the thin or upper limb of *Kappa*. In Cod. D a fine horizontal stroke runs a little to the left from the bottom of the vertical line. Compare also the initial letter in Cod. M, No. 32.

Lambda much resembles *alpha*, but is less complicated. All our models (except Harl. 5598, No. 7), from the Rosetta stone downwards, have the right limb longer than the left, which thus leans against its side, but the length of the projection varies even in the same passage (e.g. No. 10). In most copies later than the Herculanean rolls and Cod. Sinaiticus the shorter line is much the thinner, and the longer slightly curved. In Cod. Z (Nos. 6, 18) the projection is curved elegantly at the end, as we saw in *delta*.

Mu varies as much as most letters. Its normal shape, resembling the English M, is retained in the Rosetta stone and most inscriptions, but at an early period there was a tendency to make the letter broader, and not to bring the re-entering or middle angle so low as in English (e.g. Codd. Vaticanus and Sinaiticus). In Cod. Ephraemi this central angle is sometimes a little rounded: in Codd. Alex. and Parham 18 the lines forming the angle do not always spring from the top of the vertical lines: in Arund. 547 (No. 16) they spring almost from their foot, forming a thick inelegant loop below the line, the letter being rather narrow: Harl. 5598 (No. 7) somewhat resembles this last, only that the loop is higher up. In the Herculanean rolls (and to a less extent in the Cotton Genesis) the two outer lines cease to be perpendicular, and lean outwards until the letter looks much like an inverted W (No. 10). In the papyrus Hyperides (No. 9) these outer lines are low curves, and the central lines rise in a kind of flourish above them. *Mu* assumes this shape also in Cod. T, and at the end of a line even in Codd. Vaticanus and Sinaiticus. This form is so much exaggerated in some examples, that by discarding the outer curves we obtain the shape seen in Cod. Z (Nos. 6, 18) and one or two others (e.g. Paul M in Harl. 5613, No. 34), almost exactly resembling an inverted *pi*. So also in the Isaiah of Cod. Z, only that the left side and base line were made by one stroke of the pen.

Nu is easier, the only change (besides the universal transition from the square to the oblong in the later uncials) being that in a few cases the thin cross line does not pass from the top of the left to the bottom of the right vertical line as in English (N), but only from about half-way or two-thirds down the left vertical in the Cotton Genesis, Codd. A, Rossanensis, Harl. 5598 (No. 7), and others; in Codd. ℵNR Parham 18 it often neither springs from the top of one, nor reaches the foot of the other (Nos. 4, 5, 11b, 12, 36); while in Cod. Claromont. (No. 41) it is here and there not far from horizontal. In a few *cursives* (e.g. 440 Evan. at Cambridge, and Tischendorf's lo^{ti} or 61 of the Acts), H and N almost interchange their shapes: so in Evan. 66 and Wake 34 at the end of a line only.

Xi in the Rosetta stone and Herculanean rolls consists of three parallel straight lines, the middle one being the shortest, as in modern printed Greek: but all our Biblical manuscripts exhibit modifications of the small printed ξ, such as must be closely inspected, but cannot easily be described. In the Cotton Genesis this *xi* is narrow and smaller than its fellows, much like an old English ʒ resting on a horizontal base which curves downwards: while in late uncials, as B of the Apocalypse, Cod. Augiensis (l. 13 Scrivener's *photographed page*), and especially in Parham 18 (No. 36), the letter and its flourished finial are continued far below the line. For the rest we must refer to our facsimile alphabets, &c. The figures in Cod. Frid.-August. (Nos. 2, 11a, ll. 3, 8) look particularly awkward, nor does the shape in Cod. Rossanensis much differ from these. In Cod. E, the Zurich Psalter of the seventh century, and Mr. W. White's fragment W^d, *xi* is the common Z with a large horizontal line over it, strengthened by knobs at each end.

Omicron is unchanged, excepting that in the latest uncials (No. 16, 36) the circle is mostly compressed, like *theta*, into a very eccentric ellipse.

Pi requires attention. Its original shape was doubtless two vertical straight lines joined at top by another horizontal, thinner perhaps but not much shorter than they. Thus we meet with it on the Rosetta stone, Codd. R, Vatican., Sinaiticus, Ephraemi, Claromontanus, Laud. of the Acts, the two Pentateuchs, Cureton's Homer, and sometimes Cod. A (No. 12). The fine horizontal line is, however, slightly produced on both sides in such early documents as the papyri of Hyperides and Herculaneum, and in the Cotton Genesis, as well as in Cod. A occasionally[1]. Both extremities of this line are fortified by strong points in Codd. N and Rossanensis, and mostly in Cod. A, but the left side only in Cod. Z, and this in Cod. Bezae occasionally becomes a sort of hooked curve. The later oblong *pi* was usually very plain, with thick vertical lines and a very fine horizontal, in Arund. 547 (No. 16) not at all produced; in Harl. 5598 (No. 7) slightly produced on both sides; in Parham 18 (No. 36) produced only on the right.

Rho is otherwise simple, but in all our authorities except inscriptions is produced below the line of writing, least perhaps in the papyri and

---

[1] Cod. A is found in the simpler form in the Old Testament, but mostly with the horizontal line produced in the New.

UNCIAL LETTERS. 39

Cod. Claromont., considerably in Codd. AX (Nos. 12, 38), most in Parham 18 (No. 36): Codd. N, Rossanensis, and many later copies have the lower extremity boldly *bevelled*. The form is P rather than Ρ in Codd. אA. In Cod. D a horizontal stroke, longer and thicker than in *kappa*, runs to the left from the bottom of the vertical line.

Sigma retains its angular shape (C or Σ) only on inscriptions, as the Rosetta, and that long after the square shapes of *omicron* and *theta* were discarded. The uncial or semicircular form, however, arose early, and to this letter must be applied all that was said of *epsilon* as regards terminal points (a knob at the lower extremity occurs even in Cod. א, e.g. Acts ii. 31), and its cramped shape in later ages.

Tau in its oldest form consists of two straight lines of like thickness, the horizontal being bisected by the lower and vertical one. As early as in Cod. Sinaiticus the horizontal line is made thin, and strengthened on the left side *only* by a point or small knob (Nos. 3, 11): thus we find it in Cod. Laud. of the Acts sometimes. In Cod. Alex. *both* ends are slightly pointed, in Codd. Ephraemi, Rossanensis, and others much more. In Cod. Bezae the horizontal is curved and flourished; in the late uncials the vertical is very thick, the horizontal fine, and the ends formed into heavy triangles (e.g. No. 16).

Upsilon on the Rosetta stone and Herculanean rolls is like our Y, all the strokes being of equal thickness and not running below the line: nor do they in Hyperides or in Codd. XZ and Augiensis, which have the upper lines neatly curved (Nos. 6, 9, 18, 38). The right limb of many of the rest is sometimes, but not always curved; the vertical line in Codd. Vatican. and Sinaiticus drops slightly below the line; in Codd. A, Ephraemi, Cotton Genesis, Cureton's Homer, Laud. of the Acts and Rossanensis somewhat more; in others (as Codd. Bezae NR) considerably. In the subscription to St. Matthew's Gospel, which may be by a somewhat later hand, a horizontal line crosses the vertical a little below the curved lines in Cod. Rossanensis. In later uncials (Nos. 7, 36) it becomes a long or awkward Y, or even degenerates into a long V (No. 16); or, in copies written by Latin scribes, into Y reversed. We have described under *iota* the custom of placing dots, &c. over *upsilon*. But in Tischendorf's Leipzig II. (fragments from Numbers to Judges of the seventh or eighth century) *upsilon* receives two dots, *iota* only one. Once in Cod. Z (Matt. xxi. 5) and oftener in its Isaiah a convex semicircle, like a circumflex, stands over *upsilon*.

Phi is a remarkable letter. In most copies it is the largest in the alphabet, quite disproportionately large in Codd. ZL (Paris 62) and others, and to some extent in Codd. AR, Ephraemi, Rossanensis, and Claromont. The circle (which in the Cotton Genesis is *sometimes* still a lozenge, see above, p. 32, note 1), though large and in some copies even too broad (e.g. No. 18), is usually in the line of the other letters, the vertical line being produced *far* upwards (Cod. Augiens. and Nos. 16, 41), or downwards (No. 10), or both (No. 36). On the Rosetta stone the circle is very small and the straight line short.

Chi is a simple transverse cross (X) and never goes above or below the line. The limb that inclines from left to right is in the uncial form for the most part thick, the other thin (with final points according to the practice stated for *epsilon*), and this limb or both (as in Cod. Z) a little curved.

Psi is a rare but trying letter. Its oldest form resembled an English V with a straight line running up bisecting its interior angle. On the Rosetta stone it had already changed into its present form (Ψ), the curve being a small semicircle, the vertical rising above the other letters and falling a little below the line. In the Cotton Genesis *psi* is rather taller than the rest, but the vertical line does not rise above the level of the circle. In Codd. ANR and Rossanensis the under line is prolonged: in R the two limbs are straight lines making an angle of about 45° with the vertical, while oftentimes in Hyperides and Cod. Augiensis (Scrivener's *photograph*, ll. 18, 23) they curve *downwards*; the limbs in N and R being strongly (slightly in Rossanensis) pointed at the ends, and the bottom of the vertical bevelled as usual. In Cod. B of the Apocalypse, in Evan. OW^{d}Ξ, and even in Hyperides, the limbs (strongly pointed) fall into a straight line, and the figure becomes a large cross (No. 7). In Evan. 66 the vertical is crossed above the semicircle by a minute horizontal line.

Omega took the form Ω, even when *omicron* and *theta* were square; thus it appears on the Rosetta stone, but in the Hyperides and Herculaneum rolls it is a single curve, much like the w of English writing, only that the central part is sometimes only a low double curve (No. 10, l. 6). In the Cotton Genesis, Codd. Vatican., Sinaiticus, Alex., Ephraemi, Bezae, Claromont., Nitriens., Rossanensis, there is little difference in shape, though sometimes Cod. Vatican. comes near the Herculanean rolls, and Cod. Alex. next to it: elsewhere their strokes (especially those in the centre) are fuller and more laboured. Yet in Cod. N it is often but a plain semicircle, bisected by a perpendicular radius, with the ends of the curve bent inwards (No. 14, l. 2). In the late uncials (Nos. 7, 16) it almost degenerates into an ungraceful W, while in Cod. Augiensis (*photograph*, l. 18) the first limb is occasionally a complete circle.

These details might be indefinitely added to by references to other codices and monuments of antiquity, but we have employed most of the principal copies of the Greek Testament, and have indicated to the student the chief points to which his attention should be drawn. Three leading principles have perhaps been sufficiently established by the foregoing examples:

First, that the uncials used in writing differ from the capitals cut in stone by the curved shapes which the writing hand naturally adopts[1].

Secondly, that the upright uncials of square dimensions

---

[1] See Maunde Thompson's 'Greek and Latin Palaeography.'

are more ancient than those which are narrow, oblong, or leaning[1].

Thirdly, that the simpler and less elaborate the style of writing, the more remote is its probable date.

Copies of a later age occasionally aim at imitating the fashion of an earlier period, or possibly the style of the older book from which their text is drawn. But this anachronism of fashion may be detected, as well by other circumstances we are soon to mention, as from the air of constraint which pervades the whole manuscript: the rather as the scribe will now and then fall into the more familiar manner of his contemporaries; especially when writing those small letters which our Biblical manuscripts of all dates (even the most venerable) perpetually crowd into the ends of lines, in order to save space.

11. We do not intend to dwell much on the cursive handwriting. No books of the Greek Scriptures earlier than the ninth century in this style are now extant[2], though it was prevalent long before in the intercourse of business or common life. The papyri of Hyperides (e.g. No. 9) and the Herculanean rolls, in a few places, show that the process had then commenced, for the letters of each word are often joined, and their shapes prove that swiftness of execution was more aimed at than distinctness. This is seen even more clearly in a petition to Ptolemy Philometor (B.C. 164) represented in the 'Paléographie Universelle' (No. 56). The same great work contains (No. 66) two really cursive charters of the Emperors

---

[1] Codd. B of Apocalypse, Θ^n Λ (No. 80) of the Gospels, and Silvestre's No. 68, all of about the eighth century, slope more or less to the right; Cod. Γ (No. 35) of the ninth century, a very little to the left. Tischendorf assigns to the seventh century the fragments comprising Leipzig II. (see p. 39), though they lean much to the right (Monum. sacra ined. tom. i, pp. xxx-xxxiv, 141-176), and those of Isaiah (ibid. pp. xxxvi, xxxvii, 187-199).

[2] The earliest cursive Biblical manuscript formerly alleged, i.e. Evan. 14, on examination proves to have no inscription whatever. 'On folio 392, in a comparatively modern hand, is rather uncouthly written ἐγράφη νικηφόρου βασιλεύοντος A. Z. What the initials A. Z. stand for I do not know.' (Dean Burgon, Guardian, Jan. 15, 1873.) The claim of priority for Cod. 14 being thus disposed of (though it must be noted that Dr. C. R. Gregory refers it without doubt to the tenth century), we may note that Cod. 429 of the Gospels is dated 978, Cod. 148 of the Acts 984, Cod. 5^{pe} 994, and Λ, written partly in cursives, and partly in uncials is of the ninth century. But the date May 7, 835 A.D. is plainly visible on Cod. 481, which is therefore indisputably the earliest.

Maurice (A.D. 600) and Heraclius (A.D. 616). Other instances of early cursive writing may be found in two Deeds of Sale, A.D. 616, and 599, a Manumission in 355, an Official Deed in 233, a Deed of Sale in 154, in Aristotle on the Constitution of Athens, about 100, in a Farm Account in 78-79, in a Receipt in A.D. 20, in the Casati contract in B.C. 114, in a Letter on Egyptian Contracts in 146, a Treasury Circular in 170, in a Steward's letter of the third century B.C., in various documents of the same century lying in the British Museum, at Paris, Berlin, Leyden, and elsewhere, of which the oldest, being amongst the papyri discovered by Dr. Flinders Petrie at Gurob is referred to B.C. 268, and the Leyden papyrus to 260[1]. Yet the earliest books of a later age known to be written in cursive letters are Cod. 481 (Scholz 461, dated A.D. 835) the Bodleian Euclid (dated A.D. 888) and the twenty-four dialogues of Plato in the same Library (dated A.D. 895)[2]. There is reason to believe, from the comparatively unformed character of the writing in them all, that Burney 19 in the British Museum (from which we have extracted the alphabet No. 8, Plate iii), and the minute, beautiful and important Codex 1 of the Gospels at Basle (of which see a facsimile No. 23), are but little later than the Oxford books, and may be referred to the tenth century. Books copied after the cursive hand had become regularly formed, in the eleventh,

[1] See Maunde Thompson, Greek and Latin Palaeology, chap. x. pp. 130, &c., and chap. viii. pp. 107, &c; Notices et Extracts des MSS. de la Bibliothèque Imperiale, Paris, plate xxiv. no. 21, pl. xlviii. no. 21 ter, xlvi. no. 69, e, xxi. no. 17, xiii. no. 5, xl. no. 62, xviii. 2, pl. xliv; Cat. Gr. Papyri in Brit. Mus. Palaeograph. Soc. ii. pl. 143, 144, Mahaffy, Petrie Papyri, pl. xiv, xxix. &c. (Cunningham Memoirs of R. Irish Academy).

[2] At the end of the Euclid we read εγραφη χειρι στεφανου κληρικου μηνι σεπτεμβριωι ινδ. ζ ετει κοσμου ϛ τ ϟ ϛ εκτησαμην αρεθας πατρευς την παρουσαν βιβλιον: of the Plato, εγραφη χειρι ιω καλλιγραφου · ευτυχως αρεθη διακονωι πατρει · νομισματων βυζαντιεων δεκα και τριων · μηνι νοεμβριωι ινδικτιωνος ιδ · ετει κοσμου ϛυδ βασιλειας λεοντος του φιλοχυ υιου βασιλειου του αειμνιστου. It should be stated that these very curious books, both written by monks, and indeed *all the dated manuscripts of the Greek Testament we have seen* except Canonici 34 in the Bodleian (which reckons from the Christian era, A.D. 1515-6), calculate from the Greek era of the Creation, September 1, B.C. 5508. To obtain the year A.D., therefore, from January 1 to August 31 in any year, subtract 5508 from the given year; from September 1 to December 31 subtract 5509. The indiction which usually accompanies this date is a useful check in case of any corruption or want of legibility in the letters employed as numerals. Both dates are given in Evan. 558, viz. A. M. 6938, and A. D. 1430.

twelfth and thirteenth centuries, are hard to be distinguished by the mere handwriting, though they are often dated, or their age fixed by the material (see p. 23), or the style of their illuminations. Colbert. 2844, or 33 of the Gospels (facsim. No. 39), is attributed to the eleventh century, and Burney 21 (No. 15)[1], is dated A.D. 1292, and afford good examples of their respective dates. *Beta* (l. 1 letter 4), *when joined to other letters*, is barely distinguishable from *upsilon*[2]; *nu* is even nearer to *mu*; the tall forms of *eta* and *epsilon* are very graceful, the whole style elegant and, after a little practice, easily read. Burney 22 (facsimile No. 37) is dated about the same time, A. D. 1319, and the four Biblical lines much resemble Burney 21[3]. In the fourteenth century a careless style came into fashion, of which Cod. Leicestrensis (No. 40) is an exaggerated instance, and during this century and the next our manuscripts, though not devoid of a certain beauty of appearance, are too full of arbitrary and elaborate contractions to be conveniently read. The formidable list of abbreviations and ligatures represented in Donaldson's Greek Grammar (p. 20, third edition)[4] originated at this period in the perverse ingenuity of the Greek emigrants in the West of Europe, who subsisted by their skill as copyists;

---

[1] The writer of Burney 21 (r^scr) A. D. 1292 (Evan. 571), ὁ ταπεινος Θεοδωρος ἁγιωπετριτης ταχα και καλλιγραφος as he calls himself (that is, as I once supposed, monk of the Convent of Sancta Petra at Constantinople, short-hand and fair writer), was the scribe of at least *five* more copies of Scripture now extant: Birch's Havn. 1, A.D. 1278 (Evan. 234); Evan. 90, A.D. 1293; Evan. 543, A.D. 1295; Scholz's Evan. 412, A.D. 1301; Evan. 74, *undated*. To this list Franz Delitzsch (1813–1890) (Zeitschr. f. luth. Theol. 1863, ii, Abhandlungen, pp. 217, 218) adds from Matthaei, Synaxarion in Mosc. Syn. Typograph. xxvi. A.D. 1295, and recognizes *Hagios Petros*, the country of Theodoros, as a town in the Morea, on the borders of Arcadia, from whose school students have attended his own lectures at Erlangen.

[2] Hence in the later uncials, some of which must therefore have been copied from earlier cursives, B and Υ (which might seem to have no resemblance) are sometimes confounded: e.g. in Parham 18 (A. D. 980), υ for β, Luke vi. 34; β for υ, John x. 1, especially where β begins or ends a line: e. g. Evan. 59, John vii. 35. Evan. 59 has β for υ very often, yet there is no extra trace that it was copied from an uncial.

[3] The full signature not easily deciphered is ἐτελειώθη τὸ παρὸν ἅγιον εὐαγγέλιον κατὰ τὴν κ̄ς τοῦ Ιαννουαρίου μηνὸς τῆς [?] ω̄ κ̄ ς ἐγχρονίας. Presuming that ϛ is suppressed before ω̄ κ̄ ς this is 6827 of the Greeks, A. D. 1319.

[4] Compare also Buttmann's Greek Grammar (Robinson's translation) p. 467; Bast in (Schaefer's Gregorius Corinthius) tabb. ad fin.; Gardthausen, Palaeographie, p. 248, &c.

and these pretty puzzles (for such they now are to many a fair classical scholar), by being introduced into early printed books[1], have largely helped to withdraw them from use in modern times.

12. We have now to describe the practice of Biblical manuscripts as regards the insertion of ι forming a diphthong with the long vowels *eta* and *omega*, also with *alpha* long, whether by being *ascript*, i. e. written by their side, or *subscript*, i. e. written under them. In the earliest inscriptions and in the papyri of Thebes ι *ascript* (the *iota* not smaller than other letters) is invariably found. In the petition to Ptolemy Philometor (*above*, p. 41) it occurs four times in the first line, three times in the third: in the fragments of Hyperides it is perpetually though not always read, even where (especially with verbs) it has no rightful place, e. g. ετωι και αντιβολωι (facsimile No. 9, ll. 3, 4) for αἰτῶ καὶ ἀντιβολῶ. A little before the Christian era it began to grow obsolete, probably from its being lost in pronunciation. In the Herculanean Philodemus (the possible limits of whose date are from B. C. 50 to A. D. 79) as in Evann. 556, 604 (Matt. ii. 12, 13), it is often dropped, though more usually written. In Codd. Vaticanus and Sinaiticus it is probably not found, and from this period it almost disappears from Biblical uncials[2]; in Cureton's Homer, of the fifth or perhaps of the sixth century, ι *ascript* is sometimes neglected, but usually inserted; sometimes also ι is placed *above* H or Ω, an arrangement neither neat nor convenient. With the cursive character ι *ascript* came in again, as may be seen from the subscriptions in the Bodleian Euclid and Plato (p. 42, note 1). The *semicursive* fragment of St. Paul's Epistles in red letters (M of St. Paul, Plate xii No. 34), used for the binding of Harleian 5613, contains ι *ascript* twice, but I have tried in vain to verify Griesbach's statement (Symbol. Crit. ii. p. 166) that it has ι *subscript* ' bis tantum aut ter.' I can find no such instance in

---

[1] Thus the type cast for the Royal Printing Office at Paris, and used by Robert Stephen, is said to have been modelled on the style of the calligrapher Angelus Vergecius, from whose skill arose the expression 'he writes like an angel.' Codd. 296 of the Gospels, 124 of the Acts, 151 of St. Paul are in his hand.

[2] Yet Tischendorf (N.T. 1859, Proleg. p. cxxxiii) cites ηδισαν from Cod. Bezae (Mark i. 34), ξυλωι (Luke xxiii. 31) from Cod. Cyprius, ωι from Cod. U (Matt. xxv. 15) and Cod. Λ (Luke vii. 4). Add Cod. Bezae πατρωιου Acts xxii. 3, Scrivener's edition, Introd. p. xix. Bentley's nephew speaks of ι *ascript* as in the first hand of Cod. B, but he seems to have been mistaken.

these leaves. The cursive manuscripts, speaking generally, either entirely omit both forms, or, if they give either, far more often neglect than insert them. Cod. 1 of the Gospels exhibits the *ascript* ι. Of forty-three codices now in England which have been examined with a view to this matter, twelve have no vestige of either fashion, fifteen represent the *ascript* use, nine the *subscript* exclusively, while the few that remain exhibit both indifferently[1]. The earliest cursive copy ascertained to exhibit ι *subscript* is Matthaei's r (Apoc. 50[2] [x]), and after that the Cod. Ephesius (Evan. 71), dated A.D. 1160. The *subscript* ι came much into vogue during the fifteenth century, and thus was adopted in printed books.

13. Breathings (*spiritus*) and accents[2] were not applied systematically to Greek Texts before the seventh century. But a practice prevailed in that and the succeeding century of inserting them in older manuscripts, where they were absent *primâ manu*. That such was done in many instances (e. g. in Codd. Vatican. and Coislin. 202 or H of St. Paul) appears clearly from the fact that the passages which the scribe who retouched the old letters for any cause left unaltered, are destitute of these marks, though they appear in all other places. Cod. ℵ exhibits breathings, apparently by the original scribe, in Tobit vi. 9; Gal. v. 21 only. The case of Cod. Alexandrinus is less easy. Though the rest of the book has neither breathings (except a few here and there) nor accents, the first four lines of *each* column of the book of Genesis (see facsimile No. 12), which are written in red, are fully furnished with them. These marks Baber, who edited the Old Testament portion of Cod. A, pronounced to be by a second hand (Notae, p. 1); Sir Frederick Madden, a more competent judge, declares them the work of the original scribe (Madden's Silvestre, Vol. i. p. 194, note), and after repeated examination we know not how to dissent from his view[3]. So too in the Sarravian Pentateuch of the fifth century

---

[1] In B-C iii. 10 (*dated* 1430), the whole manuscript being written by the same hand, we have ι *ascript* twenty-five times up to Luke i. 75, then on the same page ι *subscript* in Luke i. 77 and eighty-five times afterwards: the two usages are nowhere mixed. In Evan. 558, *subscript* and *ascript* are mixed in the same page, Luc. i. 75, 77.

[2] The invention of breathings, accents, and stops is attributed to Aristophanes of Byzantium, 260 B.C.

[3] See below vol. ii. c. ix. 9. note, end. Dr. Scrivener appears not to have formed a positive opinion, which indeed in some of these cases is hardly possible.

we read τονΫν (Lev. xi. 7) by the first hand. The Cureton palimpsest of Homer also has them, though they are occasionally obliterated, and some few are evidently inserted by a corrector; the case is nearly so with the Milan Homer edited by Mai; and the same must be stated of the Vienna Dioscorides (Silvestre, No. 62), whose date is fixed by internal evidence to about A.D. 500. In the papyrus fragment of the Psalms, now in the British Museum, the accents are very accurate, and the work of the original scribe. These facts, and others like these, may make us hesitate to adopt the notion generally received among scholars on the authority of Montfaucon (Palaeogr. Graec. p. 33), that breathings and accents were not introduced *primâ manu* before the seventh or eighth century; although up to that period, no doubt, they were placed very incorrectly, and often omitted altogether. The breathings are much the more ancient and important of the two. The *spiritus lenis* indeed may be a mere invention of the Alexandrian grammarians of the second or third century before Christ, but the *spiritus asper* is in fact the substitute for a real letter (H) which appears on the oldest inscriptions; its original shape being the first half of the H (⊢), of which the second half was subsequently adopted for the *lenis* (⊣). This form is sometimes found in manuscripts of about the eleventh century (e.g. Lebanon, B.M. Addit. 11300 or k^{scr}, and usually in Lambeth 1178 or d^{scr}) ed. of 1550, but even in the Cod. Alexandrinus the comma and inverted comma are several times substituted to represent the *lenis* and *asper* respectively (facsimile No. 12): and at a later period this last was the ordinary, though not quite the invariable, mode of expressing the breathings. Aristophanes of Byzantium (keeper of the famous Library at Alexandria under Ptolemy Euergetes, about B.C. 240), though probably not the inventor of the Greek accents, was the first to arrange them in a system. Accentuation must have been a welcome aid to those who employed Greek as a learned, though not as their vernacular tongue, and is so convenient and suggestive that no modern scholar can afford to dispense with its familiar use: yet not being, like the rough breathing, an essential portion of the language, it was but slowly brought into general vogue. It would seem that in Augustine's age [354–430] the distinction between the smooth and rough breathing in the manuscripts was just such a point as a careful reader would mark, a hasty one overlook[1]. Hence it is not surprising that though these marks are entirely absent both from the Theban and Herculanean papyri, a few breathings are apparently by the first hand in Cod. Borgianus or T (Tischendorf, N. T. 1859, Proleg. p. cxxxi). One rough breathing is just visible in that early palimpsest of St. John's Gospel, I^b or N^b. Such as appear, together with some accents, in the Coislin Octateuch of the sixth or seventh century, may not the less be *primâ manu* because many pages are destitute of them; those of Cod. Claromontanus, which were once deemed original, are now pronounced by its editor Tischendorf to be a later addition. Cod. N, the purple fragment so often spoken of already, exhibits *primâ manu* over certain vowels a kind of smooth breathing or slight acute accent, sometimes little larger than a point, but inserted on no intelligible principle, so far as we can see, and far oftener omitted entirely. All copies of Scripture which have not been specified, down to the end of the seventh century, are quite destitute of breathings and accents. An important manuscript of the eighth or ninth century, Cod. L or Paris 62 of the Gospels, has them for the most part, but not always; though often in the wrong place, and at times in utter defiance of all grammatical rules. Cod. B of the Apocalypse, however, though of the same age, has breathings and accents as constantly and correctly as most. Codices of the ninth century, with the exception of three written in the West of Europe (Codd. Augiensis or Paul F, Sangallensis or Δ of the Gospels, and Boernerianus or Paul G, which will be particularly described afterwards), are all accompanied with these marks in full, though often set down without any precise rule, so far as our experience has enabled us to observe. The uncial Evangelistaria (e.g. Arundel 547; Parham 18; Harleian 5598), especially, are much addicted to prefixing the *spiritus asper* improperly; chiefly, perhaps, to words beginning with H, so that documents of that age are but slender authorities on such points. Of the cursives the general tendency is to be more and more accurate as regards the accentua-

[1] He is speaking (Quaestion. super Genes. clxii) of the difference between ῥάβδου αὐτοῦ and ῥάβδου αὑτοῦ, Gen. xlvii. 31. 'Fallit enim eos verbum Graecum, quod eisdem literis scribitur, sive *ejus*, sive *suae* : sed accentus [he must mean the breathings] dispares sunt, et ab eis, qui ista noverunt, in codicibus non contemnuntur' (Opera, Tom. iv. p. 53, ed. 1586, Lugdun.); adding that 'suae' *might* be expressed by ἑαυτοῦ.

tion, the later the date: but this is only a general rule, as some that are early are as careful, and certain of the latest as negligent, as can well be imagined. All of them are partial to placing accents or breathings over both parts of a word compounded with a preposition (e.g. ἐπισυνάξαι), and on the other hand often drop them between a preposition and its case (e.g. ἐπάροτρον).

14. The punctuation in early times was very simple. In the papyri of Hyperides there are no stops at all, in the Herculanean rolls exceeding few: Codd. Sinaiticus and Vaticanus (the latter very rarely by the first hand) have a single point here and there on a level with the top of the letters, and occasionally a very small break in the continuous uncials, with or (as always in Cod. I^b of the sixth century) without the point, to denote a pause in the sense. Codd. A N have the same point a little oftener; in Codd. C W^a (Paris 314) Z and the Cotton Genesis the single point stands indiscriminately at the head, middle, or foot of the letters, while in E (Basil. A. N. iii. 12) of the Gospels and B of the Apocalypse, as in Cod. Marchalianus of the Prophets (sixth or seventh century), this change in the position of the point indicates a full-stop, half stop, or comma respectively. In Cod. L, of the same date as Codd. E and B (Apoc.), besides the full point we have the comma (:.) and semicolon (::), with a cross also for a stop. In Codd. Y Θ^a (of about the eighth century) the single point has its various powers as in Cod. E, &c., but besides this are double, treble, and in Cod. Y quadruple, points with different powers. In late uncials, especially Evangelistaria, the chief stop is a cross, often in red (e.g. Arund. 547); while in Harleian 5598 ⁊ seems to be the note of interrogation[1]. When the continuous writing came to be broken up into separate words (of which Cod. Augiensis in the ninth century affords one of the earliest examples) the single point was intended to be placed after the last letter of each word, on a level with the middle of the letters. But even in this copy it is often omitted in parts, and in Codd. ΔG, written on the same plan, more frequently still. Our statements refer only to the Greek portions of these

---

[1] In the Gale Evangelistarium (Trin. Coll. Camb. O. 4. 22) the interrogative clause is set between two such marks in red. Hence it seems not so much a stop as a vocal note. In the Armenian and Spanish languages the note of interrogation is set before the interrogative clause, and very conveniently too.

PUNCTUATION. 49

copies; the Latin semicolon (;) and the note of interrogation (?) occur in their Latin versions. The Greek interrogation (;) first occurs about the ninth century, and (,) used as a stop a little later. The Bodleian Genesis of this date, or a little earlier, uses (,) also as an interrogative: so in later times B–C. iii. 5 [xii], and Evan. 556 [xii]. In the earliest cursives the system of punctuation is much the same as that of printed books: the English colon (:) not being much used, but the upper single point in its stead[1]. In a few cursives (e. g. Gonville or 59 of the Gospels), this upper point, set in a larger space, stands also for a full stop: indeed (·) is the only stop found in Tischendorf's lo^ti or 61 of the Acts (Brit. Mus. Add. 20,003): while (;) and (·) are often confused in 440 of the Gospels (Cantab. Mm. 6. 9). The English comma, placed above a letter, is used for the apostrophus, which occurs in the very oldest uncials, especially at the end of proper names, or to separate compounds (e. g. απ' ορφανισθεντες in Cod. Clarom.), or when the word ends in ξ or ρ (e. g. σαρξ' in Cod. B, θυγατηρ' in Codd. Sinait. and A, χειρ' in Cod. A, ὡσπερ' in the Dioscorides, A.D. 500), or even to divide syllables (e. g. συριγ'γας in Cod. Frid.-August., πολ'λα, κατεστραμ'μενη, αναγ'γελι in Cod. Sinaiticus). In Cod. Z it is found only after αλλ and μεθ, but in Z's Isaiah it indicates other elisions (e. g. επ). This mark is more rare in Cod. Ephraemi than in some others, but is used more or less by all, and is found after εξ, or ουχ, and a few like words, even in the most recent cursives. In Cod. Bezae and others it assumes the shape of > rather than that of a comma.

15. Abbreviated words are perhaps least met with in Cod. Vatican., but even it has θσ̄, κσ̄, ισ̄, χσ̄, π̄να for θεός, κύριος, Ιησοῦς, χριστός, πνεῦμα, &c. and their cases. The Cotton Genesis has θο̄υ ch. i. 27 by a later hand, but θεου ch. xli. 38. Besides these Codd. Sinaiticus, Alex., Ephraemi and the rest supply ᾱνοσ, ο̄υνοσ, π̄ηρ (π̄ρ Cod. Sarrav. Num. xii. 14, &c., π̄ηρ Cod.

---

[1] The earliest known example of the use of two dots occurs in the Artemisia papyrus at Vienna (Maunde Thompson, p. 69), and other early instances are found in a letter of Dionysius to Ptolemy about B.C. 160, published by the French Institute, 1865, in 'Papyrus grecs du Musée du Louvre,' &c. tom. xviii. 2° ptie, pl. xxxiv, pap. 49, and in fragments of the Phaedo of Plato discovered at Gurob. The same double points are also occasionally set in the larger spaces of Codd. Sinaiticus, Sarravianus, and Bezae, but in the last-named copy for the most part in a later hand.

50   GREEK MANUSCRIPTS.

Rossanensis), $\overline{\mu\eta\rho}$, $\overline{\iota\lambda\eta\mu}$ or $\overline{\iota\eta\lambda\mu}$ or $\overline{\iota\lambda\mu}$ or $\overline{\iota\eta\mu}$ ($\overline{\iota\epsilon\lambda\mu}$ Cod. Sarrav.), $\overline{\iota\eta\lambda}$ or $\overline{\iota\sigma\lambda}$ or $\overline{\iota\sigma\eta\lambda}$, $\overline{\delta\alpha\delta}$, and some of them $\overline{\sigma\eta\rho}$ for $\sigma\omega\tau\eta\rho$, $\overset{\theta}{\overline{\nu\sigma}}$ for $\upsilon\iota\acute{o}s$, $\overline{\pi\alpha\rho\nu os}$ for $\pi\alpha\rho\theta\acute{\epsilon}\nu os$ (Bodleian Genesis), $\overline{\sigma\rho\sigma}$ for $\sigma\tau\alpha\upsilon\rho\acute{o}s$: Cod. L has $\pi\nu\epsilon^{\nu}$, and Cod. Vatican. in the *Old* Testament $\overline{\alpha\nu os}$ and $\overline{\pi\rho\sigma}$ occasionally, $\overline{\iota\sigma\lambda}$ and $\overline{\iota\lambda\eta\mu}$ or $\overline{\iota\lambda\mu}$ often [1]; Evan. 604 has $\overline{\sigma\eta\rho}$ for $\sigma\omega\tau\acute{\eta}\rho$, and $\acute{\epsilon}\theta\nu$ for $\acute{\epsilon}\theta\nu\hat{\omega}\nu$ [2]. Cod. Bezae always writes at length $\alpha\nu\theta\rho\omega\pi os$, $\mu\eta\tau\eta\rho$, $\upsilon\iota os$, $\sigma\omega\tau\eta\rho$, $o\upsilon\rho\alpha\nu os$, $\delta\alpha\upsilon\epsilon\iota\delta$, $\iota\sigma\rho\alpha\eta\lambda$, $\iota\epsilon\rho o\upsilon\sigma\alpha\lambda\eta\mu$; but abridges the sacred names into $\overline{\chi\rho\sigma}$, $\overline{\iota\eta\sigma}$ [3] &c. and their cases, as very frequently, but by no means invariably, do the kindred Codd. Augiens., Sangall., and Boerner. Cod. Z seldom abridges, and all copies often set $\upsilon\iota os$ in full. A few dots sometimes supply the place of the line denoting abbreviation (e. g. $\overset{\cdot\cdot}{\theta\sigma}$ Cotton Genesis, $\overset{\cdot\cdot}{\alpha\nu o\sigma}$ Colbert. Pentateuch). A straight line over the last letter of a line, sometimes over any vowel, indicates N (or also M in the Latin of Codd. Bezae and Claromont.) in all the Biblical uncials, but is placed only over numerals in the Herculanean rolls: κ_1, τ_1, and less often θ_1 for $\kappa\alpha\iota$ (see p. 16, note 1), -$\tau\alpha\iota$, -$\theta\alpha\iota$ are met with in Cod. Sinaiticus and all later except Cod. Z: Ȣ for $o\upsilon$ chiefly in Codd. L, Augiensis, B of the Apocalypse, and the more recent uncials. Such *compendia scribendi* as ꝫ in the Herculanean rolls (above p. 33) occur mostly at the end of lines: that form, with M°Y (No. 11 a, l. 4), and a few more even in the Cod. Sinaiticus; in Cod. Sarrav. Ḿ stands for both $\mu o\upsilon$ and $\mu o\iota$; in Cureton's Homer we have Πˢ for $\pi o\upsilon s$, Cˢ for -$\sigma\alpha s$ and such like. In later books they are more numerous and complicated, particularly in cursive writing. The terminations ° for os, ¯ for ν, ` or " for $o\nu$, " for $\alpha\iota s$, ~ for $\omega\nu$ or ω or ωs, ˢ for ηs, ᵛ for $o\upsilon$ are familiar; besides others, peculiar to one or a few copies, e. g. τy for $\tau\tau$ in Burney 19, and Burdett-Coutts i. 4, h for $\alpha\upsilon$, b for $\epsilon\rho$, ¯ for α, ⱴ for $\alpha\rho$ in the Emmanuel College copy of the Epistles (Paul 30, No. 33), and : for α, C or σ for $\alpha\nu$, ✓ for αs in Parham 17 of the Apocalypse. Other more rare abridgements are ʽʽ for $\epsilon\iota s$ in Wake 12, ✓ (Burdett-Coutts I. 4) or < or ᵃ for $\epsilon\nu$, ·· for ι and ö for $\epsilon\sigma$ (B-C. iii. 37), ∵ for $\epsilon\sigma$ and ⁻ϵ for $\sigma\epsilon$ and $\frac{\tau}{\eta}$ for $\tau\eta\sigma$ (B-C.

---

[1] Abbot, ubi supra.
[2] Hoskier, Cod. 604, p. xiii.
[3] Even Codex Sinaiticus has $\overline{\iota\eta\nu}$ and $\overline{\iota\nu}$ in consecutive lines (Apoc. xxii. 20, 21), and $\overline{\chi\rho\nu}$ Rom. vii. 4.

ii. 26), π for ται and Ϛ for ωσ (B-C. iii. 42), ∧ for ην (B-C. iii. 10), Ʊ for ισ and ꝯ or ⳍ for ουν (B-C. iii. 41), Λ̈ for ιν or ἐστι, ͨ for αν, ͮ or ᵈ for οις, ͝ for ας, ⁊ or ᷒ for οις, ͭ for τε or -τες or την or τον, " for ειν, ἐ for ους or ως (Gale O. iv. 22). The mark > is not only met with in the Herculanean rolls, but in the Hyperides (facsimile 9, l. 6), in Codd. Vaticanus and Sinaiticus, the two Pentateuchs, Codd. Augiensis, Sangall. and Boernerianus, and seems merely designed to fill up vacant space, like the flourishes in a legal instrument [1].

16. Capital letters of a larger size than the rest at the beginning of clauses, &c. are freely met with in all documents excepting in the oldest papyri, the Herculanean rolls, Codd. Vaticanus, Sinaiticus, the Colbert Pentateuch, Isaiah in Cod. Z, and one or two fragments besides [2]. Their absence is a proof of high antiquity. Yet even in Codd. Vaticanus, Sinaiticus, and Sarravianus, which is the other part of the Colbert Pentateuch (in the first most frequently in the earlier portions of the Old Testament), the initial letter stands a little outside the line of writing after a break in the sense, whether the preceding line had been quite filled up or not. Such breaks occur more regularly in Codex Bezae, as will appear when we come to describe it [3]. Smaller capitals occur in the middle of lines in Codd. Bezae and Marchalianus, of the sixth and seventh centuries respectively. Moreover, all copies of whatever date are apt to crowd small

---

[1] See below p. 64, note 4.

[2] 'Fragmenta pauca evangelii Johannis palimpsesta Londinensia [Evan. I^b or N^b]. In ceteris haec fere tria: Dionis Cassii fragmenta Vaticana—vix enim qui in his videntur speciem majorum litterarum habere revera differunt—item fragmenta palimpsesta [Phaëthontis] Euripidis Claromontana et fragmenta Menandri Porphiriana' (Tischendorf, Cod. Vatic. Proleg. p. xviii, 1867).

[3] The English word *paragraph* is derived from the παραγραφαί, which are often straight lines, placed in the margin to indicate a pause in the sense. Professor Abbot, ubi supra, p. 195, alleges not a few instances where these dashes are thus employed. A specimen is given in Scrivener's Cod. Sinaiticus, facsimile 3: see his Cod. Sin., Introduction, p. xl and note. Thus also they appear in Cod. Sarravianus (Tischendorf, Mon. sacra ined. vol. iii. pp. xiv, xx). In Cod Bezae Γ is set in the margin forty-nine times by a later hand, and must be designed for the same purpose, though the mark sometimes occurs where we should hardly look for it (Scrivener, Cod. Bezae, Introduction, p. xxviii and note). In Cod. Marchalianus the dash stands over the capital at the beginning of a line, or over the first letter where there is no capital. Lastly, in Codd. Vatic. and Sinait. Γ is sometimes set in the middle of a line to indicate a paragraph break, followed by ⌐ in the margin of the next line.

letters into the end of a line to save room, and if these small letters preserve the form of the larger, it is reasonable to conclude that the scribe is writing in a natural hand, not an assumed one, and the argument for the antiquity of such a document, derived from the shape of its letters, thus becomes all the stronger. The continuous form of writing separate words must have prevailed in manuscripts long after it was obsolete in common life: Cod. Claromont., whose text is continuous even in its Latin version, divides the words in the inscriptions and subscriptions to the several books.

17. The stichometry of the sacred books has next to be considered. The Greeks and Romans measured the contents of their MSS. by lines, not only in poetry, but also artificially in prose for a standard line of fifteen or sixteen syllables, called by the earliest writers ἔπος, afterwards στίχος[1]. Not only do Athanasius [d. 373], Gregory Nyssen [d. 396], Epiphanius [d. 403], and Chrysostom [d. 407] inform us that in their time the Book of Psalms was already divided into στίχοι, while Jerome [d. 420?] testifies the same for the prophecies of Isaiah; but Origen also [d. 254] speaks of the second and third Epistles of St. John as both of them not exceeding one hundred στίχοι, of St. Paul's Epistles as consisting of few, St. John's first Epistle as of very few (Euseb. Hist. Eccles. vi. 25, cited by Tischendorf, Cod. Sinait., Proleg. p. xxi, note 2, 1863). Even the apocryphal letter of our Lord to Abgarus is described as ὀλιγοστίχου μέν, πολυδυνάμου δὲ ἐπιστολῆς (Euseb. H. E. i. 13): while Eustathius of Antioch in the fourth century reckoned 135 στίχοι between John viii. 59 and x. 41. More general is the use of the word in Ephraem the Syrian [d. 378], Ὅταν δὲ ἀναγινώσκῃς, ἐπιμελῶς καὶ ἐμπόνως ἀναγίνωσκε, ἐν πολλῇ καταστάσει διερχόμενος τὸν στίχον (tom. iii. 101). As regards the

---

[1] Many other examples of the use of στίχοι and versus in this sense will be found in that admirable monument of exact learning, now so little read, Prideaux Connections, An. 446. Stichometry can be traced back to nearly a century before Callimachus, who (B.C. 260) has been credited with the invention (Palaeography, p. 79). The term στίχοι, like the Latin versus, originally referring whether to rows of trees, or to the oars in the trireme (Virg. Aen. v. 119), would naturally come to be applied to lines of poetry, and in this sense it is used by Pindar (ἐπέων στίχες Pyth. iv. 100) and also by Theocritus (γράψον καὶ τόδε γράμμα, τύ σοι στίχοισι χαράξω Idyl. xxiii. 46), if the common reading be correct.

Psalms, we may see their arrangement for ourselves in Codd. Vaticanus and Sinaiticus, wherein, according to the true principles of Hebrew poetry, the verses do not correspond in metre or quantity of syllables, but in the parallelism or relationship subsisting between the several members of the same sentence or stanza[1]. Such στίχοι were therefore not 'space-lines,' but 'sense-lines.' It seems to have occurred to Euthalius, a deacon of Alexandria, as it did long afterwards to Bishop Jebb when he wrote his 'Sacred Literature,' that a large portion of the New Testament might be divided into στίχοι on the same principles: and that even where that distribution should prove but artificial, it would guide the public reader in the management of his voice, and remove the necessity for an elaborate system of punctuation. Such, therefore, we conceive to be the use and design of stichometry, as applied to the Greek Testament by Euthalius[2], whose edition of the Acts and Epistles was published A.D. 490. Who distributed the στίχοι of the Gospels (which are in truth better suited for such a process than the Epistles) does not appear. Although but few manuscripts now exist that are written στοιχηδόν or στιχηρῶς (a plan which consumed too much vellum to become general), we read in many copies, added usually to the subscription at the foot of each of the books of the New Testament, a calculation of the number of στίχοι it contained, the numbers being sufficiently unlike to show that the arrangement was not the same in all codices, yet near enough to prove that they were divided on the same principle[3]. In the few documents written στιχηρῶς that survive, the length of the clauses is very unequal; some (e.g. Cod. Bezae, *see* the description below

---

[1] That we have rightly understood Epiphanius' notion of the στίχοι is evident from his own language respecting Psalm cxli. 1, wherein he prefers the addition made by the Septuagint to the second clause, because by so doing its authors ἀχώλωτον ἐποίησαν τὸν στίχον: so that the passage should run 'O Lord, I cry unto Thee, make haste unto me ‖ Give ear to the voice of my request,' τῆς δεήσεώς μου to complete the rhythm. This whole subject is admirably worked out in Suicer, Thesaur. Eccles. tom. ii. pp. 1025-37.

[2] In the Epistles of St. Paul, Euthalius seems to have followed a Syrian writer. Gregory, Prolegomena, p. 113; Zacagnius, Collectanea Monumentorum Veterum Ecclesiae, Rome, A.D. 1698, pp. 404, 409.

[3] At the end of 2 Thess., in a hand which Tischendorf states to be very ancient, but not that of the original scribe, the Codex Sinaiticus has στιχων ρπ [180; the usual number is 106]: at the end of Rom., 1 Cor., 1 Thess., and the Catholic Epistles, there is no such note; but in all the other Pauline Epistles the στίχοι are numbered.

and the facsimile, No. 42) containing as much in a line as might be conveniently read aloud in a breath, others (e.g. Cod. Laud. of the Acts, Plate x. No. 25) having only one or two words in a line. The Cod. Claromontanus (facsim. No. 41) in this respect lies between those extremes, and the fourth great example of this class (Cod. Coislin. 202, H of St. Paul), of the sixth century, has one of its few surviving pages (of sixteen lines each) arranged *literatim* as follows (1 Cor. x. 22, &c.): εσμεν | παντα μοι εξεστι | αλλ ου παντα συμφερει | παντα μοι εξεστιν | αλλ ου παντα οικοδομει | μηδεισ το εαυτου ζη|(*ob necessitatem spatii*) τειτω | αλλα το του ετερου | παν το εν μακελλω πω | (*ob necessitatem*) λουμενον | εσθιετε μηδεν ανα | κρινωντες δια την | συνειδησιν | του γαρ κ̄ῡ η γη και το πλη | ρωμα αυτης. Other manuscripts written στιχηρῶς are Matthaei's V of the eighth century (though with verses like ours more than with ordinary στίχοι), Bengel's Uffenbach 3 of St. John (Evan. 101), Alter's Forlos. 29 (36 of the Apocalypse), and, as it would seem, the Cod. Sangallensis Δ. In Cod. Claromontanus there are scarcely any stops (the middle point being chiefly reserved to follow abridgements or numerals), the stichometry being of itself an elaborate scheme of punctuation; but the longer στίχοι of Cod. Bezae are often divided by a single point.

18. In using manuscripts of the Greek Testament, we must carefully note whether a reading is *primâ manu* (*) or by some subsequent corrector (**). It will often happen that these last are utterly valueless, having been inserted even from printed copies by a modern owner (like some marginal variations of the Cod. Leicestrensis)[1], and such as these really ought not to have been extracted by collators at all; while others by the second hand are almost as weighty, for age and goodness, as the text itself. All these points are explained by critical editors for each document separately; in fact to discriminate the different corrections in regard to their antiquity and importance is often the most difficult portion of such editor's task (e.g. in Codd. Bezae and Claromontanus), and one on which he often feels it hard to satisfy his own judgement. Corrections by the original scribe, or

---

[1] So the margin of Gale's Evan. 66 contains readings cited by Mill and his followers, which a hand of the sixteenth century took, some of them from the Leicester manuscript, others from early editions.

by a contemporary reviser, where they can be satisfactorily distinguished, must be regarded as a portion of the testimony of the manuscript itself, inasmuch as every carefully prepared copy was reviewed and compared (ἀντεβλήθη), if not by the writer himself, by a skilful person appointed for the task (ὁ διορθῶν, ὁ διορθωτής), whose duty it was to amend manifest errors, sometimes also to insert ornamental capitals in places which had been reserved for them; in later times (and as some believe at a very early period) to set in stops, breathings and accents; in copies destined for ecclesiastical use to arrange the musical notes that were to guide the intonation of the reader. Notices of this kind of revision are sometimes met with at the end of the best manuscripts. Such is the note in Cod. H of St. Paul: εγραψα και εξεθεμην προσ το εν Καισαρια αντιγραφον τησ βιβλιοθηκησ του αγιου Παμφιλου, the same library of the Martyr Pamphilus to which the scribe of the Cod. Frid.-August. resorted for his model[1]; and that in Birch's most valuable Urbino-Vatican. 2 (157 of the Gospels), written for the Emperor John II (1118–1143), wherein at the end of the first Gospel we read κατὰ Ματθαῖον ἐγράφη καὶ ἀντεβλήθη ἐκ τῶν ἐν ἱεροσολύμοις παλαιῶν ἀντιγράφων τῶν ἐν ἁγίω ὄρει [Athos] ἀποκειμένων: similar subscriptions are appended to the other Gospels. See also Evan. Λ. 20, 164, 262, 300, 376; Act. 15, 83, in the list of manuscripts below.

[1] The following subscription to the book of Ezra (and a very similar one follows Esther) in the Cod. Frid.-August. (fol. 13. 1), though in a hand of the seventh century, will show the care bestowed on the most ancient copies of the Septuagint: Αντεβληθη προσ παλαιωτατον λιαν αντιγραφον δεδιορθωμενον χειρι του αγιου μαρτυροσ Παμφιλου· ὑπερ αντιγραφον προσ τω τελει υποσημειωσισ τισ ἰδιοχειροσ αυτου ὑπεκειτο εχουσα οντωσ· μετελημφθη και διορθωθη προσ τα εξαπλα ωριγενουσ· Αντωνινοσ αντεβαλεν· Παμφιλοσ διορθωσα. Tregelles suggests that the work of the διορθωτὴς or *corrector* was probably of a critical character, the office of the ἀντιβάλλων or *comparer* being rather to eliminate mere clerical errors (Treg. Horne's Introd., vol. iv. p. 85). Compare Tischendorf, Cod. Sinait. Proleg. p. xxii.

CHAPTER III.

DIVISIONS OF THE TEXT, AND OTHER PARTICULARS.

WE have next to give some account of ancient divisions of the text, as found in manuscripts of the New Testament; and these must be carefully noted by the student, since few copies are without one or more of them.

1. So far as we know at present, the oldest sections still extant are those of the Codex Vaticanus. These seem to have been formed for the purpose of reference, and a new one always commences where there is some break in the sense. Many, however, at least in the Gospels, consist of but one of our modern verses, and they are so unequal in length as to be rather inconvenient for actual use. In the four Gospels only the marginal numerals are in red, St. Matthew containing 170 of these divisions, St. Mark 62, St. Luke 152, St. John 80. In the Acts of the Apostles are two sets of sections, thirty-six longer and in an older hand, sixty-nine smaller and more recent[1]. Each of these also begins after a break in the sense, but they are quite independent of each other, as a larger section will sometimes commence in the middle of a smaller, the latter being in no wise a subdivision of the former. Thus the greater Γ opens Acts ii. 1, in the middle of the lesser β, which extends from Acts i. 15 to ii. 4. The first forty-two of the lesser chapters, down to Acts xv. 40, are found also with slight variations in the margin of Codex Sinaiticus, written by a very old hand. As in most manuscripts, so in Codex Vaticanus, the Catholic Epistles follow the Acts, and in them also and in St. Paul's Epistles there are two sets of sections, only that in the Epistles the older sections are the more numerous. The Pauline Epistles are reckoned throughout as one book in the

---

[1] 'Simile aliquid invenitur in codice Arabico epp. Pauli anno 892, p. Chr., quem ex oriente Petropolin pertulimus.' Tischendorf, Cod. Vat. Proleg. p. xxx. n. 3.

elder notation, with however this remarkable peculiarity, that though in the Cod. Vatican. itself the Epistle to the Hebrews stands next after the second to the Thessalonians, *and on the same leaf with it*, the sections are arranged as if it stood between the Epistles to the Galatians and Ephesians. For whereas that to the Galatians ends with § 58, that to the Ephesians begins with § 70, and the numbers proceed regularly down to § 93, with which the second to the Thessalonians ends. The Epistle to the Hebrews which then follows opens with § 59; the last section extant (§ 64) begins at Heb. ix. 11, and the manuscript ends abruptly at καθα ver. 14. It plainly appears, then, that the sections of the Codex Vaticanus must have been copied from some yet older document, in which the Epistle to the Hebrews preceded that to the Ephesians. It will be found hereafter (vol. ii) that in the Thebaic version the Epistle to the Hebrews preceded that to the Galatians, instead of following it, as here. For a list of the more modern divisions in the Epistles, see the Table given below. The Vatican sections of the Gospels have also been discovered by Tregelles in one other copy, the palimpsest Codex Zacynthius of St. Luke (Ξ), which he published in 1861.

2. Hardly less ancient, and indeed ascribed by some to Tatian the Harmonist, the disciple of Justin Martyr, is the division of the Gospels into larger chapters or κεφάλαια *majora* [1]. It may be noticed that in none of the four Gospels does the first chapter stand at its commencement. In St. Matthew chapter A begins at chap. ii. verse 1, and has for its title περὶ τῶν μάγων: in St. Mark at chap. i. ver. 23 περὶ τοῦ δαιμονιζομένου: in St. Luke at chap ii. ver. 1 περὶ τῆς ἀπογραφῆς: in St. John at chap. ii. ver. 1 περὶ τοῦ ἐν Κανᾶ γάμου. Mill accounts for this circumstance by supposing that in the first copies the titles at the head of each Gospel were reserved till last for more splendid illumination, and were thus eventually forgotten (Proleg. N. T. § 355); Griesbach holds, that the general inscriptions of each Gospel, Κατὰ Ματθαῖον, Κατὰ Μάρκον, &c., were regarded as the special titles of the first chapters also. On either supposition, however, it would

---

[1] Lat. *breves*, or τίτλοι: but τίτλος means properly the brief summary of the contents of a κεφάλαιον placed at the top or bottom of a page, or with the κεφάλαια in a table to each Gospel. The κεφ. *minora* = Ammonian Sections.

be hard to explain how what was really the second chapter came to be *numbered* as the first; and it is worth notice that the same arrangement takes place in the κεφάλαια (though these are of a later date) of all the other books of the New Testament except the Acts, 2 Corinth., Ephes., 1 Thess., Hebrews, James, 1 and 2 Peter, 1 John, and the Apocalypse: e.g. the first chapter of the Epistle to the Romans opens ch. i. ver. 18 Πρῶτον μετὰ τὸ προοίμιον, περὶ κρίσεως τῆς κατὰ ἐθνῶν τῶν οὐ φυλασσόντων τὰ φυσικά. But the fact is that this arrangement, strange as it may seem, is conformable to the practice of the times when these divisions were finally settled. Both in the Institutes and in the Digest of Justinian the first paragraph is always cited as pr. (i.e. *principium*, προοίμιον, *Preface*), and what we should regard as the second paragraph is numbered as the first, and so on throughout the whole work [1].

The τίτλοι in St. Matthew amount to sixty-eight, in St. Mark to forty-eight, in St. Luke to eighty-three, in St. John to eighteen. This mode of division, although not met with in the Vatican and Sinaitic manuscripts, is found in the Codices Alexandrinus and Ephraemi of the fifth century, and in the Codex Nitriensis of the sixth, each of which has tables of the τίτλοι prefixed to the several Gospels: but the Codices Alexandrinus, Rossanensis, and Dublinensis of St. Matthew, and that portion of the purple Cotton fragment which is in the Vatican, exhibit them in their usual position, at the top and bottom of the pages. Thus it appears that they were too generally diffused in the fifth century not to have originated at an earlier period; although we must concede that the κεφάλαιον spoken of by Clement of Alexandria (Stromat. i) when quoting Dan. xii. 12, or by Athanasius (contra Arium) on Act. ii, and the *Capitulum* mentioned by Tertullian (ad Uxorem ii. 2) in reference to 1 Cor. vii. 12, contain no certain allusions to any specific divisions of the sacred text, but only to the particular paragraphs or passages in which their citations stand. Except that the contrary habit has grown inveterate [2], it were much to be desired that the term τίτλοι should be applied to these longer

---

[1] This full explanation of a seeming difficulty was communicated to me independently by Mr. F. W. Pennefather of Dublin, and Mr. G. A. King of Oxford.

[2] And this too in spite of the lexicographer Suidas: Τίτλος διαφέρει κεφαλαίου· καὶ ὁ μὲν Ματθαῖος τίτλους ἔχει ξη΄, κεφάλαια δὲ τνε΄. And of Suicer, s. v.

divisions, at least in the Gospels; but since usage has affixed the term κεφάλαια to the larger chapters and sections to the smaller, and τίτλοι only to the subjects or headings of the former, it would be useless to follow any other system of names.

3. The Ammonian Sections were not constructed, like the Vatican divisions and the τίτλοι, for the purpose of easy reference, or distributed like them according to the breaks in the sense, but for a wholly different purpose. So far as we can ascertain, the design of Tatian's Harmony was simply to present to Christian readers a single connected history of our Lord, by taking from the four Evangelists indifferently whatsoever best suited his purpose[1]. As this plan could scarcely be executed without *omitting* some portions of the sacred text, it is not surprising that Tatian, possibly without any evil intention, should have incurred the grave charge of mutilating Holy Scripture[2]. A more scholar-like and useful attempt was subsequently made by Ammonius of Alexandria, early in the third century [A.D. 220], who, by the side of St. Matthew's Gospel, which he selected as his standard, arranged in parallel columns, as it would seem, the corresponding passages of the other three Evangelists, so as to exhibit them all at once to the reader's eye; St. Matthew in his proper order, the rest as the necessity of abiding by St. Matthew's order prescribed. This is the account given by the celebrated Eusebius, Bishop of Caesarea, the Church

---

[1] Ὁ Τατιανός, συνάφειάν τινα καὶ συναγωγὴν οὐκ οἶδ' ὅπως τῶν εὐαγγελίων συνθείς, τὸ διὰ τεσσάρων τοῦτο προσωνόμασεν· ὃ καὶ παρά τισιν εἰσέτι νῦν φέρεται. Euseb. Hist. Eccl. iv. 29.

[2] Ambros. in Prooem. Luc. seems to aim at Tatian when he says 'Plerique etiam ex quatuor Evangelii libris in unum ea quae venenatis putaverunt assertionibus convenientia referserunt.' Eusebius H. E. iv. 29 charges him on report with *improving* not the Gospels, but the Epistles: τοῦ δὲ ἀποστόλου φασὶ τολμῆσαί τινας αὐτὸν μεταφράσαι φωνάς, ὡς ἐπιδιορθούμενον αὐτῶν τὴν τῆς φράσεως σύνταξιν. Dr. Westcott's verdict is rather less favourable than might have been anticipated: 'The heretical character of the Diatessaron was not evident on the surface of it, and consisted rather of faults of defect than of erroneous teaching' (History of the Canon, p. 354). From the Armenian version of Ephraem the Syrian's Exposition of Tatian's Harmony, printed in 1836, translated in 1841 by Aucher of the Melchitarist Monastery at Venice, but buried until it was published with notes by Moesinger in 1876, a flood of light is thrown upon this question, and it is now clear 'that Tatian habitually abridged the language of the passages which he combined' (Hort, Gk. Test. Introduction, p. 283), and that apparently in perfect good faith.

historian, who in the fourth century, in his letter to Carpianus, described his own most ingenious system of Harmony, as founded on, or at least as suggested by, the labours of Ammonius[1]. It has been generally thought that the κεφάλαια, of which St. Matthew contains 355, St. Mark 236[2], St. Luke 342, St. John 232, in all 1165, were made by Ammonius for the purpose of his work, and they have commonly received the name of the Ammonian sections: but this opinion was called in question by Bp. Lloyd (Nov. Test. Oxon. 1827, Monitum, pp. viii–xi), who strongly urges that, in his Epistle to Carpianus, Eusebius not only refrains from ascribing these numerical divisions to Ammonius (whose labours in this particular, as once seemed the case with Tatian's, must in that case be deemed to have perished utterly), but he almost implies that they had their origin at the same time with his own ten canons, with which they are so intimately connected[3]. That they were essential to Eusebius' scheme is plain enough; their place in Ammonius' parallel Harmony is not easily understood, unless indeed (what is nowhere stated, but rather the contrary) he did not set the passages from the other Gospels at full length by the side of St. Matthew's, but only these numerical references to them[4].

---

[1] Ἀμμώνιος μὲν ὁ Ἀλεξανδρεύς, πολλήν, ὡς εἰκός, φιλοπονίαν καὶ σπουδὴν εἰσαγηοχώς, τὸ διὰ τεσσάρων ἡμῖν καταλέλοιπεν εὐαγγέλιον, τῷ κατὰ Ματθαῖον τὰς ὁμοφώνους τῶν λοιπῶν εὐαγγελιστῶν περικοπὰς παραθείς, ὡς ἐξ ἀνάγκης συμβῆναι τὸν τῆς ἀκολουθίας εἱρμὸν τῶν τριῶν διαφθαρῆναι, ὅσον ἐπὶ τῷ ὕφει τῆς ἀναγνώσεως. Ἵνα δὲ σωζομένου καὶ τοῦ τῶν λοιπῶν δι' ὅλου σώματός τε καὶ εἱρμοῦ, εἰδέναι ἔχοις τοὺς οἰκείους ἑκάστου εὐαγγελιστοῦ τόπους, ἐν οἷς κατὰ τῶν αὐτῶν ἠνέχθησαν φιλαλήθως εἰπεῖν, ἐκ τοῦ πονήματος τοῦ προειρημένου ἀνδρὸς εἰληφὼς ἀφορμάς ('taking the hint from Ammonius' as Dean Burgon rightly understands the expression), καθ' ἑτέραν μέθοδον κανόνας δέκα τὸν ἀριθμὸν διεχάραξά σοι τοὺς ὑποτεταγμένους. Epist. ad Carpian. initio. I have thankfully availed myself on this subject of Burgon's elaborate studies in The Last Twelve Verses of St. Mark, pp. 125–132; 295–312.

[2] This is the number given for St. Mark by Suidas and Stephen. It is an uncertain point: thirty-four manuscripts give 233, reckoning only to xvi. 8; while thirty-six give 341. See Burgon Twelve Last Verses, p. 311.

[3] I subjoin Eusebius' own words (Epist. ad Carpian.) from which no one would infer that the *sections* were not his, as well as the *canons*. Αὕτη μὲν οὖν ἡ τῶν ὑποτεταγμένων κανόνων ὑπόθεσις· ἡ δὲ σαφὴς αὐτῶν διήγησις, ἔστιν ἥδε. Ἐφ' ἑκάστῳ τῶν τεσσάρων εὐαγγελίων ἀριθμός τις πρόκειται κατὰ μέρος, ἀρχόμενος ἀπὸ τοῦ πρώτου, εἶτα δευτέρου, καὶ τρίτου, καὶ καθεξῆς προϊὼν δι' ὅλου μέχρι τοῦ τέλους τοῦ βιβλίου [the sections]. Καθ' ἕκαστον δὲ ἀριθμὸν ὑποσημείωσις διὰ κινναβάρεως πρόκειται [the canons], δηλοῦσα ἐν ποίῳ τῶν δέκα κανόνων κείμενος ὁ ἀριθμὸς τυγχάνει.

[4] Something of this kind, however, must be the plan adopted in Codex E (see Plate xi. No. 27) of the Gospels, as described by Tregelles, who himself collated it. '[It has] the Ammonian sections; but instead of the Eusebian

There is, however, one ground for hesitation before we ascribe the sections, as well as the canons, to Eusebius; namely, that not a few ancient manuscripts (e. g. Codd. FHY) contain the former, while they omit the latter. Of palimpsests indeed it might be said with reason, that the rough process which so nearly obliterated the ink of the older writing, would completely remove the coloured paint (κιννάβαρις, *vermilion*, prescribed by Eusebius, though blue or green is occasionally found) in which the canons were invariably noted; hence we need not wonder at their absence from the Codices Ephraemi, Nitriensis (R), Dublinensis (Z), Codd. IW^b of Tischendorf, and the Wolfenbüttel fragments (PQ), in all which the sections are yet legible in ink. The Codex Sinaiticus contains both; but Tischendorf decidedly pronounces them to be in a later hand. In the Codex Bezae too, as well as the Codex Cyprius (K), even the Ammonian sections, without the canons, are by later hands, though the latter has prefixed the list or table of the canons. Of the oldest copies the Cod. Alex. (A), Tischendorf's Codd. W^{a}Θ, the Cotton frag. (N), and Codd. Beratinus and Rossanensis alone contain both the sections and the canons. Even in more modern cursive books the latter are often deficient, though the former are present. This peculiarity we have observed in Burney 23, in the British Museum, of the twelfth century, although the Epistle to Carpianus stands at the beginning; in a rather remarkable copy of about the twelfth century, in the Cambridge University Library (Mm. 6. 9, Scholz Evan. 440), in which, however, the table of canons but not the Epistle to Carpianus precedes; in the Gonville and Caius Gospels of the twelfth century (Evan. 59), and in a manuscript of about the thirteenth century at Trinity

canons there is a kind of harmony of the Gospels noted at the foot of each page, by a reference to the parallel sections of the other Evangelists.' Horne's Introd. vol. iv. p. 200. Yet the canons *also* stand in the margin of this copy under the so-called Ammonian sections: only the *table* of Eusebian canons is wanting. The same kind of harmony at the foot of the page appears in Cod. W^d at Trinity College, Cambridge, but in this latter the sections in the margin are not accompanied by the canons. Tischendorf states that the same arrangement prevails in the small fragment T^b at St. Petersburg; Dean Burgon adds to the list Codd. M. 26², 264 at Paris, and conceives that this method of harmonizing, which he regards as far simpler than the tedious and cumbersome process of resorting to the Eusebian canons (ubi supra, p. 304), was in principle, though not in details, derived to the Greek Church from early Syriac copies of the Gospels, some of which still survive (p. 306).

College, Cambridge (B. x. 17)[1]. These facts certainly seem to indicate that in the judgement of critics and transcribers, whatever that judgement may be deemed worth, the Ammonian sections had a previous existence to the Eusebian canons, as well as served for an independent purpose[2].

In his letter to Carpianus, their inventor clearly yet briefly describes the purpose of his canons, ten in number. The first contains a list of seventy-one places in which all the four Evangelists have a narrative, discourse, or saying in common: the second of 111 places in which the three Matthew, Mark, Luke agree: the third of twenty-two places common to Matthew, Luke, John: the fourth of twenty-six passages common to Matthew, Mark, John: the fifth of eighty-two places in which the two Matthew, Luke coincide: the sixth of forty-seven places wherein Matthew, Mark agree: the seventh of seven places common to Matthew and John: the eighth of fourteen places common to Luke and Mark: the ninth of twenty-one places in which Luke and John agree: the tenth of sixty-two passages of Matthew, twenty-one of Mark, seventy-one of Luke, and ninety-seven of John which have no parallels, but are peculiar to a single Evangelist. Under each of the 1165 so-named Ammonian sections, in its proper place in the margin of a manuscript, is put in coloured ink the number of that Eusebian canon to which it refers. On looking for that section in the proper table or canon, there will also be found the parallel place or places in the other Gospels, each indicated by its proper numeral, and so

---

[1] To this list of manuscripts of the Gospels which have the Ammonian sections without the Eusebian canons add Codd. 38, 54, 60, 68, 117; Brit. Mus. Addit. 16184, 18211, 19389; Milan Ambros. M. 48 *sup.*; E. 63 *sup.*; Burdett-Coutts I. 4; II. 18; 26[2]; III. 9. Now that attention has been specially directed to the matter, it is remarkable how many copies have the Ammonian sections without the corresponding Eusebian canons under them, sometimes even when (as in Codd. 572, 595, 597) the letter to Carpianus and the Eusebian tables stand at the beginning of the volume. To the list here given must now be added Codd. O, Υ, 185, 187, 190, 193, 194, 207, 209, 214, 217, 367, 406, 409, 410, 414, 418, 419, 456, 457, 494, 497, 501, 503, 504, 506, 508, 518, 544, 548, 550, 555, 558, 559, 564, 573, 575, 584, 586, 591, 592, 601, 602, 620: in all seventy-one manuscripts.

[2] No doubt they do serve, in the manuscripts which contain them and omit the canons, for marks of reference, like in kind to our modern chapters and verses; but in consequence of their having been constructed for a wholly different purpose, they are so unequal in length (as Burgon sees very clearly, pp. 297, 303), that they answer that end as ill as any the most arbitrary divisions of the text well could do.

readily searched out. A single example will serve to explain our meaning. In the facsimile of the Cotton fragment (Plate v. No. 14), in the margin of the passage (John xv. 20) we see $\overline{\dfrac{P\Lambda\Theta}{\Gamma}}$, where $P\Lambda\Theta$ (139) is the proper section of St. John, Γ (3) the number of the canon. On searching the third Eusebian table we read MT. $\bar{\zeta}$, Λ. $\overline{\nu\eta}$, ΙΩ. $\overline{\rho\lambda\theta}$, and thus we learn that the first clause of John xv. 20 is parallel in sense to the ninetieth ($\bar{\zeta}$) section of St. Matthew (x. 24), and to the fifty-eighth ($\overline{\nu\eta}$) of St. Luke (vi. 40). The advantage of such a system of parallels to the exact study of the Gospels is too evident to need insisting on.

4. The Acts of the Apostles and the Epistles are also divided into *chapters* (κεφάλαια), in design precisely the same as the κεφάλαια or τίτλοι of the Gospels, and nearly like them in length. Since there is no trace of these chapters in the two great Codices Alexandrinus and Ephraemi, of the fifth century (which yet exhibit the τίτλοι, the sections, and one of them the canons), it seems reasonable to assume that they are of later date. They are sometimes connected with the name of Euthalius, deacon of Alexandria, afterwards Bishop of Sulci[1], whom we have already spoken of as the reputed author of Scriptural stichometry (*above*, p. 53). We learn, however, from Euthalius' own Prologue to his edition of St. Paul's Epistles (A. D. 458,) that the 'summary of the chapters' (and consequently the numbers of the chapters themselves) was taken from the work of 'one of our wisest and pious fathers[2],' i. e. some Bishop that he does not wish to particularize, whom Mill (Proleg. N. T. § 907) conjectures to be Theodore of Mopsuestia, who lay under the censure of the Church. Soon after[3] the publication of St. Paul's Epistles, on

---

[1] Sulci in Sardinia is the only Bishop's see of the name I can find in Carol. a Sancto Paulo's Geographia Sacra (1703), or in Bingham's Antiquities, Bk. ix. Chapp. II, VII. Horne and even Tregelles speak of Sulca in Egypt, but I have searched in vain for any such town or see. Euthalius is called Bishop of Sulce both in Wake 12 (infra, note 4), and in the title to his works as edited by L. A. Zacagni (Collectanea Monument. Veter. Eccles. Graec. ac Latin., Rom. 1698, p. 402). But one of Zacagni's manuscripts reads Σούλκης once, and he guesses Ψέλχη near Syene, which appears in no list of Episcopal sees.

[2] Καθ' ἑκάστην ἐπιστολὴν προτάξομεν τὴν τῶν κεφαλαίων ἔκθεσιν, ἑνὶ τῶν σοφωτάτων τινὶ καὶ φιλοχρίστων πατέρων ἡμῶν πεπονημένην.

[3] Αὐτίκα δῆτα is his own expression.

the suggestion of one Athanasius, then a priest and afterwards Patriarch of Alexandria, Euthalius put forth a similar edition of the Acts and Catholic Epistles [1], also divided into chapters, with a summary of contents at the head of each chapter. Even these he is thought to have derived (at least in the Acts) from the manuscript of Pamphilus the Martyr [d. 308], to whom the same order of chapters is ascribed in a document published by Montfaucon (Bibliotheca Coislin. p. 78); the rather as Euthalius fairly professes to have compared his book in the Acts and Catholic Epistles 'with the copies in the library at Caesarea' which once belonged to 'Eusebius the friend of Pamphilus [2].' The Apocalypse still remains. It was divided, about the end of the fifth century, by Andreas, Archbishop of the Cappadocian Caesarea, into twenty-four *paragraphs* (λόγοι), corresponding to the number of the elders about the throne (Apoc. iv. 4); each paragraph being subdivided into three *chapters* (κεφάλαια)[3]. The summaries which Andreas wrote of his seventy-two chapters are still reprinted in Mill's and other large editions of the Greek Testament.

5. To Euthalius has been also referred a division of the Acts into sixteen lessons (ἀναγνώσεις) and of the Pauline Epistles into thirty-one (see table on p. 68); but these lessons are quite different from the much shorter ones adopted by the Greek Church. He is also said to have numbered in each Epistle of St. Paul the quotations from the Old Testament [4], which are

---

[1] E.g. in Wake 12, of the eleventh century, at Christ Church, the title at the head of the list of chapters in the Acts is as follows: Εὐθαλίου ἐπισκόπου ζουλκῆς ἔκθεσις κεφαλαίων τῶν Πράξεων σταλῆσα (-εῖσα) πρὸς 'Αθανάσιον ἐπίσκοπον 'Αλεξανδρείας.

[2] In Wake 12 certain of the longer κεφάλαια are subdivided into μερικαὶ ὑποδιαιρέσεις in the Acts, 1 Peter, 1 John, Romans, 1, 2 Corinthians, Colossians, 2 Thessalonians, 1 Timothy, Hebrews only. For a similar subdivision in the Gospels, see Evan. 443 in the list of cursive MSS. given below.

[3] Διὰ τὴν τριμερῆ τῶν εἴκοσι τεσσάρων πρεσβυτέρων ὑπόστασιν, σώματος καὶ ψυχῆς καὶ πνεύματος. See Matthaei, N. T. Gr. et Lat. vii. 276, note 4.

[4] Many manuscripts indicate passages of the Old Testament cited in the New by placing > (as in Codd. Vatican. W^d, &c., but in Sinait. more rarely), or ≥, or some such mark in the margin before every line. Our quotation-marks are probably derived from this sign, the angle being rounded into a curve. Compare the use of " in the margin of the Greek Testament of Colinaeus, 1534, and Stephen's editions of 1546, -49, -50, &c. Evan. 348 and others have ※. In Codd. Bezae, as will appear hereafter, the words cited are merely thrown a letter or two back in each line.

still noted in many of our manuscripts, and is the first known to have used that reckoning of the στίχοι which was formerly annexed we know not when to the Gospels and Epistles, as well as to the Acts. Besides the division of the text into στίχοι or *lines* (*above*, p. 52) we find in the Gospels alone another division into ῥήματα or ῥήσεις 'sentences,' differing but little from the στίχοι in number. Of these last the precise numbers vary in different copies, though not considerably: whether that variation arose from the circumstance that ancient numbers were represented by letters and so easily became corrupted, or from a different mode of arranging the στίχοι and ῥήματα adopted by the various scribes.

6. It is proper to state that the *subscriptions* (ὑπογραφαί) appended to St. Paul's Epistles in many manuscripts, and retained even in the Authorized English version of the New Testament, are also said to be the composition of Euthalius. In the best copies they are somewhat shorter in form, but in any shape they do no credit to the care or skill of their author, whoever he may be. 'Six of these subscriptions,' writes Paley in that masterpiece of acute reasoning, the Horae Paulinae, 'are false or improbable;' that is, they are either absolutely contradicted by the contents of the epistle [1 Cor., Galat., 1 Tim.], or are difficult to be reconciled with them [1, 2 Thess., Tit.].

The *subscriptions* to the Gospels have not, we believe, been assigned to any particular author, and being seldom found in printed copies of the Greek Testament or in modern versions, are little known to the general reader. In the earliest manuscripts the subscriptions, as well as the *titles* of the books, were of the simplest character. Κατὰ Ματθαῖον, κατὰ Μάρκον, &c. is all that the Codd. Vaticanus and Sinaiticus have, whether at the beginning or the end. Εὐαγγέλιον κατὰ Ματθαῖον is the subscription to the first Gospel in the Codex Alexandrinus; εὐαγγέλιον κατὰ Μάρκον is placed at the beginning of the second Gospel in the same manuscript, and the self-same words at the end of it by Codices Alex. and Ephraemi: in the Codex Bezae (in which St. John stands second in order) we merely read εὐαγγέλιον κατὰ Ματθαῖον ἐτελέσθη, ἄρχεται εὐαγγέλιον κατὰ Ἰωάννην. The same is the case throughout the New Testament. After a while the titles become more elaborate, and the subscriptions afford more information, the truth of which it would hardly be safe to vouch for. The earliest worth notice are found in the Codex Cyprius (K) of the eighth or ninth century, which, together with those of several other copies, are given in Scholz's Prolegomena N. T. vol. i. pp. xxix, xxx. *ad fin. Matthaei*: Τὸ κατὰ Ματθαῖον εὐαγγέλιον ἐξεδόθη ὑπ' αὐτοῦ ἐν ἱεροσολύμοις μετὰ χρόνους ἢ [ὀκτὼ] τῆς τοῦ Χριστοῦ ἀναλήψεως. *Ad fin. Marci*: Τὸ κατὰ Μάρκον εὐαγγέλιον ἐξεδόθη μετὰ χρόνους δέκα τῆς τοῦ Χριστοῦ ἀναλήψεως. Those to the other two Gospels exactly resemble St. Mark's, that of St. Luke however being dated fifteen, that of St. John thirty-two years after our Lord's Ascension, periods in all probability far too early to be correct.

7. The foreign matter so often inserted in later manuscripts has more value for the antiquarian than for the critic. That splendid copy of the Gospels Lambeth 1178, of the tenth or eleventh century, contains more such than is often found, set off by fine illuminations. At the end of each of the first three Gospels (but not of the fourth) are several pages relating to them extracted from Cosmas Indicopleustes, who made the voyage which procured him his cognomen about A.D. 522; also some iambic verses of no great excellence, as may well be supposed. In golden letters we read: *ad fin. Matth.* ἰστέον ὅτι τὸ κατὰ Ματθαῖον εὐαγγέλιον ἐβραΐδι διαλέκτωι γραφὲν ὑπ' αὐτοῦ· ἐν ἱερουσαλὴμ ἐξεδόθη· ἑρμηνεύθη δὲ ὑπὸ Ἰωάννου· ἐξηγεῖται δὲ τὴν κατὰ ἄνθρωπον τοῦ χυ γένεσιν, καί ἐστιν ἀνθρωπόμορφον τοῦτο τὸ εὐαγγέλιον. The last clause alludes to Apoc. iv. 7, wherein the four living creatures were currently believed to be typical of the four Gospels [1]. *Ad fin. Marc.* ἰστέον ὅτι τὸ κατὰ Μάρκον εὐαγγέλιον ὑπηγορεύθη ὑπὸ Πέτρου ἐν ῥώμηι· ἐποιήσατο δὲ τὴν ἀρχὴν ἀπὸ τοῦ προφητικοῦ λόγου τοῦ ἐξ ὕψους ἐπιόντος τοῦ Ἡσαΐου· τὴν πτερωτικὴν εἰκόνα τοῦ εὐαγγελίου δεικνύς. *Ad fin. Luc.* ἰστέον ὅτι τὸ κατὰ Λουκᾶν εὐαγγέλιον ὑπηγορεύθη ὑπὸ Παύλου ἐν ῥώμηι· ἅτε δὲ ἱερατικοῦ χαρακτῆρος ὑπάρχοντος

---

[1] The whole mystery is thus unfolded (apparently by Cosmas) in Lamb. 1178, p. 159: Καὶ γὰρ τὰ χερουβὶμ τετραπρόσωπα· καὶ τὰ πρόσωπα αὐτῶν εἰκόνες τῆς πραγματείας τοῦ υἱοῦ τοῦ θεοῦ· τὸ γὰρ ὅμοιον λέοντι, τὸ ἔμπρακτον καὶ βασιλικὸν καὶ ἡγεμονικὸν [John i. 1-3] χαρακτηρίζει· τὸ δὲ ὅμοιον μόσχωι, τὴν ἱερουργικὴν καὶ ἱερατικὴν [Luke i. 8] ἐμφανίζει· τὸ δὲ ἀνθρωποειδές, τὴν σάρκωσιν [Matt. i. 18] διαγράφει. τὸ δὲ ὅμοιον ἀετῶι, τὴν ἐπιφοίτησιν τοῦ ἁγίου πνεύματος [Mark i. 2] ἐμφανίζει. More usually the lion is regarded as the emblem of St. Mark, the eagle of St. John.

ἀπὸ Ζαχαρίου τοῦ ἱερέως θυμιῶντος ἤρξατο. The reader will desire no more of this.

8. The oldest manuscript known to be accompanied by a *catena* (or continuous commentary by different authors) is the palimpsest Codex Zacynthius (Ξ of Tregelles), an uncial of the eighth century. Such books are not common, but there is a very full commentary in minute letters, surrounding the large text in a noble copy of the Gospels, of the twelfth century, which belonged to the late Sir Thomas Phillipps (Middle Hill 13975, since removed to Cheltenham), yet uncollated; another of St. Paul's Epistles (No. 27) belongs to the University Library at Cambridge (Ff. 1. 30). The Apocalypse is often attended with the exposition of Andreas (p. 64), or of Arethas, also Archbishop of the Cappadocian Caesarea in the tenth century, or (what is more usual) with a sort of epitome of the two (e.g. Parham No. 17), above, below, and in the margin beside the text, in much smaller characters. In *cursive* manuscripts only the subject (ὑπόθεσις), especially that written by Oecumenius in the tenth century, sometimes stands as a *Prologue* before each book, but not so often before the Gospels or Apocalypse as the Acts and Epistles. Before the Acts we occasionally meet with Euthalius' Chronology of St. Paul's Travels, or another Ἀποδημία Παύλου. The Leicester manuscript contains between the Pauline Epistles and the Acts (1) An Exposition of the Creed and statement of the errors condemned by the seven general Councils, ending with the second at Nice. (2) Lives of the Apostles, followed by an exact description of the limits of the five Patriarchates. The Christ Church copy Wake 12 also has after the Apocalypse some seven or eight pages of a Treatise Περὶ τῶν ἁγίων καὶ οἰκουμενικῶν ζ συνόδων, including some notice περὶ τοπικῶν συνόδων. Similar treatises may be more frequent in manuscripts of the Greek Testament than we are at present aware of.

9. We have not thought it needful to insert in this place either a list of the τίτλοι of the Gospels, or of the κεφάλαια of the rest of the New Testament, or the tables of the Eusebian canons, inasmuch as they are all accessible in such ordinary books as Stephen's Greek Testament 1550 and Mill's of 1707, 1710. The Eusebian canons are given in Bishop Lloyd's Oxford

TABLE OF ANCIENT AND MODERN DIVISIONS OF THE NEW TESTAMENT.

	Vatican MS. older sections	Vatican MS. later sections	τίτλοι	κεφάλαια Ammon.	στίχοι	ῥήματα	Modern chapters	Modern verses
Matthew	170	—	68	355	2560	2522	28	1071
Mark	62	—	48	236	1616	1675	16	678
Luke	152	—	83	342	2740	3803	24	1151
John	80	—	18	232¹	2024	1938	21	880 / A.V. 879
				Euthal. κεφ λ.		ἀναγνώσματα		
Acts	36	69	40		2524	16	28	1007 / A.V. 1008
James	9	5	6		242		5	108
1 Peter	8	3	8		236		5	105
2 Peter	desunt	2	4		154		3	61
1 John	14	3	7		274		5	105
2 John	1	2	2		30		1	13
3 John	2	desunt	3		32		1	15 / A.V. 14
Jude	2	desunt	4		68		1	25
Romans		8	19		920	5	16	433
1 Corinth.		}19	9		870	5	16	437
2 Corinth.			11		590	4	13	256 / A.V. 257
Galat.		3	12		293	2	6	149
Ephes.		3	10		312	2	6	155
Philipp.		2	7		208	2	4	104
Coloss.		3	10		208	2	4	95
1 Thess.		2	7		193	1	5	89
2 Thess.		2	6		106	1	3	47
1 Tim.		—	18		230	1	6	113
2 Tim.		—	9		172	1	4	83
Titus		—	6		98 (97, Mill)	1	3	46
Philem.		—	2		38	1	1	25
Hebrews		5 to ch. ix. 11.	22		703	3	13	303
Apocalypse	24 λόγοι, 72 κεφάλαια, 1800 στίχοι.						22	405 / A.V. 404

N.B. The στίχοι of the Acts and of all the Epistles except Hebr. are taken from the Codex Passionei (G or L), an uncial of the ninth century.

93 sections in Rom. 1, 2 Corinth. Gal. Eph. Coloss. 1, 2 Thess. to Hebr. ix. 14.

[ἀναγνώσματα of Matt. 116, Mark 71, Luke 114, John 67, in Wake 25, Mutin. [5] ii. A. 5].

¹ The Ammonian κεφάλαια in the Gospels vary from the normal number in many copies, especially in SS. Matthew and Mark, but not considerably. The ἀναγνώσματα of the Gospels set down in column seven are also given in Mendham, Evan. 562. See p. 75, note 1.

Greek Test. of 1827 &c. and in Tischendorf's of 1859. We exhibit, however, for the sake of comparison, a tabular view of 'Ancient and Modern Divisions of the New Testament.' The numbers of the ῥήματα and στίχοι in the Gospels are derived from the most approved sources, but a synopsis of the variations of manuscripts in this respect has been drawn up by Scholz, Prolegomena N. T. vol. i. Cap. v, pp. xxviii, xxix [1]. A computation of their number, as also of that of the ἀναγνώσματα, is often given in the subscription at the end of a book.

10. On the divisions into chapters and verses prevailing in our modern Bibles we need not dwell long. For many centuries the Latin Church used the Greek τίτλοι (which they called *breves*) with the Euthalian κεφάλαια, and some of their copies even retained the calculation by στίχοι: but about A.D. 1248 Cardinal Hugo de Sancto Caro, while preparing a Concordance, or index of declinable words, for the *whole Bible*, divided it into its present chapters, subdividing them in turn into several parts by placing the letters A, B, C, D &c. in the margin, at equal distances from each other, as we still see in many old printed books, e. g. Stephen's N. T. of 1550. Cardinal Hugo's divisions, unless indeed he merely adopted them from Lanfranc or some other scholar, such as was very probably Stephen Langton the celebrated Archbishop of Canterbury, soon took possession of copies of the Latin Vulgate; they gradually obtained a place in later Greek manuscripts, especially those written in the West of Europe, and are found in the earliest printed and all later editions of the Greek Testament, though still unknown to the Eastern Church. They certainly possess no strong claim on our preference, although they cannot now be superseded. The chapters are inconveniently and capriciously unequal in length; occasionally too they are distributed with much lack of judge-

---

[1] The numbers of the Gospel στίχοι in our Table are taken from the uncial copies Codd. GS and twenty-seven cursives named by Scholz: those of the ῥήματα from Codd. 9, 13, 124 and seven others. In the ῥήματα he cites no other variation than that Cod. 339 has 2822 for St. Matthew: but Mill states that Cod. 48 (Bodl. 7) has 1676 for Mark, 2507 for Luke (Proleg. N. T. § 1429). In Cod. 56 (Lincoln Coll.) the ἀναγνώσματα of St. Matthew are 127, of St. Mark 74, of St. Luke 130 (Mill).

In the στίχοι, a few straggling manuscripts fluctuate between 3397 ? and 1474 for Matthew; 2006 and 1000 for Mark; 3827 and 2000 for Luke; 2300 and 1300 for John. But the great mass of authorities stand as we have represented.

ment. Thus Matt. xv. 39 belongs to ch. xvi, and perhaps ch. xix. 30 to ch. xx; Mark ix. 1 properly appertains to the preceding chapter; Luke xxi. 1–4 had better be united with ch. xx, as in Mark xii. 41–44; Acts v might as well commence with Acts iv. 32; Acts viii. 1 (or at least its first clause) should not have been separated from ch. vii; Acts xxi concludes with strange abruptness. Bp. Terrot (on Ernesti's Institutes, vol. ii. p. 21) rightly affixes 1 Cor. iv. 1–5 to ch. iii. Add that 1 Cor. xi. 1 belongs to ch. x; 2 Cor. iv. 18 and vi. 18 to ch. v and ch. vii respectively: Col. iv. 1 must clearly go with ch. iii.

In commendation of the modern verses still less can be said. As they are stated to have been constructed after the model of the ancient στίχοι (called '*versus*' in the Latin manuscripts), we have placed in the Table the exact number of each for every book in the New Testament. Of the στίχοι we reckon 19241 in all, of the modern verses 7959[1], so that on the average (for we have seen that the manuscript variations in the number of στίχοι are but inconsiderable) we may calculate about five στίχοι to every two modern verses. The fact is that some such division is simply indispensable to every accurate reader of Scripture; and Cardinal Hugo's divisions by letters of the alphabet, as well as those adopted by Sanctes Pagninus in his Latin version of the whole Bible (1528), having proved inconveniently large, Robert Stephen, the justly celebrated printer and editor of the Greek Testament, undertook to form a system of verse-divisions, taking for his model the short verses into which the Hebrew Bible had already been divided, as it would seem by Rabbi Nathan, in the preceding century. We are told by Henry Stephen (Praef. Concordantiae) that his father Robert executed this design on a journey from Paris to Lyons '*inter equitandum*[2];' that is, we

---

[1] Our English version divides 2 Cor. xiii. 12 of the Greek into two, and unites John i. 38, 39 of the Greek. The English and Greek verses begin differently in Luke i. 73, 74; vii. 18, 19. Acts ix. 28, 29; xi. 25, 26; xiii. 32, 33; xix. 40, 41; xxiv. 2, 3. 2 Cor. ii. 12, 13; v. 14, 15; xi. 8, 9. Eph. i. 10, 11; iii. 17, 18. Phil. iii. 13, 14. 1 Thess. ii. 11, 12. Heb. vii. 20, 21; x. 22, 23. 1 Jo. ii. 13, 14. 3 Jo. 14, 15. Apoc. xii. 18 or xiii. 1; xviii. 16, 17. In a few of these places editions of the Greek vary a little. The whole subject of the verses is discussed in Dr. Ezra Abbot's tract 'De Editionibus Novi Testamenti Graece in versuum quos dicunt distinctione inter se discrepantibus' 1882, included in the Prolegomena for Tischendorf's N. T., eighth edition, pp. 167, &c.

[2] 'I think it would have been better done on one's knees in the closet,' is

presume, while resting at the inns on the road. Certain it is that, although every such division must be in some measure arbitrary, a very little care would have spared us many of the disadvantages attending that which Robert Stephen first published at Geneva in his Greek Testament of 1551, from which it was introduced into the text of the Genevan English Testament of 1557, into Beza's Greek Testament of 1565, and thence into subsequent editions. It is now too late to correct the errors of the verse-divisions, but they can be neutralized, at least in a great degree, by the plan adopted by modern critics, of banishing both the verses and the chapters into the margin, and breaking the text into paragraphs, better suited to the sense. The *pericopae* or sections of Bengel[1] (whose labours will be described in their proper place) have been received with general approbation, and adopted, with some modification, by several recent editors. Much pains were bestowed on their arrangement of the paragraphs by the Revisers of the English version of 1881.

11. We now come to the *contents* of manuscripts of the Greek Testament, and must distinguish regular copies of the sacred volume or of parts of it from Lectionaries, or Church-lesson books, containing only extracts, arranged in the order of Divine Service daily throughout the year. The latter we will consider presently: with regard to the former it is right to bear in mind, that comparatively few copies of the whole New Testament remain; the usual practice being to write the four Gospels in one volume, the Acts and Epistles in another: manuscripts of the Apocalypse, which was little used for public worship, being much rarer than those of the other books. Occasionally the Gospels, Acts, and Epistles form a single volume; sometimes the Apocalypse is added to other books; as to the Pauline Epistles in Lambeth 1186, or even to the Gospels, in a later hand (e.g. Cambridge University Libr. Dd. 9. 69: Gospels No. 60, dated A.D. 1297). The Apocalypse, being a short work, is often

---

Mr. Kelly's quaint and not unfair comment (Lectures on the Minor Prophets, p. 324), unless, as is not unlikely, he copied what was done before.

[1] Novum Testamentum Graecum. Edente Jo. Alberto Bengelio. Tubingae 1734. 4to. The practice of the oldest Greek manuscripts in regard to paragraphs has been stated above (p. 49, note 2), and will be further explained in the next section under our descriptions of Codd. ℵBD.

found bound up in volumes containing very miscellaneous matter (e. g. Vatican. 2066 or B; Brit. Mus. Harleian. 5678, No. 31; and Oxon. Barocc. 48, No. 28). The Codex Sinaiticus of Tischendorf is the more precious, in that it happily exhibits the whole New Testament complete: so would also the Codices Alexandrinus and Ephraemi, but that they are sadly mutilated: no other uncial copies have this advantage, and very few cursives. In England only five such are known, the great Codex Leicestrensis, which is imperfect at the beginning and end; Butler 2 (Evan. 201) Additional 11837, dated A.D. 1357, and (Evan. 584) Additional 17469, both in the British Museum; Canonici 34 (Evan. 488) in the Bodleian, dated A.D. 1515-16. Additional MS. 28815 (Evan. 603, and Paul 266, and Apoc. 89) in the British Museum and B-C. II. 4 at Sir Roger Cholmely's School, Highgate, are separated portions of one complete copy. The Apocalypse in the well-known Codex Montfortianus at Dublin is usually considered to be by a later hand. Besides these Scholz enumerates only nineteen foreign copies of the whole New Testament[1]; making but twenty-four in all, as far as was then known, out of the vast mass of extant documents.

12. Whether copies contain the whole or a part of the sacred volume, the general *order* of the books is the following: Gospels, Acts, Catholic Epistles, Pauline Epistles, Apocalypse. A solitary manuscript of the fifteenth century (Venet. 10, Evan. 209) places the Gospels between the Pauline Epistles and the Apocalypse[2]; in the Codices Sinaiticus, Leicestrensis, Fabri (Evan. 90), and Montfortianus, as in the Bodleian Canonici 34, the copy in the King's Library Brit. Mus. (Act. 20), and the

---

[1] Coislin. 199 (Evan. 35); Vatic. 2080 (Evan. 175); Palat. Vat. 171 (Evan. 149); Lambec. 1 at Vienna (Evan. 218); Vatic. 1160 (Evan. 141); Venet. 5 (Evan. 205); its alleged duplicate Venet. 10 (Evan. 209); Matthaei k (Evan. 241); Moscow Synod. 380 (Evan. 242); Paris, Reg. 47 (Evan. 18); Reg. 61 (Evan. 263); Vat. Ottob. 66 (Evan. 386); Vat. Ottob. 381 (Evan. 390); Taurin. 302 (Evan. 339); S. Saba, 10 and 20 (Evan. 462 and 466); Laurent. 53 (Evan. 367); Vallicel. F. 17 (Evan. 394); Phillipps 7682 (Evan. 531); perhaps Scholz ought to have added Venet. 6 (Evan. 206) which he states to contain the whole New Testament, Proleg. N. T. vol. i. p. lxxii. In Evan. 180 all except the Gospels are by a later hand. Add (Evan. 622) also copies at Poictiers, Ferrara, and Toledo. Lagarde (Genesis, pp. 7, 8) describes another copy at Zittau, collated by Matthaei in 1801-2, apparently unpublished.

[2] I presume that the same order is found in Evan. 393, whereof Scholz states 'sec. xvi. continet epist. cath. paul. ev.' Proleg. N. T. vol. i. p. xc.

Complutensian edition (1514), the Pauline Epistles precede the Acts. The Pauline Epistles stand between the Acts and the Catholic Epistles in Phillipps 1284, Evan. 527; Parham 71. 6, Evan. 534; Upsal, Sparfwenfeldt 42, Acts 68; Paris Reg. 102 A, Acts 119; Reg. 103 A, Acts 120. In Oxford Bodl. Miscell. 74 the order is Acts, Cath. Epp., Apocalypse, Paul. Epp., but an earlier hand wrote from 3 John onwards. In Evan. 51 Dr. C. R. Gregory points out minute indications that the scribe, not the binder, set the Gospels last. In the Memphitic and Thebaic the Acts follow the Catholic Epistles (see below, vol. ii, chap. iii). The Codex Basiliensis (No. 4 of the Epistles), Acts Cod. 134, Brit. Mus. Addl. 19388, Lambeth 1182, 1183, and Burdett-Coutts III. 1, have the Pauline Epistles immediately after the Acts and before the Catholic Epistles, as in our present Bibles. Scholz's Evan. 368 stands thus, St. John's Gospel, Apocalypse, then all the Epistles; in Havniens. 1 (Cod. 234 of the Gospels, A.D. 1278) the order appears to be Acts, Paul. Ep., Cath. Ep., Gospels; in Ambros. Z 34 *sup.* at Milan, Dean Burgon testifies that the Catholic and Pauline Epistles are followed by the Gospels; in Basil. B. VI. 27 or Cod. 1, the Gospels have been bound after the Acts and Epistles; while in Evan. 175 the Apocalypse stands between the Acts and Catholic Epistles; in Evan. 51 the binder has set the Gospels last: these, however, are mere accidental exceptions to the prevailing rule [1]. The four Gospels are almost invariably found in their familiar order, although in the Codex Bezae (as we partly saw above, p. 65) they stand Matthew, John, Luke, Mark [2]; in the Codex Monacensis (X) John, Luke,

---

[1] Hartwell Horne in the second volume of his Introduction tells us that in some of the few manuscripts which contain the whole of the New Testament the books are arranged thus: Gospels, Acts, Catholic Epistles, Apocalypse, Pauline Epistles (p. 92, ed. 1834). This statement may be true of some of the foreign MSS. named in p. 69 note, but of the English it can refer to none, although Wake 34 at Christ Church commences with the Acts and Catholic Epistles, followed by the Apocalypse beginning on the same page as Jude ends, and the Pauline Epistles on the same page as the Apocalypse ends. The Gospels, which come last, may have been misplaced by an early binder.

[2] This is the true *Western* order (Scrivener, Cod. Bezae, Introd. p. xxx and note), and will be found in the copies of the Old Latin a_1, a_2, b, e, f_1, f_2, i, n, g, r to be described in vol. ii, and in the Gothic version. In Burdett-Coutts II. 7, p. 4, also, prefixed to the Gospels, we read the following rubric-title to certain verses of Gregory Nazianzen: $\overline{\chi\upsilon}$ θαύματα· παρὰ ματθαίω ἰωάννη τὲ καὶ λουκᾶ καὶ μάρκω· κ.τ.λ.

Mark, Matthew (but two leaves of Matthew *also* stand before John), also in the Latin *k*; in Cod. 90 (Fabri) John, Luke, Matthew, Mark; in Cod. 399 at Turin John, Luke, Matthew, an arrangement which Dr. Hort refers to the Commentary of Titus of Bostra on St. Luke which accompanies it; in the Curetonian Syriac version Matthew, Mark, John, Luke. In the Pauline Epistles that to the Hebrews immediately follows the second to the Thessalonians in the four great Codices Vaticanus, Sinaiticus, Alexandrinus, and Ephraemi[1]: in the copy from which the Cod. Vatican. was taken the Hebrews followed the Galatians (*above*, p. 57). The Codex Claromontanus, the document next in importance to these four, sets the Colossians appropriately enough next to its kindred and contemporaneous Epistle to the Ephesians, but postpones that to the Hebrews to Philemon, as in our present Bibles: an arrangement which at first, no doubt, originated in the early scruples prevailing in the Western Church, with respect to the authorship and canonical authority of that divine epistle.

13. We must now describe the *Lectionaries* or Service-books of the Greek Church, in which the portions of Scripture publicly read throughout the year are set down in chronological order, without regard to their actual places in the sacred volume. In length and general arrangement they resemble not so much the Lessons as the Epistles and Gospels in our English Book of Common Prayer, only that every day in the year has its own proper portion, and the numerous Saints' days independent services of their own. These Lectionaries consist either of lessons from the Gospels, and are then called *Evangelistaria* or *Evangeliaria* (εὐαγγελιστάρια)[2]; or from the Acts and Epistles, termed *Praxapostolos* (πραξαπόστολος) or *Apostolos*[3]: the general name of Lectionary is often, though incorrectly, confined to the latter class. A few books called ἀποστολοευαγγέλια have lessons

---

[1] Tischendorf cites the following copies in which the Epistle to the Hebrews stands in the same order as in Codd. ℵABC, 'H [Coislin. 202], 17, 23, 47, 57, 71, 73 aliique.' Add 77, 80, 166, 189, 196, 264, 265, 266 (Burdett-Coutts II. 4). So in Zoega's Thebaic version. Epiphanius (adv. Haer. i. 42) says: ἄλλα δὲ ἀντίγραφα ἔχει τὴν πρὸς Ἑβραίους δεκάτην, πρὸ τῶν δύο τῶν πρὸς Τιμόθεον καὶ Τίτον. So Paul 166, 281, and also Bp. Lightfoot's MSS. of the Memphitic except 7 and 16. In the Thebaic it follows 2 Cor. See below.

[2] They are also termed Εὐαγγέλια—evidently a popular, as well as a misleading name.   [3] Suicer, s. v.

taken both from the Gospels and the Apostolic writings. In *Euchologies*, or Books of Offices, wherein both the *Apostolos* and the *Gospels* are found, the former always precede in each Office, just as the Epistle precedes the Gospel in the Service-books of Western Christendom. The peculiar arrangement of Lectionaries renders them very unfit for the hasty, partial, cursory collation which has befallen too many manuscripts of the other class, and this circumstance, joined with the irksomeness of using Service-books never familiar to the habits even of scholars in this part of Europe, has caused these documents to be so little consulted, that the contents of the very best and oldest among them have until recently been little known. Matthaei, of whose elaborate and important edition of the Greek Testament (12 tom. Riga 1782–88) we shall give an account hereafter, has done excellent service in this department; two of his best copies, the uncials B and H (Nos. 47, 50), being Evangelistaria. The present writer also has collated three noble uncials of the same rank, Arundel 547 being of the ninth century, Parham 18 bearing date A.D. 980, Harleian 5598, A.D. 995. Not a few other uncial Lectionaries remain quite neglected, for though none of them perhaps are older than the eighth century, the ancient character was retained for these costly and splendid Service-books till about the eleventh century (Montfaucon, Palaeogr. Graec. p. 260), before which time the cursive hand was generally used in other Biblical manuscripts. There is, of course, no place in a Lectionary for divisions by κεφάλαια, for the so-called Ammonian sections, or for the canons of Eusebius.

The division of the New Testament into Church-lessons was, however, of far more remote antiquity than the employment of separate volumes to contain them. Towards the end of the fourth century, that golden age of Patristic theology, Chrysostom recognizes some stated order of the lessons as familiar to all his hearers, for he exhorts them to peruse and mark beforehand the passages (περικοπαί[1]) of the Gospels which were to be publicly read to them the ensuing Sunday or Saturday[2]. All the infor-

[1] This was the word for a lection or lesson, and Suicer tells us that ἀνάγνωσις and ἀνάγνωσμα were employed as equivalents. But in modern textual criticism, ἀναγνώσματα is used to signify the marks indicating lections, which are found in the margin or at the head or foot of pages, or the computation of their number which is often appended at the end of a book. See pp. 68, note 1, 69.

[2] Chrysost. in Joan. Hom. x κατὰ μίαν σαββάτων ἢ καὶ κατὰ σάββατον. Traces

mation we can gather favours the notion that there was no great difference between the calendar of Church-lessons in earlier and later stages. Not only do they correspond in all cases where such agreement is natural, as in the proper services for the great feasts and fasts, but in such purely arbitrary arrangements as the reading of the book of Genesis, instead of the Gospels, on the week days of Lent; of the Acts all the time between Easter and Pentecost[1]; and the selection of St. Matthew's history of the Passion alone at the Liturgy on Good Friday[2]. The earliest formal *Menologium*, or Table of proper lessons, now extant is prefixed to the Codex Cyprius (K) of the eighth or ninth century; another is found in the Codex Campianus (M), which is perhaps a little later; they are more frequently found than the contrary in later manuscripts of every kind; while there are comparatively few copies that have not been accommodated to ecclesiastical use either by their original scribe or a later hand, by means of noting the proper days for each lesson (often in red ink) at the top or bottom or in the margin of the several pages. Not only in the margin, but even in the text itself are perpetually interpolated, mostly in vermilion or red ink, the beginning (ἀρχή or αρχ) and ending (τέλος or τε^λ) of each lesson, and the several words to be inserted or substituted in order to suit the purpose of public reading; from which source (as we have stated above, p. 11) various readings have almost unavoidably sprung: e.g. in Acts iii. 11 τοῦ ἰαθέντος χωλοῦ of the Lectionaries ultimately displaced αὐτοῦ from the text itself.

of these Church-lessons occur in manuscripts as early as the fifth and sixth centuries. Thus Cod. Alexandrinus reads Rom. xvi. 25-27 not only in its proper place, but also at the end of ch. xiv where the Lectionaries place it (see p. 84). Codex Bezae prefixes to Luke xvi. 19 εἶπεν δὲ καὶ ἑτέραν παραβολήν, the proper introduction to the Gospel for the 5th Sunday in St. Luke. To John xiv. 1 the same manuscript prefixes καὶ εἶπεν τοῖς μαθηταῖς αὐτοῦ, as does our English Prayer Book in the Gospel for May 1. Even τέλος or τὸ τέλος, which follows ἀπέχει in Mark xiv. 41 in the same manuscript and other authorities, probably has the same origin.

[1] See the passages from Augustine Tract. VI. in Joan.; and Chrysost. Hom. VII ad Antioch.; Hom. LXIII, XLVII in Act. in Bingham's Antiquities, Book XIV, Chap. III. Sect. 3. Chrysostom even calls the arrangement τῶν πατέρων ὁ νόμος. The strong passage cited from Cyril of Jerusalem by Dean Burgon (Last Twelve Verses of St. Mark, p. 195) shows the confirmed practice as already settled in A.D. 348.

[2] August. Serm. CXLIII de Tempore. The few verses Luke xxiii. 39-43, John xix. 31-37 are merely wrought into one narrative with Matt. xxvii, each in its proper place. See p. 85.

We purpose to annex to this Chapter a table of lessons throughout the year, according to the use laid down in Synaxaria, Menologies, and Lectionaries, as well to enable the student to compare the proper lessons of the Greek Church with our own, as to facilitate reference to the manuscripts themselves, which are now placed almost out of the reach of the inexperienced. On comparing the manner in which the terms are used by different scribes and authors, we conceive that *Synaxarion* (συναξάριον) is, like Eclogadion, a name used for a table of daily lessons for the year beginning at Easter, and that these have varied but slightly in the course of many ages throughout the whole Eastern Church; that tables of Saints' day lessons, called *Menologies*, (μηνολόγιον), distributed in order of the months from September (when the new year and the indiction began) to August, differed widely from each other, both in respect to the lessons read and the days kept holy [1]. While the great feasts remained entirely the same, different generations and provinces and even dioceses had their favourite worthies, whose memory they specially cherished; so that the character of the menology (which sometimes forms a larger, sometimes but a small portion of a Lectionary) will often guide us to the country and district in which the volume itself was written. The Parham Evangelistarium 18 affords us a conspicuous example of this fact: coming from a region of which we know but little (Ciscissa in Cappadocia Prima), its menology in many particulars but little resembles those usually met with [2].

14. It only remains to say a few words about the *notation* adopted to indicate the several classes of manuscripts of the Greek Testament. These classes are six in number; that con-

---

[1] Besides this special meaning, Synaxarion was also employed in a general sense for any catalogue of Church-lessons, both for daily use and for Saints' days.

[2] This was naturally even more the case in countries where the Liturgy was not in Greek. Thus in the 'Calendar of the Coptic Church' translated from the Arabic by Dr. S. C. Malan (1873), the only Feast-days identical with those given below (pp. 87-89) are Sept. 14; Oct. 8; Nov. 8, 13, 14, 17, 25, 30; Dec. 20, 24, 25, 29; Jan. 1, 6 (the Lord's Baptism), 22; Feb. 2, 24; March 25; April 25; May 2; June 19, 24, 29; July 22; Aug. 6, 25. Elsewhere the day is altered, even if the festival be the same; e.g. St. Thomas' Day is Oct. 6 with the Greeks, Oct. 23 with the Copts; St. Luke's Day (Oct. 18), and the Beheading of the Baptist (Aug. 29), are kept by the Copts a day later than by the Greeks, since Aug. 29 is their New Year's Day.

taining the Gospels (*Evangelia* or *Evan.*), or the Acts and Catholic Epistles (*Act.* and *Cath.*), or the Pauline Epistles (*Paul.*), or the Apocalypse (*Apoc.*), or Lectionaries of the Gospels (*Evangelistaria* or *Evst.*), or those of the Acts and Epistles (*Apostolos* or *Apost.*). When one manuscript (as often happens) belongs to more than one of these classes, its distinct parts are numbered separately, so that a copy of the whole New Testament will appear in four lists, and be reckoned four times over. All critics are agreed in distinguishing the documents written in the uncial character by capital letters; the custom having originated in the accidental circumstance that the Codex Alexandrinus was designated as Cod. A in the lower margin of Walton's Polyglott. Lectionaries in uncial letters are not marked by capitals, but by Arabic numerals, like cursive manuscripts of all classes [1]. Of course no system can escape some attendant evils. Even the catalogue of the later manuscripts is often upon its first appearance full of mis-statements, of repetitions and loose descriptions, which must be remedied and supplied in subsequent examination, so far as opportunity is granted from time to time. In describing the uncials (as we purpose to do in the two next chapters) our course is tolerably plain; but the lists that comprise the last eight chapters of this volume, and which respectively detail the cursive manuscripts and the Lectionaries of the Greek Testament, must be regarded only as an approximation to what such an enumeration ought to be, though much pains and time have been spent upon them: the comparatively few copies which seem to be sufficiently known are distinguished by an asterisk from their less fortunate kindred.

For indeed the only method of grappling with the perplexity produced by the large additions of manuscripts, especially of the cursive character, which constant discovery has effected during late years, is to enumerate arithmetically those which have been supplied from time to time, as was done in the last edition of this work, carefully noting if they have been examined by a competent judge or especially if they have been properly collated. In the Appendix of the third edition, the late Dean Burgon continued his work in this direction by adding a list of some

---

[1] This system was introduced by Wetstein (N. T. 1751-52). Mill used to cite copies by abridgements of their names, e.g. Alex. Cant. Mont. &c.

three hundred and seventy-four cursives, besides the others with which he had previously increased the number before known. That list, as was stated in the Postcript to the Preface, awaited an examination and collation by competent persons. Such an examination has been made in many instances by Dr. C. R. Gregory, who also, whether fired by Dean Burgon's example as shown in his published letters in the *Guardian* or not, has in his turn added with most commendable diligence in research a very large number of MSS. previously unknown. Some more have been added in this edition, but much work is still required of scholars, before this mass of materials can be used with effect by Textual students.

APPENDIX TO CHAPTER III.

SYNAXARION AND ECLOGADION OF THE GOSPELS AND APOSTOLIC WRITINGS DAILY THROUGHOUT THE YEAR.

[Gathered chiefly from Evangelist. Arund. 547, Parham 18, Harl. 5598, Burney 22, Gale O. 4. 22, Christ's Coll. Camb. F. 1. 8, compared with the Liturgical notes in Wake 12, and those by later hands in Cod. Bezae (D). Use has been made also of Apostolos B-C. III. 24, B-C. III. 53, and the Euchology, or Book of Offices, B-C. III. 42.]

Ἐκ τοῦ κατὰ Ἰωάννην [Arundel 547]

Τῇ ἁγίᾳ καὶ μεγάλῃ κυριακῇ τοῦ πάσχα.

Easter-day	John i. 1-17.	Acts i. 1-8.
2nd day of Easter week (τῆς διακινησίμου)	18-28.	12-26.
3rd	Luke xxiv. 12-35.	ii. 14-21
4th	John i. 35-52.	38-43.
5th	iii. 1-15.	iii. 1-8.
6th (παρασκευῇ)	ii. 12-22.	ii. 12-36.
7th (σαββάτῳ)	iii. 22-33.	iii. 11-16.

Ἀντίπασχα or 1st Sunday after Easter (τοῦ Θωμᾶ, B-C. III. 42)

	xx. 19-31.	v. 12-20.
2nd day of 2nd week	ii. 1-11.	iii. 19-26.
3rd	iii. 16-21.	iv. 1-10.
4th	v. 17-24.	13-22.
5th	24-30.	23-31.
6th (παρασκευῇ)	v. 30—vi. 2.	v. 1-11.
7th (σαββάτῳ)	vi. 14-27.	21-32.

Κυριακῇ γ΄ or 2nd after Easter (τῶν μυροφόρων, B-C. III. 42)

Mark xv. 43—xvi. 8.		vi. 1-7.
2nd day of 3rd week	John iv. 46-54.	8—vii. 60.
3rd	vi. 27-33.	viii. 5-17.
4th (6th, Gale)	48-54.	18-25.
5th	40-44.	26-39.
6th (παρασκευῇ)		
(4th, Gale)	35-39.	40—ix. 19.
7th (σαββάτῳ) xv. 17—xvi. 1.		19-31.

Κυριακῇ δ΄ or 3rd Sunday after Easter (τοῦ παραλύτου sic, B-C. III. 42) John v. 1-15. Acts ix. 32-42.

2nd day of 4th week	vi. 56-69.	x. 1-16.
3rd	vii. 1-13.	21-33.
4th (τῆς μεσοπεντηκοστῆς, B-C. III. 42)	14-30.	xiv. 6-18.
5th	viii. 12-20.	x. 34-43.
6th (παρασκευῇ)	21-30.	44—xi. 10.
7th (σαββάτῳ)	31-42.	xii. 1-11.

Κυριακῇ ε΄ or 4th Sunday after Easter (τῆς σαμαρείτιδος) iv. 5-42. xi. 19-30.

2nd day of 5th week	viii. 42-51.	xii. 12-17.
3rd	51-59.	25—xiii. 12.
4th	vi. 5-14.	xiii. 13-24.
5th	ix. 39—x. 9.	xiv. 20-27 (-xv. 4, B-C. III. 24).
6th (παρασκευῇ)	x. 17-28.	xv. 5-12.
7th (σαββάτῳ)	27-38.	35-41.

Κυριακῇ Ϛ΄ or 5th Sunday after Easter (τοῦ τυφλοῦ) ix. 1-38. xvi. 16-34.

2nd day of 6th week	xi. 47-54.	xvii. 1-9.
3rd	xii. 19-36.	19-27.
4th	36-47.	xviii. 22-28.

SYNAXARION. 81

5th 'Αναλήψεως, Ascension Day
Matins, Mark xvi. 9-20.
Liturgy, Lukexxiv.36-53. Acts i. 1-12.
6th (παρασκευῇ) John xiv. 1-10
   (11, Gale, Wake 12).   xix. 1-8.
7th (σαββάτῳ) 10-21 (om.
        18-20, Gale).   xx. 7-12.

Κυριακῇ ζ' or 6th Sunday
after Easter τῶν ἁγίων τιη πατέρων ἐν
Νικαίᾳ.   xvii. 1-13.   16-38.
2nd day of 7th
week   xiv. 27—xv. 7.   xxi. 8-14.
3rd   xvi. 2-13.   26-32.
4th   15-23.   xxiii. 1-11.
5th   23-33.   xxv. 13-19.
6th (παρασκευῇ)   [1.
    xvii. 18-26.   xxvii.1-xxviii.
7th (σαββάτῳ) xxi. 14-25. xxviii.1-31.

Κυριακῇ τῆς πεντηκοστῆς
Whitsunday
Matins,   xx. 19-23.
Liturgy, vii. 37—viii. 12¹.   ii. 1-11.

Ἐκ τοῦ κατὰ Ματθαῖον.
2nd day of 1st week Τῇ ἐπαύριον τῆς πεντηκοστῆς.
    Matt. xviii. 10-20.   Eph. v. 8-19.
3rd   iv. 25—v. 11.
4th   20-30.
5th   31-41.
6th (παρασκευῇ) vii. 9-18.
7th (σαββάτῳ) v. 42-48. Rom. i. 7-12.

Κυριακῇ α' τῶν } x. 32-33 ; } Heb. xi. 33-
ἁγίων πάντων   37-38 ;   xii. 2.
               xix. 37-30 ;
2nd day of 2nd   vi. 31-34 ;
week   vii. 9-14. Rom. ii. 1-6.
3rd   vii. 15-21.   13, 17-27.
4th   11-23.   28—iii. 4.
5th   viii. 23-27.   iii. 4-9.
6th (παρασκευῇ) ix. 14-17.   9-18.
7th (σαββάτῳ) vii. 1-8.   iii. 19-26.

Κυριακῇ β' Matt. iv. 18-23. Rom. ii. 10-16.
2nd day of 3rd
week   ix. 36—x. 8.   iv. 4-8.
3rd   9-15.   8-12.
4th   16-22.   13-17.
5th   23-31.   18-25.
6th (παρασκευῇ) 32-36; xi. 1. v. 12-14.
7th (σαββάτῳ)
    vii. 24—viii. 4. iii. 28—iv. 3.

Κυριακῇ γ'   vi. 22-23.   v. 1-10.
2nd day of 4th
week   xi. 2-15.   15-17.
3rd   16-20.   17-21.
4th   20-26.   vii. 1. . . . .
5th   27-30.
6th (παρασκευῇ)   xii. 1-8.
7th (σαββάτῳ) viii. 14-23
  (om. 19-22, Gale).   vi. 11-17.

Κυριακῇ δ'   viii. 5-13.   vi. 18-23.
2nd day of 5th
week   xii. 9-13. vii. 19-viii. 3.
3rd   14-16 ; 22-30. viii. 2-9.
4th   38-45.   8-14.
5th   xii. 46—xiii. 3.   22-27.
6th (παρασκευῇ)   3-12.   ix. 6-13.
7th (σαββάτῳ) ix. 9-13. viii. 14-21.

Κυριακῇ ε'   viii. 28—ix. 1.   x. 1-10.
2nd day of 6th
week   xiii. 10-23.   ix. 13-19.
3rd   24-30.   17-28.
4th   31-36.   29-33.
5th   36-43.   ix. 33 ; x.
                      12-17.
6th (παρασκευῇ)   44-54. x. 15—xi. 2.
7th (σαββάτῳ) ix. 18-26. ix. 1-5.

Κυριακῇ ς'   ix. 1-8.   xii. 6-14.
2nd day of 7th
week   xiii. 54-58.   xi. 2-6.
3rd   xiv. 1-13.   7-12.
4th   xiv. 35—xv. 11.   13-20.
5th   12-21.   19-24.
6th (παρασκευῇ)   29-31.   25-28.
7th (σαββάτῳ) x. 37-xi. 1.   xii. 1-3.

---

¹ The *pericope adulterae* John vii. 53—viii. 11 is omitted in all the copies we know on the feast of Pentecost. Whenever read it was on some Saint's Day (vid. infra, p. 87, notes 2, 3).

VOL. I.   G

Κυριακῇ ζ'   Matt. ix. 27-35. Rom. xv.1-7.
2nd day of 8th
  week   xvi. 1-6.   xi. 29-36.
  3rd   6-12.   xii. 14-21.
  4th   20-24.   xiv. 10-18.
  5th   24-28.   xv. 8-12.
  6th (παρασκευῇ) xvii.10-18.   13-16.
  7th (σαββάτῳ)   xii. 30-37.   xiii. 1-10.

Κυριακῇ η'   xiv. 14-22. 1 Cor. i.10-18.
2nd day of 9th
  week   xviii. 1-11. Rom. xv. 17-25.
  3rd   xviii. 18-20 (al. 22);
                 xix. 1-2;   13-15.   26-29.
  4th   xx. 1-16.   xvi. 17-20.
  5th   17-28.   1 Cor. ii. 10-15.
  6th (παρασκευῇ) xxi. 12-14;
                 17-20.   16—iii. 8.
  7th (σαββάτῳ) xv. 32-39. Rom.xiv.6-9.

Κυριακῇ θ'   xiv. 22-34. 1Cor.iii.9-17.
2nd day of 10th
  week   xxi. 18-22.   18-23.
  3rd   23-27.   iv. 5-8.
  4th   28-32.   v. 9-13.
  5th   43-46.   vi. 1-6.
  6th (παρασκευῇ) xxii. 23-33. 7-11.
  7th (σαββάτῳ)
                 xvii. 24—xviii. 1. Rom. xv. 30-33.

Κυριακῇ ι'   xvii. 14-23. 1 Cor. iv. 9-16.
2nd day of 11th
  week   xxiii. 13-22. vi. 20-vii.7.
  3rd   23-28.   vii. 7-15.
  4th   29-39.
  5th xxiv. 13 (14, Wake 12 ;
             15 Cod. Bezae) -28.
  6th (παρασκευῇ) 27-35 (33
     Sch. and Matt.) ; 42-51. —vii. 35.
  7th (σαββάτῳ)   xix. 3-12.   i. 3-9.

Κυριακῇ ια'   xviii. 23-35.   ix. 2-12.

Ἐκ τοῦ κατὰ Μάρκον.

2nd day of 12th
  week   Mark i. 9-15. vii. 37—viii. 3.

  3rd   16-22.   viii. 4-7.
  4th   23-28.   ix. 13-18.
  5th   29-35.   x. 2-10.
  6th (παρασκευῇ) ii. 18-22.   10-15.
  7th (σαββάτῳ)
       Matt. xx. 29-34.   i. 26-29.

Κυριακῇ ιβ'
       Matt. xix. 16-26. 1 Cor. xv. 1-11.
2nd day of 13th
  week   Mark iii. 6-12.   x. 14-23.
  3rd   13-21.   31—xi. 3.
  4th   20-27.   xi. 4-12.
  5th   28-35.   13-23.
  6th (παρασκευῇ) iv. 1-9.   31. xii. 6.
  7th (σαββάτῳ)
       Matt. xxii. 15-22.   ii. 6-9.

Κυριακῇ ιγ'
       Matt. xxi. 33-42. 1 Cor. xvi. 13-24.
2nd day of 14th
  week   Mark iv. 10-23.   xii. 12-18.
  3rd   24-34.   18-26.
  4th   35-41. xiii.8—xiv.1.
  5th   v. 1-20 (al. 17). xiv. 1-12.
  6th (παρασκευῇ) v. 22-24 ; 35-vi. 1. 12-20.
  7th (σαββάτῳ)
       Matt. xxiii. 1-12.   iv. 1-5.

Κυριακῇ ιδ'
       Matt. xxii. 2-14. 2 Cor. i. 21—ii. 4.
2nd day of 15th
  week Mark v. 24-34. 1 Cor. xiv. 26-33.
  3rd   vi. 1-7.   33-40.
  4th   7-13.   xv. 12-20.
  5th   30-45.   29-34.
  6th (παρασκευῇ) 45-53.   34-40.
  7th (σαββάτῳ)
       Matt. xxiv. 1-13 (om. 10-12, Gale).
                                iv. 7—v. 5.

Κυριακῇ ιε'
       Matt. xxii. 35-40. 2 Cor. iv. 6-11
                           (15, B-C. III. 24).
2nd day of 16th
  week Mark vi. 54 (al. 56)
                 —vii. 8. 1 Cor. xvi.-3-13.
  3rd   5-16.   2 Cor. i. 1-7.
  4th   14-24.   12-20.
  5th   24-30.   ii. 4-15.

SYNAXARION.

6th (παρασκευῇ) viii. 1-10.	15—iii. 3.	[Κυριακῇ ιϚ´(16th) Matt. xxv. 14-30	
7th (σαββάτῳ)		(29, Gale).	2 Cor. vi. 1-10¹.
Matt. xxiv. 34-37 ; 42-44.		σαββάτῳ ιζ´ (17th) Matt. xxv. 1-13.	
	1 Cor. x. 23-28.	Κυριακῇ ιζ´ (17th) Matt. xv. 21-28].	

Ἀρχὴ τῆς ἰνδικτοῦ τοῦ νέου ἔτους, ἤγουν τοῦ εὐαγγελιστοῦ λουκᾶ [Arund. 547, Parham 18].		Κυριακῇ δ´ Luke viii. 5-8,	3rd	Luke xiv. 25-35.
			9-15.	4th xv. 1-10.
		2nd day of 5th		5th xvi. 1-9.
		week	ix. 18-22.	6th (παρασκευῇ)
		3rd	23-27.	xvi. 15-18 ; xvii. 1-4.
Ἐκ τοῦ κατὰ Λουκᾶν [Christ's Coll. F. 1. 8].		4th	43-50.	7th (σαββάτῳ) ix. 57-62.
		5th	49-56.	
2nd day of 1st		6th (παρασκευῇ) v. 1-15.		Κυριακῇ θ´ xii. 16-21.
week	Luke iii. 19-22.	7th (σαββάτῳ) vii. 1-10.		2nd day of 10th
3rd	23—iv. 1.			week xvii. 20-25.
4th	1-15.	Κυριακῇ ε´	xvi. 19-31.	3rd xvii. 26-37 ; xviii. 18.
5th	16-22.	2nd day of 6th		4th xviii. 15-17 ; 26-30.
6th (παρασκευῇ)	22-30.	week	x. 22-24.	5th 31-34.
7th (σαββάτῳ)	31-36.	3rd	xi. 1-10 (Mt.).	6th (παρασκευῇ) xix. 12-28.
		4th	9-13.	7th (σαββάτῳ) x. 19-21.
Κυριακῇ α´	v. 1-11.	5th	14-23.	
2nd day of 2nd		6th (παρασκευῇ)	23-26.	Κυριακῇ ι´ xiii. 10-17.
week	iv. 38-44.	7th (σαββάτῳ) viii. 16-21.		2nd day of 11th
3rd	v. 12-16.			week xix. 37-44.
4th	33-39.	Κυριακῇ Ϛ´ viii. 27 (26, Gale)		3rd 45-48.
5th	vi. 12-16 (al. 19).	-35 ; 38-39.		4th xx. 1-8.
6th (παρασκευῇ)	17-23.	2nd day of 7th		5th 9-18.
7th σαββάτῳ).	v. 17-26.	week	xi. 29-33.	6th (παρασκευῇ) 19-26.
		3rd	34-41.	7th (σαββάτῳ) xii. 32-40.
Κυριακῇ β´	v. 31-36.	4th	42-46.	
2nd day of 3rd		5th	47—xii. 1.	Κυριακῇ ια´ xiv. 16-24.
week	24-30.	6th (παρασκευῇ) xii. 2-12.		2nd day of 12th
3rd	37-45.	7th (σαββάτῳ)	ix. 1-6.	week xx. 27-44.
4th	vi. 46—vii. 1.			3rd xxi. 12-19.
5th	vii. 17-30.	Κυριακῇ ζ´	viii. 41-56.	4th xxi. 5-8 ; 10-11 ; 20-24.
6th (παρασκευῇ)	31-35.	2nd day of 8th		5th xxi. 28-33.
7th (σαββάτῳ)	v. 27-32.	week xii. 13-15 ; 22-31.		6th (παρασκευῇ)
		3rd	xii. 42-48.	xxi. 37—xxii. 8.
Κυριακῇ γ´	vii. 11-16.	4th	48-59.	7th (σαββάτῳ) xiii. 19-29.
2nd day of 4th		5th	xiii. 1-9.	
week	36-50.	6th (παρασκευῇ)	31-35.	Κυριακῇ ιβ´ xvii. 12-19.
3rd	vii. 1-3.	7th (σαββάτῳ)	ix. 37-43.	2nd day of 13th
4th	22-25.			week Mark viii. 11-21.
5th	ix. 7-11.	Κυριακῇ η´	x. 25-37.	3rd 22-26.
6th (παρασκευῇ)	12-18.	2nd day of 9th		4th 30-34.
7th (σαββάτῳ)	vi. 1-10.	week	xiv. 12-51.	5th ix. 10-16.

¹ Lessons for the week in B-C, III. 24 are (2) 2 Cor. iii. 4-12. (3) iv. 1-6. (4) 11-18. (5) v. 10-15. (6) 15-21.

6th (παρασκευῇ)	[2nd day of 15th	7th (σαββάτῳ)
Mark ix. 33-41.	week Mark x. 46-52.	Luke xviii. 1-8.
7th (σαββάτῳ)	3rd xi. 11-23.	
Luke xiv. 1-11.	4th 22-26.	Κυριακῇ ις' (of the Publican)
	5th 27-33.	Luke xviii. 9-14].
Κυριακῇ ιγ' Luke xviii. 18-27.	6th (παρασκευῇ) xii. 1-12.	Apost. 2 Tim. iii. 10-15
2nd day of 14th	7th (σαββάτῳ)	(B-C. III. 42).
week Mark ix. 42.—x. 1.	Luke xvii. 3-10.	2nd day of 17th
3rd x. 2-11.		week Mark xiii. 9-13.
4th 11-16.	Κυριακῇ ιε' Luke xix. 1-10.	3rd 14-23.
5th 17-27.	2nd day of 16th	4th 24-31.
6th (παρασκευῇ) 24-32.	week Mark xii. 13-17.	5th xiii. 31—xiv. 2.
7th (σαββάτῳ)	3rd 18-27.	6th (παρασκευῇ) xiv. 3-9.
Luke xvi. 10-15.	4th 28-34.	7th (σαββάτῳ)
	5th 38-44.	Luke xx. 46—xxi. 4.
Κυριακῇ ιδ' Luke xviii. 35-43.	6th (παρασκευῇ) xiii. 1-9.	

Κυριακῇ ιζ' (of the Canaanitess) Matt. xv. 21-28.

σαββάτῳ πρὸ τῆς ἀποκρέω, Luke xv. 1-10.

Κυριακῇ πρὸ τῆς ἀποκρέω (of the Prodigal)
Luke xv. 11-32. 1 Thess. v. 14-23
(1 Cor. vi. 12-20, B-C. III. 42).

2nd day of the week of the
Carnival Mark xi. 1-11. 2 Tim. iii. 1-10.
3rd xiv. 10-42. iii. 14-iv. 5.
4th 43—xv. 1. iv. 9-18.
5th xv. 1-15. Tit. i. 5-12.
6th (παρασκευῇ) xv. 20 ; 22 ; 25 ; 33-41.
Tit. i. 15-ii. 10.
7th (σαββάτῳ) Luke xxi. 8-9 ; 25-27 ;
33-36 ; 1 Cor. vi. 12-20 (2 Tim. ii.
11-19, B-C. III. 24).

Κυριακῇ τῆς ἀποκρέω   Matt. xxv. 31-46.
1 Cor. viii. 8—ix. 2 (1 Cor. vi. 12-20,
B-C. III. 24).

2nd day of the week of the cheese-eater
Luke xix. 29-40 ; xxii. 7-8 ; 39. Heb.
iv. 1-13.
3rd xxii. 39—xxiii. 1. Heb. v. 12-vi. 8.
4th   deest.
5th xxiii 1-33 ; 44-56. Heb. xxii. 14-27.
6th (παρασκευῇ)   deest.
7th (σαββάτῳ) Matt. vi. 1-13. Rom. xiv.
19-23 ; xvi. 25-27.

Κυριακῇ τῆς τυροφάγου Matt. vi. 14-21.
Rom. xiii. 11—xiv. 4.

Παννυχὶς τῆς ἁγίας νηστείας.
Vigil of Lent (Parh., Christ's) Matt. vii. 7-11.

Τῶν νηστειῶν (Lent).
σαββάτῳ α'
  Mark ii. 23—iii. 5.   Heb. i. 1-12.
Κυριακῇ α' John i. 44-52. Heb. xi. 24-40.
σαββάτῳ β' Mark i. 35-44.   iii. 12-14.
Κυριακῇ β'   ii. 1-12.   i. 10—ii. 3.
σαββάτῳ γ'   14-17.   x. 32-37.
Κυριακῇ γ'   viii. 34—ix 1.   iv. 14—v. 6.
σαββάτῳ δ'   vii. 31-37.   vi. 9-12.
Κυριακῇ δ'   ix. 17-31.   13-20.
σαββάτῳ ε'   viii. 27-31.   ix. 24-28.
Κυριακῇ ε'   x. 32-45.   11-14.
σαββάτῳ ς' (of Lazarus)
  John xi. 1-45. xii. 28—xiii. 8.
Κυριακῇ ς' τῶν Βαΐων, Matins, Matt. xxi.
1-11 ; 15-17 [εἰς τὴν λιτήν, Mark x.
46—xi. 11, Burney 22]. Liturgy, John
xii. 1-18. Phil. iv. 4-9.

Τῇ ἁγίᾳ μεγάλῃ (Holy Week).
2nd { Matins, Matt. xxi. 18-43.
     { Liturgy,   xxiv. 3-35.
3rd { Matins,   xxii. 15—xxiv. 2.
     { Liturgy, xxiv. 36—xxvi. 2.

SYNAXARION. 85

4th { Matins, John (xi. 47-53 (al. 56) Gale) xii. 17 (al. 19)-47 (al. 50).
Liturgy, Matt. xxvi. 6-16.

5th { Matins, Luke xxii. 1-36 (39, Gale).
Liturgy, Matt. xxvi. 1-20.

Εὐαγγέλιον τοῦ νιπτῆρος, John xiii. 3-10. μετὰ τὸ νίψασθαι 12-17[1];
Matt. xxvi. 21-39; Luke xxii. 43, 44;
Matt. xxvi. 40—xxvii. 2. 1 Cor. xi. 23-32.

Εὐαγγέλια τῶν ἁγίων παθῶν ῑῡ χῡ (Twelve Gospels of the Passions).

(1) John xiii. 31—xviii.1. (2) John xviii.1-28. (3) Matt.xxvi.57-75. (4) John xviii. 28—xix. 16. (5) Matt. xxvii. 3-32. (6) Mark xv. 16-32. (7) Matt. xxvii. 33-54. (8) Luke xxiii. 32-49. (9) John xix. 25-37. (10) Mark xv. 43-47. (11) John xix. 38-42. (12) Matt. xxvii. 62-66.

Εὐαγγέλια τῶν ὡρῶν τῆς ἁγίας παραμονῆς (Night-watches of Vigil of Good Friday).

Hour (1) Matt. xxvii. 1-56. (3) Mark xv. 1-41. (6) Luke xxii. 66—xxiii. 49. (9) John xix. 16 (al. 23 or xviii. 28)-37.

Τῇ ἁγίᾳ παρασκευῇ (Good Friday) εἰς τὴν λειτουργίαν (ἑσπέρας, B-C. III. 42).
Matt. xxvii. 1-38; Luke xxiii. 39-43;
Matt. xxvii. 39-54; John xix. 31-37:
Matt. xxvii. 55-61. 1 Cor. i. 18—ii. 2.

Τῷ ἁγίῳ καὶ μεγάλῳ σαββάτῳ (Easter Even).

Matins, Matt. xxvii. 62-66. 1 Cor. v. 6-8 (Gal. iii. 13, 14, B-C. III. 24).
Evensong, Matt. xxviii. 1-20. Rom. vi. 3-11 (λειτουργ. Matt. xxviii. 1-20, ἑσπέρας Rom. vi. 3-11, B-C. III. 42).

Εὐαγγέλια ἀναστάσιμα ἑωθινά (vid. Suicer Thes. Eccles. i. 1229), eleven Gospels, used in turn, one every Sunday at Matins, beginning with All Saints' Day (B-C. III. 42). In some Evst. these are found at the end of the book.

(1) Matt. xxviii. 16-20. (2) Mark xvi. 1-8. (3) ib. 9-20. (4) Luke xxiv. 1-12. (5) ib. 12-35. (6) ib. 36-53. (7) John xx. 1-10. (8) ib. 11-18. (9) ib. 19-31. (10) John xxi. 1-14. (11) ib. 15-25.

We have now traced the daily service of the Greek Church, as derived from the Gospels, throughout the whole year, from Easter Day to Easter Even, only that in Lent the lessons from the 2nd to the 6th days inclusive in each week are taken from the book of Genesis. The reader will observe that from Easter to Pentecost St. John and the Acts are read for seven weeks, or eight Sundays. The first Sunday after Pentecost is the Greek All Saints' Day, their Trinity Sunday being virtually kept a fortnight earlier; but from the Monday next after the day of Pentecost (Whit-Monday) St. Matthew is used continuously every day for eleven weeks and as many Sundays. For six weeks more, St. Matthew is appointed for the Saturday and Sunday lessons, St. Mark for the other days of the week. But inasmuch as St. Luke was to be taken up with the new year, the year of the

---

[1] In B-C. III. 42 all the Gospels for this day run into each other without break, e.g. John xiii. 3-17 being read *uno tenore*. Just so in the same manuscript stands the mixed lesson for Good Friday evening.

APPENDIX TO CHAPTER III.

indiction [Arund. 547], which in *this* case must be September 24 [1], if all the lessons in Matthew and Mark were not read out by this time (which, unless Easter was very early, would not be the case), they were at once broken off, and (after proper lessons had been employed for the Sunday before and the Saturday and Sunday which followed [2] the feast of the Elevation of the Cross, Sept. 14) the lessons from St. Luke (seventeen weeks and sixteen Sundays in all) were taken up and read on as far as was necessary : only that the 17th Sunday of St. Matthew (called from the subject of its Gospel *the Canaanitess*) was always resumed on the Sunday preceding that before the Carnival (πρὸ τῆς ἀποκρέω), which is also named from its Gospel that of *the Prodigal*, and answers to the Latin *Septuagesima*. Then follow the Sunday of the Carnival (ἀποκρέω) or *Sexagesima*, that of *the Cheese-eater* (τυροφάγου) or *Quinquagesima*, and the six Sundays in Lent. The whole number of Sunday Gospels in the year (even reckoning the two interpolated about September 14) is thus only fifty-three, *the Canaanitess* coming twice over : but in the Menology or Catalogue of immoveable feasts will be found proper lessons for three Saturdays and Sundays about Christmas and Epiphany, which could either be substituted for, or added to the ordinary Gospels for the year, according as the distance from Easter in one year to Easter in the next exceeded or fell short of fifty-two weeks. The system of lessons from the Acts and Epistles is much simpler than that of the Gospels : it exhibits fifty-two Sundays in the year, without any of the complicated arrangements of the other scheme. Since the Epistles from the Saturday of the 16th week after Pentecost to the Sunday of the Prodigal could not be set (like the rest) by the side of their corresponding Gospels, they are given separately in the following table [3].

Κυριακῇ ιϛ'	2 Cor. vi. 1-10.	Κυριακῇ κα'	Gal. ii. 16-20.
σαββάτῳ ιζ'	1 Cor. xiv. 20-25.	σαββάτῳ κβ'	2 Cor. v. 1-10 (1-4 in B-C. III. 24).
Κυριακῇ ιζ'	2 Cor. vi. 16—viii. 1.		
σαββάτῳ ιη'	1 Cor. xv. 39-45.	Κυριακῇ κβ'	Gal. vi. 11-18.
Κυριακῇ ιη'	2 Cor. ix. 6-11.	σαββάτῳ κγ'	2 Cor. viii. 1-5.
σαββάτῳ ιθ'	1 Cor. xv. 58—xvi. 3.	Κυριακῇ κγ'	Eph. ii. 4-10.
Κυριακῇ ιθ'	2 Cor. xi. 31—xii. 9.	σαββάτῳ κδ'	2 Cor. xi. 1-6.
σαββάτῳ κ'	2 Cor. i. 8-11.	Κυριακῇ κδ'	Eph. ii. 14-22.
Κυριακῇ κ'	Gal. i. 11-19.	σαββάτῳ κε'	Gal. i. 3-10.
σαββάτῳ κα'	2 Cor. iii. 12-18.	Κυριακῇ κε'	Eph. iv. 1-7.

[1] The more usual indiction, which dates from Sept. 1, is manifestly excluded by the following rubric (Burney, 22, p. 191, and in other copies): Δέον γινώσκειν ὅτι ἄρχεται ὁ Λουκᾶς ἀναγινώσκεσθαι ἀπὸ τῆς Κυριακῆς μετὰ τὴν ὕψωσιν· τότε γὰρ καὶ ἡ ἰσημερία [i. e. ἰσημερία] γίνεται, ὃ καλεῖται νέον ἔτος. Ἢ ὅτι ἀπὸ τὰς [τῆς] κγ' τοῦ σεπτεμβρίου ὁ Λουκᾶς ἀναγινώσκεται.
[2] The lesson for the Sunday after Sept. 14 is the same as that for the 3rd Sunday in Lent.
[3] The ordinary lessons for week days stand thus in B-C. III. 24. Week ιϛ'. (2) 2 Cor. iii. 4-12. (3) iv. 1-6. (4) 11-18. (5) v. 10-15. (6) 15-21. ιζ'. (2) vi. 11-16. (3) vii. 1-11. (4) 10-16. (5) viii. 7-11. (6) 10-21. ιη'. (2) viii. 20—ix. 1. (3) ix. 1-5. (4) 12—x. 5. (5) 4-12. (6) 13-18. ιθ'. (2) xi. 5-9. (3) 10-18. (4) xii. 10-14. (5) 14-19. (6) 19—xiii. 1. κ'. (2) xiii. 2-7. (3) 7-11. (4) Gal. i. 18—ii. 5. (5) ii. 6-16. (6) ii. 20—iii. 7. κα'. (2) iii. 15-22. (3) 23—iv. 5. (4) iv. 9-14. (5) 13-26. (6) 28—v. 5. κβ'. (2) v. 4-14. (3) 14-21. (4) vi. 2-10. (5) Eph. i. 9-17. (6) 16-23. κγ'. (2) ii. 18—iii. 5. (3) 5-12. (4) 13-21. (5) iv. 12-16. (6) 17-25. κδ'. (2) v. 19-26. (3) 25-31. (4) 28—vi. 6. (5) 7-11. (6) 17-21. κε'. (2) Phil. i. 2. *Iliat codex nsque ad* λ'. (1) 1 Thess. i. 6-10. (3) 9—ii. 4. (4) 4-8. (5) 9-14. (6) 14-20. λα'. (2) iii. 1-8. (3) 6-11. (4) 11—iv. 6. (5) 7-11. (6) 17—v. 5. λβ'. (?) v. 4-11. (3) 11-15. (4) 15-23. (5) 2 Thess. i. 1-5. (6) 11—ii. 5. λγ'. (2) ii. 13—iii. 5. (3) 3-9. (4) 10-18. (5) 1 Tim. i. 1-8. (6) 8-14. λδ'. (2) 1 Tim. ii. 5-15. (3) iii. 1-13. (4) iv. 4-9. (5) 14—v. 10. (6) 17—vi. 2. λε'. (2) vi. 2-11. (3) 17-21. (4) 2 Tim. i. 8-14. (5) 14—ii. 2. (6) 22-26.

σαββάτῳ κϛ'	Gal. iii. 8-12.	Κυριακῇ λα'	2 Tim. i. 3-9.
Κυριακῇ κϛ'	Eph. v. 8-19.	σαββάτῳ λβ'	Col. ii. 8-12.
σαββάτῳ κζ'	Gal. v. 22—vi. 2.	Κυριακῇ λβ'	1 Tim. vi. 11-16.
Κυριακῇ κζ'	Eph. vi. 10-17.	σαββάτῳ λγ'	1 Tim. ii. 1-7.
σαββάτῳ κη'	Col. i. 9-18.	Κυριακῇ λγ'	as Κυρ. λα'. (2 Tim. i.
Κυριακῇ κη'	2 Cor. ii. 14—iii. 3.		3-9 in B-C. III. 24).
σαββάτῳ κθ'	Eph. ii. 11-13.	σαββάτῳ λδ'	1 Tim. iii. 13—iv. 5.
Κυριακῇ κθ'	Col. iii. 4-11.	Κυριακῇ λδ'	2 Tim. iii. 10-15.
σαββάτῳ λ'	Eph. v. 1-8.	σαββάτῳ λε'	1 Tim. iv. 9-15.
Κυριακῇ λ'	Col. iii. 12-16.	Κυριακῇ λε'	2 Tim. ii. 1-10.
σαββάτῳ λα'	Col. i. 2-6.	σαββάτῳ λϛ'	2 Tim. ii. 11-19.

ON THE MENOLOGY, OR CALENDAR OF IMMOVEABLE FESTIVALS AND SAINTS' DAYS.

We cannot in this place enter very fully into this portion of the contents of Lectionaries, inasmuch as, for reasons we have assigned above, the investigation would be both tedious and difficult. All the great feast-days, however, as well as the commemorations of the Apostles and of a few other Saints, occur alike in all the books, and ought not to be omitted here. We commence with the month of September (the opening of the year at Constantinople, as do all the Lectionaries and Synaxaria we have seen [1].

Sept. 1. Simeon Stylites, Luke iv. 16-22; Col. iii. 12-16 (1 Tim. ii. 1-7, B-C. III. 53).
2. John the Faster, Matt. v. 14-19 (Wake 12). (John xv. 1-11, Parham 18.)
8. Birthday of the Virgin, Θεοτόκος, Matins, Luke i. 39-49, 56 (B-C. III. 24 and 42). Liturgy, Luke x. 38-42; xi. 27, 28; Phil. ii. 5-11.
Κυριακῇ πρὸ τῆς ὑψώσεως, John iii. 13-17; Gal. vi. 11-18.
14. Elevation of the Cross, Matins, John xii. 28-36. Liturgy, John xix. 6-35 (diff. in K and some others); 1 Cor. i. 18-24.

σαββάτῳ { μετὰ | John viii. 21-30; 1 Cor. i. 26-29.
Κυριακῇ { τὴν ὕψωσιν | Mark viii. 34—ix.1; Gal. ii. 16-20.

18. Theodora[2], John viii. 3-11 (Parham).
24. Thecla, Matt. xxv. 1-13; 2 Tim. i. 3-9.

Oct. 3. Dionysius the Areopagite, Matt. xiii. 45-54; Acts xvii. 16 (19, Cod. Bezae)—34 (16-23, 30, B-C, III. 24) (diff. in K).
6. Thomas the Apostle, John xx. 19-31; 1 Cor. iv. 9-16.
8. Pelagia, John viii. 3-11 [3].
9. James son of Alphaeus, Matt. x. 1-7, 14, 15.
18. Luke the Evangelist, Luke x. 16-21; Col. iv. 5-9, 14, 18.
23. James, ὁ ἀδελφόθεος, Mark vi. 1-7; James i. 1-12.

Nov. 8. Michael and Archangels, Matins, Matt. xviii. 10-20. Liturgy, Luke x. 16-21; Heb. ii. 2-10.
13. Chrysostom, Matins, John x. 1-9.

---

[1] In the *Menology*, even Arund. 547 has μηνὶ σεπτεμβρίῳ ἀ· ἀρχὴ τῆς ἰνδίκτου. So Burn. 22 nearly.
[2] *Theodosia* in Codex Cyprius (*see* p. 73), with the cognate lesson, Luke vii. 36-50, which lesson is read in Gale for Sept. 16, Euphemia and in Evst. 261 (D.M. Addit. 11,840). In Burdett-Coutts II. 7, John viii. 3-11 is used εἰς μετανοούντας: B-C. II. 30 adds καὶ γυναικῶν.
[3] So Cod. Cyprius, but the Christ's Coll. Evst. removes Pelagia to Aug. 31, and reads John viii. 1-11.

APPENDIX TO CHAPTER III.

Liturgy, John x. 9-16; Heb. vii. 26—viii. 2.

Nov. 14. Philip the Apostle, John i. 44-55; Acts viii. 26-39.

16. Matthew the Apostle, Matt. ix. 9-13; 1 Cor. iv. 9-16.

17. Gregory Thaumaturgus, Matt. x. 1-10 (Wake 12); 1 Cor. xii. 7, 8, 10, 11.

25. Clement of Rome, John xv. 17—xvi. 1; Phil. iii. 20—iv. 3.

30. Andrew the Apostle, John i. 35-52; 1 Cor. iv. 9-16.

Dec. 20. Ignatius, ὁ θεόφορος, Mark ix. 33-41; Heb. iv. 14—v. 6 (Rom. viii. 28-39, B·C. III. 24).

Saturday before Christmas, Matt. xiii. 31-58 (Luke xiii. 19-29, Gale); Gal. iii. 8-12.

Sunday before Christmas, Matt. i. 1-25; Heb. xi. 9-16 (9, 10, 32-40, B-C. III. 24).

24. Christmas Eve, Luke ii. 1-20; Heb. i. 1-12. Προεόρτια, 1 Pet. ii. 10 (B-C. III. 24).

25. Christmas Day, Matins, Matt. i. 18-25. Liturgy, Matt. ii. 1-12; Gal. iv. 4-7.

26. εἰς τὴν σύναξιν τῆς θεοτόκου, Matt. ii. 13-23; Heb. ii. 11-18.

27. Stephen[1], Matt. xxi. 33-42 (Gale); Acts vi. 1-7.

Saturday after Christmas, Matt. xii. 15-21; 1 Tim. vi. 11-16.

Sunday after Christmas, Mark i. 1-8; Gal. i. 11-19. The same Lessons for

29. Innocents (Gale).

Saturday πρὸ τῶν φώτων, Matt. iii. 1-6; 1 Tim. iii. 13—iv. 5.

Sunday πρὸ τῶν φώτων, Mark i. 1-8; 1 Tim. iii. 13—iv. 5 (2 Tim. iv. 5-8, B-C. III. 24).

Jan. 1. Circumcision, Luke ii. 20, 21, 40-52; 1 Cor. xiii. 12—xiv. 5.

5. Vigil of θεοφανία, Luke iii. 1-18; 1 Cor. ix. 19—x. 4.

6. θεοφανία (Epiphany) { Matins, Mark i. 9-11. { Titus ii. 11-14 (B-C. III. 42 adds iii. 4-7). Liturgy, Matt. iii. 13-17.

7. John, ὁ πρόδρομος, John i. 29-34.

Saturday μετὰ τὰ φῶτα, Matt. iv. 1-11; Eph. vi. 10-17.

Sunday μετὰ τὰ φῶτα, Matt. iv. 12-17; Eph. iv. 7-13.

16. Peter ad Vincula, John xxi. 15-19 (B-C. III. 42).

22. Timothy, Matt. x. 32, 33, 37, 38; xix. 27-30; 2 Tim. i. 3-9.

Feb. 2. Presentation of Christ, Matins, Luke ii. 25-32. Liturgy, Luke ii. 22-40; Heb. vii. 7-17.

3. Simeon ὁ θεοδόχος and Anna, Luke ii. 25-38; Heb. ix. 11-14.

23. Polycarp, John xii. 24-36,

24. Finding of the Head of John the Baptist { Matins, Luke vii. 18-29 (17-30, B-C. III. 42). Liturgy, Matt. xi. 5-14; 2 Cor. iv. 6-11.

March 24. Vigil of Annunciation, Luke i. 39-56 (Gale).

25. Annunciation, Luke i. 24-38; Heb. ii. 11-18.

April 23. St. George, Matins, Mark xiii. 9-13. Liturgy, Acts xii. 1-11 (Cod. Bezae)[2].

25. (Oct. 19, B-C. III. 24). Mark the Evangelist, Mark vi. 7-13; Col. iv. 5, 10, 11, 18.

30. James, son of Zebedee, Matt. x. 1-7, 14, 15.

May 2. Athanasius, Matt. v. 14-19; Heb. iv. 14.—v. 6.

8. (Sept. 26, B-C. III. 42). John, ὁ θεόλογος, John xix. 25-27; xxi. 24, 25; 1 John i. 1-7 (iv. 12-19, B-C. III. 42).

21. Helena, Luke iv. 22, &c., Evst. 298.

26. Jude the Apostle, John xiv. 21-24.

---

[1] The Proto-martyr Stephen is commemorated on August 2 in Evst. 3 (Wheeler 3).

[2] The same Saint is commemorated in the fragment of a Golden Evangelistarium seen at Sinai by the Rev. E. M. Young in 1864, and in B-C. III. 42 as μεγαλόμαρτυς ὁ τροπαιοφόρος; which (Evst. 286) is described in its place below.

MENOLOGY.

June 11. Bartholomew and Barnabas the Apostles, Mark vi. 7-13; Acts xi. 19-30.
19. Jude, brother of the Lord, Mark vi. 7-13, or εὐαγγέλιον ἀποστολικόν (Matt. x. 1-8 ? June 30).
24. Birth of John the Baptist, Luke i. 1-25; 57-80; Rom. xiii. 11—xiv. 4.
29. Peter and Paul the Apostles, Matins, John xxi. 15-31. Liturgy, Matt. xvi. 13-19; 2 Cor. xi. 21—xii. 9.
30. The Twelve Apostles, Matt. x. 1-8.
July 20. Elijah, Luke iv. 22, &c., Evst. 229.
22. Mary Magdalene, ἡ μυροφόρος, Mark xvi. 9-20; 2 Tim. ii. 1-10.
Aug. 1. τῶν ἁγίων μακκαβαίων, Matt. x. 16, &c., Evst. 228 and others.

Aug. 6. Transfiguration { Matins, Luke ix. 29-36 or Mark ix. 2-9. Liturgy, Matt. xvii. 1-9; 2 Pet. i. 10-19.
15. Assumption of the Virgin, Luke x. 38-42 (Gale, Codex Bezae).
20. Thaddaeus the Apostle, Matt. x. 16-22; 1 Cor. iv. 9-16.
25. Titus, Matt. v. 14-19 (Gale); 2 Tim. ii. 1-10.
29. Beheading of John the Baptist. Matins, Matt. xiv. 1-13. Liturgy. Mark vi. 14-30; Acts xiii. 25-32 (39, B.C. III. 24).
Εἰς τὰ ἐγκαίνια, Dedication, John x. 22 (17, Gale)—28 (Gale, Cod. Bezae); 2 Cor. v. 15-21; Heb. ix. 1-7.

At Cambridge (Univ. Libr. II. 28. 8) is a rare volume containing the Greek Gospel Church-Lessons, Θεῖον καὶ ἱερὸν εὐαγγέλιον, Venice, 1615-24, once belonging to Bishop Hacket: also the Apostolos of a smaller size. Another edition appeared in 1851, also at Venice.

For a comparison of the Greek with the Coptic Calendar, see p. 77, note 2. For the Monology in the Jerusalem Syriac Lectionary, see Vol. II, Chap. I.

on his subsequent visit in 1853, could he gain any tidings of the leaves he had left behind;—he even seems to have concluded that they had been carried into Europe by some richer or more fortunate collector. At the beginning of 1859, after the care of the seventh edition of his N.T. was happily over, he went for a third time into the East, under the well-deserved patronage of the Emperor of Russia, the great protector of the Oriental Church; and the treasure which had been twice withdrawn from him as a private traveller, was now, on the occasion of some chance conversation, spontaneously put into the hands of one sent from the champion and benefactor of the oppressed Church. Tischendorf touchingly describes his surprise, his joy, his midnight studies over the priceless volume ('*quippe dormire nefas videbatur*') on that memorable 4th of February, 1859. The rest was easy; he was allowed to copy his prize at Cairo, and ultimately to bring it to Europe, as a tribute of duty and gratitude to the Emperor Alexander II. To that monarch's wise munificence both the larger edition (1862), and the smaller of the New Testament only (1863), are mainly due.

The Codex Sinaiticus is $13\frac{1}{2}$ inches in length by $14\frac{7}{8}$ inches high, and consists of $346\frac{1}{2}$ leaves of the same beautiful vellum as the Cod. Friderico-Augustanus which is really a part of it whereof 199 contain portions of the Septuagint version, $147\frac{1}{2}$ the whole New Testament, Barnabas' Epistle, and a considerable fragment of Hermas' Shepherd. It has subsequently appeared that the Russian Archimandrite (afterwards Bishop) Porphyry had brought with him from Sinai in 1845 some pieces of Genesis xxiii, xxiv, and of Numbers v, vi, and vii, which had been applied long before to the binding of other books [1]. Each page comprises four columns (*see* p. 27), with forty-eight lines in each column, of those continuous, noble, simple uncials (*compare* Plate IV. 11 a *with* 11 b). The poetical books of the Old Testament,

---

[1] These fragments were published by Tischendorf in his Appendix Codd. cel. Sin. Vat. Alex. 1867. They consist of Gen. xxiii. 19—xxiv. 4; 5-8; 10-14; 17, 18; 25-27; 30-33; 36-41; 43-46; Num. v. 26-30; vi. 5, 6, 11, 12, 17, 18; 22-27; vii. 4, 5, 12, 13; 15-26. Another leaf of the same manuscript, containing Lev. xxii. 3—xxiii. 22, was also found at Sinai by Dr. H. Brügsch Bey, of Göttingen, and published by him in his Neue Bruchstücke des Codex Sinaiticus aufgefunden in der Bibliothek des Sinai Klosters, 1875, but is not, after all, part of Cod. ℵ. Another morsel, containing Gen. xxiv. 9, 10, and 41-43, now at St. Petersburg, really belongs to it.

however, being written in στίχοι, admit of only two columns on a page (*above*, p. 52). 'In the Catholic Epistles the scribe has frequently contented himself with a column of forty-seven lines[1].' The order of the sacred books is remarkable, though by no means unprecedented. St. Paul's Epistles precede the Acts, and amongst them, that to the Hebrews follows 2 Thess., standing on the same page with it (p. 74). Although this manuscript has hitherto been inspected by few Englishmen (Tregelles, however, and Dean Stanley were among the number), yet its general aspect has grown familiar to us by the means of photographs of its most important pages taken for the use of private scholars[2], as well as from the facsimiles contained in Tischendorf's several editions. Breathings and accents there are none except in Tobit vi. 9, and Gal. v. 21, as has been already mentioned: the apostrophus and the single point for punctuation are entirely absent for pages together, yet occasionally are rather thickly studded, not only in places where a later hand has been unusually busy (e.g. Isaiah i. 1—iii. 2, two pages), but in some others (e.g. in 2 Cor. xii. 20 there are eight stops). Even words very usually abridged (except θσ̄, κσ, ισ̄, χσ, πνα which are constant) are here written in full though the practice varies, πατηρ, υιος, ουρανος, ανθρωπος, δαυειδ: we find ισραηλ', ισλ̄, or ιηλ̄: ϊερουσαλημ', ιημ̄, ιλμ̄, ιηλμ'. Tischendorf considers the two points over *iota* and *upsilon* (which are sometimes wanting) as seldom from the first hand: the mark >, besides its rather rare marginal use in citations (*see* p. 64, note 4), we notice in the text oftener in the Old Testament than in the New. Words are divided at the end of a line: thus K in OYK, and X in OYX are separated[3]. Small

---

[1] J. Rendel Harris, New Testament Autographs, Baltimore (without date), an original and ingenious contribution to textual criticism; as is the Origin of the Leicester Codex (1887) Camb. Synd. by the same author, Fellow of Clare College, and Reader in Palaeography at Cambridge. Curious results in Bradshaw's spirit. Identity of hand with Caius Psalter.

[2] Abbot, Comparative Antiquity of the Sinaitic and Vatican Manuscripts, p. 195. Dean Burgon surrendered the position maintained in The Last Twelve Verses of St. Mark.

[3] It has been suggested that this strange mode of division originated in the reluctance of scribes to begin a new line with any combination of letters which could not commence a Greek word, and to end a line with any letter which is not a vowel, or a liquid, or σ, or γ before another consonant, except in the case of Proper Names (Journal of Sacred Literature, April 1863, p. 8). Certainly the general practice in Cod. ℵ bears out the rule thus laid down, though a few

letters, of the most perfect shape, freely occur in all places, especially at the end of lines, where the—*superscript* (*see* p. 50) is almost always made to represent Ν (e.g. seventeen times in Mark i. 1-35). Other *compendia scribendi* are Κ for και, and ΗΝ written as in Plate I. No. 2[1]. Numerals are represented by letters, with a straight line placed over them, e.g. μ̄ Mark i. 13[1]. Although there are no capitals, the initial letter of a line which begins a paragraph generally (not always) stands out from the rank of the rest, as in the Old Testament portion of Cod. Vaticanus, and less frequently in the New, after the fashion of certain earlier pieces on papyrus. The titles and subscriptions of the several books are as short as possible (*see* p. 65). The τίτλοι or κεφάλαια *majora* are absent; the margin contains the so-called Ammonian sections and Eusebian canons, but Tischendorf is positive that neither they nor such notes as στιχων ρ̄π̄ (*see* p. 53, note 3) appended to 2 Thessalonians, are by the original scribe, although they may possibly be due to a contemporary hand. From the number of ὁμοιοτέλευτα and other errors, one cannot affirm that it is very carefully written. Its itacisms are of the oldest type, and those not constant; chiefly ι for ει, and δε and ε, and much more rarely η and υ and οι interchanged. The grammatical forms commonly termed Alexandrian occur, pretty much as in other manuscripts of the earliest date. The whole manuscript is disfigured by corrections, a few by the original scribe, or by the usual comparer or διορθώτης (*see* p. 55); very many by an ancient and elegant hand of the sixth century (ℵ^a), whose emendations are of great importance; some again by a hand but little later (ℵ^b); far the greatest number by a scholar of the seventh century (ℵ^c), who often cancels the changes introduced by ℵ^a; others by as many as eight several later writers, whose varying styles Tischendorf has carefully discriminated and illustrated by facsimiles[2].

---

instances to the contrary occur here and there (Scrivener, Collation of Cod. Sinaiticus, Introd. p. xiv, note). Hort refers it to a grammatical rule not to end a line with οὐκ or οὐχ, or a consonant preceding an elided vowel, as ἀπ', οὐδ'. New Testament in Greek, p. 315.

[1] But ΜΙ ΝΙ, for μη, νη occur even in the Septuagint Cod. Sarravianus, also of the fourth century, in which copy numerals are quite constantly expressed by letters.

[2] Tischendorf, however, describes ℵ^a as 'et formis et atramento primam

The foregoing considerations were bringing even cautious students to a general conviction that Cod. ℵ, if not, as its enthusiastic discoverer had announced, 'omnium antiquissimus' in the absolute sense of the words, was yet but little lower in date than the Vatican manuscript itself, and a veritable relic of the middle of the fourth century—the presence in its margin of the sections and canons of Eusebius [d. 340?], by a hand nearly if not quite contemporaneous, seems to preclude the notion of higher antiquity[1]—when Constantine Simonides, a Greek of

manum tantum non adaequans,' and its writer has been regarded by some as little inferior in value to the first scribe. Thus Dr. Hort (Introd. p. 271), calling him the 'corrector' proper, states that he 'made use of an excellent exemplar, and the readings which he occasionally uses take high rank as authority.' Hort considers ℵ^b as mixed, ℵ^c as still more so.

[1] I am indebted for the following Memoranda on Cod. ℵ to the kindness of the Dean of Derry and Raphoe.

i. It is demonstrable that the Eusebian Sections and Canons on the margin are contemporaneous with the text. For they are wanting from leaves 10 and 15. Now these leaves are conjugate; and they have been (on other grounds) noted by Tischendorf as written not by the scribe of the body of the N. T., but by one of his colleagues ('D') who wrote part of the O. T. and acted as Diorthota of the N. T. It thus appears that, after the marginal numbers had been inserted, the sheet containing leaves 10 and 15 was cancelled, and rewritten by a contemporary hand. The numbers must therefore have been written before the MS. was completed and issued.

ii. The exemplar whence these numbers were derived, differed considerably from that which the text follows. For, in some cases, the sectional numbers indicate the presence of passages which are absent from the text. E. g. St. Matt. xvi. 2, 3, which is sect. 162, is wanting; and 162 is assigned to ver. 4, while the wrong canon (5 for 6) betrays the presence in the canonizer's exemplar of the passage omitted by the scribe. The same is true of St. Mark xv. 28 (in which case the scribe is 'D').

iii. The scribe who wrote the text was unacquainted with the Eusebian sections. For the beginning of a section is not marked, as in A and most subsequent MSS., by a division of the text and a larger letter. On the contrary the text is divided into paragraphs quite independent of the Eusebian divisions, which often begin in the middle of a line, and are marked merely by two dots (:) in vermilion, inserted no doubt by the rubricator as he entered the numbers in the margin. The fact that the numbers of the sections as well as of the canons (not as in other MSS. of the Canons only) are in vermilion, points the same way.

iv. From the above it follows, (1) That while Cod. ℵ proves the absence from its exemplar of certain passages, its margin proves the presence of some of them in a contemporaneous exemplar; (2) that while on the one hand the Eusebian numbers, coeval with the text, show that the MS. cannot be dated before the time of Eusebius, on the other hand the form of the text, inasmuch as it is not arranged so as to suit them, and as it differs from the text implied in them, marks for it a date little, if at all, after his time—certainly many years earlier than A.

v. As regards the omission of the verses of St. Mark xvi. 9-20, it is not correct to

Syme, who had just edited a few papyrus fragments of the New Testament alleged to have been written in the first century of the Christian era, suddenly astonished the learned world in 1862 by claiming to be himself the scribe who had penned this manuscript in the monastery of Panteleemon on Mount Athos, as recently as in the years 1839 and 1840. The writer of these pages must refer to the Introduction to his Collation of the Codex Sinaiticus (pp. lx—lxxii, 2nd edition, 1867) for a statement of the reasons which have been universally accepted as conclusive, why the manuscript which Simonides may very well have written under the circumstances he has described neither was nor possibly could be that venerable document. The discussion of the whole question, however, though painful enough in some aspects, was the means of directing attention to certain peculiarities of Cod. א which might otherwise have been overlooked. While engaged in demonstrating that it could not have been transcribed from a Moscow-printed Bible, as was 'Cod. Simoneidos' (to borrow the designation employed by its author), critics came to perceive that either this copy or its immediate prototype must have been derived from a papyrus *exemplar*, and that probably of Egyptian origin (Collation, &c. pp. viii*; xiv; lxviii), a confirmation of the impression conveyed to the reader by a first glance at the eight narrow columns of each open leaf (p. 28). The claim of Simonides to be the sole writer of a book which must have consisted when complete of about 730 leaves, or 1460 pages of very large size (Collation, &c. p. xxxii), and that too within the compass of eight or ten months[1] (he inscribed on

assert that Cod. א betrays no sign of consciousness of their existence. For the last line of ver. 8, containing only the letters τοᴦαρ, has the rest of the space (more than half the width of the column) filled up with a minute and elaborate 'arabesque' executed with the pen in ink and vermilion, nothing like which occurs anywhere else in the whole MS. (O. T. or N. T.), such spaces being elsewhere invariably left blank. By this careful filling up of the blank, the scribe (who here is the diorthota 'D'), distinctly shows that the omission is not a case of 'non-interpolation,' but of deliberate excision. John Gwynn, May 21, 1883.

[1] He would have written about 20,000 separate uncial letters every day. Compare the performance of that veritable Briareus, Nicodemus ὁ ξένος, who transcribed the Octateuch (in cursive characters certainly) now at Ferrara (Holmes, Cod. 107), beginning his task on the 8th of June, and finishing it the 15th of July, A. D. 1334, 'working very hard'—as he must have done indeed (Burgon, *Guardian*, Jan. 29, 1873).

his finished work, as he tells us, the words Σιμωνίδου τὸ ὅλον ἔργον), made it important to scrutinize the grounds of Tischendorf's judgement that four several scribes had been engaged upon it, one of whom, as he afterwards came to persuade himself, was the writer of its rival, Codex Vaticanus[1]. Such an investigation, so far as it depends only on the handwriting, can scarcely be carried out satisfactorily without actual examination of the manuscript itself, which is unfortunately not easily within the reach of those who could use it independently; but it is at all events quite plain, as well from internal considerations as from minute peculiarities in the writing, such as the frequent use of the apostrophus and of the mark > (*see above*, p. 50) on some sheets and their complete absence from others (Collation, &c. pp. xvi–xviii; xxxii; xxxvii), that at least two, and probably more, persons have been employed on the several parts of the volume[2].

It is indeed a strange coincidence, although unquestionably it can be nothing more, that Simonides should have brought to the West from Mount Athos some years before one genuine fragment of the Shepherd of Hermas in Greek, and the transcript of a second (both of which materially aided Tischendorf in editing the remains of that Apostolic Father), when taken in connexion with the fact that the worth of Codex Sinaiticus is vastly enhanced by its exhibiting next to the Apocalypse, and on the same page with its conclusion, the only complete extant copy, besides the one discovered by Bryennios in 1875, of the Epistle of Barnabas in Greek, followed by a considerable portion of this

---

[1] This opinion, first put forth by Tischendorf in his N.T. Vaticanum 1867, Proleg. pp. xxi–xxiii, was minutely discussed in the course of a review of that book in the *Christian Remembrancer*, October 1867, by the writer of these pages. Although Dr. Hort labours to show that no critical inferences ought to be drawn from this identity of the scribe of Cod. B with the writer of six conjugate leaves of Cod. ℵ (being three pairs in three distinct quires, one of them containing the conclusion of St. Mark's Gospel', he is constrained to admit that 'the fact appears to be sufficiently established by concurrent peculiarities in the form of one letter, punctuation, avoidance of contractions, and some points of orthography' (Introduction, p. 213'. The internal evidence indeed, though relating to minute matters, is cumulative and irresistible, and does not seem to have been noticed by Tischendorf, who drew his conclusions from the handwriting only.

[2] Prothero (Memoir of H. Bradshaw, pp. 92–118) reprints a letter of Bradshaw from *Guardian*, Jan. 28, 1863, worth studying:—'Simonides died hard, and to the very end was supported by a few dupes of his ingenious mendacity.' (p. 99.)

self-same Shepherd of Hermas, much of which, as well as of Barnabas, was previously known to us only in the Old Latin translation. Both these works are included in the list of books of the New Testament contained in the great Codex Claromontanus D of St. Paul's Epistles, to be described hereafter, Barnabas standing there in an order sufficiently remarkable; and their presence, like that of the Epistles of Clement at the end of Codex Alexandrinus (p. 99), brings us back to a time when the Church had not yet laid aside the primitive custom of reading publicly in the congregation certain venerated writings which have never been regarded exactly in the same light as Holy Scripture itself. Between the end of Barnabas and the opening of the Shepherd are lost the last six leaves of a quaternion (which usually consists of eight) numbered 91 at its head in a fairly ancient hand. The limited space would not suffice for the insertion of Clement's genuine Epistle, since the head of the next quaternion is numbered 92, but might suit one of the other uncanonical books on the list in Cod. Claromontanus, viz. the Acts of Paul and the Revelation of Peter.

With regard to the deeply interesting question as to the critical character of Cod. ℵ, although it strongly supports the Codex Vaticanus in many characteristic readings, yet it cannot be said to give its exclusive adherence to any of the witnesses hitherto examined. It so lends its grave authority, now to one and now to another, as to convince us more than ever of the futility of seeking to derive the genuine text of the New Testament from any one copy, however ancient and, on the whole, trustworthy, when evidence of a wide and varied character is at hand.

A. CODEX ALEXANDRINUS in the British Museum, where the open volume of the New Testament is publicly shown in the Manuscript room. It was placed in that Library on its formation in 1753, having previously belonged to the king's private collection from the year 1628, when Cyril Lucar, Patriarch of Constantinople (whose crude attempts to reform the Eastern Church on the model of Geneva ultimately provoked the untoward Synod of Bethlehem in 1672 [1]), sent this most precious

[1] A more favourable estimate of the ecclesiastical policy of Cyril (who was murdered by order of the Sultan in 1638, aet. 80) is maintained by Dr. Th. Smith, 'Collectanea de Cyrillo Lucario, Patriarcha Constantinopolitano,' London 1707.

document by our Ambassador in Turkey, Sir Thomas Roe, as a truly royal gift to Charles I. An Arabic inscription, several centuries old, at the back of the Table of Contents on the first leaf of the manuscript, and translated into Latin in another hand, which Mr. W. Aldis Wright recognizes as Bentley's (Academy, April 17, 1875), states that it was written by the hand of Thecla the Martyr[1]. A recent Latin note on the first page of the first of two fly-leaves declares that it was given to the Patriarchal Chamber in the year of the Martyrs, 814 [A.D. 1098]. Another, and apparently the earliest inscription, in an obscure Moorish-Arabic scrawl, set at the foot of the first page of Genesis, was thus translated for Baber by Professor Nicoll of Oxford, 'Dicatus est Cellae Patriarchae in urbe munitâ Alexandriâ. Qui cum ex eâ extraxerit sit anathematizatus, vi avulsus. Athanasius humilis' (Cod. Alex. V. T., Prolegomena, p. xxvi, note 92). That the book was brought from Alexandria by Cyril (who had been Patriarch of that see from 1602 to 1621) need not be disputed, although Wetstein, on the doubtful authority of Matthew Muttis of Cyprus, Cyril's deacon, concludes that he procured it from Mount Athos. In the volume itself the Patriarch has written and subscribed the following words: 'Liber iste scripturae sacrae N. et V. Testamenti, prout ex traditione habemus, est scriptus manu Theclae, nobilis foeminae Aegyptiae, ante mile [sic] et trecentos annos circiter, paulò post Concilium Nicenum. Nomen Theclae in fine libri erat exaratum, sed extincto Christianismo in Aegypto a Mahometanis, et libri unà Christianorum in similem sunt reducti conditionem. Extinctum ergo est Theclae nomen et laceratum, sed memoria et traditio recens observat.' Cyril seems to lean wholly on the Arabic inscription on the first leaf of the volume: independent testimony he would appear to have received none.

This celebrated manuscript, the earliest of first-rate importance applied by scholars to the criticism of the text, and yielding in value to but one or two at the utmost, is now bound in four volumes, whereof three contain the Septuagint version of

---

[1] I.e. 'Memorant hunc Librum scriptū fuisse ma-nu Theclae Martyris.' On the page over against Cyril's note the same hand writes 'videantur literae ejusdē Cyrill: Lucar: ad Georgium Episco Cant' [Abbot]; *Harl:* 823, 2. quae extant in Clementis Epistolis ad Corinthios editionis Colomesii Lond. 1687 8° page 354 &c.'

Plate V

(12)

ἘΝ ἀρχῇ ἐποίησεν ὁ θ͞ς τὸν ο͞υ
ρανὸν καὶ τὴν γῆν · ἡ δὲ γῆ ἦν ἀό
ρατος κὰι ἀκατασκεύαστος ·
κἀι σκότος ἐπάνω τῆς ἀβύσσου ·

(13)

προσεχετε ἐαυτοις και παντι τῶ
ποιμνιω ἐν ὡ ὑμας το π͞να το
ἁγιον ἐθετο ἐπισκοπους ·
ποιμαινειν την ἐκκλησιαν
του κ͞υ ην περιεποιησατο δια
του ἁιματος του ιδιου ·

(14)

λθ ΤΟΥ ΛΟΓΟΥ ΟΥ
 Γ
    ΕΓѠ ΕΙΠΤΟΝ ΥΜ
    ΙΝ · ΟΥΚ ΕCΤΙΝ
    ΔΟΥΛΟC ΜΙΖѠΝ
    ΤΟΥ Κ͞Υ ΑΥ ΤΟΥ

the Old Testament almost complete[1], the fourth volume the New Testament with several lamentable defects. In St. Matthew's Gospel some twenty-five leaves are wanting up to ch. xxv. 6 ἐξέρχεσθε, from John vi. 50 ἵνα to viii. 52 καὶ σύ[2] two leaves are lost, and three leaves from 2 Cor. iv. 13 ἐπίστευσα to xii. 6 ἐξ ἐμοῦ. All the other books of the New Testament are here entire, the Catholic Epistles following the Acts, that to the Hebrews standing before the Pastoral Epistles (*see above,* p. 74). After the Apocalypse we find what was till very recently the only known extant copy of the first or genuine Epistle of Clement of Rome, and a small fragment of a second of suspected authenticity, both in the same hand as the latter part of the New Testament. It would appear also that these two Epistles of Clement were designed to form a part of the volume of Scripture, for in the Table of Contents exhibited on the first leaf of the manuscript under the head Η ΚΑΙΝΗ ΔΙΑΘΗΚΗ, they are represented as immediately following the Apocalypse: next is given the number of books, ΟΜΟΥ ΒΙΒΛΙΑ, the numerals being now illegible; and after this, as if distinct from Scripture, the eighteen Psalms of Solomon. Such uncanonical works (ἰδιωτικοὶ ψαλμοὶ . . . ἀκανόνιστα βιβλία) were forbidden to be read in churches by the 59th canon of the Council of Laodicea (A.D. 363?); whose 60th canon, which seems to have been added a little later, enumerates the books of the N. T. in the precise order seen in Cod. A, only that the Apocalypse and Clement's Epistles do not stand on the list.

This manuscript is in quarto, 12¾ inches high and 10¼ broad, and consists of 773 leaves (of which 639 contain the Old Testament), each page being divided into two columns of fifty or fifty-one lines each, having about twenty letters or upwards in a line. These letters are written continuously in uncial charac-

---

[1] Not to mention a few casual *lacunae* here and there, especially in the early leaves of the manuscript, the lower part of one leaf has been cut out, so that Gen. xiv. 14-17; xv. 1-5; 16-20; xvi. 6-9 are wanting. The leaf containing 1 Sam. xii. 20—xiv. 9, and the nine leaves containing Ps. l. 20—lxxx. 10 (Engl.) are lost.

[2] Yet we may be sure that these two leaves did not contain the Pericope Adulterae, John vii. 53—viii. 11. Taking the Elzevir N. T. of 1624, which is printed without breaks for the verses, we count 286 lines of the Elzevir for the two leaves of Cod. A preceding its defect, 288 lines for the two which follow it; but 317 lines for the two missing leaves. Deduct the thirty lines containing John vii. 53—viii. 11, and the result for the lost leaves is 287.

ters, without any space between the words, the uncials being of an elegant yet simple form, in a firm and uniform hand, though in some places larger than in others. Specimens of both styles may be seen in our facsimiles (Plate v, Nos. 12, 13)[1], the first, Gen. i. 1, 2, being written in vermilion, the second, Acts xx. 28, in the once black, but now yellowish-brown ink of the body of the Codex. The punctuation, which no later hand has meddled with, consists merely of a point placed at the end of a sentence, usually on a level with the top of the preceding letter, but not always; and a vacant space follows the point at the end of a paragraph, the space being proportioned to the break in the sense. Capital letters of various sizes abound at the beginning of books and sections, not painted as in later copies, but written by the original scribe in common ink. As these capitals stand entirely outside the column in the margin (excepting in such rare cases as Gen. i. 1), if the section begins in the middle of a line, the capital is necessarily postponed till the beginning of the next line, whose first letter is always the capital, even though it be in the middle of a word (see p. 51). Vermilion is freely used in the initial lines of books, and has stood the test of time much better than the black ink: the first four lines of each column on the first page of Genesis are in this colour, accompanied with the only breathings and accents in the manuscript (see above, pp. 45, 46). The first line of St. Mark, the first three of St. Luke, the first verse of St. John, the opening of the Acts down to δι, and so on for other books, are in vermilion. At the end of each book are neat and unique ornaments in the ink of the first hand: see especially those at the end of St. Mark and the Acts. As we have before stated this codex is the earliest which has the κεφάλαια proper, the so-called Ammonian sections, and the Eusebian canons complete. Lists of the κεφάλαια precede each Gospel, except the first, where they are lost. Their titles stand or have stood at the top of the pages, but the binder has often ruthlessly cut them short, and committed other yet more serious mutilation at the edges. The

---

[1] An excellent facsimile of A is given in the Facsimiles of the Palaeographical Society, Plate 106; others in Woide's New Testament from this MS. (1786), and in Baber's Old Test. (1816). Two specimens from the first Epistle of Clement are exhibited in Jacobson's Patres Apostolici, vol. i. p. 110, 1838 (1863); and one in Cassell's Bible Dict. vol. i. p. 49.

places at which they begin are indicated throughout, and their numbers are moreover set in the margin of Luke and John. The sections and Eusebian canons are conspicuous in the margin, and at the beginning of each of these sections a capital letter is found. The rest of the New Testament has no division into κεφάλαια, as was usual in later times, but paragraphs and capitals occur as the sense requires.

The palaeographic reasons for assigning this manuscript to the beginning or middle of the fifth century (the date now very generally acquiesced in, though it may be referred even to the end of the fourth century, and is certainly not much later) depend in part on the general style of the writing, which is at once firm, elegant and simple; partly on the formation of certain letters, in which respect it holds a middle place between copies of the fourth and sixth centuries. The reader will recall what we have already said (pp. 33-40) as to the shape of *alpha, delta, epsilon, pi, sigma, phi,* and *omega* in the Codex Alexandrinus. Woide, who edited the New Testament, believes that two hands were employed in that volume, changing in the page containing 1 Cor. v—vii, the vellum of the latter portion being thinner and the ink more thick, so that it has peeled off or eaten through the vellum in many places. This, however, is a point on which those who know manuscripts best will most hesitate to speak decidedly[1].

The external arguments for fixing the date are less weighty, but all point to the same conclusion. On the evidence for its being written by St. Thecla, indeed, no one has cared to lay much stress, though some have thought that the scribe might belong to a monastery dedicated to that holy martyr[2], whether

---

[1] Notice especially what Tregelles says of the Codex Augiensis (Tregelles' Horne's Introd. vol. iv. p. 198), where the difference of hand in the leaves removed from their proper place is much more striking than any change in Cod. Alexandrinus. Yet even in that case it is likely that one scribe only was engaged. It should be stated, however, that Mr. E. Maunde Thompson, who edits the autotype edition, believes that the hand changed at the beginning of St. Luke, and altered again at 1 Cor. x. 8. His reasons appear to us precarious and insufficient, and he seems to cut away the ground from under him when he admits (Praef. p. 9) that 'sufficient uniformity is maintained to make it difficult to decide the exact place where a new hand begins.'

[2] Tischendorf, Septuagint, Proleg. p. lxv, cites with some approval Grabe's references (Proleg. Cap. i. pp. 9-12) to Gregory Nazianzen [d. 389], three of whose Epistles are written to a holy virgin of that name (of course not the

the contemporary of St. Paul be meant, or her namesake who suffered in the second year of Diocletian, A.D. 286 (Eusebius de Martyr. Palaestin. c. iii). Tregelles explains the origin of the Arabic inscription, on which Cyril's statement appears to rest, by remarking that the New Testament in our manuscript at present commences with Matt. xxv. 6, this lesson (Matt. xxv. 1–13) *being that appointed by the Greek Church for the festival of St. Thecla* (see above, Menology, p. 87, Sept. 24). Thus the Egyptian who wrote this Arabic note, observing the name of Thecla in the now mutilated upper margin of the Codex, where such rubrical notes are commonly placed by later hands, may have hastily concluded that she wrote the book, and so perplexed our Biblical critics. It seems a fatal objection to this shrewd conjecture, as Mr. E. Maunde Thompson points out, that the Arabic numeration of the leaf, set in the *verso* of the lower margin, itself posterior in date to the Arabic note relating to Thecla, is 26[1]; so that the twenty-five leaves now lost must have been still extant when that note was written.

Other more trustworthy reasons for assigning Cod. A to the fifth century may be summed up very briefly. The presence of the canons of Eusebius [A.D. 268–340?], and of the epistle to Marcellinus by the great Athanasius, Patriarch of Alexandria [300?–373], standing before the Psalms, place a limit in one direction, while the absence of the Euthalian divisions of the Acts and Epistles (*see above*, p. 64), which came into vogue very soon after A.D. 458, and the shortness of the ὑπογραφαί (*above*, p. 65), appear tolerably decisive against a later date than A.D. 450. The insertion of the Epistles of Clement, like that of the treatises of Barnabas and Hermas in the Cod. Sinaiticus (p. 92), recalls us to a period when the canon of Scripture was in some particulars a little unsettled, that is, about the age of the Councils of Laodicea (363?) and of Carthage (397). Other arguments have been urged both for an earlier and a later date, but they scarcely deserve discussion. Wetstein's objection to the name Θεοτόκος as

---

martyr', to whose παρθενών at Seleucia he betook himself, the better to carry out his very sincere *nolo episcopari* on the death of his father Gregory, Bishop of Nazianzus: Πρῶτον μὲν ἦλθον εἰς Σελεύκειαν φυγὰς | Τὸν παρθενῶνα τῆς ἀοιδίμου κόρης | Θέκλας· κ.τ.λ. 'De vitâ suâ.'

[1] The last Arabic numeral in the Old Testament is 641, the first in the New Testament 667.

applied to the Blessed Virgin in the title to her song, added to the Psalms, is quite groundless: that appellation was given to her by both the Gregories in the middle of the fourth century (*vid.* Suicer, Thesaur. Eccles. i. p. 1387), as habitually as it was a century after: nor should we insist much on the contrary upon Woide's or Schulz's persuasion that the τρισάγιον (ἅγιος ὁ θεός, ἅγιος ἰσχυρός, ἅγιος ἀθάνατος) would have been found in the ὕμνος ἑωθινός after the Psalms, had the manuscript been written as late as the fifth century.

Partial and inaccurate collations of the New Testament portion of this manuscript were made by Patrick Young, Librarian to Charles I[1], who first published from it the Epistles of Clement in 1633: then by Alexander Huish, Prebendary of Wells, for Walton's Polyglott, and by some others[2]. The Old Testament portion was edited in 1707-20, after a not very happy plan, but with learned Prolegomena and notes, by the Prussian J. E. Grabe, the second and third of his four volumes being posthumous.

In 1786, Charles Godfrey Woide, preacher at the Dutch Chapel Royal and Assistant Librarian in the British Museum, a distinguished Coptic scholar [d. 1790], published, by the aid of 456 subscribers, a noble folio edition of the New Testament from this manuscript, with valuable Prolegomena, a copy of the text which, so far as it has been tested, has been found reasonably accurate, together with notes on the changes made in the codex by later hands, and a minute collation of its readings with the common text as presented in Kuster's edition of Mill's N. T. (1710). In this last point Woide has not been taken as a model by subsequent editors of manuscripts, much to the inconvenience of the student. In 1816-28 the Old Testament portion of the

---

[1] Very interesting is Whitelock's notice of a design which was never carried out, under the date of March 13, 1645. 'The Assembly of Divines desired by some of their brethren, sent to the House [of Commons] that Mr. Patrick Young might be encouraged in the printing of the Greek Testament much expected and desired by the learned, especially beyond seas; and an ordinance was read for printing and publishing the Old Testament of the Septuagint translation, wherein Mr. Young had formerly taken pains and had in his hand, as library keeper at St. James's, an original *Teeta* [sic] Bible of that translation' (Memorials, p. 197, ed. 1732).

[2] 'MS^m Alexand^m accuratissime ipse contuli, A. D. 1716. Rich: Bentleius.' Trin. Coll. Camb. B. xvii. 9, in a copy of Fell's Greek Testament, 1675, which contains his collation. Ellis, Bentleii Critica Sacra, p. xxviii.

Codex Alexandrinus was published in three folio volumes at the national expense, by the Rev. Henry Hervey Baber, also of the British Museum, the Prolegomena to whose magnificent work are very inferior to Woide's, but contain some additional information. Both these performances, and many others like them which we shall have to describe, are printed in an uncial type, bearing some general resemblance to that of their respective originals, but which must not be supposed to convey any adequate notion of their actual appearance. Such quasi-facsimiles (for they are nothing more), while they add to the cost of the book, seem to answer no useful purpose whatever; and, if taken by an incautious reader for more than they profess to be, will seriously mislead him. In 1860 Mr. B. H. Cowper put forth an octavo edition of the New Testament pages in common type, but burdened with modern breathings and accents, the lacunae of the manuscript being unwisely supplied by means of Kuster's edition of Mill, and the original paragraphs departed from, wheresoever they were judged to be inconvenient. These obvious faults are the more to be regretted, inasmuch as Mr. Cowper has not shrunk from the labour of revising Woide's edition by a comparison with the Codex itself, thus giving to his book a distinctive value of its own. An admirable autotype facsimile of the New Testament was published in 1879, and afterwards of the Old Testament, by Mr. E. Maunde Thompson. then the Principal Keeper of Manuscripts, now the Principal Librarian, of the British Museum.

The Codex Alexandrinus has been judged to be carelessly written; many errors of transcription no doubt exist, but not so many as in some copies (e.g. Cod. ℵ), nor more than in others (as Cod. B). None other than the ordinary abridgements are found in it (*see* pp. 49–50): numerals are not expressed by letters except in Apoc. vii. 4; xxi. 17: ι and υ have usually the dots over them at the beginning of a syllable. Of itacisms it may be doubted whether it contains more than others of the same date: the interchange of ι and ει, η and ι, ε αι, are the most frequent; but these mutations are too common to prove anything touching the country of the manuscript. Its external history renders it very likely that it was written at Alexandria, that great manufactory of correct and elegant copies, while Egypt was yet a Christian land: but such forms as λήμψομαι,

ΜΙΝ ΤΟΝ ΛΑΙΘΟΝ ΕΚ ΤΗϹ
ΘΥΡΑϹ ΤΟΥ ΜΝΗΜΕΙΟΥ
ΚΑΙ ΑΝΑΒΛΕΨΑϹΑΙ ΘΕΩ
ΡΟΥϹΙΝ ΟΤΙ ΑΝΑΚΕΚΥ
ΛΙϹΤΑΙ Ο ΛΙΘΟϹ ΗΝ ΓΑΡ
ΜΕΓΑϹ ϹΦΟΔΡΑ ΚΑΙ ΕΛ
ΘΟΥϹΑΙ ΕΙϹ ΤΟ ΜΝΗΜΕΙ
ΟΝ ΕΙΔΟΝ ΝΕΑΝΙϹΚΟΝ
ΚΑΘΗΜΕΝΟΝ ΕΝ ΤΟΙϹ
ΔΕΞΙΟΙϹ ΠΕΡΙΒΕΒΛΗΜΕ
ΝΟΝ ϹΤΟΛΗΝ ΛΕΥΚΗΝ
ΚΑΙ ΕΞΕΘΑΜΒΗΘΗϹΑΝ
Ο ΔΕ ΛΕΓΕΙ ΑΥΤΑΙϹ ΜΗ
ΕΚΘΑΜΒΕΙϹΘΕ ΙΝ ΖΗΤΕΙ
ΤΕ ΤΟΝ ΝΑΖΑΡΗΝΟΝ ΤΟΝ
ΕϹΤΑΥΡΩΜΕΝΟΝ ΗΓΕΡ
ΘΗ ΟΥΚ ΕϹΤΙΝ ΩΔΕ ΙΔΕ
Ο ΤΟΠΟϹ ΟΠΟΥ ΕΘΗΚΑ
ΑΥΤΟΝ ΑΛΛΑ ΥΠΑΓΕΤΕ
ΕΙΠΑΤΕ ΤΟΙϹ ΜΑΘΗΤΑΙϹ
ΑΥΤΟΥ ΚΑΙ ΤΩ ΠΕΤΡΩ
ΟΤΙ ΠΡΟΑΓΕΙ ΥΜΑϹ ΕΙϹ
ΤΗΝ ΓΑΛΙΛΑΙΑΝ ΕΚΕΙ ΑΥ
ΤΟΝ ΟΨΕϹΘΕ ΚΑΘΩϹ ΕΙ
ΠΕΝ ΥΜΙΝ ΚΑΙ ΕΞΕΛΘΟΥ
ϹΑΙ ΕΦΥΓΟΝ ΑΠΟ ΤΟΥ
ΜΝΗΜΕΙΟΥ ΕΙΧΕΝ ΓΑΡ
ΑΥΤΑϹ ΤΡΟΜΟϹ ΚΑΙ ΕΚ
ϹΤΑϹΙϹ ΚΑΙ ΟΥΔΕΝΙ ΟΥ
ΔΕΝ ΕΙΠΟΝ ΕΦΟΒΟΥΝ
ΤΟ ΓΑΡ :⁊

ΚΑΤΑ
ΜΑΡΚΟΝ

ἐλάβαμεν, ἤλθαν, ἔνατος, ἐκαθερίσθη, and others named by Woide, are peculiar to no single nation, but are found repeatedly in Greek-Latin codices which unquestionably originated in Western Europe. This manuscript is of the very greatest importance to the critic, inasmuch as it exhibits (especially in the Gospels) a text more nearly approaching that found in later copies than is read in others of its high antiquity, although some of its errors are portentous enough, e.g. θυ̅ for ιυ̅ in John xix. 40. This topic, however, will be discussed at length in another place, and we shall elsewhere consider the testimony Codex A bears in the celebrated passage 1 Tim. iii. 16.

B. CODEX VATICANUS 1209 is probably the oldest large vellum manuscript in existence, and is the glory of the great Vatican Library at Rome. To this legitimate source of deep interest must be added the almost romantic curiosity which was once excited by the jealous watchfulness of its official guardians. But now that an acquaintance with it has been placed within the reach of scholars through the magnificent autotype edition issued by the authorities of the Vatican, it may be hoped that all such mystic glamour will soon be left with the past. This book seems to have been brought into the Vatican Library shortly after its establishment by Pope Nicolas V in 1448, but nothing is known of its previous history[1]. It is entered in the earliest catalogue of that Library, made in 1475. Since the missing portions at the end of the New Testament are believed to have been supplied in the fifteenth century from a manuscript belonging to Cardinal Bessarion, we may be allowed to conjecture, if we please, that this learned Greek brought the Codex into the west of Europe. It was taken to Paris by Napoleon I, where it was studied by Hug in 1809. Although this book has not even yet been as thoroughly collated, or rendered as available as it might be to the critical student, its general character and appearance are sufficiently well known. It is a quarto volume, arranged in quires of five sheets or ten leaves each, like Codex Marchalianus of the Prophets written in the sixth or seventh century and Cod. Rossanensis of

---

[1] See Bibliothèque du Vatican au Xme siècle, par Eugène Müntz et Paul Fabre, Paris. Thorn. 824 Lat., 400 Gr.

the Gospels to be described hereafter, not of four or three sheets as Cod. ℵ, the ancient, perhaps the original, numbering of the quires being often found in the margin. The New Testament fills 142 out of its 759 thin and delicate vellum leaves, said to be made of the skins of antelopes: it is bound in red morocco, being 10½ inches high, 10 broad, 4½ thick. It once contained the whole Bible in Greek, the Old Testament of the Septuagint version (a tolerably fair representation of which was exhibited in the Roman edition as early as 1587[1]), except the books of the Maccabees and the Prayer of Manasses. The first forty-six chapters of Genesis (the manuscript begins at πολιν, Gen. xlvi. 28) and Psalms cv—cxxxvii, also the books of the Maccabees, are wanting. The New Testament is complete down to Heb. ix. 14 καθα: the rest of the Epistle to the Hebrews (the Catholic Epistles had followed the Acts, see p. 74), and the Apocalypse, being written in the later hand alluded to above. The peculiar arrangement of three columns on a page, or six on the opened leaf of the volume, is described by eye-witnesses as very striking: in the poetical books of the Old Testament (since they are written στιχηρῶς) only two columns fill a page. Our facsimile (Plate viii, No. 20) comprises Mark xvi. 3 μιν τον λιθον to the end of verse 8, where the Gospel ends abruptly; both the arabesque ornament and the subscription KATA MAPKON being in a later hand (for M see p. 37). All who have inspected the Codex are loud in their praises of the fine thin vellum, the clear and elegant hand of the first penman, the simplicity of the whole style of the work: capital letters, so frequent in the Codex Alexandrinus, were totally wanting in this document for some centuries. In several of these particulars our manuscript resembles the Herculanean rolls, and thus asserts a just claim to high antiquity, which the absence of the divisions into κεφάλαια, of the sections and canons, and the substitution in their room of another scheme of chapters of its own (described above, p. 56), beyond question

---

[1] The 'Epistle' of Cardinal Carafa to Sixtus V, and the Preface to the Reader by the actual editor Peter Morinus, both of which Tischendorf reprints in full (Septuagint, Proleg. pp. xxi—xxvii), display an amount of critical skill and discernment quite beyond their age, and in strange contrast with the signal mismanagement in regard to the revision of the Latin Vulgate version under the auspices of the same Pope.

tend very powerfully to confirm. Each column contains ordinarily forty-two lines [1], each line from sixteen to eighteen letters, of a size somewhat less than in Cod. A, much less than in Cod. ℵ (though they all vary a little in this respect), with no intervals between words, a space of the breadth of half a letter being left at the end of a sentence, and a little more at the conclusion of a paragraph; the first letter of the new sentence occasionally standing a little out of the line (*see* pp. 51, 93). It has been doubted whether any of the stops are *primâ manu*, and (contrary to the judgement of Birch and others) the breathings and accents are now universally allowed to have been added by a later hand. This hand, referred by some to the eighth century (although Tischendorf, with Dr. Hort's approval, assigns it to the tenth or eleventh [2]), retraced, with as much care as such an operation would permit, the faint lines of the original writing (the ink whereof was perhaps never quite black), the remains of which can even now be seen by a keen-sighted reader by the side of the thicker and more modern strokes; and, anxious at the same time to represent a critical revision of the text, the writer left untouched such words or letters as he wished to reject. In these last places, *where no breathings or accents and scarcely any stops*[3] *have ever been detected*, we have an opportunity of seeing the manuscript in its primitive condition, before it had been tampered with by the later scribe. There are occasional breaks in the continuity of the writing, every

---

[1] In Pentateuch, Joshua, Judges, Ruth, and 1 Kings i. 1—xix. 11, there are forty-four lines in a column; and in 2 Paralip. x. 16—xxvi. 13, there are forty lines in a column.

[2] The writer of the Preface to the sixth volume of the Roman edition of 1881 (apparently Fabiani), is jubilant over his discovery of the name of this retracer ('eruditissimi et patientissimi viri,' as he is pleased to call him, p. xviii) in the person of Clement the Monk, who has written his name twice in the book in a scrawl of the fifteenth century. But mere resemblance in the ink is but a lame proof of identity, and Fabiani recognizes some other correctors, whom he designates as B¹, posterior to the mischievous 'instaurator.'

[3] Hug says *none*, but Tischendorf (Cod. Frid.-Aug. Proleg. p. 9) himself detected two in a part that the second scribe had left untouched; and not a very few elsewhere (N. T. Vatican. Proleg. pp. xx, xxi, 1867); though a break often occurs with no stop by either hand. In the much contested passage Rom. ix. 5, Dr. Vance Smith ('Revised Texts and Margins,' p. 34, note*), while confidently claiming the stop after σαρκα in Cod. A as *primâ manu*, and noticing the space after the word in Cod. Ephraemi (C), admits that 'in the Vatican the originality of the stops may be doubtful.' In the judgement of Fabiani, 'vix aliqua primo exscriptori tribuenda' (Praef. N. T. Vat. 1881, p. xviii).

descent in the genealogies of our Lord (Matt. i, Luke iii [1]), each of the beatitudes (Matt. v), of the parables in Matt. xiii, and the salutations of Rom. xvi, forming a separate paragraph; but such a case will oftentimes not occur for several consecutive pages. The writer's plan was to proceed regularly with a book until it was finished: then to break off from the column he was writing, and to begin the next book on the very next column. Thus only *one* column perfectly blank is found in the whole New Testament [2], that which follows ἐφοβοῦντο γάρ in Mark xvi. 8: and since Cod. B is the only one yet known, except Cod. ℵ, that actually omits the last twelve verses of that Gospel, by leaving such a space the scribe has intimated that he was fully aware of their existence, or even found them in the copy from which he wrote. The capital letters at the beginning of each book are likewise due to the corrector, who sometimes erased, sometimes merely touched slightly. the original initial letter, which (as in the Herculanean rolls) is no larger than any other. The *paragraph* marks (usually straight lines, but sometimes Γ [3]) are seen quite frequently in some parts; whether from the first hand is very doubtful. The note of citation > [3] is perpetual, not occasional as in Cod. ℵ. Fewer abridgements than usual occur in this venerable copy [3]. The formation of *delta, pi, chi*; the loop-like curve on the left side of *alpha*; the absence of points at the extremities of *sigma* or *epsilon*; the length and size of *rho, upsilon, phi*, all point to the FOURTH century as the date of this manuscript. The smaller letters so often found at the end of lines preserve

[1] The publication of the Roman edition (1868-81) enables us to add (Abbot, *ubi supra*, p. 193) that the blessings of the twelve patriarchs in Gen. xlix are in separate paragraphs numbered from A to IB, that the twenty-two names of the unclean birds Deut. xiv. 12-18, twenty-five kings in Josh. xii. 10-22, eleven dukes in 1 Chr. i. 51-54, each stand in a separate line. In Cod. ℵ, especially in the New Testament, this arrangement στιχηρῶς is much more frequent than in Cod. B, although the practice is in some measure common to both.

[2] The Roman edition (1868-81) also makes known to us that in the Old Testament two columns are left blank between Nehemiah and the Psalms, which could not have been otherwise, inasmuch as the Psalms are written στιχηρῶς with but two columns on a page. Between Tobit and Hosea (which book stands first of the Prophetical writings) a column is very naturally left blank, and two columns at the end of Daniel, with whose prophecy the Old Testament concludes. But these peculiarities obviously bear no analogy to the case of the end of St. Mark's Gospel.

[3] See above, pp. 49-51.

the same firm and simple character as the rest; of the use of the apostrophus, so frequent in Codd. ℵ, A and some others, Tischendorf enumerates ten instances in the New Testament (N. T. Vatican. Proleg. p. xxi), whereof four are represented in the Roman edition of 1868, with two more which Tischendorf considers as simple points (Acts vii. 13, 14).

Tischendorf says truly enough that something like a history might be written of the futile attempts to collate Cod. B, and a very unprofitable history it would be. The manuscript is first distinctly heard of (for it does not appear to have been used for the Complutensian Polyglott[1]) through Sepulveda, to whose correspondence with Erasmus attention has been seasonably recalled by Tregelles. Writing in 1533, he says, 'Est enim Graecum exemplar antiquissimum in Bibliothecâ Vaticanâ, in quo diligentissimè et accuratissimè literis majusculis conscriptum utrumque Testamentum continetur longè diversum a vulgatis exemplaribus': and, after noticing as a weighty proof of excellence its agreement with the Latin version (multum convenit cum vetere nostrâ translatione) against the common Greek text (vulgatam Graecorum editionem), he furnishes Erasmus with 365 readings as a convincing argument in support of his statements. It would probably be from this list that in his Annotations to the Acts, published in 1535, Erasmus cites the reading καῖδα, ch. xxvii. 16 ('quidam admonent' is the expression he uses), from a Greek codex in the Pontifical Library, since for this reading Cod. B is the only known *Greek* witness, except a corrector of Cod. ℵ. It seems, however, that he had obtained some account of this manuscript from the Papal Librarian Paul Bombasius as early as 1521 (*see* Wetstein's Proleg. N. T., vol. i. p. 23). Lucas Brugensis, who published his Notationes in S. Biblia in 1580, and his Commentary on the Four Gospels (dedicated to Cardinal Bellarmine) in 1606, made known some twenty extracts from Cod. B taken by Werner of Nimeguen ; that most imperfect collection being the only source from which Mill and even Wetstein had any acquaintance with the contents of this first-rate document.

[1] The writer of the Preface to the Roman edition (vol. vi. Praef. p. 9, 1881) vainly struggles to maintain the opposite view, because the Cardinal, in his Preface to the Complutensian N. T., speaks about 'adhibitis Vaticanis libris,' as if there was but one there.

More indeed might have been gleaned from the Barberini readings gathered in or about 1625 (of which we shall speak in the next section), but their real value and character were not known in the lifetime of Wetstein. In 1698 Lorenzo Alexander Zacagni, Librarian of the Vatican, in his Preface to the Collectanea Monumentorum Veterum Eccles., describes Cod. B, and especially its peculiar division into sections, in a passage cited by Mill (Proleg. § 1480). In 1669 indeed the first real collation of the manuscript with the Aldine edition (1518) had been attempted by Bartolocci, then Librarian of the Vatican; from some accident, however, it was never published, though a transcript under the feigned name of Giulio a Sta. Anastasia yet remains in the Imperial Library of Paris (MSS. Gr. Supplem. 53), where it was first discovered and used by Scholz in 1819, and subsequently by Tischendorf and Muralt, the latter of whom (apparently on but slender grounds) regards it as the best hitherto made; others have declared it to be very imperfect, and quite inferior to those of Bentley and Birch. The collation which bears Bentley's name (Trin. Coll. B. xvii. 3, in Cephalaeus' N. T. 1524) was procured about 1720 by his money and the labour of the Abbate Mico, for the purpose of his projected Greek Testament. When he had found out its defects, by means of an examination of the original by his nephew Thomas Bentley in 1726, our great critic engaged the Abbate Rulotta in 1729 for forty scudi (Bentley's Correspondence, p. 706) to revise Mico's sheets, and especially to note the changes made by the second hand. Rulotta's papers came to light in 1855 among the Bentley manuscripts in the Library of Trinity College, Cambridge (B. xvii. 20), and have lately proved of signal value[1]; Mico's were published in 1799 at Oxford, by Henry Ford, Lord Almoner's Reader in Arabic there (1783–1813), together with some Thebaic fragments of the New Testament, in a volume which (since it was chiefly drawn from Woide's posthumous papers) he was pleased to call an Appendix to the Codex Alexandrinus. A fourth collation of the Vatican MS. was made about 1780 by Andrew Birch of Copenhagen, and is included in the notes to the first volume of his Greek Testament 1788, or published separately in three volumes which

[1] Rulotta's labours are now printed in Bentleii Critica Sacra by Mr. A. A. Ellis, 1862, pp. 121-154.

were issued successively 1798 (Acts, Cath. Epp., Paul.), 1800 (Apoc.), and 1801 (Evans). Birch's collation does not extend to the Gospels of St. Luke and St. John, and on the whole is less full and exact than Mico's. In 1810, however, when, with the other best treasures of the Vatican, Codex B was at Paris, the celebrated critic J. L. Hug sent forth his treatise 'de Antiquitate Vaticani Codicis Commentatio,' and though even he did not perceive the need of a new and full collation when he examined it in 1809, he has the merit of first placing it in the paramount rank it still holds as one of the oldest and most venerable of extant monuments of sacred antiquity. His conclusion respecting its date, that it is not later than the middle of the fourth century, has been acquiesced in with little opposition, though Tischendorf declares rather pithily that he holds this belief 'non propter Hugium sed cum Hugio' (Cod. Ephraem. Proleg. p. 19). Some of his reasons, no doubt, are weak enough[1]; but the strength of his position depends on an accumulation of minute particulars, against which there seems nothing to set up which would suggest a lower period. On its return to Rome, this volume was no longer available for the free use and reference of critics. In 1843 Tischendorf, after long and anxious expectation during a visit to Rome that lasted some months, obtained a sight of it for two days of three hours each[2]. In 1844 Edward de Muralt was admitted to the higher privilege of three days or nine hours enjoyment of this treasure, and on the strength of the favour published an edition of the New Testament, *ad fidem codicis principis Vaticani*, in 1846. Tregelles, who went to Rome in 1845 for the special purpose of consulting it, was treated even worse. He had forearmed himself (as he fondly imagined) with recommendatory letters from Cardinal Wiseman, and was often

---

[1] Thus the correspondence of Codex B with what St. Basil (c. Eunom. ii. 19) states he found in the middle of the fourth century, ἐν τοῖς παλαιοῖς τῶν ἀντιγράφων, in Eph. i. 1, viz. τοῖς οὖσιν without ἐν Ἐφέσῳ, though now read only in this and the Sinaitic manuscript *primâ manu*, and in one cursive copy (Cod. 67) *secundâ manu*, seems in itself of but little weight. Another point that has been raised is the position of the Epistle to the Hebrews. But this argument can apply only to the elder document from which the Vatican MS. was taken, and wherein this book unquestionably followed that to the Galatians. In Cod. B it *always* stood in its present place, after 2 Thess., as in the Codices cited p. 74, note.

[2] Besides the twenty-five readings Tischendorf observed himself, Cardinal Mai supplied him with thirty-four more for his N. T. of 1849. His seventh edition of 1859 was enriched by 230 other readings furnished by Albert Dressel in 1855.

allowed to *see* the manuscript, but hindered from transcribing any of its readings[1].

What the Papal authorities would not entrust to others, they had at least the merit of attempting and at length accomplishing themselves. As early as 1836 Bishop Wiseman announced in his Lectures on the Connection between Science and Revelation, vol. ii. pp. 187–191, that Cardinal Mai, whose services to classical and ecclesiastical literature were renowned throughout Europe, was engaged on an edition of the Codex Vaticanus, commenced under the immediate sanction of Pope Leo XII (1823–29). As years passed by and no such work appeared, adverse reports and evil surmises began to take the place of hope, although the Cardinal often spoke of his work as already finished, only that he desired to write full Prolegomena before it should appear. In September 1854 he died, honoured and ripe in years; and at length, when no more seemed to be looked for in that quarter, five quarto volumes issued from the Roman press in 1857, the New Testament comprising the fifth volume, with a slight and meagre preface by the Cardinal, and a letter to the reader by 'Carolus Vercellone, Sodalis Barnabites,' which told in a few frank manly words how little accuracy we had to expect in a work, by the publication of which he still persuaded himself he was decorating Mai's memory 'novâ usque gloriâ atque splendidiore coronâ' (tom. i. p. iii). The cause of that long delay now required no explanation. In fact so long as Mai lived the edition never would have appeared; for though he had not patience or special skill enough to accomplish his task well, he was too good a scholar not to know that he had done it very ill. The text is broken up into paragraphs, the numbers of the modern chapters and verses being placed in the margin; the peculiar divisions of the Codex Vaticanus (*see* p. 56) sometimes omitted, sometimes tampered with. The Greek type employed is not an imitation of the uncials in the manuscript (of which circumstance we do not complain), but has modern stops, breathings, accents, *ι subscript*, &c., as if the venerable document were written yesterday. As regards the orthography

---

[1] 'They would not let me open it,' he adds, 'without searching my pocket, and depriving me of pen, ink, and paper... If I looked at a passage too long the two *prelati* would snatch the book out from my hand.' Tregelles, Lecture on the Historic Evidence of the N. T., p. 84.

it is partially, and only partially, modernized; clauses or whole passages omitted in the manuscript are supplied from other sources, although the fact is duly notified[1]; sometimes the readings of the first hand are put in the margin, while those of the second stand in the text, sometimes the contrary: in a word, the plan of the work exhibits all the faults such a performance well can have. Nor is the execution at all less objectionable. Although the five volumes were ten years in printing (1828-38), Mai devoted to their superintendence only his scanty spare hours, and even then worked so carelessly that after cancelling a hundred pages for their incurable want of exactness, he was reduced to the shift of making *manual* corrections with moveable types, and projected huge tables of errata, which Vercellone has in some measure tried to supply. When once it is stated that the type was set up from the common Elzevir or from some other printed Greek Testament, the readings of the Codex itself being inserted as corrections, and the whole revised by means of an assistant who read the proof-sheets to the Cardinal while he inspected the manuscript; no one will look for accuracy from a method which could not possibly lead to it. Accordingly, when Mai's text came to be compared with the collations of Bartolocci, of Mico, of Rulotta, and of Birch, or with the scattered readings which had been extracted by others, it was soon discovered that while this edition added very considerably to our knowledge of the Codex Vaticanus, and often enabled us to form a decision on its readings when the others were at variance; it was in its turn convicted by them of so many errors, oversights, and inconsistencies, that its single evidence could never be used with confidence, especially when it agreed with the commonly received Greek text. Immediately after the appearance of Mai's expensive quartos, an octavo reprint of the New Testament was struck off at Leipsic for certain London booksellers, which proved but a hasty, slovenly, unscholarlike performance, and was put aside in 1859 by a cheap Roman edition in octavo, prepared, as was the quarto, by Mai, prefaced by another graceful and sensible epistle of Vercellone[2]. This

---

[1] The great gap in the Pauline Epistles is filled up from Vatic. 1761 (Act. 158, Paul. 192) of the eleventh century.

[2] Other editions of the Vatican N. T. appeared at Ratisbon; at Leyden (1860) by A. Kuenen and C. G. Cobet, with a masterly Preface by the latter; and at

last edition was undertaken by the Cardinal, after sad experience had taught him the defects of his larger work, and he took good care to avoid some of the worst of them: the readings of the second hand are usually, though not always, banished to the margin, their number on the whole is increased, gross errors are corrected, omissions supplied, and the Vatican chapters are given faithfully and in full. But Mai's whole procedure in this matter is so truly unfortunate, that in a person whose fame was less solidly grounded, we should impute it to mere helpless incapacity[1]. Not only did he split up the paragraphs of his quarto into the modern chapters and verses (in itself a most undesirable change, see above, p. 70), but by omitting some things and altering others, he introduced almost as many errors as he removed. When Dean Burgon was permitted to examine the Codex for an hour and a half in 1860, on consulting it for sixteen passages out of hundreds wherein the two are utterly at variance, he discovered that the quarto was right in seven of them, the octavo in nine: as if Mai were determined that neither of his editions should supersede the use of the other. Dean Alford also collated numerous passages in 1861[2], and his secretary Mr. Cure in 1862, especially with reference to the several correcting hands: 'in errorem quidem et ipse haud raro inductus,' is Tischendorf's verdict on his labours. Thus critics of every shade of opinion became unanimous on one point, that

Berlin (1862) by Philip Buttmann, furnished with an Appendix containing the varying results of no less than nine collations, eight of which we have described in the text, the ninth being derived from Lachmann's Greek Testament (1742, 1850), whose readings were all obtained second-hand. Tischendorf does not much commend the accuracy of Buttmann's work.

[1] 'Angelus Mai, quamquam, ut in proverbio est, ἐν τυφλῶν πόλει γλαμυρὸς βασιλεύων, non is erat cui tanta res rectò mandari posset:' Kuenen and Cobet, N. T. Vat. Praef. p. 1. Tischendorf too, in his over querulous Responsa ad Calumnias Romanas &c., 1870, p. 11, is not more than just in alleging 'Angelum Maium in editionibus suis Codicis Vaticani alienissimum se praebuisse ab omni subtiliore rei palaeographicae scientiâ, ac tantum non ignarum earum legum ad quas is codex in usum criticum edendus esset.' The defence set up for Mai in the Preface to the Roman volume of 1881, was that he intended to produce only a new edition of the 'authentic' Septuagint of 1586-7, chiefly for the use of Greek-speaking Catholics.

[2] The Dean himself on Feb. 20, 1861, and for four subsequent days, 'went twice over the doubtful passages and facsimilized most of the important various readings,' in spite of much opposition from the Librarian, who 'insisted that our order from Antonelli, although it ran "per verificare," to verify passages, only extended to seeing the Codex, not to using it.' (Life by his Widow, pp. 310, 315.)

a new edition of the Codex Vaticanus was as imperatively needed as ever; one which should preserve with accuracy all that the first hand has written (transcriptural errors included), should note in every instance the corrections made by the second hand, and, wherever any one of the previous collators might be found in error, should expressly state the true reading.

It would have been a grievous reproach had no efforts been made to supply so great and acknowledged a want. Early in 1866, Tischendorf again visited Rome, and when admitted into the presence of Pope Pius IX, boldly sought permission to edit at his own cost such an edition of Cod. B as he had already published of Cod. ℵ. The request was denied by his Holiness, who obscurely hinted his intention of carrying out the same design on his own account. Tischendorf, however, obtained permission to use the manuscript so far as to consult it in such parts of the New Testament as presented any special difficulty, or respecting which previous collators were at variance. He commenced his task February 28, and in the course of it could not refrain from copying at length twenty pages of the great Codex—nineteen from the New Testament, and one from the Old. This licence was not unnaturally regarded as a breach of his contract, so that, after he had used the manuscript for eight days, it was abruptly withdrawn from him on March 12. An appeal to the generosity of Vercellone, who had been entrusted with the care of the forthcoming edition, procured for him the sight of this coveted treasure for six days longer between March 20 and 26, the Italian being always present on these latter occasions, and receiving instruction for the preparation of his own work by watching the processes of a master hand. Thus fourteen days of three hours each, used zealously and skilfully, enabled Tischendorf to put forth an edition of Cod. B far superior to any that preceded it[1]. The Prolegomena are full of matter from which we have drawn freely in the foregoing description, the text is in cursive type, the nineteen pages which cost him so dearly being arranged in their proper lines, the remainder according to columns. Much that ought to have been noted was doubtless passed over by Tischendorf for mere pressure of time; but he takes great

---

[1] 'Novum Testamentum Vaticanum post Angeli Maii aliorumque imperfectos labores ex ipso codice edidit Ae. F. C. Tischendorf.' Lipsiae, 4to, 1867.

pains to distinguish the readings of the original writer or his διορθωτής (see p. 55)[1], both of whom supplied words or letters here and there in the margin or between the lines[2], from the corrections of a second yet ancient scribe (B²), and those of the person (B³) who retraced the faded writing at a later period[3]. One notion, taken up by Tischendorf in the course of his collation in 1866, was received at first with general incredulity by other scholars. He has pronounced a decided opinion, not only that Codd. ℵ and B are documents of the same age, but that the scribe who wrote the latter is one of the four [D] to whose diligence we owe the former. That there should be a general similarity in the style of the two great codices is probable enough, although the letters in Cod. ℵ are about half as large again as those of its fellow, but such as are aware of the difficulty of arriving at a safe conclusion as to identity of penmanship after close and repeated comparison of one document with another, will hardly attach much weight to the impression of any person, however large his experience, who has nothing but memory to trust to. Tregelles, who has also seen both copies, states that Cod. ℵ looks much the fresher and clearer of the two. Yet the reasons alleged above, which are quite independent of the appearance of the handwriting, leave scarcely a doubt that Tischendorf's judgement was correct.

The Roman edition, projected by Vercellone and Cozza

---

[1] To his hand Tischendorf assigns seven readings, Matt. xiii. 52; xiv. 5; xvi. 4; xxii. 10; xxvii. 4. Luke iii. 1 (*bis*), 7. 'For some six centuries after it was written B appears to have undergone no changes in its text except from the hand of the "corrector," the "second hand"' (Hort, Introd. p. 270). What then of B²?

[2] It must surely be to these, the earliest scribes, that Cobet refers when he uses language that would not be at all applicable to the case of B² or B³: 'In Vaticano duorum librorum veterum testimonia continentur, et nihilo plus in primâ manu quam in secundâ inest auctoritatis ac fidei. Utriusque unaquaeque lectio ex se ipsâ spectanda ponderandaque est, et si hoc ages, modo hanc modo illam animadvertes esse potiorem. Hoc autem in primis firmiter tenendum est, non esse secundae manûs lectiones correctoris alicujus suspiciones aut conjecturas, sive illae sunt acutiores sive leviores, sed quidquid a secundâ manu correctum, mutatum, deletum esse Maius referat, id omne haud secus atque id quod prior manus dederit, perantiqui cujusdam Codicis fide nixum esse.' (N. T. Vat. Praef. p. xxvi.)

[3] It may be mere oversight that in Matt. xxvii. 4 he does not say in 1867 of what hand the marginal δικαιον is : in his eighth edition (1865) he adjudges it to B². In Matt. xxiv. 23 πιστευητε and ver. 32 εκφύη he gives to B³ in 1867 what he had assigned to B² in 1865. The Roman Commentary gives no light in the other places, but assigns πιστεύητε to B², B³.

under the auspices of Pius IX, was designed to consist of six volumes, four containing the Old Testament, one the New, another being devoted to the notes and discrimination of corrections by later hands. The New Testament appeared in 1868 [1]. a second volume in 1869, containing the text from Genesis to Joshua; three more have since completed the Old Testament (1870, 1871, 1872). The learned, genial, and modest Vercellone (b. 1814) died early in 1869, so that the later volumes bear on their title-page the mournful inscription 'Carolum Vercellone excepit Caietanus Sergio Sodalis Barnabites' as Cozza's associate. These editors fared but ill whether as Biblical critics or as general scholars, under the rough handling of Tischendorf, whom the wiser policy of Vercellone had kept in good humour, but whose powers his successors greatly undervalued. There seems, however, to be no great cause, in spite of their adversary's minute diligence in fault-finding (Appendix N. T. Vatic. 1869, p. xi, &c.) [2], for doubting their general correctness, although they persist in placing on the page with the rest of their text readings which are known or credibly stated to be of decidedly later date, in spite of the incongruousness of the mixture of what was original with matter plainly adscititious [3]. Thus in the Roman edition αδελφων μου των Matt. xxv. 40, imputed by Tischendorf to B² and B³, stands in the margin just in the same way as ο γαμος Matt. xxii. 10, which he refers to the first hand. But this is only one instance of a lack of judgement which deforms every page of their performance: e.g. Matt. xix. 12; xxiii. 26; 37; xxv. 16; xxvii. 12; 13; 45; xxviii. 15; Acts xv. 1: all which places exhibit, undistinguished from emendations of the original scribe or his 'corrector,' readings

---

[1] 'Bibliorum Sacrorum Graecus Codex Vaticanus, Auspice Pio IX Pontifice Maximo, collatis studiis Caroli Vercellone Sodalis Barnabitae, et Josephi Cozza Monachi Basiliani editus. Romae typis et impensis S. Congregationis de Propaganda Fide,' square folio, 1868.

[2] The feeble rejoinder of the Roman editors was followed up in 1870 by Tischendorf's Responsa ad Calumnias Romanas, &c., the tone of which pamphlet we cannot highly praise.

[3] This practice is plainly confessed to in the Preface to the volume of 1881 (p. xvi) without any consciousness of the fatal mistake which it involves: 'Facies libri Vaticani repraesentata est [ut] ea primum omnia apparerent, quae a priore codicis notario profecta adhuc manifesto perspiciuntur, tum ea tantum a posterioribus sive emendatoribus, sive instauratoribus commutata adderentur, quae sine scripturae confusione legi possent.'

in the margin or between the lines which Tischendorf asserts to belong mostly to B³, a few to B².[1]

At length, after baffling delays only too readily accounted for by the public calamities of the Papal state, the concluding volume of this sumptuous and important work was published late in 1881. Sergius had now retired through failing eyesight, and his place was taken by 'Henricus Canonicus Fabiani,' Cozza (who is now Abbot of the Grotta Ferrata at Tusculum near Frascati, the chief seat of the monks of the Greek order of St. Basil) still holding the second place. From the laudatory tone in which the latter is spoken of (p. xiv), it would seem that the Preface was written by his new colleague, who acknowledges the help of U. Ubaldi and the Basilian monk Ant. Rocchi, all three 'adjutoribus et administris miratis equidem se tantis viris adjutores et successores datos' (p. xv). This Preface consists of twenty-two pages, and contains almost nothing that is interesting to the critic, much that displays superficial and newly-acquired acquaintance with the whole subject. Fabiani assigns the end of the fourth century as the date of the manuscript, regarding it as only a few years older than the Sinaitic copy[2], whose discovery he

---

[1] In 1 Cor. vii. 29 Vercellone joins ἐστιν and τὸ closely, but Tischendorf leaves a space between them, with a middle point, which he expressly states to be *primâ manu*. Again, in ver. 34 Vercellone joins μεμέρισται with the following καί. Tischendorf in 1867 (but not in his last edition of the N. T.) interposes a point and space. In these *minutiae* Vercellone, who was not working against time, may be presumed to be the more accurate of the two. The editors of the sixth volume have no note at either place. Tischendorf detects an error of Vercellone, εἴτε for εἶχε Heb. ix. 1, but this has been corrected by the hand in some copies of the Roman volume, as also in the Commentary.

[2] His reasons for regarding the Sinaitic manuscript as the younger (*see* p. 89, note 2) are valid enough so far as they go (Praef. p. vi) : its initial letters stand out more from the line of the writing ; abridgements of words are fewer and less simple ; it contains the Ammonian sections and Eusebian canons instead of the antiquated divisions of its rival, and the text is broken up into smaller paragraphs. Tregelles, who had seen both copies, used to plead the fresher appearance of the Sinaitic, contrasted with the worn look of the Vatican MS.; but then its extensive hiatus proves that the latter had been less carefully preserved.

Eusebius sent to Constantine's new city (Euseb. Vit. Const. Lib. iv) πεντήκοντα σωμάτια ἐν διφθέραις (c. 36)... ἐν πολυτελῶς ἠσκημένοις τεύχεσι τρισσὰ καὶ τετρασσά (c. 37) : on which last words Valesius notes, 'Codices enim membranacei ferè per quaterniones digerebantur, hoc est quatuor folia simul compacta, ut terniones tria sunt folia simul compacta. Et quaterniones quidem sedecim habebant paginas, terniones vero duodenas.' But now that we have come to know that Cod. B is arranged in quires of five sheets (*see* p. 105), that manuscript will hardly answer to the description τρισσὰ καὶ τετρασσά (*see* p. 27, note 1)

hails without a vestige of ungenerous jealousy: 'Quorum tale est demum par, ut potius liber Vaticanus gaudere debeat quod tam sui similem invenerit fratrem, quam expavescere quod aemulum' (p. viii). Since that time a splendid edition has been issued of the New Testament in 1889, and the Old in 1890, under the care of the Abbate Cozza-Luzi, in which the whole is beautifully exhibited in photograph: so that all students can now examine for themselves the readings and characteristics of this celebrated manuscript with all but the advantage which is given in an examination of the original vellum itself (Novum Testamentum e Codd. Vat. 1209, &c. Rom. 1889, 4to): and gratitude is due from all textual scholars to the authorities of the Vatican.

Those who agree the most unreservedly respecting the age of the Codex Vaticanus, vary widely in their estimate of its critical value. By some it has been held in such undue esteem that its readings, if probable in themselves, and supported (or even though not supported) by two or three other copies and versions, have been accepted in preference to the united testimony of all

as Cod. ℵ does. Indeed Canon Cook (Revised Version, &c., p. 162) objects to Valesius' explanation altogether, on the ground that his sense would rather require τριπλύα καὶ τετραπλύα, and that the rare words τρισσά ('three by three') and τετρασσά ('four by four') exactly describe the arrangement of three columns on a page in Cod. B, and four on a page in Cod. ℵ. The Canon has since observed that the same view is maintained by O. von Gebhardt ('Bibel-text' in Herzog's Real-Encyklopädie, Leipsic 1878, second edition). On the other hand Archdeacon Palmer, in an obliging communication made to me, comparing the words πεντήκοντα σωμάτια ἐν διφθέραις ἐγκατασκεύοις (c. 36) with ἐν πολυτελῶς ἠσκημένοις τεύχεσιν τρισσὰ καὶ τετρασσὰ διαπεμψάντων ἡμῶν, and interpreting Eusebius' compliance (c. 37) by means of Constantine's directions (c. 36), is inclined to refer τρισσὰ καὶ τετρασσά to σωμάτια, as if it were 'we sent abroad the collections [of writings] in richly adorned cases, three or four in a case.' It will probably be thought that the expression is on the whole too obscure to be depended on for any controversial purposes. It is safer to argue that if the sections and canons extant in Cod. ℵ be by a contemporary hand (see p. 93, and Dean Gwynn's *Memoranda* in our *Addenda* for that page), that circumstance, the great antiquity of the manuscript considered, will confirm the probability of Eusebius' connexion with it. Eusebius agrees also with ℵ in omitting ἡ πύλη, Matt. vii. 13, and knew of copies, not however the best or with his approval, which inserted ἡσαΐου before τοῦ προφήτου in Matt. xiii. 35 : ℵ being the only uncial which exhibits that reading. So again Eusebius after Origen maintains the impossible number ἑκατὸν ἑξήκοντα of ℵ and a few others in Luke xxiv. 13. Dr. C. R. Gregory, Prolegomena, pp. 347, 348, inclines to the belief that B and ℵ were among the fifty MSS. sent by Eusebius to Constantine about A.D. 331-2. Canon Cook's entire argument (Revised Version of the First Three Gospels (1882), pp. 160-165) should be consulted.

authorities besides: while others, admitting the interest due to age, have spoken of its text as one of the most vicious extant. Without anticipating what must be discussed hereafter we may say at once, that, while we accord to Cod. B at least as much weight as to any single document in existence, we ought never to forget that it is but one out of many, several of them being nearly (and one quite) as old, and in other respects not less worthy of confidence than itself. One marked feature, characteristic of this copy, is the great number of its omissions, which has induced Dr. Dobbin to speak of it as presenting 'an abbreviated text of the New Testament:' and certainly the facts he states on this point are startling enough[1]. He calculates that Codex B leaves out words or whole clauses no less than 330 times in Matthew, 365 in Mark, 439 in Luke, 357 in John, 384 in the Acts, 681 in the surviving Epistles; or 2,556 times in all. That no small proportion of these are mere oversights of the scribe seems evident from the circumstance that this same scribe has repeatedly written words and clauses *twice over*, a class of mistakes which Mai and the collators have seldom thought fit to notice, inasmuch as the false addition has not been retraced by the second hand, but which by no means enhances our estimate of the care employed in copying this venerable record of primitive Christianity[2]. Hug and others have referred the origin of Codex B to Egypt, but (unlike in this respect to Codex A) its history does not confirm their conjecture, and the argument derived from orthography or grammatical forms, is now well understood to be but slight and ambiguous[3]. Dr. Hort, on no very substantial

[1] Dublin University Magazine, Nov. 1859, p. 620. Even Bishop Lightfoot, a strong and consistent admirer of the manuscript, speaks of its 'impatience of apparently superfluous words' (Epistle to the Colossians, p. 316). Dr. Hort (Introduction, p. 235) pleads that such facts 'have no bearing on either the merits or the demerits of the scribe of B, except as regards the absolutely singular readings of B,' whereas multitudes of these omissions are found in other good documents.

[2] Dean Burgon cites four specimens of such repetitions: Matt. xxi. 4, five words written twice over; ib. xxvi. 56-7, six words; Luke i. 37, three words or one line; John xvii. 18, six words. These, however, are but a few out of many. Nor is Tischendorf's judgement at variance with our own. Speaking of some supposed or possible gross *errata* of the recent Roman edition, he puts in the significant proviso 'tamen haec quoque satis cum universâ scripturae Vaticanae vitiositate conveniunt' (Appendix N. T. Vaticani, 1869, p. xvii).

[3] The latest Roman editors incline to an Egyptian origin, rather than one suggested in Magna Graecia, but the only fresh reason they allege can have very slight weight, namely, that two of the damaged leaves have been repaired by

(24)

(25)

ΠΟΙΜΕΝΕΙΝ
ΤΗΝΕΚΚΛΗΣΙΑΝ
ΤΟΥΥΙΥ
Α Ξ Ψ

REGERE
ECCLESIAM
DOMINI
B Θ Φ

(26)

Τὸ κατὰ ᵇ ματθαῖον ᶜ ἅγιορ ᵈ εὐαγγέλιορ. Cap. 1.
ἰβλὸς ᵇ γενεσεως ᶜ ἰησοῦ ᵈ χρισ =
τοῦ ᶜ υἱοῦ ᵇ δαυιδ᾽ υἱοῦ ᵇ ἀβραάμ.
ἱ ἀβραὰμ ᵏ ἐγέννησε/ Τὸν ᶦ ἰσαάκ. ᵐ Ἰ
σαὰκ ᵑ δὲ ᵒ ἐγέννησε./ Τὸν ᴾ ιακώβ. ᵠ Ἰα
κὼβ ʳ δὲ ˢ ἐγέννησε / Τὸν ᵗ ἰούδαν.
"καὶ ᵘ τοὺς ᵛ ἀδελφοὺς ʷ αὐτοῦ. ˣ ἰούδας ʸ δὲ ᶻ ἐγέν-

Euangelium ᵃ ſcdm ᵇ Matthei.   Cap. j.
Iber ᵇ gnatiõis ᶜ ieſu ᵈ chri
ſti ᵉ filij ᶠ dauid ᵍ filij ʰ abraã.
ⁱ Abraã ᵏ genuit ᶦ yſaac. ᵐ Ⱥ
ſaac ⁿ āt ᵒ genuit ᴾ iacob. ᵠ Ja
cob ʳ aūt ˢ genuit ᵗ iudam:
"et ᵘ fratreſ ᵛ eius.ʷ Judas ˣ autem ʸ genuit

grounds, is 'inclined to surmise that B and ℵ were both written in the West, probably at Rome' (Introduction, pp. 265-7).

C. CODEX EPHRAEMI, No. 9, in the Royal Library of Paris, is a most valuable palimpsest containing portions of the Septuagint version of the Old Testament on sixty-four leaves, and fragments of every part of the New on 145 leaves, amounting on the whole to less than two-thirds of the volume [1]. This manuscript seems to have been brought from the East by Andrew John Lascar [d. 1535], a learned Greek patronized by Lorenzo de' Medici; it once belonged to Cardinal Nicolas Ridolphi of that family, was brought into France by Queen Catherine de' Medici of evil memory, and so passed into the Royal Library at Paris [2]. The ancient writing is barely legible, having been almost removed about the twelfth century to receive some Greek works of St. Ephraem, the great Syrian Father [299-378]. A chemical preparation applied at the instance of Fleck in 1834, though it revived much that was before illegible, has defaced the vellum with stains of various colours, from green and blue to black and brown. The older writing was first noticed by Peter Allix

pieces of papyrus. The learned Ceriani of Milan believes that Cod. B was written in Italy, Cod. ℵ in Palestine or Syria (Quarterly Review, April, 1882, p. 355). The supposed Eusebian origin of both has been already stated.

[1] As this manuscript is of first-rate importance it is necessary to subjoin a full list of the passages it contains, that it may not be cited *e silentio* for what it does not exhibit : Matt. i. 2—v. 15 ; vii. 5—xvii. 26 ; xviii. 28—xxii. 20 ; xxiii. 17—xxiv. 10 ; xxiv. 45—xxv. 30 ; xxvi. 22—xxvii. 11 ; xxvii. 47—xxviii. 14 : Mark i. 17—vi. 31 ; viii. 5—xii. 29 ; xiii. 19—xvi. 20 : Luke i. 2—ii. 5 ; ii. 42—iii. 21 ; iv. 25—vi. 4 ; vi. 37—vii. 16 or 17 ; viii. 28—xii. 3 ; xix. 42—xx. 27 ; xxi. 21—xxii. 19 ; xxiii. 25—xxiv. 7 ; xxiv. 46-53 : John i. 1-41 ; iii. 33—v. 16 ; vi. 38—vii. 3 ; viii. 34—ix. 11 ; xi. 8-46 ; xiii. 8—xiv. 7 ; xvi. 21—xviii. 36 ; xx. 26—xxi. 25 : Acts i. 2—iv. 3 ; v. 35—x. 42 ; xiii. 1—xvi. 36 ; xx. 10—xxi. 30 ; xxii. 21—xxiii. 18 ; xxiv. 15—xxvi. 19 ; xxvii. 16—xxviii. 4 : James i. 1—iv. 2 : 1 Pet. i. 2—iv. 6 : 2 Pet. i. 1—1 John iv. 2 : 3 John 3-15 : Jude 3-25 : Rom. i. 1—ii. 5 ; iii. 21—ix. 6 ; x. 15—xi. 31 ; xiii. 10—1 Cor. vii. 18 ; ix. 6—xiii. 8 ; xv. 40—2 Cor. x. 8 : Gal. i. 20—vi. 18 : Eph. ii. 18—iv. 17 : Phil. i. 22—iii. 5 : Col. i. 1—1 Thess. ii. 9 : Heb. ii. 4—vii. 26 ; ix. 15—x. 24 ; xii. 15—xiii. 25 : 1 Tim. iii. 9—v. 20 ; vi. 21—Philem. 25 : Apoc. i. 2—iii. 19 ; v. 14—vii. 14 ; vii. 17—viii. 4 ; ix. 17—x. 10 ; xi. 3—xvi. 13 ; xviii. 2—xix. 5. Of all the books only 2 John and 2 Thess. are entirely lost ; about thirty-seven chapters of the Gospels, ten of the Acts, forty-two of the Epistles, eight of the Apocalypse have perished. The order of the books is indicated, p. 74.

[2] The following Medicean manuscripts seem to have come into the Royal Library by the same means ; Evan. 16, 19, 42, 317. Act. 12, 126. Paul. 164. It appears therefore that Cod. C was not one of the manuscripts bought of Marshal Strozzi (Pattison, Life of Is. Casaubon, p. 202), which were only 800 out of the 4,500 which belonged to the Queen (ibid. p. 204).

nearly two centuries ago; various readings extracted from it were communicated by Boivin to Kuster, who published them (under the notation of Paris 9) in his edition of Mill's N.T., 1710. A complete collation of the New Testament was first made in 1716 by Wetstein, then very young, for Bentley's projected edition, for which labour (as he records the fact himself) he paid Wetstein £50. This collation Wetstein of course used for his own Greek Testament of 1751-2, and though several persons subsequently examined the manuscript, and so became aware that more might be gathered from it, it was not until 1843 that Tischendorf brought out at Leipsic his full and noble edition of the New Testament portion; the Old Testament he published in 1845. Although Tischendorf complains of the typographical errors made in his absence in the former of these two volumes, and has corrected them in the other, they probably comprise by far the most masterly production of this nature up to that date published; it is said too that none but those who have seen Codex C can appreciate the difficulty of deciphering some parts of it [1], in fact, whatever is not patent at first sight. The Prolegomena are especially valuable; the uncial type does not aim at being an imitation, but the facsimile faithfully represents the original, even to the present colour of the ink. In shape Codex C is about the size of Cod. A, but not quite so tall; its vellum is hardly so fine as that of Cod. A and a few others, yet sufficiently good. In this copy there is but one column in a page, which contains from forty to forty-six lines (usually forty-one), the characters being a little larger than those of either A or B, and somewhat more elaborate [2]. Thus the points at the ends of *sigma*, *epsilon*, and especially of the horizontal line of *tau*, are more decided than in Codex A; *delta*, though not so fully formed as in later books, is less simple than in A, the strokes being of less equal thickness, and the base more

[1] Bp. Chr. Wordsworth (N. T. Part iv. p. 159) reminds us of Wetstein's statement (Bentley's Correspondence, p. 501) that it had cost him two hours to read one page; so that his £50 were not so easily earned, after all. This collation is preserved in Trinity College Library, B. xvii. 7, 9.

[2] Dr. Hort, with his ever ready acuteness, draws certain inferences to be discussed hereafter from the fact that a displacement in the leaves of the exemplar wherefrom the Apocalypse in Cod. C was copied, which the scribe of C did not notice, proves it to have been a book of nearly 120 small leaves, and accordingly that it 'formed a volume either to itself or without considerable additions' (Introduction, p. 268).

ornamented. On the other hand, *alpha* and *pi* are nearer the model of Codex B. *Iota* and *upsilon*, which in Cod. A and many other copies have two dots over them when they commence a syllable, and are sometimes found with one dot, have here a small straight line in their place (*see* p. 36). There are no breathings or accents by the first hand: the apostrophus is found but rarely, chiefly with Proper names, as $\overline{δαδ}'$. The uncial writing is continuous; the punctuation of Cod. C, like that of A and B, consisting only of a single point, mostly but not always put level with the top of the preceding letter; wherever such a point was employed, a space of one letter broad was usually left vacant: these points are most common in the later books of the N.T. The κεφάλαια are not placed in the upper margin of the page as in Cod. A, but a list of their τίτλοι preceded each Gospel: the so-called Ammonian sections stand in the margin, but not at present the Eusebian canons; though, since lines of the text written in vermilion have been thoroughly washed out, the canons (for which that colour was commonly employed) may easily have shared the same fate (*see* p. 61). There is no trace of chapters in the Acts, Epistles, or Apocalypse, and both the titles and subscriptions to the various books are very simple. Capital letters are used quite as freely as in Cod. A, both at the commencement of the (Ammonian) sections, and in many other places. All these circumstances taken together indicate for Cod. C as early a date as the fifth century, though there is no sufficient cause for deeming it at all older than Cod. A. Alexandria has been assigned as its native country, for the very insufficient reasons stated when we were describing A and B. It is carefully transcribed, and of its great critical value there is no doubt; its text seems to stand nearly midway between A and B, somewhat inclining to the latter. Two correctors have been very busily at work on Cod. C, greatly to the perplexity of the critical collator: they are respectively indicated by Tischendorf as C**, C***. The earliest, or the second hand, may have been of the sixth century, and his corrections are for some cause regarded by Dr. Hort as almost equally valuable for critical purposes with the manuscript itself: the second corrector, or the third hand, is perhaps of the ninth century, and he revised such portions as were adapted to ecclesiastical use, inserting many accents, the *rough* breathing, and some vocal notes. By him or more probably by a fourth hand (who did not change the text, but added some liturgical directions in the margin) small crosses were interpolated as stops, agreeably to the fashion of their times.

D OF THE GOSPELS AND ACTS, CODEX BEZAE GRAECO-LATINUS, belongs to the University Library at Cambridge, where the open volume is conspicuously exhibited to visitors in the New Building (Nn. II. 41). It was presented to the University in 1581 by Theodore Beza, for whom and his master Calvin the heads of that learned body then cherished a veneration which already boded ill for the peace of the English Church [1]. Between the Gospels (whose order was spoken of above, pp. 72-4) and the Acts, the Catholic Epistles once stood, of which only a few verses remain in the Latin translation (3 John ver. 11-15), followed by the words 'epistulae Johannis III explicit, incipit actus apostolorum,' as if St. Jude's Epistle were displaced or wanting. There are not a few hiatus both in the Greek and Latin texts [2]. The contents of this remarkable document were partially made known by numerous extracts from it, under the designation of β', in the margin of Robert Stephen's Greek Testament of 1550, whose account of it is that it was collated for him in Italy by his friends (τὸ δὲ β' ἐστὶ τὸ ἐν Ἰταλίᾳ ὑπὸ τῶν ἡμετέρων ἀντιβληθὲν φίλων. Epistle to the Reader) [3]. It is not very easy to reconcile this statement with Beza's account pre-

[1] Very remarkable is the language of the University in returning thanks for the gift: 'Nam hoc scito, post unicae scripturae sacratissimam cognitionem, nullos unquam ex omni memoriâ temporum scriptores extitisse, quos memorabili viro Johanni Calvino tibique praeferamus.' Scrivener's Codex Bezae, Introd. p. vi.

[2] Matt. i. 1-20; vi. 20—ix. 2; xxvii. 2-12: John i. 16—iii. 26: Acts viii. 29—x. 14; xxi. 2-10; 15-18 (though Ussher, Mill, Wetstein and Dickinson cite several readings from these verses, which must have been extant in their time); xxii. 10-20; 29—xxviii. 31 in the *Greek*: Matt. i. 1-11; vi. 8—viii. 27; xxvi. 65—xxvii. 1: John i. 1—iii. 16: Acts viii. 20—x. 4; xx. 31—xxi. 2; 7-10; xxii. 2-10; xxii. 20—xxviii. 31 in the *Latin*. The original writing has perished in the following, which are supplied by a scribe of not earlier than the ninth century: Matt. iii. 7-16: Mark xvi. 15-20: John xviii. 14—xx. 13 in the *Greek*: Matt. ii. 21—iii. 7: Mark xvi. 6-20: John xviii. 2—xx. 1 in the *Latin*. A fragment, containing a few words of Matt. xxvi. 65-67 (Latin) and xxvii. 2 (Greek), (Fol. 96, Scrivener), was overlooked by Kipling.

[3] It is surprising that any one should have questioned the identity of Cod. D with Stephen's β'. No other manuscript has been discovered which agrees with β' in the many singular readings and arbitrary additions in support of which it is cited by Stephen. That he omitted so many more than he inserted is no argument against their identity, since we know that he did the same in the

ΟΥΚΑΣΧΗΜΟΝΕΙ
ΟΥΖΗΤΕΙΤΑΕΑΥΤΗΣ
ΟΥΠΑΡΟΞΥΝΕΤΑΙ
ΟΥΛΟΓΙΖΕΤΑΙΤΟΚΑΚΟΝ
ΟΥΧΑΙΡΕΙΕΠΙΤΗΑΔΙΚΙΑ
ΣΥΝΧΑΙΡΕΙΔΕΤΗΑΛΗΘΕΙΑ
ΠΑΝΤΑΣΤΕΓΕΙ
ΠΑΝΤΑΠΙΣΤΕΥΕΙ
ΠΑΝΤΑΕΛΠΙΖΕΙ
ΠΑΝΤΑ ΥΠΟΜΕΝΕΙ
Η ΑΓΑΠΗ
ΟΥΔΕΠΟΤΕΕΚΠΙΠΤΕΙ ⳨

ΚΑΤ ΙΩΑΝ

CΗΜΕΝΩΝΠΟΙΩΘΑΝΑΤΩΔΟΞΑCΕΙΤΟΝΘΝ
ΚΑΙΤΟΥΤΟΕΙΠΩΝΛΕΓΕΙΑΥΤΩΑΚΟΛΟΥΘΕΙΜΟΙ
ΕΠΙΣΤΡΑΦΕΙΣΔΕΟΠΕΤΡΟΣΒΛΕΠΕΙΤΟΝΜΑΘΗΤΗΝ
ΟΝΗΓΑΠΑ ΙΗΣ ΑΚΟΛΟΥΘΟΥΝΤΑ
ΟΣΚΑΙΑΝΕΠΕΣΕΝΕΝΤΩΔΕΙΠΝΩ
ΕΠΙΤΟΣΤΗΘΟΣΑΥΤΟΥ ΚΑΙΕΙΠΕΝΑΥΤΩ
ΚΕ ΤΙΣΕΣΤΙΝΟΠΑΡΑΔΙΔΩΝΣΕ
ΤΟΥΤΟΝΟΥΝΕΙΔΩΝΟΠΕΤΡΟΣΛΕΓΕΙΑΥΤΩΙΗΥ·
ΚΕ ΟΥΤΟΣΔΕΤΙ· ΛΕΓΕΙΑΥΤΩΟΙΗΣ
ΕΑΝΑΥΤΟΝΘΕΛΩΜΕΝΕΙΝΟΥΤΩΣ
ΕΩΣΕΡΧΟΜΑΙΤΙΠΡΟΣΣΕ ΣΥΜΟΙΑΚΟΛΟΥΘΕΙ
ΕΞΗΛΘΕΝΟΥΝΟΥΤΟΣΟΛΟΓΟΣΕΙΣΤΟΥΣ

NON AMBITIOSA EST
NON QUAERIT QUAE SUA SUNT
NON INRITATUR
NON COGITAT MALUM
NON GAUDET SUPER INIQUITATEM
CONGAUDET AUTEM UERITATI
OMNIA SUFFERIT
OMNIA CREDIT   (43)
OMNIA SPERAT   ΠΟΝΗΡΟΥ ΟΤΙ
OMNIA SUSTENET   CΟΥ ΕϹΤΙΝ ΗΒΑ
                       ϹΙΛΕΙΑ ΚΑΙ ΗΔΥ
CARITAS   ΝΑΜΙϹ ΚΑΙ ΗΔΟ
NUMQUAM EXCIDET   ΞΑ ΕΙϹ ΤΟΥϹ ΑΙ–
                       ΝΑϹ ΑΜΗΝ·
                       ΕΑΝ ΓΑΡ ΑΦΗΤΕ
     sec͞ iohan͞   ΤΟΙϹ ΑΝΟΙϹ ΤΑ
                       ΠΑΡΑΠΤΩΜΑΤΑ

SIGNIFICANS QUA MORTE HONORIFICABIT d͞m
:T HOC CUM DIXISSET DICIT ILLI SEQUERE ME
CONUERSUS AUTEM PETRUS UIDET DISCIPULUM
QUEM DILIGEBAT IH͞S SEQUENTEM
QUI ET RECUBUIT IN CENA
SUPER PECTUS EIUS ET DIXIT ILLI
d͞m̄e QUIS EST QUI TRADIDIT TE
HUNC ERGO UIDENS PETRUS DICIT AD IH͞M
d͞m̄e HIC AUTEM QUID · DICIT ILLI IH͞S
SI EUM UOLO SIC MANERE
USQUE DUM UENIO QUID AD TE TU ME SEQUERE
EXIUIT ERGO HIC UERBUS APUT FRATRES

fixed to the manuscript and still extant in his own cramped handwriting, wherein he alleges that he obtained the volume in 1562 from the monastery of St. Irenaeus at Lyons ('oriente ibi civili bello'), where it had long lain buried ('postquam ibi in pulvere diu jacuisset'). This great city, it must be remembered, was sacked in that very year by the infamous Des Adrets, whom it suited to espouse for a while the cause of the Huguenots; and we can hardly doubt that some one who had shared in the plunder of the abbey[1] conveyed this portion of it to Beza, whose influence at that juncture was paramount among the French Reformed[2].

case of his α′ (the Complutensian Polyglott) and η′ (Codex L, Paris 62). The great inaccuracy of Stephen's *margin* (the text is much better revised) is so visible from these and other well-ascertained instances that no one ought to wonder if β′ is alleged occasionally (not often) for readings which D does not contain. On a careful analysis of all the variations imputed to β′ by Stephen, they will be found to amount to 389 in the parts written in the original hand, whereof 309 are alleged quite correctly, forty-seven a little loosely, while in eight instances corrected readings are regarded in error as from the original scribe. Of the twenty-five places which remain, all but three had been previously discovered in other copies used by Stephen, so that β′ in their case has been substituted by mistake for some other numeral. One of the three remaining has recently been accounted for by Mr. A. A. Vansittart, who has found καὶ περισσευθήσεται added to δοθήσεται αὐτῷ (Luke viii. 18 from Matt. xiii. 12) in Stephen's θ′ or Coislin 200 at Paris (No. 38, of the Gospels). I do not find β′ cited by Stephen after Acts xx. 24, except indeed in Rom. iii. 10 (with α′), in manifest error, just as in the Apocalypse xix. 14 ε′ (No. 6 of the Gospels), which does not contain this book, is cited instead of ιε′; or as ια′ is quoted in xiii. 4, *but not elsewhere in the Apocalypse*, undoubtedly in the place of ις′; or as ις′, which had broken off at xvii. 8, reappears instead of ιε′ in xx. 3. In the various places named in the last note, wherein the Greek of Cod. D is lost, β′ is cited only at Matt. xxvii. 3, beyond question instead of η′; and for *part* of the reading in Acts ix. 31, δ′ (to which the whole rightly belongs) being alleged for the other part. In John xix. 6, indeed, where the original Greek is missing, β′ is cited, but it is for a reading actually extant in the modern hand which has there supplied Codex D's defects.

[1] 'Ils s'emparèrent des portes et de tous les lieux forts . . . non pas sans leur impiétés et barbaries accoutumées envers les choses saintes' (Mézeray, Hist. de France, tom. iii. p. 87, 1685). Accordingly, travellers are shown to this day the bones of unclean animals which the Huguenots, in wanton mockery, then mingled with the presumed remains of St. Irenaeus and the martyrs of Lyons.

[2] One cannot understand why Wetstein (N. T. Proleg. vol. i, 30) should have supposed that Beza *prevaricated* as to the means whereby he procured his manuscript. He was not the man to be at all ashamed of spoiling the Philistines, and the bare mention of Lyons in connexion with the year 1562 would have been abundantly intelligible scarce twenty years afterwards. It is however remarkable that in the last edition of his Annotations (1598) he nowhere calls it Codex Lugdunensis, but *Claromontanus* (notes on Luke xix. 26; Acts xx. 3); for, though it might be natural that Beza, at eighty years of age and after the

Beza in his editions of the Greek Testament published in 1582, 1589, and 1598, made some occasional references to the readings of his manuscript. Archbishop Whitgift borrowed it from Cambridge in 1583, and caused a poor transcript to be made of its Greek text, which he bequeathed to Trinity College (whereof he had been Master), in whose Library it still remains (B. x. 3).

Patrick Young, of whom we have heard in connexion with Cod. A (p. 103 and note 1), sent extracts from Cod. D to the brothers Dupuy at Paris, through whom they reached Morinus and Steph. Curcellaeus. An unusually full collation was made for Walton's Polyglott (Tom. vi, Num. xvi, 1657) by pious Archbishop Ussher, who devoted to these studies the doleful leisure of his latter years. Mill collated and Wetstein transcribed (1716) this document for their great editions of the Greek Testament, but they both did their work carelessly; and though Bentley was allowed to keep it at home for seven years, his notices of its readings, as represented by Mr. Ellis (Bentleii Critica Sacra, pp. 2-26), or preserved in Stephen's N.T. of 1549 (Trin. Coll. B. xvii. 4), were put to no practical use. The best collation by far was made about 1732 by John Dickinson of St. John's College for John Jackson of Leicester, with whose other books it came into Jesus College Library (O. θ. 2), where it has lain neglected. But a manuscript replete as this is with variations from the sacred text beyond all other example could be adequately represented only by being published in full; a design entrusted by the University of Cambridge to Dr. Thomas Kipling, Senior Wrangler in 1768 and afterwards Dean of Peterborough [d. 1822], whose 'Codex Theodori Bezae Cantabrigiensis' 1793, 2 vols. fol. (in type imitating the original handwriting much more closely than in Cod. A and the rest), is a not unfaithful transcript of the text[1],

---

lapse of so long a time, should confound the Lyons copy with his own Codex Claromontanus of St. Paul's Epistles (D); yet the only way in which we can account for the Codex Bezae being collated in *Italy* for Stephen, is by adopting Wetstein's suggestion that it was the actual copy ('antiquissimum codicem Graecum') taken to the Council of Trent in 1546 by William a Prato, Bishop of *Clermont* in Auvergne, to confirm the Latin reading in John xxi. 22 '*sic* eum volo,' which D alone may seem to do. Some learned man (ὑπὸ τῶν ἡμετέρων φίλων does not well suit his son Henry) might have sent to Robert Stephen from Tren the readings of a manuscript to which attention had been thus specially directed.

[1] Not more than eighty-three typographical errors have been detected in

though the Prolegomena too plainly testify to the editor's pitiable ignorance of sacred criticism, while his habit of placing the readings of the several later hands (very loosely distinguished from each other) in the text, and those of the first hand in the notes (a defect we have also noted in the Roman editions of Cod. B), renders his volumes very inconvenient for use. Let Kipling be praised for the care and exact diligence his work evinces, but Herbert Marsh [1757–1839] was of all Cambridge men of that period the only one known to be competent for such a task. In 1864 the present writer was aided by the Syndics of the Cambridge Press in publishing an edition of Codex Bezae in common type, illustrated by a copious Introduction and critical notes, to which work the reader is referred for fuller information respecting this manuscript.

The Codex Bezae is a quarto volume 10 inches high by 8 broad, with one column on a page, the Greek text and its Latin version being parallel, the Greek on the left, or *verso* of each leaf, and the Latin on the right, opposite to it, on the *recto* of the next. Notwithstanding the Alexandrian forms that abound in it as much as in any other copy, and which have been held by some to prove the Egyptian origin of Codd. ABC, the fact of its having a Latin version sufficiently attests its Western origin. The vellum is not quite equal in fineness to that of a few others. There are thirty-three lines in every page, and these of unequal length, as this manuscript is arranged in στίχοι, being the earliest in date that is so (*see* p. 53). The Latin is placed in the same line and as nearly as possible in the same order as the corresponding Greek. It has not the larger κεφάλαια or Eusebian canons, but only the so-called Ammonian sections, often incorrectly placed, and obviously in a later hand of about the ninth century. The original absence of these divisions is no proof that the book was not at first intended for ecclesiastical use (as some have stated), inasmuch as the sections and canons were constructed for a very different purpose (*see above*, pp. 59–63), but is another argument for its being copied in the West, perhaps not far from the place where it rested so long. Other proofs of its Occidental, perhaps of its Gallican origin, especially that derived from the style of the Latin version, are

Kipling throughout his difficult task, whereof sixteen are in his Annotations, &c.

collected in Scrivener's edition (Introd. pp. xxxi, xl—xlv). The characters are of the same size as in C, larger on the whole than in AB, but betray a later age than any of these, although the Latin as well as the Greek is written continuously, excepting that in the titles and subscriptions of the several books (as in Codd. DH of St. Paul) the words are separated. This copy has paragraph divisions of unequal length peculiar to itself[1]. They are indicated by placing the initial letter out in the margin, that letter being usually of the same size with the rest, though sometimes a little larger. Cod. D appears to be the earliest which exhibits larger letters after a pause in the middle of a line; but these are not very frequent. Instances of each case may be noticed in our facsimile (No. 42), wherein the shapes of *kappa*, *rho* and *phi*, as indicated before (pp. 32, note 1, 37, 39), are very observable. The Greek and Latin writing on the opposite pages are much like each other in appearance, the Latin letters being round and flowing, not square as in codices a little earlier in date, such as the Medicean and Vatican fragments of Virgil. This manuscript has been corrected, first by the original penman with a light stroke made by a pen nearly empty; after him by not less than eight or nine different revisers, some nearly coeval with the Codex itself, others not many centuries old. The changes they have made, especially when they employed a knife to scrape away the primitive reading, render too many places almost illegible. The first scribe often used a sponge to wash out his error before the ink was well dried in (*see* p. 27). In addition to the single point about three-fourths of the height of a letter up, which often subdivides the στίχοι in both languages (facsimile, No. 42, l. 9) the coarse late hand which inserted the Ammonian sections placed double dots (:) after the numerals, and often inserted similar points in the text, before or over the first letter of a section. Each member of the genealogy in Luke iii forms a separate στίχος, as in Cod. B: quotations are indicated by throwing the commencement of the lines which contain them, both Greek and Latin, about an inch back or less

---

[1] In St. Luke 136 (143 Lat.): in what remains of St. Matthew 583 (590 Lat.), of St. Mark 148, of St. John 165 (168 Lat.), of the Acts 235. The later παραγραφαί, indicated by ʃ (*see* p. 51, note 3), though forty-five out of the forty-nine are firmly and neatly made, and often resemble in colour the ink of the original scribe, can be shown to be full four centuries later (Scrivener, Cod. Bezae, Introd. p. xxviii).

(e.g. Matt. xxvi. 31; Mark i. 2, 3; Acts ii. 34, 35; iv. 25, 26). The first three lines of each book, in both languages, were written in bright red ink, which was also employed in the alternate lines of the subscriptions, and in other slight ornaments. The traces of the scribe's needle and lines (see p. 27) are very visible, the margin ample, and the volume on the whole in good keeping, though its first extant page (Latin) is much decayed, and it is stained in parts by some chemical mixture that has been applied to it. The portions supplied by a later hand are of course in the uncial Greek and cursive Latin characters usual at the dates assigned to them. The liturgical notes in the margin of the Saturday and Sunday lessons (αυυαγυοσμα is the form often used) are in thick letters, of a yet later date than the Ammonian sections. A few others for the great Feasts and Fast days occur; and, in a hand of about the twelfth century, lessons for the Festivals of St. George and St. Dionysius, the patron saints of England and France, as may be seen in the table of Menology.

The vellum employed for Codex Bezae is arranged in quires of four sheets (or eight leaves) each even throughout[1], the numeral signatures of which are set *primâ manu* so low down in the margin at the foot of the last page of each, that they are mostly cut off, in whole or partly, by the binder. Assuming that it ended with the Acts of the Apostles, it originally consisted of upwards of sixty-four (probably of sixty-seven) quires, of which the first, forty-fourth, and sixty-fourth, have each lost some leaves, the thirty-fourth is entire though containing but six leaves, while those signed Γ (3), IΔ (14), KB (22), ME (45), down to NB (52), NZ (57), and all after ΞΔ (64), are wholly wanting. The result is that out of the 534 leaves it originally contained, only 406 now survive, about twelve of them being more or less mutilated. It is not easy to surmise what may have been written on the sixty-seven leaves that intervened between MΔ 5 and NΓ 1; the gap ends with 3 John ver. 11

---

[1] Bradshaw (Prothero's Memoirs, p. 97) in a letter to the *Guardian*, Jan. 28, 1863, writes thus :—'I saw Cod. ℵ at Leipsig *per* Tischendorf. I had been curious to know whether it was written in even quaternions throughout, like the Cod. Bezae, or in a series of fasciculi, each ending with a quire of varying size, like the Cod. Alexandrinus, and I found the latter to be the case. This, by-the-bye, is sufficient to prove'—why, is not quite clear—'that it cannot be the volume which Dr. Simonides speaks of having written at Mount Athos.'

(Greek), but the space is apparently too great for the Catholic Epistles alone, even though we suppose that Jude was inserted (as appears in some catalogues) otherwise than in the last place. The leaves added by later hands are nine in number. The Greek portion of the supplement to St. John (xviii. 14—xx. 13) much resembles in text the style of the original manuscript, and is often supported by Codd. ℵAB(C). The Latin of this portion is taken from the Vulgate version.

The internal character of the Codex Bezae is a most difficult and indeed an almost inexhaustible theme. No known manuscript contains so many bold and extensive interpolations (six hundred, it is said, in the Acts alone), countenanced, where they are not absolutely unsupported, chiefly by the Old Latin and the Curetonian version: its own parallel Latin translation is too servilely accommodated to the Greek text to be regarded as an independent authority, save where the corresponding Greek is lost.

This passage was penned by Dr. Scrivener before the publication of the highly ingenious treatise by Mr. Rendel Harris, entitled 'A Study of the Codex Bezae' (1891), being the beginning of the second volume of the Cambridge 'Texts and Studies.' Mr. Harris from curious internal evidence, such as the existence in the text of a vitiated rendering of a verse of Homer which bears signs of having been retranslated from a Latin translation, infers that the Greek has been made up from the Latin, and traces the latter to the second century. He shows its affinity with the text of Irenaeus, and discovers traces in it of Montanism. He opens up many points of interest for any one who would examine this 'singular Codex': but injustice must not be done to the fertile author by supposing that in what is evidently 'a Study' he concludes that he has settled all the numerous questions which he broaches. No one however can really investigate the Codex Bezae without studying this work, which will be found both instructive in the highest degree and amusing.

(27)

ΠΡΟCΑΥΤΟΝ. ΠΑCΑΗ ΙΟΥΔΑΙΑ Plate X
ΧѠΡΑ. ΚΑΙΟΙΙΕΡΟCΟΛΥΜΙΤΑΙ.
ΚΑΙΕΒΑΠΤΙΖΟΝΤΟΠΑΝΤΕC.
ΕΝΤѠΙΟΡΔΑΝΗΠΟΤΑΜѠΝ
ΠΑΥΤΟΥ. ΕΞΟΜΟΛΟΓΟΥΜΕ
ΝΟΙΤΑCΑΜΑΡΤΙΑCΑΥΤѠΝ·
ΗΝΔΕΟΙѠΑΝΝΗCΕΝΔΕΔΥΜΕΝΟC

(28)

ΚΑΙΠΡΟCΕΦΕΡΟΝ
ΑΥΤѠΠΑΙΔΙΑ
ΙΝΑΤΗΤΑΙΑΥ
ΤѠΝ· ΟΙΔΕΜΑΘΗ
ΤΑΙΕΠΕΤΙΜѠΝ

(29)

ΒΛΗΘΗ· ΕΙCΓΕΕΝ
ΝΑΝ· ΤΕΤΗCΛ.
ΕΡΡΗΘΗΔΕ· ΟΤΙΟC
ΑΝΑΠΟΛΥCΗΤΗΝ
ΓΥΝΑΙΚΑΑΥΤΟΥ·

(30)

ϹΑΝΤΕϹ· ΚΑΙΤΙϹ   ΠΟΥΤѠΝ· ΚΑΙΕΝ
ΔΥΝΑΤΑΙϹѠΘΗΝΑΙ   ΤѠΑΙѠΝΙΤѠΕΡ
ΟΔΕΙϹ· ΕΙΠΕΝ·   ΧΟΜΕΝѠΖѠΗΝ

CHAPTER V.

UNCIAL MANUSCRIPTS OF THE GOSPELS.

OF the manuscripts hitherto described, Codd. אABC for their presumed critical value, Cod. D for its numberless and strange deviations from other authorities, and all five for their high antiquity, demanded a full description. Of those which follow many contain but a few fragments of the Gospels, and others are so recent in date that they hardly exceed in importance some of the best cursive copies (e.g. FGHS)[1]. None of these need detain us long.

E. CODEX BASILIENSIS (B vi. 21, now A. N. iii. 12) ($κεφ. τ.$, $κεφ.$, $Am.$, $Eus.$ at foot of the pages) contains the four Gospels, excepting Luke iii. 4–15; xxiv. 47–53, and was written about the middle of the eighth century, unless (with Dean Burgon) we refer it to the seventh. It measures $9 \times 6\frac{1}{2}$ inches, and contains 318 folios. There are 247 folios *verso*, and 71 *recto*[2]. Three leaves (160, 207, 214) on which are Luke i. 69—ii. 4; xii. 58—xiii. 12; xv. 8-20 are in a cursive and later hand, above the obliterated fragments of a homily as old as the main body of the manuscript. There is a 'liber praedicatorum' on the first folio. This copy is one of the most notable of the later uncials, and might well have been published at length. It was given to a religious house in Basle by Cardinal John de Ragusio, who was sent on a mission to the Greeks by the Council of Basle (1431), and probably brought it from Constantinople. Erasmus much overlooked it for later books when preparing his Greek Testament at Basle; indeed it was not brought into the Public Library there before 1559. A collation was sent to Mill by John Battier, Greek Professor at Basle: Mill named it B. I, and truly declared it to

---

[1] Yet Φ (Beratinus) and Σ (Rossanensis) contain St. Matthew and St. Mark, and are probably a little older than D.

[2] H. C. Hoskier, Collation of Cod. 604, &c. Appendix F. Mr. Hoskier saw the MS. on May 18, 1886.

be 'probatae fidei et bonae notae.' Bengel (who obtained a few extracts from it) calls it Basil. *a*: but its first real collator was Wetstein, whose native town it adorns. Since his time, Tischendorf in 1843, Professor Müller of Basle and Tregelles in 1846, have independently collated it throughout. Judging from the specimen sent to him, Mill (N. T. Proleg. § 1118) thought the hand much like that of Cod. A; the uncial letters (though not so regular or neat) are firm, round, and simple: indeed 'the penmanship is exceedingly tasteful and delicate throughout. The employment of green, blue, and vermilion in the capitals I do not remember to have met with elsewhere' (Burgon, *Guardian*, Jan. 29, 1873). There is but one column of about twenty-four lines on the page; it has breathings and accents pretty uniformly, and not ill placed; otherwise, from the shape of most of the letters (e.g. *pi*, facsimile No. 27, lines 1, 3), it might be judged of earlier date: observe, however, the oblong form of *omicron* where the space is crowded in the last line of the facsimile, when the older scribes would have retained the circular shape and made the letter very small (*see* facsimile No. 11 b. l. 6): *delta* also and *xi* betray a less ancient scribe. The single stop in Cod. E, as was stated above (p. 48), changes its place according to the variation of its power, as in other copies of about the same age. The capitals at the beginning of sections stand out in the margin as in Codd. AC. The lists of the larger κεφάλαια together with the numbers of the sections in the margin and the Eusebian canons beneath them, as well as harmonizing references to the other Gospels at the foot of the page, names of Feast days with their Proper lessons, and other liturgical notices, have been inserted (as some think, but erroneously in Burgon's judgement) by a later hand. Under the text (Mark i. 5, 6) are placed the harmonizing references, in the order (varying in each Gospel) Mark, Luke, John, Matthew. I⁾ (John) furnishes no parallel on this page. The first section (a) of Mᵒ (Mark i. 1, 2) corresponds to the seventieth (o) of Λᵒ (Luke vii. 27), and to the 103rd (ργ) of M (Matt. xi. 10). Again the second (β) of Mark (i. 3) is parallel to the seventh (ζ) of Luke (iii. 3), and to the eighth (η) of Matt. (iii. 3). The passage given in our facsimile (No. 27) is part of the third (γ) of Mark (i. 4-6), and answers to nothing in Luke, but to the ninth (θ) of Matt. (iii. 4-6). See p. 60, note 4. The value of this codex, as supplying materials for criticism, is considerable. It approaches more nearly than some others of its date to the text now commonly received, and is an excellent witness for it. The asterisk is much used to indicate disputed passages: e.g. Matt. xvi. 2, 3: Luke xxii. 43, 44; xxiii. 34: John viii. 2-11. (For the fragments attached to this Codex, see Apoc. 15.)

F. CODEX BOREELI, now in the Public Library at Utrecht, once belonged to John Boreel [d. 1629], Dutch ambassador at the court of King James I. Wetstein obtained some readings from it in 1730, as far as Luke xi, but stated that he knew not where it then was. In 1830 Professor Heringa of Utrecht discovered it in private hands at Arnheim, and procured it for his University Library, where in 1850 Tregelles found it, though with some difficulty, the leaves being torn and all loose in a box, and he then made a facsimile; Tischendorf had looked through it in 1841. In 1843, after Heringa's death, H. E. Vinke published that scholar's 'Disputatio de Codice Boreeliano,' which includes a full and exact collation of the text. Cod. F contains the Four Gospels with many defects, some of which have been caused since the collation was made which Wetstein published: hence the codex must still sometimes be cited on his authority as F^w. In fact there are but 204 leaves and a few fragments remaining, written with two columns of about nineteen lines each on the page, in a tall, oblong, upright form; it was referred by Mr. H. Deane in 1876 to the eighth, by Tischendorf to the ninth, by Tregelles to the tenth century. In St. Luke there are no less than twenty-four gaps: in Wetstein's collation it began at Matt. vii. 6, but now at Matt. ix. 1. Other hiatus are Matt. xii. 1–44; xiii. 55—xiv. 9; xv. 20–31; xx. 18—xxi. 5: Mark i. 43—ii. 8; ii. 23—iii. 5; xi. 6–26; xiv. 54—xv. 5; xv. 39—xvi. 19: John iii. 5–14; iv. 23–38; v. 18–38; vi. 39–63; vii. 28—viii. 10; x. 32—xi. 3; xi. 40—xii. 3; xii. 14–25: it ends at John xiii. 34. Few manuscripts have fallen into such unworthy hands. The Eusebian canons are wanting, the sections standing without them in the margin. Thus in Mark x. 13 (see facsimile No. 28) the section ρϛ (106) has not under it the proper canon β (2). The letters *delta, epsilon, theta, omicron*, and especially the cross-like *psi* (see p. 40), are of the most recent uncial form, *phi* is large and bevelled at both ends; the breathings and accents are fully and not incorrectly given.

F*. CODEX COISLIN. I is that great copy of the Septuagint Octateuch, the glory of the Coislin Library, first made known by Montfaucon (Biblioth. Coislin., 1715), and illustrated by a facsimile in Silvestre's Paléogr. Univ. No. 65. It contains 227 leaves in two columns, 13 inches by 9: the fine massive uncials of the sixth or seventh century are much like Cod. A's in general appearance. In the margin *primâ manu* Wetstein found Acts ix. 24, 25, and so inserted this as Cod. F in his list of MSS. of the Acts. In 1842 Tischendorf observed nineteen other passages of the New Testament, which he published in his Monumenta sacra inedita (1846, p. 400, &c.) with a facsimile. The texts are Matt. v. 48; xii. 48; xxvii. 25: Luke i. 42; ii. 24; xxiii. 21: John v. 35; vi. 53, 55: Acts iv. 33, 34; ix. 24, 25; x. 13, 15; xxii. 22: 1 Cor. vii. 39; xi. 29: 1 Cor. iii. 13; ix. 7; xi. 33: Gal. iv. 21, 22: Col. ii. 16, 17; Heb. x. 26.

G. COD. HARLEIAN. 5684 \
   or WOLFII A,   } These two copies were brought from the East by Andrew Eras-\
H. COD. WOLFII B.   } mus Seidel, purchased by La Croze, and by him presented to J. C. Wolff, who published loose extracts from them both in his 'Anecdota Graeca' (vol. iii. 1723), and barbarously mutilated them in 1721 in order to send pieces to Bentley, among whose papers in Trinity College Library (B. XVII. 20) Tregelles found the fragments in 1845 (Account of the Printed Text, p. 160). Subsequently Cod. G came with the rest of the Harleian collection into the British Museum; Cod. H, which had long been missing, was brought to light in the Public Library of Hamburg, through Petersen the Librarian, in 1838. Codd. GH have now been thoroughly collated both by Tischendorf and Tregelles. Cod. G appears to be of the tenth, Cod. H of the ninth century, and is stated to be of higher critical value. Besides the mutilated fragments at Trinity College (Matt. v. 29-31; 39-43 of Cod. G; Luke i. 3-6; 13-15 of Cod. H), many parts of both have perished: viz. in Cod. G 372 verses; Matt. i. 1—vi. 6; vii. 25—viii. 9; viii. 23—ix. 2; xxviii. 18—Mark i. 13; xiv. 19-25: Luke i. 1-13; v. 4—vii. 3; viii. 46—ix. 5; xii. 27-41; xxiv. 41-53: John xviii.

(31.)

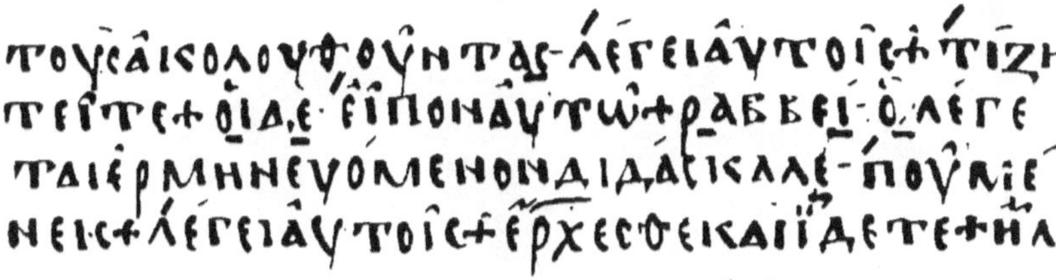

ΤΟΥϹΑΚΟΛΟΥΘΟΥΝΤΑϹ·ΛΕΓΕΙΑΥΤΟΙϹ·ΤΙΖΗ
ΤΕΙΤΕ+ΟΙΔΕΕΙΠΟΝΑΥΤΩ·ΡΑΒΒΕΙ·ΟΛΕΓΕ
ΤΑΙΕΡΜΗΝΕΥΟΜΕΝΟΝΔΙΔΑϹΚΑΛΕ·ΠΟΥΜΕ
ΝΕΙϹ+ΛΕΓΕΙΑΥΤΟΙϹ+ΕΡΧΕϹΘΕΚΑΙΙΔΕΤΕ+ΗΛ

(32.)

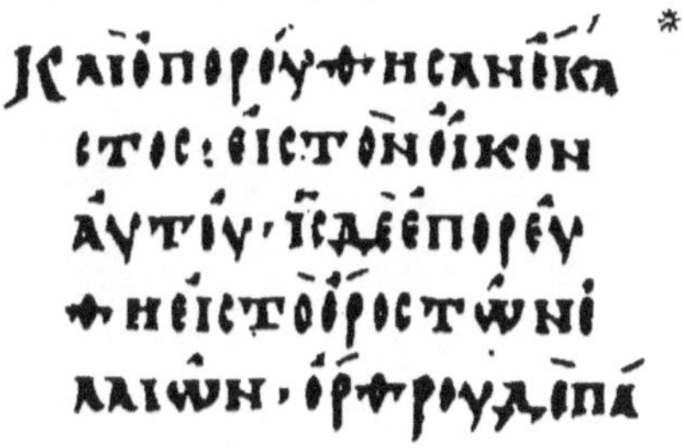

ΚΑΙΟΠΟΡΕΥ+ΗϹΑΝΕΚΑ
ϹΤΙϹ·ΕΙϹΤΟΝΟΙΚΟΝ
ΑΥΤΟΥ·ΙϹΔΕΕΠΟΡΕΥ
+ΗΕΙϹΤΟΟΡΟϹΤΩΝΕ
ΛΑΙΩΝ·ΟΡΘΡΟΥΔΕΠΑ

(33)

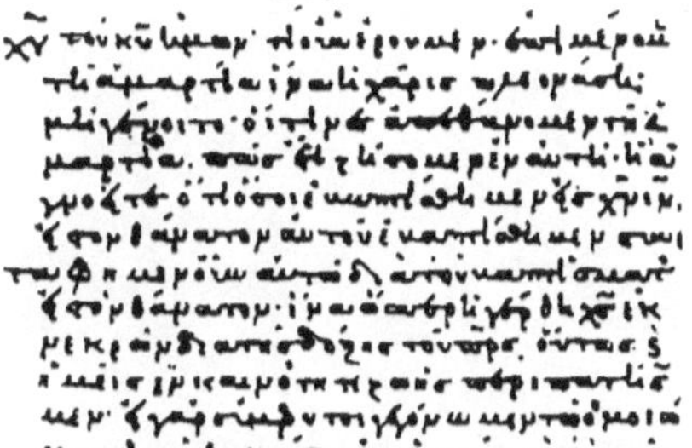

[minuscule Greek text, largely illegible]

(34)

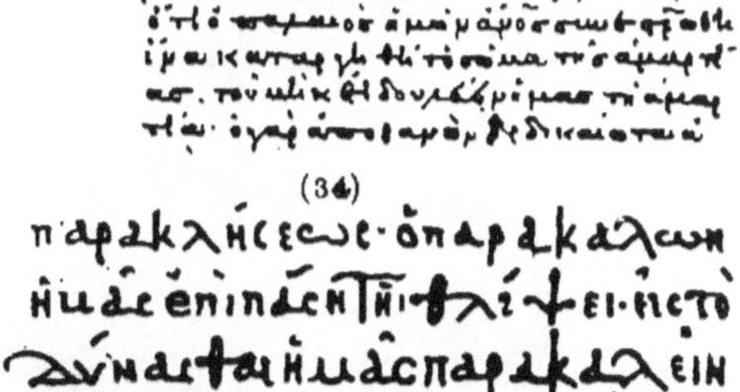

ΠΑΡΑΚΛΗϹΕΩϹ·ΟΠΑΡΑΚΑΛΩΝ
ΗΜΑϹΕΠΙΠΑϹΗΤΗΘΛΙΨΕΙ·ΕΙϹΤΟ
ΔΥΝΑϹΘΑΙΗΜΑϹΠΑΡΑΚΑΛΕΙΝ
ΤΟΥϹΕΝΠΑϹΗΘΛΙΨΕΙ·ΔΙΑΤΗϹΠΑ
ΡΑΚΛΗϹΕΩϹΗϹΠΑΡΕΚΑΛΟΥΜΕ
ΤΑΑΥΤΟΙΥ̅Π̅ΟΤ̅Ο̅Υ̅Τ̅Υ̅·ΟΤΙΚΑΘΩϹ

(35)

ΠΙϹΤΡΑΦΕΙϹΚΑΙΙΔΩΝΤΟΥϹΜΑ
ΘΗΤΑϹΑΥΤΟΥ·ΕΠΕΤΙΜΗϹΕΝΤΩ
ΠΕΤΡΩΛΕΓΩΝ·ΥΠΑΓΕΟΠΙϹΩΜΟΥ

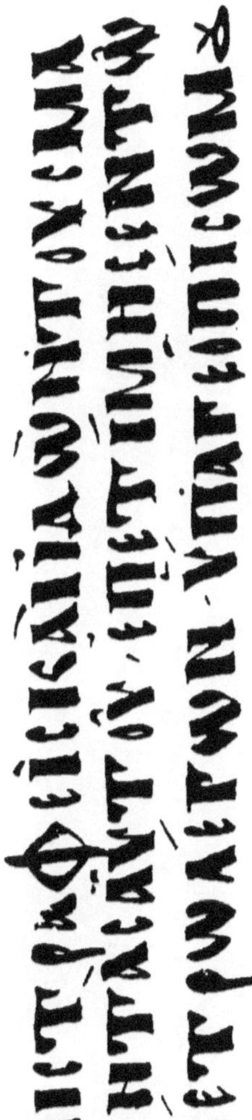

5-19; xix. 4-27 (of which one later hand supplies Matt. xxviii. 18—Mark i. 8: John xviii. 5-19; another Luke xii. 27-41): in Cod. H 679 verses; Matt. i. 1—xv. 30; xxv. 33—xxvi. 3; Mark i. 32—ii. 4; xv. 44—xvi. 14; Luke v. 18-32; vi. 8-22; x. 2-19: John ix. 30—x. 25; xviii. 2-18; xx. 12-25. Cod. G has some Church notes in the margin; Cod. H the sections without the Eusebian canons; G however has both sections and canons; its τίτλοι and larger κεφάλαια are in red (those of St. John being lost), and the Church notes seem *primâ manu*. Each member of the genealogy in Luke iii forms a separate line. Both G and H are written in a somewhat rude style, with breathings and accents rather irregularly placed, as was the fashion of their times; G in two columns of twenty-two lines each on a page, H in one column of twenty-three lines. In each the latest form of the uncial letters is very manifest (e.g. *delta, theta*), but G is the neater of the two. In G the single point, in H a kind of Maltese cross, are the prevailing marks of punctuation. Our facsimiles (Nos. 29 of G, 31 of H) are due to Tregelles; that of G he took from the fragment at Trinity College. Inasmuch as beside Matt. v. 30, 31 in Cod. G A͞Р (ἀρχή) is conspicuous in the margin, and T͞Ε T͞HC Λ͞. (τέλος τῆς λέξεως) stands in the text itself, good scholars may be excused for having mistaken it for a scrap of some Evangelistarium.

I. Cod. Tischendorfian. II at St. Petersburg, consists of palimpsest fragments found by Tischendorf in 1853 'in the dust of an Eastern library,' i.e. in the Convent of St. Saba near the Red Sea, and published in his new series of 'Monumenta sacra inedita,' vol. i, 1855. On the twenty-eight vellum leaves (eight of them on four double leaves) Georgian writing covers the partially obliterated Greek, which is for the most part very hard to read. They compose portions of no less than seven different manuscripts; the first two, of the fifth century, are as old as Codd. AC (the first having scarcely any capital letters and those very slightly larger than the rest); the third fragment seems of the sixth century, nearly of the date of Cod. N (p. 139), about as old as Cod. P (*see* p. 143); the fourth scarcely less ancient: all four, like other palimpsests, have the pseudo-Ammonian sections without the Eusebian canons (*see* p. 61). Of the

Gospels we have 190 verses: viz. (*Frag.* 1 or I_a) John xi. 50—xii. 9; xv. 12—xvi. 2; xix. 11–24: (*Frag.* 2 or I_b) Matt. xiv. 13–16; 19–23; xxiv. 37—xxv. 1; xxv. 32–45; xxvi. 31–45: Mark ix. 14–22; xiv. 58–70: (*Frag.* 3 or I_c) Matt. xvii. 22—xviii. 3; xviii. 11–19; xix. 5–14: Luke xviii. 14–25: John iv. 52—v. 8; xx. 17–26: (*Frag.* 4 or I_d) Luke vii. 39–49; xxiv. 10–19. The fifth fragment (I_e), containing portions of the Acts and of St. Paul's Epistles (1 Cor. xv. 53—xvi. 9: Tit. i. 1–13: Acts xxviii. 8–17) is as old as the third, if not as the first. The sixth and seventh fragments are of the seventh century: viz. (*Frag.* 6 or I_f, *of two leaves*) Acts ii. 6–17; xxvi. 7–18: (*Frag.* 7 or I_g, *of one leaf*) Acts xiii. 39–46. In all seven are 255 verses. All except *Frag.* 6 are in two columns of from twenty-nine to eighteen lines each, and unaccentuated; *Frag.* 6 has but one column on a page, with some accents. The first five fragments, so far as they extend, must be placed in the highest rank as critical authorities. The first, as cited in Tischendorf's eighth edition of his Greek Testament, agrees with Cod. A thirty-four times, four times with Cod. B, and twenty-three times with the two united; it stands alone eleven times. The text of the second and third is more mixed though they incline more to favour Codd. ℵB; not, however, so decidedly as the first does Cod. A. Tischendorf gives us six facsimiles of them in the 'Monumenta sacra inedita,' Nova Collect. vol. i (1855), a seventh in 'Anecdota sacra et profana,'1855. From the same Armenian book, as Tischendorf thinks (and he was very likely to *know*), are taken the three palimpsest leaves of 2 and 3 Kings, and the six of Isaiah published by him in the same volume of the 'Monumenta.'

I^b. See N^b, below.

K. COD. CYPRIUS, or No. 63 of the Royal Library at Paris, shares only with Codd. ℵBMSU the advantage of being a *complete* uncial copy of the Four Gospels. It was brought into the Colbert Library from Cyprus in 1673; Mill inserted its readings from Simon; it was re-examined by Scholz, whose inaccuracies (especially those committed when collating Cod. K for his 'Curae Criticae in Historiam textûs Evangeliorum,' Heidelberg, 1820) have been strongly denounced by later editors, and it must be feared with too good reason. The indepen-

(21)

ΚΑΙΕΞΕΛΘΟΥΣΑΙΕ ΕΣΤΙΝΔΕΚΑΙ
ΦΥΓΟΝΑΠΟΤΟΥ ΤΑΥΤΑΦΕΡΟ
ΜΝΗΜΕΙΟΥ· ΕΙ ΜΕΝΑΜΕΤΑΤΟ
ΧΕΝΔΕΑΥΤΑΣΤΡΟ ΕΦΟΒΟΥΝΤΟ
ΜΟΣΚΑΙΕΚΣΤΑΣΕΙΣ· ΓΑΡ+
ΚΑΙΟΥΔΕΝΙΟΥΔΕΝ
ΕΙΠΟΝ·ΕΦΟΒΟΥΝ ΝΑΣΤΑΣΔΕΠΡΩΙ
ΤΟΓΑΡ· ΠΡΩΤΗΣΑΒΒΑΤΟΥ

(22)

ΒΑΝΤΟΣΑΥΤΟΥ
ΕΙΣΤΟΠΛΟΙΟ
ΠΑΡΕΚΑΛΕΙΑΥ
ΤΟΝΟΔΑΙΜΟ
ΝΙΣΘΕΙΣΙΝΑ

(23)

dent collations of Tischendorf and Tregelles have now done all that can be needed for this copy. It is an oblong quarto, in compressed uncials, of about the middle of the ninth century at the latest, having one column of about twenty-one lines on each page, but the handwriting is irregular and varies much in size. A single point being often found where the sense does not require it, this codex has been thought to have been copied from an older one arranged in στίχοι; the ends of each στίχος may have been indicated in this manner by the scribe. The subscriptions, τίτλοι, the sections, and indices of the κεφάλαια of the last three Gospels are believed to be the work of a later hand: the Eusebian canons are absent. The breathings and accents are *primâ manu*, but often omitted or incorrectly placed. Itacisms and permutations of consonants are very frequent, and the text is of an unusual and interesting character. Scholz regards the directions for the Church lessons, even the ἀρχαί and τέλη in the margin at the beginning and end of lessons, as by the original scribe. He transcribes at length the ἐκλογάδιον τῶν δ' εὐαγγελιστῶν and the fragments of a menology prefixed to Cod. K (N. T. vol. i, pp. 455–493), of which tables it affords the earliest specimen. The second hand writes at the end προσδέξηται αὐτὴν [τὴν δέλτον] ἡ παναγία θεοτόκος καὶ ὁ ἅγιος εὐτύχιος. The style of this copy will be seen from our facsimile (No. 19) taken from John vi. 52, 53: the number of the section (ξϛ') or 66 stands in the margin, but the ordinary place of the Eusebian canon (ι or 10) under it is filled by a simple flourish. The stop in l. 1 after λεγοντεσ illustrates the unusual punctuation of this copy, as may that after ὁ ι̅σ̅ in l. 3.

L. COD. REGIUS, No. 62 in the Royal Library at Paris, is by far the most remarkable document of its age and class. It contains the Four Gospels, except the following passages, Matt. iv. 22—v. 14; xxviii. 17-20: Mark x. 16-30; xv. 2-20: John xxi. 15-25. It was written in about the eighth century and consists of 257 leaves quarto, of thick vellum, 9 inches high by 6½ broad, with two columns of twenty-five lines each on a page, regularly marked, as we so often see, by the *stilus* and ruler (p. 27). This is doubtless Stephen's η', though he cites it erroneously in Acts xxiv. 7 bis; xxv. 14; xxvii. 1; xxviii. 11: it was even then in the Royal Library, although 'Roberto Stephano' is marked in the volume. Wetstein collated Cod. L but loosely; Griesbach, who set a very high value on it, studied it with peculiar care; Tischendorf published it in full in his 'Monumenta sacra inedita,' 1846. It is but carelessly written, and abounds with errors of the ignorant scribe, who was more probably an Egyptian than a native Greek. The breathings and accents are often deficient, often added wrongly, and placed throughout without rule or propriety. The apostrophus also is common, and frequently out of place; the points for stops are quite irregular, as we have elsewhere stated (p. 48). Capitals occur plentifully, often painted and in questionable taste (see facsimile No. 21, column 2), and there is a tendency throughout to inelegant ornament. This codex is in bad condition through damp, the ink brown or pale, the uncial letters of a debased oblong shape: *phi* is enormously large and sometimes quite angular; other letters are such as might be looked for from its date, and are neither neat nor remarkably clear. The lessons for Sundays, festivals, &c. and the ἀρχαί and τέλη are marked everywhere in the margin, especially in St. Matthew; there are also many corrections and important critical notes (e.g. Mark xvi. 8) in the text or margin, apparently *primâ manu*. Our facsimile is taken from a photograph of its most important page, Mark xvi. 8, 9, with part of the note cited at length below. Before each Gospel are indices of the κεφάλαια, now imperfect: we find also the τίτλοι at the head and occasionally at the foot of the several pages; the numbers of the κεφάλαια (usually pointed out by the sign of the cross), the sections and Eusebian canons stand in the inner margin [1], often ill put, as if only half understood. The critical weight of this copy may best be discussed hereafter; it will here suffice barely to mention its strong resemblance to Cod. B (less, however, in St. John's Gospel than elsewhere), to the citations of Origen [186-253], and to the margin of the Harkleian Syriac version [A.D. 616]. Cod. L abounds in what are termed Alexandrian forms, beyond any other copy of its date.

M. COD. CAMPIANUS, No. 48 in the Royal Library at Paris,

---

[1] In our facsimile (No. 21), over against the beginning of Mark xvi. 8, is set the number of the section (ϹΑΓ or 233), above the corresponding Eusebian canon (Β or 2).

contains the Four Gospels complete in a small quarto form, written in very elegant and minute uncials of the end of the ninth century, with two columns of twenty-four lines each on a page. The Abbé François de Camps gave it to Louis XIV, Jan. 1, 1707. This document is Kuster's 2 (1710); it was collated by Wetstein, Scholz, and Tregelles; transcribed in 1841 by Tischendorf. Its synaxarion and menology have been published by Scholz in the same place as those of Cod. K, and obviously with great carelessness. Ἀναγνώσματα, i. e. notes of the Church Lessons, abound in the margin (Tischendorf thinks them *primâ manu*) in a very small hand, like in style to the Oxford Plato (Clarke 39, *above*, p. 42). We find too Hippolytus' Chronology of the Gospels, Eusebius' letter to Carpianus with his canons, and some Arabic scrawl on the last leaf, of which the name of Jerusalem alone has been read, a note in Slavonic, and others in a contemporaneous cursive hand. Dean Burgon also observed at the foot of the several pages the same kind of harmony as we described for Cod. E. It has breathings, accents pretty fairly given, and a musical notation in red, so frequent in Church manuscripts of the age. Its readings are very good; itacisms and ν ἐφελκυστικόν are frequent. Tischendorf compares the form of its uncials to those of Cod. V; which, judging from the facsimile given by Matthaei, we should deem somewhat less beautiful. From our facsimile (No. 32) it will be seen that the round letters are much narrowed, the later form of *delta* and *theta* quite decided, while *alpha* and *pi* might look earlier. Our specimen (John vii. 53—viii. 2) represents the celebrated Pericope adulterae in one of its earliest forms.

N. CODEX PURPUREUS. Only twelve leaves of this beautiful copy were till recently believed to survive, and some former possessor must have divided them in order to obtain a better price from several purchasers than from one. Four leaves are now in the British Museum (Cotton, Titus C. xv), six in the Vatican (No. 3785), two at Vienna (Lambec. 2), at the end of a fragment of Genesis in a different hand. The London fragments (Matt. xxvi. 57–65; xxvii. 26–34: John xiv. 2–10; xv. 15–22) were collated by Wetstein on his first visit to England in 1715, and marked in his Greek Testament by the letter J: Scrivener transcribed them in 1845, and announced that they contained fifty-seven various readings, of which Wetstein had given but five. The Vienna fragment (Luke xxiv. 13-21; 39-49) had long been known by the descriptions of Lambecius: Wetstein had called it N; Treschow in 1773 and Alter in 1787 had given imperfect collations of it. Scholz first noticed the Vatican leaves (Matt. xix. 6-13; xx. 6-22; xx. 29—xxi. 19), denoted them by Γ, and used some readings extracted by Gaetano Marini. It was reserved for Tischendorf (Monumenta sacra inedita, 1846) to publish them all in full, and to determine by actual inspection that they were portions of the same manuscript, of the date of about the end of the sixth century. Besides these twelve leaves John Sakkelion the Librarian saw in or about 1864 at the Monastery of St. John in Patmos thirty-three other leaves containing portions of St. Mark's Gospel (ch. vi. 53—xv. 23)[1], whose readings were communicated to Tischendorf, and are included in his eighth edition of the N. T. The others were probably stolen from the same place. This book is written on the thinnest vellum (see pp. 23, 25), dyed purple, and the silver letters (which have turned quite black) were impressed in some way upon it, but are too varied in shape, and at the end of the lines in size, to admit the supposition of moveable type being used, as some have thought to be the case in the Codex Argenteus of the Gothic Gospels. The abridgements $\overline{\Theta C}$, $\overline{XC}$, &c. are in gold; and some changes have been made by an ancient second hand. The so-called Ammonian sections and the Eusebian canons are faithfully given (see p. 59), and the Vatican portion has the forty-first, forty-sixth, and forty-seventh τίτλοι of St. Matthew at the head of the pages. Each page has two columns of sixteen lines, and the letters (about ten or twelve in a line) are firm, uniform, bold, and unornamented, though not quite so much so as in a few older documents; their lower extremities are bevelled. Their size is at least four times that of the letters in Cod. A, the punctuation quite as simple, being a single point (and that usually neglected) level with the top of the letter (see our facsimile, Plate v, No. 14,

---

[1] Dr. Hort more exactly reckons that these leaves apparently contain Mark vi. 53—vii. 4; vii. 21—viii. 32; ix. 1—x. 43; xi. 7—xii. 19; xiv. 25—xv. 22 (*Addenda and Corrigenda* to Tregelles's N. T., p. 1019), adding that Tischendorf had access also to a few verses preserved in the collections of the Russian Bishop Porphyry. They are published in Duchesne's 'Archives des Missions scientifiques et littéraires' (Paris, 1877), 3ᵉ sér. tom. iii. pp. 386-419.

l. 3), and there is no space left between words even after stops. A few letters stand out as capitals at the beginning of lines; of the breathings and accents, if such they be, we have spoken above (p. 47). Letters diminished at the end of a line do not lose their ancient shape, as in many later books: *compendia scribendi* are rare, yet ⊢ stands for N at the end of a line no less than twenty-nine times in the London leaves alone, but ϗ for αι only once. I at the beginning of a syllable has two dots over it, Υ but one. We have discussed above (pp. 32-39) the shape of the alphabet in N (for by that single letter Tischendorf denotes it), and compared it with others of nearly the same date; *alpha, omega, lambda* look more ancient than *delta* or *xi* (see Plate ii. No. 4). It exhibits strong Alexandrian forms, e. g. παραλήμψομε, ειχοσαν (the latter condemned *secundâ manu*), and not a few such itacisms as the changes of ι and ει, αι and ε.

Cod. N^b (Γ^b of Tischendorf's N. T., eighth edition), MUSEI BRITANNICI (Addit. 17136), is a 12mo volume containing the hymns of Severus in Syriac, and is one of the books brought thither from the Nitrian desert. It is a palimpsest, with a second Syriac work written below the first, and, under both, *four* leaves (117, 118, 127, 128) contain fragments of seventeen verses of St. John (xiii. 16; 17; 19; 20; 23; 24; 26; 27; xvi. 7; 8; 9) although only one word—περί—is preserved; 12; 13; 15; 16; 18; 19). These Tischendorf (and Tregelles about the same time) deciphered with great difficulty, as every one who has examined the manuscript would anticipate, and published in the second volume of his new collection of 'Monumenta sacra inedita.' Each page contained two columns. We meet with the sections without the Eusebian canons, the earliest form of uncial characters, no capital letters (*see* p. 51, note 2), and only the simplest kind of punctuation, although one rough breathing is legible. Tischendorf hesitates whether he shall assign the fragment to the fourth or fifth century. It agrees with Cod. A five or six times, with Cod. B five, with the two together six, and is against them both thrice.

O. No less than nine small fragments have borne this mark. O of Wetstein was given by Anselmo Banduri to Montfaucon, and contains only Luke xviii. 11-14: *this* Tischendorf discards as taken from an Evangelistarium (of the tenth century, as he judges from the writing) chiefly because it wants the number of the section at ver. 14. In its room he puts for Cod. O Moscow Synod. 120 (Matthaei, 15), a few leaves of about the ninth century (containing the fifteen verses, John i. 1, 3, 4; xx. 10-13; 15-17; 20-24, with some scholia), which had been used for binding a copy of Chrysostom's Homilies on Genesis, brought from the monastery of Dionysius at Mount Athos, and published in Matthaei's Greek Testament with a facsimile (see ix. 257 &c., and facsimile in tom. xii). Further portions of this fragment were seen at Athos in 1864 by Mr. Philip E. Pusey. Tregelles has also appended it to his edition of Cod. Ξ. In this fragment we find the cross-like *psi*, the interrogative; (John xx. 13), and the comma (ib. ver. 12). Alford's Frag. Ath. b = Tisch. W^o—p. 145—and Frag. Ath. a are probably parts of O. The next five comprise N. T. hymns.

Cod. O^a. *Magnificat* and *Benedictus* in Greek uncials of the eighth or ninth century, in a Latin book at Wolfenbüttel, is published by Tischendorf, Anecdota sacr. et prof. 1855; as is also O^b, which contains these two and *Nunc Dimittis*, of the ninth century, and is at Oxford, Bodleian, Misc. Gr. 5, ff. 313-4[1]. O^c. *Magnificat* in the Verona Psalter of the sixth century (the Greek being written in Latin letters), published by Bianchini (Vindiciae Canon. Script. 1740). O^1, O^c, both contain the three hymns, O^d in the great purple and silver Zurich Psalter of the seventh century (Tischendorf, Monum. sacra inedita, tom. iv, 1869)[2]; O^e of the ninth century at St. Gall (Cod. 17), partly written in Greek, partly in Latin. O^f, also of the ninth century, is described by Tischendorf (N. T., eighth edition) once as 'Noroff. Petrop.,' once as 'Mosquensis.' O^g (IX) in the Arsenal Library at Paris (MS. Gr. 2), containing, besides the Psalms and Canticle of the Old Testament, the *Magnificat*, *Benedictus*, and *Nunc Dimittis*, besides the *Lord's Prayer*, the *Sanctus* and other such pieces. O^h. Taurinensis Reg. B. vii.

[1] These songs, with thirteen others from the Old Testament and Apocrypha, though *partially* written in uncial letters, are included in a volume of Psalms and Hymns, whose prevailing character is early cursive.

[2] From Tischendorf's copy of O^d Dr. Caspar René Gregory has gathered readings in Heb. v. 8—vi. 10, and sent them to Dr. Hort.

30 (viii or ix), 5¾ × 4, ff. 303 (20)[1]. Psalter with Luke i. 46-55; ii. 29-31. See Gregory, Prolegomena, p. 441.

P. CODEX GUELPHERBYTANUS A. } These are two palim-
Q. .... B. } psests, discovered by F. A. Knittel, Archdeacon of Wolfenbüttel, in the Ducal Library of that city, which (together with some fragments of Ulphilas' Gothic version) lie under the more modern writings of Isidore of Seville. He published the whole in 1762[2], so far at least as he could read them, though Tregelles believed more might be deciphered, and Tischendorf, with his unconquerable energy, collating them both in 1854, was able to re-edit them more accurately, Cod. Q in the third volume (1860) and Cod. P in the sixth (1869) of his Monumenta sacra inedita. The volume (called the Codex Carolinus) seems to have been once at Bobbio, and has been traced from Weissenburg to Mayence and Prague, till it was bought by a Duke of Brunswick in 1689. Codex P contains, on forty-three or forty-four leaves, thirty-one fragments of 518 verses, taken from all the four Evangelists[3]; Codex Q, on thirteen leaves, twelve fragments of 247 verses from SS. Luke and John[4]; but all can be traced only with great difficulty. A few portions, once written in vermilion, have quite departed, but Tischendorf has made material additions to Knittel's labours, both in extent and accuracy. He assigns P to the sixth, Q to the fifth century. Both are written in two columns, the uncials being bold, round or square, those of Q not a little the smaller. The letters in P, however, are sometimes compressed at the end of a line. The capitals in P are large and frequent, and both have the sections without the canons of

---

[1] I.e., twenty lines on a page, according to the form used in this edition.

[2] They had been previously described in a tract 'Jac. Frid. Heusinger, de quatuor Evan. Cod. Graec. quem antiqua manu membrana scriptum Guelferbytana bibliotheca servat.' Guelf. 1752.

[3] Codex P contains Matt. i. 11-21; iii. 13—iv. 19; x. 7-19; x. 42—xi. 11; xiii. 40-50; xiv. 15—xv. 3; xv. 29-39; Mark i. 1-11; iii. 5-17; xiv. 13-24; 48-61; xv. 12-37; Luke i. 1-13; ii. 9-20; vi. 21-42; vii. 32—viii. 2; viii. 31-50; ix. 26-36; x. 36—xi. 4; xii. 34-45; xiv. 14-25; xv. 13—xvi. 22; xviii. 13-39; xx. 21—xxi. 3; xxii. 3-16; xxiii. 20-33; 45-56; xxiv. 1, 14-37; John i. 29-41; ii. 13-25; xxi. 1-11.

[4] Codex Q contains Luke iv. 34—v. 4; vi. 10-26; xii. 6-43; xv. 14-31; xvii. 34—xviii. 15; xviii. 34—xix. 11; xix. 47—xx. 17; xx. 34—xxi. 8; xxii. 27-46; xxiii. 30-49: John xii. 3-20; xiv. 3-22.

Eusebius (*see* p. 59). The table of τίτλοι found in the volume is written in oblong uncials of a lower date, as Knittel thought, possibly without good reason. Itacisms, what are termed Alexandrian forms, and the usual contractions ($\overline{\text{IC}}$, $\overline{\text{XC}}$, $\overline{\text{KC}}$, $\overline{\Theta\text{C}}$, $\overline{\text{ΥC}}$, $\overline{\text{ΠΗΡ}}$, $\overline{\text{ΠΝΑ}}$, $\overline{\text{ΙΛΗΜ}}$, $\overline{\text{ΑΝΟC}}$, $\overline{\Delta\text{ΑΔ}}$, $\overset{s}{\text{M}}$) occur in both copies. Breathings also are seen here and there in Q. From Tischendorf's beautiful facsimiles of Codd. PQ we observe that while *delta* is far more elaborate in P than in Q, the precise contrary is the case with *pi*. *Epsilon* and *sigma* in P have strong points at all the extremities; *nu* in each is of the ancient form exhibited in Codd. אNR (*see* p. 37); while in P *alpha* resembles in shape that of our alphabet in Plate ii. No. 5, *eta* that in Plate iii. No. 7. As regards their text we observe that in the first hundred verses of St. Luke which are contained in both copies, wherein P is cited for various readings 216 times, and Q 182 times, P stands alone fourteen times, Q not once. P agrees with other manuscripts against AB twenty-one times, Q nineteen: P agrees with AB united fifty times, Q also fifty: P sides with B against A twenty-nine times, Q thirty-eight: but P accords with A against B in 102 places, Q in seventy-five.

R. This letter, like some that precede, has been used to represent different books by various editors, a practice the inconvenience of which is very manifest. (1) R of Griesbach and Scholz is a fragment of one quarto leaf containing John i. 38–50, at Tübingen, with musical notes, which from its thick vellum, from the want of the sections and Eusebian canons, and the general resemblance of its uncials to those of late Service Books, Tischendorf pronounces to be an Evangelistarium, and puts in its room (2) in his N.T. of 1849, fourteen leaves of a palimpsest in the Royal Library of Naples (Borbon. ii. C. 15) of the eighth century, under a *Typicum* (see Suicer, Thes. Eccles. tom. ii. p. 1335), or Ritual of the Greek Church, of the fourteenth century. These are fragments from the first three Evangelists, in oblong uncials, leaning to the right. Tischendorf, by chemical applications, was able in 1843 to read one page, in two columns of twenty-five lines each (Mark xiv. 32–39)[1], and saw the sections in the margin; the Eusebian canons he thinks have been washed out (*see* p. 59): but

[1] Published in the Jahrbücher (Vienna) d. Lit. 1847.

(15) προ καταγμοῦ· ἀμ̅νωαμ̅νωλ̅γωὑμ̅ν ὅτι ἐὰν μὴ ὁ κόκκος τ̅ϛ βαῆϛ π̅σ ... αὐτομ̅ · ἰω̅ φοβερε πατ̅ϛ ὁ πω̅νὴ ἀθ̅ λ̅τοϛ· ὁ τιμῶν τ̅ με εμε τι̅μϛ· ε̅κ τ̅ γ̅εῖοϛ

(16)
ΑΥΤΩΟΙΦΑΡΙΣΑΙ
ΟΙΒΥΠΕΡΕΣΕΑΥΤΟΥ
ΜΑΡΤΥΡΕΙΣΗΜΑΡ
ΤΥΡΙΑΣΟΥΟΥΚΕΣ
ΤΙΝΑΛΗΘΗΣΑΠΕ

(17)
ΖΑΖΟΝΤΟΝΟΝ
ΚΑΙΕΠΛΗΣΘΗ
ΣΑΝΦΟΒΟΥΛΕ
ΓΟΝΤΕΣΟΤΙ

in 1859 he calls this fragment W^b, reserving the letter R for (3) CODEX NITRIENSIS, Brit. Museum, Additional 17211, the very important palimpsest containing on forty-eight (53) leaves about 516 verses of St. Luke in twenty-five fragments [1], under the black, broad Syriac writing, being a treatise of Severus of Antioch against Johannes Grammaticus, of the eighth or ninth century. There are two columns of about twenty-five lines each on a page; for their boldness and simplicity the letters may be referred to the end of the sixth century; we have given a facsimile of the manuscript (which cannot be read in parts but with the utmost difficulty), and an alphabet collected from it (Nos. 5, 17). In size and shape the letters are much like those of Codd. INP, only that they are somewhat irregular and straggling: the punctuation is effected by a single point almost level with the top of the letters, as in Cod. N. The pseudo-Ammonian sections are there without the Eusebian canons, and the first two leaves are devoted to the τίτλοι of St. Luke. This most important palimpsest is one of the 550 manuscripts brought to England, about 1847, from the Syrian convent of S. Mary Deipara, in the Nitrian Desert, seventy miles N.W. of Cairo. When examined at the British Museum by the late Canon Cureton, then one of the Librarians, he discovered in the same volume, and published in 1851 (with six pages in facsimile), a palimpsest of 4000 lines of Homer's Iliad not in the same hand as St. Luke, but quite as ancient. The fragments of St. Luke were independently transcribed, with most laudable patience, both by Tregelles in 1854, and by Tischendorf in 1855, who afterwards re-examined the places wherein he differed from Tregelles (e.g. chh. viii. 5; xviii. 7, 10), and discovered by the aid of Dr. Wright a few more fragments of chh. vi-viii. Tischendorf published an edition of Cod. R in his 'Monumenta sacra inedita,' vol. ii, with a facsimile: the amended readings, together with the newly-discovered variations in chh. vi. 31-36, 39, vii. 44, 46, 47, are inserted in the eighth edition of his Greek Testament. In this palimpsest as at present bound

---

[1] Codex R contains Luke i. 1-13; i. 69—ii. 4; 16-27; iv. 38—v. 5; v. 25—vi. 8; 18-36, 39; vi. 49—vii. 22; 44, 46, 47; viii. 5-15; viii. 25—ix. 1; ix. 12-43; x. 3-16; xi. 5-27; xii. 4-15; 40-52; xiii. 26—xiv. 1; xiv. 12—xv. 1; xv. 13—xvi. 16; xvii. 21—xviii. 10; xviii. 22—xx. 20; xx. 33-47; xxi. 12—xxii. 15; 42-56; xxii. 71—xxiii. 11; xxiii. 38-51. A second hand has supplied ch. xv. 19-21.

up in the Museum the fragments of St. Luke end on f. 48, and the rest of the Greek in the volume is in later, smaller, sloping uncials, and contains propositions from the tenth and thirteenth books of Euclid. On the critical character of the readings of this precious fragment we shall make some comments below.

S. CODEX VATICANUS 354 contains the four Gospels entire, and is amongst the earliest dated manuscripts of the Greek Testament (p. 41, note 2). This is a folio of 234 leaves, written in large oblong or compressed uncials: the Epistle to Carpianus and Eusebian canons are prefixed, and it contains many later corrections (e.g. Luke viii. 15) and marginal notes (e.g. Matt. xxvii. 16, 17). Luke xxii. 43, 44; John v. 4; vii. 53—viii. 11 are obelized. At the end we read ἐγράφει ἡ τιμία δέλτος αὕτη διὰ χειρὸς ἐμοῦ Μιχαὴλ μοναχοῦ ἁμαρτωλοῦ μηνὶ μαρτίω α'. ἡμέρα ε', ὥρα ς', ἔτους ϛυνζ. ινδ. ζ': i.e. A.D. 949. 'Codicem bis diligenter contulimus,' says Birch: but collators in his day (1781–3) seldom noticed orthographical forms or stated where the readings *agree* with the received text, so that a more thorough examination was still required. Tregelles only inspected it, but Tischendorf, when at Rome in 1866, carefully re-examined it, and has inserted many of its readings in his eighth edition and its supplementary leaves. He states that Birch's facsimile (consisting of the obelized John v. 4) is coarsely executed, while Bianchini's is too elegant; he made another for himself.

T. CODEX BORGIANUS I, now in the Propaganda at Rome (*see below*, Evan. 180), contains thirteen or more quarto leaves of SS. Luke and John, with a Thebaic or Sahidic version at their side, but on the opposite and left page. Each page consists of two columns: a single point indicates a break in the sense, but there are no other divisions. The fragment contains Luke xxii. 20—xxiii. 20; John vi. 28—67; vii. 6—viii. 31 (179 verses, since John vii. 53—viii. 11 are wanting). The portion containing St. John, both in Greek and Egyptian, was carefully edited at Rome in 1789 by A. A. Giorgi, an Augustinian Eremite; his facsimile, however (ch. vii. 35), seems somewhat rough, though Tischendorf (who has inspected the codex) says that its uncials look as if written by a Copt, from their resemblance to Coptic letters [1] : the shapes of *alpha* and *iota* are specially noticeable. Birch had previously collated the Greek text. Notwithstanding the occasional presence of the rough and smooth breathing in this copy (p. 47)[2], Giorgi refers it to the fourth century, Tischendorf to the fifth. The Greek fragment of St. Luke was first collated by Mr. Bradley H. Alford, and inserted by his brother, Dean Alford, in the fourth edition of his Greek Testament, vol. i (1859). Dr. Tregelles had drawn Mr. Alford's attention to it, from a hint thrown out by Zoega, in p. 184 of his 'Catalogus codd. Copt. MSS. qui in Museo Borgiano Velitris adservantur.' Romae, 1810.

T⁸ or T^woi is used by Tischendorf to indicate a few leaves in Greek and Thebaic, which once belonged to Woide, and were published with his other Thebaic fragments in Ford's Appendix to the Codex Alexandrinus, Oxon. 1799. They contain Luke xii. 15—xiii. 32 ; John viii. 33-42 (eighty-five verses). From the second fragment it plainly appears (what the similarity of the facsimiles had suggested to Tregelles) that T and T⁸ are parts of the same manuscript, for the page of T⁸ which contains John viii. 33 in Greek exhibits on its reverse the Thebaic version of John viii. 23-32, of which T affords us only the Greek text. This fact was first noted by Tischendorf (N.T. 1859), who adds that the Coptic scribe blundered much over the Greek: e.g. $\beta\alpha\beta o\upsilon\sigma\alpha$ Luke xiii. 21 ; so $\delta\epsilon\kappa\alpha\iota$ for $\delta\epsilon\kappa\alpha$ $\kappa\alpha\iota$, ver. 16. He transcribed T and T^woi (as well as T^b, T^c, T^d, which we proceed to describe), for publication in the ninth volume of his 'Monumenta sacra inedita' (1870), but owing to his death they never appeared. But Bp. Lightfoot gives reasons (*see below*, vol. ii.

---

[1] For the Coptic style of the letters Tischendorf compares a double palimpsest leaf in the British Museum, containing 1 Kings viii. 58—ix. 1, which he assigns to the fifth century, although the capital letters stand out a little, and are slightly larger than the rest (Monum. sacr. ined. vol. ii. Proleg. p. xliv). But both Dr. Wright and Mr. E. Maunde Thompson, from their great experience in this style of writing, have come to suspect that it is usually somewhat less ancient than from other indications might be supposed.

[2] Tischendorf found breathings also in the palimpsest Numbers (Monum. sac. ined. *ubi supra*, p. xxv).

c. 2) for thinking that this fragment was not originally a portion of T.

T^b at St. Petersburg much resembles the preceding in the Coptic-like style of writing, but is not earlier than the sixth century. It contains on six octavo leaves John i. 25–42; ii. 9—iv. 50, spaces left in the text answering the purpose of stops. T^b has a harmony of the Gospels at the foot of the page.

T^c is a fragment of about twenty-one verses between Matt. xiv. 19 and xv. 8, also of the sixth century, and at St. Petersburg, in the collection of Bishop Porphyry. Its text in the twenty-nine places cited by Tischendorf in his eighth edition accords with Cod. ℵ twenty-four times, with Cod. B twenty times, with Codd. C and D sixteen times each, with Cod. 33 nine times. Cod. A is wanting here. Compared with these primary authorities severally, it agrees with ℵ alone once, with 33 alone twice, with ℵB united against the rest four times: so that its critical character is very decided.

T^d is a fragment of a Lectionary, Greek and Sahidic, of about the seventh century, found by Tischendorf in 1866 among the Borgian manuscripts at Rome. It contains Matt. xvi. 13–20; Mark i. 3–8, xii. 35–37; John xix. 23–27; xx. 30–31: twenty-four verses only. This fragment and the next have been brought into this place, rather than inserted in the list of Evangelistaria, because they both contained fragments of the Thebaic version.

T^e is a fragment of St. Matthew at Cambridge (Univ. Libr. Addit. 1875). Dr. Hort communicated its readings to Dr. C. R. Gregory, for his Prolegomena to the eighth edition of Tischendorf's N. T. It is 'a tiny morsel' of an uncial Lectionary of the sixth century, containing only Matt. iii. 13–16, the parallel column probably in the Thebaic version having perished. It was brought, among other Coptic fragments, from Upper Egypt by Mr. Greville Chester. Dr. Hort kindly enables me to add to his description of T^e (Addenda to Tregelles' N. T. p. 1070) that this 'tiny morsel' is irregular in shape, frequently less than four inches in width and height, the uncial Greek letters being three-eighths of an inch high. There seem to have been two columns of either eight or more probably of twenty-four lines each on a page, but no Coptic portions survive. 'If of twenty-four lines the fragment might belong to the inner column of a bilingual MS. with the two languages in parallel columns, or to the outer column of a wholly Greek MS. or of a bilingual MS. with the section in the two languages consecutively, as in Mr. Horner's Graeco-Thebaic fragment (Evst. 299: *see* p. 398). In the latter case it might belong to the inner column of a wholly Greek MS. or of a bilingual MS. with the section in two consecutive languages. The size of the letters renders it improbable, however, that the columns were of eight lines only.' (Hort.)

T^f Horner. See below under Thebaic or Sahidic MSS. at the end.

T^g Cairo, Cod. Papadopulus Kerameus [vi or vii], $9\frac{1}{2} \times 8\frac{1}{4}$, ff. 3 (27), two cols., written in letters like Coptic. Matt. xx. 3–32; xxii. 4–16. Facsimile by the Abbate Cozza-Luzi in 'N.T. e Cod. Vat. 1209 nativi textus Graeci primo omnium phototypice representatum'—Danesio, Rome, 1889. See Gregory, Prolegomena, p. 450.

U. CODEX NANIANUS I, so called from a former possessor, is now in the Library of St. Mark, Venice (I. viii). It contains the four Gospels entire, carefully and luxuriously written in two columns of twenty-one lines each on the quarto page, scarcely before the tenth century, although the 'letters are in general an imitation of those used before the introduction of compressed uncials; but they do not belong to the age when full and round writing was customary or natural, so that the stiffness and want of ease is manifest' (Tregelles' Horne, p. 202). It has *Carp., Eus. t.,* κεφ. *t.,* τίτλ., κεφ., *pict.,* with much gold ornament. Thus while the small o in l. 1 of our facsimile (No. 22) is in the oldest style, the oblong *omicrons* creep in at the end of lines 2 and 4. Münter sent some extracts from this copy to Birch, who used them for his edition, and states that the book contains the Eusebian canons. Accordingly in Mark

v. 18, B (in error for H) stands under the proper section $\overline{\mu\eta}$ (48). Tischendorf in 1843 and Tregelles in 1846 collated Cod. U thoroughly and independently, and compared their work at Leipsic for the purpose of mutual correction.

V. CODEX MOSQUENSIS, of the Holy Synod, is known almost[1] exclusively from Matthaei's Greek Testament: he states, no doubt most truly, that he collated it 'bis diligentissimè,' and gives a facsimile of it, assigning it to the eighth century. Judging from Matthaei's plate, it is hard to say why others have dated it in the ninth. It contained in 1779, when first collated, the Four Gospels in 8vo with the sections and Eusebian canons, in uncial letters down to John vii. 39, ουπω γαρ ην, and from that point in cursive letters of the thirteenth century, Matt. v. 44—vi. 12; ix. 18—x. 1 being lost: when re-collated but four years later Matt. xxii. 44—xxiii. 35; John xxi. 10-25 had disappeared. Matthaei tells us that the manuscript is written in a kind of stichometry by a diligent scribe: its resemblance to Cod. M has been already mentioned. The cursive portion is Matthaei's V, Scholz's Evan. 250.

W[a]. COD. REG. PARIS 314 consists of but two leaves at the end of another book, containing Luke ix. 34–47; x. 12–22 (twenty-three verses). Its date is about the eighth century; the uncial letters are firmly written, *delta* and *theta* being of the ordinary oblong shape of that period. Accents and breathings are usually put; all the stops are expressed by a single point, whose position makes no difference in its power. This copy was adapted to Church use, but is not an Evangelistarium, inasmuch as it exhibits the sections and Eusebian canons[2], and τίτλοι twice at the head of the page. This fragment was brought to light by Scholz, and published by Tischendorf, Monumenta sacra inedita, 1846.

---

[1] I say *almost*, for Bengel's description makes it plain that this is the Moscow manuscript from which F. C. Gross sent him the extracts that Wetstein copied and numbered Evan. 87. Bengel, however, states that the cursive portion from John vii onwards bears the date of 6508 or A. D. 1000. Scholz was the first to notice this identity (*see* Evan. 250).

[2] Notwithstanding, the Eusebian canons have been washed out of W[b], a strong confirmation of what was conjectured above, p. 61.

W^b. Tischendorf considers the fragment at Naples he had formerly numbered R (2) as another portion of the same copy, and therefore indicates it in his seventh edition of the N. T. (1859) as W^b. It has seventy-nine leaves, of which the fourteen last are palimpsest, is written in two columns, with twenty-five lines in each page; has the Ammonian sections and lections, and contains Matt. xix. 14-28; xx. 23—xxi. 2; xxvi. 52—xxvii. 1; Mark xiii. 21—xiv. 67; Luke iii. 1—iv. 20. (Prolegomena to Tischendorf, p. 395.)

W^c is assigned by Tischendorf to three leaves containing Mark ii. 8-16; Luke i. 20-32; 64-79 (thirty-five verses), which have been washed to make a palimpsest, and the writing erased in parts by a knife. There are also some traces of a Latin version, but all these were used up to bind other books in the library of St. Gall. They are of the eighth century, or the ninth according to Tischendorf, edd. 7 and 8, and have appeared in vol. iii of 'Monumenta sacra inedita,' with a facsimile, whose style closely resembles that of Cod. Δ, and its kindred FG of St. Paul's Epistles.

W^d was discovered in 1857 by Mr. W. White, sub-librarian of Trinity College, Cambridge, in the College Library, and was afterwards observed and arranged by Mr. H. Bradshaw, University Librarian, its slips (about twenty-seven in number) having been worked into the binding of a volume of Gregory Nazianzen: they are now carefully arranged under glass (B. viii. 5). They comprise portions of four leaves, severally containing Mark vii. 3-4; 6-8; 30-36; 36—viii. 4; 4-10; 11-16; ix. 2; 7-9, in uncial letters of the ninth century, if not rather earlier, slightly leaning to the right. The sections are set in the margin without the Eusebian canons, with a table of harmony at the foot of each page of twenty-four lines. The τίτλοι are in red at the top and bottom of the pages, their corresponding numerals in the margin. The breathings and accents are often very faint: lessons and musical notes, crosses, &c. are in red, and sometimes cover the original stops. In text it much resembles Codd. אBDLΔ: one reading (Mark vii. 33) appears to be unique. Dr. Scrivener has included it in a volume of fresh collations of manuscripts and editions which is shortly to appear under the accomplished editorship of Mr. J. Rendel Harris.

W^e is a fragment containing John iv. 7-14, in three leaves, found by the Very Rev. G. W. Kitchin, Dean of Winchester, in Christ Church Library, when Tischendorf was at Oxford in 1865. It much resembles O at Moscow, and, like it, had a commentary annexed, to which there are numeral references set before each verse.

W^f is a palimpsest fragment of St. Matt. xxv. 31-36, and vi. 1-18 (containing the doxology in the Lord's Prayer), of about the ninth century, underlying Wake 13 at Christ Church, Oxford (Acts 192, Paul. 246), discovered by the late Mr. A. A. Vansittart (Journal of Philology, vol. ii. no. 4, p. 241, note 1).

X. CODEX MONACENSIS, in the University Library at Munich (No. $\frac{1}{20}$), is a valuable folio manuscript of the end of the ninth or early in the tenth century, containing the Four Gospels (in the order described above, with serious omissions[1], and a commentary (chiefly from Chrysostom) surrounding and interspersed with the text of all but St. Mark, in early cursive letters, not unlike (in Tischendorf's judgement) the celebrated Oxford Plato dated 895. The very elegant uncials of Cod. X 'are small and upright; though some of them are compressed, they seem as if they were *partial* imitations of those used in very early copies' (Tregelles' Horne, p. 195). Each page has two columns of about forty-five lines each. There are no divisions by κεφάλαια or sections, nor notes to serve for ecclesiastical use. From a memorandum we find that it came from Rome to Ingoldstadt, as a present from Gerard Vossius [1577-1649]; from Ingoldstadt it was taken to Landshut in 1803, thence to Munich in 1827. When it was at Ingoldstadt Griesbach obtained some extracts from it through Dobrowsky; Scholz first collated it, but in his usual unhappy way; Tischendorf in 1844, Tregelles in 1846. Dean Burgon examined it in 1872.

---

[1] Codex X contains Matt. vi. 6, 10, 11; vii. 1—ix. 20; ix. 34—xi. 24; xii. 9—xvi. 28; xvii. 14—xviii. 25; xix. 22—xxi. 13; 28—xxii. 22; xxiii. 27—xxiv. 2; 23-35; xxv. 1-30; xxvi. 69—xxvii. 12; Mark vi. 47—Luke i. 37; ii. 19—iii. 38; iv. 21—x. 37; xi. 1—xviii. 43; xx. 46—John ii. 22; vii. 1—xiii. 5; xiii. 20—xv. 25; xvi. 23—xxi. 25. The hiatus in John ii. 22—vii. 1 is supplied on paper in a hand of the twelfth century; Mark xiv. 61-64; xiv. 72—xv. 4; xv. 33—xvi. 6 are illegible in parts, and xvi. 6-8 have perished. Matt. v. 45 survives only in the commentary.

(18)

ΑΝΟΙΓΩΣΙΝΟΙΟΦΘΑΛ
ΜΟΙΗΜΩΝ
ΣΠΛΑΓΧΝΙΣΘΕΙΣΔΕΟΙ͞Σ
ΗΨΑΤΟΤΩΝΟΜΜΑΤΩ͞
Α͞Υ͞ΤΩΝ Κ ΑΙΕΥΘΕΩΣ

(19)

ΕΜΑΧΟΝΤΟΟΥΝΠΡΟΣΑΛΛΗΛΟΥΣΟΙΪΟΥΔΑΙΟΙΛΕ
ΓΟΝΤΕΣ·ΠΩΣΔΥΝΑΤΑΙΟΥΤΟΣΗΜΙΝΤΗΝΣΑΡ
ΚΑ͜ ΔΟ͞Υ͞ΝΑΙΦΑΓΕΙΝ·ΕΙΠΕΝΟΥ͞ΝΑΥΤΟΙΣΟ Ι͞Σ·Α̅

Y. CODEX BARBERINI 225 at Rome (in the Library founded by Cardinal Barberini in the seventeenth century) contains on six large leaves the 137 verses John xvi. 3—xix. 41, of about the eighth century. Tischendorf obtained access to it in 1843 for a few hours, after some difficulty with the Prince Barberini, and published it in his first instalment of 'Monumenta sacra inedita,' 1846. Scholz had first noticed, and loosely collated it. A later hand has coarsely retraced the letters, but the ancient writing is plain and good. Accents and breathings are most often neglected or placed wrongly: $κ_1$ $θ_1$ $η$ are frequent at the end of lines. For punctuation one, two, three or even four points are employed, the power of the single point varying as in Codd. E Θ^a and B of the Apocalypse. The pseudo-Ammonian sections are without the Eusebian canons: and such forms as λήμψεται xvi. 14, λήμψεσθε ver. 24 occur. These few uncial leaves are prefixed to a cursive copy of the Gospels with Theophylact's commentary (Evan. 392): the text is mixed, and lies about midway between that of Cod. A and Cod. B.

Z. CODEX DUBLINENSIS RESCRIPTUS, one of the chief palimpsests extant, contains 295 verses of St. Matthew's Gospel in twenty-two fragments [1]. It is of a small quarto size, originally 10½ inches by 8, now reduced to 8¾ inches by 6, once containing 120 leaves arranged in quaternions, of which the first that remains bears the *signature* 13 (ΙΓ): fourteen sheets or double leaves and four single leaves being all that survive. It was discovered in 1787 by Dr. John Barrett, Senior Fellow of Trinity College, Dublin, under some cursive writing of the tenth century or later, consisting of Chrysostom de Sacerdotio, extracts from Epiphanius, &c. In the same volume are portions of Isaiah (eight leaves) and of Gregory Nazianzen, in erased uncial letters, the latter not so ancient as the fragment of St. Matthew. All the thirty-two leaves of this Gospel that remain were engraved in copper-plate facsimile [2] at the expense of Trinity College, and

---

[1] Codex Z contains Matt. i. 17—ii. 6 ; ii. 13-20 ; iv. 4-13 ; v. 45—vi. 15 ; vii. 16—viii. 6 ; x. 40—xi. 18 ; xii. 43—xiii. 11 ; 57—xiv. 19 ; xv. 13-23 ; xvii. 9-17 ; 26—xviii. 6 ; xix. 4-12 ; 21-28 ; xx. 7—xxi. 8 ; 23-30 ; xxii. 16-25 ; 37—xxiii. 3 ; 15-23 ; xxiv. 15-25 ; xxv. 1-11 ; xxvi. 21-29 ; 62-71.

[2] Not in moveable type, as a critic in the *Saturday Review* (Aug. 20, 1881) seems to suppose.

published by Barrett in 1801, furnished with Prolegomena, and the contents of each facsimile plate in modern Greek characters, on the opposite page. The facsimiles are not very accurate, and the form of the letters is stated to be less free and symmetrical than in the original: yet from these plates (for the want of a better guide) our alphabet (No. 6) and specimen (No. 18) have been taken. The Greek type on the opposite page was not very well revised, and a comparison with the copper-plate will occasionally convict it of errors, which have been animadverted upon more severely than was quite necessary. The Prolegomena were encumbered with a discussion of our Lord's genealogies quite foreign to the subject, and the tone of scholarship is not very high; but Barrett's judgement on the manuscript is correct in the main, and his conclusion, that it is as old as the sixth century, has been generally received. Tregelles in 1853 was permitted to apply a chemical mixture to the vellum, which was already miserably discoloured, apparently from the purple dye: he was thus enabled to add a little (about 200 letters) to what Barrett had read long since [1], but he found that in most places which that editor had left blank, the vellum had been cut away or lost: it would no doubt have been better for Barrett to have stated, in each particular case, why he had been unable to give the text of the passage. A far better edition of the manuscript, including the fragment of Isaiah, and a newly-discovered leaf of the Latin Codex Palatinus (e), with Prolegomena and two plates of real facsimiles, was published in 1880 by T. K. Abbott, B.D., Professor of Biblical Greek in the University of Dublin. He has read 400 letters hitherto deemed illegible, and is inclined to assign the fifth century as the date of the Codex. Codex Z, like many others, and for the same orthographical reasons, has been referred to Alexandria as its native country. It is written with a single column on each page of twenty-one or twenty-three lines [2]. The so-named Ammonian sections are given, but not the

---

[1] Mr. E. H. Hansell prints in red these additional readings thus fresh brought to light in the Appendix to his 'Texts of the oldest existing manuscripts of the New Testament,' Oxford, 1864.

[2] 'Barrett's edition shows that of the sixty-four pages of the MS. fifty had originally twenty-one lines to the page, and fourteen had twenty-three.' Dr. Ezra Abbot.

Eusebian canons: the τίτλοι are written at the top of the pages by a later hand according to Porter and Abbott, though this may be questioned (Gebhardt and Harnack's 'Texte,' &c., I. iv. p. xxiii ff., 1883), their numbers being set in the margin. The writing is continuous, the *single* point either rarely found or quite washed out: the abbreviations are very few, and there are no breathings or accents. Like Cod. B, this manuscript indicates citations by > in the margin, and it represents N by —, but only at the end of a word and line. A space, proportionate to the occasion, is usually left when there is a break in the sense, and capitals extend into the margin when a new section begins. The letters are in a plain, steady, beautiful hand: they yield in elegance to none, and are never compressed at the end of a line. The shape of *alpha* (which varies a good deal), and especially that of *mu*, is very peculiar: *phi* is inordinately large: *delta* has an upper curve which is not usual: the same curves appear also in *zeta, lambda,* and *chi*. The characters are less in size than in N, about equal to those in R, much greater than in AB. In regard to the text, it agrees much with Codd. אBD: with Cod. A it has only twenty-three verses in common: yet in them A and Z vary fourteen times. Mr. Abbott adds that while אBZ stand together ten times against other uncials, BZ are never alone, but אZ against B often. It is freer than either of them from transcriptural errors. Codd. אBCZ combine less often than אBDZ. On examining Cod. Z throughout twenty-six pages, he finds it alone thirteen times, differing from א thirty times, from B forty-four times, from Stephen's text ninety-five times. Thus it approaches nearer to א than to B.

Γ. CODEX TISCHENDORFIAN. IV was brought by Tischendorf from an 'eastern monastery' (he usually describes the locality of his manuscripts in such like general terms), and was bought of him for the Bodleian Library (Misc. Gr. 313) in 1855. It consists of 158 leaves, 12 inches × $9\frac{1}{4}$, with one column (of twenty-four not very straight or regular lines) on a page, in uncials of the ninth century, leaning slightly back, but otherwise much resembling Cod. K in style (facsimile No. 35).

St. Luke's Gospel is complete; the last ten leaves are hurt by damp, though still legible. In St. Mark only 105 verses are wanting (iii. 35—vi. 20); about 531 verses of the other Gospels survive[1]. Tischendorf, and Tregelles by his leave, have independently collated this copy, of which Tischendorf gives a facsimile in his 'Anecdota sacra et profana,' 1855. Some of its peculiar readings are very notable, and few uncials of its date deserve that more careful study, which it has hardly yet received. In 1859 Tischendorf, on his return from his third Eastern journey, took to St. Petersburg ninety-nine additional leaves of this self-same manuscript, doubtless procured from the same place as he had obtained the Bodleian portion six years before (Notitia Cod. Sinait. p. 53). This copy of the Gospels, though unfortunately in two distant libraries, is now nearly perfect[2], and at the end of St. John's Gospel, in the more recently discovered portion, we find an inscription which seems to fix the date : ετελειωθη ἡ δέλτος αὕτη μηνι νοεμβριω κ̅ζ̅, ιυδ. η̅, ἡμερα ε̅, ωρα β̅. Tischendorf, by the aid of Ant. Pilgrami's 'Calendarium chronologum medii potissimum aevi monumentis accommodatum,' Vienn. 1781, pp. vii, 11, 105, states that the only year between A.D. 800 and 950, on which the Indiction was eight, and Nov. 27 fell on a Thursday, was 844[3]. In the Oxford sheets we find tables of κεφάλαια before the Gospels of SS. Matthew and Luke; the τίτλοι at the heading of the pages; their numbers *rubro* neatly set in the margin; capitals in red at the commencement of these chapters; the ἀρχαὶ καὶ τέλη of lections; the sections and Eusebian canons in their usual places, and some liturgical directions. Over the original breathings and accents some late scrawler has in many places put others, in a very careless fashion.

Δ. CODEX SANGALLENSIS, was first inspected by Gerbert (1773), named by Scholz (N. T. 1830), and made fully known

---

[1] These are Matt. vi. 16–29; vii. 26—viii. 27; xii. 18—xiv. 15; xx. 25—xxi. 19; xxii. 25—xxiii. 13; John vi. 14—viii. 3; xv. 24—xix. 6.

[2] In the St. Petersburg portion are all the rest of St. John, and Matt. i. 1—v. 31; ix. 6—xii. 18; xiv. 15—xx. 25; xxiii. 13—xxviii. 20; or all St. Matthew except 115 verses.

[3] Dr. Gregory, Tisch. Prolegomena, p. 401, quotes Gardthausen, Griechische Palaeogr., Lipsiae, 1879, pp. 159, 344, as assigning A. D. 979 as the date.

to us by the admirable edition in lithographed facsimile of every page, by H. Ch. M. Rettig [1799-1836], published at Zurich, 1836 [1], with copious and satisfactory Prolegomena. It is preserved and was probably transcribed a thousand years since in the great monastery of St. Gall in the north-east of Switzerland (Stifts bibliothek, 48). It is rudely written on 197 leaves of coarse vellum quarto, $8\frac{7}{8}$ inches by $7\frac{1}{2}$ in size, with from twenty to twenty-six (usually twenty-one) lines on each page, in a very peculiar hand, with an interlinear Latin version, and contains the four Gospels complete except John xix. 17-35. Before St. Matthew's Gospel are placed Prologues, Latin verses, the Eusebian canons in Roman letters, tables of the κεφάλαια both in Greek and Latin, &c. Rettig thinks he has traced several different scribes and inks employed on it, which might happen easily enough in the Scriptorium of a monastery; but, if so, their style of writing is very nearly the same, and they doubtless copied from the same archetype, about the same time. He has produced more convincing arguments to show that Cod. Δ is part of the same book as the Codex Boernerianus, G of St. Paul's Epistles. Not only do they exactly resemble each other in their whole arrangement and appearance, but marginal notes by the first hand are found in each, of precisely the same character. Thus the predestinarian doctrines of the heretic Godeschalk [d. 866] are pointed out for refutation at the hard texts, Luke xiii. 24; John xii. 40 in Δ, and six times in G [2]. St. Mark's Gospel represents a text different from that of the other

---

[1] The edition was posthumous, and has prefixed to it a touching 'Life' of two pages in length, by his brother and pupil, dwelling especially on Rettig's happy change in his later days from rationalism to a higher and spiritual life.

[2] Viz. Rom. iii. 5 ; 1 Cor. ii. 8 ; 1 Tim. ii. 4; iv. 10; vi. 4; 2 Tim. ii. 15. Equally strong are the notices of Aganon, who is cited eight times in Δ, about sixteen in G. This personage was Bishop of Chartres, and a severe disciplinarian, who died A.D. 941 ; a fact which does not hinder our assigning Cod. Δ to the ninth century, as Rettig states that all notices of him are by a later hand. There is the less need of multiplying proofs of this kind, as Tregelles has observed, a circumstance which demonstrates to a certainty the identity of Cod. Δ and G. When he was at Dresden he found in Cod. G twelve leaves of later writing in precisely the same hand as several that are lithographed by Rettig, because they were attached to Cod. Δ. 'Thus,' he says, 'these MSS. once formed ONE BOOK ; and when separated, some of the superfluous leaves with additional writing attached to the former part, and some to the latter' (Tregelles' Horne's Introd. vol. iv. p. 197).

Evangelists, and the Latin version (which is clearly *primâ manu*) seems a mixture of the Vulgate with the older Italic, so altered and accommodated to the Greek as to be of little critical value. The penmen seem to have known but little Greek, and to have copied from a manuscript written continuously, for the divisions between the words are sometimes absurdly wrong. There are scarcely any breathings or accents, except about the opening of St. Mark, and once an aspirate to ἑπτα; what we do find are often falsely given; and a dot is set in most places regularly at the end of every *Greek* word. The letters have but little tendency to the oblong shape, but *delta* and *theta* are decidedly of the latest uncial type. Here, as in Paul. Cod. G, the mark >>> is much used to fill up vacant spaces. The text from which Δ was copied seems to have been arranged in στίχοι, for almost every line has at least one Greek capital letter, grotesquely ornamental in colours [1]. We transcribe three lines, taken almost at random, from pp. 80-1 (Matt. xx. 13-15), in order to explain our meaning:

dixit   uni   eor̄   amice   non ījusto tibi   n̄ne
ειπεν · μοναδι · αυτων · Εταιρε · ουκ · αδικω · σε · Ουχι

ex denario   conveniesti mecū tolle   tuū   et vade
δηναριου   συνεφωνησασ · μοι · Αρον · το · σον και υπαγε

       volo autē huic   novissimo   dare sicut et tibi antā non li
Θελω δε τουτω τω εσχατω δουναι ωσ και · σοι · II · ουκ εξ

It will be observed that, while in Cod. Δ a line begins at any place, even in the middle of a word; if the capital letters be assumed to commence the lines, the text divides itself into regular στίχοι. See above, pp. 52-54. Here are also the τίτλοι, the sections and canons. The letters N and Π, Z and Ξ, T and Θ, P and the Latin R are perpetually confounded. Facsimiles of Luke i. 1-9 may be seen in Pal. Soc. xi. 179. As in the kindred Codd. Augiensis and Boernerianus the Latin f is much like r. Tregelles has noted ι ascript in Cod. Δ, but this is rare. There is no question that this document was written by Latin (most probably by Irish) monks, in the west of Europe, during the ninth century (or the tenth, Pal. Soc.). *See below*, Paul. Cod. G.

---

[1] The portion of this manuscript contained in Paul. G was divided into στίχοι on the same principle by Hug (Introduction, vol. i. p. 283, Wait's translation).

Θᵃ. CODEX TISCHENDORFIAN. I was brought from the East by Tischendorf in 1845, published by him in his 'Monumenta sacra inedita,' 1846, with a few supplements in vol. ii of his new collection (1857), and deposited in the University Library at Leipsic. It consists of but four leaves (all imperfect) quarto, of very thin vellum, almost too brittle to be touched, so that each leaf is kept separately in glass. It contains about forty-two verses; viz. Matt. xii. 17-19; 23-25; xiii. 46-55 (in mere shreds); xiv. 8-29; xv. 4-14, with the greater κεφάλαια in red; the sections and Eusebian canons stand in the inner margin. A few breathings are *primâ manu*, and many accents by two later correctors. The stops (which are rather numerous) resemble those of Cod. Y, only that four points are not found in Θᵃ. Tischendorf places its date towards the end of the seventh century, assigning Mount Sinai or lower Egypt for its country. The uncials (especially ΕΘΟC) are somewhat oblong, leaning to the right (see p. 41 note), but the writing is elegant and uniform; *delta* keeps its ancient shape, and the diameter of *theta* does not extend beyond the curve. In regard to the text, it much resembles אB, and stands alone with them in ch. xiv. 12 (αὐτόν).

Seven other small fragments, of which four and part of another are from the manuscripts of Bishop Porphyry at St. Petersburg, were intended to be included in Tischendorf's ninth volume of 'Monumenta sacra inedita' (1870), but owing to Tischendorf's death they never appeared. That active critic had brought two (Θᵇ, ᵈ) and part of another (Θᶜ) from the East, and deposited them in the Library at St. Petersburg. They are described by him as follows:

Θᵇ, six leaves in large 8vo, of the sixth or seventh century, torn piecemeal for binding and hard to decipher, contains Matt. xxii. 16—xxiii. 13; Mark iv. 24-35; v. 14-23.

Θᶜ, one folio leaf, of the sixth century, much like Cod. N, contains Matt. xxi. 19-24. Another leaf contains John xviii. 29-35.

Θᵈ, half a leaf in two columns, of the seventh or eighth century, with accents by a later hand, contains Luke xi. 37-41; 42-45.

Θᵉ, containing fragments of Matt. xxvi. 2–4; 7–9: Θᶠ, of Matt. xxvi. 59–70; xxvii. 44–56; Mark i. 34—ii. 12 (not continuously throughout): Θᵍ, of John vi. 13, 14; 22–24; are all of about the sixth century.

Θʰ, consisting of three leaves, in Greek and Arabic of the ninth or tenth centuries, contains imperfect portions of Matt. xiv. 6–13; xxv. 9–16; 41—xxvi. 1.

Λ. CODEX TISCHENDORFIAN. III[1], whose history, so far as we know it, exactly resembles that of Cod. Γ, and like it is now in the Bodleian (Auct. T. Infra I. 1). It contains 157 leaves, written in two columns of twenty-three lines each, in small, oblong, clumsy, sloping uncials of the eighth or rather of the ninth century (see p. 41, note 1, and facsimile No. 30). It has the Gospels of St. Luke and St. John complete, with the subscription to St. Mark, each Gospel being preceded by tables of κεφάλαια, with the τίτλοι at the heads of the pages; the numbers of the κεφάλαια, of the sections, and of the Eusebian canons (these last *rubro*) being set in the margin. There are also scholia interspersed, of some critical value; a portion being in uncial characters. This copy also was described (with a facsimile) by Tischendorf, Anecdota sacra et profana, 1855, and collated by himself and Tregelles. Its text is said to vary greatly from that common in the later uncials, and to be very like Scholz's 262 (Paris 53). For ι *ascriptum* see p. 44, note 2.

Here again the history of this manuscript curiously coincides with that of Cod. Γ. In his Notitia Cod. Sinaitici, p. 58, Tischendorf describes an early cursive copy of St. Matthew and St. Mark (*the subscription to the latter being wanting*), which he took to St. Petersburg in 1859, so exactly corresponding in general appearance with Cod. Λ (although that be written in uncial characters), as well as in the style and character of the marginal scholia, which are often in small uncials, that he pronounces them part of the same codex. Very possibly he *might* have added that he procured the two from the same source: at any rate the subscription to St. Matthew at St. Petersburg precisely resembles the other three subscriptions at Oxford, and

---

[1] Λ (1) is really an Evangelistary. See Evst. 493.

those in Paris 53 (Scholz's 262)[1], with which Tischendorf had previously compared Cod. Λ (N. T. Proleg. p. clxxvii, seventh edition). These cursive leaves are preceded by Eusebius' Epistle to Carpianus, his table of canons, and a table of the κεφάλαια of St. Matthew. The τίτλοι in uncials head the pages, and their numbers stand in the margin.

From the marginal scholia Tischendorf cites the following notices of the Jewish Gospel, or that according to the Hebrews, which certainly have their value as helping to inform us respecting its nature: Matt. iv. 5 το ιουδαικον ουκ εχει εις την αγιαν πολιν αλλ εν ιλημ. xvi. 17 Βαριωνα· το ιουδαικον υιε ιωαννου. xviii. 22 το ιουδαικον εξης εχει μετα το ἑβδομηκοντακις ἑπτα· και γαρ εν τοις προφηταις μετα το χρισθηναι αυτους εν π̄ν̄ι ἁγιω εὑρισκετω (*sic*) εν αυτοις λογος ἁμαρτιας :—an addition which Jerome (contra Pelag. III) expressly cites from the Gospel of the Nazarenes. xxvi. 47 το ιουδαικον· και ηρνησατο και ωμοσεν και κατηρασατο. It is plain that this whole matter requires careful discussion, but at present it would seem that the first half of Cod. Λ was written in cursive, the second in uncial letters; if not by the same person, yet on the same plan and at the same place.

Ξ. CODEX ZACYNTHIUS is a palimpsest in the Library of the British and Foreign Bible Society in London, which, under a cursive Evangelistarium written on coarse vellum in or about the thirteenth century, contains large portions (342 verses) of St. Luke, down to ch. xi. 33[2], in full well-formed uncials, but surrounded by and often interwoven with large extracts from the Fathers, in a hand so cramped and, as regards the round letters (ΕΘΟC), so oblong, that it cannot be earlier than the eighth century, although some such compressed forms occur in Cod. P of the sixth (*see* p. 144). The general absence of accents and breathings also would favour an earlier date. As the

---

[1] The subscription to St. Matthew stands in *both* : ευαγγελιον κατα ματθαιον. εγραφη και αντεβληθη εκ των [*sic*] ιεροσολυμοις παλαιων αντιγραφων· των εν τω ἁγιω ορει αποκειμενων· εν στιχοις β̄φιδ̄· κεφφ. τ̄ν̄ε. Very similar subscriptions occur in Codd. 20, 215, 300, 376, 428, 573.

[2] Cod. Ξ contains Luke i. 1-9; 19-23; 27, 28; 30-32; 36-66; 77—ii. 19; 21, 22; 33-39; iii. 5-8; 11-20; iv. 1, 2; 6-20; 32-43; v. 17-36; vi. 21—vii. 6; 11-37; 39-47; viii. 4-21; 25-35; 43-50; ix. 1-28; 32, 33; 35; 41—x. 18; 21-40; xi. 1, 2; 3, 4; 24-30; 31; 32, 33.

arrangement of the matter makes it certain that the commentary is contemporaneous, Cod. Ξ must be regarded as the earliest known, indeed as the only uncial, copy furnished with a catena. This volume, which once belonged to 'Il Principe Comuto, Zante,' and is marked as Μνημόσυνον σεβάσματος τοῦ Ἱππέος Ἀντωνίου Κόμητος 1820, was presented to the Bible Society in 1821 by General Macaulay, who brought it from Zante. Mr. Knolleke, one of the Secretaries, seems first to have noticed the older writing, and on the discovery being communicated to Tregelles in 1858 by Dr. Paul de Lagarde of Berlin, with characteristic eagerness that critic examined, deciphered, and published the Scripture text, together with the Moscow fragment O, in 1861: he doubted whether the small Patristic writing could all be read without chemical restoration. Besides the usual τίτλοι above the text and other notations of sections, and numbers running up from 1 to 100 which refer to the catena, this copy is remarkable for possessing also the division into chapters, hitherto as has been stated deemed unique in Cod. B. To this notation is commonly prefixed γκί, formed like a cross, in the fashion of the eighth century. The ancient volume must have been a large folio (14 inches by 11), of which eighty-six leaves and three half-leaves survive: of course very hard to read. Of the ecclesiastical writers cited by name Chrysostom, Origen, and Cyril are the best known. In text it generally favours the B and ℵ and their company. In the 564 places wherein Tischendorf cites it in his eighth edition, it supports Cod. L in full three cases out of four, and those the most characteristic. It stands alone only fourteen times, and with Cod. L or others against the five great uncials only thirty times. In regard to these five, Cod. Ξ sides plainly with Cod. B in preference to Cod. A, following B alone seven times, BL twenty-four times, but ℵ thirteen times, A fifteen times, C (which is often defective) five times, D fourteen times, with none of these unsupported except with ℵ once. Their combinations in agreement with Ξ are curious and complicated, but lead to the same result. This copy is with ℵB six times, with ℵBL fifty-five; with ℵBC twenty, but with ℵBD as many as fifty-four times, with ℵBCD thirty-eight times; with BCD thrice, with BC six times, with BD thirteen. It combines with ℵA ten times, with AC fifteen, with AD eleven, with ℵAC sixteen, with ACD twelve, with ℵAD six, with ℵACD twelve. Thus Cod. Ξ favours B against A 226 times, A against B ninety-seven. Combinations of its readings opposed to both A and B are ℵC six, ℵD eight, CD two, ℵCD three. In the other passages it favours ABC against ℵD eleven times, ABCD against ℵ eight times, ℵABC against D eighteen times, ℵABD against C, or where C is defective, thirty-nine times, and is expressly cited twenty-seven times as standing with ℵABCD against later copies. The character of the variations of Cod. Ξ from the Received text may be judged of by the estimate made by some scholar, that forty-seven of them are transpositions in the order of the words, 201 are substitutions of one word for another, 118 are omissions, while the additions do not exceed twenty-four (*Christian Remembrancer*, January, 1862). The cursive Evangelistarium written over the uncial is noticed below, and bears the mark 200*.

Π. CODEX PETROPOLITANUS consists of 350 vellum leaves in small quarto, and contains the Gospels complete except Matt. iii. 12—iv.18; xix.12—xx.3; John viii. 6-39; seventy-seven verses. A century since it belonged to Parodus, a noble Greek of Smyrna, and its last possessor was persuaded by Tischendorf, in 1859, to present it to the Emperor of Russia. Tischendorf states that it is of the age of the later uncials (meaning the ninth century), but of higher critical importance than most of them, and much like Cod. K in its rarer readings. There are many marginal and other corrections by a later hand, and John v. 4; viii. 3-6 are obelized. In the table of κεφάλαια before St. Mark, there is a gap after $\overline{\lambda\varsigma}$: Mark xvi. 18-20; John xxi. 22-25 are in a later hand. At the end of St. Mark, the last section inserted is $\overline{\sigma\lambda\delta}$ by the side of ἀναστὰς δέ ver. 9, with ῆ under it for the Eusebian canon. Tischendorf first used its readings for his Synopsis Evangelica 1864, then for the eighth edition of his Greek Testament 1865, &c. This manuscript in the great majority of instances sides with the later uncials (whether supported by Cod. A or not) against Codd. ℵBCD united.

Σ. COD. ROSSANENSIS, like Cod. N described above, is a manuscript written on thin vellum leaves stained purple, in silver letters, the first three lines of each Gospel being in gold. Like

Cod. D it probably dates from the sixth century, if not a little sooner, and is the earliest known copy of Scripture which is adorned with miniatures in watercolours, seventeen in number, very interesting and in good preservation. The illustrated Dioscorides at Vienna bears about the same date. Attention was called to the book by Cesare Malpica in 1846, but it was not seen by any one who cared to use it before March, 1879, when Oscar von Gebhardt of Göttingen and Adolf Harnack of Giessen, in their search for codices of Hippolytus, of Dionysius of Alexandria, and of Cyril of Jerusalem, described by Cardinal Sirlet in 1582, found it in the Archbishop's Library at Rossano, a small city in Calabria, and published an account of it in 1880 in a sumptuous form, far more satisfactory to the artist than to the Biblical critic. Their volume is illustrated by two facsimile leaves, of one of which a reduction may be seen in our Plate xiv, No. 43. A copy of the manuscripts was published at Leipsic in 1883 with an Introduction by Oscar von Gebhardt, the Text being edited by Adolf Harnack [1]. The page we have exhibited gives the earliest MS. authority, except Φ, for the doxology in the Lord's Prayer, Matt. vi. 13. The manuscript is in quarto, 13½ inches high by 10¼ broad, and now contains only the Gospels of St. Matthew and St. Mark on 188 leaves of two columns each, there being twenty lines in each column of very regular writing, and from nine to twelve letters in each line. It ends abruptly at Mark xvi. 14, and the last ten leaves have suffered from damp; otherwise the writing (especially on the inner or smooth side of the vellum) is in good preservation, and the colours of the paintings wonderfully fresh. The binding is of strong black leather, about 200 years old. As in Cod. B, the sheets are ranged in quinions, the *signatures* in silver by the original scribe standing at the lower border of each quire on the right, and the pages being marked in the upper border in modern black ink. In Cod. Σ there is no separation between the words, it has no breathings or accents. Capital letters stand outside the columns, being about twice the size of the rest, and the smaller letters at the end of lines are not compressed, as we

---

[1] Texte und Untersuchungen zur Geschichte der altchristlichen Literatur, 1. Bd. 4. Hft., 1883, Leipsig. Also see *Church Quarterly*, Jan. 1884. Prof. Sanday in Studia Biblica, i. p. 111. 'Would delight the heart of the Dean of Chichester.' *Athenaeum*, No. 302, Sept. 19, 1885.

find them even in Cod. P (*see* pp. 144, 163). The letters are round and square, and, as was abundantly seen above (pp. 33-40), belong to the older type of writing. The punctuation is very simple: the full stop occurs half up the letter. There are few erasures, but transcriptural errors are mostly corrected in silver letters by the original scribe. To St. Matthew's Gospel is prefixed Eusebius' Epistle to Carpianus and his Tables of Canons, both imperfect; also lists of the κεφάλαια *majora* and τίτλοι in the upper margins of the several leaves, with a subscription to the first Gospel (Єυαγγελιον κατα ματθαιον). This supplementary matter is written somewhat smaller, but (as the editors judge) by the same hand as the text, although the letters are somewhat more recent in general appearance, and ι *ascriptum* occurs, as it never does in the body of the manuscript: κ also is only twice abridged in the text, but often in the smaller writing. In the margin of the Greek text the Ammonian sections stand in minute characters over the numbers of the Eusebian canons. The text agrees but slightly with א or B, and rather with the main body of uncials and cursives, which it favours in about a proportion of three to one. With the cognate purple manuscript Cod. N it accords so wonderfully, that although one of them cannot have been copied directly from the other, they must have been drawn directly or indirectly from the same source. Strong proofs of the affinity between N and Σ are Matt. xix. 7 ἡμῖν added to ἐνετείλατο: xxi. 8 ἐκ (for ἀπό): Mark vi. 53 ἐκεῖ added to προσω(ο in Σ)ρμισθησαν: vii. 1 οἱ prefixed to ἐλθόντες: *ibid.* 29 ὁ ἰσ added to εἶπεν αὐτῇ: viii. 3 ἐγλυθήσονται: *ibid.* 13 καταλιπών for ἀφείς: *ibid.* 18 οὔπω νοεῖτε for καὶ οὐ μνημονεύετε: ix. 3 λευκᾶναι οὕτως: x. 5 ἐπέτρεψεν for ἔγραψεν: xiv. 36 πλήν before ἀλλ': xv. 21 omit παράγοντα: in all which places the two manuscripts are either virtually or entirely alone. Generally speaking, the Codex Rossanensis follows the Traditional Text, but not invariably. We find here the usual itacisms, as ει for ι, αι for ε, η for ει and ι, ου for ω, and vice versa; even ο for ω, which is rarer in very ancient copies. The so-called Alexandrian forms ἤλθατε, ἐλθάτω, ἴδαμεν, ἴδαν for verbs, τρίχαν and νύκταν for nouns, ἐκαθερίσθη, λήμψομαι, δεκατέσσερες, τεσσεράκοντα, it has in common with all copies approaching it in age.

Υ. CODEX BLENHEIMIUS. Brit. Mus. Additional 31919,

formerly Blenheim 3. D. 13, purchased at Puttick's from the Sunderland sale in April, 1882. Under a Menaeum (*see* our Evst. 282) for the twenty-eight days of February [A.D. 1431], 12⅞ × 8½, containing 108 leaves, Professors T. K. Abbott and J. P. Mahaffy of Trinity College, Dublin, discovered at Blenheim in May, 1881, *palimpsest* fragments of the Gospels of the eighth century, being seventeen passages scattered over thirty-three of the leaves: viz. Matt. i. 1–14; v. 3–19; xii. 27–41; xxiii. 5—xxv. 30; 43—xxvi. 26; 50—xxvii. 17. Mark i. 1–42; ii. 21—v. 1; 29—vi. 22; x. 50—xi. 13. Luke xvi. 21—xvii. 3; 19–37; xix. 15–31. John ii. 18—iii. 5; iv. 23–37; v. 35—vi. 2: in all 484 verses. In 1883, Dr. Gregory discovered two more leaves, making thirty-six in all, with a reduction of the passages to sixteen by filling up an hiatus, and giving a total of 497 verses. It is probable that writing lies under all the 108 leaves. It exhibits *Am.* (not *Eus.*) in gold, ἀρχαί and τέλη, but is very hard to read, and has not yet been collated. Of less account are palimpsest pieces of the eleventh century on some of the leaves, containing Matt. xi. 13, &c.; Luke i. 64, &c.; ii. 25–34, and a later cursive patch (fol. 23) containing Mark vi. 14–20.

Φ. CODEX BERATINUS. This symbol was taken by Herr Oscar von Gebhardt to denote the imaginary parent of Cursives 13, 69, 124, 346, of which the similarity has been traced by the late W. H. Ferrar and Dr. T. K. Abbott in 'A Collection of Four Important MSS.' (1877). But it is now permanently affixed to an Uncial MS. seen by M. Pierre Batiffol on the instigation of Prof. Duchesne in 1875 at Berat or Belgrade in Albania. This manuscript had been previously described by Mgr. Anthymus Alexoudi, Orthodox Metropolitan of Belgrade, in an account of his diocese published in 1868 in Corfu. According to M. Batiffol, it is a purple manuscript, written in silver letters on vellum, an *édition de grande luxe*, and therefore open to the charge brought by St. Jerome in his Prolegomena to Job against the great adornment of manuscripts, as being far from constituting an index of accuracy. It contains 190 unpaged leaves in quaternions, firmly sewn together, having two columns in a page of seventeen lines each, and from eight to twelve words in a line. The leaves are in size about 12¼ inches by 10½, and

Plate XV.

ωϲϲγΝΕΤΑΖΕ
ΑΥΤΟΙϹΟΙϹΚΑΙ   Γ
ΗΤΟΙΜΑϹΑΝΤο   Κ
ΠΑϲΧΑ·   Μ
ΟΥΙΑϹΔΕΓΕΝο   Μ
ΜΕΝΗϹΑΝΕ   ϹΠΑΔ
                Β
ΚΕΙΤΟΜΕΤΑτ   Ε Υ ω Τ
ΔΦΔΕΚΑΜΑΘΗ
ΤωΝ· ΚΑΙΑΙϹΘΙ

the columns measure 8¼ inches high by rather more than 4¼ broad. The pages have the κεφάλαια marked at the top, and the sections and canons in writing of the eighth century at the side. The letters are in silver, very regular, and clearly written. None are in gold, except the title and the first line in St. Mark, and the words Πατήρ, 'Ιησοῦς, and some others in the first six folios. There is no ornamentation, but the first letters of paragraphs are twice as large as the other letters. The letters have no decoration, except a cross in the middle of the initial O's. The writing is continuous in full line without stichometry. Quotations from the Old Testament are marked with a kind of inverted comma. There are no breathings, or accents. Punctuation is made only with the single comma or double comma, consisting of a point slightly elongated much like a modern written comma, and placed at about mid-height, or else with a vacant space, or by passing to the next line. The apostrophe is not always used to mark elisions, but is generally put after P final. Abbreviations are of the most ancient kind. The character of the letters may be seen in the specimen given above, No. 43. Altogether, the Codex Beratinus (Φ) may probably be placed at the end of the fifth century, a little before the Dioscorides (506 A. D.), and before the Codex Rossanensis.

As to the character of the text, it inclines to the large body of Uncials and Cursives, and is rarely found with Bא and Z of St. Matthew or Δ of St. Mark. A specimen examination of fifty passages at the beginning of St. Matthew gives forty-four instances in which it agrees with the larger body of Uncials and Cursives, six when it passes over to the other side, whilst in thirty-eight it agrees with Σ. In the same passages, Σ agrees thirty-eight times with the larger body, and twelve times with א or B. Like Σ it contains the doxology in Matt. vi. 13.

Codex Φ has gone through many vicissitudes. It has perhaps been at Patmos, where it may have been mutilated by some of the Crusaders, and at Antioch. It contains only St. Matthew and St. Mark; a note says that the disappearance of St. Luke and St. John is due to the Franks of Champagne. The first six folios are in a bad state, so that the text as we have it does not begin till St. Matt. vi. 3 η αριστερα σου κ.τ.λ. Hiatus occurs Matt. vii. 26—viii. 7, in xviii. 23—xix. 3, and in Mark xiv. 62-fin. So that Cod. Φ presents no direct evidence—only the testimony to the general character of its companions derived from its own character and general coincidence—upon the last twelve verses of St. Mark. Part of folio 112, at the end of St. Matthew, is blank, and folios 113, 114, contain the κεφάλαια of St. Mark.

It was handsomely bound in 1805 in wood covered with chased silver.

Ψ. In the Monastery of Laura at Mount Athos [viii or ix], $8\frac{1}{4}$ × 6, ff. 261 (31), κεφ. t., Am., Eus., lect. Mark ix. 5-end; Luke, John, Acts, 1, 2 Peter, James, 1, 2, 3 John, Romans, Hebrews viii. 13; ix. 19–end. Inserts the supplement of L to St. Mark before the last twelve verses, and the lectionary τέλος after ἐφοβοῦντο γάρ. See Gregory, Prolegomena, p. 445.

Ω. In the Monastery of Dionysius at Athos [viii or ix], $8\frac{3}{4}$ × $6\frac{1}{2}$, ff. 289 (22), two columns. Whole four Gospels. Gregory, p. 446.

ב. In the Monastery of St. Andrew at Athos [ix or x], 8 × $6\frac{1}{4}$, ff. 152 (37). The four Gospels. Gregory, p. 446.

CHAPTER VI.

UNCIAL MANUSCRIPTS OF THE ACTS AND CATHOLIC EPISTLES, OF ST. PAUL'S EPISTLES, AND OF THE APOCALYPSE.

I. *Manuscripts of the Acts and Catholic Epistles.*

ℵ. COD. SINAITICUS.   B. COD. VATICANUS.
A. COD. ALEXANDRINUS.   C. COD. EPHRAEMI.
                D. CODEX BEZAE.

E. CODEX LAUDIANUS 35 is one of the most precious treasures preserved in the Bodleian at Oxford. It is a Latin-Greek copy, with two columns on a page, the Latin version holding the post of honour on the left, and is written in very short στίχοι, consisting of from one to three words each, the Latin words always standing opposite to the corresponding Greek. This peculiar arrangement points decisively to the West of Europe as its country, notwithstanding the abundance of Alexandrian forms has led some to refer it to Egypt. The very large, bold, thick, rude uncials, without break in the words and without accents, lead us up to the end of the sixth century as its date. The Latin is not of Jerome's or the Vulgate version, but is made to correspond closely with the Greek, even in its interpolations and rarest various readings. The contrary supposition that the Greek portion of this codex *Latinised*, or had been altered to coincide with the Latin, is inconsistent with the facts of the case. This manuscript contains only the Acts of the Apostles (from ch. xxvi. 29 παυλος to ch. xxviii. 26 λέγον being lost), and exhibits a remarkable modification of the text, of which we shall speak in Chapter VII. That the book was once in Sardinia, appears from an edict of Flavius Pancratius, συν θεω απο επαρχων δουξ σαρδινιας, appended (as also is the Apostles' Creed in Latin, and some other foreign matter) in a later hand: Imperial governors ruled in that island with the title of *dux* from the reign of Justinian, A.D. 534 to A.D. 749. It was probably among the Greek volumes brought into England by the fellow-countryman of St. Paul, Theodore of Tarsus[1], 'the grand old man' as he has been called by one of kindred spirit to his own (Dean Hook, Lives of the Archbishops of Canterbury, vol. i. p. 150), who came to England as Primate at the age of sixty-six, A.D. 668, and died in 690. At all events, Mill (N. T. Proleg. §§ 1022-6)[2] has rendered it all but certain, that the Venerable Bede [d. 735] had this very codex before him when he wrote his 'Expositio Retractata' of the Acts[3], and Woide (Notitia Cod. Alex., p. 156, &c.) has since alleged six additional instances of agreement between them. The manuscript, however, must have been complete when Bede used it, for he cites in the Latin ch. xxvii. 5; xxviii. 2. Tischendorf (Proleg. p. xv) adds ch. xxvii. 1, 7, 14, 15, 16, 17: but these last instances are somewhat uncertain. This manuscript, with many others, was presented to the University of Oxford in the year 1636, by its munificent Chancellor, Archbishop Laud. Thomas Hearne, the celebrated antiquary, published a full edition of it in 1715, which is now very scarce, and was long known to be far from accurate. Sabatier in 1751 gave the Latin of it taken from Hearne. Tischendorf has published a new edition, from two separate collations made by himself in 1854 and 1865, in the ninth volume by way of Appendix to his 'Monumenta sacra inedita,' 1870. It is also found in vol. ii of Hansell's edition of the Ancient Texts, published at the Clarendon Press in 1864. Cod. E

---

[1] Dean Gywnn of Raphoe is so good as to remind me that among the other proper names enumerated by Wetstein and Semler as written on the reverse of the last leaf of this manuscript, θεωδοροc stands by itself in a hand which may be as old as the seventh century. Common as the name is, the fact is interesting and suggestive. For the orthography compare κωλονια Acts xvi. 12 in Cod. E.

[2] It is probable that Mill got this from 'Nouvelles Observations sur le Texte et les Versions du Nouveau Testament,' par R. Simon, Paris, 1695.

[3] I see no force in Tischendorf's objection, that if Theodore had brought Cod. E to England, Bede would have used it before he came to write his 'Expositio Retractata.'

has been stated to have capital letters at the commencement of each of the Euthalian sections, but as the capitals occur at other places where the sense is broken but slightly (e.g. ch. xvii. 20), this circumstance does not prove that those sections were known to the scribe. It is in size $10\frac{1}{4}$ inches by $8\frac{1}{2}$, and consists of 227 leaves of twenty-three, twenty-four, twenty-five, or twenty-six lines each; about fifteen leaves are lost: the vellum is rather coarse in quality, and the ink in many places very faint. There seem to be no stops nor breathings, except an aspirate over initial *upsilon* (ῠ or ὐ, sometimes ῡ or ὔ) almost invariably. The shape of *xi* is more complicated than usual (see our facsimile, No. 25); the other letters (e.g. *delta* or *psi*) are such as were common in the sixth or early in the seventh century. There are also many changes by a later uncial hand. Mr. Hansell (Ancient Texts, Oxford, 1864), as well as Tischendorf, exhibits one whole page in zinco-photography.

F[a]. COD. COISLIN. I.

G. Tischendorf, in his eighth edition of the N. T., assigns this letter (formerly appropriated to Cod. L) to one octavo leaf of the seventh century, now at St. Petersburg, written in thick uncials without accents, torn from the wooden cover of a Syriac book, and containing Acts ii. 45—iii. 8. It has a few rare and valuable readings. Dr. Hort (Supplement to Tregelles, p. 1021) cites it as G[a].

G[b]. VATICANUS ROMANUS 9671 [iv?] fol., ff. 5 (22), palimpsest. *See* Gregory, Prolegomena, p. 414.

H. COD. MUTINENSIS [cxcvi] ii. G. 3, of the Acts, in the Grand Ducal Library at Modena, is an uncial copy of about the ninth century, defective in Acts i. 1—v. 28; ix. 39—x. 19; xiii. 36—xiv. 3, all supplied by a cursive hand [h], 'in my judgement... scarcely later' (Burgon), and in xxvii. 4—xxviii. 31 (written in uncials of about the eleventh century). The Epistles are in cursive letters of the twelfth century, indicated in the Catholic Epistles by h, in the Pauline by 179. Scholz first collated it loosely, as usual; then Tischendorf in 1843,

Tregelles in 1846, afterwards comparing their collations for mutual correction.

I. Cod. Petropolit. or Tischendorfian. II.

K. Cod. Mosquensis, S. Synodi No. 98, is Matthaei's g, and came from the monastery of St. Dionysius on Mount Athos. It contains the Catholic Epistles entire, but not the Acts; and the Pauline Epistles are defective only in Rom. x. 18—1 Cor. vi. 13; 1 Cor. viii. 7–11. Matthaei alone has collated this document, and judging from his facsimile (Cath. Epp. 1782) it seems to belong to the ninth century. This copy is Scholz's Act. 102, Paul. 117. It is not so thoroughly known but that it is often necessary to cite its readings *ex silentio*.

L (formerly G). Cod. Biblioth. Angelicae A. 2. 15, belonging to the Augustinian monks at Rome, formerly 'Cardinalis Passionei,' contains the Acts from ch. viii. 10, μισ του θεου to the end, the Catholic Epistles complete, and the Pauline down to Heb. xiii. 10, οὐκ ἔχουσιν, of a date not earlier than the middle of the ninth century. It was collated in part by Bianchini and Birch, in full by Scholz (1820, J. Paul) and by F. F. Fleck (1833). Tischendorf in 1843, Tregelles in 1845, collated it independently, and subsequently compared their papers, as they have done in several other instances.

M of Gregory (G^b), fol., ff. 5 (22), palimpsest, containing fragments of Acts xvi—xviii of the eighth or ninth century, was published by Cozza (Sacr. Bibl. Vetust. Frag. iii: Rome, 1877). It was transferred to the Vatican (No. 9671) from the Greek convent of Grotta Ferrata.

P. Cod. Porphyrianus is a palimpsest containing the Acts, all the Epistles, the Apocalypse, and a few fragments of 4 Maccabees, of the ninth century, found by Tischendorf in 1862 at St. Petersburg in the possession of the Archimandrite (now Bishop) Porphyry, who allowed him to take it to Leipsic to decipher. He has published it at length in his 'Monumenta sacra inedita,' vol. v, vi, whence Tregelles derived its readings for the Pauline Epistles and the Apocalypse. In the latter book it is especially useful, and generally confirms Codd. AC, though it is often with

Cod. ℵ, sometimes against all the rest. It has the $\overset{x}{\alpha\rho}$ and $\overset{.}{\tau\epsilon}$ of Church lessons in the margin, and is defective (besides a few words or letters lost here and there) in Acts i. 1—ii. 15; 1 John iii. 20—v. 1; Jude 4-15; Rom. ii. 16—iii. 5; viii. 33—ix. 11; xi. 22—xii. 1; 1 Cor. vii. 16, 17; xii. 23—xiii. 5; xiv. 23-39; 2 Cor. ii. 14, 15; Col. iii. 16—iv. 8; 1 Thess. iii. 5—iv. 17; Apoc. xvi. 13—xvii. 1; xx. 1-9; xxii. 6-21. Moreover James ii. 12-21; 2 Pet. i. 20—ii. 5 are barely legible. Mr. Hammond (Outlines of Textual Criticism) has taken from Tischendorf's fifth volume a neat facsimile of it in Acts iv. 10-15, comprising uncials of the latest form, leaning to the right, lying under cursive writing (Heb. vii. 17-25), some four centuries more recent. Dr. Hort (Supplement to Tregelles, p. xxx) states that in the Acts the text of Cod. P is almost exclusively of a very late type, but that it contains a much larger though varying proportion of various readings elsewhere, except in 1 Peter. The upper or later writing in this manuscript is, for once, available for critical purposes, since it consists of fragments of the labours of Euthalius (*see* p. 64), and is cited by Tischendorf under the notation of Euthal.^{cod.}

S. From the monastery of Laura at Mount Athos [viii or ix], 11 × 8½, ff. 120 (30), Acts, Cath. Rom. 1 Cor. i. 1—v. 8; xiii. 8—xvi. 24; 2 Cor. i. 1—xi. 23; Eph. iv. 20—vi. 20. *See* Gregory, p. 447.

ב. Rom. Vat. Gr. 2061, formerly Basil 100, before Patiriensis 27 [v], palimpsest, ff. 21 out of 316. Fragments of Acts, Cath., and Paul. Came from the monastery of St. Mary of Patirium, a suburb of Rossana in Calabria. Discovered by M. Pierre Batiffol, the investigator of Cod. Φ. *See* Gregory, p. 447.

II. *Manuscripts of the Pauline Epistles.*

ℵ. Cod. Sinaiticus.
A. Cod. Alexandrinus.
B. Cod. Vaticanus.
C. Cod. Ephraemi.

D. Cod. Claromontanus, No. 107 of the Royal Library at Paris, is a Greek-Latin copy of St. Paul's Epistles, one of the most ancient and important in existence. Like the Cod. Ephraemi in the same Library it has been fortunate in such an editor as Tischendorf, who published it in 1852 with complete Prolegomena, and a facsimile traced by Tregelles. This noble volume is in small quarto, written on 533 leaves of the thinnest and finest vellum: indeed its extraordinary delicacy has caused the writing at the back of every page to be rather too visible on the other side. The words, both Greek and Latin, are written continuously (except the Latin titles and subscriptions), but in a stichometrical form (see p. 52): the Greek, as in Cod. Bezae, stands on the left or first page of the opened book, not on the right, as in the Cod. Laudianus. Each page has but one column of about twenty-one lines, so that in this copy, as in the Codex Bezae, the Greek and Latin are in parallel lines, but on separate pages. The ink is dark and clear, and otherwise the book is in good condition. It contains all St. Paul's Epistles (the Hebrews after Philemon), except Rom. i. 1-7; 27-30, both Greek and Latin: Rom. i. 24-27 in the Latin is supplied in a later but very old hand, as also are Rom. i. 27-30 and 1 Cor. xiv. 13-22 in the Greek: the Latin of 1 Cor. xiv. 8-18; Heb. xiii. 21-23 is lost. The Epistle to the Hebrews has been erroneously imputed by some to a later scribe, inasmuch as it is not included in the list of the sacred books and in the number of their στίχοι or *versus*, which stand immediately *before* the Hebrews in this codex [1]: but the same list overlooks the Epistle to the Philippians, which has never been doubted to be St. Paul's: in this manuscript, however, the Epistle to the Colossians precedes that to the Philippians. Our earliest notice of it is derived from the Preface to Beza's third edition of the N. T. (Feb. 20, 1582): he there describes it as of equal antiquity with his copy of the Gospels (D), and states that it had been found 'in Claromontano apud Bellovacos coenobio,' at Clermont near Beauvais. Although Beza sometimes through inadvertence calls his codex of the Gospels Claromontanus, there seems no reason for disputing with Wetstein the correctness of his account (*see*

---

[1] The names and order of the books of the New Testament in this most curious and venerable list stand thus: Matthew, John, Mark, Luke, Romans, 1, 2 Corinth., Galat., E*fes.*, 1, 2 Tim., Tit., Colos., *Filimon*, 1, 2 Pet., James, 1, 2, 3 John, Jude, Barnabas' Ep., John's Revelation, Act. Apost., Pastor [Hermas], Actus Paul., Revelatio Petri.

p. 125, note 2), though it throws no light on the manuscript's early history. From Beza it passed into the possession of Claude Dupuy, Councillor of Paris, probably on Beza's death [1605]: thence to his sons Jacques and Pierre Dupuy: before the death of Jacques (who was the King's Librarian) in 1656, it had been bought by Louis XIV for the Royal Library at Paris. In 1707, John Aymont, an apostate priest, stole thirty-five leaves; one, which he disposed of in Holland, was restored in 1720 by its possessor Stosch; the rest were sold to that great collector, Harley, Earl of Oxford, but sent back in 1729 by his son, who had learnt their shameful story. Beza made some, but not a considerable, use of this document; it was amongst the authorities consulted for Walton's Polyglott; Wetstein collated it twice in early life (1715-16); Tregelles examined it in 1849, and compared his results with the then unpublished transcript of Tischendorf, which proved on its appearance (1852) the most difficult, as well as one of the most important, of his critical works; so hard it had been found at times to determine satisfactorily the original readings of a manuscript which had been corrected by *nine* different hands, ancient and modern. The date of the codex is doubtless the sixth century, in the middle or towards the end of it. The Latin letters, especially *d*, are the latest in form (facsimile No. 41, 1 Cor. xiii. 5-8), and are much like those in the Cod. Bezae (No. 42), which in many points Cod. Claromontanus strongly resembles. Leaves 162, 163 are palimpsest, and contain part of the Phaethon, a lost play of Euripides. We have already noticed many of its peculiarities (pp. 33-40), and need not here repeat them. *Delta* and *pi* look more ancient even than in Cod. A: the uncials are simple, square, regular and beautiful, of about the size of those in Codd. CD, and larger than in Cod. B. The stichometry forbids our assigning it to a period earlier than the end of the fifth century while other circumstances connected with the Latin version tend to put it a little lower still. The apostrophus is frequent, but there are few stops or abridgements; no breathings or accents are *primâ manu*. Initial letters, placed at the beginning of books or sections, are plain, and not much larger than the rest. The comparative correctness of the Greek text, and its Alexandrian forms, have caused certain critics to refer us as usual to Egypt for its country: the Latin text is more faulty, and shows comparative ignorance of the language: yet of what use a Latin version could be except in Africa or western Europe it were hard to imagine. This Latin is more independent of the Greek, and less altered from it than in Codd. Bezae or Laudian., wherein it has little critical value: that of Cod. Claromont. better represents the African type of the Old Latin. Of the corrections, a few were made by the original scribe when revising; a hand of the seventh century went through the whole (D**); two others follow; then in sharp black uncials of the ninth or tenth century another made more than two thousand critical changes in the text, and added stops and all the breathings and accents (D***); another D*** (among other changes) added to the Latin subscriptions. D^b supplied Rom. i. 27–30 very early; D^c, a later hand, 1 Cor. xiv. 13–22. Tischendorf distinguishes several others besides these.

E. COD. SANGERMANENSIS is another Greek-Latin manuscript and takes its name from the Abbey of St. Germain des Prez near Paris. Towards the end of the last century the Abbey (which at the Revolution had been turned into a saltpetre manufactory) was burnt down, and many of its books were lost. In 1805 Matthaei found this copy, as might almost have been anticipated, at St. Petersburg, where it is now deposited. The volume is a large quarto, the Latin and Greek in parallel columns on the same page, the Greek standing on the left; its uncials are coarse, large, and thick, not unlike those in Cod. E of the Acts, but of later shape, with breathings and accents *primâ manu*, of about the tenth, or late in the ninth, century[1]. It was used for the Oxford New Testament of 1675: Mill obtained some extracts from it, and noted its obvious connexion with Cod. Claromontanus: Wetstein thoroughly collated it; and not only he but Sabatier and Griesbach perceived that it was, at least in the Greek, nothing better than a mere transcript of Cod. Claromontanus, made by some ignorant person later than the corrector indicated by D***. Muralt's endeavours to shake this conclusion have not satisfied

---

[1] Facsimiles of this manuscript are given by Semler in his edition of Wetstein's Prolegomena (1764, Nos. 8, 9). Bianchini's estimate of its age (Evangeliarium Quadruplex, tom. ii. fol. 591, 2), as of the seventh century, is certainly too high.

better judges; indeed the facts are too numerous and too plain to be resisted. Thus, while in Rom. iv. 25 Cod. D reads δικαιωσιν (accentuated δικαίωσιν by D***), in which D*‡ changes ν into νην, the writer of Cod. E adopts δικαίωσινην with its monstrous accent: in 1 Cor. xv. 5 Cod. D reads μετα ταυτα τοις ενδεκα, D*** εἶτα τοῖς δώδεκα (again observe the accents), out of which Cod. E makes up μετα ταυεῖτα τοῖς δώενδεκα. In Gal. iv. 31 Cod. D has διο, which is changed by D*** into ἆρα: Cod. E mixes up the two into διᾶραο. Compare Tischendorf's notes on Eph. ii. 19; Heb. x. 17, 33, and Dr. Hort's longer specimen, Rom. xv. 31-3 (Introd. p. 254). The Latin version also is borrowed from Cod. D, but is more mixed, and may be of some critical use: the Greek is manifestly worthless, and should long since have been removed from the list of authorities. This copy is defective, Rom. viii. 21-33; ix. 15-25; 1 Tim. i. 1—vi. 15; Heb. xii. 8—xiii. 25.

Fᵃ. COD. COISLIN. I.

F. COD. AUGIENSIS in the Library of Trinity College, Cambridge (B. xvii. 1), is another Greek-Latin manuscript on 136 leaves of good vellum 4to (the *signatures* proving that seven more are lost, *see* p. 28), 9 inches by 7¼, with the two languages in parallel columns of twenty-eight lines on each page, the Greek being always inside, the Latin next the edge of the book. It is called from the monastery of Augia Dives or Major (Reichenau, or *rich meadow*), on a fertile island in the lower part of Lake Constance, to which it long appertained, and where it may even have been written, a thousand years since. By notices at the beginning and end we can trace it through the hands of G. M. Wepfer of Schaffhausen and of L. Ch. Mieg, who covered many of its pages with Latin notes wretchedly scrawled, but allowed Wetstein to examine it. In 1718 Bentley was induced by Wetstein to buy it at Heidelberg for 250 Dutch florins, and both he and Wetstein collated the Greek portion, the latter carelessly, but Bentley somewhat more fully in the margin of a Greek Testament (Oxon. 1675) still preserved in Trinity College (B. xvii. 8). Tischendorf in 1842, Tregelles in 1845, re-examined the book (which had been placed where it now is on the death of Bentley's nephew in 1787), and drew attention to the Latin version: in 1859 Scrivener published an edition of the Codex in common type, with Prolegomena and a photograph of one page (1 Tim. iii. 14—iv. 5)[1]. The Epistles of St. Paul are defective in Rom. i. 1—iii. 19; and the Greek only in 1 Cor. iii. 8-16; vi. 7-14; Col. ii. 1-8; Philem. 21-25; in which four places the Latin stands in its own column with no Greek over against it. In the Epistle to the Hebrews, the Greek being quite lost, the Latin occupies both columns: this Epistle alone has an Argument, almost verbatim the same as we read in the great Cod. Amiatinus of the Vulgate. At the end of the Epistle, and on the same page (fol. 139, *verso*), commences a kind of Postscript (having little connexion with the sacred text), the larger portion of which is met with under the title of Dicta Abbatis Pinophi, in the works of Rabanus Maurus, Archbishop of Mayence, who died in A.D. 856; from which circumstance the Cod. Augiensis has been referred to the ninth century. Palaeographical arguments also would lead us to the same conclusion. The Latin version (a modification of the Vulgate in its purest form, though somewhat tampered with in parts to make it suit the Greek text[2]) is written in the cursive minuscule character common in the age of Charlemagne. The Greek must have been taken from an archetype with the words continuously written; for not only are they miserably ill divided by the unlearned German[3] scribe, but his design (not always acted upon) was to put a single middle point at the end of each word. The Latin is exquisitely written, the Greek uncials are neat, but evidently the work of an unpractised hand, which soon changes from weariness. The shapes of *eta, theta, pi,* and other testing letters are such as we might have expected from the date; some others have an older look. Contrary to the more ancient custom, capitals, small but numerous, occur in the *middle* of the lines in both languages. Of the ordinary breathings[4] and accents there are no traces. Here and there we meet with a straight line, inclined between the horizontal and the acute accent, placed over an initial vowel, usually when it should be aspirated, but not always (e.g. ἰδιον 1 Cor. vi. 18).

[1] Facsimile of 1 Tim. vi. 19—2 Tim. i. 5 is given in Pal. Soc. Pt. ix (1879), Pl. 127.
[2] So 1 Cor. xii. 2. For ἄφωνα, Vulg. *muta*, Cod. Aug. ἄμορφα. Rom. viii. 26. For ἀσθενείαις, Vulg. *infirmitatem orationis nostrae*, Cod. Aug. τῆς δεήσεως, cf. 1 Cor. vii. 11. Infinitives for Imperatives.
[3] He betrays his nationality by placing 'waltet' *primâ manu* over the first εξουσειαζει, 1 Cor. vii. 4.
[4] In 1 Tim. iv. 2 the Latin h is inserted *secundâ manu* before υποκρισι.

Over ι and υ double or single points, or a comma, are frequently placed, especially if they begin a syllable; and occasionally a large comma or kind of circumflex over ι, ει, and some other vowels and diphthongs. The arrangement of the Greek forbids punctuation there; in the Latin we find the single middle point as a colon or after an abridgement, the semicolon (;) sometimes, the note of interrogation (?) when needed. Besides the universal forms of abridgement (see p. 49), ϗ and ƀ are frequent in the Greek, but no others: in the Latin the abbreviations are numerous, and some of them unusual: Scrivener (Cod. Augiensis Proleg. pp. xxxi–ii) has drawn up a list of them. This copy abounds as much as any with real variations from the common text, and with numberless errors of the pen, itacisms of vowels, and permutations of consonants. It exhibits many corrections, a few *primâ manu*, some unfortunately very recent, but by far the greater number in a hand almost contemporary with the manuscript, which has also inserted over the Greek, in 106 places, Latin renderings differing from those in the parallel column, but which in eighty-six of these 106 instances agree with the Latin of the sister manuscript.

G. Cod. Boernerianus, so called from a former possessor, but now in the Royal Library at Dresden. In the sixteenth century it belonged to Paul Junius of Leyden: it was bought dear at the book-sale of Peter Francius, Professor at Amsterdam, in 1705, by C. F. Boerner, a Professor at Leipsic, who lent it to Kuster to enrich his edition of Mill (1710), and subsequently to Bentley. The latter so earnestly wished to purchase it as a companion to Cod. F, that though he received it in 1719, it could not be recovered from him for five years, during which he was constantly offering high sums for it[1]: a copy, but not in Bentley's hand, had been already made (Trin. Coll. B. xvii. 2). Cod. G was published in full by Matthaei in 1791, in common type, with two facsimile

---

[1] Boerner's son tells the tale thirty years afterwards with amusing querulousness in his Catalogus Bibl. Boern. Lips. 1754, p. 6, cited by Matthaei Cod. Boern. p. xviii. But there must have been some misunderstanding on both sides, for it appears from a manuscript note in his copy of the Oxford N.T. of 1675 (Trin. Coll. B. xvii. 8), that Bentley considered Cod. G his own property; since after describing Cod. F before the Epistle to the Romans as his own, and as commencing at Rom. iii. 19, he adds 'Variae lectiones ex altero *nostro* MSto, ejusdem veteris exemplaris apographo.'

pages (1 Cor. ii. 9—iii. 3; 1 Tim. i. 1-10), and his edition is believed to be very accurate; Anger, Tischendorf, Tregelles, Böttiger and others who have examined it have only expressly indicated three errors [1]. Rettig has abundantly proved that, as it is exactly of the same size, so it once formed part of the same volume with Cod. Δ (*see* p. 157 and note): they must date towards the end of the ninth century, and may very possibly have been written in the monastery of St. Gall (where Δ still remains) by some of the Irish monks who flocked to those parts. That Cod. G has been in such hands appears from some very curious Irish lines at the foot of one of Matthaei's plates (fol. 23), which, after having long perplexed learned men, have at length been translated for Dr. Reeves, the eminent Celtic scholar [2]. All that we have said respecting the form of Cod. Δ applies to this portion of it: the Latin version (a specimen of the Old Latin, but as in Codd. Bezae and Laudianus much changed to suit the Greek) is cursive and interlinear; the Greek uncials coarse and peculiar; the punctuation chiefly a stop at the end of the words, which have no breathings nor accents. Its affinity to the Cod. Augiensis has no parallel in this branch of literature. Scrivener has noted all the differences between them at the foot of each page in his

[1] viz. ημας for υμας, Rom. xvi. 17; μετρους for μερους, Eph. iv. 16; εσκοτισμενος for -μενοι, iv. 18. Add to these στωμα for σωμα, 1 Cor. ix. 27, as cited by Bentley (Ellis, Critica Sacra, p. 36).

[2] By John O'Donovan, Editor of Irish Annals. I have been favoured with corrections by the late Dr. Todd, of Trinity College, Dublin, and recently by the Rev. Robert King of Ballymena, whose version I have ventured to adopt.

Téicht do róim [téicht do róim]	To come to Rome, to come to Rome,
Mór saido becic torbai	Much of trouble, little of profit,
Inrí chondaigi hifoss	The thing thou seekest here,
Manimbera latt ni fog bai	If thou bring not with thee, thou findest not.
Mór báis mór baile	Great folly, great madness,
Mór coll ceille mór mire	Great ruin of sense, great insanity,
Olais airchenn teicht dóecaib	Since thou hast set out for death,
Beith fó étoil maic Maire.	That thou shouldest be in disobedience to the Son of Mary.

The second stanza intimates that as the pilgrimage to Rome is at the risk of life, it is folly not to be at peace with Christ before we set out. The opening words 'To come to Rome' imply that the verses were written there by some disappointed pilgrim. Since the handwriting resembles that of the interlinear Latin, Mr. King suggests that both may have been the work of the Scottish Bishop Marcus, or of his nephew Moengal (Rettig, Cod. Δ, Prolegomena, p. xx), who called at St. Gall on their return from Rome, whence Marcus went homewards, leaving his books and Moengal behind him.

edition of Cod. F: they amount to but 1,982 places, whereof 578 are mere blunders of the scribe, 967 changes of vowels or itacisms, 166 interchanges of consonants, seventy-one grammatical or orthographical forms; the remaining 200 are real various readings, thirty-two of them relating to the article. While in Cod. F (whose first seven leaves are lost) the text commences at Rom. iii. 19, μω· λεγει, this portion is found complete in Cod. G, except Rom. i. 1–5; ii. 16–25. All the other lacunae of Cod. F occur also in Cod. G, which ends at Philem. 20 ἐν χρω: there is no Latin version to supply these gaps in Cod. G, but a blank space is always left, sufficient to contain what is missing. At the end of Philemon G writes Προσ λαουδακησασ¹ ᵃᵈ ˡᵃᵘᵈⁱᶜᵉⁿˢᵉˢ αρχεται ⁱⁿᶜⁱᵖⁱᵗ επιστολη ᵉᵖⁱˢᵗᵒˡᵃ, but neither that writing nor the Epistle to the Hebrews follows. It seems tolerably plain that one of these manuscripts was not copied immediately from the other, for while they often accord even in the strangest errors of the pen that men unskilled in Greek could fall into, their division of the Greek words, though equally false and absurd, is often quite different: it results therefore that they are independent transcripts of the same venerable archetype (probably stichometrical and some centuries older than themselves) which was written without any division between the words². From the form of the letters

---

¹ Here αου standing to represent *au* shows that the Greek is derived from the Latin, not *vice versá*.

² That Cod. G cannot have been taken from Cod. F appears both from matters connected with their respective Latin versions, and because F contains no trace of the vacant lines left in G at the end of Rom. xiv to receive ch. xvi. 25–27. But Dr. Hort (Journal of Philology, vol. iii. No. 5, pp. 67, 68 note) has come to think that F is a mere transcript of G, the scribe of the former being by far the more ignorant of the two. He meets our argument to the contrary stated above in the text, by alleging that in respect to the division of words F is free from no outrageous portent found in G, while it has to answer for many of its own. But (to take our examples from one open leaf) if the writer of F were so helplessly ignorant as Dr. Hort represents, how could he have set right G's error in 1 Tim. iv. 7, reading και · γρωδεις for G's και αιγρωδεις? Again, if F had before him an undivided manuscript, one can easily account for such monsters as in 1 Tim. iv. 2 και · καυτη ριασ μενων· F (*photographed page*), but no one could possibly have so written with G's κεκαυτηριασμενων before him. That the two copies were compared together in after times seems evident from the fact stated in p. 179, that Latin renderings from G stand in eighty-six places above the Greek of F. It was at the same time perhaps that some ill-divided words in F were corrected by means of a loop from the Greek of G: e.g. 2 Cor. i. 3 οικτιρμων G, οικ ͜ τιρμων F; ii. 14 θριαμβευοντι G, θριαμ ͜ βευοντι F; iv. 9 ενκαταλιμπαννομενοι G, εν · καταλιμπαν ͜ νομενοι F; ver. 15 πλεονασασα G, πλεονα ͜ σασα F. 'Mr. Hort's

and other circumstances Cod. F may be deemed somewhat but not much the older; its corrector *secundâ manu* evidently had both the Greek and the Latin of Cod. G before him, and Rabanus, in whose works the Dicta Pinophi are preserved (p. 178), was the great antagonist of Godeschalk, on whom the annotator of Codd. ΔG bears so hard. Cod. G is in 4to, of ninety-nine leaves, with twenty-one lines in each. The line indicating breathing (if such be its use, *see* p. 178) and the mark > employed to fill up spaces (p. 51), more frequent in it than in F.

Since Dr. Scrivener wrote the above, a very valuable little treatise—a 'specimen primum'—has been given to the learned world by Herr P. Corssen[1], and a most clear and carefully argued paper has been sent to the editor by the Rev. Nicholas Pocock of Clifton. Both Herr Corssen and Mr. Pocock agree in showing that F was not derived from G, nor G from F, but that they come from the same original. Both agree, again, that the Greek version is derived, at least in large measure, from the Latin, as in such instances as the following, which are supplied by Mr. Pocock, who holds, and appears to prove, that F and G were copied from an interlinear manuscript: *ut sciatis*, ινα οιδαται (F, G), 1 Thess. iii. 3; *sicut cancer ut serpat*, ως γαγγρα, ινα νομηνεξει (G), 2 Tim. ii. 17, F having the same reading, only dividing the last word; Gal. iv. 3 *eramus autem servientes*, ημεθα δε δουλωμενοι (F, G). Herr Corssen considers that a Latin was the scribe of the original, that it was written in Italy, and that it was better than the Claromontanus (D), to which it had affinities, this last having an amended text with corrections from the Greek. The original of all three he supposes to date from not before the fifth century. But in some of these last suppositions we are getting upon the ocean of conjecture.

view, that F was copied directly from G' (writes Bishop Lightfoot very gently, Journal of Philology, vol. iii. No. 6, p. 210, note), 'deserves consideration, and may prove true, though his arguments do not seem quite conclusive.' Lightfoot elsewhere pronounces that 'the divergent phenomena of the two Latin texts' seem unfavourable to Dr. Hort's hypothesis (Ep. to Coloss. p. 355, note 2). But the latter still adheres to it with characteristic firmness : 'we believe F to be as certainly in its Greek text a transcript of G [as E is of D]; if not, it is an inferior copy of the same immediate exemplar' (Introd. p. 150). Yet why 'inferior'?

[1] Epistularum Paulinarum codd. Gr. et Lat. scriptas Augiensem Boernerianum Claromontanum examinavit, &c. Petrus Corssen, H. Fienche Kiliensis, 1889.

H. COD. COISLIN. 202 is a very precious fragment, of which twelve leaves are in the Imperial Library at Paris; nine are in the monastery or laura of St. Athanasius at Mount Athos, and have been edited by M. Duchesne in the 'Archives des missions scientifiques et littéraires' (1876); two more are at Moscow, and have been described by Matthaei (D. Pauli Epp. ad Hebr. et Col. Riga, 1784, p. 58); some others are in the Antonian Library of St. Petersburg (three); some more in the Imperial Library as described by Muralt (two), or in that of Bishop Porphyry (one), or at Turin (two). The leaves at Paris contain 1 Cor. x. 22–29; xi. 9–16; 1 Tim. iii. 7–13; Tit. i. 1–3; 15—ii. 5; iii. 13–15; Heb. ii. 11–16; iii. 13–18; iv. 12–15. At Mount Athos are 2 Cor. x. 18—xi. 6; xi. 12—xii. 2; Gal. i. 1–4; ii. 4–17; iv. 30—v. 5. At Moscow, Heb. x. 1–7; 32–38. At St. Petersburg, 2 Cor. iv. 2–7; 1 Thess. ii. 9–13; iv. 5–11 (Antonian; Gal. i. 4–10; ii. 9–14 (Imperial). In the Library of Bishop Porphyry, Col. iii. 4–11; and at Turin, 1 Tim. vi. 9–13; 2 Tim. ii. 1–9. They are in quarto, with large square uncials of about sixteen lines on a page, and date from the sixth century. Breathings and accents are added by a later hand, which retouched this copy (*see* Silvestre, Paléographie Universelle, Nos. 63, 64). These leaves, which comprise one of our best authorities for stichometrical writing, were used in A.D. 1218 to bind some other manuscripts on Mount Athos, and thence came into the library of Coislin, Bishop of Metz. Montfaucon has published Cod. H in his 'Bibliotheca Coisliniana,' but Tischendorf, who transcribed it, projected a fuller and more accurate edition. He observed at Paris in 1865 an additional passage, 2 Cor. iv. 4–6 (Monum. sacr. ined. vol. ix. p. xiv, note), and cites Cod. H in his eighth edition on 1 Tim. vi. 19; Heb. x. 1–6; 34–38. The subscriptions, which appear due to Euthalius of Sulci [1], written in vermilion, are not retouched, and consequently have neither breathings nor accents. Besides arguments to the Epistles, we copy the following final subscription from Tischendorf (N. T. 1859, p. clxxxix): ἔγραψα καὶ ἐξεθέμην κατὰ δύναμιν στειχηρὸν· τόδε τὸ τεῦχος παύλου τοῦ ἀποστόλου πρὸς ἐγγραμμὸν καὶ εὐκατάλημπτον ἀνάγνωσιν. τῶν καθ' ἡμᾶς ἀδελφῶν· παρῶν ἀπάντων τολμης συγγνώμην αἰτῶ. εὐχὴ τῇ ὑπὲρ ἐμῶν· τὴν

---

[1] *See* p. 63, note 1.

συνπεριφοράν κομιζόμενος· ἀντεβλήθη δὲ ἡ βίβλος· πρὸς τὸ ἐν καισαρία ἀντίγραφον τῆς βιβλιοθήκης τοῦ ἁγίου παμφίλου χειρὶ γεγραμμένον αὐτοῦ (see p. 55, note 1). From this subscription we may conclude with Dr. Field (Proleg. in Hexapla Origenis, p. xcix) that the noble Library at Caesarea was still safe in the sixth century, though it may have perished A.D. 638, when that city was taken by the Saracens.

I. COD. TISCHENDORFIAN. II, at St. Petersburg. Add also two large leaves of the sixth century, elegantly written, without breathings or accents, containing 2 Cor. i. 20—ii. 12. Described by Tischendorf, Notitia Cod. Sin. Append. p. 50, cited as O in his eighth edition of the N. T.

K. COD. MOSQUENSIS.

L. COD. ANGELICUS at Rome.

M. CODEX RUBER is peculiar for the beautifully bright red colour of the ink [1], the elegance of the small uncial characters, and the excellency and critical value of the text. Two folio leaves, containing Heb. i. 1—iv. 3; xii. 20—xiii. 25, once belonged to Uffenbach, then to J. C. Wolff, who bequeathed them to the Public Library (Johanneum) of Hamburg (see Cod. H of the Gospels. To the same manuscript pertain fragments of two leaves used in binding Cod. Harleian. 5613 in the British Museum, and seen at once by Griesbach, who first collated them (Symbol. Crit. vol. ii. p. 164, &c.), to be portions of the Hamburg fragment [2]. Each page in both contains two columns, of forty-five lines in the Hamburg, of thirty-eight in the London leaves. The latter comprise 1 Cor. xv. 52—2 Cor. i. 15; x. 13—xii. 5; reckoning both fragments, 196 verses in all. Tischendorf has since found one leaf more. Henke in 1800 edited the Hamburg portion, Tregelles collated it twice, and Tischendorf in 1855 published the text of both in full in his 'Anecdota Sacra et Profana,' but corrected in the second edition, 1861 (Praef. xvi),

---

[1] Scholz describes Codd. 196, 362, 366 of the Gospels as also written in red ink. See too Evan. 254.

[2] Dr. C. R. Gregory has read a few words more of this MS. Griesbach and Scholz number the London part as 64, the Hamburg part as 53.

five mistakes in his printed text. The letters are a little unusual in form, perhaps about the tenth century in date; but though sometimes joined in the same word, can hardly be called *semicursive*. Our facsimile (Plate xii, No. 34) is from the London fragment: the graceful, though peculiar, shapes both of *alpha* and *mu* (*see* p. 37, ter) closely resemble those in some writing of about the same age, added to the venerable Leyden Octateuch, on a page published in facsimile by Tischendorf (Monum. sacr. ined. vol. iii). Accents and breathings are given pretty correctly and constantly: *iota* ascript occurs three times (2 Cor. i. 1; 4; Heb. xiii. 21)[1]; only ten *itacisms* occur, and ν ἐφελκυστικόν (as it is called) is rare. The usual stop is the single point in its three positions, with a change in power, as in Cod. E of the Gospels. The interrogative (;) occurs once (Heb. iii. 17), and > is often repeated to fill up space, or, in a smaller size, to mark quotations. After the name of each of the Epistles (2 Cor. and Heb.) in their titles we read ἐκτεθεισα ὡς ἐν πινακι, which Tischendorf thus explains; that whereas it was customary to prefix an argument to each Epistle, these words, originally employed to introduce the argument, were retained even when the argument was omitted. Henke's account of the expression looks a little less forced, that this manuscript was set forth ὡς ἐν πινακι, that is, in vermilion, after the pattern of Imperial letters patent.

N. (O^d Hort.) Two leaves of the ninth century at St. Petersburg, containing Gal. v. 14—vi. 2; Heb. v. 8—vi. 10.

O. (N^c Tisch.) FRAGMENTA MOSQUENSIA used as early as A.D. 975 in binding a volume of Gregory Nazianzen now at Moscow (S. Synodi 61). Matthaei describes them on Heb. x. 1: they contain only the twelve verses Heb. x. 1–3; 3–7; 32–34; 35–38. These very ancient leaves may possibly be as old as the sixth century, for their letters resemble in shape those in Cod. H

---

[1] Griesbach (Symbol. Critic. vol. ii. p. 166) says that in the Harleian fragment 'Iota bis tantum aut ter subscribitur, semel postscribitur, plerumque omittitur,' overlooking the second ascript. Scrivener repeats this statement about *ι* subscript (Cod. Augiens. Introd. p. lxxii), believing he had verified it: but Tischendorf cannot see the subscripts, nor can Scrivener on again consulting Harl. 5613 for the purpose. Tregelles too says, 'I have not seen a *sub*scribed iota in any uncial document' (Printed Text, p. 158, note).

which the later hand has so coarsely renewed; but they are more probably a little later.

O^a. One unpublished double leaf brought by Tischendorf to St. Petersburg from the East, of the sixth century, containing 2 Cor. i. 20—ii. 12.

O^b of the same date, at Moscow, contains Eph. iv. 1–18.

P. Cod. Porphyrianus.

Q. Tischendorf also discovered in 1862 at St. Petersburg five or six leaves of St. Paul, written on papyrus of the fifth century. From the extreme brittleness of the leaves only portions can be read. He cites them at 1 Cor. vi. 13, 14; vii. 3, 13, 14. These also Porphyry brought from the East. It contains 1 Cor. i. 17–20; vi. 13–15; 16–18; vii. 3, 4, 10, 11, 12–14, with defects. This is the only papyrus manuscript of the New Testament written with uncials.

R. Cod. Cryptoferratensis Z. β. 1. is a palimpsest fragment of the end of the seventh or the eighth century, cited by Caspar René Gregory as first used by Tischendorf. It is one leaf, containing 2 Cor. xi. 9-19. Edited by Cozza, and published amongst other old fragments at Rome in 1867 with facsimile (Greg., p. 435).

S. From Laura of Athos.

T. Paris, Louvre, Egyptian Museum, 7332 [iv–vi], $5\frac{3}{4} \times 4$, two small fragments, 1 Tim. vi. 3; iii. 15, 16. *See* Gregory, p. 441, who, however, unconsciously classes it as an Evan.

ℶ. Rom. Vat. Gr. 2061.

III. *Manuscripts of the Apocalypse.*

א. Cod. Sinaiticus.

A. Cod. Alexandrinus.

B. Cod. Vaticanus 2066 (formerly 105 in the Library of the Basilian monks in the city) was judiciously substituted by Wetstein for the modern portion of the great Vatican MS., collated by Mico, and published in 1796 by Ford in his 'Appendix' to Codex Alexandrinus, as also in 1868 by Vercellone and Cozza[1]. It is an uncial copy of about the end of the eighth century, and the volume also contains in the same hand Homilies of Basil the Great and of Gregory of Nyssa, &c. It was first known from a notice (by Vitali) and facsimile in Bianchini's Evangeliarium Quadruplex (1749), part i. vol. ii. p. 524 (facs. p. 505, tab. iv): Wetstein was promised a collation of it by Cardinal Quirini, who seems to have met with unexpected hindrances, as the papers only arrived after the text of the New Testament was printed, and then proved very loose and defective. When Tischendorf was at Rome in 1843, though forbidden to collate it afresh (in consequence, as we now know, of its having been already printed in Mai's then unpublished volumes of the Codex Vaticanus), he was permitted to make a facsimile of a few verses, and while thus employed he so far contrived to elude the watchful custodian, as to compare the whole manuscript with a modern Greek Testament. The result was given in his Monumenta sacra inedita (1846), pp. 407-432, with a good facsimile; but (as was natural under the unpromising circumstances—'*arrepta potius quam lecta*' is his own confession) Tregelles in 1845 was able to observe several points which he had overlooked, and more have come to light since Mai's edition has appeared. In 1866, however, Tischendorf was allowed to transcribe this document at leisure, and re-published it in full in his Appendix N. T. Vaticani, 1869, pp. 1-20.

This Codex is now known to contain the whole of the Apocalypse, a fact which the poor collation that Wetstein managed to procure had rendered doubtful. It is rather an octavo than a folio or quarto; the uncials being of a peculiar kind, simple and unornamented, leaning a little to the right (*see* p. 41, note): they hold a sort of middle place between square and oblong characters. The shape of *beta* is peculiar, the two loops to the right nowhere touching each other, and *psi* has degenerated into

---

[1] Tregelles, wishing to reserve the letter B for the great Codex Vaticanus 1209, called this copy first L (N. T. Part iv. p. iii), and afterwards Q (N. T. Part vi. p. i). Surely Mr. Vansittart was right (Journal of Philology, vol. ii. No. 3, p. 41) in protesting against a change so needless and inconvenient; nor has Tischendorf adopted it in his eighth edition of the N. T.

the form of a cross (*see* Plate iii, No. 7): *delta, theta, xi* are also of the latest uncial fashion. The breathings and accents are *primâ manu*, and pretty correct; the rule of the grammarians respecting the change of power of the single point in punctuation according to its change of position is now regularly observed. The scarcity of old copies of the Apocalypse renders this uncial of some importance, and it often confirms the readings of the older codices ℵAC, though on the whole it resembles them considerably less than does Cod. P, and agrees in preference with the later or more ordinary cursives.

C. CODEX EPHRAEMI.

P. CODEX PORPHYRIANUS.

Note. Of the three large uncials which contain the Apocalypse, ℵA are complete, but C has lost 171 verses out of 405. In the 286 places wherein the three are available, and Lachmann, Tregelles, and Tischendorf, one or all, depart from the Received text, ℵAC agree fifty-two times, ℵA seventeen, ℵC twenty-six, AC eighty-two, and this last combination supplies the best readings: ℵ stands alone twenty-three times, A fifty-nine, C twenty-seven. When C has failed us ℵA agree fifty-two times and differ eighty-eight.

CHAPTER VII.

CURSIVE MANUSCRIPTS OF THE GOSPELS.

Part I.

THE later manuscripts of the Greek Testament, written in cursive characters from the tenth down to the fifteenth century or later, are too numerous to be minutely described in an elementary work like the present. We shall therefore speak of them with all possible brevity, dwelling only on a few which present points of especial interest, and employing certain abbreviations, a list of which we subjoin for the reader's convenience [1].

Abbreviations used in the following Catalogue.

Act. MS. of Acts and Catholic Epistles.
Am. Ammonian Sections (so-called) in the margin of MSS.
Apoc. MS. of the Apocalypse.
Apost. MS. of Apostolos.
'Αναγν. 'Αναγνώσματα or ἀναγνώσεις, readings or *lections*: here marks of the lections in the margin or at the head or foot of pages, or the computation of them at the end of the book.
Argent. Written in silver letters, either capitals or all.

'Αρχή and τέλος, see *Lect.*
Aur. Written in gold letters, either capitals (*l. l.*) or all.
Carp. Epistle to Carpianus.
Chart. Written on paper.
Chart. by itself = linen paper.
Chart. b. = *bombycina*, or cotton paper.
Cols. Columns. When the MS. is written only in one, no notice is given.
Coll. Collated.
Curs. Cursive MSS.
Eus. Eusebian Canons standing in the margin under Ammonian Sections.

---

[1] Very many corrections have been made in the following Catalogue as well from investigations of my own as from information kindly furnished to me by Mr. H. Bradshaw, University Librarian at Cambridge, by Professor Hort, by Mr. A. A. Vansittart, late Fellow of Trinity College there [d. 1882], by Mr. W. Kelly, and especially by Dean Burgon, to whom the present edition is more deeply indebted than it would be possible to acknowledge in detail. His series of Letters addressed to me in the *Guardian* newspaper (1873) contains but a part of the help he has afforded towards the preparation of this and the second edition. Ed. iii.

Eus. t. Tables of so-called Eusebian Canons prefixed to the Gospels.
Euthal. κεφ. Euthalian κεφάλαια found in Acts and Epistles.
Evan. Evangelia.
Evst. Evangelistaria.
Ff. Folia, or leaves. The figures in brackets immediately appended denote the number of lines on a page.
Harm. Harmony, sometimes given with κεφ. t.
Insp. Inspected.
Κεφ. Letters in the margin denoting the κεφάλαια majora.
Κεφ. t. Tables of κεφ. prefixed to each book.
Lect. Notices of proper lessons for feasts, &c., in the margin, or above, or below, or interspersed with the text. Often marked with ἀρχή and τέλος at beginning and end.
Membr. On vellum.

Men. A menology, or calendar, of Saints' Days at the beginning or end of a book.
Mus. Musical notes, especially in Evangelistaria.
Mut. That the copy is mutilated.
Orn. Ornamented.
Paul. MS. of St. Paul's Epistles.
Pict. Illuminated with pictures.
Prol. Contains a prologue or ὑπόθεσις.
'Ρήμ. Where the ῥήματα, or phrases are numbered.
Syn. A synaxarion, or calendar, of daily lessons—also called *eclogadion*.
Στίχ. Where the στίχοι, or lines, are numbered.
Subscr. Subscriptions (ὑπογραφαί) at the end of books.
Τίτλ. Titles of κεφ. at the head or foot of the pages.
Vers. Greek or Latin metrical verses at beginning or end of books.
Unc. Uncial MS.

The other Abbreviations will be evident upon perusing this work. Where *Chart.* is not printed, the MS. is written on vellum. The Latin numeral within square brackets denotes the date of the book, whether fixed by a subscription in the book itself, or approximated by other means, e. g. [xiii] indicates a book of the thirteenth century. The Arabic numerals within ordinary brackets denote the number of lines on a page. Thus 297 (38) = 297 leaves and thirty-eight lines in a page. The names within parentheses indicate the *collators* or *inspectors* of each manuscript, and if it has been satisfactorily examined, an asterisk is prefixed to the number by which it is known. If the copy contain other portions of the New Testament, its notation in those portions is always given. Measurements where given are in inches [1].

(1) *Manuscripts of the Gospels.*

*1. (Act. 1, Paul. 1.) Basiliensis A. N. iv. 2 at Basle [x, Burgon xii or xiii], 7¾ × 4½, ff. 297 (38); *prol., pict., τίτλ., syn., ἀναγν.* in Acts and Epp. by later hand. Hebrews last in Paul. Gospels bound up last of all. Among the illuminations were what have been said to be pictures of the Emperor Leo the Wise [886–911] and his son Constantine Porphyrogenitus, but all the beautiful miniatures were stolen prior to 1860–2, except one before St. John's Gospel. Its later history is the same as that of Cod. E of the Gospels: it was known to Erasmus; it was borrowed by Reuchlin, a few extracts given by Bengel

---

[1] For the Authorities chiefly consulted in the list of Cursive Manuscripts given in this edition, see Appendix A to this volume; and for a list of Facsimiles, see Appendix B.

(Bas. γ), collated by Wetstein, and recently in the Gospels by C. L. Roth and Tregelles, who have compared their results. Our facsimile (No. 23) gives an excellent notion of the elegant and minute style of writing, which is fully furnished with breathings, accents, and ι ascript. The initial letters are gilt, and on the first page of each Gospel the full point is a large gilt ball. In the Gospels the text adheres frequently to the uncials Codd. ℵB, BL and such cursives as 118, 131, and especially 209 (Insp. by Burgon, Hoskier, Greg.).

2. Basil. A. N. iv. 1 [xv or earlier], $7\frac{3}{4} \times 6$, ff. 248 (20), *subscr.*, κεφ. t., κεφ.(not John), τίτλ., *Am.*, is the inferior manuscript chiefly used by Erasmus for his first edition of the N. T. (1516), with press corrections by his hand, and barbarously scored with red chalk to suit his pages. The monks at Basle had bought it for two Rhenish florins (Bengel, Wetstein, Burgon, Hoskier, Greg.).

3. (Act. 3, Paul. 3.) Cod. Corsendonck. [xii], 4to, $9\frac{3}{4} \times 7$, ff. 451 (24), *Carp., Eus. t.,* κεφ. *t., prol., pict.,* κεφ., τίτλ., *Am., Eus., syn.*, once belonging to a convent at Corsendonck near Turnhout, now in the Imperial Library at Vienna (Forlos. 15, Kollar. 5). It was lent to Erasmus for his second edition in 1519, as he testifies on the first leaf (Alter). It had been collated before Alter by J. Walker for Bentley, when in 'the Dominican Library, Brussels.' This collation is unpublished (Trin. Coll. B. xvii. 34): Ellis, Bentleii Critica Sacra, p. xxix (Greg.).

4. Cod. Regius 84 [xii], $7\frac{1}{4} \times 5\frac{3}{4}$, ff. 212 (27), κεφ. t., κεφ., τίτλ., *Am., Eus., lect., syn., men., subscr.,* στίχ., in the Royal Library at Paris (designated RI by Tischendorf), was rightly recognized by Le Long as Robert Stephen's γ' (*see* Chap. V). Mill notices its affinity to the Latin versions and the Complutensian edition (N. T. Prol. § 1161); *mut.* in Matt. ii. 9–20; John i. 49—iii. 11; forty-nine verses. It is clumsily written and contains *syn.* from some Fathers (Scholz, Greg.).

5. (Act. 5, Paul. 5.) Paris, National (Library), Greek 106 [xii or later], is Stephen's δ' : $8\frac{1}{4} \times 6\frac{1}{4}$, ff. 348 (28), *prob.,* κεφ. t., κεφ., τίτλ., *Am., Eus.* Carefully written and full of flourishes (Wetstein, Scholz, Greg.).

6. (Act. 6, Paul. 6.) Par. Nat. Gr. 112 [xi or later], is Stephen's ε' ; in text it much resembles Codd. 4, 5, and 75. 12mo, $5\frac{1}{2} \times 4\frac{1}{8}$, ff. 235, *prol.,* κεφ. *t.,* κεφ., τίτλ., *Am., syn.* with St. Chrysostom's Liturgy, *men.* (Wetstein, Griesbach, Scholz). This exquisite manuscript is written in characters so small, that some pages require a glass to read them. Scholz collated Matt., Mark i—iv, John vii, viii (Greg.).

7. Par. Nat. Gr. 71 [xi], is Stephen's ϛ'. $8 \times 6\frac{1}{4}$, ff. 186 (29), *prol., syn., Carp., Eus. t., pict.,* τίτλ. with metrical paraphrase, *Am., Eus., men.*, very full *lect.* In style not unlike Cod. 4, but neater (Wetst., Scholz, Abbé Martin, Greg.).

8. Par. Nat. Gr. 49 [xi], $11\frac{1}{4} \times 8\frac{1}{2}$, ff. 199 (22), two columns, proved by Mr. Vansittart to be Stephen's ζ'[1]: beautifully written in two columns

---

[1] Stephen's margin cites ζ' eighty-four times in the Gospels, usually in company with several others, but alone in Mark vi. 20; xiv. 15; Luke i. 37. Since Evan. 18 or Reg. 47 contains the whole N. T., and Stephen cites ζ' in the Acts

on the page. *Carp., Eus. t., prol., pict.,* κεφ., τίτλ., *lect., men., Am., Eus., syn.* (Wetst., Scholz, Greg.).

9. Par. Nat. Gr. 83 [A.D. 1167, when 'Manuel Porphyrogenitus was ruler of Constantinople, Amauri of Jerusalem, William II of Sicily': this note (derived from Wetstein) is now nearly obliterated], $9\frac{1}{4} \times 6\frac{3}{4}$, ff. 298(20), is probably Stephen's ιβ'. *Carp., Eus. t., pict.,* κεφ., τίτλ., *Am., syn., mut., men., subscr.,* στίχ. (first leaf of St. John). It once belonged to Peter Stella. The style is rather barbarous, and ornamentation peculiar (Kuster's Paris 3, Scholz, Greg.).

10. Par. Nat. Gr. 91 [xiii or later], $7\frac{1}{2} \times 5\frac{7}{8}$, ff. 275 (24), given in 1439 to a library of Canons Regular at Verona by Dorotheus Archbishop of Mitylene, when he came to the Council of Florence. Scholz tells us that it was 'antea Joannis Huraultii Boistallerii.' Griesbach mistook this copy for Reg. 95, olim $\frac{2865}{3}$, which is Kuster's Paris 1 and Wetstein's Cod. 10, being Cod. 285 of Scholz and our own list (Burgon, *Guardian,* Jan. 15, 1873). *Carp., Eus. t., pict.,* κεφ., τίτλ., *Am., Eus., lect., syn., men.* (Griesbach, Scholz, Greg.).

11. Par. Nat. Gr. 121–2 [xii or earlier], in two small volumes, $6\frac{3}{8} \times 3\frac{5}{8}$, neatly written, ff. 230 and 274 (16), *Eus. t.,* κεφ., τίτλ., *Am., Eus.* It also once belonged to Teller (Kuster's Paris 4, Scholz, Greg.).

12. Par. Nat. Gr. 230 [xi], $10\frac{3}{8} \times 8\frac{1}{8}$, 294 (21), *prol., pict., Eus. t.,* κεφ. *t.,* κεφ., τίτλ., with a commentary, that on St. Mark being Victor's of Antioch (Greg.).

13. Par. Nat. Gr. 50 [xii], $9\frac{1}{4} \times 7\frac{1}{2}$, ff. 170 (29), κεφ. *t.,* κεφ., τίτλ., *Am. lect., syn., men., subscr.,* στίχ., is Kuster's Paris 6, who says that it supplied him with more various readings than all the rest of his Paris manuscripts put together. This, like Codd. 10, 11, once belonged to Teller: it is not correctly written. *Syn., mut.* in Matt. i. 1—ii. 20; xxvi. 33–53; xxvii. 26—xxviii. 10; Mark i. 20–45; John xxi. 3–25; 163 verses (Kuster, Wetstein, Griesbach, Begtrup in 1797). This manuscript was collated in 1868 by Professor W. H. Ferrar, Fellow of Trinity College, Dublin [d. 1871], who regarded Codd. 13, 69, 124, 346 as transcripts of one archetype, which he proposed to restore by comparing the four copies together. His design was carried out by Professor T. K. Abbott, Fellow and Tutor of Trinity College. For facsimiles of them all, &c., *see* 'Collation of Four Important Manuscripts of the Gospels,' &c. Dublin, 1877 (Greg.).

14. Par. Nat. Gr. 70 [xii or xiii, Greg. x], $6\frac{7}{8} \times 4\frac{5}{8}$, ff. 392 (17), once Cardinal Mazarin's; was Kuster's Paris 7. A facsimile of this beautiful copy, with round conjoined minuscule letters, regular breathings and

---

once (ch. xvii. 5), in the Catholic Epistles seven times, in the Pauline twenty-seven, in the Apocalypse never; Reg. 47 has been suggested to have been Stephen's ζ', rather than Cod. 8 or Reg. 49. On testing the two with Steph. ζ' in eight places, Mr. Vansittart found that they both agreed with it in five (Matt. xx. 12; Mark vi. 20; x. 52; Luke vi. 37; John vi. 58), but that in the remaining three (Mark xii. 31; Luke i. 37; John x. 32) Reg. 49 agreed with ζ', while Reg. 47 did not.

accents, is given in the 'Paléographie Universelle,' No. 78, and in Montfaucon, Pal. Gr., p. 282. *Mut.* Matt. i. 1-9; iii. 16—iv. 9. Κεφ. *t.*, *pict.*, Paschal Canon, *Carp.*, *Eus. t.*, *κεφ. t.*, *κεφ.*, *τίτλ.*, *Am.*, *Eus.* (Kuster, Scholz).

15. Par. Nat. Gr. 64 [x], $7\frac{1}{4} \times 5\frac{3}{8}$, ff. 225 (23), *Carp.*, *prol.*, *κεφ. t.*, *κεφ.*, *τίτλ.*, *Am.*, *lect.*, *men.*, is Kuster's Paris 8. *Eus. t.*, *syn.*, *pict.* very superb: the first three pages are written in gold, with exquisite miniatures, four on p. 2, four on p. 3, Burgon. (Kuster, Scholz, Greg.)

16. Par. Nat. Gr. 54, formerly 1881 [xiv], $12\frac{3}{8} \times 10$, ff.?, 2 cols., *Eus. t.* (Latin), *pict.*, *κεφ.*, *τίτλ.*, *Am.* (Matt. and Mark), *lect.*, *subscr.*; once belonged to the Medici; it has a Latin version in parts; *mut.* Mark xvi. 6-20. *Eus. t.*, *syn.*, *pict.* (Wetstein, Scholz). This gorgeous and 'right royal' copy was never quite finished, but is unique in respect of being written in four colours, vermilion, lake, blue, and black, according to the character of the contents (Burgon, Greg.).

17. Par. Nat. Gr. 55 [xvi], $11\frac{3}{4} \times 8\frac{1}{4}$, ff. 353 (25), 2 cols., has the Latin Vulgate version: it was neatly written, not by George Hermonymus the Spartan (but see Greg.), as Wetstein guesses, but by a Western professional scribe, Burgon. It once belonged to Cardinal Bourbon. *Syn.*, *pict.* very elegant, *lect.* (Wetstein, Griesbach, Scholz).

18. (Act. 113, Paul. 132, Apoc. 51.) Par. Nat. Gr. 47, formerly 2241 [A.D. 1364], $11\frac{1}{2} \times 8\frac{3}{4}$, ff. 444 (23), *prol.*, *κεφ. t.*, *κεφ.*, *lect.*, *ἀναγν.*, *subscr.*, *στίχ.*, *syn.*, *men.*; bought in 1687, and written at Constantinople. It is one of the few copies of the whole New Testament (*see* p. 72, note), and was given by Nicephorus Cannabetes to the monastery τοῦ ζωοδότου χριστοῦ ἐν τῷ τοῦ Μυζιθρᾶ (Misitra) τῆς Λακεδαίμονος κάστρῳ. Two *syn.* between the Pauline Epistles and the Apocalypse, psalms, hymns (Scholz, Greg., Reiche).

19. Par. Nat. Gr. 189, formerly 1880 [xii], $12\frac{1}{2} \times 9\frac{1}{4}$, ff. 387, *κεφ. t.*, *κεφ.*, *τίτλ.*, *Am.*, *Eus.*, *subscr.*, Wetstein's 1869, once belonged to the Medici, *pict.*, with Victor's commentary on St. Mark, a catena to St. John, and scholia to the other Gospels. In marvellous condition, with much gold ornamentation (Scholz, Greg.).

20. Par. Nat. Gr. 188, formerly 1883 [xii], $13\frac{1}{8} \times 9\frac{5}{8}$, a splendid folio, ff. 274, *κεφ. t.*, *κεφ.*, *τίτλ.*, *Am.*, *Eus.*, *lect.*, *subscr.*, *στίχ.*—all by second hand (Greg.), brought from the East in 1669. It is beautifully written, and contains catenae, Victor's commentary on St. Mark, and other treatises enumerated by Scholz, who collated most of it. At the end of SS. Mark, Luke, and John 'dicitur etiam hoc evangelium ex accuratis codicibus esse exscriptum, nec non collatum' (Scholz). A second (or perhaps the original) hand has been busy here to assimilate the text to that of Codd. 215, 300, or to some common model. In Cod. 215 the foregoing subscription is appended to all the Four Gospels, and the other contents correspond exactly (Burgon, Last Twelve Verses of St. Mark, pp. 119, 279). See on Evann. Λ, 428. Collated by W. F. Rose.

21. Par. Nat. Gr. 68, formerly 2860 [x], $9 \times 7\frac{1}{8}$, ff. 203, 2 cols., *pict.*, *κεφ.*, *τίτλ.*, *Am.*, *men.*, with *syn.* on paper in a later hand (Scholz, Greg.).

22. Par. Nat. Gr. 72, once Colbert. 2467 [xi], $10\frac{1}{4} \times 7\frac{1}{2}$, ff. 232 (22),

contains remarkable readings. John xiv. 22—xvi. 27. Fully collated by the Rev. W. F. Rose (*see* Evan. 563). It begins Matt. ii. 2, six leaves containing Matt. v. 25—viii. 4 being misplaced before it. Κεφ. *t.*, τίτλ., κεφ., *Am.*, *Eus.* partial, *subscr.* No *lect.*, ἀρχ., or *mut.* Matt. iv. 20—v. 25; τέλ. p. m. A beautiful copy, singularly free from itacisms and errors from homœoteleuton, and very carefully accentuated, with slight illuminated headings to the Gospels, which I recently had the pleasure of inspecting (Wetstein, Scholz, Scriv., Greg.).

23. Par. Nat. Gr. 77, Colbert. 3947 [xi], 9 × 7¼, 4to, ff. 230, κεφ. *t.*, κεφ., τίτλ., *Am.*, *lect.*, with the Latin Vulgate version down to Luke iv. 18. *Mut.* Matt. i. 1–17; Luke xxiv. 46—John ii. 20; xxi. 24, 25; ninety-six verses (Scholz).

24. Par. Nat. Gr. 178, Colbert. 4112 [xi, Greg. x], 10¼ × 5⅞, ff. 240, with a commentary (Victor's on St. Mark), *prol.*, κεφ. *t.*, κεφ., τίτλ., *Am.*, *Eus.*, and also *syn.*, but in a later hand. *Mut.* Matt. xxvii. 20—Mark iv. 22; 186 verses (Griesb., Scholz). See Burgon, *ubi supra*, p. 228. Used in Cramer's Cat. on St. Mark, 1840 (Greg.).

25. Par. Nat. Gr. 191, Colbert. 2259 [x, Greg. xi], 11¾ × 9⅛, ff. 292, with Victor's commentary on St. Mark, and scholia, κεφ. *t.*, κεφ., τίτλ., *lect.* (partial). 'Grandly written,' but very imperfect, wanting about 715 verses, viz. Matt. xxiii. 1—xxv. 42; Mark i. 1—vii. 36; Luke viii. 31–41; ix. 44–54; x. 39—xi. 4; John xiii. 19?—xxi. 25 (Griesbach, Scholz, Greg., Martin).

26. Par. Nat. Gr. 78, Colbert. 4078 [xi], 9½ × 7¼, ff. 179 (27), neatly and correctly written by Paul a priest. *Carp.*, *Eus. t.*, κεφ. *t.*, τίτλ., *Am.*, *lect.*, *syn.*, *men.* (Wetstein, Scholz, Greg.).

27. Par. Nat. Gr. 115, Colbert. 6043 [xi, Greg. x], 6¼ × 4¾, ff. 460 (19), is Mill's Colb. 1. That critic procured Larroque's collation of Codd. 27–33 (a very imperfect one) for his edition of the New Testament. From John xviii. 3 the text is supplied, cotton *chart.* [xiv]. κεφ. *t.*, *pict.*, κεφ., τίτλ., *Am.*, *Eus.* (*syn.*, *men.* later), *syn.*, *pict.* Extensively altered by a later hand (Wetstein, Scholz, Greg.).

28. Par. Nat. Gr. 379, Colbert. 4705 [xi], 9⅛ × 7⅛, ff. 292 (19), is Mill's Colb. 2, most carelessly written by an ignorant scribe; it often resembles Cod. D, but has many unique readings and interpolations, with 'many relics of a very ancient text hereabouts' (Hort on Mark vi. 43, Introd. p. 242). Κεφ. *t.* (inaccurate), κεφ., τίτλ., *Am.*, *Eus.*, *subscr.* (*lect.* later), *syn.* *Mut.* in 334 verses, viz. Matt. vii. 17—ix. 12; xiv. 33—xvi. 10; xxvi. 70—xxvii. 48; Luke xx. 19—xxii. 46; John xii. 40—xiii. 1; xv. 24—xvi. 12; xviii. 16–28; xx. 20—xxi. 5; 18–25 (Scholz, Greg.).

29. Par. Nat. Gr. 89, Colbert. 6066 [xii, Greg. x], 7⅝ × 5½, ff. 169, is Mill's Colb. 3, correctly written by a Latin scribe, with very many peculiar corrections by a later hand. Lost leaves in the three later Gospels are supplied [xv]. Scholia, *Eus. t.*, *prol.*, κεφ., τίτλ., *Am.*, *Eus.*, *subscr.*, *syn.*, *men.* *Mut.* Matt. i—xv. Mill compares its text with that of Cod. 71 (Scholz, Greg.).

30. Par. Nat. Gr. 100, Colbert. 4444 [xvi, Greg. xv], 8⅜ × 5⅞, *chart.*,

ff. 313 (18), κεφ. (Gr. and Lat.), τίτλ., is Mill's Colb. 4, containing all the Gospels, by the writer of Cod. 70. In text it much resembles Cod. 17 (Scholz, Greg.).

31. Par. Nat. Gr. 94, Colbert. 6083 [xiii], $7\frac{1}{4} \times 5\frac{1}{2}$, ff. 188, *pict.*, κεφ. *t.*, κεφ., τίτλ., is also Mill's Colb. 4, but contains all the Gospels with prayers. This copy has many erasures (Scholz, Greg.).

32. Par. Nat. Gr. 116, Colbert. 6511 [xii], $5\frac{3}{4} \times 4\frac{1}{4}$, ff. 244 (21), *prol.*, κεφ. *t.*, κεφ., τίτλ., *Am.* (*lect.* and ἀναγν. later), is Mill's Colb. 5. It begins Matt. x. 22. *Mut.* Matt. xxiv. 15–30; Luke xxii. 35—John iv. 20 (Scholz). Mill misrepresented the contents of Codd. 30–32, through supposing that they contained no more than the small portions which were collated for his use.

*33. (Act. 13, Paul 17.) Par. Nat. Gr. 14, Colbert. 2844 [xi, Greg. ix or x], fol., $14\frac{3}{4} \times 9\frac{3}{4}$, ff. 143 (52), κεφ., τίτλ., is Mill's Colb. 8, containing some of the Prophets and all the New Testament, except Mark ix. 31— xi. 11; xiii. 11—xiv. 60; Luke xxi. 38—xxiii. 26; and the Apocalypse. In text it resembles Codd. BDL more than any other cursive manuscript. After Larroque, Wetstein, Griesbach, Begtrup, and Scholz, it was most laboriously collated by Tregelles in 1850. There are fifty-two long lines in each page, in a fine round hand, the accents being sometimes neglected, and *eta* unusually like our English letter h. The ends of the leaves are much damaged, and greatly misplaced by the binder; so that the Gospels now stand last, though on comparing the style of handwriting (which undergoes a *gradual* change throughout the volume) at their beginning and end with that in the Prophets which stand first, and that in the Epistles which should follow them, it is plain that they originally occupied their usual place. The ink too, by reason of the damp, has often left its proper page blank, so that the writing can only be read *set off* on the opposite page, especially in the Acts. Hence it is no wonder that Tregelles should say that of all the manuscripts he has collated 'none has ever been so wearisome to the eyes, and exhaustive of every faculty of attention.' (Account of the Printed Text, p. 162.)

The next eight copies, like Cod. H of St. Paul, belonged to that noble collection made by the Chancellor Seguier, and on his death in 1672 bequeathed to Coislin, Bishop of Metz. Montfaucon has described them in his 'Bibliotheca Coisliniana,' fol. 1715, and all were slightly collated by Wetstein and Scholz.

34. Par. Nat. Coislin. 195, formerly 306 [xi, Greg. x], $11\frac{1}{4} \times 7\frac{1}{2}$, ff. 469 (22), *Carp., Eus. t., prol., pict.*, κεφ., τίτλ., *Am., subscr.*, στίχ.; 'a grand folio, splendidly written and in splendid condition' (Burgon), from Mount Athos, has a catena (Victor's commentary on St. Mark) resembling that of Cod. 194. Fresh as from the artist's hand.

35. (Act. 14, Paul. 18. Apoc. 17.) Par. Nat. Coislin. 199, formerly 44 [xi], $7\frac{3}{8} \times 5\frac{1}{2}$, ff. 328 (27), κεφ. *t., lect.*, ἀναγν., *syn., men., subscr.*, στίχ., contains the whole New Testament (*see* p. 72, note), with many corrections.

36. Par. Nat. Coislin. 20, formerly 26 [xi, Greg. x], 11½ × 8¾, ff. 509 (19), *Carp.*, *Eus. t.*, κεφ. t., *prol.*, *pict.*, κεφ., τίτλ., *Am.*, *Eus. t.*, *prol.*, with a commentary (Victor's on St. Mark), from the *laura* [i. e. convent, Suicer, Thes. Eccles. tom. ii. 205] of St. Athanasius in Mount Athos, very sumptuous.

37. Par. Nat. Coislin. 21, formerly 238 [xii], 12⅛ × 9½, ff. 357, *Eus. t.*, κεφ. t., *prol.*, *pict.*, κεφ., τίτλ., *Am.*, *Eus.*, with short scholia, Victor's commentary on St. Mark, *Eus. t.*, *syn.*, *prol.*, *pict.* (Montfaucon).

38. (Act. 19, Paul. 23.) Par. Nat. Coislin. 200, formerly 500 [xiii], 6¾ × 5¾, ff 300 (30), copied for the Emperor Michael Palaeologus [1259–1282], and by him sent to St. Louis [d. 1270], containing all the N. T. except St. Paul's Epistles, has been rightly judged by Wetstein to be Stephen's θ'[1]. *Pict.*, κεφ., τίτλ., *Am.* (not *Eus.*), *mut.* 143 verses; Matt. xiv. 15—xv. 30; xx. 14—xxi. 27; Mark xii. 3—xiii. 4. A facsimile of this beautiful book is given in the 'Paléographie Univers.,' No. 84 (collated by Wetstein). Burgon has also a photograph of it, and, like Wetstein and Silvestre, notices that it was Ex Bibl. Pattr. Cadomensium [Caen] Soc. Jesu, 1640.

39. Par. Nat. Coislin. 23, formerly 315 [xi], 13⅛ × 10⅜, ff. 288, κεφ. t. (see Greg.), κεφ., τίτλ.. *Am.*, *subscr.*, στίχ., written at Constantinople with many abbreviations εἰς τὸ πατριαρχεῖον, ἐπὶ Σεργίου [II] τοῦ πατριάρχου, and in 1218 conveyed to the convent of St. Athanasius on Mount Athos. With a commentary (Victor's on St. Mark, from the same original as that in Cod. 34). Not *written by* Sergius, as Scholz says (Burgon).

40. Par. Nat. Coislin. 22, formerly 375 [xi], 11¾ × 8½, ff. 312, *Carp.*, *Eus. t.*, *prol.*, κεφ. t., κεφ., τίτλ., *Am.*, *Eus.*, once belonged to the monastery of St. Nicholas σταυρονικήτας, with a commentary (Victor's on St. Mark) and *Eus. t.* Ends at John xx. 25.

41. Par. Nat. Coislin. 24, formerly 241 [xi], 4to, 12 × 9½, ff. 224 (32), κεφ. t. (Mark), κεφ., τίτλ., *lect.*, *subscr.*, στίχ., contains SS. Matthew and Mark with a commentary (Victor's on St. Mark).

42. Cod. Medicaeus exhibits many readings of the same class as Codd. 1, 13, 33, but its authority has the less weight, since it has disappeared under circumstances somewhat suspicious. Edward Bernard communicated to Mill these readings, which he had found in the hand of Peter Pithaeus, a former owner, in the margin of Stephen's N. T. of 1550: they professed to be extracted from an 'exemplar Regium Medicaeum' (which may be supposed to mean that portion of the King's Library which Catherine de' Medici brought to France: above, p. 117, note 3), and were inserted under the title of *Med.* in Mill's great work, though he remarked their resemblance to the text of Cod. K (N. T., Proleg. § 1462). The braggart Denis Amelotte [1606–78] professes to

---

[1] Stephen includes his θ' among the copies that αὐτοὶ πανταχόθεν συνηθροίσαμεν, which might suit the case of Coislin. 200, as St. Louis would have brought or sent it to France. Mr. Vansittart tested Cod. 38 in Matt. xxvi. 45; Luke viii. 18; xix. 26; James v. 5; 2 Pet. ii. 18, and found it agree in all with Stephen's θ'. What of ἀγγελία, 1 John i. 5? In Luke viii. 18 that most careless editor misprints β' when he means θ'. See above, p. 124, note 3.

have used the manuscript about the middle of the seventeenth century, and states that it was in a college at Troyes; but Scholz could find it neither in that city nor elsewhere.

43. (Act. 54, Paul. 130.) Par. Biblioth. Armament. 8409, 8410, formerly Gr. 4 [xi], in two volumes; the first containing the Gospels with *Eus. t.*, the second the Acts and Epistles, 8¼ × 6¾, ff. 199 (23) and 190 (25), *Carp., Eus. t., prol., κεφ. t., κεφ., τίτλ., Am., Eus., subscr. (lect.* and ἀναγν. later, *see* Greg.). Perhaps written at Ephesus; given by P. de Berzi in 1661 to the Oratory of San Maglorian (Amelotte, Simon, Scholz).

44. Lond. British Museum, Add. 4949 [xi], 12 × 9½, ff. 259 (21), *syn., men., pict., κεφ., τίτλ., Am., Eus., lect.* (ἀρχή and τέλος later), *subscr.* and στίχ. in John, brought from Mount Athos by Caesar de Missy [1703-75], George III's French chaplain, who spent his life in collecting materials for an edition of the N. T. His collation, most imperfectly given by Wetstein, is still preserved with the manuscript (Bloomfield, 1860).

45. Oxford Bodleian Barocc. 31 [xii or xiii], 7⅛ × 5¼, ff. 399 (20), is Mill's Bodl. 1, a very neat copy, with *Eus. t., κεφ. t., κεφ., τίτλ.* (occasional), *Am., Eus., lect.* (here and there), *subscr., στίχ. Mut.* Mark ii. 5-15 (Mill, Griesbach).

46. Oxf. Bodl. Barocc. 29 [xi], Mill's Bodl. 2, 7¼ × 5, ff. 342 (18), with τὸ νομικόν and τὸ κυριακὸν πάσχα, *Carp., Eus. t., κεφ. t., pict., κεφ., τίτλ., Am., Eus., lect., syn., men., vers., subscr., στίχ.,* ἀναγν. Preliminary matter in later hand (Mill, Griesbach).

47. Oxf. Bodl. Gr. Misc. 9 [xv], 4¾ × 3¼, ff. 554 (30), *prol., κεφ. t., κεφ., τίτλ., subscr., στίχ.* (Mark), *vers.* (Polyglott, Mill, Greg.), in a vile hand, κεφ. t., and much foreign matter, is Mill's Bodl. 6 and Bodl. 1 of Walton's Polyglott (Polyglott, Mill).

48. Oxf. Bodl. Misc. Gr., formerly 2044 (Mill's Bodl. 5) [xii], 11⅛ × 8¾, ff. 145 (50), 2 cols., *pict., Eus. t., κεφ., subscr., ῥήμ., στίχ.,* scholia in a later hand (Mill).

49. Oxf. Bodl. Roe 1, formerly 247 [xi], 5¾ × 4½, ff. 223 (26), ll. rubr., is also Mill's Roe 1, brought by Sir T. Roe from Turkey about 1628; it has *Eus. t., κεφ. t., κεφ., τίτλ., Am.,* some *Eus., lect., subscr., στίχ.* (Luke) (Mill).

50. Oxf. Bodl. Laud. Gr. 33, formerly D. 122 [xi], 11 × 8¾, ff. 241, *prol.* (Mark), *κεφ. t., pict., κεφ., τίτλ., Am.,* some *Eus., στίχ.,* is Mill's Laud. 1 (*see* p. 170), surrounded by a catena (Victor's or Cyril's of Alexandria in St. Mark), and attended with other matter. *Mut.* Matt. i. 1—ix. 35; xii. 3-23; xvii. 12-24; xxv. 20-32; John v. 29-end; and Mark xiv. 40—xvi. 20 is by a later hand. It contains many unusual readings (Mill, Griesbach).

51. (Act. 32, Paul. 38.) Oxf. Bodl. Laud. Gr. 31, formerly C. 63 [xiii], 11¾ × 8¾, ff. 325 (28), 2 cols., Mill's Laud. 2, whose resemblance to the Complutensian text is pointed out by him (N. T., Proleg. § 1437), though, judging from his own collation of Cod. 51, his statement 'per omnia penè respondet' is rather too strong. *Prol., κεφ. t., κεφ., τίτλ., Am.* (not Eus.), *lect., syn., men., subscr.* The *present* order of the

contents (*see* p. 72) is Act., Paul., Cath., Evangelia (Mill, Griesbach): but it ought to be collated afresh. This is Bentley's γ in the unpublished margin of B. xvii. 5 at Trin. Coll., Cambridge. He calls it a quarto, 400 years old. *Mut.* 2 Pet. iii. 2–17; Matt. xviii. 12–35; Mark ii. 8— iii. 4 (*see* Codd. 54, 60, 113, 440, 507, 508, Acts 23, Apoc. 28, Evst. 5).

52. Oxf. Bodl. Laud. Gr. 3, formerly C. 28 [dated A.D. 1286], 6½ × 5, ff. 158 (27), elegant, written by νικητας ὁ μαυρωνης, is Mill's Laud. 5, with *Pict.*, *prol.*, κεφ. *t.*, κεφ., τίτλ., *Am.*, *Eus.*, *lect.*, *subscr.*, *mut.* in initio (Mill, Griesbach).

53. Oxf. Bodl. Seld. supr. 28, formerly 3416 [xiv], 6 × 4¾, ff. 140, is Mill's Seld. 1, who pronounces it much like Stephen's γ' (Cod. 4), having *prol.*, κεφ. *t.*, κεφ., τίτλ., *subscr.*, ἀναγν., beautifully written (Mill, Griesbach).

54. Oxf. Bodl. Seld. supr. 29 (Coxe 54), formerly 3417, Mill's Seld. 2[1] [dated A.D. 1338], 4to, 6⅜ × 4¾, ff. 230 (sic), *Syn.*, *men.*, *Eus. t.*, κεφ. *t.*, τίτλ., *Am.*, *lect.*, *vers.* (Mill). This is Bentley's κ (*see* Cod. 51). See under 58.

55. Oxf. Bodl. Seld. supr. 6 (Coxe 5), formerly 3394, Mill's Seld. 3 [xiii], 4to, 7½ × 5½, ff. 349 (21), containing also Judges vi. 1–24 (Grabe, Prol. V. T., tom. i. cap. iii. § 6), has *prol.* in Matt., κεφ. *t.*, *pict.*, κεφ., *lect.*, *syn.*, *men.*, ἀναγν., *subscr.*, στίχ. (Mill).

56. Oxf. Lincoln Coll. II (Gr.) 18 [xv or xvi], 4to, 8¼ × 5⅝, ff. 232 (24), *chart.*, was presented about 1502, by Edmund Audley, Bishop of Salisbury: *prol.* (Mark, Luke), κεφ. *t.*, κεφ., some τίτλ., ἀναγν., *vers.*, titles to Gospels, *subscr.*, στίχ. (John). Walton gives some various readings, but confounds it with Act. 33, Paul. 39, speaking of them as if one 'vetustissimum exemplar.' It has been inspected by Dobbin, Scrivener, and Mill, but so loosely that the late Rev. R. C. Pascoe, Fellow of Exeter College, detected thirty-four omissions for thirty-one citations (one of them being an error) in four chapters.

57. (Act. 85, Paul. 41.) Oxf. Magdalen Coll., Greek 9 [xii, opening], 9 × 7½, ff. 291 (25), *aur.* beautiful, in a small and beautiful hand, with abbreviations. *Mut.* Mark i. 1–11, and at end. Psalms and Hymns follow the Epistles. It has κεφ. *t.*, κεφ., τίτλ. (*lect.* in red, *vers.* later). Collated twice by Dr. Hammond, the great commentator, whose papers seem to have been used for Walton's Polyglott (Magd. 1): also examined by Dobbin (Mill).

58. Oxf. New Coll. 68 [xv], 7¾ × 5¼, ff. 342 (20), is Walton and Mill's N. 1. This, like Codd. 56–7, has been accurately examined by Dr. Dobbin, for the purpose of his 'Collation of the Codex Montfortianus' (London, 1854), with whose readings Codd. 56, 58 have been compared in 1922 places. He has undoubtedly proved the close connexion

---

[1] 'Textus ipse distinctus est in clausulas majores, seu Paragraphos; ad initium notatos singulos literâ majusculâ miniatâ,' Mill (N. T. Proleg. § 1445). Yet since Burgon testifies that its text 'is not broken up into Paragraphs after all,' Mill can only intend to designate in a roundabout way the presence of the larger chapters (p. 55) with their appropriate capitals.

subsisting between the three manuscripts (which had been observed by Mill, N. T. Proleg. § 1388), though he may not have quite demonstrated that they must be direct transcripts from each other. *Prol.*, κεφ. *t.*, κεφ. (partially), τίτλ., *Am.* (partial), ἀναγν. (partial), *syn., subscr.* (Mark), *vers.*, with scholia. The writing is very careless, and those are in error who follow Walton in stating that it contains the Acts and Epistles (Walton's Polyglott, Mill, Dobbin). Mr. C. Forster rightly asks for photographs and a thorough re-collation of Codd. 56, 58, 61, 'to throw light upon their direct relationship, or non-relationship to each other' ('A New Plea for the Three Heavenly Witnesses,' 1867, p. 139). Dr. C. R. Gregory has expressed the opinion that Codd. 47, 56, 58 are in the same hand, and one of them copied from Cod. 54.

*59. Cambridge, Gonville and Caius Coll. 403 [xii], 8 × 6, ff. 238 (23), an important copy, 'textu notabili,' as Tischendorf states (much like D, 61, 71), but carelessly written, and exhibiting no less than eighty-one omissions by ὁμοιοτέλευτον (*see* p. 9). It was very poorly examined for Walton's Polyglott, better though defectively by Mill, seen by Wetstein in 1716, minutely collated by Scrivener in 1860. It once belonged to the House of Friars Minor at Oxford, from whence Richard Brynkley borrowed it and took it to the Grey Friars at Cambridge, whence it went to Thomas Hatcher, who gave it to the College in 1867 (J. Rendel Harris, The origin of the Leicester Codex, 1887). It has τίτλ., κεφ., *Am.* (but not *Eus.*), and exhibits (many and rare *compendia scribendi.*

60. (Apoc. 10.) Camb. University Library, Dd. ix. 69 [A.D. 1297], 8 × 6, ff. 324 = 293 + 1 + 30 (24), but the Apocalypse is later, and has a few scholia from Arethas about it. This copy is Mill's Moore 1¹, and is still badly known. *Carp., Eus. t.,* κεφ. *t., pict.,* κεφ., τίτλ., *lect.* (later), *Am.* without *Eus., subscr.,* and it is an elegant copy (Mill). The Gospels appear to have been written in the East, the Apocalypse in the West of Europe. This is Bentley's є (*see* Cod. 51).

*61. (Act. 34, Paul. 40, Apoc. 92.) Codex Montfortianus at Trinity College, Dublin, G. 97 [xv or xvi], 6¼ × 4¾, ff. 445 (21), *chart.,* so celebrated in the controversy respecting 1 John v. 7. Its last collator, Dr. Orlando Dobbin (*see* on Cod. 58), has discussed in his Introduction every point of interest connected with it. It contains the whole New Testament, apparently the work of three or four successive scribes, paper leaves, only one of them—that on which 1 John v. 7 stands—being glazed[2],

---

[1] On the death of Dr. John Moore, Bishop of Ely (whose honesty as a book-collector is impeached, on no fair grounds, by Tew in Bridge's 'Northamptonshire,' vol. ii. p. 45, Oxon. 1791), in 1714, George I was induced to buy his books and manuscripts for the Library at Cambridge, amounting to 30,000 volumes, in acknowledgement of the attachment of the University to the House of Hanover. Every one remembers the epigram which this royal gift provoked. *See* 'Cap and Gown,' p. 15.

[2] 'We often hear,' said a witty and most reverend Irish Prelate, 'that the text of the Three Heavenly Witnesses is a *gloss;* and any one that will go into the College Library may see as much for himself.' It was a little bold in Mr. Charles Forster ('A New Plea,' &c., pp. 119, 120, 139), whose zeal in defence of what he held to be the truth I heartily revere, to urge the authority of Dr. Adam Clarke for assigning this manuscript to the thirteenth century, the rather since almost in the same breath, he stigmatizes the Wesleyan minister

as if to protect it from harm. This manuscript was first heard of between the publication of Erasmus' second (1519) and third (1522) editions of his N. T., and after he had publicly declared, in answer to objectors, that if any *Greek* manuscript could be found containing the passage, he would insert it in his revision of the text; a promise which he fulfilled in 1522. Erasmus describes his authority as 'Codex Britannicus,' 'apud Anglos repertus,' and there is the fullest reason to believe that the Cod. Montfortianus is the copy referred to (*see* Vol. II. Chap. XI). Its earliest known owner was Froy[1], a Franciscan friar, then Thomas Clement [fl. 1569], then William Chark [fl. 1582], then Thomas Montfort, D.D. of Cambridge, from whom it derives its name, then Archbishop Ussher, who caused the collation to be made which appears in Walton's Polyglott (Matt. i. 1— Acts xxii. 29; Rom. i), and presented the manuscript to Trinity College. Dr. Barrett appended to his edition of Cod. Z a full collation of the parts left untouched by his predecessors; but since the work of Ussher's friends was known to be very defective, Dobbin has re-collated the whole of that portion which Barrett left unexamined, comparing the readings throughout with Codd. 56, 58 of the Gospels, and Cod. 33 of the Acts. This copy has *prol.*, κεφ. τ., κεφ., τίτλ., *Am., Eus., subscr.*, στίχ., besides which the division by the Latin chapters in St. Mark is employed, a sure proof—if any were needed—of the modern date of the manuscript. There are many corrections by a more recent hand, erasures by the pen, &c. It has been supposed that the Gospels were first written; then the Acts and Epistles (transcribed, in Dobbin's judgement, from Cod. 33, Acts); the Apocalypse last; having been added about 1580, as Tregelles and Dr. Dobbin think, from Cod. 69, when they were both in Chark's possession. The text, however, of the Apocalypse is not quite the same in the two codices, nor would it be easy, without seeing them together, to verify Dobbin's conjecture, that the titles to the sacred books, in pale red ink, were added by the same person in both manuscripts. In the margin of this copy, as of Cod. 69, are inserted many readings in Chark's handwriting, even the misprint of Erasmus, ἐμαῖς for ἐν αἷς, Apoc. ii. 13.

62. Walton's *Goog.*, which was brought from the East, and once belonged to Dr. Henry Googe, Fellow of Trinity College. The collations of Codd. D, 59, 61, 62 made for the London Polyglott were given in 1667 to Emmanuel College, where they yet remain. *Goog.* was identified with the Cambridge Kk. v. 35 by Bp. Marsh, who was a little careless in this kind of work.

62². Camb. Univ. Lib. Kk. v. 35 [xv], $9\frac{1}{4} \times 5\frac{3}{4}$, ff. 403 (14), *chart.*, κεφ., (κεφ. Lat.), τίτλ., *subscr., vers.* Mr. Bradshaw has pointed out that Kk. v. 35 is a mere transcript by George Hermonymus from Cod. 70 also for a 'self-taught philomath' (p. 122). Dr. Clarke tells us fairly the grounds on which he arrived at his strange conclusion (Observations on the Text of the Three Divine Witnesses, Manchester. 1805, pp. 8-10), and marvellously unsound they are. But what avails authority, *quum res ipsa per se clamat?* The facsimile made for Dr. Clarke nearly seventy years ago has been copied in Horne's Introduction and twenty other books, and leaves no sort of doubt about the date of Codex Montfortianus.

[1] This Froy or Roy is believed by Mr. Rendel Harris (Origin of Cod. Leic., p. 48) to be the forger of Cod. 61.

in his handwriting, and hastily copied from it, errors of the pen and all. It has no *men.*, *lect.*, as *Goog.* had, but the ordinary κεφάλαια and *Latin* chapters. Again, *Goog.*, as Walton says, 'ex Oriente advectus est,' and must have been in England before 1657; whereas Bp. Moore got Kk. v. 35 from France in 1706, with other books from the collection of J. B. Hantin, the numismatist.

63. Cod. Ussher 1, Trin. Coll. Dublin, A. i. 8, formerly D. 20 [x], fol., with a commentary, $12\frac{3}{4} \times 9\frac{1}{2}$, ff. 237 (18–24), *prol.*, *κεφ. t.*, *pict.*, *κεφ.*, τίτλ., *Am.*, *Eus.* (*lect.*, *later.*), *subscr.* Henry Dodwell made a few extracts for Bishop Fell's N.T. of 1675; Richard Bulkeley loosely collated it for Mill, Dr. Dobbin in 1855 examined St. Matthew, and the Rev. John Twycross, of the Charter House, re-collated the whole manuscript in 1858. The last leaf, containing John xxi. 25, is lost; but (*see* Scrivener, Cod. Sin., Introd., p. lix, note, and an admirable paper by Dr. Gwynn in *Hermathena*, xix, 1893, p. 368) it originally contained the verse and witnesses to it. Dr. C. R. Gregory has noticed in Cod. 63 a mutilated double leaf of an Evangelistarium in two columns [ix or x], containing part of ὥρα γ'.

64. Bute, formerly Ussher 2. This MS. belonged, like the preceding, to the illustrious Primate of Ireland, but has been missing from Trin. Coll. Library in Dublin ever since 1742, or, as Dr. C. R. Gregory thinks on the authority of Dr. T. K. Abbott, 1702. It was collated, like Cod. 63, by Dodwell for Fell, by Bulkeley for Mill. It once belonged to Dr. Thomas Goad, and was very neatly, though incorrectly, written in octavo. As the Emmanuel College copy of the Epistles (Act. 53, Paul. 30) never contained the Gospels, for which it is perpetually cited in Walton's Polyglott as *Em.*, the strong resemblance subsisting between *Usser.* 2 and *Em.* led Mill to suspect that they were in fact the same copy. The result of an examination of Walton's with Mill's collations is that they are in numberless instances cited together in support of readings, in company with other manuscripts; often with a very few or even alone (e. g. Matt. vi. 22; viii. 11; xii. 41; Mark ii. 2; iv. 1; ix. 10; 25; Luke iv. 32; viii. 27; John i. 21; iv. 24; v. 7; 20; 36; vii. 10; xvi. 19; xxi. 1). That *Usser.* 2 and *Em.* are sometimes alleged separately is easily accounted for by the inveterate want of accuracy exhibited by all early collators. But all doubt is at an end since Dean Burgon in 1880 found this celebrated copy in the library of the Marquis of Bute, and has traced the curious history of its rovings. From Dr. Goad (d. 1638) it came into the keeping of Primate Ussher, by whose hand the modern chapters seem to have been written in the margin. Then towards the end of the seventeenth century (as his signature proves) it belonged to one John Jones: a later hand puts in the date Saturday, May 25, 1728. It has also the book plate of John Earl of Moira (d. 1793). Then we trace it to James Verschoyle, afterwards Bishop of Killala from 1793 to 1834, thence to the Earls of Huntingdon for two generations, when it was purchased at the Donnington Park sale by Lord Bute. Without doubt this is the long lost Cod. 64, the *Usser.* 2 and *Em.* of Mill: it was recognized at once by the reading in John viii. 8. Dean Burgon describes it as [xii or xiii] now in two volumes, bound in red morocco about 150 years since. It has 440 leaves, $4\frac{3}{5}$ inches by $3\frac{2}{5}$ in size. *Carp.*,

Eus. t., κεφ. t., τίτλ., κεφ., *Am.* (gilt), *Eus.* (carmine), *lect.*, ἀρχαί and τέλη. At the end are fourteen leaves of *syn.* Though beautifully written, it has no *pict.* or elaborate headings. Previous collators had done their work very poorly, as we have reason to know. Out of about sixty variations in Mark i—v, Mill has recorded only twenty-six. Over each proper name of a *person* stands a little waved stroke: cf. Evan. 530. (Collated for Burgon.)

65. Lond. Brit. Mus. Harleian 5776 [xiii], 9 × 7, ff. 309 (22), is Mill's Cov. 1, brought from the East in 1677 with four other manuscripts of the Greek Testament by Dr. John Covell [1637–1722], once English Chaplain at Constantinople, then Chaplain to Queen Mary at the Hague, afterwards Master of Christ's College, Cambridge. *Carp., Eus. t.*, κεφ. t., κεφ., τίτλ., *Am., Eus.*, στίχ., *subscr.* (Mill). This book was presented to Covell in 1674 by Daniel, Bishop of Proconnesus. The last verse is supplied by a late hand, the concluding leaf being lost, as in Cod. 63.

*66. Camb. Trin. Coll. O. viii. 3, Cod. Galei Londinensis [xii], 8¾ × 6, *chart.*, ff. 282 (21), *pict.*, *syn.*, *men.*, *Carp.* ten blank pages, κεφ., no τίτλ., *lect.*, *Am.*, *Eus.*, *subscr.* (later), ἀναγν., κεφ. t., στίχ., once belonged to Th. Gale [1636–1702], High Master of St. Paul's School, Dean of York (1697), with some scholia in the margin by a recent hand, and other changes in the text by one much earlier. Known to (Mill), but for a time lost sight of. Collated by Scrivener, 1862. Inserted in the great printed Catalogue of Manuscripts, Oxford, 1697.

67. Oxf. Bodl. Misc. Gr. 76 [x or xi], 9 × 7, ff. 202 (20), 2 cols., is Mill's Hunt. 2, brought from the East by Dr. Robert Huntington, Chaplain at Aleppo, Provost of Trinity College, Dublin, and afterwards Bishop of Raphoe [d. 1701]. *Mut.* John vi. 64—xxi. 25. *Eus. t., pict.*, κεφ. t., κεφ., τίτλ., *Am., Eus.*, *lect.*, *subscr.* On f. 3, the Athanasian Creed is on *rect.* on gold ground (Mill).

68. Oxf. Lincoln Coll. (Evst. 199) II. Gr. 17 [xii], 8 × 5, ff. 29 (23), *Carp., Eus. t.*, κεφ. t., *orn.*, κεφ., τίτλ. (gold), *Am., lect.*, στίχ., besides *syn., men.*, and verses at the end of each Gospel by Theodulos Hieromonachus, is Mill's Wheel. 1, brought from Zante in 1676, with two other copies, by George Wheeler, Canon of Durham. Between the Gospels of SS. Luke and John are small fragments of two leaves of a beautiful Evangelistarium [ix ?], with red musical notes (Mill, Scr.).

*69. (Act. 31, Paul. 37, Apoc. 14.) Codex Leicestrensis [xiv Harris; end of xv], 14½ × 10⅜, ff. 213 (38), like Codd. 206 and 233, and Brit. Mus. Harl. 3161; rapidly written on 83 leaves of vellum and 130 of paper, the vellum being outside the quinion at beginning and end, and three paper leaves within (*see* p. 24), apparently with a reed (*see* p. 27), is now in the library of the Town Council of Leicester. It contains the whole New Testament, except Matt. i. 1—xviii. 15; Acts x. 45—xiv. 17; Jude 7—25; Apoc. xviii. 7—xxii. 21, but with fragments down to xix. 10. The original order was Paul., Acts, Cath. Epp., Apoc., Gospels last and missing when the MS. came into Chark's hands. Written in the strange hand which our facsimile exhibits (No. 40), *epsilon* being recumbent and almost like *alpha*, and with accents placed over the succeeding consonant instead of the vowel[1]. The words Ειμι Ιλερμου Χαρκου at the top of the first page, in the same beautiful hand that wrote many (too many) marginal notes, prove that this codex once belonged to the William Chark, mentioned under Cod. 61 (p. 201) who got it from Brynkley, who probably got it like the Caius MS. (Evan. 59) from the Convent of Grey Friars at Cambridge. In 1641 (Wetstein states 1669) Thomas Hayne, M.A., of Trussington, in that county, gave this MS. with his other books to the Leicester Library. Mill was permitted to use it at Oxford, and collated it there in 1671. A collation also made by John Jackson and William Tiffin was lent to Wetstein through Caesar de Missy and Th. Gee, a Presbyterian minister of But Close, Leicester. Tregelles re-collated it in 1852 for his edition of the Greek Testament, and Scrivener very minutely in 1855; the latter published his results, with a full description of the book itself, in the Appendix to his 'Codex Augiensis.' No manuscript of its age has a text so remarkable as this, less however in the Acts than in the Gospels. Though none of the ordinary divisions into sections, and scarcely any liturgical marks, occur throughout, there is evidently a close connexion between Cod. 69 and the Church Service-books, as well in the interpolations of proper names, particles of time, or whole passages (e.g. Luke xxii. 43, 44 placed after Matt. xxvi. 39) which are common to both, as especially in the titles of the Gospels: ἐκ τοῦ κατὰ μάρκον εὐαγγέλιον (sic), &c., being in the very language of the Lectionaries[2]. Codd. 178, 443 have the same peculiarity. Tables of κεφάλαια stand before the three later Gospels, with very unusual variations; for which, as well as for the foreign matter inserted and other peculiarities of Cod. 69, consult Scrivener's Cod. Augiensis (Introd. pp. xl–xlvii). See also Mr. J. Rendel Harris, Origin of the Leicester Codex, 1887.

70. Camb. Univ. Lib. Ll. ii. 13 [xv], $11\frac{1}{4} \times 7\frac{1}{4}$, ff. 186 (23), *orn.*, τίτλ. in margin, κεφ. Lat., *vers.*, was written, like Codd. 30, 62^2, 287, by G. Hermonymus the Spartan (who settled at Paris, 1472, and became the Greek teacher of Budaeus and Reuchlin), for William Bodet; there are marginal corrections by Budaeus, from whose letter to Bp. Tonstall we may fix the date about A.D. 1491–4. It once belonged to Bunckle of London, then to Bp. Moore. Like Cod. 62^2 it has the Latin chapters (Mill).

*71. Lambeth 528 [A.D. 1100], $6\frac{1}{2} \times 4\frac{3}{4}$, ff. 265 (26), is Mill's *Eph.* and Scrivener's g. This elegant copy, which once belonged to an Archbishop of Ephesus, was brought to England in 1675 by Philip Traberon, English Chaplain at Smyrna. Traberon made a careful collation of his manuscript, of which both the rough copy (B. M., Burney 24) and a fair one (Lambeth 528 b) survive. This last Scrivener in

---

[1] Another facsimile (Luke xxi. 36—John viii. 6) is given by Abbott in his 'Collation of Four Important Manuscripts' (*see* Cod. 13). In all four the *pericope adulterae* follows Luke xxi. 38.

[2] See the style of the Evangelistaria, as cited above, pp. 80–83; Matthaei's uncials BII and Birch's 178 of the Gospels, described below. So B.-C. ii. 13, to be described hereafter, reads in St. Matthew only ἀρχ' ἐκ τοῦ κατὰ ματθαίον ἀγίου εὐαγγελίου. Compare also Codd. 211, 261, 357, and B.-C. iii. 5 in SS. Matthew and Mark.

1845 compared with the original, and revised, especially in regard to later corrections, of which there are many. Mill used Traheron's collation very carelessly. *Carp., Eus. t., κεφ. t.* [xv], *κεφ., τίτλ., Am., Eus., lect.* This copy presents a text full of interest, and much superior to that of the mass of manuscripts of its age. See Cod. 29.

72. Brit. Mus. Harleian. 5647 [xi], large 4to, 10 × 8, ff. 268 (22, 24), an elegant copy, with a catena on St. Matthew, *κεφ. t., pict., κεφ., τίτλ., lect., Am., Eus., subscr., στίχ.* (Mark), various readings in the ample margin. Lent by T. Johnson to (Wetstein).

73. Christ Church, Oxford, Wake 26 [xi], 4to, $9\frac{7}{8} \times 8\frac{1}{8}$, ff. 291, *κεφ. t., Eus. t., vers., κεφ., Am., Eus., τίτλ., pict.,* few *lect.* It is marked ʻEx dono Mauri Cordati Principis Hungaro-Walachiae, A⁰ 1724.' This and Cod. 74 were once Archbishop Wake's, and were collated for Wetstein by (Jo. Walker, *Wake MS.* 35)[1].

74. Christ Church, Oxford, Wake 20 [xiii], 8 × 6, ff. 204, written by Theodore (*see* p. 42, note 3). *Mut.* Matt. i. 1–14; v. 29—vi. 1; thirty-two verses. It came in 1727 from the Monastery of Παντοκράτωρ, on Mount Athos. *Carp., Eus. t., κεφ. t., syn., men., κεφ., τίτλ., Am., Eus., lect., subscr., vers.*

75. Cod. Genevensis 19 [xi], $9 \times 6\frac{1}{2}$, ff. 500 (19), *Carp., Eus. t., prol., κεφ. t., Am., τίτλ., Eus., lect., pict., men.* In text it much resembles that of Cod. 6. Seen in 1714 by Wetstein, examined by Scholz (collated Matt. i—vi, John vii, viii), collated (Matt. i—xviii, Mark i—v) by Cellérier, a Professor at Geneva, whose collation (Matt. i—xviii) is corrected and supplemented with Matt. xix—end by H. C. Hoskier, though his visit to the MS. was unfortunately short. The first diorthota made corrections and additions as regards breathings and stops. Other corrections made not much later (Hoskier, Collation of 604, App. G).

76. (Act. 43, Paul. 49.) Cod. Caesar-Vindobonensis, Nessel. 300, Lambec. 28 [xi–xiii], $7\frac{1}{2} \times 5\frac{3}{4}$, ff. 358 (27), *prol., κεφ. t., κεφ., τίτλ., Am., lect., syn., men., pict.* This copy (the only one known to read αὐτῆς with the Complutensian and other editions in Luke ii. 22) is erroneously called an uncial by Mill (Gerhard à Mastricht 1690; Ashe 1691; F. K. Alter 1786) (Greg.).

77. Caesar-Vindobon. Nessel. 114, Lambec. 29 [xi], $9\frac{1}{4} \times 8$, ff. 300 (21), very neat; with a commentary (Victor's on St. Mark), *Carp., Eus. t., prol., κεφ. t., κεφ., τίτλ., Am., Eus.* (*lect.* and *syn.* by a later hand). It once belonged to Matthias Corvinus, the great king of Hungary (1458–90). Collated in ʻTentamen descriptionis codicum,' &c. 1773 by (Treschow, and also by Alter) (Greg.).

---

[1] Of the 183 manuscript volumes bequeathed by William Wake, Archbishop of Canterbury [1657-1737] to Christ Church (of which he had been a Canon), no less than twenty-eight contain portions of the Greek Testament. They are all described in this list from a comparison of Dean Gaisford's MS. Catalogue (1837) with the books themselves, to which Bp. Jacobson's kindness gave me access in 1861. Corrected by E. M., to whom similar kindness has been shown. See also ʻAccount of some MSS. at Christ Church, Oxford,' by the Rev. Charles H. Hoole, Student.

78. Cod. Nicolae Jancovich de Vadass, now in Hungary [xii], 9¼ × 5¾, ff. 293 (22), *Eus. t.*, κεφ. t., τίτλ., κεφ., *lect.*, *syn.*, *pict.* It was once in the library of king Matthias Corvinus: on the sack of Buda by the Turks in 1527, his noble collection of 50,000 volumes was scattered, and about 1686 this book fell into the hands of S. B., then of J. G., Carpzov of Leipsic, at whose sale it was purchased and brought back to its former country. A previous possessor, in the seventeenth century, was Γεώργιος δεσμοφύλαξ Ναυπλίου. (Collated by C. F. Boerner for Kuster, and 'in usum' of Scholz.)

79. Leyden, Bibl. Univ. 74 [xv], Latin version older, 6½ × 4¾, ff. 208 (26–28), 2 cols., κεφ., *lect.*, ἀναγν. (all partial). *Mut.* Matt. i. 1—xiv. 13. Brought by Georg. Douze from Constantinople in 1597, consulted by Gomar in 1644 (Greg.).

80. Paris, Lesoeuf [xii], 9¼ × 6⅜, ff. 309 (23), *prol.*, κεφ. t., κεφ. (also Lat. cent. xv), τίτλ. This MS. belonged to J. G. Graevius, and was collated by Bynaeus in 1691: then it passed into the hands of J. Van der Hagen, who showed it to Wetstein in 1739: afterwards it was bought by Ambrose Didot at a sale, and sold to Mons. Lesoeuf, where Dr. C. R. Gregory saw it. (*See* Proleg. to Tisch. ed. viii. p. 485.)

81. Oxf. Bodl. Misc. Gr. 323, Auct. T. Infr. i. 5 [xiii], 7 × 5, ff. 182. Κεφ., τίτλ., some *Am.* Bought in 1883 from Mr. William Ward who brought it from Ephesus. Contains Matt. xix. 15—xxi. 19; 31-41; xxii. 7—xxviii. 20; Mark i. 9—iii. 18; 35—xv. 15; 32—xvi. 14; Luke i. 18—ii. 19; iii. 7—iv. 40; v. 8—xxii. 5; 36—xxiii. 10; John viii. 4—xxi. 18. This place has been hitherto occupied by Greek MSS. cited in a Correctorium Bibliorum Latinorum of the thirteenth century[1]. Dr. Hort appropriates this numeral to Muralt's 2pe. (Evan. 473.)

82. Oxf. Bodl. MS. Bibl. Gr. c. 1. Some fragments: (1) John iii. 23; (2) 26, 27; (3) 2 Cor. xi. 3: Chart. (1, 2) [xiii], (3) [vi or vii] uncials and minuscules intermixed, and some Coptic and Arabic words.

In this place other fragments have been placed till now. Seven unknown Greek manuscripts of St. John, three of St. Matthew and (apparently) of the other Gospels, cited in Laurentius Valla's 'Annotationes in N.T., ex diversorum utriusque linguae, Graecae et Latinae, codicum collatione,' written about 1440, edited by Erasmus, Paris 1505. His copies seem modern, and have probably been used by later critics. The whole subject, however, is very carefully examined in the Rev. A. T. Russell's 'Memoirs of the life and works of Bp. Andrewes,' pp. 282-310. Hort's Cod. 82 is Burgon's Venet. xii, to be described hereafter.

[1] These formal revisions of the Latin Bible were mainly two, one made by the University of Paris with the sanction of the Archbishop of Sens about 1230, and a rival one undertaken by the Mendicant Orders, through Cardinal Hugo de St. Caro (*see* above, p. 69 , and adopted by their general Chapter held at Paris in 1256. A previous revision had been made by Cardinal Nicolaus and the Cistercian Abbot Stephanus in 1150. A manuscript of that of 1256 was used by Lucas Brugensis and Simon (Wetstein, N. T. Prol. vol. i. p. 85). Canon Westcott calls attention to a *Correctorium* in the British Museum, King's Library, 1 A. viii.

83. Cod. Monacensis 518 [xi], 8½ × 6½, ff. 321 (20), beautifully written, *prol.*, κεφ. τ., κεφ., *lect.*, ἀναγν., *syn.*, *men.*, *subscr.*, στίχ., in the Royal Library at Munich, whither it was brought from Augsburg (Bengel's August. 1, Scholz, Greg.).

84. Monacensis 568 [xii], 6⅜ × 5¼, ff. 65, κεφ., τίτλ., *Am.* (not *Eus.*), *lect.* both in the text and margin, contains SS. Matthew and Mark. *Mut.* Matt. i. 18—xiii. 10; xiii. 27-42; xiv. 3—xviii. 25; xix. 9-21; xxii. 4—Mark vii. 13 (Burgon, Greg.).

85. Monacensis 569 [xiii], 5½ × 3¾, ff. 30, κεφ., *lect.* in vermilion, τίτλ., *Am.* (not *Eus.*), contains only Matt. viii. 15—ix. 17; xvi. 12—xvii. 20; xxiv. 26-45; xxvi. 25-54; Mark vi. 13—ix. 45; Luke iii. 12—vi. 44; John ix. 11—xii. 5; xix. 6-24; xx. 23—xxi. 9 (Bengel's August. 3, Scholz).

86. Posoniensis Lycaei Aug. [x], 9½ × 7¼, ff. 280, *prol.*, *Eus. t.*, *pict.*, *syn.* Once at Buda, but it had been bought in 1183 at Constantinople for the Emperor Alexius II Comnenus (Bengel, Endlicher). It was brought by Rayger, a doctor of medicine, from Italy, where it had been carried, to Pressburg, to his brother-in-law Gleichgross, who was a pastor in that place, amongst whose books it was sold to the library of the Lycaeum in Pressburg. (*See* Gregory, Proleg. p. 486.)

87. Trevirensis [xii], fol., contains St. John's Gospel with a catena, published at length by Cordier at Antwerp. It once belonged to the eminent philosopher and mathematician, Cardinal Nicolas of Cuza, on the Moselle, near Trèves [1401–64: *see* Cod. 129 Evan., and Cod. 59 Acts]; previously at the monastery of Petra or of the Fore-runner of Constantinople[1] (Scholz). Wetstein's 87 is our 250.

88. Codex of the Gospels, 4to, on vellum, cited as ancient and correct by Joachim Camerarius (who collated it) in his Annotations to the New Testament, 1642. It resembles in text Codd. 63, 72, 80.

*89. Gottingensis Cod. Theol. 53 [1006], fol., ff. 172, *Carp.*, *Eus. t.*, κεφ. τ., κεφ., *Eust.*, *lect.*, with corrections. Collated by A. G. Gehl in 1729 (?), and by Matthaei (No. 20) in 1786-7.

90. (Act. 47, Paul. 14.) Cod. Jac. Fabri, a Dominican of Deventer, now in the library of the church of the Remonstrants at Amsterdam, 186 [xvi, but copied from a manuscript written by Theodore and dated 1293], 4to, *chart.*, 2 vols., κεφ. (Lat.), *lect.*, *syn.* The Gospels stand John, Luke, Matthew, Mark (*see* p. 70); the Pauline Epistles precede the Acts; and Jude is written twice, from different copies. This codex (which has belonged to Abr. Hinckelmann of Hamburg, and to Wolff) was collated by Wetstein. Faber [1472—living in 1515] had also compared it with another 'very ancient' vellum manuscript of the Gospels presented by Sixtus IV (1471-84) to Jo. Wessel of Groningen, but which was then at Zvolle. As might be expected, this

---

[1] On fol. 4 we read ἡ βίβλος αὕτη (ἥδε 178) τῆς μονῆς τοῦ Προδρόμου | τῆς κειμένης ἔγγιστα τῆς Ἀε'αι'τίου | ἀρχαϊκὴ δὲ τῇ μονῇ κλῆσις Πέτρα. Compare Cod. 178 and Montfauc., Palaeogr. Graeca, pp. 39, 110, 305.

copy much resembles Cod. 74. See Delitzsch, Handschr. Funde, ii. pp. 54–57.

91. Perronianus [x], of which extracts were sent by Montfaucon to Mill, had been Cardinal Perron's [d. 1618], and before him had belonged to 'S. Taurini monasterium Ebroicense' (Evreux). Hort suggests, and Gregory favours the suggestion, that this is the same as Evan. 299 (Cod. Par. Reg. 177), which came from Evreux.

92. Faeschii 1 (Act. 49) [xiv or xv] ⎫ The former, $10\frac{1}{4} \times 8$, ff. 141,
94. Faeschii 2 [xvi or xvii] ⎭ κεφ. t., τίτλ., pict., contains St. Mark with Victor's commentary on vellum, and scholia on the Catholic Epistles, with the authors' names, Didymus, Origen, Cyril, &c., and is referred by Gregory to the tenth century; the latter, $8\frac{1}{2} \times 5\frac{1}{2}$, ff. 172 (22), SS. Mark and Luke, with Victor's commentary on St. Mark, that of Titus of Bostra on St. Luke, on paper [xv or xvi, Greg.]. Both belonged to Andrew Faesch, of Basle, and were collated by Wetstein. Dean Burgon found them both at Basle (O. ii. 27 and O. ii. 23).

93. Graevii [1632–1703] of the Gospels, cited by Vossius on the Genealogy, Luke iii, but not known (Cod. 80 ? Greg.).

95. Oxf. Lincoln Coll. II. Gr. 16 [xii or earlier], $10\frac{1}{2} \times 8$, ff. 110 (20), is Mill's Wheeler 2[1]. It contains SS. Luke and John with commentary, mut. Luke i. 1—xi. 2; John vii. 2–17; xx. 31—xxi. 10. With full scholia neatly written in the margin, κεφ., Am. (later), syn., men. (Mill, Professor Nicoll).

96. Bodl. Misc Gr. 8 (Auct. D. 5. 1) [xv], $5\frac{3}{4} \times 3\frac{3}{4}$, ff. 62 (18), chart., is Walton's and Mill's Trit., with many rare readings, containing St. John with a commentary, beautifully written by Jo. Trithemius, Abbot of Spanheim [d. 1516]. Received from Abraham Scultet by Geo. Hackwell, 1607 (Walton's Polyglott, Mill, Griesbach).

97. Hirsaugiensis [1500, by Nicolas, a monk of Hirschau in Bavaria], 12mo, ff. 71, on vellum, containing St. John, seems but a copy of 96. Collated by Maius, and the collation given in J. D. Michaelis, Orientalische und exegetische Bibliothek, ii. p. 243, &c. (Greg., Bengel[2], Maius, Schulz).

98. Oxf. Bodl. E. D. Clarke 5 [xii], $8\frac{1}{2} \times 6$, ff. 222 (25), pict., κεφ. t., κεφ., τίτλ., Am., lect., subscr., στίχ., brought by Clarke from the East. It was collated in a few places for Scholz, who substituted it here for Cod. R (see p. 139) of Griesbach.

99. Lipsiensis, Bibliothec. Paul. [xvi], $8\frac{1}{4} \times 7\frac{1}{8}$, ff. 22 (22, 23), Matthaei's 18, contains Matt. iv. 8—v. 27; vi. 2—xv. 30; Luke i. 1–13; Carp., κεφ. t., κεφ., τίτλ., Am., Eus., lect., syn. (Matthaei, Greg.). Wetstein's 99 is our 155.

---

[1] Noted 'Ex libris Georgii Wheleri Westmonasteriensis peregrinatione ejus Constantinopolitanâ collect. Anno Domini 1676.' See Evan. 68; Evst. 3.

[2] Cod. 101 better suits Bengel's description of Uffen. 3 than 97: they are written on different materials, and the description of their respective texts will not let us suspect them to be the same. Wetstein never cites Cod. 101, but the addition of τὸν θεόν at the end of John viii. 27, the reading of the margin of Uffen. 3, has been erroneously ascribed in the critical editions to 97, not to 101.

100. Paul. L. B. de Eubeswald [x], 4to, 9¼ × 7½, ff. 374, κεφ., τίτλ., *Am.*, *Eus.*, *lect.* (*syn.*, *men.*, ἀναγν. later); vellum, *mut.* John xxi. 25; *pict.*, κεφ. *t.*, *Eus. t.*, and in a later hand many corrections with scholia, *chart.* J. C. Wagenseil used it in Hungary for John viii. 6. Now in the University of Pesth, but in the fifteenth century belonging to Bp. Jo. Pannonius. Edited at Pesth in 1860 'cum interpretatione Hungaria' by S. Markfi.

101. Uffenbach. 3 [xvi], 12mo, *chart.*, St. John στιχήρης. So near the Basle (that is, we suppose, Erasmus') edition, that Bengel scarcely ever cites it. With two others (Paul. M. and Acts 45) it was lent by Z. C. Uffenbach, Consul of Frankfort-on-the-Main, to Wetstein in 1717, and afterwards to Bengel. (Gregory would omit it.)

102. Bibliothecae Medicae, an unknown manuscript with many rare readings, extracted by Wetstein at Amsterdam for Matt. xxiv—Mark viii. 1, from the margin of a copy of Plantin's N. T. 1591, in the library of J. Le Long. Canon Westcott is convinced that the manuscript from which these readings were derived is none other than Cod. B itself, and Dr. Gregory agrees with him. In St. Matthew's Gospel he finds the two authorities agree seventy times and differ only five times, always in a manner to be easily accounted for: in St. Mark they agree in eighty-four out of the eighty-five citations, the remaining one (ch. ii. 22) being hardly an exception. Westcott, New Test., Smith's 'Dictionary of the Bible.' Hort's Cod. 102 is w^scr (Evan. 507), to be described hereafter.

103. Regius 196 [xi], fol., once Cardinal Mazarin's, seems the same manuscript as that from which Emericus Bigot gave extracts for Curcellaeus' N. T. 1658 (Scholz). Burgon supposes some mistake here, as he finds Reg. 196 to be a copy of Theophylact's commentary on SS. Matthew and Mark, written over an older manuscript [viii or ix]. Perhaps the same as 14 or 278 (Greg.).

104. Hieronymi Vignerii [x], from which also Bigot extracted readings, which Wetstein obtained through J. Drieberg in 1744, and published. Perhaps 697 (Greg.).

105. (Act. 48, Paul. 24.) Cod. Ebnerianus, Bodl. Misc. Gr. 136, a beautiful copy [xii], 8 × 6¼, ff. 426 (27), formerly belonging to Jerome Ebner von Eschenbach of Nuremberg. *Pict.*, *Carp.*, *Eus. t.*, κεφ. *t.*, τίτλ., κεφ., *Am.* (not *Eus.*), *subscr.*, στίχ., the Nicene Creed, all in gold: with *lect.* throughout and *syn.*, *men.* prefixed by Joasaph, a calligraphist, A.D. 1391, who also added John viii. 3-11 at the end of that Gospel. Facsimile in Horne's Introduction, and in Tregelles' Horne, p. 220 (Schoenleben 1738, Rev. H. O. Coxe, by whom the collation was lent before 1845 to the Rev. R. J. F. Thomas, Vicar of Yeovil [d. 1873], together with one of Canon. Graec. 110 of the Acts and Epistles, both of which are mislaid).

106. Winchelsea [x], with many important readings, often resembling the Harkleian Syriac: not now in the Earl of Winchelsea's Library (Jackson collated it for Wetstein in 1748).

107. Bodl. E. D. Clarke 6 [xiv and later], 8½ × 6¾, ff. 351, κεφ. *t.*, *pict.*,

κεφ., τίτλ., containing the Gospels in different hands. (Like 98, 111, 112, *partially* collated for Scholz.) Griesbach's 107 is also 201.

108. Vindobonensis Caesarei, Suppl. Gr. 2, formerly Kollar. 4 [xi], 12¾ × 9¼, ff. 426, 2 vols. With a commentary (Victor's on St. Mark: Burgon, Last Twelve Verses, &c., p. 288), *Carp., Eus. t., prol., κεφ. t., pict., κεφ., τίτλ., Am., Eus., subscr., στίχ.* It seems to have been written at Constantinople, and formerly belonged to Parrhasius, then to the convent of St. John de Carbonaria at Naples (Treschow, Alter, Birch, Scholz).

109. Brit. Mus. Addit. 5117 [A.D. 1326], 7¼ × 5¾, ff. 225 (24–30), ll. rubr., *Carp., prol., κεφ. t., Eus. t., syn., men., lect., Am., τίτλ., subscr., στίχ.*, Mead. 1, then Askew (5115 is Act. 22, and 5116 is Paul. 75, these two in the same hand; different from that employed in the Gospels).

110[1]. Brit. Mus. Addit. 19,386 [xiv], 11 × 8, ff. 267 (?), *Carp., Eus. t.* (faded), *κεφ. t., prol., κεφ., τίτλ., lect., syn.*, with a dial of the year. Four Gospels with commentary by Theophylact. Purchased from Constantine Simonides in 1853. (Greg. 1260.)

111[2]. Bodl. Clarke 7 [xii], 8¼ × 6, ff. 181 (31), *κεφ. t. (mut. Matt.)*,

---

[1] Cod. Ravianus, Bibl. Reg. Berolinensis [xvi], 4to, 2 vols., on parchment, once belonging to Jo. Rave of Upsal, has been examined by Wetstein, Griesbach, and by G. G. Pappelbaum in 1796. It contains the whole New Testament, and has attracted attention because it has the disputed words in 1 John v. 7, 8. It is now, however, admitted by all to be a mere transcript of the N. T. in the Complutensian Polyglott with variations from Erasmus or Stephen, and as such has no independent authority.

[2] (Wetstein.) THE VELESIAN READINGS. The Jesuit de la Cerda in his 'Adversaria Sacra,' cap. xci (Lyons, 1626), a collection of various readings, written in vermilion in the margin of a *Greek* Testament (which from its misprint in 1 Pet. iii. 11 we know to be R. Stephen's of 1550) by Petro Faxardo, Marquis of Velez, a Spaniard, who had taken them from sixteen manuscripts, eight of which were in the king's library, in the Escurial. It is never stated what codices or how many support each variation. De la Cerda had received the readings from Mariana, the great Jesuit historian of Spain, then lately dead, and appears to have inadvertently added to Mariana's account of their origin, that the sixteen manuscripts were in Greek. These Velesian readings, though suspected from the first even by Mariana by reason of their strange resemblance to the Latin Vulgate and the manuscripts of the Old Latin, were repeated as critical authorities in Walton's Polyglott, 1657, and (contrary to his own better judgement) were retained by Mill in 1707. Wetstein, however (N. T. Proleg. vol. i. pp. 59–61), and after him Michaelis and Bp. Marsh, have abundantly proved that the various readings must have been collected by Velez from *Latin* manuscripts, and by him translated into Greek, very foolishly perhaps, but not of necessity with a fraudulent design. Certainly, any little weight the Velesian readings may have, must be referred to the Latin, not to the Greek text. Among the various proofs of their Latin origin urged by Wetstein and others, the following establish the fact beyond the possibility of doubt:

	Greek Text.	Vulgate Text.	Vulgate various reading.	Velesian reading.
Mark viii. 38	ἐπαισχυνθῇ	confusus fuerit	confessus fuerit	ὁμολογήσῃ
Heb. xii. 18	κεκαυμένῳ	accensibilem	accessibilem	προσίτῳ
— xiii. 2	ἔλαθον	latuerunt	placuerunt	ἤρεσαν
James v. 6	κατεδικάσατε	addixistis	adduxistis	ἠγάγετε
Apoc. xix. 6	ὄχλου	turbae	tubae	σάλπιγγος
— xxi. 12	ἀγγέλους	angelos	angelos	γωνίας

κεφ., τίτλ., Am., vers., subscr., στίχ. *Mut.* John xvi. 27—xvii. 15; xx. 25-end, and

112[1]. Bodl. Clarke 10 [xi], 5½ × 4¼, ff. 167 (33), *Carp., Eus. t., prol., pict., syn., men.,* κεφ. t., κεφ., τίτλ., *lect.,* with commencement and large letters in gold, having both *Am.* and *Eus.,* in Matt. i—Mark ii, in the same line (a very rare arrangement; see Codd. 192, 198, 212, and Wake 21 *below*), a very beautiful copy. These two, very partially collated for Scholz, were substituted by him and Tischendorf for collations whose history is not a little curious.

113. Brit. Mus. Harleian. 1810 [xi], 8 × 7¼, ff. 270 (26), *prol., syn.* (later), *Carp., Eus. t.,* κεφ. t., *pict.,* κεφ., τίτλ., *Am., Eus., lect.* (Griesbach, Bloomfield). Apparently this is Bentley's θ 'membr. 4to 600 annorum,' collated by him in the margin of Trin. Coll. B. xvii. 5 (*see* Cod. 51). Its readings are of more than usual interest, as are those of

114. Brit. Mus. Harl. 5540 [x], 5¼ × 4¼, ff. 280 (20) (facsimile in a Greek Testament, published in 1837 by Taylor, London), very elegant, with more recent marginal notes and Matt. xxviii. 19—Mark i. 12 in a later hand. *Mut.* Matt. xvii. 4-18; xxvi. 59-73 (Griesbach, Bloomfield). *Carp.,* τίτλ., κεφ., *Am.* (not *Eus.*), κεφ. t. (Luke, John). See Canon Westcott's article, 'New Test.,' in Smith's 'Dictionary of the Bible.'

115. Brit. Mus. Harl. 5559 [xii], 6¾ × 5¾, ff. 271 (19), κεφ., some τίτλ., *Am.,* frequently *Eus.*[2], once Bernard Mould's (Smyrna, 1724), with an unusual text. *Mut.* Matt. i. 1—viii. 10; Mark v. 23-36; Luke i. 78—ii. 9; vi. 4-15; John xi. 2—xxi. 25 (Griesbach, Bloomfield). A few more words of John xi survive.

116. Brit. Mus. Harl. 5567 [xii], 6¼ × 5, ff. 300 (23), *Syn., Eus. t.,* κεφ. t., κεφ., τίτλ., *Am., lect., subscr.,* ἀναγν., στίχ., *men.,* of some value.

---

[1] (Wetstein.) THE BARBERINI READINGS must also be banished from our list of critical authorities, though for a different reason. The collection of various readings from twenty-two manuscripts (ten of the Gospels, eight of the Acts and Epistles, and four of the Apocalypse), seen by Isaac Vossius in 1642 in the Barberini Library at Rome, was made about 1625, and first published in 1673 by Peter Possinus (Poussines), a Jesuit, at the end of a catena of St. Mark. He alleged that the collations were made by John M. Caryophilus [d. 1635], a Cretan, while preparing an edition of the Greek Testament, under the patronage of Paul V [d. 1621] and Urban VIII [d. 1644]. As the Barberini readings often favour the Latin version, they fell into the same suspicion as the Velesian: Wetstein especially (N. T. Proleg. vol. i. pp. 61, 62`, after pressing against them some objections more ingenious than solid, declares 'lis haec non aliter quam ipsis libris Romae inventis et productis, *quod nunquam credo fiet*, solvi potest.' The very papers Wetstein thus called for were discovered by Birch (Barberini Lib. 209) more than thirty years later, and besides them Caryophilus' petition for the loan of six manuscripts from the Vatican (Codd. BS, 127, 129, 141, 144`, which he doubtless obtained and used. The good faith of the collator being thus happily vindicated, we have only to identify his eleven { Cod. 141 of the Gospels being also Act. 75, Paul. 86, Apoc. 40. Another of his manuscripts was Act. 73, Paul. 80] remaining codices, most of them probably being in that very Library, and may then dismiss the Barberini readings as having done their work, and been fairly superseded.

[2] In Codd. 115 and 202 *Eus.* is usually, in Codd. 116, 117, 417, 422, and B. M. Addit. 15,581 but rarely, written under *Am.*: these copies therefore were probably never quite finished. See p. 62, and note 1.

It belonged in 1649 to Athanasius a Greek monk, then to Bernard Mould (Griesbach, Bloomfield).

117. (Apost. 6.) Brit. Mus. Harl. 5731 [xv], 8 × 6, ff. 202 (28), carelessly written, once belonged to Bentley. *Mut.* Matt. i. 1–18: *pict., prol., Eus. t., κεφ. t., κεφ., τίτλ., lect., Am., syn.*, fragments of a Lectionary on the last twenty leaves (Griesbach, Bloomfield).

*118. Oxf. Bodl. Misc. Gr. 13 [xiii], 7¾ × 5¼, ff. 257, an important palimpsest (with the Gospels *uppermost*) once the property of Archbishop Marsh of Armagh [d. 1713]. *Eus. t., κεφ. t., τίτλ., lect., Am., Eus., στίχ., ῥήμ. (syn., men.* later), and some of the Psalms on paper. Later hands also supplied Matt. i. 1—vi. 2; Luke xiii. 35—xiv. 20; xviii. 8—xix. 9; John xvi. 25—xxi. 25. Well collated by (Griesbach).

119. Paris Nat. Gr. 85 [xii], 9 × 6⅜, ff. 237 (23), formerly Teller's of Rheims, is Kuster's Paris 5 (Griesbach, Gregory), *prol., κεφ. t., κεφ., τίτλ., Am., lect., subscr., στίχ., pict.*

120. Par. Nat. Suppl. Gr. 185 [xiii], 7½ × 5¾, ff. 177, *κεφ., τίτλ., Am.*, formerly belonged to St. Victor's on the Walls, and seems to be Stephen's ιδ', whose text (1550) and Colinaeus' (1534) it closely resembles. St. Mark is wanting (Griesbach).

121. Par. St. Geneviève, A. O. 34 [Sept. 1284, Indiction 12], 7⅞ × 6, ff. 241, *κεφ. t., κεφ., τίτλ., Am., lect., syn., men. Mut.* Matt. v. 21—viii. 24 (Griesbach).

122. (Act. 177, Paul. 219.) Lugdunensis-Batavorum Bibl. publ. Gr. 74 A [xii], 7⅛ × 5½, ff. 222, *Eus. t., κεφ. t., κεφ., τίτλ., Am., Eus., lect., vers., στίχ., men.*, once Meerman's[1] 116. *Mut.* Acts i. 1–14; xxi. 14—xxii. 28; 1 John iv. 20—Jude 25; Rom. i. 1—vii. 13; 1 Cor. ii. 7—xiv. 23 (J. Dermout, Collectanea Critica in N. T., 1825). Griesbach's 122 is also 97. See Cod. 435.

123. Vindobon. Caesar. Nessel. 240, formerly 30 [xi], 4to, 8⅛ × 6, ff. 328 (18), brought from Constantinople about 1562 by the Imperial Ambassador to the Porte, Ogier de Busbeck; *Carp., Eus. t., prol., κεφ. t., pict., κεφ., τίτλ., Am., subscr.*, corrections by another hand (Treschow, Alter, Birch).

*124. Vind. Caes. Ness. 188, formerly 31 [xii], 4to, 8½ × 7⅛, ff. 180 (25), *Carp., Eus. t., harm., κεφ. t., κεφ., τίτλ., Am., Eus., syn., men.*, an eclectic copy, with corrections by the first hand (Mark ii. 14; Luke iii. 1, &c.). This manuscript was written in Calabria, where it belonged to a certain Leo, and was brought to Vienna probably in 1564. It resembles the Harkleian Syriac, Old Latin, Codd. DL. i. 13, and especially 69 (Treschow, Alter, Birch). Collated by Dr. Em. Hoffmann for Professor Ferrar where Alter and Birch disagree. See Cod. 13, for Abbott's recent edition.

125. Vind. Caes. Suppl. G. 50, formerly Kollar. 6 [x], 8¾ × 6⅞, ff. 306 (23), *κεφ. t., κεφ., τίτλ., Am., Eus., pict. (lect., subscr., στίχ., vers.* later), with many corrections in the margin and between the lines (Treschow, Alter, Birch).

---

[1] Meerman's other manuscript of the N. T., sold at his sale in 1824, is No. 562.

126. Guelpherbytanus xvi. 6, Aug. Quarto [xi], 8¼ × 6⅝, ff. 219 (26), carelessly written, *Eus. t.*, *κεφ. t.*, *prol.*, *pict.*, with *lect.*, *syn.* in a later hand, and some quite modern corrections. Matt. xxviii. 18–20 is cruciform, capitals often occur in the middle of words, and the text is of an unusual character. Inspected by (Heusinger 1752, Knittel, Tischendorf).

N.B. Codd. 127–181, all at Rome, were inspected, and a few (127, 131, 157) really collated by Birch, about 1782. Of 153 Scholz collated the greater part, and small portions of 138–44; 146–52; 154–57; 159–60; 162; 164–71; 173–75; 177–80.

127. Rom. Vatican. Gr. 349 [xi], 12⅜ × 9⅝, ff. 370 (16), ll. rubr., *Carp.*, *Eus. t.*, *prol.*, *κεφ. t.*, *κεφ.*, *τίτλ.*, *Am.*, *lect.*, a neatly written and important copy, with a few later corrections (e. g. Matt. xxvii. 49).

128. Rom. Vat. Gr. 356 [xi Birch, xiii or xiv Greg.], 12½ × 9⅝, ff. 370 (18), ll. rubr., *prol.*, *κεφ. t.* with harmony, *κεφ.*, *τίτλ.*, *subscr.*, *στίχ.* (p. 69, note).

129. Rom. Vat. Gr. 358 [xii], 11¼ × 8⅞, ff. 355, ll. rubr., *Carp.* (with addition), *Eus. t.*, *prol.*, *κεφ. t.*, *κεφ.*, *τίτλ.*, *Am.*, *Eus.*, *syn.*, *men.*, *pict.*, with scholia, Victor's commentary on St. Mark, and a note on John vii. 53, such as we read in Cod. 145 and others. Bought at Constantinople in 1438 by Nicolas de Cuza, Eastern Legate to the Council of Ferrara (*see* Cod. 87).

130. Rom. Vat. Gr. 359 [xiii Birch, xv or xvi Greg.], 11⅛ × 8¼, *chart.*, ff. 229 (26), ll. rubr., *κεφ.* lat., a curious copy, with the Greek and Latin in parallel columns, and the Latin chapters.

131. (Act. 70, Paul. 77.) Rom. Vat. Gr. 360 [xi Birch, xiv or xv Greg.], 9¼ × 7, ff. 233 (37), 2 cols., contains the whole New Testament except the Apoc. (Birch), with many remarkable variations, and a text somewhat like that of Aldus' Greek Testament (1518). The manuscript was given to Sixtus V [1585–90] for the Vatican by 'Aldus Manuccius Paulli F. Aldi.' The Epistle to the Hebrews stands before 1 Tim. *Carp.*, *Eus. t.*, *κεφ. t.*, of an unusual arrangement (viz. Matt. 74, Mark 46, Luke 57). *Am.*, *syn.*, *men.*, *subscr.*, *στίχ.* (*lect.* with *init.* later). This copy contains many itacisms, and corrections *primâ manu*.

132. Rom. Vat. Gr. 361 [xi Birch, xii or xiii Greg.], 10⅝ × 6¼, ff. 289 (20), *Eus. t.*, *prol.*, *κεφ. t.*, *κεφ.*, *Am.*, *Eus.*, *subscr.*, *pict. in aur.*, *lect.* (later).

133. (Act. 71, Paul. 78.) Rom. Vat. Gr. 363 [xi?], 7⅞ × 6⅜, ff. 332 (29), *prol.*, *κεφ. t.*, *κεφ.*, *τίτλ.*, *Am.*, *lect.*, *subscr.*, *syn.*, *men.*, *pict.*, Euthalian prologues.

134. Rom. Vat. Gr. 364 [xi or xii], 4to, elegant, 8½ × 6⅛, ff. 297 (20), *Carp.*, *Eus. t.*, *κεφ. t.*, *κεφ.*, *τίτλ.*, *Am.*, *Eus.*, *syn.*, *men.*, *pict.*, titles in gold.

135. Rom. Vat. Gr. 365 [xi?], 9⅝ × 7⅞, *κεφ. t.*, *pict.* The first 26 of its 174 leaves are later and *chart.*

136. Rom. Vat. Gr. 665 [xiii], 9¾ × 6¾, ff. 235 (32), on cotton paper;

contains SS. Matthew and Mark with Euthymius' commentary. *Mut.* Mark xv. 1–end.

137. Rom. Vat. Gr. 756 [xi or xii], $11\frac{1}{4} \times 8\frac{1}{2}$, ff. 300 (19), *κεφ. t.*, *κεφ.*, *τίτλ.*, *Am.*, *syn.*, *men.*, *pict.*, with a commentary (Victor's on St. Mark). At the end we read *κσ φραγκισκος ακκιδας ευγενης κολασσευς . . . ρωμη ηγαγε το παρον βιβλιον ετει απο αδαμ ζφο* [A. D. 1583], *μηνι ιουλιω*, *ινδ. ια.*

138. Rom. Vat. Gr. 757 [xii], $11\frac{3}{4} \times 9\frac{1}{8}$, ff. 380 (37), *κεφ. t.*, with commentary from Origen, &c., and that of Victor on St. Mark, mixed up with the text, both in a slovenly hand (Burgon). Comp. Cod. 374.

139. Rom. Vat. Gr. 758 [dated 1173 by a somewhat later hand (Greg.)], $14\frac{3}{4} \times 10\frac{7}{8}$, ff. 233, contains SS. Luke and John with a commentary.

140. Rom. Vat. Gr. 1158 [xii], $9\frac{1}{4} \times 6\frac{3}{4}$, ff. 408 (22), 2 cols., beautifully written, and given by the Queen of Cyprus to Innocent VII (1404–6). *Eus. t.*, *κεφ.*, *τίτλ.*, *Am.*, *Eus.*, *pict.* In Luke i. 64 it supports the Complutensian reading, *καὶ ἡ γλῶσσα αὐτοῦ διηρθρώθη.*

141. (Act. 75, Paul. 86, Apoc. 40.) Rom. Vat. Gr. 1160 [xiii], 2 vols., $9\frac{1}{4} \times 6\frac{1}{2}$, ff. 400 (26), *prol.*, *κεφ. t.*, *κεφ.*, *τίτλ.*, *lect.*, *ἀναγν.*, *syn.*, *men.*, *subscr.*, *στίχ.*, *pict.*, *Euthal.*, contains the whole New Testament, *syn.*, *pict.* The leaves are arranged in quaternions, but separately numbered for each volume (Birch).

142. (Act. 76, Paul. 87.) Rom. Vat. Gr. 1210 [xi], $4\frac{3}{4} \times 3\frac{1}{4}$, ff. 324 (30), very neat, *κεφ. t.* at end, *κεφ.*, *τίτλ.*, *subscr.*, *pict.*, *Euthal.* (*syn.*, *men.*, A. D. 1447), containing also the Psalms. There are many marginal readings in another ancient hand.

143. Rom. Vat. Gr. 1229 [xi], $12\frac{1}{2} \times 9\frac{3}{4}$, ff. 275 (24), *κεφ. t.*, *κεφ.*, *τίτλ.*, *Am.*, *Eus.*, *pict.*, with a marginal commentary (Victor's on St. Mark). On the first leaf is read *της ορθης πιστεως πιστῳ οικονομῳ και φυλακι Παυλῳ τετάρτῳ* [1555—59].

144. Rom. Vat. Gr. 1254 [xi], $6\frac{1}{8} \times 4\frac{5}{8}$, ff. 267, *Eus. t.*, *κεφ. t.*, *κεφ.*, *τίτλ.*, *Am.*, *lect.*

145. Rom. Vat. Gr. 1548 [xi Greg., xiii Birch], $7 \times 5\frac{1}{8}$, ff. 161 (17), *prol.*, *κεφ. t.*, *κεφ.*, *τίτλ.*, *Am.*, *Eus.*, *lect.*, contains SS. Luke and John. *Mut.* Luke iv. 15—v. 36; John i. 1–26. A later hand has written Luke xvii—xxi, and made many corrections.

146. Rom. Palatino-Vatican. 5[1] [xii], $12\frac{1}{8} \times 9\frac{1}{8}$, ff. 265 (13), *κεφ. t.*, Mark, *Am.*, *Eus.*, contains SS. Matt. and Mark with a commentary (Victor's on St. Mark?).

147. Rom. Pal.-Vat. 89 [xi Birch, xiv Greg.], $6\frac{1}{2} \times 5\frac{1}{8}$, ff. 351 (20), *prol.*, *κεφ. t.*, *κεφ.*, *τίτλ.*, *syn.*, *men.*, *subscr.*, *στίχ.*

148. Rom. Pal.-Vat. 136 [xi Greg., xiii Birch], $7\frac{1}{2} \times 4\frac{1}{8}$, ff. 153, *κεφ. t.*, *κεφ.*, *τίτλ.*, *Am.*, *Eus.*, *syn.*, with some scholia and unusual readings.

[1] A collection presented to Urban VIII (1623–44) by Maximilian, Elector of Bavaria, from the spoils of the unhappy Elector Palatine, titular king of Bohemia.

149. (Act. 77, Paul. 88, Apoc. 25.) Rom. Pal.-Vat. 171 [xiv or xv], fol., ff. 179, *prol.* in Cath. and Paul., *lect.*, contains the whole New Testament (*see* p. 69, note).

150. Rom. Pal.-Vat. 189 [xi or xii], $4\frac{1}{2} \times 3\frac{3}{8}$, ff. 331 (23), *Eus. t., prol.*, κεφ. t., *Am., Eus., lect., syn., men., subscr.,* στίχ., *pict.*

151. Rom. Pal.-Vat. 220 [x or xi], $9\frac{5}{8} \times 7$, ff. 224 (28), ll. black and gold, *Carp., Eus. t.,* κεφ. t., κεφ., τίτλ., *Am., pict.,* scholia in the margin, and some rare readings (e. g. John xix. 14). The sheets are in twenty-one quaternions. After St. Matthew stands εκλογη εν συντομω εκ των συν- τεθεντων υπο Ευσεβιου προς Στεφανον λ.

152. Rom. Pal.-Vat. 227 [xiii], $8\frac{1}{2} \times 6\frac{1}{4}$, ff. 308 (20), κεφ. t., κεφ., τίτλ., *pict.*

153. Rom. Pal.-Vat. 229 [xiii], 4to, $8\frac{1}{4} \times 5\frac{3}{8}$, ff. 266 (25), ll. rubr., *chart., prol.,* κεφ. t., κεφ., τίτλ., *Am., lect., men., subscr.* (full), στίχ.

154. Rom. Alexandrino-Vatican. vel Christinae 28 [dated April 14, 1442], written in Italy on cotton paper, $10\frac{3}{8} \times 8\frac{1}{8}$, ff. 355 (40), ll. rubr., κεφ., *Am.* (*lect., syn., men.,* and date later, true date xiii, Greg.), with Theophylact's commentary. This and the two next were given by Christina, Queen of Sweden, to Card. Azzolini, and bought from him by Alexander VIII (1689-91).

155. Rom. Alex.-Vat. 79 [xi? Birch, xiv Scholz], $6 \times 4\frac{3}{8}$, ff. 306 (20), κεφ., τίτλ., *Am., syn., subscr.,* στίχ., with some lessons from St. Paul prefixed. Given by Andrew Rivet to Rutgersius, Swedish Ambassador to the United Provinces. This copy is Wetstein's 99, the codex Rutgersii cited by Dan. Heinsius in his Exercitat. sacr. in Evangel.

156. Rom. Alex.-Vat. 189 [xii], $4\frac{3}{4} \times 4$, ff. 244 (23), κεφ. t., κεφ., τίτλ., *Am.*; ' ex bibliothecâ Goldasti' is on the first page.

157. Rom. Urbino-Vat. 2 [xii], $7\frac{3}{8} \times 5\frac{1}{4}$, ff. 325 (22), *Carp., prol., Eus. t.,* κεφ. t., κεφ., τίτλ., *lect., subscr., pict.* It belonged to the Ducal Library at Urbino, and was brought to Rome by Clement VII (1523-34). It is very beautifully written (Birch, N. T. 1788, gives a facsimile), certain chronicles and rich ornaments in vermilion and gold. On fol. 19 we read underneath two figures respectively Ιωαννης εν χω τω θω πιστος βασιλευς πορφυρογεννητος και αυτοκρατωρ ρωμαιων, ὁ Κομνηνος, and Αλεξιος εν χω τω θω πιστος βασιλευς πορφυρογεννητος ὁ Κομνηνος. The Emperor John II the Handsome succeeded his father, the great Alexius, A.D. 1118. This MS. is remarkable for its eclectic text, which is said by Zahn to approach sometimes that of Marcion (Geschichte d. N. T. Kanons, i. 456, note 2, and 457, note 1). It is often in agreement with Codd. BDL, 69, 106, and especially with 1.

158. Cod. Pii II, Rom. Vat. 55 [xi], $3\frac{1}{2} \times 3$, ff. 235 (20), κεφ. t., κεφ., τίτλ., *Am., Eus., lect.* (partial), and readings in the margin, *primâ manu*. This copy was given to the Library by Pius II (1458-64).

159. Rom. Barberinianus 464, formerly 8 [xi], $10\frac{3}{8} \times 8\frac{1}{2}$, ff. 203 (23), 2 cols., κεφ. t., κεφ., τίτλ., *Am., Eus., lect., subscr.* (*Carp., Eus. t.,* κεφ. t. Matt., *syn., men.* xvi), in the Barberini Library, at Rome,

founded above two centuries since by the Cardinal, Francis II, of that name.

160. Rom. Barb. iv. 27, formerly 9 [dated 1123], $8\frac{7}{8} \times 7\frac{1}{8}$, ff. 216, κεφ. τ., κεφ., τίτλ., Am., lect., syn., men., subscr.

161. Rom. Barb. iii. 17, formerly 10 [x or xi], $8 \times 6\frac{1}{2}$, ff. 203 (24), 2 cols., κεφ. τ., κεφ., τίτλ., Am., Eus. (lect. later), ending at John xvi. 4. This copy follows the Latin version both in its text (John iii. 6) and marginal scholia (John vii. 29). Various readings are often thus noted in its margin.

162. Rom. Barb. iv. 31, formerly 11 [dated May 13, 1153 (ςχξά), Indict. 1], $9\frac{1}{4} \times 6\frac{3}{4}$, written by one Manuel: ff. 248 (23), Carp., Eus. t., κεφ., τίτλ., Am., pict., subscr.

163. Rom. Barb. v. 16, formerly 12 [xi], $11\frac{1}{2} \times 8$, ff. 173 (33), 2 cols., Eus. t., κεφ. t., κεφ., Am., Eus., lect., syn., men., subscr., pict., written in Syria. Scholz says it contains only the portions of the Gospels read in Church-lessons, but Birch the four Gospels, with the numbers of ῥήματα and στίχοι to the first three Gospels.

164. Rom. Barb. iii. 38, formerly 13 [dated Oct. 1039], $6\frac{7}{8} \times 5\frac{3}{8}$, ff. 214 (27), Carp., Eus. t., κεφ. t., κεφ., τίτλ., Am., Eus., lect., subscr., pict. (syn., men. later), and the numbers of στίχοι. The subscription states that it was written by Leo, a priest and calligrapher, and bought in 1168 by Bartholomew, who compared it with ancient Jerusalem manuscripts on the sacred mount.

165. Rom. Barb. v. 37, formerly 14 [dated 1291], $11\frac{7}{8} \times 8$, ff. 215, 2 cols., Carp., Eus. t., κεφ. t., κεφ., τίτλ., Am., Eus., syn., with the Latin Vulgate version. Written for one Archbishop Paul, and given to the Library by Eugenia, daughter of Jo. Pontanus.

166. Rom. Barb. iii. 131, formerly 115 [xiii], 4to, $8\frac{3}{8} \times 6\frac{1}{2}$, ff. 75 (27), κεφ., τίτλ., Am., Eus., lect., containing only SS. Luke ix. 33—xxiv. 24 and John.

167. Rom. Barb. iii. 6, formerly 208 [xiii], $4\frac{7}{8} \times 3\frac{1}{4}$, ff. 264 (25), κεφ. t., κεφ., τίτλ., pict. (later).

168. Rom. Barb. vi. 9, formerly 211 [xiii], $13\frac{3}{8} \times 8\frac{5}{8}$, ff. 217, 2 cols., κεφ. t., κεφ., τίτλ., Am., Eus. (Mark subscr., στίχ.).

169. Rom. Vallicellianus B. 133 [xi], $4\frac{3}{4} \times 4$, ff. 249 (19), prol., κεφ. t., κεφ., τίτλ., Am., Eus., subscr., syn., men., pict., once the property of Achilles Statius, as also was Cod. 171. This codex and the next three are in the Library of St. Maria in Vallicella at Rome, and belong to the Fathers of the Oratory of St. Philippo Neri.

170. Rom. Vallicell. C. 61 [xiii–xv], $8\frac{1}{2} \times 6\frac{1}{4}$, ff. 277 (23), prol., κεφ. t. κεφ., τίτλ., Am., Eus., lect., ἀναγν., subscr., στίχ. (occasionally in later hand). The end of St. Luke and most of St. John is in a later hand.

171. Rom. Vallicell. C. 73 [xiv, Montfaucon xi], $5\frac{3}{4} \times 4\frac{1}{4}$, ff. 253 (20), prol., κεφ. t., κεφ., τίτλ., Am., Eus., lect., subscr.

172. Rom. Vallicell. F. 90 [xii], 4to, ff. 217, now only contains the

Pentateuch, but from Bianchini, I. ii. pp. 529-30, we infer that the Gospels were once there.

173. Rom. Vat. Gr. 1983, formerly Basil. 22, ending John xiii. 1, seems to have been written in Asia Minor [xi Birch and Burgon, xii or xiii Greg.], $7\frac{7}{8} \times 5\frac{1}{4}$, ff. 155 (20), 2 cols., *Carp.*, *Eus. t.*, κεφ. t., κεφ., τίτλ., *Am.*, *lect.*, *men.*, *subscr.*; ῥήμ., στίχ. as in Codd. 163, 164, 167. This codex, and the next four, were brought from the Library of the Basilian monks.

174. Rom. Vat. Gr. 2002, formerly Basil. 41 [dated second hour of Sept. 7, A.D. 1052], $9\frac{3}{4} \times 7\frac{1}{2}$, ff. 132 (30), 2 cols., κεφ. t., κεφ., τίτλ., *Am.*, *Eus.*, *lect.*, *subscr.*, στίχ. *Mut.* Matt. i. 1—ii. 1 ; John i. 1–27; ending John viii. 47. Written by the monk Constantine 'tabernis habitante,' ' cum pracesset praefecturae Georgilas dux Calabriae' (Scholz).

175. (Act. 41, Paul. 194, Apoc. 20.) Rom. Vat. Gr. 2080, formerly Basil. 119 [x–xii], $8 \times 5\frac{3}{4}$, ff. 247, *subscr.*, contains the whole New Testament, beginning M tt. iv. 17, with scholia to the Acts, between which and the Catholic Epistles stands the Apocalypse. There are some marginal corrections *primâ manu* (e. g. Luke xxiv. 13). The Pauline Epistles have Euthalius' subscriptions. Also inspected by Bianchini.

176. Rom. Vat. Gr. 2113, formerly Basil. 152 [x or xi], $8\frac{1}{4} \times 5\frac{3}{4}$, ff. 77, ll. coloured, John ii. 1, κεφ., τίτλ., *Am.*, *lect.* Begins Matt. x. 13, ends John ii. 1.

177. Rom. Vat. Gr. ? formerly Basil. 163 [xi]. 8vo, *mut.* John i. 1–29. Dr. Gregory thinks that it is 2115, his Evan. 870.

178. Rom. Angelicus A. 1. 5 [xii], $14\frac{7}{8} \times 11\frac{3}{8}$, ff. 272 (23), 2 cols., *Eus. t.*, κεφ., τίτλ. with harmony, *Am.*, *mut.* Jo. xxi. 17–25. Arranged in quaternions, and the titles to the Gospels resemble those in Cod. 69. Codd. 178-9 belong to the Angelica convent of Augustinian Eremites at Rome. It has on the first leaf the same subscription as we gave under Cod. 87, and which Birch and Scholz misunderstand.

179. Rom. Angelic. A. 4. 11 [xii], $7\frac{3}{4} \times 6\frac{1}{2}$, ff. 248 (22), *Eus. t.*, κεφ. t., κεφ., τίτλ., *Am.*, *Eus.*, *lect.* (*syn.*, *men.*, xv or xvi, *chart.*). The last five leaves (214–18) and two others (23, 30) are *chart.*, and in a later hand.

180. (Act. 82, Paul. 92, Apoc. 44.) Rom. Propagandae L. vi. 19, formerly 251, before Borgiae 2 [Gospels xi, Greg. xiv], $8\frac{1}{8} \times 5\frac{1}{4}$, ff. ? κεφ. t., κεφ., τίτλ., *Am.*, *Eus.*, *lect.* (*syn.*, *men.*, xv *chart.*) ; the Gospels were written by one Andreas: the rest of the New Testament and some apocryphal books by one John, November, 1284 [1]. This manuscript, with Cod. T and Evst. 37, belonged to the Velitrant Museum of ' Praesul Steph. Borgia, Collegii Urbani de Propaganda Fide a secretis.'

181. Cod. Francisci Xavier, Cardinal. de Zelada [xi], fol., ff. 596, with scholia in the margin. This manuscript (from which Birch took

---

[1] Or rather A.D. 1274. According to Engelbreth the letters stand ψτψπβ, which can only mean A.M. 6782 (see p. 42, note 2).

extracts) is now missing. Compare Birch, N. T., Proleg. p. lviii; Burgon, Last Twelve Verses &c., pp. 284, 288.

Codd. 182-198, all in that noble Library at Florence, founded by Cosmo de' Medici [d. 1464], increased by his grandson Lorenzo [d. 1492], were very slightly examined by Birch, and subsequently by Scholz. Dean Burgon has described his own researches at Florence in the *Guardian* for August 20 and 27, 1873, from which I have thankfully corrected the statements made in my first edition respecting all the manuscripts there. They have been examined since then more leisurely by Dr. Gregory, from whose careful account some particulars have been added in this edition (*see* Greg., Prolegomena (ii), pp. 505-509).

182. Flor. Laurentianus Plut. vi. 11 [xii], $10 \times 7\frac{1}{2}$, ff. 226 (24), κεφ. t., κεφ., τίτλ. to St. John only, *subscr.* (in Luke). The titles of the Gospels in lake, forming a kind of imitation of ropework.

183. Flor. Laur. vi. 14 [xiv, xii Greg.], $6\frac{1}{2} \times 5\frac{1}{8}$, ff. 349 (19), *Eus. t.*, κεφ. t., κεφ., τίτλ., *Am., Eus.* in gold; and in a later hand, *capp. Lat.*, ἀναγν., *lect., syn., men.,* at the end of which is τέλος σὺν Θεῷ ἁγίῳ τοῦ μηνολογίου, ἀμήν· αυιη΄, i.e. A.D. 1418. This mode of reckoning is very rare (*see* p. 42, note 2), and tempted Scholz to read ϛυιη΄ of the Greek era, i.e. A.D. 910.

184. Flor. Laur. vi. 15 [xiii], $11\frac{1}{4} \times 5\frac{1}{2}$, ff. 72 (49), 2 cols., *Carp., prol., κεφ. t., Am., Eus., lect.* Left in an unfinished state.

185. Flor. Laur. vi. 16 [xii], $14 \times 6\frac{3}{4}$, ff. 341 (21), *prol.*, κεφ. t., κεφ., τίτλ., *Am., lect.,* ἀναγν., *subscr.,* στίχ. The summary of the Synaxarion is subscribed Πόνος Βασιλείου, καὶ Θῦ λόγου λόγοι (Burgon).

186. Flor. Laur. vi. 18 [xi], fol., $11\frac{3}{8} \times 8\frac{1}{2}$, ff. 260 (20), *Carp., Eus. t., prol.,* κεφ. t., κεφ., τίτλ., *Am., Eus., syn., men., pict.* (Matt.), commentary (Victor's on St. Mark); written by Leontius, a calligrapher. Burgon cites Bandini's Catal. i. 130-3, where the elaborate *syn.* are given in full.

187. Flor. Laur. vi. 23 [xii], $7\frac{7}{8} \times 6\frac{1}{4}$, ff. 212 (25), *pict.* very rich and numerous. *Carp., Eus. t.,* κεφ. t., τίτλ., *Am.* (not *Eus.*), all in gold. A peculiar kind of asterisk occurs very frequently in the text and margin, the purpose of which is not clear.

188. Flor. Laur. vi. 25 [xi], $6 \times 4\frac{1}{2}$, ff. 228 (26), *syn.* and *men.* full and beautiful. *Prol.,* κεφ. t., κεφ., τίτλ., *Am., Eus., lect., subscr.,* στίχ.

189. (Act. 141, Paul. 239.) Flor. Laur. vi. 27 [xii], $4\frac{1}{2} \times 3\frac{7}{8}$, ff. 452 (24), κεφ. t., κεφ., *lect.,* ἀναγν., *Euthal.* in Cath. and Paul., minute and beautifully written, *mut.* from John xix. 38.

190. Flor. Laur. vi. 28 [July, 1285, Ind. 13], 8vo, $5\frac{3}{8} \times 4\frac{3}{8}$, ff. 439 (17), *prol.,* κεφ. t., κεφ., τίτλ., *Am., lect., pict.*

191. Flor. Laur. vi. 29 [xiii], $5\frac{1}{4} \times 3\frac{3}{4}$, ff. 180 (27), *prol.,* κεφ. *Lat., subscr.,* with στίχοι numbered: ἀναγνώσματα marked in a more recent hand.

192. Flor. Laur. vi. 30 [xiii], $4\frac{3}{4} \times 3\frac{1}{2}$, ff. 200 (28), *prol.,* κεφ. t., κεφ.,

τίτλ., *lect.*, *subscr.*, *Am.* and *Eus.* in one line, the latter later (*see* Cod. 112): ἀρχή of *lect.*, never τέλος.

193. Flor. Laur. vi. 32 [xi], 8vo, 6¼ × 5, ff. 165 (27), *Carp.*, *Eus. t.*, *pict.*, *κεφ.*, *Am.* (not *Eus.*), (ἀναγν., *lect.* in later hand).

194. Flor. Laur. vi. 33 [xi], 11¾ × 9¾, ff. 263 (22), *pict.*, and a marginal catena (Victor's on St. Mark) resembling that of Cod. 34: e.g. on Luke xxiv. 13. *Κεφ.*, *Am.* (not *Eus.*), *subscr.*, *στίχ.*, *pict.* Begins Matt. iii. 7.

195. Flor. Laur. vi. 34 [xi], 10⅞ × 8⅝, ff. 277 (25), once belonged to the Cistercian convent of S. Salvator de Septimo. *Prol.* (the same as in Cod. 186 but briefer, attributed to Eusebius), *syn.*, and a commentary (Victor's on St. Mark). The date of the year is lost, but the month (May) and indiction (8) remain. *Κεφ. t.*, *κεφ.*, *τίτλ.*, *Am.*, *Eus.*, *syn.*, *men.*

196. Flor. Laur. viii. 12 [xii], 9¾ × 7¼, ff. 369 (44), *prol.*, *κεφ. t.* (all together at the beginning), *κεφ.*, *τίτλ.*, the text in red letters (*see* p. 184, note 1), *pict.*, with a catena in black. Given by a son of Cosmo de' Medici in 1473 to the Convent of St. Mark at Florence.

197. (Act. 90.) Flor. Laur. viii. 14 [xi], fol., 11¾ × 9¼, ff. 154 (29), *prol.*, *κεφ. t.*, *κεφ.*, *τίτλ.*, contains the Epistle of St. James with a marginal gloss: also portions of SS. Matthew and Mark, with Chrysostom's commentary on St. Matthew, and Victor's on St. Mark, all imperfect.

198. Flor. Laur. Ædil. 221 [xiii], 4to, 9¾ × 6⅝, ff. 171 (29), *chart.*, *Carp.*, *Eus. t.*, *κεφ. t.*, *Am.*, *Eus.*, *lect.*, *subscr.*: from the library 'Aedilium Flor. Ecc.' Here again *Am.* and *Eus.* are in the same line (*see* Cod. 112): the ἀναγνώσματα also are numbered.

Codd. 199–203 were inspected, rather than collated, by Birch at Florence before 1788; the first two in the Benedictine library of St. Maria; the others in that of St. Mark, belonging to the Dominican Friars. Scholz could not find any of them, but 201 is Wetstein's 107, Scrivener's m; 202 is now in the British Museum, Addit. 14,774. The other two Burgon found in the Laurentian Library, whither they came at the suppression of monasteries in 1810. They were examined afterwards by Gregory.

199. Flor. Laur. Conv. Sopp. 160, formerly Badia 99 or S. Mariae 67 [xii], 5⅝ × 4¾, ff. 229 (25), *Eus. t.*, *κεφ. t.* with *harm.*, *κεφ.*, *τίτλ.*, *subscr.*, *pict.*, *lect.*, with iambic verses and various scholia. The στίχοι are numbered and, besides *Am.*, *Eus.*, there exists in parts a Harmony at the foot of the pages, such as is described in p. 58, note 2.

200. Flor. Laur. Conv. Sopp. 159, formerly Badia 69 or S. Mariae 66 [x], 8¾ × 6⅞, ff. 229 (25), *pict.*, *Carp.*, *Eus. t.*, *κεφ. t.*, *Am.*, all in gold: *Eus.* in red, *κεφ.*, *τίτλ.*, with fragments of Gregory of Nyssa against the Arians (*syn.* and *men.* xiv). There are many scholia in vermilion scattered throughout the book. Codd. 199, 200 were presented to St. Maria's by Antonia Corbinelli [d. 1423]: the latter from St. Justina's, another Benedictine house.

*201. (Act. 91, Paul. 104, Apoc. 94.) Lond. Brit. Mus. Addit. 11,837, formerly Praedicator. S. Marci 701 [Oct. 7, 1357, Ind. 11], 13½ × 11, ff. 492 (22), is m^scr. in the Gospels, p^scr. in Act., Paul., and b^scr. in Apoc. This splendid copy was purchased for the British Museum from the heirs of Dr. Samuel Butler, Bishop of Lichfield. It contains the whole New Testament; was first cited by Wetstein (107) from notices by Jo. Lamy, in his 'de Eruditione Apostolorum,' Florence, 1738; glanced at by Birch, and stated by Scholz (N. T. vol. ii. pp. xii, xxviii) to have been cursorily collated by himself: how that is possible can hardly be understood, as he elsewhere professes his ignorance whither the manuscript had gone (N. T. vol. i. p. lxxii). Scrivener collated the whole volume. There are many changes by a later hand, also *syn.*, κεφ. *t.*, κεφ., τίτλ., *Am.*, some *Eus.*, *lect.*, *prol.*, ἀναγν., *subscr.*, στίχ., *vers.*, and some foreign matter.

202. Brit. Mus. Addit. 14,774, formerly Praed. S. Marci 705 [xii], 10 × 8, ff. 278 (21), κεφ. *t.* (in red and gold), *orn.*, κεφ., τίτλ., *Am.*, *Eus.* (the last often omitted), *lect.*, *subscr.*, στίχ., *men.*, *syn.* This splendid copy cost the Museum £84 (Bloomfield).

203. Flor. Bibl. Nat. Convent. i. 10, 7, formerly Praed. S. Marci 707 [xv], 8⅜ × 5¾, *chart.*, is really in modern Greek. Birch cites it for John vii. 53, but it ought to be expunged from the list.

204. (Act. 92, Paul. 105.) [xi or xiii] Bologna, Bibl. Univ. 2775, formerly Bononiensis Canonicor. Regular. St. Salvador 640. After the suppression of the house in 1867, it was moved to its present place. 7¾ × 5¾, ff. 443 (25). *Syn.*, κεφ., ἀναγνώσματα numbered (without *Am.*, *Carp.*), *lect.*, *pict.* (Birch, Scholz, corrected by Burgon). Also τίτλ., *men.*, *subscr.*, στίχ.

Codd. 205-215, 217 in the Ducal palace at Venice, were slightly examined by Birch in 1783, carefully by Burgon in 1872, and by Gregory in 1886.

205. (Act. 93, Paul. 106, Apoc. 88.) Venice, Mark 5 [xv], large fol., 15½ × 11, ff. 441 (55, 56), *prol.* (Cath., Paul.), κεφ. *t.*, κεφ. (Gr. and Lat.), τίτλ., *subscr.*, contains both Testaments, with many peculiar readings. It was written for Cardinal Bessarion (apparently by John Rhosen his librarian), the donor of all these books. This is Dean Holmes' No. 68 in the Septuagint, and contains a note in the Cardinal's hand: τόπος μκ. Ἡ θεία γραφὴ παλαιά τε καὶ νέα πᾶσα· κτῆμα Βησσαρίωνος Καρδηνάλεως Ἐπισκόπου Οαβίνων τοῦ (*sic*) καὶ Νικαίας. By τόπος μκ Holmes understands the class mark of the volume in Bessarion's Library. W. F. Rinck considers it in the *Gospels* a copy of Cod. 209 ('Lucubratio Critica in Act. Apost. Epp. C. et P.,' Basileae, 1830). Burgon, who fully admits their wonderful similarity in respect to the text, judges that Cod. 205, which is much more modern than Cod. 209, was transcribed from the same *uncial* archetype.

206. (Act. 94, Paul. 107, Apoc. 101.) Ven. Mark 6 [xv or xvi], 15 × 10⅜, ff. 431, like Codd. 69 and 233, is partly on parchment, partly on paper. It contains both Testaments, but is not numbered for the Apocalypse. A mere duplicate of Cod. 205, as Holmes saw clearly: it is his No. 122.

207. Ven. Mark 8 [xi or xii], 10⅞ × 8⅜, ff. 267 (22), 2 cols., *Carp.*,

prol., pict., κεφ. *t.*, τίτλ., κεφ., *Am.* (not *Eus.*) in gold, *syn.*, *men.*, *mut.* in Matt. i. 1–13 ; Mark i. 1–11, for the sake of the gorgeous illuminations. Written in two columns. Once owned by A. F. R.

208. Ven. Mark 9 [xi or xii], 7⅛ × 5¾, ff. 239 (23), *Carp., Eus. t.*, κεφ. *t.*, κεφ., τίτλ., *Am., Eus.*, of some value.

209. (Act. 95, Paul. 108, Apoc. 46.) Ven. Mark 10 [xi, xiv Greg.], 7¾ × 4¾, ff. 411 (27), of the whole New Testament, once Bessarion's, who had it with him at the Council of Florence, 1439. There are numerous minute marginal notes in vermilion, obviously *primâ manu*. In its delicate style of writing this copy greatly resembles Cod. 1 (facsimile No. 23). Κεφ. *t.*, τίτλ., κεφ., *Am.* (not *Eus.*), also the modern chapters in the margin. *Prol.* to Epistles, *lect.*, but not much in the Gospels, before each of which stands a blank leaf, as if for *pict*. A good collation of Codd. 205 and 209 is needed; Birch did little, Engelbreth gave him some readings, and Fleck has published part of a collation by Heimbach. Rinck collated Apoc. i–iii. In the Gospels they are very like Codd. B, 1. The Apocalypse is in a later hand, somewhat resembling that of Cod. 205, and has *prol.* For the unusual order of the books, *see* above, p. 72.

210. Ven. Mark 27 [xi or xii], a noble fol., 14 × 11⅞, ff. 372, with a catena (Victor's commentary on St. Mark). *Mut.* Matt. i. 1—ii. 18, from the same cause as in Cod. 207. Rich blue and gold illuminations, and pictures of SS. Mark and Luke. Τίτλ., κεφ., *pict*.

211. Ven. Mark 539 [xii], fol., 11½ × 9½, ff. 280 (29–26), 2 cols., *mut*. Luke i. 1—ii. 32 ; John i. 1—iv. 2, with an Arabic version in the right-hand column of each page. Κεφ. *t., Am., Eus.* (irregularly inserted), *lect., syn., men.*, *subscr.*, ῥήμ., στίχ.

Burgon cites Zanetti, Graeca D. Marc. Bibl. Codd. MSS., Venet. 1740, p. 291, for the enumeration of the five Patriarchates (*see* above, p. 67), and other curious matter appended to St. John. The heading of the second Gospel is εὐαγγέλιον ἐκ τοῦ κατὰ Μάρκον.

212. Ven. Mark 540 [xi or xii], 6⅜ × 5, ff. 273 (23), the first page in gold, with *pict.* and most elaborate illuminations. Much *mut.*, twenty leaves being supplied in a modern hand. *Carp., Eus. t.*, κεφ., *vers.*, τίτλ., *lect., Am.* with *Eus.* in a line with them (*see* Cod. 112), a little later, carried only to the end of St. Mark.

213. Ven. Mark 542 [xi], 8vo, 8⅜ × 6¼, ff. 356 (18), *mut.* John xviii. 40—xxi. 25. *Eus. t.*, τίτλ., κεφ. (*Am., Eus.* most irregularly inserted), few ἀρχαί and τέλη, ἀναγν., heroic verses as colophons to the Gospels. Large full stops are found in impossible places.

214. Ven. Mark 543 [xiv], 8vo, 9¾ × 6¼, ff. 227 (27), *chart., argent., prol.*, κεφ. *t.* with *harm.*, κεφ., *Am.* (not *Eus.*), ἀναγν., *lect., syn., men., subscr., vers*.

215. Ven. Mark 544 [xi], fol., 12¾ × 9½, ff. 271 (24), *Carp., Eus. t.*, κεφ. *t.* with *harm.*, τίτλ., κεφ., *Am., Eus., lect., syn., pict.* (later). This copy is a duplicate of Codd. 20, 300, as well in its text as in the subscriptions and commentary, being without any of the later corrections

seen in Cod. 20. The commentary on St. John is Chrysostom's, those on the other Gospels the same as in Cod. 300 (Burgon).

216. Codex Canonici, brought by him from Corcyra, written in a small character [no date assigned], never was at St. Mark's, as Scholz alleges: Griesbach inserted it in his list through a misunderstanding of Birch's meaning. It is probably one of those now at Oxford, to be described hereafter (*see* Codd. 489, 490).

217. Ven. Mark, Gr. i. 3, given in 1478 by Peter de Montagnana to the monastery of St. John in Viridario, at Padua (viii. A.) [xii or xiii], $8\frac{1}{8} \times 6\frac{1}{8}$, ff. 306 (21), in fine condition. *Carp., Eus. t., κεφ. t., τίτλ., κεφ., Am.* (not *Eus.*), full *syn.*, few *lect., prol., vers.*

Codd. 218-225 are in the Imperial Library at Vienna. Alter and Birch collated them about the same time, the latter but cursorily, and Gregory examined them in 1887.

*218. (Act. 65, Paul. 57, Apoc. 33.) Vindobon. Caesar. Nessel. 23, formerly 1 [xiii], fol., $12\frac{1}{2} \times 8\frac{1}{4}$, ff. 623 (49, 50), 2 cols., κεφ. t., κεφ., τίτλ., *Am., subscr.*, Euthal. in Acts, Cath., Paul., contains both Testaments. *Mut.* Apoc. xiii. 5—xiv. 8; xv. 7—xvii. 2; xviii. 10—xix. 15; ending at xx. 7 λυθήσεται. This important copy, containing many peculiar readings, was described by Treschow, and comprises the text of Alter's inconvenient, though fairly accurate N. T. 1786-7, to be described in Vol. II. Like Cod. 123 it was brought from Constantinople by De Busbeck.

219. Vind. Caes. Ness. 321, formerly 32 [xiii], $6\frac{1}{4} \times 4\frac{3}{4}$, ff. 232 (21), κεφ. t., κεφ., τίτλ., *Am., Eus., subscr.*

220. Vind. Caes. Ness. 337, formerly 33 [xiv], 12mo, $3\frac{7}{8} \times 2\frac{5}{8}$, ff. 303 (22), in very small letters, κεφ., τίτλ., *Am., lect., syn.*

221. Vind. Caes. Ness. 117, formerly 38 [x or xi], $11 \times 7\frac{5}{8}$, ff. 251 (41-43), with commentaries (Chrysostom on Matt., John; Victor on Mark, Titus of Bostra on Luke), to which the *fragments* of text here given are accommodated.

222. Vind. Caes. Ness. 180, formerly 39 [xiv], $8\frac{1}{2} \times 6$, ff. 346 (32), on cotton paper, *mut.* Contains *fragments* of the Gospels, with a commentary (Victor's on St. Mark). This and the last were brought from Constantinople by De Busbeck.

223. Vind. Caes. 301, formerly 40 [xiv, Greg. x], $7 \times 5\frac{1}{2}$, ff. 115 (32), contains fragments of SS. Matthew, Luke, and John, with a catena. Codd. 221-3 must be cited cautiously: Alter appears to have made no systematic use of them.

224. Vind. Caes. Suppl. Gr. 97, formerly Kollar. 8 [xii], $5\frac{1}{2} \times 4\frac{3}{8}$, ff. 97 (19), κεφ. t., κεφ., τίτλ., *Am., lect., syn., men., subscr.*, only contains St. Matthew. This copy came from Naples.

225. Vind. Caes. Suppl. Gr. 102, formerly Kollar. 9 [dated ϛψ' or A. D. 1192], $5\frac{3}{8} \times 3\frac{7}{8}$, ff. 171 (29), *pict., lect., ἀναγν., syn., men.*

Codd. 226-233 are in the Escurial, described by D. G. Moldenhawer, who collated them about 1783, loosely enough, for Birch's edition. In 1870 the Librarian, José Fernandez Montana (in order to correct Haenel's errors) sent to Mr. Wm. Kelly, who obligingly communicated it to me, a complete catalogue of the four copies of the Greek Bible, and of nineteen of the New Testament 'neither more or less,' then at the Escurial, with their present class-marks. I do not recognize, either in his list or in that subjoined, the 'Codex Aureus containing the Four Gospels in letters of gold, a work of the early part of the eleventh century,' spoken of in the *Globe* newspaper of Oct. 3, 1872, on occasion of the fire at the Escurial on Oct. 2, which however did not touch the manuscripts. Perhaps that Codex is in Latin, unless it be Evst. 40. *See* also Emmanuel Miller, Cat. des MSS. Gr. de la Bibl. de l'Escurial, Paris, A.D. 1848.

226. (Act. 108, Paul. 228.) Cod. Escurialensis χ. iv. 17 [xi], 8vo, ff. ?, on the finest vellum, richly ornamented, in a small, round, very neat hand. *Eus. t., κεφ. t., lect., pict., τίτλ., κεφ., Am., Eus.* Many corrections were made by a later hand, but the original text is valuable, and the readings sometimes unique. Fairly collated.

227. Escurial. χ. iii. 15 [xiii], 4to, ff. 158, *prol., κεφ. t., Am., pict.* A later hand, which dates from 1308, has been very busy in making corrections.

228. (Act. 109, Paul. 229.) Escurial. χ. iv. 12 [xiv, Montana xvi], 8vo, ff. ?, *chart*. Once belonged to Nicolas Nathanael of Crete, then to Andreas Damarius of Epidaurus, a calligrapher. *Eus. t., syn.*[1]

229. Escurial. χ. iv. 21 [dated 1140], 8vo, ff. 296, written by Basil Argyropolus, a notary. *Mut.* Mark xvi. 15–20; John i. 1–11. *Pict., lect.*; the latter by a hand of about the fourteenth century, which retraced much of the discoloured ink, and corrected in the margin (since mutilated by the binder) very many important readings of the first hand, which often resemble those of ADK. i. 72. This copy must be mislaid, as it is not in Montana's list.

230. Escurial. φ (Montana ψ).[2] iii. 5 [dated Oct. 29, 1013, with the wrong Indiction, 11 for 12: Montana's date is 1014, and the error is probably not his: *see* p. 42, note 2], 4to, ff. 218, written by Luke a monk and priest, with double *syn.*[3], *Carp., κεφ. t., subscr., ῥήμ., στίχ.*: see p. 67, note. An interesting copy, deemed by Moldenhawer worthy of closer examination.

231. Escurial. φ (Montana ψ).[2] iii. 6 [xii], 4to, ff. 181, *lect., Eus. t.* torn, *κεφ. t.*, a picture 'quae Marcum mentitur,' *subscr., στίχ., syn., men.* There are some marginal glosses by a later hand (which obelizes John vii. 53 *seq.*), and a Latin version above parts of St. Matthew.

232. Escurial. φ (Montana ψ).[2] iii. 7 [xiii: dated 1292, Montana], 4to, ff. 288, very elegant but otherwise a poor copy. Double *syn., τίτλοι* in the margin of SS. Matthew and Luke, but elsewhere kept apart.

233. Escurial. Y. ii. 8 [xi ?, Montana xiii], ff. 279, like Codd. 69 and 206, is partly of parchment, partly paper, in bad condition, and once

---

[1] Thus, at least, I understand Moldenhawer's description, 'Evangeliis et Actis λέξεις subjiciuntur dudum in vulgus notae.'

[2] Others F.

[3] By double *syn.* Moldenhawer may be supposed to mean here and in Cod. 232 both *syn.* and *men.*

belonged to Matthew Dandolo, a Venetian noble. It has a catena, and by reason of ligatures, &c. (*see* p. 43), is hard to read. *Prol.*, κεφ. t., *Eus. t.* (apart), vers., ῥήμ., στίχ.

234. (Act. 57, Paul. 72.) Cod. Havniensis reg. theol. 1322, formerly 1 [dated 1278], 10 × 7⅜, ff. 315 (35), 2 cols., one of the several copies written by Theodore (*see* p. 43, note 1). This copy and Cod. 235 are now in the Royal Library at Copenhagen, but were bought at Venice by F. Rostgaard in 1699. The order of the books in Cod. 234 is described p. 73. *Carp., Eus. t., lect., syn., men.*, with many corrections. (C. G. Hensler, 1784.)

235. Havniens. reg. theol. 1323, formerly 2 [dated 1314], 4to, ff. 279, *chart.*, written by the ἱερομόναχος Philotheus, though very incorrectly; the text agrees much with Codd. DK. i. 33 and the Harkleian Syriac. Κεφ. t., lect.; the words are often ill divided and the stops misplaced (Hensler).

236[1]. London, J. Bevan Braithwaite 3 [xi], 6½ × 4¾, ff. 256 (20), 7 *chart., syn., men., Eus. t., Am.,* κεφ., some τίτλ., some *lect.,* κεφ. t. *Mut.* at beginning and at end after John ix. 28. Beautifully written. Bought at Athens in 1889. Collated by W. C. Braithwaite.

Codd. 237-259 are nearly all Moscow manuscripts, and were thoroughly collated by C. F. Matthaei, for his N. T., to be described in Vol. II. These Russian codices were for the most part brought from the twenty-two monasteries of Mount Athos by the monk Arsenius, on the suggestion of the Patriarch Nico, in the reign of Michael, son of Alexius (1645-76), and placed in the Library of the Holy Synod, at Moscow.

*237. Mosc. S. Synod 42 [x], fol., ff. 288, Matthaei's d, from Philotheus (a monastery), *pict.*, with scholia, and Victor's commentary on St. Mark.

*238. Mosc. Syn. 48 (Mt. e) [xi], fol., ff. 355, *Eus. t.* (*mut.*), κεφ. t., *pict.*, with a catena and scholia; contains only SS. Matthew and Mark, but is of good quality. This copy formed the basis of Matthaei's edition of Victor's commentary on St. Mark, 1775 (Burgon).

*239. Mosc. Syn. 47 (Mt. g) [xi], fol., ff. 277, *Eus. t.*, κεφ. t. (Luke, John), contains Mark xvi. 2-8; Luke; John to xxi. 23, with scholia.

*240. Mosc. Syn. 49 (Mt. i) [xii], fol., ff. 410, κεφ. t., once belonging to Philotheus, then to Dionysius (monasteries) on Athos, with the commentary of Euthymius Zigabenus. *Mut.* Mark viii. 12-34; xiv. 17-54; Luke xv. 32—xvi. 8.

*241. Mosc. (Act. 104, Paul. 120, Apoc. 47) Dresdensis Reg. A. 172 (Tregelles), once Matthaei's (k) [xi], 4to, 8⅞ × 6¾. ff. 356 (31), *prol.*, κεφ. t., κεφ., τίτλ., *syn., men.* (Gregory); Epp. *prol.*, κεφ. t., the whole N. T. (p. 69, note), beautifully written, with rare readings. Bought by Alexius for fifty-two *aspri* at the siege of Constantinople (A.D. 1453), after-

---

[1] Readings extracted by Griesbach (Symb. Crit. i. pp. 247-304) from the margin of a copy of Mill's Greek Testament in the Bodleian, in his own or Thomas Hearne's handwriting, were placed here, but are omitted. Scrivener (Cod. Augiensis, Introd. p. xxxvi) has shown that they were derived from Evan. 440.

wards given by Pachonius to a monastery at Athos, and thence called δοχειαρίου.

*242. Mosc. (Act. 105, Paul. 121, Apoc. 48) Syn. 380 (Mt. 1) [xii], 8vo, ff. 510, the whole N. T., with Psalms, ᾠδαί, prol., pict., Am.

243. Mosc. Cod. Typographei S. Syn. 13 (Mt. m) [xiv], fol., chart., ff. 224, from the Iberian monastery on Athos, contains SS. Matthew and Luke with Theophylact's commentary.

*244. Mosc. Typograph. 1 (Mt. n) [xii], fol., ff. 274, pict., with Euthymius Zigabenus' commentary.

*245. Mosc. Syn. 265, 278, formerly (Greg.) (Mt. o) [dated 1199], 4to, ff. 246, from the famous monastery of Batopedion, written by John, a priest.

*246. Mosc. Syn. 261 (Mt. p) [xiv], 4to, chart., ff. 189, syn., κεφ. τ., with marginal various readings. *Mut.* Matt. xii. 41—xiii. 55; John xvii. 24—xviii. 20.

*247. Mosc. Syn. 373 (Mt. q) [xii], 8vo, ff. 223, syn., men., κεφ. τ., κεφ., Am., Eus., lect., prol., from Philotheus.

*248. Mosc. Syn. 264 (Mt. r) [dated 1275], 4to, ff. 260 (8 chart. + 252), κεφ. τ. (chart.), Eus., lect., written by Meletius a Beraean for Cyrus Alypius, οἰκόνομος of St. George's monastery, in the reign of Michael Palaeologus (1259–82).

*249. Mosc. Syn. 94 (Mt. s) [xi], fol.. ff. 809 (more likely 309 as Greg.), from Παντοκράτωρ monastery (as Cod. 74). Contains St. John with a catena.

*250. Mosc. Syn. in a box (Mt. v) [xiii], small 8vo, ff. 225, Carp., Eus. t., κεφ. τ., Am., Eus., syn., is the cursive portion of Cod V (see p. 144, and note), John vii. 39—xxi. 25. It is also Wetstein's Cod. 87.

*251. Mosc. Tabularii Caesarei (Mt. x) [xi], 4to, ff. 270, Carp., Eus. t., pict., Am., presented to a monastery in A. D. 1400.

*252. Dresd. Reg. A. 145 (Tregelles), once Matthaei's (z) [xi], 8⅜ × 7, ff. 123 (31), κεφ. τ., κεφ., τίτλ., Am., Eus., lect., ἀναγν. (Greg.), with corrections and double readings (as from another copy), but *prima manu*.

*253. Mosc. of Nicephorus Archbishop of Cherson 'et Slabinii' (Slaviansk ?)[1], formerly belonged to the monastery of St. Michael at Jerusalem (Mt. 10) [xi], fol., ff. 248, prol., κεφ. τ., Am., Eus., with scholia, Victor's commentary on St. Mark, and rare readings, much resembling those of Cod. 259.

*254. Dresd. A. 100 (Matthaei 11) (Tregelles) [xi], 11⅝ × 9¼, ff. 247 (24), κεφ. τ., κεφ., Am., Eus., pict., from the monastery of St. Athanasius. Contains SS. Luke and John with scholia.

---

[1] Holmes, Praefatio ad Pentateuchum, describes his Cod. 32 as 'e Codicibus Eugenii, olim Archiepiscopi Slabinii et Chersonis.' Nicephorus also is named by Holmes as the editor of a Catena on the Octateuch and the four books of Kings from the Constantinopolitan manuscripts (Leipzig, 1772-3), and is described as 'primo Hieromonachus, et postea Archiepiscopus Slabiniensis et Chersonensis, sedem Astracani habens' (ubi supra, cap. iv).

*255. Mosc. Syn. 139 (Mt. 12) [xiii], fol., ff. 299 *chart.* +9, once 'Dionysii monachi rhetoris *et amicorum.*' Commentaries of Chrysostom and others (ἐξηγητικαὶ ἐκλογαί), with fragments of the text interspersed.

*256. Mosc. Typogr. Syn. 3 (Mt. 14) [ix?], fol., ff. 147, scholia on SS. Mark and Luke, with portions of the text. The commentary on St. Mark is *ascribed* to Victor, but in this copy and the preceding the scholia are but few in number (Burgon).

*257. Mosc. Syn. 120 (Mt. 15) is Evan. O, described above.

*258. Dresd. Reg. A. 123 (Tregelles), (Mt. 17) [xiii], $8\frac{1}{2} \times 6\frac{1}{2}$, ff. 126, barbarously written; *pict., lect., syn.*

*259. Mosc. Syn. 45 (Mt. a) [xi], fol., ff. 263, *Carp., Eus. t., prol.,* κεφ. *t., Am., Eus., syn., men.,* from the Iberian monastery, with a commentary (Victor's on St. Mark). This is one of Matthaei's best manuscripts. His other twenty-two copies contain portions of Chrysostom, and therefore come under the head of Patristic Quotations.

Codd. 260–469 were added to the list by Scholz: the very few he professes to have collated thoroughly will be distinguished by an asterisk.

260. Paris National. Gr. 51 [xiii], $12 \times 8\frac{3}{4}$, ff. 241 (24), *prol., argent.,* κεφ. *t.,* κεφ., τίτλ., *Am., Eus., pict.,* once (like Cod. 309) 'domini du Fresne'; correctly written.

261. Par. Nat. Gr. 52 [xiv], $11 \times 8\frac{7}{8}$, ff. 175, κεφ. *t.,* τίτλ., κεφ., *Am., lect.,* ἀναγν. (*subscr.,* στίχ. later), once at the monastery of the Forerunner at Constantinople. *Mut.* Luke xxiv. 39–53. Matt. i. 1—xi. 1 supplied [xiv] *chart.*

*262. Par. Nat. Gr. 53 [x], $12\frac{3}{4} \times 9\frac{7}{8}$, ff. 212 (27), 2 cols., κεφ. *t.,* κεφ., some τίτλ. (*Am., Eus., harm.* at bottom of page, except in Luke, John, where too *Am.* is later), *subscr.,* with rare readings, like those of Evan. Λ and Evann. 300, 376, 428.

263. (Act. 117, Paul. 137.) Par. Nat. Gr. 61 [xiii], $8\frac{1}{4} \times 6\frac{1}{4}$, ff. 294 (28, 29), κεφ. *t.,* κεφ., τίτλ., *Am., lect., subscr.,* στίχ. Probably from Asia Minor. It once belonged to Jo. Hurault Boistaller, as did Codd. 301, 306, 314.

264. Par. Nat. Gr. 65 [xiii], 4to, $8 \times 5\frac{3}{8}$, ff. 287 (20), κεφ. *t.,* τίτλ., κεφ., *Am., Eus., harm., subscr.,* στίχ., *syn.,* with what have been called Coptic-like letters, but brought from the East in 1718 by Paul Lucas. The leaves are misplaced in binding, as are those of Cod. 272. At the foot of every page is a harmony like those in Codd. E, W[d]. *See* p. 58, note 2 (Burgon).

Of these copies, 265–270, Burgon states that the grand 4to Cod. 265 seems to contain an important text, 270 a peculiar text, though less beautiful externally than 266, 267, 269. Cod. 268 in double columns has *Eus. t.* very superb, but *pict.* of Evangelists only sketched in ink. Cod. 269, once belonging to Henry IV (in which the last leaf of St. Luke is missing), is in its ancient binding, and is full of very uncommon representations of Gospel incidents.

VOL. I.   Q

265. Par. Nat. Gr. 66 [x], $9\frac{7}{8} \times 7\frac{1}{2}$, ff. 372, *κεφ. t.*, *τίτλ.*, *κεφ.*, *Am.*, *Eus.*, once belonged to Philibert de la Mare.

266. Par. Nat. Gr. 67 [x], $9\frac{1}{2} \times 6\frac{1}{2}$, ff. 282 (23), *κεφ. t.*, *τίτλ.*, *κεφ.*, *Am.*, *lect.*, *subscr.*, *vers.*, *syn.*, *men.*

267. Par. Nat. Gr. 69 [x], $8 \times 6\frac{1}{8}$, ff. 396 (19), *prol.*, *κεφ. t.*, *Am.*. *Eus.* in same line, *lect.*, *ἀναγν.*, *subscr.*, *στίχ.* *Mut.* Matt. i. 1–8; Mark i. 1–7; Luke i. 1–8; xxiv. 50—John i. 12.

268. Par. Nat. Gr. 73 [xii], $9\frac{3}{4} \times 7\frac{3}{4}$, ff. 217 (25), 2 cols., *Carp.*, *Eus. t.*, *κεφ. t.*, *κεφ.*, *τίτλ.*, *Am.*, *Eus.*, *lect.*, *syn.*, *men.*, *pict.*

269. Par. Nat. Gr. 74 [xi], $9\frac{1}{4} \times 7\frac{3}{4}$, ff. 215 (28), *prol.*, *κεφ. t.*, *κεφ.*, *τίτλ.*, *Am.*, *vers.*, *pict.*, *Eus. t.* (later).

270. Par. Nat. Gr. 75 [xi], $7\frac{1}{4} \times 5\frac{1}{4}$, ff. 346 (19), *κεφ.*, *τίτλ.*, *Am.*, *Eus.*, *pict.*, *syn.*, *men.*, with a mixed text.

271. Par. Nat. Gr. Suppl. Gr. 75 [xii], 8vo, $7\frac{3}{8} \times 5\frac{1}{4}$, ff. 252 (22), 2 cols., *Carp.*, *Eus. t.*, *κεφ. t.*, *τίτλ.*, *κεφ.*, *Am.*, *Eus.*, *pict.*

272. Brit. Mus. Addit. 15,581 [xii], $5\frac{1}{2} \times 4\frac{3}{4}$, ff. 218 (21), *κεφ. t.*, *κεφ.*, few *τίτλ.*, *Am.*, *Eus.* (mostly omitted). Once Melchisedek Thevenot's. Gregory traces it through the Paris Nat. Library and Th. Rodd to the Brit. Museum, which purchased it.

273. Par. Nat. Gr. 79, 4to, $8\frac{5}{8} \times 6\frac{1}{4}$, ff. 201 (29–31), *Carp.*, *Eus. t.*, *κεφ. t.* with *harm.*, *κεφ.*, *τίτλ.*, *Am.*, *Eus.*, *syn.*, *men.*, *subscr.*, *vers.*, and *syn.*, *men.* again in the later hand, on vellum [xii], but partly on cotton paper [xiv]. contains also some scholia, extracts from Severianus' commentary, annals of the Gospels, a list of the Gospel parables, with a mixed text.

274. Par. Nat. Gr. Suppl. Gr. 79 [x], $9\frac{3}{8} \times 6\frac{1}{2}$, ff. 232 (26), *κεφ.*, *τίτλ.*, *Am.*, *lect.*, *syn.*, *men.*, once belonged to Maximus Panagiotes, *protocanon* of the Church at Callipolis (there were many places of this name: but *see* Evan. 346). *Mut.* (but supplied in a later hand) Mark i. 1–17; vi. 21–54; John i. 1–20; iii. 18—iv. 1; vii. 23–42; ix. 10–27; xviii. 12–29. Dean Burgon had a photograph of this manuscript, which he regarded as a specimen of the transition period between uncial and cursive writing. The subscription, resembling that of Cod. L, set in the margin of Cod. 274, he judges to look as old as that of L: *see* Chapter IX, Mark xvi. 9–20.

275. Par. Nat. Gr. 80 [xi], $10\frac{1}{8} \times 8\frac{1}{8}$, ff. 230 (24), *prol.*, *argent.*, *κεφ. t.*, *κεφ.*, *τίτλ.*, *Am.*, *Eus.*, antea Mcmmianus.

276. Par. Nat. Gr. 81 [A.D. 1092], $7\frac{7}{8} \times 5\frac{3}{4}$, ff. 307, *Eus. t.*, *κεφ. t.*, *κεφ.*, *τίτλ.*, *Am.*, *Eus.*, *lect.*, *pict.*, *vers.*, written by Nicephorus of the monastery Meletius.

277. Par. Nat. Gr. 81 A [xi], $6\frac{3}{4} \times 5\frac{1}{8}$, ff. 261, *Carp.*, *Eus. t.*, *κεφ. t.*, *κεφ.*, *τίτλ.*, *lect.*, *Am.*, *Eus.*, *subscr.*, *στίχ.* (*ἀναγν.*, *syn.*, *men.*, *pict.* later).

278. Par. Nat. Gr. 82 [xii, Greg. A.D. 1072], $8 \times 5\frac{7}{8}$, ff. 305 (21), *Carp.*, *Eus. t.*, *κεφ.*, *τίτλ.*, *lect.*, *Am.*, *Eus.*, *syn.*, *men.*, *vers.*, *pict.*, once Mazarin's, with Armenian inscriptions. Matt. xiii. 43—xvii. 5 is in a later hand.

279. Par. Nat. Gr. 86 [xii], $7 \times 5\frac{3}{8}$, ff. 250, *Eus. t.*, κεφ. *t.*, κεφ., τίτλ., *lect.*, *Am.*, *Eus.*, *syn.*; this copy and Cod. 294 were brought from Patmos and given to Louis XIV in 1686 by Joseph Georgirenus, Archbishop of Samos.

280. Par. Nat. Gr. 87 [xii], $7\frac{3}{4} \times 5\frac{1}{2}$, ff. 177 (25, 26), κεφ. *t.*, κεφ., τίτλ., *Am.*, *Eus.*, *syn.*, *subscr.*, στίχ. *Mut.* Mark viii. 3—xv. 36.

281. Par. Nat. Gr. 88 [xii], $8\frac{3}{4} \times 6\frac{1}{8}$, ff. 249 (22, 23), *Eus. t.*, κεφ., τίτλ., *Am.*, *subscr.* (*lect.* later). *Mut.* Matt. xxviii. 11–20; Luke i. 1–9. Given to the Monastery 'Deiparae Hieracis' by the eremite monk Meletius.

282. Par. Nat. Gr. 90 [A.D. 1176], 7×5, ff. 150 (33), 2 cols., *argent.*, κεφ. *t.*, κεφ., τίτλ., *lect.*, *subscr.* (*Am.* later).

283. Par. Nat. Gr. 92 [xiv], $7\frac{1}{2} \times 5$, ff. 159 (32), κεφ., τίτλ.

284. Par. Nat. Gr. 93 [xiii], $7\frac{5}{8} \times 5\frac{7}{8}$, ff. 254 (22), *Carp.*, *Eus. t.*, *argent.*, κεφ. *t.*, κεφ., τίτλ., some *lect.*, *Am.*, *Eus.*, *subscr.*, *pict.* Once Teller's of Rheims and Peter Stella's.

285. Par. Nat. Gr. 95, olim $\frac{2865}{3}$ [xiv], $7\frac{3}{4} \times 5\frac{3}{8}$, ff. 246 (22), κεφ. *t.*, κεφ., *subscr.*, *pict.*, once Teller's (58): given by Augustin Justinian to Jo. Maria of Catana. This codex is Kuster's Paris 1 and Wetstein's 10. *See* Evan. 10.

286. Par. Nat. Gr. 96 [April 12, 1432, Indiction 10], $8\frac{1}{2} \times 5\frac{1}{2}$, by the monk Calistus, with the Paschal canon for the years 1432–1502. Ff. 264 (21), *chart.*, *Carp.*, κεφ. *t.*, κεφ., τίτλ., *Am.*, *Eus.*

287. Par. Nat. Gr. 98 [A.D. 1478], $9\frac{3}{8} \times 5\frac{1}{2}$, *chart.*, ff. 322 (18), κεφ., τίτλ., *Am.*, *pict.* Written by Hermonymus (*see* Evan. 70), with a most interesting personal memorandum by its original owner D. Chambellan, and a portrait of his betrothed, 1479. Burgon, *Guardian*, Jan. 22, 1873.

288. According to Dr. C. R. Gregory, the following three fragments are parts of the same MS.—

(1) Oxf. Bodl. Canon. Gr. 33 (Scriv. Ed. iii. Evan. 487), St. Matthew; once belonged to Antony Dizomaeus.

(2) Par. Nat. Gr. 99, once German Brixius'. St. Luke.

(3) Par. Institut. III in Quarto (Scriv. Ed. iii. Evan. 471), St. John. On the first page is written 'C. Emmerci Sanguntiniani, emptus 40 assibus.' M. Tardieu, the librarian, informed Dean Burgon that it came from the City Library, to which it was bequeathed by 'M. Morrian, procureur du roi et de la ville de Paris.'

[xv], $9\frac{1}{2} \times 6\frac{1}{4}$, *chart.*, ff. 90 + 93 + 67 (18), κεφ. (Gr. et Lat.), τίτλ. (κεφ. Lat. only in Luke): written by George Hermonymus. (F. Madan from Omont, Bulletin de la société de l'histoire, Paris, tome xii, 1885, and Gregory.)

289. Par. Nat. Gr. 100 A [A.D. Feb. 15, 1625], *chart.*, ff. 336, *capp. Lat.*, written by Lucas ἀρχιθύτης.

290. Par. Nat. Suppl. Gr. 108 a [xiii], $8\frac{5}{8} \times 5\frac{3}{4}$, *chart.*, ff. 259 (22), *argent.*, κεφ. *t.* with *harm.*, κεφ., *lect.*, ἀναγν., *syn.*, *subscr.*, στίχ., *vers.*, from the Sorbonne.

291. Par. Nat. Gr. 113 [xii], $8\frac{3}{8} \times 5\frac{1}{4}$, ff. 290 (20), *prol.*, *argent.*, *κεφ. t.*, *κεφ.*, *τίτλ.*, *lect.*, *ἀναγν.*, belonged to one Nicolas.

292. Par. Nat. Gr. 114 [xi], $7\frac{1}{4} \times 4\frac{3}{8}$, ff. 290, *κεφ.*, *τίτλ.*, *Am.*, *Eus.*, *lect.*, *syn.* (later), *pict.* *Mut.* Matt. i. 1—vii. 14; John xix. 14—xxi. 25.

293. Par. Nat. Gr. 117 [Nov. 1262], $5\frac{3}{8} \times 3\frac{7}{8}$, ff. 340 (20), *prol.*, *argent.*, *κεφ. t.*, *κεφ.*, *τίτλ.*, *Am.*, *syn.*, *subscr.*, *στίχ.*, *pict.*, written by Manuel for Blasius a monk.

294. Par. Nat. Gr. 118 [A.D. 1291], ff. 238, *κεφ.*, *τίτλ.*, *Am.*, *Eus.*, *lect.*, *pict.* *Mut.* Matt. i. 18—xii. 25. *See* Evan. 279.

295. Par. Nat. Gr. 120 [xiii], $4\frac{1}{2} \times 2\frac{3}{4}$, ff. 239, *κεφ. t.*, *κεφ.*, *τίτλ.* *Mut.* Matt. i. 1–11.

296. (Act. 124, Paul. 49, Apoc. 57.) Par. Nat. Gr. 123 and 124 [xvi], $4\frac{7}{8} \times 3\frac{1}{2}$, ff. 257 and 303 (20), *capp. Lat.*, written by Angelus Vergecius (*see* p. 44, note 1).

297. Par. Nat. Suppl. Gr. 140 [xii], $5\frac{3}{8} \times 3\frac{1}{2}$, ff. 196, *κεφ. t.*, some *Am.*, *lect.*, *syn.*, *men.*

298. Par. Nat. Suppl. Gr. 175 [xii], $7\frac{1}{2} \times 5\frac{1}{2}$, ff. 222 (27), *κεφ. t.*, *κεφ.*, *τίτλ.*, *Am.*, *lect.*, *ἀναγν.*, *syn.*, *men.*, from the Jesuits' Public Library, Lyons.

*299. Par. Nat. Gr. 177 [xi], $10\frac{7}{8} \times 8\frac{1}{4}$, ff. 328 (24), *Carp.*, *Eus. t.*, *prol.*, *κεφ. t.*, *κεφ.*, *τίτλ.*, *Am.*, *Eus.*, *subscr.*, *pict.*, an accurately written copy with a mixed text, Victor's commentary on St. Mark, and scholia which seem to have been written in Syria by a partisan of Theodore of Mopsuestia: and other fragments.

*300. Par. Nat. Gr. 186 [xi], $13 \times 9\frac{3}{8}$, ff. 209 (36), *Eus. t.*, *κεφ. t.*, *κεφ.*, *τίτλ.*, *Am.*, *Eus.*, more roughly written than the sister-copy, Evan. 20, 'olim Fonte-Blandensis' (Fontainbleau), contains the first three Gospels, with subscriptions like that of Cod. 262. Contains catena, '*πάρεργα* de locis selectis,' and in the outer margin commentaries in a later hand, Chrysostom's on St. Matthew, Victor's or Cyril's of Alexandria on St. Mark (Evann. 20, 300 mention both names), and that of Titus of Bostra on St. Luke. *See* Evan. 428, and especially Evan. 215. Collated by Scholz and W. F. Rose.

301. Par. Nat. Gr. 187 [xi], $13\frac{3}{8} \times 10\frac{1}{2}$, ff. 221 (22), *κεφ. t.*, *Am.*, *subscr.*, *στίχ.*, once Boistaller's, a mixed text with a catena (Victor on St. Mark).

302. Par. Nat. Gr. 193 [xvi]. *chart.*, ff. 172, once Mazarin's: contains fragments of SS. Matthew and Luke with a commentary. Poor.

303. Par. Nat. Gr. 194 A [xi], $11\frac{1}{2} \times 9\frac{3}{8}$, ff. 321 (33), *syn.* (later), contains vellum fragments of John i–iv; and on cotton paper, dated 1255. Theophylact's commentary, and some iambic verses written by Nicander, a monk.

304. Par. Nat. Gr. 194 [xiii], $10\frac{7}{8} \times 8\frac{1}{2}$, ff. 242 (31–33), once Teller's; contains SS. Matthew and Mark with a catena, that of St. Mark possibly a modification of Victor's (Burgon).

305. Par. Nat. Gr. 195 [xiii], $12\frac{1}{4} \times 9$, *chart.*, ff. 261 (51, 54), *κεφ. t.* all together, *κεφ.*, *τίτλ.* (*Am.*, *lect.* later), once Mazarin's. Burgon states that this copy contains nothing but the commentary of Euthymius Zigabenus.

306. Par. Nat. Gr. 197 [xii], 11×8, ff. 559 (25), *mut.* John xxi. 1–8, 24, 25, once Boistaller's, contains SS. Matthew and John with Theophylact's commentary.

307. Par. Nat. Gr. 199 [xi], $11\frac{3}{8} \times 8\frac{3}{4}$, ff. 306 (30), *mut.*, contains only Chrysostom's Homilies on SS. Matthew and John (Burgon).

308. Par. Nat. Gr. 200 [xii], $11 \times 8\frac{7}{8}$, ff. 187 (27), once Mazarin's; *mut.*, contains the same as Cod. 307.

309. Par. Nat. Gr. 201 [x–xii], $10\frac{1}{4} \times 7\frac{3}{4}$, ff. 303 (37), 'very peculiar in its style and beautifully written,' *pict.*, once Du Fresne's, has SS. Matthew and John with Chrysostom's commentary, Luke with that of Titus of Bostra, Mark with Victor's. 'This is not properly a text of the Gospel: but parts of the text (*κείμενον*) interwoven with the commentary (*ἑρμήνεια*)' (Burgon, Last Twelve Verses, pp. 282, 287).

310. Par. Nat. Gr. 202 [xi], $12\frac{1}{8} \times 8\frac{1}{8}$, ff. 378 (27), has St. Matthew with a catena, once Colbert's (as also were Evann. 267, 273, 279, 281–3, 286–8, 291, 294, 296, 315, 318–9). Formerly given to St. Saba's monastery by its Provost Arsenius.

311. Par. Nat. Gr. 203 [xii], $14 \times 11\frac{1}{2}$, ff. 357 (28), once Mazarin's; this also has St. Matthew with a catena.

312. Par. Nat. Gr. 206 [A.D. 1308], $10\frac{1}{4} \times 8$, ff. 87 (30), Victor's commentary without the text, like that in Cod. 20, which (and Cod. 300) it closely resembles (Burgon, *ibid.* p. 279, note).

313. Par. Nat. Gr. 208 [xiv or xv], $12 \times 8\frac{1}{4}$, *chart.*, ff. 460, *mut.*, once Mazarin's; contains St. Luke with a catena.

314. Par. Nat. Gr. 209 [x–xii], 11×8, ff. 349 (32), once Boistaller's, contains St. John with a remarkable catena (quite different from that published by Cramer), with the names of the several authors (Burgon).

315. Par. Nat. Gr. 210 [xiii], $10\frac{7}{8} \times 7\frac{3}{8}$, ff. 156, has the same contents as Cod. 314. *Mut.* John i. 1–21; xiv. 25—xv. 16; xxi. 22–25.

316. Par. Nat. Gr. 211 [xii], $13\frac{3}{8} \times 8\frac{5}{8}$, *chart.*, ff. 129 (33), *κεφ.*, *τίτλ.*, brought from Constantinople. Contains SS. John and Luke with a commentary.

317. Par. Nat. Gr. 212 [xii], $12\frac{3}{4} \times 9\frac{1}{4}$, ff. 352 (29), 'olim Medicaeus' (*see* p. 121, note 2), contains John x. 9—xxi. 25 with a catena.

318. Par. Nat. Gr. 213 [xiv], $13\frac{3}{8} \times 9\frac{3}{8}$, ff. 16, 2 cols., has John vii. 1—xxi. 25 with a commentary.

319. Par. Nat. Gr. 231 [xii], $8\frac{1}{4} \times 6\frac{1}{4}$, ff. 203 (33), with a commentary, *mut.*

320. Par. Nat. Gr. 232 [xi], $9 \times 7\frac{1}{4}$, ff. 392 (21), *κεφ. t.*, *κεφ.*, *τίτλ.*, has St. Luke with a commentary.

321, 322 are Evst. 101 and 14 (Burgon, Greg.). Instead of these—

321. Brit. Mus. Addit. 34,107 [xi–xii], $5\frac{1}{4} \times 4\frac{1}{4}$, ff. 213 (21-24), *mut.* at beginning (five leaves); κεφ., κεφ. *t.*, *Am.* Very minute. Purchased of H. L. Dupuis, Esq., in 1891.

322. Brit. Mus. Addit. 34,108 [xiii], $8\frac{1}{2} \times 6\frac{1}{2}$, ff. 175 (28), (148 *membr.* + 17 *chart.*), *Carp.*, *Eus. t.*, *prol.*, κεφ. *t.*, κεφ., τίτλ., *lect.*, *Am.*, *Eus.*, *subscr.*, στίχ., *syn.* Seventeen leaves of paper are added at the end containing Luke iv. 3—viii. 19, *syn.*, *men.* [xv]. The writing is clear and firm, injured in part. Belonged to monastery of 'Ρενδήνη: purchased of H. L. Dupuis in 1891.

323. Par. Nat. Suppl. Gr. 118 [xv or xvi], $8\frac{1}{4} \times 5\frac{5}{8}$, *chart.*, ff. 94, contains Matt. vi, vii, and a Greek version of some Arabic fables.

324. (Evst. 97, Apost. 32.) Par. Nat. Gr. 376 [xiii or xiv], $7\frac{3}{8} \times 5$, ff. 315 (29), *Carp.*, *Eus. t.*, κεφ. *t.*, κεφ., τίτλ., *Am.*, *Eus.*, *lect.* (*syn.*, *men.* later), once Mazarin's, together with lessons from the Acts, Epistles, and Gospels, contains also Gospels complete (on cotton paper), and a list of Emperors from Constantine to Manuel Porphyrogenitus (A.D. 1143).

325. Instead of 325 (Ed. 3), which is Evst. 99—

Brit. Mus. Addit. 32,341 [xi], $7\frac{3}{4} \times 6$, ff. 222 (23), *prol.*, κεφ. *t.*, κεφ., τίτλ., *lect.*, *Am.*, *Eus.*, *subscr.*, *syn.* *Mut.* Matt. vi. 56—vii. 17; Luke xi. 17–32; xxiv. 26—John i. 22; end of *syn.* worn and faded. Purchased of the Rev. G. J. Chester in 1884.

326. Par. Nat. Gr. 378 [xiv], *chart.*, ff. 255, contains commentaries (ἑρμήνεια) on certain ecclesiastical lessons or texts (τὸ κείμενον). This is not a manuscript of the Gospels, properly so called.

327 and 328 are Evst. 99 and 100 (Burg. Greg.). Instead—

327. London, J. Bevan Braithwaite 1 [xii], 8×7, ff. 98 (21), τίτλ., κεφ., *Am.*, *Eus.*, *subscr.*, *prol.*, κεφ. *t.* *Mut.* beg. and end. Contains St. Mark and St. Luke. Bought at Athens in 1884 with the next. (Collated, as also the next, by W. C. Braithwaite.) (Greg. 531.)

328. J. Bevan Braithwaite 2 [xiii–xiv], $4\frac{3}{8} \times 3$, 2 vols., ff. 97 + 113 = 210 (29), *lect.*, τίτλ., κεφ. *Mut.* Matt. i. 1–12. Well written. (Greg. 573.)

329. Par. Nat. Coisl. Gr. 19 [xi], $12\frac{3}{4} \times 9\frac{1}{4}$, ff. 321 (25), κεφ. *t.* (John), *subscr.* (Luke), στίχ. (Luke, John), with a commentary (Victor's on St. Mark). Described (as is also Cod. 331) by Montfaucon.

330. (Act. 132, Paul. 131.) Formerly Petrop. Muralt. 101–xi. 1, 2, 330. (8 pe.) Coislin. 196 [xi], 9×7, ff. 289 (30), *Eus. t.*, *prol.* κεφ. *t.*, κεφ., *Am.*, *Eus.*, *men.*, *subscr.*, *Euthal.*, *subscr.* (Paul.), from Athanasius at Athos.

331. Par. Nat. Coisl. Gr. 197 [x–xii], $9\frac{1}{2} \times 7$, ff. 275 (20), *Carp.*, *Eus. t.*, *prol.*, κεφ. *t.*, κεφ., τίτλ., *Am.*, *Eus.*, *lect.*, once Hector D'Ailli's, Bishop of Toul.

332. Taurinensis Univ. C. ii. 4 (20) [xi], at Turin, $12\frac{1}{8} \times 9\frac{1}{8}$, ff. 304 (33), κεφ. *t.*, κεφ., τίτλ., *pict.*, with a commentary (Victor's on St. Mark). Bound in A.D. 1258. Burgon cites Pasinus' Catalogue, P. i. p. 91.

333. Taurin. B. i. 9 (4) [A.D. 1214], $13\frac{3}{8} \times 10\frac{1}{4}$, ff. 377, *chart.*, once belonged to Arsenius, Abp. of Monembasia in the Morea, then to Gabriel, metropolitan of Philadelphia; SS. Matthew and John with Nicetas' catena.

334. Taurin. B. iii. 8 (43) [xiv], $11\frac{1}{4} \times 8\frac{1}{2}$, ff. 267, SS. Matthew and Mark with a commentary; *prol.*, *κεφ. t.*, *κεφ.*, *τίτλ.*

335. Taurin. B. iii. 2 (44) [xvi], *chart.*, $11\frac{1}{2} \times 8\frac{1}{8}$, ff. 110 (29), *prol.*, *argent.*, *στίχ.* (Matt.).

336. Taurin. B. ii. 17 (101) [xvi], *chart.*, $11\frac{3}{4} \times 8\frac{3}{8}$, ff. 191 +, St. Luke with a catena.

337. Taurin. B. iii. 25 (52) [xii], $11\frac{1}{2} \times 8\frac{7}{8}$, ff. 114 (28), 2 cols., parts of St. Matthew with a commentary.

338. Taurin. B. vii. 33 (335) [xii], $5\frac{1}{2} \times 4\frac{1}{4}$, ff. 362 (18), *Carp.*, *Eus. t.*, *κεφ. t.*, *κεφ.*, *τίτλ.*, *Am.*, *Eus.*, *pict.*

339. (Act. 135, Paul. 170, Apoc. 83.) Taurin. B. v. 8 (302) [xiii], $8\frac{1}{2} \times 6\frac{1}{8}$, ff. 200, 2 cols., *Carp.*, *Eus. t.*, *κεφ. t.*, *κεφ.*, *τίτλ.*, *Am.*, *Eus.*, *syn.*, *men.*, *Euthal.* (Act., Cath., Paul.), and other matter[1].

340. Taurin. B. vii. 16 (344) [xiv], $5\frac{3}{4} \times 4\frac{1}{8}$, ff. 243 (21), *κεφ. t.* (*κεφ.*, *τίτλ.*, *Am.*, *lect.* later), with later corrections.

341. Taurin. B. vii. 14 (350) [dated 1296], $6 \times 4\frac{3}{4}$, ff. 268 (24), *Carp.*, *κεφ. t.*, *lect.* Written by Nicetas Mauron, a reader.

342. Taurin. B. v. 24 (149) [xiii], $8 \times 6\frac{1}{8}$, ff. 300 (21), *Carp.*, *Eus. t.*, *κεφ. t.*, *κεφ.*, *τίτλ.*, *Am.*, *Eus.*, *pict.*

343. Mediolani Ambrosianus H. 13 Sup. [xi or xii], $7 \times 4\frac{3}{4}$, ff. 263, *Carp.*, *Eus. t.*, *κεφ. t.*, *κεφ.*, *τίτλ.*, *Am.*, *Eus.*, *lect.* (later), *pict.* Written by Antony, a priest, on Sunday, Sept. 1, of the third Indiction, which in the twelfth century, might be A.D. 1140 or 1185. Seen by Burgon.

344. Med. Ambros. G. 16 Sup. [x–xii], $6\frac{7}{8} \times 4\frac{3}{4}$, ff. 327 (19), *Carp.* (later), *κεφ. t.*, *κεφ.*, *τίτλ.*, *Am.* (*lect.*, *syn.* later), *subscr.* *Mut.* John xxi. 12–25. But Luke xiii. 21—xvi. 23; xxi. 12[?]; xxii. 12–23; xxiii. 45—John xxi. 25 are [xiv] *chart.* First page of St. Matthew, and several of the early pages of St. Luke, have been re-written over the original text. (Burgon.)

345. Med. Ambros. 17 Sup. [xi or xii], $5\frac{3}{4} \times 4\frac{1}{2}$, ff. 375 (15), 2 cols., *κεφ.*, *τίτλ.*, *Am.*, *Eus.*, *lect.*, *subscr.*, *ῥήμ.*, *στίχ.*, *vers.*, *pict.* (John), (*syn.*, *men.* later). *Mut.* Matt. i. 1–11.

*346. Med. Ambros. S. 23 Sup. [xii], $8\frac{3}{4} \times 6\frac{1}{2}$, ff. 168, *κεφ. t.*, *κεφ.*, *τίτλ.*, *Am.*, *lect.*, *subscr.*, *ῥήμ.*, *στίχ.*, *syn.*, *men.*, carelessly written, with very unusual readings[2]. *Mut.* John iii. 26—vii. 52. Bought in 1606 at Gallipoli. Collated by Ceriani for Professor Ferrar, by Burgon and Rose from Luke xxi. 37 . . . . xxiv. 53. Last of Abbott's four (*see* Evan. 13). He gives a facsimile of Luke xi. 49–51.

347. Med. Ambros. 35 Sup. [xii], $9 \times 6\frac{1}{2}$, ff. 245 (15), 2 cols., *Carp.*,

[1] Written in three several and minute hands (Hort):—A for the Gospels, the Epistle of Pilate and its Answer, and a treatise on the genealogy of the Virgin; B for the Apocalypse and a Synaxarion; C the Acts, Cath. Paul. (Hebrews last), and Lives of the Apostles, followed on the same page by the Psalter by B, so that Apoc. and *syn.* probably stood last.

[2] This manuscript appears to be the only Greek witness for the Old Latin and Curetonian Syriac variation Matt. i. 16 ἰωσὴφ ᾧ μνηστευθῆσα παρθένος μαριὰμ ἐγέννησεν ι̅ν̅ τὸν λεγόμενον χ̅ν̅. But then it was written in Italy, as Ceriani judges.

κεφ. t., vers., κεφ., τίτλ., Am., Eus., lect., correctly written by Constantine Chrysographus.

348. Med. Ambros. B. 56 Sup. [Dec. 29, 1022], $7\frac{3}{4} \times 5\frac{7}{8}$, ff. 187, 2 cols., Carp., Eus. t., prol., κεφ., τίτλ., Am., Eus., lect., syn., men., once 'J. V. Pinelli.' Citations from the O. T. are asterisked. Burgon had a photograph.

349. Med. Ambros. F. 61 Sup. [1322], chart., $8\frac{7}{8} \times 5\frac{7}{8}$, ff. 399, κεφ., τίτλ., Am., subscr., syn., men., vers., bought at Corfu.

350. Med. Ambros. B. 62 Sup. [xi], $7\frac{7}{8} \times 6\frac{1}{4}$, ff. 305 (21), κεφ., τίτλ., Am., lect., pict. (syn., men. later). The first four leaves [xvi], chart. Mut. John xxi. 9-25.

351. Med. Ambros. B. 70 Sup. [xi or xii], $8\frac{1}{2} \times 6$, ff. 268 (22), Carp., Eus. t., κεφ. t., Am., Eus., subscr., with a Latin version [xv] here and there written above the text 'school-boy fashion.' Burgon.

352. Med. Ambros. B. 93 Sup. [xii], $9\frac{3}{8} \times 7\frac{3}{4}$, ff. 219 (20), κεφ., τίτλ., Am. (later), brought from Calabria, 1607. Mut. Matt. i. 1-17 ; Mark i. 1-15; xvi. 13-20; Luke i. 1-7; xxiv. 43-53; John i. 1-10; xxi. 3-25. Lect. in margin, and the faded ink retouched [xiv].

353. Med. Ambros. M. 93 Sup. [xiii], $11\frac{1}{4} \times 6\frac{1}{4}$, ff. 194 (23), κεφ., τίτλ., Am., Eus., lect. (in latter parts, later), with the same commentary as Evan. 181. Mut. John xxi. 24, 25.

354. Venetiis Marcianus 29 [xi], ff. $9\frac{3}{8} \times 6\frac{1}{4}$, ff. 442 (22), Matt. with Theophylact; ch. xxviii is wanting. Written in a very large hand, and bought at Constantinople in 1419 (Burgon, Guardian, Oct. 29, 1873).

355. Ven. Marc. 541 [xi ?], $6\frac{1}{2} \times 4\frac{7}{8}$, ff. 410 (18), Carp., Eus. t., κεφ. t., κεφ., τίτλ., Am., Eus., lect. (later), syn. (later still), a sumptuous and peculiar copy.

356. Ven. Marc. 545 [xvi], chart., $8\frac{7}{8} \times 6\frac{1}{4}$, ff. 176 (21), with Titus of Bostra's catena on St. Luke. A note runs thus : Ἀντωνίου τοῦ Ἀγγελίου καὶ χρήσει καὶ κτήσει, pro quo solvit librario qui descripserat HS. cxxvi. l. Δ'. 3.

357. Ven. Marc. 28 [xi], $12\frac{1}{2} \times 8\frac{1}{2}$, ff. 281 (35), κεφ. t. (rather later), κεφ., τίτλ., lect., SS. Luke and John with a catena. The titles resemble those of Evan. 69.

358. Mutinensis ii. A. 9 [xiv], $6 \times 4\frac{7}{8}$, ff. ?, κεφ. t., κεφ., τίτλ., Am., Eus., lect. (later), subscr., at Modena, in a small hand with rude illuminations.

359. Mutin. [242], iii. B. 16 [xiv], $7\frac{1}{4} \times 4\frac{7}{8}$, ff. ?, with slight decorations, on brownish paper, having scribe's name on last page. Carp., Eus. t., prol., κεφ. t., κεφ., τίτλ., Am., Eus. (later), lect., syn., men.

360. Parmae reg. 2319 [xi], $7\frac{3}{8} \times 6\frac{1}{8}$, ff. ?, κεφ. t., κεφ., τίτλ., Am., Eus., lect. (later), vers., pict. (syn., men. later still), with an unusual text, in double columns, collated by De Rossi, who once possessed this codex and

361. Parmae reg. 1821 [xiii], $4\frac{1}{4} \times 3\frac{1}{8}$, ff. ?, κεφ. t. with harm., lect.,

ἀναγν., *subscr.*, *στίχ.*, *syn.*, *men.*, faded. *Mut.* Luke viii. 14—xi. 20. Fully described (as also Cod. 360) in De Rossi's printed Catalogue.

362. Florentiae Laurentianus Conv. Soppr. 176, formerly Cod. Biblioth. S. Mariae No. 74 [xiii], $13\frac{1}{8} \times 9\frac{1}{4}$, ff. 314 (32), Luke vi. 29—xii. 10, with a fuller catena than Cramer's, citing the names of Greek expositors. Text in vermilion, commentary in black (Burgon). Described, like Evann. 201, 370, by Jo. Lamy, 'De eruditione Apostolorum,' Florent. 1738, p. 239.

363. (Act. 144, Paul. 180.) Flor. Laur. vi. 13 [xiii], a beautiful small 4to, $8\frac{1}{4} \times 5\frac{5}{8}$, ff. 306 (32), *argent.*, *κεφ. t.* with *harm.*, *lect.*, *ἀναγν.*, *subscr.*, *στίχ.*, *vers.*; *Euthal.* (Paul., Cath.).

364. Flor. Laur. vi. 24 [xiii, Greg. x], 8vo, $5\frac{3}{8} \times 4$, ff. 224 (20), *ἀναγν.* (*κεφ.*, *τίτλ.*, *Am.*, *Eus.* only in Matt., *lect.* later), (*syn.*, *men.* xv), the style of the characters rather peculiar, without the usual breaks between the Gospels; some leaves at the beginning and end [xiv].

365. (Act. 145, Paul. 181.) Flor. Laur. vi. 36 [xiii], 4to, $7\frac{1}{2} \times 5\frac{3}{8}$, ff. 358 (33), *Eus. t.*, *κεφ.*, *τίτλ.*, *Am.*, *vers.*, *pict.*, contains also the Psalms. Scholz collated it in select passages. *See* Gregory, who saw it.

366. Flor. Laur. Conv. Soppr. 171 (St. Maria's No. 20), [xii], a grand fol., $11\frac{1}{2} \times 8\frac{7}{8}$, ff. 323 (31), *κεφ.*, *τίτλ.*, with *harm.*, St. Matthew in vermilion with catena in black. *Mut.* ch. i. 1—ii. 16, with many later marginal notes. Entirely dissimilar in style from Cod. 362.

367. (Act. 146, Paul. 182, Apoc. 23.) Flor. Laur. Conv. Soppr. 53 (St. Maria's No. 6 [dated 26 Decembr. 1332], 4to, *chart.*, $9\frac{3}{4} \times 7$, ff. 349 (32), *prol.*, *κεφ. t.*, *κεφ.*, *τίτλ.*, *Am.*, *lect.*, *subscr.*, *vers.*, *στίχ.*, *syn.*, *men.*, written by one Mark. Bought in 1482 for three aurei by the Benedictines of St. Maria (Burgon).

368. (Act. 150, Apoc. 84.) Flor. Riccardianus 84, in the Libreria Riccardi, 'olim Cosmae Oricellarii *et amicorum*' (Evan. 255) [xv], 8vo, *chart.*, $6\frac{1}{8} \times 4\frac{1}{8}$, ff. 124 (21), contains St. John's Gospel, the Apocalypse, the Epistles and lessons from them, with Plato's Epistles, carelessly written.

369. Flor. Ricc. 90 [xii or xiv], 4to, $5\frac{3}{8} \times 4\frac{1}{4}$, ff. 23 + (25), *κεφ.*, *τίτλ.*, *Am.*, *Eus.*, *lect.*, contains Mark vi. 25—ix. 45; x. 17—xvi. 9, with part of a Greek Grammar and 'Avieni Fabulae.' The text is much rubricated.

370. Flor. Ricc. 5 [xiv], fol., *chart.*, $10\frac{7}{8} \times 7\frac{3}{4}$, ff. 424, *κεφ.*, *τίτλ.*, *Am.*, *lect.*, with Theophylact's commentary. *Mut.* Matt. i. 1—iv. 17; John xvi. 29—xxi. 25. Described by Lamy, *see* Evan. 362.

371. Rom. Vatican. Gr. 1159 [x], 4to, $8 \times 6\frac{1}{2}$, ff. 315 (21), *Eus. t.*, *κεφ. t.*, *κεφ.*, *τίτλ.*, *Am.*, *Eus.*, *pict.*

372. Rom. Vat. Gr. 1161 [xv], 4to, $9\frac{1}{2} \times 6\frac{1}{2}$, ff. 199 (30), *capp. Lat.*, ends John iii. 1. Beautifully written.

373. Rom. Vat. Gr. 1423 [xv], fol., *chart.*, $16\frac{3}{8} \times 11$, ff. 221 (46), *Am.*, *subscr.*, *στίχ.*, 'olim Cardinalis Sirleti,' with a catena, *mut.* in fine. G. Sirlet [1514–85] became Librarian of the Vatican 1573.

374. Rom. Vat. Gr. 1445 [xii], fol., $11\frac{1}{2} \times 8\frac{3}{8}$, ff. 173 (45), *pict.* (*κεφ. t.*, *κεφ.*, *τίτλ.* later), with a commentary ascribed to Peter of Laodicea, who is also named on the fly-leaf of Cod. 138. Burgon, however, says, 'This is simply a mistake. No such work exists: and the commentary on the second Evangelist is that of Victor,' *ubi supra*, p. 286. In 1221 one John procured it from Theodosiopolis; there were at least five cities of that name, three of them in Asia Minor.

375. Rom. Vat. Gr. 1533 [xii], $6\frac{3}{4} \times 5\frac{1}{2}$, ff. 199 (26), 2 cols., *Eus. t.*, *κεφ. t.*, *κεφ.*, *τίτλ.*, *Am.*, *Eus.*, *pict.*

376. Rom. Vat. Gr. 1539 [xi], $4\frac{1}{4} \times 3$, ff. 185 (28), *κεφ. t.*, *κεφ.*, *τίτλ.*, *Am.*, *subscr.*, given by Francis Accidas. With subscriptions resembling those of Codd. Λ, 262, 300 (*see* pp. 160, 161, and note).

377. Rom. Vat. Gr. 1618 [xv], *chart.*, $12 \times 8\frac{1}{4}$, ff. 339 (30), St. Matthew with a catena, the other Gospels with questions and answers.

378. Rom. Vat. Gr. 1658 [xiv], $12\frac{1}{8} \times 8\frac{5}{8}$, ff.?, portions from St. Matthew with Chrysostom's Homilies, and from the prophets.

379. Rom. Vat. Gr. 1769 [xv], *chart.*, $11\frac{5}{8} \times 8$, ff. 437 (27), *κεφ. t.*, *κεφ.*, *τίτλ.*, with a commentary.

380. Rom. Vat. Gr. 2139 [xv], *chart.*, $9\frac{5}{8} \times 6$, ff. 202 (23), *Carp.*, *Eus. t.*, *prol.*, *κεφ. t.* (*capp. Lat.*), *Am.*, *Eus.*, *subscr.*

381. Rom. Palatino-Vat. Gr. 20 [xiv], *chart.*, $12\frac{1}{4} \times 9\frac{7}{8}$, ff. 226 (33), St. Luke with a catena.

382. Rom. Vat. Gr. 2070 [xiii], $8\frac{1}{2} \times 7\frac{1}{4}$, ff. 167 (24), 2 cols., *κεφ. t.*, *κεφ.*, *τίτλ.*, *Am.*, *lect.*, *subscr.*, *στίχ.*; 'olim Basil.,' carelessly written, fragments of SS. John and Luke are placed by the binder before SS. Matthew and Mark. Much is lost.

383, 384, 385 are all Collegii Romani [xvi], 4to, *chart.*, with a commentary.

386. (Act. 151, Paul. 199, Apoc. 70: *see* p. 72, note.) Rom. Vat. Ottobon. 66 [xv], $11\frac{1}{2} \times 8\frac{3}{8}$, ff. 393 (24), *Eus. t.*, *κεφ. t.*, *lect.*, *ἀναγν.*, *subscr.*, *στίχ.*, *syn.*, *men.*, *Euthal.* (Cath., Paul.), once 'Jo. Angeli ducis ab Altamps,' as also Codd. 388, 389, 390, Paul. 202.

387. Rom. Vat. Ottob. 204 [xii], $8\frac{1}{2} \times 6\frac{1}{2}$, ff. 298 (21), *lect.*, *subscr.*, *στίχ.*

388. Rom. Vat. Ottob. 212 [xii], $8\frac{3}{4} \times 6\frac{1}{4}$, ff. 315 (21), *argent.*, *κεφ. t.*, *κεφ.*, *τίτλ.*, *Am.*, *Eus.*, *lect.*, *ἀναγν.*, *subscr.*, *στίχ.*, *pict.*, *syn.*, *men.*, once belonged to Alexius and Theodora.

389. Rom. Vat. Ottob. 297 [xi], $6\frac{3}{4} \times 5\frac{3}{8}$, ff. 192 (23), *Eus. t.*, *κεφ. t.*, *κεφ.*, *τίτλ.* with *harm.*, *Am.*, *Eus.*, *subscr.*, *στίχ.*

390. (Act. 164, Paul. 203.) Rom. Vat. Ottob. 381 [dated 1282], 4to, $8\frac{5}{8} \times 6$, ff. 336 (29), *Carp.*, *Eus. t.*, *prol.*, *κεφ. t.*, *κεφ.*, *τίτλ.*, *Am.*, *Eus.*, *lect.*, *subscr.*, *vers.*, *syn.*, *men.*; *Euthal.* (Paul.), with scholia, was in a church at Scio A.D. 1359.

391. Rom. Vat. Ottob. 432 [xi, April 13, Indiction 8], $11\frac{3}{8} \times 9\frac{1}{8}$, ff.

232 (17), *Carp., prol.*, κεφ. t., κεφ., τίτλ., *Am., Eus.*, with a commentary. Given to Benedict XIII (1724-30) by Abachum Andriani, an abbot of Athos. Matt. i. 1-8; Luke i; John vii. 53—viii. 11 were written [xv].

392. Rom. Barberin. v. 17, formerly 225, is the cursive portion of Evan. Y [xii], 11¼ × 8, ff. (391 — 8 =) 383 (36), κεφ., τίτλ., with Theophylact's commentary.

393. (Act. 167, Paul. 185.) Rom. Vallicell. E. 22 [xvi], *chart.*, 10½ × 6⅞, ff. 222 (34), κεφ., τίτλ. (*lect.* later).

394. (Act. 170, Paul. 186.) Rom. Vallicell. F. 17 [July 4, 1330, Indict. 13], *chart.*, 9¼ × 6¼, ff. 344 (29), *argent.*, κεφ. t., *lect.*, ἀναγν., *syn.*, *men.*, written by Michael, a priest.

395. Rom. Casanatensis G. iv. 1 [xii], 11 × 8¼, ff. ?, κεφ. t., τίτλ., *Am., Eus., pict.*, with marginal corrections, bought about 1765.

396. Rom. Chisianus R. iv. 6 [xii], 8¾ × 6½, ff. 115 (27), *argent.*, κεφ. t., κεφ., τίτλ., *Am., Eus.*, begins Matt. xxiii. 27.

397. Rom. Vallicell. E. 40 [xv], 9⅝ × 8¼, ff. 295 (10), St. John with a catena (described by Bianchini).

398. Taurin. Univ. C. ii. 5 [xiii, or xvi in Pasinus' Catalogue], select passages with a catena, 12⅛ × 8½, *chart.*, ff. 310 (30), 2 cols.

399. Taurin. C. ii. 14 [xv, or xvi in Pasinus' Cat.], *chart.*, 11⅝ × 8, ff. 404 (22), *prol.*, κεφ. t., *vers.*, commentary, sometimes without the text. Found by Dr. Hort to contain SS. John, Luke (with Titus of Bostra's commentary), Matthew, *hoc ordine*. See p. 73.

400. (Act. 181, Paul. 200.) Berolinensis Reg. A. Duodec. 10, Diezii [xv], 5 × 3¾, ff. 249 (14–16), *Euthal.*, *mut.*, damaged by fire and water, contains Matt. xii. 29—xiii. 2: and the Acts and Epistles, except Acts i. 11—ii. 11; Rom. i. 1-27; 1 Cor. xiv. 12—xv. 46; 2 Cor. i. 1-8; v. 4-19; 1 Tim. iv. 1—Heb. i. 9. This copy belonged to Henry Benzil, Archbishop of Upsal, then to Laurence Benzelstierna, Bishop of Arosen: it was described by C. Aurivill (1802), collated by G. T. Pappelbaum (1815).

401. Neapolit. Bibl. Nat. II. Aa. 3 [xi or xii], 8⅜ × 6⅜, ff. 113 (23), κεφ. t., κεφ., τίτλ., *Am., vers.* (later), contains Matthew, Mark vi. 1— xvi. 20, Luke, John i. 1—xii. 1.

402. Neapol. Nat. II. Aa. 5 [xiv or xv], 6¼ × 4½, ff. 253 (24), κεφ. t., *lect.*, ἀναγν., *subscr.*, στίχ., *pict.*

403. Neapol. Nat. II. Aa. 4 [xii or xiii], *chart.*, 7 × 4⅞, ff. 212 (22), *argent.*, κεφ. t., *Am., lect., men.* Contains Matt. xii. 23—xix. 12; 28— xxviii. 20; Mark; Luke i. 1—v. 21; 36—xxiv. 53; John i. 1— xviii. 36.

404. Neapol. 'Abbatis Scotti' [xi], 8vo, *prol.* Not known.

The manuscripts once belonging to the Nani family, which include Evan. U, were catalogued by J. A. Mingarelli ('Graeci codices manu scripti apud Nanios Patricios Venetos asservati,' Bononiae, 1784), and, being now at St. Mark's, were inspected by Burgon.

405. Venet. Marc. i. 10, 'olim Nan. 3, antea monasterii SS. Cosmae et Damiani urbis Prusiens.s,' i.e. Brusa or Prusa [xi], 8¼ × 7, ff. 228 (22), *Carp.*, *Eus. t.*, κεφ. *t.*, τίτλ., κεφ., *Am.*, *Eus.*, *lect.*, *subscr.*, the leaves utterly disarranged by the binder. (Wiedmann and J. G. J. Braun collated portions of 405–417 for Scholz.)

406. Ven. Marc. i. 10, Nan. 4 [xi], 6¾ × 5⅞, ff. 297 (18), κεφ. *t.*, κεφ., τίτλ., *Am.* (not *Eus.*), few *lect.* *Mut.* Mark iv. 41—v. 14; Luke iii. 16—iv. 4.

407. Ven. Marc. i. 12, Nan. 5 [xi], 6 × 5⅛, ff. 87 (21), contains Luke v. 30—John ix. 2. Κεφ. *t.*, κεφ., τίτλ., *Am.*, *lect.*, *pict.*, στίχοι βῶ at the end of St. Luke, *subscr.*, *vers.*

408. Ven. Marc. i. 14, Nan. 7 [xii], 9¼ × 5⅛, ff. 261 (22), once belonged to St. John Chrysostom's monastery, by the Jordan, as stated in a note of the original scribe. *Carp.*, *Eus. t.*, κεφ. *t.*, κεφ., τίτλ., *Am.*, *Eus.*, few *lect.*, στίχ., *subscr.*, *vers.*, *pict.*, full stops very numerous in the text. Matt. i. 1–13 and *syn.* later.

409. Ven. Marc. i. 15, Nan. 8 [xii or xiv], 8⅛ × 5¾, ff. 210 (28), the writing and *pict.* very rough, the stops being mostly red crosses. *Carp.*, *Eus. t.*, *prol.*, κεφ. *t.*, τίτλ., κεφ., *Am.* (not *Eus.*), *lect.*, *vers.*, *subscr.*, στίχ., *syn.*, *men.*, foreign matter by Cosmas, &c. (*see* p. 66).

410. Ven. Marc. i. 17, Nan. 10 [xiii or xiv], 9¼ × 6¾, *chart.*, ff. 212, written by one Joasaph a monk, *Carp.*, *Eus. t.*, *prol.* [xiii] on parchment, κεφ. *t.* on paper. Κεφ., τίτλ., *Am.* (not *Eus.*), *lect.*, *prol.*, *vers.*, *subscr.*, στίχ., *syn.*, *men.*

411. Ven. Marc. i. 18, Nan. 11 [x or xi], 6½ × 4⅞, ff. 375 (20), very beautifully written in upright characters. *Carp.*, *Eus. t.*, *prol.*, matter by Cosmas (*see* p. 66), κεφ. *t.*, τίτλ., κεφ., *Am.*, *Eus.*, *lect.*, *syn.*, *men.*, *vers.* *Pict.* torn out.

412. Ven. Marc. i. 19, Nan. 12 [1301], 7 × 5¼, ff. 327 (22), written by Theodore (*see* p. 43, note 1). *Carp.*, *Eus. t.*, *prol.*, κεφ. *t.*, τίτλ., κεφ., *Am.*, *Eus.*, *lect.*, *syn.*, *men.*, στίχ., *vers.* In text it much resembles Scrivener's q and r by the same hand, without being identical with either.

413. Ven. Marc. i. 20, Nan. 13 [1302, Indiction 15], 8¾ × 6¾, ff. 270 (24), once belonged to St. Catherine's monastery on Sinai, where Cod. ℵ was found, and is elegantly written by one Theodosius ῥακενδύτης. *Carp.*, *Eus. t.*, *prol.*, κεφ. *t.*, τίτλ., κεφ., *Am.*, *Eus.*, rude *pict.*, *lect.*, *subscr.*, στίχ., *syn.*, *men.*

414. Ven. Marc. i. 21, Nan. 14 [xiv], 9¼ × 6½, ff. 225 (26), κεφ., τίτλ., *Am.*, *lect.*, *subscr.*, *syn.*, *men.*, written by Philip, a monk.

415. Ven. Marc. i. 22, Nan. 15 [dated January, 1356], 7¼ × 5¼, ff. ?, *syn.*, *men.*, rude *pict.*, κεφ. *t.*, κεφ., τίτλ., ἀναγν., *subscr.*

416. Ven. Marc. i. 24, Nan. 17 [xiv], 7¾ × 5⅞, ff. 225 (22), very roughly written, begins Matt. xxv. 36, ends John xviii. 7. *Mut.* Matt. xxvi. 17—xxvii. 17; 35—Mark ii. 27. Κεφ. *t.* (κεφ., τίτλ. later), *Am.*, *Eus.*, *lect.* (later), ἀναγν, with changes by different hands.

417. Ven. Marc. i. 25, Nan. 18 [xii–xiv], $9\frac{1}{8} \times 5\frac{7}{8}$, ff. 112 (27, 26), begins Matt. v. 44, ends Luke vi. 9. Κεφ., τίτλ., *Am.*, *Eus.*, *lect.* (later), *subscr.*

418. Ven. Marc. i. 28, Nan. 21 [xv], *chart.*, $8\frac{3}{4} \times 6\frac{1}{4}$, ff. 110 (17), 2 cols., contains SS. Matthew and Mark, down to ch. xiii. 32, unfinished, in two columns. Κεφ. *t.* with *harm.*, κεφ., τίτλ., *Am.* (not *Eus.*), *lect.*, many red crosses for stops.

419. Ven. Marc. i. 60, formerly at St. Michael's, Venice, 'prope Murianum,' 241 [xi or xii], $7\frac{5}{8} \times 6$, ff. 260 (22), ends John xxi. 7 (described by J. B. Mittarelli, Venice, 1779). *Mut.* John viii. 44—xi. 32, supplied by a later hand. Κεφ. *t.*, τίτλ., κεφ., *Am.* (not *Eus.*), *lect.*, with red musical notes.

420. Messanensis Univ. 18 (Schulz's 237) [xiv], $6\frac{7}{8} \times 4\frac{7}{8}$, ff. 127 (22), *Carp.*, *Eus. t.*, *prol.* (πρόγραμμα), κεφ. *t.*, κεφ., τίτλ. with *harm.*, also *harm.* at bottom of the page, *Am.*, *Eus.*, *subscr.*, στίχ., *vers.*, *pict.*, by different hands, with readings from other copies (inspected by Munter, as was Cod. 421).

421. (Act. 176, Paul. 218.) Syracusanus (Schulz's 238) [xii]?, once Landolini's; *prol.*, *Eus. t.* Dr. Gregory could not find it.

422. Monacensis Reg. 210, at Munich [xi or later], $9\frac{1}{4} \times 6\frac{1}{2}$, ff. 256 (28), 2 cols., *Carp.*, *prol.*, κεφ. *t.*, τίτλ., κεφ., *Am.*, *Eus.* (partially), *lect.* (later), *subscr.*, στίχ., *syn.*, *men.*, roughly written in two columns by the monk Joseph, but St. John in a somewhat more recent hand; described by Ignatius Hardt and Dean Burgon. It abounds with itacisms and strange blunders, and other tokens of great ignorance on the part of the scribe.

423. Mon. Reg. 36 [1556]. *chart.*, $13\frac{3}{8} \times 9\frac{1}{4}$, ff. 465 (30), contains St. Matthew with Nicetas' catena. Marked Τόμος Α and superbly bound, as in Cod. 432. The same scribe wrote Codd. 424, 425, 432 (Burgon).

424. Mon. Reg. 83 [xvi], *chart.*, $13\frac{3}{8} \times 8\frac{3}{4}$, ff. 399, contains St. Luke with the commentary of Titus of Bostra and others.

425. Mon. Reg. 37 [xvi] *chart.*, $13\frac{3}{8} \times 9\frac{1}{4}$, ff. 576 (30), second volume of 423, contains St. John with a very full catena of Nicetas. Marked Τόμος Β.

426. Mon. Reg. 473, once Augsburg 9 [xiv], $9\frac{3}{4} \times 6\frac{3}{4}$, *chart.*, ff. 208 (26), κεφ. *t.*, contains Luke vi. 17—xi. 26 with Nicetas' catena, the second of four volumes (δεύτερον τῶν τεσσάρων τεῦχος τῶν εἰς τὸ κατὰ Λουκᾶν ἅγιον εὐαγγέλιον κατὰ συναγωγὴν ἐξηγήσεων).

427. Mon. Reg. 465, Augsburg 10 [xii or xiii], $10\frac{1}{2} \times 8\frac{1}{8}$, ff. 140 (34), *Am.*, *lect.* (ῥήμ., στίχ. Luke), written by one Maurus, contains SS. Luke and Mark with Theophylact's (and Victor's?) commentary.

428. Mon. Reg. 381, Augsburg 11 [xiii], $12\frac{1}{2} \times 9\frac{1}{4}$, *chart.*, ff. 335 (33), with rude pictures of the Evangelists on a vellum leaf. Its subscriptions are like those of Evann. Λ, 262, &c. The commentary is Theophylact's.

429. Mon. Reg. 208 [xii or xiii], a superb 4to, $10\frac{7}{8} \times 9\frac{1}{8}$, ff. 234 (35),

2 cols., written by John, a priest and '*ἔκδικος* magnae ecclesiae,' contains Luke i. 1—ii. 39 with a catena, questions and answers from SS. Matthew and John, with the text. Burgon declares that the date June 20, A.D. 978, Indiction 6, which we took from Scholz (*see* above, p. 41, note 2), is that of the manuscript this was copied from, not of Cod. 429 itself. In that case we have another early dated cursive the less. Gregory, Prolegomena, p. 449, inclines to the placing of this MS. amongst the uncials.

430. Mon. Reg. 437 [xi], 11⅝ × 8⅝, ff. 354 (24), contains John i–viii with the catena of Nicetas, metropolitan of Heraclia Serrarum in Macedonia, now *Xerosna*. Martin Crusius of Tübingen procured it from Leontius, a Cyprian monk, in 1590, and sent it to the Library at Augsburg.

431. (Act. 180, Paul. 238.) Molsheimensis [xii], *Eus. t., prol.* with many unusual readings, was brought to Strasburg from the Jesuits' College at Molsheim in Alsace. Extracts were made from it by the Jesuit Hermann Goldhagen (N. T. Mogunt. 1753), and it was collated by Arendt, 1833. ' Periit a. 1870,' Gregory.

432. Mon. Reg. 99 [xvi], *chart.*, 13¼ × 8¼, ff. 572 (30), contains St. Mark with the commentary of Victor of Antioch, being the same copy as Peltanus used for his Latin edition of that work, Ingolstad, 1580.

433. Berolinensis Reg. MS. 4to, 12 (kn) (Schulz's 239) [xi or xii], 8 × 5¾, ff. 80 (24), κεφ. t., κεφ., τίτλ., Am., Eus., lect., brought from the East by W. Ern. de Knobelsdorf, with a mixed text and many errors in very minute letters. It contains Matt. i. 1-21; vi. 12-32; xxii. 25—xxviii. 20; Mark i. 1—v. 29; ix. 21—xiii. 12; Luke viii. 27—John ix. 21; xx. 15—xxi. 25. (G. T. Pappelbaum, 1824.)

434. Vindobon. Caes. 71, formerly 42 [xiv], 11¾ × 7¾, ff. 424 (29), contains St. Luke with a catena. Like Codd. 218, &c., bought at Constantinople by De Busbeck.

435. Lugd.-Bat. Bibl. Univ. Gronovii 137 (Schulz's 245) [x], 8⅝ × 6¼, ff. 284 (24), *pict. Mut.* Matt. i. 20—ii. 13; xxii. 4-9 (John x. 14—xxi. 25 in a rather later hand). It has a somewhat unusual text (collated, as was also Evan. 122, by J. Dermout, Collectanea Critica in N.T., 1825).

436. Meerman. 117 [A.D. 1322], ff. 277. Dr. Gregory has traced this MS. to No. 54 in the library of the Jesuit College at Clermont, then to Meerman, then to Payne a London bookseller, who bought it in 1824. It is not known now. For the MS. once in Dean Burgon's possession but in the Bodleian Library, *see* Evan. 562.

437. Petropol. Caes. [xi], like Cod. E of the Pauline Epistles, one leaf of the Colbert Pentateuch, and some other manuscripts, has found its way from the Coislin library and the Abbey of St. Germain des Prés near Paris, to St. Petersburg. It was written by Michael Cerularius, Patriarch of Constantinople, and noticed by Matthaei (N. T. iii. p. 99, 2nd ed.). Not in Muralt's List.

438. Brit Mus. Addit. 5111, 5112 (Askew 621) [A. D. 1189], 10 × 7, ff. 211 and 241 (18), *Carp.*, *Eus. t.*, κεφ. t., *pict.*, κεφ., τίτλ., *Am.*, *Eus.* (no *subscr.*). It was written by Gregory a monk, and is in two volumes, containing severally Matt. and Mark, Luke and John.

439. Brit. Mus. Addit. 5107 (Askew 622) [dated April, 1159, Ind. 7], 12¼ × 9½, ff. 219 (23), 2 cols., written by the monk Nepho, at Athos, *Carp.*, *Eus. t.*, κεφ. t., *pict.*, τίτλ., κεφ., *Am.*, *Eus.* (Bloomfield).

440. (Act. 111, Paul. 221.) Camb. Univ. Libr. Mm. vi. 9 [xii], 7 × 5½, ff. 288 (28), *Eus. t.*, κεφ., τίτλ., *lect.*, *Am.*, *syn.* (later); *prol.* (Cath. and Paul.), *subscr.* (Paul.). From this copy Griesbach's readings in Cod. 236 were derived. Described below under Scrivener's v before Evan. 507.

441, 442, at Cambridge, must be removed from Scholz's list; they are *printed* editions with manuscript notes. Cod. 441 is Act. 110, Paul. 222; Cod. 442 is Act. 152, Paul. 223.

443. Camb. Univ. Libr. Nn. ii. 36, once Askew 624 [xii], 11 × 8¼, ff. 235 (24), 2 cols, *Carp.*, *Eus. t.*, κεφ. t., τίτλ., *Am.*, *Eus.*, some *lect.* (later), *syn.*, *men.*, *prol.* The κεφάλαια proper are subdivided in this copy, e.g. the 19th of St. Matthew, into no less than thirteen parts (see p. 64, note 2). For the titles of the Gospels, see Evan. 69. Evan. 443 was bought for the University Library in 1775 for £20, at the celebrated book-sale of Anthony Askew [1722-74], the learned physician who projected an edition of Aeschylus. See Marsh on Michaelis, vol. ii. pp. 661-2.

444. (Act. 153, Paul. 240.) Brit. Mus. Harl. 5796 [xv], 10¼ × 7½, ff. 324 (26-29), κεφ. t., τίτλ., *lect.*, άναγν., *subscr.*, στίχ., *syn.*, *men.*, neatly written, sold in 1537 'aspris 500:¹' bought at Smyrna in 1722 by Bernard Mould.

445. Brit. Mus. Harl. 5736 [A.D. 1506], *chart.*, 8¼ × 6, ff. 194 (24), κεφ., τίτλ., *Am.*, *lect.*, in the hand ' Antonii cujusdam eparchi,' once (like Apoc. 31) in the Jesuits' College, Agen, on the Garonne.

446. Brit. Mus. Harl. 5777 [xv], 9 × 6, ff. 228 or 231 (25), κεφ., τίτλ., *Am.*, *lect.*, κεφ. t. (not Matt.), *subscr.* (Luke), *syn.*, *men.* *Mut.* Matt. i. 1-17; Mark i. 7-9; Luke i. 1-18; John i. 1-22, by a person who mischievously cut out the ornaments. It is clearly but unskilfully written, and Covell states on the outer leaf that it seems a copy from his manuscript, noted above as Evan. 65. This codex is Cov. 5 (Bloomfield).

447. Brit. Mus. Harl. 5784 [xv], 7¼ × 5¾, ff. 329 (21), *Eus. t.*, *prol.*, κεφ. t., *orn.*, κεφ., τίτλ., *lect.*, *subscr.*, στίχ., *prol.* (Paul.); well written, and much like

448. Brit. Mus. Harl. 5790 [dated Rome, April 25, 1478], 12¼ × 8½, ff. 299 (22), κεφ. t., *pict.*, κεφ., τίτλ. in margin, *subscr.*, beautifully written by John Rhosus of Crete a priest for Francis Gonzaga Cardinal of S. Maria Nuova: belonged to Giovanni Pietro Arrivabene.

449. Brit. Mus. Addit. 4950-1 [xiii], 5 × 3½, 2 vols., ff. 146 and 171,

¹ The aspor or asprum was a mediaeval Greek silver coin (derived from άσπρος, *albus*); we may infer its value from a passage cited by Ducange from Vincentius Bellovac. xxx. 75 'quindecim drachmas seu asperos.'

(23), *prol.*, κεφ. t., *pict.*, κεφ., τίτλ., *lect.*, *Am.*, *Eus.*, *men.*, *syn.*, clearly and carefully written ; once Caesar de Missy's (*see* Evan. 44).

Out of this whole mass of 190 manuscripts, Scholz collated five entire (262, 299, 300, 301, 346), eleven in the greater part (260, 270, 271, 277, 284, 285, 298, 324, 353, 382, 428), many in a few places, and not a few seem to have been left by him untouched. His list of Oriental manuscripts (Evann. 450–469), as it is given in the first volume of his Greek Testament (Proleg. pp. xcvi–xcvii)[1], has been withdrawn from the catalogue of cursive copies of the Gospels, in deference to the wish of the Dean of Chichester (Letter iii addressed to myself in the *Guardian* newspaper, July 5, 1882). It must be confessed indeed that Scholz's account of what he had seen in the East about 1823 cannot be easily reconciled with the description of the Rev. H. O. Coxe of the Bodleian Library thirty-five years later ('Report to Her Majesty's Government of the Greek Manuscripts yet remaining in the Libraries of the Levant, 1858'); that most of the books which Scholz catalogued at St. Saba on the Dead Sea were removed before 1875, as Mr. F. W. Pennefather informs us, to the Great Greek Convent of the Cross at Jerusalem ; and that at least four of them were brought to Parham in Sussex from St. Saba in 1834 by the late Lord de la Zouche. Instead of Scholz's seven (450–6), Coxe saw fourteen copies of the Gospels at Jerusalem ; twenty of the Gospels (besides a noble palimpsest of the Orestes and Phoenissae) at St. Saba after the four had been subtracted, instead of Scholz's ten (457–466); at Patmos five instead of Scholz's three (467–469). In spite of one's respect for the memory of that zealous and worthy labourer, M. A. Scholz, with whom I had a personal conference regarding our common studies in 1845, I cannot help acquiescing in Dean Burgon's decision, though not, perhaps, without some natural reluctance.

---

[1] 450. Great Gr. Monastery at Jerusalem 1 [July 1, 1043], 8vo, *syn.*, *Eus. t.*, first three Gospels with an Arabic version, neatly written by a reader, Euphemius. This appears to be Coxe's 6, 4to, St. Luke only.
451. Jerusalem 2 [xii], 8vo.   452. Jerusalem 3 [xiv], 8vo.
453. Jerusalem 4 [xiv], 8vo.   454. Jerusalem 5 [xiv], 8vo.
455. Jerusalem 6 [xiv], 4to, with a commentary.
456. Jerusalem 7 [xiii], 4to, St. Matthew with a commentary, neatly written. *Perhaps* Coxe's 43 [xi], in gold *uncial* letters.
457. St. Saba 2 [xiii], 4to, *syn.*, *men.*, is Act. 186, Paul. 234.
458. St. Saba 3 [dated 1272, Indiction 15], 16mo.
459. St. Saba 7 [xii], 8vo.   460. St. Saba 8 [xii], 8vo.
461. *See* Evan. 481.
462. St. Saba 10 [xiv], 4to, is also Act. 187, Paul. 235, Apoc. 86.
463. St. Saba 11 [xiv], 4to, *chart*.   464. St. Saba 12 [xi], 4to.
465. St. Saba 19 [xiii], 8vo.
466. St. Saba 20 [xiii], 8vo, is Act. 189, Paul. 237, Apoc. 86[2] or 89. Also 'from a monastery in the island of Patmos.'
467. [xi], 4to.   468. [xii], 8vo, with a commentary.   469. [xiv], 4to.

CHAPTER VIII.

CURSIVE MANUSCRIPTS OF THE GOSPELS.

PART II.

WE have already intimated that Tischendorf has chosen to make no addition to the numerical list of cursive manuscripts furnished by Scholz, preferring to indicate the fresh materials which have since come to light by another notation, derived from the names of the collators or the places where they are deposited. As this plan has proved in practice very inconvenient, it is no wonder that Dean Burgon, after casting away Scholz's numbers from 450 to 469, on account of their evident inaccuracy, which has since then received definite proof, should have assigned numerals to the cursives unknown to Scholz from 450 to 737, still excluding, as far as was then possible, those whose location or character was uncertain. Burgon's method, as laid down in his Letters in the *Guardian* for July 5, 12, 19, 26, 1882, having the priority of publication, and being arranged with regard to the places where the manuscripts are deposited rather than to their actual collators, may as well be adopted as any other that might be made. The only important point to be secured is that all scholars should employ the SAME NUMBERS when speaking of the SAME MANUSCRIPTS.

It is greatly to be regretted that Dr. C. R. Gregory, even upon advice tendered by other critics, if such was the case, should have neglected the important principle laid down in the preceding sentence, and in Part II of his very valuable Prolegomena to Tischendorf's eighth edition, published seven years after the third edition of this work, should have helped to make confusion worse confounded in this large and increasing field. But it is not my object to assail one who has done this study very great service, but only to point out an inconvenience which I shall endeavour to minimize as far as I can. It is clear that Dr. Scrivener's order, being the first out, and having been followed since then in quotations in books, and notably by the late learned Abbé Martin, cannot be allowed to drop. I have therefore followed it in the succeeding pages. But it has been my object to bring together the two lists as soon as possible after the close of Dr. Scrivener's, and the end of the supplementary lists of Dean Burgon and the Abbé Martin, and to follow, as far as the case will admit, the lead of Dr. Gregory, where he has every right to prescribe the series of numbers. Unfortunately, this course is not always open, because when the time has arrived it is found that some MSS. have been already forestalled, and others are in arrear.

It should be added, that the number of the MSS. as standing in Dr. Gregory's list, where it varies from the present, is given at the end of the account of each manuscript; and reversely a table is added at the end of this volume of the varying numbers in this list which answer to the numbers in Dr. Gregory's list.

We begin with the following twenty Italian manuscripts, added to our previous list of cursive copies of the Gospels by Burgon in Letters addressed to Dr. Scrivener and inserted in the *Guardian* of Jan. 29 and Feb. 5, 1873.

450. Ferrara, Univ. 119, NA. 4 [xiv], 8vo, ff. ?, κεφ. t. (Lat. later), Am., lect., syn., men. (Lat. syn. later). (Greg. 581.)

451. (Act. 194, Paul. 222, Apoc. 102.) Ferr. Univ. 187, 188, NA. 7 [A. D. 1334], $6\frac{3}{4} \times 4\frac{3}{4}$, chart., ff. ?, capp. Lat., containing the whole New Testament: the only divisions recognized are those of the modern chapters in vermilion. (Greg. 582.)

452. Parma, Reg. 5 [xi or xii], $13\frac{1}{2} \times 9\frac{1}{2}$, ff. 284 (21), *Carp.*, *Eus. t.*, argent., κεφ. t., κεφ., τίτλ., Am., Eus., lect., pict., syn., men., once belonging to the Bonvisi family, then transferred to the Public Library at Lucca. As superb a copy as any known, the illuminations gorgeous, the first page of the Gospel and other portions in gold, with a 'luxurious prodigality' of miniatures. (Greg. 583.)

453. Parma, Reg. 95 [xi, or older], $7\frac{3}{8} \times 5\frac{1}{5}$, ff. 318. κεφ. t., κεφ., τίτλ., Am., Eus., lect., subscr., very tastefully decorated. *Mut.* Matt. i. 1–20. Lect. and marginal corrections by the first hand in vermilion. (Greg. 584.)

454. Modena, Bibl. Estensis ii. A. 1 [xi or xii], a beautiful copy, $7\frac{1}{2} \times 4\frac{1}{2}$, ff. ?, syn. at beginning and end, κεφ. t., κεφ., τίτλ., Am., Eus., superb pict., men., with slight marginal corrections of the text. (Greg. 585.)

455. Mod. Bibl. Est. ii. A. 5 [xiv], 6½ × 4⅞, ff. 239 (20), *argent.*, κεφ t., κεφ., *lect.*, ἀναγν., *subscr.*, στίχ., *vers.*, *syn.*, *men.*, small and neat, without *pict.* or illuminations. (Greg. 586.)

Here also is a late copy of Victor of Antioch's commentary on St. Mark.

456. Milan, in the great Ambrosian Library, M. 48 sup., 8¾ × 7⅜, ff. 183, *prol.*, *argent.*, κεφ. t., κεφ., τίτλ., *Am.*, *pict.*, beautifully written, *pict.* almost obliterated. *Am.* (not *Eus.*). The last leaf more recent. (Greg. 587.)

457. Milan, Ambros. E. 63 sup. [May, 1321, Indiction 4], 8½ × 5¾, ff. 221, *Eus. t.*, *prol.*, κεφ. t., κεφ., τίτλ., *Am.*, *Eus.*, *lect.*, ἀναγν., *subscr.*, *pict. Mut.* Luke xxiv. 5—John i. 8, and the early part of John v. *Am.* (not *Eus.*), *lect.*, *pict.* (Greg. 588.)

458, 459, 460. For these Dr. Gregory inserts Milan, Ambr. A. 178 sup., Parmae Reg. 15, Rom. Corsin. 41. G. 16, but without explanation. *See* below, Evann. 830, 831, 837.

458. Milan, Ambros. D. 161 inf. [xvi], transcribed from an original in the Vatican, *chart.* St. Mark's Gospel with Victor of Antioch's commentary.

459. Milan, Ambros. D. 282 inf., transcribed by John Sancta Maura, a one-eyed Cyprian, aged 74, June 9, 1612: *chart.*, with a catena.

460. Milan, Ambros. D. 298 inf., transcribed by the same, fol., *chart.* These two codices purport to be commentaries of Peter of Laodicea on St. John and St. Mark respectively: but 'such titles are quite misleading.' *See* Burgon, Letter to *Guardian*, Feb. 5, 1873.

461. (Act. 197, Paul. 223.) Milan, Ambros. Z. 34 sup. [xiii or xiv], *chart.*, 6½ × 4¾, ff. 295 (31), κεφ. t., κεφ., τίτλ., *Am.*, *syn.*, *men.*, *subscr.*, ῥήμ., στίχ., *vers.*, with *pict.* on vellum not belonging to it. The order of its contents is Catholic Epp., Pauline Epp., *syn.*, Gospels. (Greg. 592.)

462. Venice, Ven. Marc. i. 58 [xiii], 9¾ × 7, ff. 153 (22), κεφ. t., κεφ., τίτλ., *Am.*, *lect.*; wrongly called an Evangelistarium in the Supplementary Catalogue, contains only Mark i. 44—Luke xxiv. 53; John i. 15—xi. 13. (Greg. 593.)

463. Instead of Ven. i. xxxix. 8, 7, or Nan. 27, which appears to be a commentary—Ven. Marc. ii. 7 [xiv], 12¾ × 9⅞, ff. 430 (31), κεφ. t. (John), κεφ., τίτλ., with Euthymius Zigabenus' commentary. (Greg. 600.)

464. Ven. Marc. i. 59 [xii, Greg. xiii], 6½ × 4⅞, κεφ. t., κεφ., τίτλ. (*lect.*, *subscr.*, στίχ. later), with very remarkable readings. Burgon collated sixteen chapters in the several Gospels. (Greg. 597.)

465. Ven. Marc. i. 57 [xi or xii], 11⅝ × 8¼, ff. 228 (29), κεφ. t., κεφ., τίτλ., ends Mark xii. 18, with Theophylact's commentary. (Greg. 596.)

466. Ven. Marc. 494 [xv, Greg. xiii], 16¾ × 11¼, *chart.*, ff. 320 (50), 2 cols., full of various Patristic matter. (Greg. 598.)

467. Ven. Marc. 495 [xv], 16 × 11¼, *chart.*, ff. 437 (42), κεφ. t., κεφ., τίτλ., *Am.*, *lect.*, *vers.*, described by Zanetti, p. 259, with a commentary (Victor's on St. Mark). (Greg. 599.)

We do not include Ven. Marc. i. 61, which is a mere catena on Matt. i—ix, or an unnumbered catena of St. Luke in the same Library, or Ven. M. 1, an uncial copy of the Old Testament [ix?], at the end of which are found *Carp., Eus. t.* of unique fullness, as if the Gospels were to follow.

468. Ven. Marc. 56 [xvi], fol., *chart.*, 11¾ × 7⅞, ff. ?, κεφ. t. (John), *capp. Lat., Am., lect., syn.*, wrongly set down by Scholz as Evst. 143, contains the Gospels, beginning Matt. v. 44. It was once 'S. Michaelis Venet. prope Murianum,' and is described in Mittarelli's Catalogue of that Library, p. 1099. (Greg. 595.)

469. Quaritch i. [xi–xii], 10¼ × 7½, ff. ? (19), *prol.*, κεφ. t., κεφ., τίτλ., *Am., Eus.*, headings. *Mut.* at beginning and at beginning of St. Luke and end of St. John. Beautifully written in gold letters. (E. M., March 18, 1893.)

470. Ven. s. Lazarus 1531 [xiii, Greg. xiv], 10 × 7¾, ff. 234 (?), κεφ. t., *prol.* (John), *lect.*, ἀναγν. (later), *subscr.*, στίχ., is a fragment of the Gospels containing Matt. i. 22—Luke xxiii. 15; 33–48. (Greg. 594.)

471. Quaritch ii. [xi], 5⅞ × 4¾, ff. ? (25), *Carp., Eus. t.*, κεφ. t., κεφ., τίτλ., *Am., Eus., lect., subscr.*, στίχ., ἀναγν. *Mut.* here and there: beautifully written, and otherwise complete. Belonged to the Hon. Frederic North. (E. M., March 18, 1893.)

472. (Act. 235, Paul. 276, Apoc. 103.) Poictiers [xvi], small folio, *chart.*, of the whole New Testament, as described to Burgon by M. Dartige, the librarian there. Two librarians named Cavou successfully robbed the library, and probably sold miniatures and pictures. (H. C. Hoskier.) G. Haenel (Catal. Librorum MSS. Lips. 1830) names this and another of the whole N. T. at Arras [xv], 8vo, but of the latter the librarian, M. Wicquot, knows nothing.

Edward de Muralt, in his N. T. 'ad fidem codicis principis Vaticani,' 1848 (p. 111), inserts a collation of eleven manuscripts (five of the Gospels, one Psalter with hymns, five Lectionaries), chiefly at St. Petersburg. He also describes them in his Preface (pp. lv–lvii), and in the Catalogue of Greek Manuscripts in the Imperial Library there. The copies of the Gospels are—

473. 2ᵖᵉ, 81 Hort (Petrop. vi. 470) [ix–x Hort], 8½ × 5¼, ff. 405 (18, 19), *Am., Eus. t., pict.*, κεφ. t., κεφ., τίτλ. (in silver uncials), *subscr.*, a purple MS. with golden letters, very beautiful, said to have been written by the Empress Theodora. *Mut.* John xi. 26–48; xiii. 2–23. St. Mark of this MS. was edited by J. Belsheim with facsimile in 1885 (Jacob Dybwad, Christiania). Highly valued by some critics. (Greg. 565.)

474. 4ᵖᵉ, Petrop. 98. Formerly Pogodini 472 [xii or xiii], ff. 194 (23, 24), *Eus. t.*, κεφ. t., *Am., Eus., lect., pict.* (Greg. 571.)

475. 7ᵖᵉ, Petrop. ix. 3. 471 [A.D. 1062], 9⅞ × 7½, ff. 357 (12), *Eus. t.*, κεφ. t., κεφ., τίτλ., στίχ., *pict., lect., syn., men.*, with Victor's Commentary on St. Mark. (Greg. 569.)

476. 8ᵖᵉ, Petrop. Muralt. 105 [xii or xiii], 7 × 4⅞, ff. 225 (27), κεφ. t., *pict.* Brought by Titoff from Turkey.

477. 11ne, Petrop. 118 (Q. v. 1, 15) [xv], 7 × 5⅝, ff. 384, *Eus. t., pict., syn., men.*, written for Demetrius Palaeologus.

478¹. tisch.¹ Leipzig, Univ. Libr. Tisch. iv. [x], 6¾ × 5¼, ff. 360 (21), *Carp., Eus. t., prol.,* κεφ., *Am., Eus., lect., men., subscr., vers.* Brought by Tischendorf from the East (Tisch., Anecdota sacra et profana, pp. 20–29). (Greg. 564.)

479. tisch.² Petrop. Muralt. 97 [xii], 7⅞ × 6½, ff. 191. *Mut.* Matt. i. 1–16; 30; John xvi. 20—xx. 25. (Tisch., Notitia Cod. Sinait., p. 60.) (Greg. 570.)

480. tisch.³ Petrop. Muralt. 99 [xii], 7⅜ × 4⅞, ff. 19 (12), Matt. viii. 3—ix. 50. (Tisch., Notitia Cod. Sinait., p. 64.) (Greg. 572.)

481. Petrop. (Scholz's 461, St. Saba 9) [May 7, 835, Indiction 13], 6₈ × 3⅞, ff. 344 (19), κεφ., τίτλ., *lect.* The date, being the earliest known of a Greek N. T. MS., is plainly visible in a photographed facsimile in 'Exempla Codicum Graecorum literis minusculis scriptorum' (fol., Heidelberg, 1878), Tab. 1, by Wattenbach and von Velsen. This precious treasure was the property of Porphyry Uspensky, Bp. of Kiow, but is now at St. Petersburg. (*See* Greg. 461.)

The five following are in the Bodleian Library, and for the most part uncollated:—

482. Oxf. Bodl. Cromwell 15 [xi], 8½ × 6¼, ff. 216 (24), exquisitely written, with textual corrections in the margin. *Carp., Eus. t., prol.,* κεφ. t., τίτλ., κεφ., *Am., Eus., lect.* (few in later hand). *Mut.* Mark xvi. 17 (ταῦτα)–end; John xix. 29–end. This copy and the next in order came in 1727 from Παντοκράτωρ on Athos. (Greg. 527.)

483. Oxf. Bodl. Crom. 16 [xi], 8 × 6, ff. 354 (20), fairly written. The Gospels are followed by the Proper Lessons for the Holy Week. *Pict., Carp., Eus. t.,* κεφ. t., *Am., Eus., syn.* (later), ἀρχαί and τέλη. Collated in 1749 by Th. Mangey, Prebendary of Durham, the editor of Philo [1684-1755]. 'It is well worth proper examination' (E. B. Nicholson, Bodley's Librarian). (Greg. 528.)

484. Oxf. Bodl. Misc. Gr. 17, Auct. D. Infra 2, 21 [xi], 5½ × 4, ff. 363 (20), *prol.,* κεφ. t., κεφ., τίτλ., *Am., lect., subscr., syn., men.*, in text said to resemble Cod. 71, once Humphrey Wanley's [1672-1726], bought in 1776 by Sam. Smalbroke, fifty-four years Canon Residentiary of Lichfield, was presented by him on his eightieth birthday, June 4, 1800. (Greg. 529.)

485. Oxf. Bodl. Misc. Gr. 141, Rawl. G. 3 [xi], 6 × 4¼, ff. 303 (20), with some foreign matter, has κεφ. t., κεφ., τίτλ., *Am.*, a few *Eus.*, ἀρχαί and τέλη, *subscr. Mut.* John xxi. 3-24. (Greg. 430.)

486. Oxf. Bodl. Misc. Gr. 293, Auct. T. V. 34 [xii or xiii], 7¼ × 5¼, ff. 213 (27), *orn.,* τίτλ., κεφ., *lect., Am., subscr.* (except in Luke), ἀναγν., στίχ., κεφ. t. (Luke). Of a very unusual style. (Greg. 706.)

To this list we must add the five following copies from the collection

---

¹ The Psalter 5pe (Petrop. ix. 1) [994], containing the hymns, Luke i. 46-55; 68-79; ii. 29-32, is like our Evan. 612, which see.

of the Abbot M. Aloy. Canonici, purchased at Venice in 1817 for the Bodleian Library by Dr. Bandinel, who secured 2045 out of the total number of 3550 manuscripts.

487. Oxf. Bodl. Canon. Gr. 33. Part of Evan. 288, which see.

488. Oxf. Bodl. Canon. Gr. 34 (Act. 211, Paul. 249, Apoc. 98) [A.D. 1515, 1516], 9 x 6¼, *chart.*, ff. 319 (25), *capp. Lat.*, written by Michael Damascenus the Cretan for John Francis Picus of Mirandola, contains the whole N. T., the Apocalypse alone being yet collated (k^{scr}) : *mut.* Apoc. ii. 11–23. It has Œcumenius' and Euthalius' *prol.* (Greg. 522.)

489. Oxf. Bodl. Canon. Gr. 36 [xi], 10 x 7½, ff. 270 (22), κεφ. t., *syn., men., pict.,* τίτλ., κεφ., *Am., Eus., lect.,* ἀναγν., Gospels: olim Georg. Phlebaris. (Greg. 523.)

490. Oxf. Bodl. Canon. Gr. 112 [xii], 5½ x 4½, ff. 186 (21 &c.), *pict., Carp.,* κεφ. t., κεφ., τίτλ., *Am., Eus., lect., syn., men.,* Gospels well written. (Greg. 524.)

491. Oxf. Bodl. Canon. Gr. 122 Cod. Sclavonicus [A.D. 1429], 12½ x 9, ff. 312 (20), 2 cols., *pict., prol., syn., men.,* κεφ. t., κεφ., τίτλ., *lect., subscr.,* στίχ., Gospels in Sclavonian with a Greek version later, written in Moldavia by Gabriel, a monk. (Greg. 525.)

*492. Oxf. Ch. Ch. Wake[1] 12 (Act. 193, Paul. 277, Apoc. 26) Cod. Dionysii (who wrote it) [xi], 12 x 9½, ff. 240 (36), 2 cols., was also noted by Scholz, on Gaisford's information, Evangelistarium 181, Apostol. 57: but this is an error, as the Gospels are contained at full length and in their proper order, with unusually full liturgical matter, *pict., Carp., Eus. t., prol.,* κεφ. t., κεφ., τίτλ., *Am., Eus., lect.,* στίχ., ἀναγν., *vers.* (*syn., men.* with synopsis). The Acts, Catholic and Pauline Epistles (Œcumenius' *prol.,* κεφ., scholia) follow them, and last of all comes the Apocalypse. *Mut.* Luke xvi. 26–30; xvii. 5–8; xxiv. 22–24; John i. 1—vii. 39; viii. 31—ix. 11; x. 10—xi. 54; xii. 36—xiii. 27; Acts i. 1—vii. 49; x. 19—xiv. 10; xv. 15—xvi. 11; xviii. 1—xxi. 25; xxiii. 18—James iii. 17; 1 Cor. xii. 11—xv. 12; xvi. 13–15; 2 Cor. xiii. 4, 5; Gal. v. 16—vi. 18 (partly); 2 Tim. iii. 10, 11; Tit. iii. 5–7; the illuminations also being often wantonly cut out. This copy contains much foreign matter besides; its contents were carefully tabulated by J. Walker; it was thoroughly collated by Scrivener in 1864. (Greg. 606.)

493. Oxf. Ch. Ch. Wake 21 [xi], 11 x 8¼, ff. 221 (26), 2 cols., *Carp.* (later), *Eus. t., prol.* (later), κεφ. t., τίτλ., κεφ., *lect.* (partly later), ῥήμ., στίχ., *syn.*, brought from Παντοκράτωρ on Athos, 1727. The scribe's name, Abraham Teudatus, a Patrician (Montfaucon, Palaeo. Gr., p. 46), is written cruciform after *Eus. t.* (Greg. 507.)

494. Oxf. Ch. Ch. Wake 22 [xiii], 10 x 8, ff. 160 (24, 27), κεφ. t.,

---

[1] In addition to Evann. 73, 74, Gaisford in 1837 catalogued, and Scrivener in 1861 inspected, these fourteen copies of the Gospels in the collection of Archbishop Wake, now at Christ Church, Oxford. They were brought from Constantinople about 1731, and have now been described in the Rev. G. W. Kitchin's Catalogue of the Manuscripts in Christ Church Library (4to, 1867).

τίτλ., κεφ., lect., subscr., ἀναγν., in a wretched hand and bad condition, begins Matt. i. 23, ends John xix. 31. Also *mut.* Matt. v. 26—vi. 23 ; Luke xxiv. 9-28 ; John iii. 14—iv. 1 ; xv. 9—xvi. 6. (Greg. 508.)

495. Oxf. Ch. Ch. Wake 24 [xi], 11¾ × 8¾, ff. 229 (24), from Παντοκράτωρ in 1727. *Eus. t., prol.,* κεφ. *t., pict.,* τίτλ., κεφ., *Am., Eus.* in gold. One leaf (John xix. 13-29), and another containing John xxi. 24, 25, are in duplicate at the beginning, *primâ manu.* (Greg. 509.) This copy (as Wake remarks) is in the same style, but less free than

496. Oxf. Ch. Ch. Wake 25 [x or xi], 10¾ × 8¼, ff. 292 (22), κεφ. *t., pict.,* κεφ., *lect.,* τίτλ., some *Eus.,* ἀναγν., *subscr.,* στίχ., *syn., men., pict.* (in red ink, nearly faded). (Greg. 510.)

497. Oxf. Ch. Ch. Wake. 27, *chart.* [xiii], 9½ × 6¼, ff. 337 (20), *pict.* (Matt.), κεφ., τίτλ., *lect.,* κεφ. *t., prol.* (Luke), *subscr.* (Mark). *Mut.* at beginning. Matt. xviii. 9—Mark xiv. 13 ; Luke vii. 4—John xxi. 13 are [xiii], the rest supplied [xv]. (Greg. 511.)

498. Oxf. Ch. Ch. Wake 28 [xiii], 9 × 6¾, ff. 210 (24), κεφ. *t.,* some τίτλ., κεφ., *syn., men., lect.,* much of this *rubro, vers., subscr.,* στίχ., ἀναγν. Subscribed Θῦ το δωρον και γρηγοριου πονος. (Greg. 512.)

499. Oxf. Ch. Ch. Wake 29 [ϛχ¹λθ or A.D. 1131, Indict. 9], 7¾ × 6¼, ff. 162-4, *chart.* in later hand (25), κεφ. *t.,* κεφ., τίτλ., *Am., Eus., lect., vers., subscr.,* στίχ. After some later fragments (Matt. i. 12—v. 3, and other matter) on paper, the older copy begins Matt. v. 29. (Greg. 513.)

500. Oxf. Ch. Ch. Wake 30 [xii], 7½ × 5½, ff. 226 (23), *Eus. t., prol.,* κεφ. *t.* (almost illegible), κεφ., τίτλ., *lect.* in red, almost obliterated from damp ; ending John xx. 18, neatly written, but in ill condition. (Greg. 514.)

501. Oxf. Ch. Ch. Wake 31 [xi], 7 × 5½, ff. 127 (34), small, in a very elegant and minute hand. *Pict.,* κεφ. *t.,* some τίτλ. (in gold), κεφ., *Am.,* (no *Eus.*), *lect.* full, some στίχ., *mut.* (Greg. 515.)

502. Oxf. Ch. Ch. Wake 32 [x or xi], 7¼ × 5½, ff. 287 (23), small, elegant, and with much gold ornament. *Pict.,* κεφ. *t.,* κεφ., some τίτλ., *Am., lect.,* some στίχ. *Mut.* in places. (Greg. 516.)

*503 (Act. 190, Paul. 244, Apoc. 27.) Oxf. Ch. Ch. Wake 34 [xi or xii], 10 × 8, ff. 201 (31, 29). This remarkable copy begins with the ὑπόθεσις to 2 Peter, the second leaf contains Acts xvii. 24—xviii. 13 misplaced, then follow the five later Catholic Epistles (*mut.* 1 John iii. 19—iv. 9) with ὑποθέσεις : then the Apocalypse on the same page as Jude ends, and the ὑπόθεσις to the Romans on the same page as the Apocalypse ends, and then the Pauline Epistles (*mut.* Heb. vii. 26—ix. 28). All the Epistles have *prol.,* κεφ. *t.,* and Œcumenius' smaller (not the Euthalian) κεφ., with much *lect. primâ manu,* and *syn.* later. Last, but seemingly misplaced by an early binder, follow the Gospels, κεφ. *t.,* κεφ., τίτλ., *Am., lect., subscr. Mut.* Mark xvi. 2-17 ; Luke ii. 15-47 ; vi. 42—John xxi. 25, and in other places. This copy is Scholz's Act. 190, Paul.

---

[1] The letter χ is quite illegible, but the Indiction 9 belongs only to A.D. 831, 1131, 1431, while the style of the manuscript leaves no doubt which to choose.

244, Apoc. 27, but unnumbered in the Gospels. Collated fully by Scrivener in 1863. (Greg. 517.)

504. Oxf. Ch. Ch. Wake 36 [xii], 6 × 5, ff. 249-6 *chart.* (23), κεφ. t., κεφ., τίτλ., *Am., lect., prol.* (Luke), *pict.* (Luke, John), *syn., men.* (Greg. 518.)

505. Oxf. Ch. Ch. Wake 39 [xiii], 5¼ × 4¼, ff. 308 (17 &c.), κεφ., some τίτλ., a poor copy, in several hands. (Greg. 567.)

506. Oxf. Ch. Ch. Wake. 40 [xii], 4½ × 3⅛, ff. 218 (22, 23), a beautiful little copy. *Syn., men.,* κεφ. *t., lect.* in the faintest red, but no other divisions. (Greg. 520.)[1]

F. H. A. Scrivener has published the following in his 'Collation of Greek Manuscripts of the Holy Gospels, 1853,' and 'Codex Augiensis' (Appendix), 1859.

*v^scr, or cant^scr. of Tischendorf. *See* Evan. 440 (Act. 111, Paul. 221 of Scholz; Evan. 236, Act. and Paul. 61 of Griesbach; Act. and Paul. o^scr), in a minute hand, with many unusual readings, especially in the Epistles, from Bp. Moore's Library. *Men.* Ὑποθέσεις Oecumenii to the Catholic and first eight Pauline Epistles: beautifully written with many contractions. This is Bentley's o (*see* Evan. 51).

*507. w^scr. (Act. 224, Paul. 260.) Camb. Trin. Coll. B. x. 16 [dated A.D. 1316], *chart.,* 7¼ × 5, ff. 363 (28, 29), was inelegantly written by a monk James on Mount Sinai. *Prol.,* κεφ. t., *Am., Eus.,* κεφ., *lect., subscr.,* ἀναγν., *vers., syn., men.;* also ὑποθέσεις, *lect., syn., men.* to Epistles; and much extraneous matter[2]. *See* Evan. 570. This is Bentley's r (Evan. 51), and, like i^scr which follows, came to him from Παντοκράτωρ. Hort makes it his Cod. 102. (Greg. 489.)

*508. i^scr. Camb. Trin. Coll. B. x. 17 [xiii], 8½ × 6, ff. 317 (20), from

---

[1] Of these manuscripts Thomas Mangey (Evan. 483) states on the fly-leaves that he collated Nos. 12, 25, 28, 34 in 1749. Caspar Wetstein collated the Apocalypse in Nos. 12 and 34 for his relative's great edition; while in the margin of No. 35, a 4to Greek Testament printed at Geneva (1620), is inserted a most laborious collation (preceded by a full description) of eight of the Wake manuscripts with Wetstein's N. T. of 1711, having this title prefixed to them, 'IIae Variae lectiones ex MSS. notatae sunt manu et opera Johannis Walkeri, A. 1732.' John Walker, most of whose labours seem never yet to have been used, although they were known to Berriman in 1741 (Critical Dissertation on 1 Tim. iii. 16, pp. 102-4), was Fellow of Trinity College, Cambridge, where so many of his critical materials accumulated for the illustrious Bentley are deposited. Walker d. 1741, Archdeacon of Hereford, after Bentley's will, six months before him. The codd. in Trinity College were bought from Bentley's heirs (not from Richard Bentley) when Wordsworth was Master (1820-41), and so were not in Bentley's hands when Walker died. Old Latin Biblical Texts, xxiv-vi. Of his eight codices, we find on investigation that Walker's C is Wake 26; Walker's 1 is Wake 20 (collations of these two, sent by Walker to Wetstein, comprise Codd. 73, 74, described above); Walker's B is Wake 21; Walker's D is Wake 24, both of Gospels; Walker's E is Wake 18, his H is Wake 19, both Evangelistaria; Walker's q is Wake 12, of which Caspar Wetstein afterwards examined the Apocalypse (Cod. 26); Walker's W is Wake 38 of the Acts and Epistles, or Scholz's Act. 191, Paul. 245.

[2] Bentley specifies 'argumenta inedita Cosmae Indicopleustae in 4 Evangelia, et versus iambici fortasse Jacobi Calligraphi: argumenta incerti ad Actus: prologus ineditus et argumenta Oecumenii ad Epistolas omnes.'

Athos, bequeathed to Trinity College by Bentley. Κεφ. τ., τίτλ., κεφ., Am. (not Eus.), lect., and (on paper) are ὑπόθεσις to St. Matthew and syn. This is Bentley's δ, who dates it 'annorum 700' [xi], and adds 'nuper in monasterio Pantocratoris in monte Atho, nunc meus.' (Greg. 477.)

*j^{scr}. Evan. N.

*509. a^{scr}. London, Lambeth 1175 [xi], 11⅞ × 9¾, ff. 220, five leaves bound up with it (23–35), 2 cols. (23, 24), 2 cols., κεφ. τ., κεφ., τίτλ., Am., Eus., lect., subscr. Mut. Matt. i. 1–13; once at Constantinople, but brought (together with the next five) from the Greek Archipelago by J. D. Carlyle, Professor of Arabic at Cambridge [d. 1804]. (Greg. 470.)

*510. b^{scr}. Lond. Lamb. 1176 [xii], 7¾ × 6, ff. 209 (24), Carp., Eus. t., syn., pict., κεφ. t. (chart.), men., τίτλ., κεφ., subscr., proll. at end, very elegant. A copy 'eximiae notae,' but with many corrections by a later hand, and some foreign matter. (Greg. 471.)

*511. c^{scr}. Lond. Lamb. 1177 [xi–xii], 7½ × 5⅝, ff. 210 (17 &c.), τίτλ., Am., lect., κεφ. t. (Luke, John), subscr., στίχ., syn., for valuable readings by far the most important at Lambeth, shamefully ill written, torn and much mutilated[1]. (Greg. 472.)

*512. d^{scr}. Lond. Lamb. 1178 [xi or xiv], 11¾ × 9¼, ff. 302 (23), Syn., lect., τίτλ., κεφ., Am., Eus., prol., κεφ. t., orn., subscr., men., in a fine hand, splendidly illuminated, and with much curious matter in the subscriptions. Mut. Matt. i. 1–8. A noble-looking copy. (Greg. 473.)

*513. e^{scr}. Lond. Lamb. 1179 [x or later], 8¾ × 6¾, ff. 176 (24), 2 cols., τίτλ., κεφ., lect., Am., Eus., subscr., κεφ. t., neatly written but in wretched condition, beginning Matt. xiii. 53, ending John xiii. 8. Also mut. Matt. xvi. 28—xvii. 18; xxiv. 39—xxv. 9; xxvi. 71—xxvii. 14; Mark viii. 32—ix. 9; John xi. 8-30. Carlyle brought it from Trinity Monastery, Chalké. (Greg. 474.)

514. v^{scr}. Constantinople, Library of Patriarch of Jerusalem, restored from Lambeth in 1817, where it was No. 1180 [xiv], ff. 246, chart., τίτλ., Am., Eus., lect., with important variations: collated by Dr. Charles Burney in Mark i. 1—iv. 16; John vii. 53—viii. 11 (Lambeth 1223). (Greg. 488.)

*515. f^{scr}. Lond. Lamb. 1192 [xiii], 8 × 6½, ff. 472-6, chart. (22), lect., τίτλ., κεφ., Am., Eus., κεφ. t., pict.; from Syria, beautifully written, but tampered with by a later hand. Mut. John xvi. 8–22, and a later hand [xv] has supplied Mark iii. 6–21; Luke xii. 48—xiii. 2; John xviii. 27—xxi. 25; at the beginning stand some texts, περὶ ἀνεξικακίας. Re-examined by Bloomfield. About Luke xix, xx its readings agree much with those of Evan. Δ, and those of the oldest uncials. (Greg. 475.)

(g^{scr} is Lamb. 528 and Evan. 71, described above.)

516. u^{scr}. Constantin. Libr. Patr. of Jerus., C. 4 of Archdeacon Todd's Lambeth Catalogue, was a copy of the Gospels, in the Carlyle

---

[1] Matt. iv. 1—vii. 6; xx. 21—xxi. 12; Luke iv. 29—v. 1; 17-33; xvi. 24—xvii. 13; xx. 19-41; John vi. 51—viii. 2; xii. 20-40; xiv. 27—xv. 13; xvii. 6—xviii. 2; 37—xix. 14.

collection, restored with six others to the Patriarch of Jerusalem[1]. The collation of SS. Matthew and Mark by the Rev. G. Bennet is at Lambeth (1255, No. 25). (Greg. 487.)

*517. tˢᶜʳ. Lond. Lamb. 1350 [xiv], 8½ × 5¾, ff. 51 (20), St. John on paper, written with a reed, appended to a copy of John Damascene 'De Fide Orthodoxa:' has ὑπόθεσις or prol., κεφ., and a few rubrical directions; carelessly written, and inscribed 'T. Wagstaffe ex dono D. Barthol. Cassano e sacerdotibus ecclesiae Graecae, Oct. 20, 1732.' (Greg. 486.)

518. Lond. Sion College Library, A. 32. 1 (Ev. 1. (3)), [xi], 11 × 8¾, ff. 152 (24), a beautiful fragment, miserably injured by damp and past neglect, consisting of 153 leaves preserved in a box, was given by 'Mr. Edward Payne, a tenant in Sion College, as were also Evst. 227, 228, and perhaps Evst. 229.' The capitals, stops, and τίτλοι are in gold, κεφ., Am. (no Eus.) in red. Full lect., ἀρχαί and τέλη in red. It begins at Matt. x. 17, ends at John ix. 14. St. Mark's Gospel only has κεφ. t. Mark i. 1–13; Luke i. 1–13; John i. 1–17 have been taken away for the sake of the illuminations, and much of the text is illegible. (Greg. 559.)

519. Edinburgh, University Library, A. C. 25 [xi], 8vo, ff. 198, κεφ. t., κεφ., τίτλ., Am., Eus., lect., subscr., pict., in bad condition, presented in 1650 by Sir John Chiesley. (Greg. 563.)

520. Glasgow, Hunterian Museum, V. vii. 2 [xii], 4to, ff. 367, Carp., Eus. t., κεφ. t., κεφ., τίτλ., Am., Eus., syn., men., pict. (Greg. 560.)

521. Glasg. Hunt. Mus. Q. 7, 10 [xi], 4to, ff. 291, prol., κεφ. t., κεφ., τίτλ., Am., subscr. Both these were once Caesar de Missy's (see Evan. 44). (Greg. 561.)

522. Glasg. Hunt. Mus. S. 8, 141 [xv], 4to, ff. 78, κεφ., Lat. Codd. 519–22 were first announced by Haenel (see under Evan. 472). (Greg. 562.)

523. Lond., Mr. White, formerly Blenheim 3. B. 14 [xiii, Greg. xiv], 7½ × 6¼, ff. 170 (22), prol., κεφ. t., κεφ., τίτλ., Am., Eus., lect., ἀναγν., syn., men. : like Apost. 52, once belonging to the Metropolitan Church of Heraclea on the Propontis, and presented in 1738 to Charles, Duke of Marlborough, amoris et observantiae ergo by Thomas Payne, Archdeacon of Brecon, once our Chaplain at Constantinople: a bright, clean copy, written in very black ink, with vermilion ornamentation, and barbarous pict. (Greg. 701.)

Mr. Bradshaw indicated in the 'Transactions of the Royal Society of Literature,' vol. ii. p. 355, two copies of the Gospels belonging to the Earl of Leicester at Holkham, to be described with facsimiles in the Catalogue of the Library there. They were examined by Dean Burgon, who thus reported of them:—

---

[1] In Mr. Coxe's 'Report to Her Majesty's Government,' we find an account (which illness compelled him to give at second hand) of several copies of the Gospels and one palimpsest Evangelistarium, all dated [xii], still remaining in this Prelate's Library.

524. Holkham 3 [xiii], 8¾ × 6⅛, of 183 leaves, four being misplaced. It is beautifully written in twenty-seven long lines on a page. *Eus. t.*, τίτλ., *Am.* (not *Eus.*), imperfectly given: no *lect.* (κεφ., *subscr.*, *pict.*). Besides five pictures of the Evangelists and gorgeous headings to the Gospels are seventeen representations of Scripture subjects, some damaged. This 'superb MS. of extraordinary interest' in the style of its writing closely resembles Evan. 38. (Greg. 557.)

525. Holkham 4 [xiii or earlier], 8½ × 6⅓, ff. 352 (20), finely written, but quite different in style from Cod. 524. Τίτλ. in gold, *lect.*, ἀρχαί and τέλη in vermilion, κεφ., στίχ. numbered. (Κεφ. *t.*, *Am.*, ἀναγν., *subscr.*, στίχ., *pict.*) (Greg. 558.)

Eight copies of the Gospels, brought together by the late Sir Thomas Phillipps, Bart., at Middle Hill, Worcestershire, are now the property of Mr. Fitzroy Fenwick, and, with the rest of this unrivalled private collection of manuscripts, are now at Thirlestaine House, Cheltenham, where Burgon examined them in 1880, and Hoskier in 1886, who quotes (Cod. 604, App. E), some of the readings. Scrivener had used some of them at Middle Hill in 1856.

526. Phillipps 13,975 [xii], 12½ × 9½, ff. 196, once Lord Strangford's 464, a grand copy, the text being surrounded with a commentary (abounding, as usual, in contractions) in very minute letters. That on St. Mark is Victor's. *Pict.* of SS. Mark and Luke, beautiful illuminations for headings of the Gospels. Κεφ., τίτλ., *Am.*, *Eus.* in gold, *pict.* (*syn.*, *men.* at end). (Greg. 556.)

527. Phillipps 1284 (Act. 200, Paul. 281) [xii], 7⅔ × 5¼, ff. 344 (28), from the library of Mr. Lammens of Ghent, a rough specimen, contains the Gospels, Acts, and Epistles, the Pauline preceding the Catholic. *Mut.* Matt. ix. 36—x. 22 ; Mark i. 21-45, and the first page of St. John. The writing varies ; that from Acts to 1 Thess. is more delicate, and looks older. No *Am.*, *Eus.* Much *lect.* in vermilion, ἀρχαί and τέλη. Τίτλ., κεφ. *t.*, ἀναγν., *subscr.*, *syn.*, and sparse *men.* (Greg. 676.)

528. Phillipps 2387 [xiii], 6¼ × 4½, ff. 222 (25), bought of Thorpe for thirty guineas : rough, but interesting. One leaf only of *Eus. t.* Wantonly *mut.* in headings of the Gospels, and in Mark i. 1-19 ; Luke i. 1-18 ; John i. 1-23. Κεφ., τίτλ., *Am.* (not *Eus.*), ἀρχαί and τέλη later, *syn.*, *men.* (xvii) at the beginning, and much marginal *lect.* by a modern hand.

529. Phillipps 3886 [xi or xii], 10½ × 8¼, ff. 326 (20), a beautiful copy, bought (as were Evann. 530, 532, 533) by Payne at Lord Guildford's sale. *Eus. t.*, *Carp.*, *pict.*, κεφ. *t.*, τίτλ., *Am.*, *Eus.* (*lect.*, ἀρχ., τέλη, ἀναγν. later). (Greg. 678.)

530. Phillipps 3887 [xii], 8¼ × 6, ff. 240 (25, 26), the first four lines in SS. Matt., Mark, Luke being of gold, with *pict.* of the four Evangelists and nineteen others, *Eus. t.*, *Am.* incomplete and irregular (no *Eus.*). No *lect.*, but marginal critical notes. As in Evan. 64, a line (~) is set over Proper Names of persons in the Genealogies (*see* at end of Evan. 64). (Greg. 679.)

531. (Acts 199, Paul. 231, Apoc. 104.) Phillipps 7682 [xi], 6⅝ × 5, ff. 190 (41 or 50), 2 cols. (two scribes, Hoskier ; several, Greg.), the hands

so minute as to require a magnifying glass, contains the whole New Testament, also from Lord Guildford's (871), being, like Evann. 532 and 583, to be described below, from the Hon. F. North's collection (319). The ink is a dull brown, the ornaments in blue, vermilion, and carmine. *Carp.*, *Eus. t.*, *prol.*, κεφ. τ., κεφ. (Gr. and Lat.), τίτλ., *Am.*, few *Eus.*, *lect.*, *subscr.* There are many important corrections in the margin, and 18½ pages from Epiphanius at the end. This copy has every appearance of having been made from a very ancient codex: observe the arrangement of the Beatitudes in Matt. v in single lines, as also the genealogy in Luke iii. (Greg. 680.)

532. Phillipps 7712, North 184 (*see* Evan. 529), [xiii], 7½ × 5½, ff. ?, in a large hand and very black ink, the first page being in gold, with many gold balls for stops. There is much preliminary matter, *Eus. t.* (two sets in different hands), *pict.* (*Carp.*, *prol.* later), κεφ., τίτλ., *Am.*, *lect.* (later), *syn.*, *men.*, *subscr.*, στίχ. The text is corrected throughout by an ancient scribe, in a hand bright, clear, and small. (Greg. 681.)

533. Phillipps 7757 [xi], 6 × 4½, ff. ?, an exquisite little manuscript, with accessories in lake, vermilion, and blue. *See* Evan. 529. *Prol.*, *Carp.*, *Eus. t.*, κεφ. τ., κεφ., τίτλ., *Am.*, *Eus.*, *subscr.*, vers.

Haenel is mistaken in supposing that a Greek Evangelistarium is included in this grand and unique collection.

The Parham copies of the New Testament are described in a 'Catalogue of materials for writing, early writings on tablets and stones, rolled and other Manuscripts and Oriental Manuscript books in the library of Robert Curzon (Lord de la Zouche of Harynworth, 1870–73) at Parham,' fol., 1849. This accomplished person collected them in the course of his visits to Eastern Monasteries from 1834 to 1837, and permitted me in 1855 to collate thoroughly three of them, and to inspect the rest. They were all examined by Dean Burgon, to whom his son, the present Lord de la Zouche, had given free access to them. The codices of the Gospels are eight in number.

534. (Act. 215, Paul. 233.) Parham lxxi. 6 [xi], 9 × 6½, ff. 348 (41), contains the Gospels, Acts, and Epistles, the Pauline preceding the Catholic, and was brought in 1837 from Caracalla on Athos. *Prol.*, κεφ. τ., τίτλ., *Am.*, *lect.* (ἀρχ. and τέλ.), ἀναγν., *subscr.*, στίχ., vers., *syn.*, *men.* The usual arabesque ornaments are in red. (Greg. 547.)

535. Parh. lxxi. 7 [xi, Greg. x], 6⅓ × 4½, ff. 167 (26), brought from St. Saba in 1834. *Pict.*, κεφ. τ., illuminated headings, τίτλ., *Am.* (not *Eus.*). *Mut.* John xvi. 27—xix. 40. There is a musical notation on the first four leaves, and the first nine lines of St. John are in gold. (Greg. 548.)

536. Parh. lxxiii. 8 [xi], 4to, 11 × 9, ff. 198, brought from Xenophon on Athos 1837. The text is surrounded by a commentary, that on St. Mark being Victor's. *Prol.*, κεφ. τ., κεφ., τίτλ., *lect.* (ἀρχ. and τέλ.), *subscr.*, *syn.*, *men.* (Greg. 549.)

537. Parh. lxxiv. 9 [xi, Greg. xii], 10¼ × 7¾, ff. 219 (28), brought from Caracalla 1837, in its old black binding. *Carp.*, *prol.* (later), κεφ. τ., κεφ., τίτλ., *Am.*, *lect.* (ἀρχ. and τέλ.), *subscr.*, στίχ., *syn.*, *men.* With faded red arabesques (no *pict.*) and lake headings to the Gospels, the

writing being large and spread. There are marginal notes here and there. (Greg. 550.)

538. Parh. lxxv. 10 [xii], 4to, ff. 233 (22, 23), from Caracalla, also in its old black binding. There are rude *pict.* of the four Evangelists, and barbarous headings to the Gospels. Κεφ. t., κεφ., τίτλ., Am., few Eus., lect., subscr., στίχ., vers. (syn., men. later). The number of Am., κεφ. varies from what is usual. (Greg. 551.)

539. Parh. lxxvi. 11 [xii], 4to, ff. 252 (27), κεφ. t. (Luke), κεφ., τίτλ., Am., ἀρχ. and τέλ., brought from St. Saba in 1834. Rough illuminations. It contains some rare and even unique readings. (Greg. 552.)

540. Parh. lxxvii. 12 [xiii], 8½ × 6, ff. 304 (21), brought from St. Saba in 1834. Externally uninteresting, with decorations in faded lake, κεφ. t., κεφ., τίτλ., subscr., στίχ. (Greg. 553.)

541. Parh. lxxviii. 13 [A.D. 1272], 5¾ × 4½, ff. 230 (21). A facsimile is given in the Catalogue. This 'singularly rough little object' was bought at St. Saba in 1834 for ten dollars. Κεφ., τίτλ., lect. (Greg. 554.)

*542. 1scr. (Act. 188, Paul. 258.) Wordsworth [xiii], 4to, ff. 231, was bought in 1837 by Dr. Christopher Wordsworth, Bishop of Lincoln, and bears a stamp 'Bibliotheca Suchtelen' (Russian Ambassador at Stockholm). Κεφ. t., τίτλ., Am., lect., syn., men., prol. or ὑποθέσεις are prefixed to the Epistles, and scholia of Chrysostom, &c. set in the margin. (Greg. 479.)

*543. 9scr. (Act. 187, Paul. 257.) Theodori, from the name of the scribe [A.D. 1295], 8vo, ff. 360, passed from Caesar de Missy into the Duke of Sussex's library: in 1845 it belonged to the late Wm. Pickering, the much-respected bookseller: its present locality is unknown. *Syn., Carp., Eus. t., κεφ. t., κεφ., Am., lect., ὑποθέσεις or prol.,* and *syn.* before Act. and all Epp., Euthalius περὶ χρόνων, men. after St. Jude; it has many later changes made in the text. (Greg. 483.)

544. Ashburnham 204 [xiii], 4to, ff. 104, 'a piteous fragment,' brought from Greece by the Earl of Aberdeen, and bought at his sale. It contains only Matt. xxv. 32–5, 40, 41—xxviii. 20; Mark i. 4—xv. 47 (but defective throughout); Luke i. 1—xxiv. 48; John i. 1—ii. 4: about Luke vi a different hand was employed. There is no heading to St. Luke's Gospel, but a blank space is left, so that perhaps the MS. was never finished. Κεφ. t., κεφ., τίτλ., Am., Eus. (partially). (Greg. 671.)

The Baroness Burdett-Coutts imported in 1870–2 from Janina in Epirus upwards of one hundred manuscripts, chiefly Greek and theological, among which are sixteen copies of the Gospels or parts of them, three of the Acts, two of the Catholic, and three of St. Paul's Epistles, one of the Apocalypse, sixteen Evangelistaria and five Praxapostoli. Those marked I and II are deposited in the Library of Sir Roger Cholmely's School, Highgate; those marked III are in the Baroness's possession. The copies of the Gospels are—

*545. B.-C. I. 3 [xii], 7⅜ × 5⅝, ff. ? *Mut.* John x. 1—xii. 10; xv. 24—xxi. 25. *Carp., Eus. t.,* κεφ. t., τίτλ., κεφ., *Am., Eus., pict., lect., vers.* (Greg. 532.)

*546. B.-C. I. 4 [xii], 6¾ × 5⅜, ff. ?, a fine copy. *Mut.* Matt. i. 1—ix. 13, with gilded illuminations. *Syn.*, κεφ. t., τίτλ., *Am.* (not *Eus.*), *lect.*, iambic verses. (Greg. 533.)

*547. B.-C. I. 7 [xiii], 6 × 4, ff. 267 (22), *chart. Mut.* Luke. i. 26–42; xx. 16—xxi. 24. *Syn.*, *men.*, *pict.*, κεφ. t., τίτλ., *lect.* (not *Am.*, *Eus.*). After the subscription to St. John follow the numerals ξ θ ϙ π. It has on the cover a curious metal tablet adorned with figures and a superscription. (Greg. 534.)

*548. B.-C. I. 9 [xii], 7 × 5, ff. 125 (18), SS. Matthew and Mark only. *Mut.* Matt. xi. 28—xiii. 34; xviii. 13—xxi. 15; 33—xxii. 10; xxiv. 46—xxv. 21; Mark iii. 11—v. 31; ix. 18—xii. 6; 34–44; ends with πανταχοῦ Mark xvi. 20. *Syn.*, *lect.*, κεφ., τίτλ., *Am.*, *Eus.* (Greg. 535.)

*549. B.-C. II. 7 [xii or xiii], 5 × 3, ff. 172 (26–31), a very curious volume in ancient binding with two metal plates on the covers much resembling that of B-C. I. 7, contains the Four Gospels and the Acts, breaking off at ch. xxvi. 24 μαίνῃ παῦλε; the writing being unusually full of abbreviations, and the margin gradually contracting, as if vellum was becoming scarce. The last five pages are in another, though contemporary hand. Seven pages containing Gregory Nazianzen's heroic verses on the Lord's genealogy, and others on His miracles and parables, partly in red, precede κεφ. t. to St. Matthew; other such verses of Gregory precede SS. Mark and Luke, and follow St. John, and κεφ. t. stand before SS. Luke and John. There are τίτλ., κεφ. (no *lect.*; and *Am.*, *Eus.*, only in the open leaf containing Luke xii): in the Gospels there is a *prol.*, and no chapter divisions in the Acts, but a few capitals in red. Pretty illuminations precede each book. (Greg. 536.)

*550. B.-C. II. 13 [xii], 7 × 5, ff. 143 (29), with poor arabesque ornamentation, complete. *Lect.*, a few τίτλ. by a later hand, as is also much of *Am.*, *Eus.*, which are only partially inserted. (Greg. 537.)

*551. B.-C. II. 16 [xiii], 6⅞ × 4⅞, ff. ? *Mut.* Matt. i. 1–17; Luke i. 1–17; John i. 1–46. *Lect.*, κεφ. t. (defective), τίτλ., κεφ., *Am.*, *Eus.*, *pict.* (Greg. 539.)

*552. B.-C. II. 18 [xii], 6 × 4⅜, ff. ?, very neat. The first leaf forms part of a Lectionary: on the second the Gospels begin with Matt. xiii. 7. *Mut.* John i. 1–15. Κεφ. t., τίτλ., κεφ., *Am.* (not *Eus.*), *men.* at the end, *lect.* in abundance, *pict.* of St. Mark washed out: arabesques at the head of each book. (Greg. 538.)

*553 & *554. B.-C. II. 26[1] and 26[2] are two fragments of the Gospels, whereof 26[1] comprises 27 leaves of St. Mark (19–21), covered with vile modern scribbling (ch. iii. 21—iv. 13; 37—vii. 29; viii. 15–27; ix. 9—x. 5; 29—xii. 32) [xiii], 7½ × 5½, neat, with τίτλ., *Am.*, *Eus.*, *lect.*; and 26[2] consists of 48 leaves [xiv], 8½ × 5½, containing Matt. xviii. 32—xxiv. 10; xxvi. 28—xxviii. 20; Mark i. 16—xiii. 9; xiv. 9–27, with κεφ. t., τίτλ., *Am.* (*Eus.* only partially). *lect.* There are many abridgements in the writing. Dated, perhaps by the first hand, A. D. 1323. (Greg. 540, 541.)

*555. B.-C. III. 4 [xiii], 7 × 5, ff. 264 (24), *prol.*, κεφ. t., τίτλ., κεφ., *Am.*, *Eus.*, *lect.*, *pict.* of the four Evangelists, *syn.* incomplete at the end.

Some leaves are misplaced in St. Matthew. *Mut.* John xix. 25—xxi. 2. (Greg. 542.)

*556. B.-C. III. 5 [xii], 11 × 8½, ff. 183 (26), 2 cols., κεφ. t., lect., syn., men., prol., κεφ., τίτλ., Am., Eus. *Mut.* Matt. xii. 11—xiii. 10; Mark viii. 4–28; Luke xv. 20—xvi. 9; John ii. 22—iv. 6; 53—v. 43; xi. 21-47, one leaf lost in each case, and one (John i. 51—ii. 22) misplaced in binding. This copy has John vii. 53—viii. 11 after Luke xxi. 38, like Ferrar's four, with which its text much agrees, and the titles to SS. Matthew and Mark only run εὐαγγέλιον ἐκ τοῦ κατὰ M ... (Greg. 543.)

*557. B.-C. III. 9 [xiii], 5½ × 3½, ff. 256 (22), κεφ. t. to the last three Gospels, τίτλ., κεφ., Am. (not Eus.), pict. of SS. Matthew, Mark, and John. This copy is remarkably free from lect. Neatly written, but four considerable passages in St. Luke are omitted, the text running on *uno tenore*. (Greg. 544.)

*558. B.-C. III. 10 [dated A. D. 1430], 8 × 5½, ff. 374 (+ 16 + 34) (16), chart., pict. of the four Evangelists, of the Saviour, and of the Virgin and Child. Carp., Eus. t., κεφ. t., prol., Am., Eus., lect., vers. The leaves are much misplaced in binding. (Greg. 545.)

*559. B.-C. III. 41 [xii or xiii], 6½ × 4½, ff. 275 (22). *Mut.* at beginning and end (John xviii. 30–end) and about Matt. xii. 16. Κεφ. t., τίτλ., pict., in a bad condition. (Greg. 546.)

The next two were purchased in 1876 of Quaritch for £120 and £50 respectively by Mr. Jonathan Peckover, and now belong to Miss Algerina Peckover, of Bank House, Wisbech. Burgon examined them, and J. R. Harris since then.

560. (Act. 222, Paul. 278.) Algerina Peckover (1) [xi], small 4to, ff. 239 (33), contains the Gospels, Acts, and Epistles in their usual Greek order, 'an exquisite specimen, in a somewhat minute character.' It begins with a picture of St. Matthew, the lost preliminary matter being prefixed chart. by a later hand. Pict., τίτλ., κεφ., Am., Eus., lect. (ἀρχ. and τέλ.), subscr., στίχ., vers., syn., men. On the last leaf is written in uncial letters: ὡς ἡδὺς τοῖς πλέουσιν ὁ εὔδιος λιμήν· | οὕτως καὶ τοῖς γράφουσιν ὁ ἔσχατος στίχος. Ἰωαννικίου μοναχοῦ. (Greg. 712.)

561. Algerina Peckover (2), [xi or a little later], 7¾ × 5¾, ff. 356 (16), with 17 (3 + 14) uncial palimpsest leaves at the beginning and end, containing Lessons from the Epistles to be described hereafter (Apost. 43). Carp., prol. (later), κεφ. t., pict., κεφ., τίτλ., Am., Eus., lect. (ἀρχ. and τέλ.), subscr., syn., men. (later). *Mut.* Matt. xxvii. 43, 44; John vii. 53—viii. 11; x. 27—xi. 14 (2 ff.); xi. 29-42 (1 f.). Marg. notes, Matt. v. 14; xvi. 15. One of the Ferrar group. See J. R. Harris, Codex Algerina Peckover (Journal of Exegetical Society). (Greg. 713.)

*562. Oxf. Bodl. MS. Bibl. Gr. L. 1. Mendham [xiv], 9½ × 7, ff. 270 [sic] (20), κεφ. t., κεφ., τίτλ., lect., subscr., στίχ., ἀναγν., vers., syn., men. Bohn became possessed of it, whether from Meerman or not is not known, and sold it to the Rev. Theodore Williams, Vicar of Hendon, for £120. The Rev. Joseph Mendham bought it of Payne for £70 in 1827. It was given by Mr. Mendham's widow to Dean Burgon for his life, afterwards to go to the Bodleian Library, where the Rev. W. F. Rose brought it upon the Dean's death. It is dated on the last leaf by a later hand, A. D. 1322. It is evenly written in pale brown ink with a reed-pen. The last twenty leaves contain the Gospels for Maundy Thursday, for Good Friday, and for St. John's Day. The ornamentation is as fresh and bright as if done yesterday, and its text is of the ordinary type, like lmn^{scr} (Evann. 201, 542, 568). It is a very beautiful MS., and an excellent specimen in all ways. (Greg. 521.)

Mr. James Woodhouse [d. 1866], Treasurer-General of the Ionian Islands, while resident fifty years at Corfu, formed a collection of manuscripts from monasteries in the Levant, which was sold in London in 1869, 1872, 1875. Among them were three copies of the Gospels, two Evangelistaria, one copy of the Acts and St. Paul.

*563. London, Brit. Mus. Egerton 2783 [xiii], 5¾ × 3½, ff. 337 (22), *Carp., Eus. t., prol., κεφ. t., pict., τίτλ., κεφ., lect.* (ἀρχαί and τέλη), *subscr., στίχ., vers., syn., men.* It was once fair, but has suffered from damp, and has been sadly cropped by the Western binder. *Mut.* John xx. 17. The headings of the Gospels are in lake. It abounds in curious and unique liturgical notes, whereof Burgon gives specimens, and it has textual corrections by the original scribe. Collated by Rose. Bought by Burgon, then belonged to Rev. W. F. Rose, and bought for the Museum in 1893. (Greg. 714.)

*564. Brit. Mus. Egerton 2785 [xiv], 10½ × 8, ff. 226 (27–29), 2 cols., *syn., men.,* scholium on τίτλος α΄, *prol., κεφ. t., pict., Am., τίτλ., κεφ. (lect.* later), *subscr., ῥήμ., στίχ.* The ornamentation is in lake, and at the end are extracts from Eulogius and Hesychius. Upon collation by Mr. Rose it exhibits here and there suggestive discrepancies from the common text. Evann. 563, 564 were respectively offered for sale in 1871 for £50 and £40. Bought by Burgon, belonged to Rose, and purchased for Museum in 1893. (Greg. 715.)

*565. Brit. Mus. Egerton 2784 [xii, Greg. xiv], 8¾ × 5¾, ff. 213 (22–25), *κεφ. t., τίτλ., κεφ., Am., Eus., lect., ἀναγν., subscr., ῥήμ., στίχ.,* fragment of *syn.* Apparently not from the Woodhouse collection. It is beautifully written and of an uncommon type. Its older binding suggests a Levantine origin. The readings are far more interesting than those of Cod. 564, some of them being quite unique. Belonged to Burgon, then Rose, then to the Museum in 1893. (Greg. 716.)

*566. h^{scr}. Brit. Mus. Arund. 524 [xi], 6¾ × 5¼, ff. 218 (27), *Carp., Eus. t., κεφ. t., κεφ., τίτλ., Am., Eus., lect., syn., men.,* was brought to England (with x^{scr} and many others) by the great Earl of Arundel in 1646. Henry Howard, Evelyn's Duke of Norfolk, presented them to the Royal Society, from whose rooms at Somerset House they were transferred to the Museum in 1831. (Greg. 476.)

567. Brit. Mus. Harl. 5538, described in the Harleian Catalogue as an Evangelistarium, and numbered by Scholz Evst. 149, is a copy of the Gospels [xiv, Greg. xii], 4¾ × 3½, ff. 226 (23), *orn., lect., Am.* (Greg. 505.)

*568. n^{scr}. (Paul. 259 or j^{scr}.) Brit. Mus., Burney 18 (purchased in 1818, with many other manuscripts, from the heirs of Dr. Charles

Burney), contains the Gospels and two leaves of St. Paul (Hebr. xii. 17—xiii. 25), written by one Joasaph A. D. 1366, 12¾ × 9, ff. 222 (23) +9 blank, κεφ. t., κεφ., lect., Am., Eus., ἀναγν., subscr., στίχ., very superb in gold letters. Codd. lmn (542, 201, 568) agree pretty closely. (Greg. 480.)

*569. o^scr. Brit. Mus. Burn. 19 [x], 8½ × 7, ff. 217 (22), pict. (Plate iii, No. 8), in the Escurial as late as 1809, is singularly void of the usual apparatus. (Greg. 481.)

*570. p^scr. Brit. Mus. Burn. 20 [A.D. 1285, Indict. 13, altered into 985, whose indiction is the same], 7½ × 6, ff. 317 (22, 23), written by a monk Theophilus : pict., Eus. t., κεφ. t., τίτλ., Am., Eus., lect., syn., men., the two last in a later hand, which has made many corrections : this copy is quite equal in value to Cod. c^scr (511), and often agrees closely with w^scr (507). (Greg. 482.)

*571. r^scr. Brit. Mus. Burn. 21, by the same scribe as Cod. 543 [A. D. 1292], 13 × 10, ff. 258 (24), on cotton paper in a beautiful but formed hand (see Plate vi, No. 15), syn., κεφ. t., prol., orn., κεφ., τίτλ., Am., lect., subscr., στίχ., men. A fine copy, much damaged. Codd. 543 and 571 differ only in 183 places. (Greg. 484.)

*572. s^scr. Brit. Mus. Burn. 23 [xii], 7¾ × 6, ff. 230 (23-25), boldly but carelessly written, ends John viii. 14 : mut. Luke v. 22—ix. 32 ; xi. 31—xiii. 25 ; xvii. 24—xviii. 4. Syn., Carp., κεφ. t., orn., κεφ., τίτλ., Am., lect., subscr., στίχ., with many later changes and weighty readings. (Greg. 485.)

573. Brit. Mus. Add. 5468 [A. D. 1338], 8¼ × 6, ff. 226 (29), Carp., Eus. t., κεφ. t., τίτλ., κεφ., Am., lect., subscr., στίχ., syn., men. It was 'John Jackson's book, bought of Conant in Fleet Street, 1777, for five guineas.' Mut. Matt. i. 1—vi. 18, and the last leaf of St. Luke (xxiv. 47-53). This copy has the subscriptions at the end of each of the Gospels of SS. Matthew and Mark. There is a probable reference to them at the end of St. John (ὁμοίως). It is coarsely written on thick vellum, with much lect. in vermilion. The breathings and accents are remarkably incorrect. (Greg. 686.)

574. Brit. Mus. Add. 7141, bought 1825, and once Claudius James Rich's [xiii, Greg. xi], 9¾ × 7½, ff. 192 (27), 2 cols., Carp., Eus. t., κεφ. t., τίτλ., Am. (partial), Eus., lect. in red, subscr. (Greg. 490.)

*575 or k^scr. Brit. Mus. Add. 11,300, Lebanon [xii], 6¾ × 4½, ff. 268 (26), Carp., Eus. t., κεφ. t., κεφ., τίτλ., Am., Eus., lect., subscr., most elegantly and correctly written, purchased in 1838, and said to come from Caesarea Philippi at the foot of Lebanon. Contains scholia: the text is broken up into paragraphs. (Re-examined by Bloomfield.) There is a beautiful facsimile page in the new 'Catalogue of Ancient Manuscripts in the British Museum' (1881), Plate 16. (Greg. 478.)

576. (Act. 226, Paul. 268.) Brit. Mus. Add. 11,836, this and the next two are from Bishop Butler's collection: [xi], 7¼ × 5¼, ff. 305 (34), Eus. t. (blank), pict., κεφ. t., κεφ., τίτλ., Am., subscr., κεφ. in Epistles, beautifully written in a minute hand and adorned with gold letters, contains Evan.,

Act., Cath., Paul., Psalms, &c.   *Mut.* Mark i. 1–28 ; Acts i. 1–23 ; vii. 8–39 ; Ps. i. 1–3. Akin to Cod. 440 in St. Paul (Vansittart). (Greg. 491.)

577. Brit. Mus. Add. 11,838[1] [A. D. 1326, Ind. 9], 9¼ × 6, ff. 269 (24), (*syn., men.* later), κεφ. τ., *pict.* (*lect.,* some ἀναγν. later), τίτλ., from Sinai, most beautifully written by Constantine, a monk. (Greg. 492.)

578. Brit. Mus. Add. 11,839 [xv], 10½ × 8, *chart.,* ff. 157 (27), *lect.* (later, and in latter part), ill-written, with later marginal notes, and no chapter divisions. Matt. iv. 13—xi. 27 ; Mark i. 1—vi. 1, are later. (Greg. 493.)

579. Brit. Mus. Add. 11,868, from the Butler collection [xi], 9½ × 7, ff. 7 (29), 2 cols. (now bound separately), containing Matt. x. 33—xi. 12 ; xiii. 44—xiv. 6 ; xv. 14–18 ; 20–22 ; 26–29 ; 30–32 ; 34—xvii. 10 ; 34—xvii. 10 ; 12–15 ; 18–20 ; 22–24 ; 25 (sic)—xviii. 16, two half-leaves being lost, beautifully written in two columns. Κεφ., τίτλ. (*mut.*), *Am., Eus.,* later *lect.* (Greg. 687.)

580. *See* Evan. 272. Instead—
Lord Herries [xiii], 8½ × 6⅛, f. 1 (26), κεφ., τίτλ., *Am.* (*lect.,* ἀναγν. later). (*See* Greg. 576.)

581. Brit. Mus. Add. 16,183 (sic) [xii], 6½ × 5¾, ff. 181 (28, 29), *Carp.* (*mut.* at beg.), space for *Eus. t.,* κεφ. τ., κεφ., τίτλ., *lect., Am., Eus., syn., men.,* in a minute hand, bought (as was Cod. 582) of Captain C. K. Macdonald in 1846. The two came probably from Sinai, where he once saw Cod. ℵ. (Greg. 495.)

582. (Act. 227, Paul. 279.) Brit. Mus. Add. 16,184 [xiii or xiv], 7½ × 5½, ff. 300 (33, 34), *Carp., prol.,* κεφ. τ., *lect.,* τίτλ., κεφ., *Am., Eus., subscr., στιχ., pict., syn., men.,* some later on paper. The whole New Testament, except the Apocalypse, in the usual Greek order. This copy contains many important various readings : e. g. it countenances Codd. ℵBL in Luke xi. 2, 4. (Greg. 496.)

583. Brit. Mus. Add. 16,943 [xi], 6 × 4¾, ff. 184 (22, 23), in a very small hand, *prol.,* κεφ. τ., *lect.,* τίτλ., κεφ., *Am., Eus., subscr., στιχ., pict., syn., men.,* from the collection made by the Hon. F. North for the University of Corfu. *See* Evann. 531–2 ; Act. 198. (Greg. 497.)

584. (Act. 228, Paul. 269, Apoc. 97 or j^{scr}.) Brit. Mus. Add. 17,469, contains the whole N. T., bought of T. Rodd in 1848 [xiv], 10¼ × 7, ff. 187 (35) (very minute writing), with much other matter. *Prol., vers.,* κεφ. τ., κεφ., τίτλ., *Am., lect., syn.* *Mut.* Matt. i. 1—ii. 13 ; Mark v. 2—vi. 11 ; Acts i. 1—v. 2 ; James i. 1—v. 4 ; 3 John ; Jude ; Rom. i. 1—iv. 9 ; 2 Thess. ii. 13—1 Tim. i. 13 ; vi. 19—2 Tim. ii. 19. In Acts τίτλ., *lect.* rubro. *Prol.* to every Epistle. Written by Gerasimus. (Greg. 498.)

585. Brit. Mus. Add. 17,470 [A.D. 1034], 8 × 6, ff. 287 (20), *syn., men., pict.,* κεφ. τ. (with *harm.*), κεφ., τίτλ. (with *harm.*), *Am., Eus., lect.,* with many marginal corrections of the text. Written by Synesius, a priest, bought of H. Rodd in 1848. 'A singularly genuine specimen.' (Greg. 504.)

---

[1] For Add. 11,837, which is m^{scr}, *see* Evan. *201.

586. Brit. Mus. Add. 17,741 [xii], 9¼ × 6¼, ff. 216 (22), begins Matt. xii. 21, ends John xvii. 13 : purchased in 1849. *Am.* (not *Eus.*), ἀρχαί and τέλη, *lect.* The genealogy in St. Luke is in three columns. (Greg. 499.)

587. Brit. Mus. Add. 17,982 [xiii], 8 × 6, ff. 244 (23), *Carp.*, space for *Eus. t.*, κεφ. *t.*, κεφ., τίτλ., *Am.*, ἀναγν., *vers.*, *syn.*, *men.*, ending John xix. 39 (eight leaves being lost, also leaf containing xviii. 1–21), and believed to contain important readings. (Greg. 500.)

588. Brit. Mus. Add. 18,211 [xiii], 9½ × 7½, ff. 157 (23), 12 *chart.* [xv] to supply hiatus : κεφ. *t.*, κεφ., *Am.*, some τίτλ., *lect.*, came from Patmos. F. V. J. Arundell, British Chaplain at Smyrna (1834), describes this copy, given him by Mr. Borrell, and a Lectionary sold to him at the same time, in his 'Discoveries in Asia Minor,' vol. ii. p. 268. He there compares it with the beautiful Cod. Ebnerianus (Evan. 105), which it very slightly resembles, being larger and far less elegant. *Mut.* Matt. i. 1–19; Mark i. 1–16; Luke ix. 14—xvii. 4; xxi. 19—John iv. 5. (Greg. 501.)

589. Brit. Mus. Add. 19,387 [xii], 8¼ × 6½, ff. 235 (22), κεφ., τίτλ., *Am.*, *Eus.*, *lect.*, *prol.*, κεφ. *t.*, *subscr.*, *syn.*, *men.*, written by one Leo, and found in a monastery of St. Maximus, begins Matt. viii. 6, and was purchased in 1853 from the well-known Constantine Simonides (Greg. 502) —as was also

590. Brit. Mus. Add. 19,389 [xiii], 4¾ × 3½, ff. 60 (26), κεφ., *Am.*, *lect.*, St. John's Gospel only, elegantly written by Cosmas Vanaretus, a monk. (Greg. 503.)

The foregoing Additional MSS. in the British Museum were examined and collated (apparently only in select passages) by Dr. S. T. Bloomfield for his 'Critical Annotations on the Sacred Text' (1860), designed as a Supplement to the ninth edition of his Greek Testament, and comprising an *opus supremum et ultimum*, the last effort of a long and honourable literary career. He has passed under review no less than seventy manuscripts of the New Testament, twenty-three at Lambeth, the rest in the British Museum. The following have been accumulated since his time.

591. Brit. Mus. Add. 22,506 [A.D. 1305], 9½ × 7, ff. 279 (22), κεφ. *t.*, *pict.*, κεφ., *lect.*, τίτλ., *Am.*, *subscr.*, στίχ., ἀναγν., written by Neophytus a monk of Cyprus, was bought at Milos by H. O. Coxe of a Greek who had it from a relative who had been ἡγούμενος of a Candian monastery. A facsimile is given in the new Museum Catalogue. (Greg. 645.)

592. Brit. Mus. Add. 22,736 [June, A.D. 1179], 9½ × 7½, ff. 226 (24), 2 cols., *syn.*, *prol.*, κεφ. *t.*, *pict.*, κεφ., *lect.*, τίτλ., *Am.*, written by John ἀναγνώστης, with peculiar, almost barbarous, illuminations. (Greg. 688.)

593. Brit. Mus. Add. 22,737 [xii], 8¼ × 6, ff. 313 (20), κεφ. *t.*, κεφ., not τίτλ., *lect.*, *subscr.*, στίχ., *syn.*, *men.*, with decorations in very deep lake. (Greg. 689.)

594. Brit. Mus. Add. 22,738 [xiii], 6¾ × 4⅝, ff. 237 (23, 24), *Carp.*, *Eus. t.*, κεφ. *t.*, κεφ. (τίτλ., *lect.*, *syn.*, *men.*, by another hand), *Am.*, *pict.*, rough and abounding with itacisms. Two rude pictures of Evangelists have been effaced. (Greg. 690.)

595. Brit. Mus. Add. 22,739, has a rather modern look [xiv?], $7\frac{3}{8} \times 5\frac{3}{8}$, ff. 275 (22), *Carp.*, *Eus. t.*, κεφ. *t.*, κεφ., *pict.*, τίτλ., *Am.*, *lect.*, στίχ., ἀναγν., with rough pictures and illuminations. (Greg. 691.)

596. Brit. Mus. Add. 22,740 [xii], 8×6, ff. 237 (23), *prol.*, κεφ. *t.*, *pict.*, κεφ., τίτλ., *Am.*, *Eus.* (in blue), exquisitely written, said to greatly resemble Cod. 71 (g^scr) in text, with illuminated headings to the Gospels. *Mut.* Luke ii. 7–21, and after τίτλ. of St. John. This MS. with Evst. 269, 270, 271, 272, and Evann. 592, 597, was bought of Sp. Lampros of Athens in 1859. (Greg. 692.)

597. Brit. Mus. Add. 22,741 [xiv], $10 \times 7\frac{3}{4}$, ff. 208 (22), *Eus. t.*, *Carp.*, κεφ. *t.*, κεφ., τίτλ., *Am.*, *subscr.*, *orn.*, *prol.* (here called προγράμματα, a term we have not noticed elsewhere). *Mut.* Mark i. 27–43; ii. 2–16. John vii. 1—xxi. 25. (Greg. 693.)

598. Brit. Mus. Add. 24,112 [xv], $11\frac{1}{2} \times 8\frac{1}{2}$, *chart.*, ff. 211 (33, 34), ($7\frac{1}{4}$ pages Gr. and Lat.), κεφ. *t.*, κεφ., *lect.*, *subscr.*, στίχ., ἀναγν., *syn.*, *men.* Bought at Puttick's, 1861. (Greg. 694.)

599. Brit. Mus. Add. 24,373 [xiii], $9\frac{1}{4} \times 7\frac{1}{2}$, ff. 299 (22), *syn.*, *men.*, *Carp.*, *Eus. t.*, κεφ. *t.*, *prol.*, *pict.*, *orn.*, κεφ., τίτλ., *lect.*, *Am.*, *Eus.*, *subscr.*, very beautiful. *Mut.* Matt. i. 11—xv. 19. Long *lect.*, ἀρχ. in marg., τέλ. in the text. Bought of H. S. Freeman, Consul at Janina, in 1862. (Greg. 695.)

600. Brit. Mus. Add. 24,376 [xiv], $10\frac{3}{4} \times 8\frac{1}{4}$, ff. 350 (19), 2 cols., κεφ. *t.*, *pict.*, κεφ., *lect.*, ἀναγν., some *Am.*, *subscr.*, στίχ., *syn.*, *men.* Remarkable *pict.* of the Annunciation and of the three later Evangelists, Gospel headings left blank. *See* Evst. 273–7. (Greg. 696.)

601. Brit. Mus. Add. 26,103 [xiv], 8×6, ff. 242 (25), *orn.*, κεφ., τίτλ., *Am.* (in gold), *pict.* (John), was found in a village near Corinth, and bought of C. L. Merlin, our Vice-Consul at Athens, in 1865. Beautifully written in very black ink, the first page of each Gospel being in gold. (Greg. 697.)

602. Brit. Mus. Add. 27,861 [xiv], $6\frac{1}{2} \times 5$, ff. 186 (19, 20, &c.), κεφ. *t.*, κεφ., τίτλ., *Am.*, *lect.*, *subscr.*, *syn.*, *men.*, from Sir T. Gage's sale, 1868, rough and dirty, with many marginal notes to supply omissions. St. Matthew's Gospel is wholly lost. No *pict.*, but ornamentation in faded lake. (Greg. 698.)

603. (Act. 231, Paul. 266 and 271.) Brit. Mus. Add. 28,815 [x or xi], $11\frac{1}{2} \times 8\frac{1}{2}$, ff. 302 (30), κεφ., τίτλ., *Am.*, *Eus.*, *lect.*, *pict.*, sumptuously bound with silver-gilt plates. This noble fragment was bought (as were Act. 232, Evst. 279, 280) of Sir Ivor B. Guest in 1871, and contains the Gospels, Acts, Catholic Epistles, Romans, 1, 2 Corinthians, Galatians, the rest of the original volume being evidently torn out of the book when already bound. In the same year 1871 the Baroness Burdett-Coutts also imported from Janina in Epirus sixty-seven leaves containing the rest of St. Paul's Epistles and the Apocalypse (B.-C. II. 4, Paul. 266, Apoc. 89), which fragments were described in the second edition of the present book. Mr. Edward A. Guy, of Miami University, Oxford, Ohio, U.S.A., on examining the Museum fragment in 1875 with my book in his hand, concluded that the two portions originally formed one magnificent copy of the whole New Testament,

and when I brought the two together, I saw that the illuminated heading and initial capital on the first page of B.-C. II. 4 (Eph. i) was worked off through damp on the *verso* of the last leaf (302) of the Museum copy, and the red κεφ. of Gal. vi on the top of B.-C. II. 4, leaf one, *recto*. In the larger fragment we find two *pict.* of St. Luke (one of them before the Acts), one of St. John, with illuminated headings. *Carp., Eus. t.,* &c. must have perished, as the first page opens with Matt. i. 1. It has τίτλ. in gold letters on purple vellum, a Harmony at the foot of fol. 17 b—18 b, and many brief marginal scholia. *See* Paul. 266 (B.-C. II. 4), which is at present five miles off, in the Library of Sir Roger Cholmeley's School, Highgate. (Greg. 699.)

604. Brit. Mus. Egerton 2610 [xii], 5¾ × 4¼, ff. 297 (19), about thirty letters to a line), *Carp., Eus. t., κεφ. t.* (Matt., Mark, Luke), τίτλ., *Am., Eus., pict.* (beautifully executed). First noticed by Dean Burgon, bought for the Museum in 1882, and collated by Mr. H. C. Hoskier, 'Full Account, &c.,' D. Nutt, 1890. According to Mr. Hoskier's analysis it contains no less than 270 quite unique readings, siding at least twenty times alone with D, eleven with B, six with ℵ, six with Evan. 1, twenty-nine with Evan. 473. It has 2724 variations from T. R. There are besides a vast number of almost unique readings, e. g. Luke xi. 2, for which Greg. Nyss. is about the only authority (Hoskier). (Greg. 700.)

605. (Act. 233, Paul. 243, Apoc. 106.) Zittaviensis A. 1 [xv], *chart.*, ff. 775 (30), *prol., κεφ. t., κεφ., τίτλ., subscr., στίχ., vers.*, given to the Senate of Zittau (Lusatian Saxony) in 1620, contains the canonical books of the Old Testament down to Esther, with 1 Esdras, 4 Maccabees, Judith, Tobit, and the whole New Testament. Matthaei collated the Old Testament portion for Dean Holmes's edition of the Septuagint (Cod. 44), and saw its great critical value. It was examined, as so many others have been, by Dr. C. R. Gregory. (Greg. 664.)

The next two were bought for the Bodleian in 1882: they came from Constantinople.

606. Oxf. Bodl. Gr. Misc. 305 [xi], 9½ × 7¼, ff. 149 (27), *pict.* (Matt., Mark), κεφ., *Am., Eus.,* few *lect.* (later). *subscr.* (Matt.), *orn. Mut.* Mark xvi. 19 (*post* καὶ) 20. The passages Matt. xvi. 2, 3 ; John v. 4 ; vii. 53 —viii. 11 are obelized in the margin. (Greg. 707.)

607. Oxf. Bodl. Gr. Misc. 306 [xi], 7¼ × 6, ff. 200 (32, &c.), *Eus. t.,* κεφ. *t., pict., κεφ., τίτλ., Am., Eus.,* much cropped in binding. *Mut.* (1), fol. 1 ; (2) tops of pages containing τίτλοι ; and (3) Quaternion of 8 ff., Matt. xx. 15—xxiv. 22. (Greg. 708.)

608. Brit. Mus. Add. 11,859-60 (palimpsest) is a Typicum or Rituale [xiv or xv], 10 × 7¾, ff. 39 + 29 (uncertain), from the Butler collection, having written under it an earlier cursive text [xiii] containing, in 11,859, Matt. xii. 33—xiii. 7 ; xvi. 21—xvii. 15 ; xx. 1-15 ; 15—xxi. 5 ; Mark x. 45— xi. 17: 198 verses; and in 11,860, only twenty-seven verses of the Catholic Epistles, James 1-16 ; Jude 4-15. This is Act. 234. (Greg. 1274 ?)

609. Camb. Univ. Libr., Hh. 6. 12 [xv], 8 × 5¾, *chart.*, ff. 182 (20, &c.),

κεφ. t., prol., subscr. This must be Scholz's 1673 (N. T., vol. i. p. cxix), but it contains the Gospels only, not the Acts, as he supposes. (Greg. 552.)

610. Oxf. Bodl. Barocc. 59 [xi], 8¼ × 5½, ff. 6 (21), 1 *chart.*, κεφ. t. (John), κεφ., τίτλ., *Am., lect.*, containing Luke xxiii. 38-50 ; xxiv. 46-53 ; John i. 30—iii. 5 in a book of other matter [xv], *chart.* (Greg. 526.)

611. Rom. Angel. D. 3. 8, olim Cardinalis Passionei [xi], 9⅝ × 6½, ff. 442 (21), *prol.*, κεφ. t. St. Luke with Theophylact's commentary, described with facsimile by Vitali in Bianchini's 'Evan. Quadr.' vol. ii. pt. 1, pp. 506-40, 563, 560. (Greg. 848.)

612. B.-C. I. 11 [xii], 3½ × 2½, ff. 112 (25-28), is a very small and beautiful 'Ωδεῖον, containing the Magnificat and Benedictus, besides the 151 Psalms of the Septuagint version, and the Hymns of Moses (Ex. xv. 1-14; Deut. xxxii. 14-43), of Hannah (1 Sam. ii), of Habakkuk (ch. iii), Isaiah (ch. xxvi), Jonah (ch. ii), with that of the Three Holy Children. Many such books are extant, of which this is inserted in our list as a specimen. *See* 5pe, note.

John Belsheim, editor of the Codex Aureus, found at Upsal in 1875, and described to Burgon in 1882, together with Act. 68, three manuscripts in the University Library there containing the Gospels only.

613. Upsala 4, Sparvenfeldt[1] 45 [xi], 5⅞ × 4½, ff. 208 (25), *Eus. t.*, κεφ. t., *pict.*, last leaf later, bought at Venice in 1678. (Greg. 899.)

614. Upsala 9 [xiii], 9½ × 7½, ff. 288 (22), *pict.*, given by a Greek priest in 1784 to A. F. Stiertzenbecker, who bequeathed it to the University Library. (Greg. 900.)

615. Upsala 12, Björnsthal 2 [xii], 6¾ × 4⅞, ff. 328 (31), *syn., men.,* contains the Gospels, Acts, and Epistles, being Act. 237, Paul. 274. (Greg. 901.)

616. Upsala 13, Björnsthal 3 [xii], 6¼ × 4¾, ff. 230 (24), *prol.*, κεφ. t. (Greg. 902.)

These two last and Act. 236 were bequeathed by Professor J. Björnsthal to the University Library.

617. Oxf. Oriel, MS. lxxxiii [xi or xii], 7¾ × 5¾, ff. 236 (22, 23), 2 cols., κεφ. t., *pict.* (cut out), τίτλ., *lect., Am., Eus., syn., men.*, written in gold letters. *Mut.* in many places. Brought in 1878 by Capt. J. Hext from Corfu, and given by him to Mr. Daniel Parsons, who gave it to the College as a ' joint gift.' (Greg. 618.)

618. Camb. Add. 720 [xi], 5½ × 4¼, ff. 278 (19, 20), *Am., Eus.,* κεφ., τίτλ. (fragments of κεφ. t.), *lect., syn., men., pict.* But *Carp., Eus. t.*, κεφ. t. of Matt., and perhaps *prol.* are apparently lost. *Mut.* Matt. xxviii. 1-20 ; Mark xv. 29—Luke iii. 33. In a later hand is Luke xxiv. 46-53. (Hort and Bradshaw.) (Greg. 672.)

---

[1] Belsheim (Cod. Aureus, Proleg. p. xvii and note 3) gives a short life of that noble Swede, John Gabriel Sparvenfeldt [1655-1727], who was sent over Europe by his master, Charles XI, to procure manuscripts for the Royal Library, and bought the Latin Codex Aureus at Madrid in 1690.

619. Camb. Add. 1837 [xii or xiii], 8⅝ × 6½, ff. 164 (19), injured in parts by damp. Κεφ., fragment of κεφ. t., lect., ἀναγν., subscr., στίχ. No Am., Eus., τίτλ., prol. Mut. Matt. i. 1—x. 42; xiii. 3–16; xxvii. 24–37; Mark xiv. 21—Luke iii. 16; iv. 35—v. 23; vii. 4–15. Ends Luke xix. 33. (Hort and Bradshaw.) (Greg. 673.)

620. Camb. Add. 1879. 11 [xii], 9 × 6¾, ff. 4 (26), containing Matt. x. 42—xii. 43. Am. (not Eus.), κεφ., τίτλ. Lect. are in a later hand. (Hort and Bradshaw.) (Greg. 674.) From Tischendorf's collection, as is also

621. Camb. Add. 1879. 24 [xiii—xiv], 8⅓ × 5¾, ff. 2 (25), containing Matt. xxvi. 20–39 and ὑπόθεσις and verses before St. Mark. Κεφ., τίτλ., lect. (Hort and Bradshaw.) (Greg. 675.)

The Rev. H. O. Coxe, late Bodley's Librarian, though quite unable to purchase any of the literary treasures he was commissioned to inspect in 1857, added considerably by his research to our knowledge of manuscripts in the East. A list of them was given in groups by Dr. Scrivener in the third edition of this work: but for various reasons they will be found separately placed amongst the ensuing MSS., to fill up gaps which have been since discovered in the supplementary list of cursive manuscripts that was bound up in the beginning of the last edition.

The Evann. 622–735 were reported to Dean Burgon from several Libraries in reply to his sedulous enquiries. Upon subsequent examination by Dr. C. R. Gregory on the spot, many of them were seen not to be Evangelia, but instead of that commentaries of St. Chrysostom, or other commentaries, or Evangelistaria, or MSS. containing other matter. Thus —including the list of the Abbé Martin, who extended Dean Burgon's numeration up to 776—the following must be excised: 643–665, 667, 673, 677–679, 681, 682, 685, 686, 688, 689, 695, 700–702, 706, 711, 712, 715–722, 724–728 (including 726 which Dr. Scrivener noticed as a duplication of 611), 731, 733, 734, 758, 760, 763, 771, 772, 775, 776. Gregory, Prolegomena, pp. 794, 795. The editor has inserted other MSS. in their places, being especially those found by the late Rev. H. O. Coxe in his travels, and enumerated in his Report to Her Majesty's Government.

622. (Act. 242, Paul. 290, Apoc. 110.) Crypta Ferrata, A. a. 1 [xiv], 11¾ × 8¼, ff. 386 (28), chart., κεφ. t. with harm., Am., Eus. (rare), lect., ἀναγν., subscr., στίχ., vers., pict., syn., men., a beautiful codex of the entire New Testament. Described by the custodian Rocchi (Codices Cryptenses, &c., 1882, pp. 1, 2). (Greg. 824.)

623. Crypta Ferrata, A. a. 2 [xi, Greg. xiii], 9 × 6⅝, ff. 337 (21), prol., κεφ. t., lect., ἀναγν., subscr., pict., syn., men., a beautiful codex brought from Corcyra in 1729. Described by Rocchi, pp. 2–4. (Greg. 825.)

*624. Crypta Ferrata, A. a. 3 [xi, Greg. xii], 8⅝ × 6¾, ff. 234 (26), in 2 cols., κεφ. t., κεφ., τίτλ., Am., Eus., lect., subscr., στίχ., syn., men. Collated by W. H. Simcox (Greg.), agrees with the Ferrar group. A beautiful codex: written probably at Rhegium. (Greg. 826.)

625. Crypta Ferrata, A. a. 4 [xi, Greg. xiii], 8¼ × 6⅝, ff. 225 (24), κεφ., τίτλ., Am., subscr., vers.; from St. John xix. 21 in a more recent hand. No Pericope de adulterâ. (Greg. 827.)

626. Crypta Ferrata, A. a. 5 [xi, Greg. xii], 10⅝ × 7⅞, ff. 176 (27), 2 cols., *Eus. t.* (beautiful), κεφ. t., κεφ., τίτλ., *Am., Eus., lect., subscr., ῥήμ., στίχ., pict., syn., men.*; with beautiful Eusebian tables. Described by Rocchi, pp. 5, 6. (Greg. 828.)

627. Crypta Ferrata, A. a. 6 [xi, Greg. xii], 8⅝ × 6¾, ff. 209 (26), 2 cols., κεφ. t., κεφ., τίτλ., *Am., Eus., lect., στίχ., syn., men., subscr.* to St. Mark like Λ. Begins at St. Matt. xiii. 28. Described by Rocchi, pp. 6, 7. (Greg. 829.)

628. Crypta Ferrata, A. a. 8 [xiii], 8⅝ × 4¾, ff. 118 (26), *prol.,* κεφ. t., κεφ., τίτλ., *Am., Eus.*; St. Luke and St. John *mut.* Described by Rocchi, p. 8. (Greg. 830.)

629. Crypta Ferrata, A. a. 17 [xii, Greg. xi], 5⅝ × 5⅛, ff. 69 (23), κεφ. t., κεφ., *Am., lect., subscr.* A fragment only, beginning at St. Luke xix. 35. The *pericope de adulterá* is supplied at the end of the codex—imperfect after verse 6. (Greg. 831.)

630. Messina, University Library 88 (Evst. 361) [xiv], 10¼ × 8½, ff. 260 (22), *chart., pict., Eus. t.* (exquisite), κεφ., τίτλ., *Am., Eus., syn., men.* All in good preservation. (Greg. 839.)

631. Messina, Univ. Libr. 100 [xiii], 10½ × 7⅞, ff. 125 (24), τίτλ. St. Luke i to xxii with a commentary. (Greg. 840.)

632. Lond. Butler, formerly Hamilton 244 [xii], 9⅝ × 6⅞, ff. ? (22), *Carp., Eus. t., pict.,* κεφ. t., κεφ., τίτλ., *Am., Eus.* (in the same line); superbly illuminated and adorned with effigies of St. Matthew and of the Virgin and Child, on gold ground. The Eusebian Canons written in gold between human figures standing on columns supporting arched arabesque friezes finely painted in gold and colours. (Greg. 662.)

633. Par. Nat. Suppl. 227 [xvi or xvii], 9¾ × 7, ff. 212 (22), κεφ., τίτλ., *Am.*; a Western codex. (Greg. 745.)

634. Par. Nat. Suppl. 911 [A. D. 1043], written by Euphemius ἀναγνώστης, in black, blue, and red ink, 6⅞ × 5⅜, ff. 315 (18), 2 cols., *Am.* St. Luke, Greek and Arabic. (Greg. 609.)

635. Berlin, Royal Gr. 4to, 39 [xii or xi], 9¾ × 7⅝, ff. 313, *Carp., Eus. t., prol.,* κεφ. t., κεφ., τίτλ., *Am., Eus., harm.* at foot, *lect., subscr., στίχ., pict.* Note that the *pericope de adulterá* is found in this Evan. as well as in Evann. 636, 637, 638, 641, and 642. (Greg. 655.)

636. Berl. R. Gr. 4to, 47 [xiii or xii], 9¼ × 5¾, ff. 220, *Carp., Eus. t.,* κεφ. t., κεφ., τίτλ., *Am., Eus.* in same line, *lect., syn., men.* (Greg. 658.)

637. Berl. R. Gr. 4to, 55 [xii], 8¼ × 6⅛, ff. 292, *prol.,* κεφ. t., *Am. Eus., lect., subscr., pict.* (Greg. 659.)

638. Berl. R. Gr. 4to, 66 [xii or xi], 8⅞ × 6½, ff. 139 (21), *Eus. t.,* κεφ. t., κεφ., τίτλ., *Am., Eus., lect., pict.* (Greg. 660.)

639. Berl. R. Gr. 4to, 67 [xi], 9⅞ × 7¾, ff. 234 (23), κεφ. t., κεφ., τίτλ., *Am., Eus., pict.* (Greg. 661.)

640. Berl. R. Gr. 8vo, 3 [A. D. 1077], 5⅞ × 4⅝, ff. 266 (16), κεφ. t., κεφ., τίτλ., *Am., Eus., lect., subscr., στίχ.* (Greg. 653.)

EVANN. 626-665.   265

641. Berl. R. Gr. 8vo, 4 [xi or xii], 4¾ × 3¾, ff. 178 (25), κεφ., τίτλ. *Mut.* in places. Contains from St. Matt. ii. 15 to St. John xix. 32. (Greg. 654.)

642. (Act. 252, Paul 302.) Berl. R. Gr. 8vo, 9 [xi, Greg. xiv], 5¾ × 4, ff. 140 (32), very minute writing, κεφ. *t.*, κεφ., τίτλ., *Am., Eus., lect., subscr., στίχ.*; probably once contained all the New Testament. It begins now with St. Luke xxiv. 53: *mut.* after 1 Thess. (Greg. 656.)

643. Cairo, Patriarchal Library 2 [xiii], Gospels, 4to. (Greg. 601.)

644. Cairo, Patr. Libr. 15 [xi]. *Mut.* Gosp., 4to. (Greg. 602.)

645. Cairo, Patr. Libr. 16 [xi], Gosp., 4to, *syn., men.*, beautifully written. (Greg. 603.)

646. Cairo, Patr. Libr. 17 [xi], Gosp., 4to. (Greg. 604.)

647. Cairo, Patr. Libr. 68 [x], Gosp., 4to. (Greg. 605.)

648. Cairo, Μετοικία of St. Katherine of Mount Sinai 7 [xvi], Synopsis of Gospels with Psalter, fol., *chart.* (Greg. 606.)

649. Jerusalem, Holy Sepulchre (monastery of) 2 [x], Gosp., 4to, beautifully written. (Greg. 607.)

650. Jerus. Holy Sepul. 5 [x], Gosp., 4to, beautifully written. (Greg. 608.)

651. Jerus. Holy Sepul. 6 (Scholz 450) [A. D. 1043], St. Luke (Gr. and Arab.), 4to, by Euphemius. Beautifully written [1]. (Greg. 450.)

652. Jerus. Holy Sepul. 14 [xii], Gosp. with scholia, large 4to. (Greg. 610.)

653. Jerus. Holy Sepul. 17 [xi], Gosp. with few scholia, 4to. (Greg. 611.)

654. Jerus. Holy Sepul. 31 [xi], Gosp., 4to, very beautiful. (Greg. 612.)

655. Jerus. Holy Sepul. 32 [xi], Gosp., 4to. (Greg. 613.)

656. Jerus. Holy Sepul. 33 [xii], Gosp., 4to. (Greg. 614.)

657. (Act. 325, Paul. 152.) Jerus. Holy Sepul. 40 [xii], N. T., except Apoc., 4to. A fine copy. (Greg. 615.)

658. Jerus. Holy Sepul. 41 [xi], Gosp., 4to, beautiful. (Greg. 616.)

659. Jerus. Holy Sepul. 43 [xi], Gosp., fol., scholia (Matt. unc. in golden letters). (Scholz 456?) (Greg. 617.)

660. Jerus. Holy Sepul. 44 [xiv], Gosp., fol. (Greg. 618.)

661. (Act. 260, Paul. 304.) Jerus. Holy Sepul. 45 [xii], Gosp., Paul., Cath., with λέξεις τῶν Πράξεων, 4to. (Greg. 619.)

662. Jerus. Holy Sepul. 46 [xi], Gosp., small 4to. (Greg. 620.)

663. Jerus. Holy Cross, 3 [xi], Gosp., 4to, *syn., men.*, κεφ. (Greg. 621.)

664. St. Saba 27 [xii], Gosp., fol. (Greg. 622.)

665. (Act. 328, Paul. 230.) St. Saba 52 [xi], Gosp., Paul., Cath., 4to, *syn., men.* (Greg. 623.)

---

[1] Gregory considers this to be (not a duplicate but) the same as Cod. 684.

666. Rom. Vat. Gr. 641 [A. D. 1287], $10 \times 6\frac{5}{8}$, ff. 467 (28), *chart.* The Gospels, with Theophylact's commentary. (Greg. 854.)

667. (Act. 317, Paul. 316.) St. Saba 53 [xi], Gosp., Paul., Cath., 4to. (Greg. 624.)

668. Rom. Vat. Gr. 643 [xii], $10\frac{1}{4} \times 8\frac{1}{4}$, ff. 584 (36), *pict.* The Gospels, with Theophylact's commentary. (Greg. 855.)

669. Rom. Vat. Gr. 644 [A. D. 1280], $13 \times 9\frac{1}{2}$, ff. 349 (44), 2 cols., *chart.*, *Am.*, written by order of Michael Palaeologus. Same contents as the preceding. (Greg. 856.)

670. Rom. Vat. Gr. 645 [xii], $11\frac{1}{2} \times 9\frac{1}{8}$, ff. 391 (28), *prol.*, *κεφ. t.*, *κεφ.*, *τίτλ.* St. Luke and St. John, with Theophylact's commentary. (Greg. 857.)

671. (Paul. 311.) Rom. Vat. Gr. 647 [xv or xiv], $13\frac{1}{2} \times 9\frac{3}{4}$, ff. 338 (48), *chart.* Gospels and Epistles, with commentary of Theophylact. (Greg. 858.)

672. Rom. Vat. Gr. 759 [xv or xvi], $8\frac{5}{8} \times 5\frac{3}{4}$, ff. 261, *chart.* St. Luke, with a commentary. (Greg. 859.)

673. (Act. 318, Paul. 317.) St. Saba 54 [xii], Gosp., Paul., Cath., 4to. (Greg. 625.) (Vat. Gr. 1068 is Evst. 122.—Greg.)

674. Rom. Vat. Gr. 1090 [xvi], $10\frac{3}{4} \times 8\frac{1}{4}$, ff. 509 (40), *chart.* The Gospels, with commentary of Peter of Laodicea. Part i and ii. (Greg. 861.)

675. Rom. Vat. Gr. 1191 [xii], $9 \times 6\frac{3}{4}$, ff. 402 (?), written by one 'Arsenius.' St. John, with Theophylact's commentary. (Greg. 862.)

676. Rom. Vat. Gr. 1221 [xii or xiii], $15\frac{1}{8} \times 10\frac{5}{8}$, ff. 400 (41), 2 cols., *κεφ. t.*, *κεφ.*, *τίτλ.*, *lect.*, *subscr.* The Gospels, with Theophylact's commentary. (Greg. 863.)

No. 677 is a Catech., 678 is Evst. 551, 679 a commentary. (Greg.)

677. St. Saba 56 [x], Gosp., 4to. (Greg. 626.)

678. St. Saba 57 [x], Gosp., 4to. (Greg. 627.)

679. St. Saba 58 [x], Gosp., 4to. (Greg. 628.)

680. Rom. Vat. Gr. 1895 [xv or xiv], $6\frac{1}{2} \times 4\frac{3}{8}$, ff. 223 (20), *prol.*, *κεφ. t.*, with *harm.*, *κεφ.*, *lect.*, *ἀναγν.*, *subscr.*, *στίχ.*, *vers.* (Greg. 867.)

681. St. Saba 59 [x], Gosp., 4to. (Greg. 629.)

682. St. Saba 60 [x], Gosp., 4to. (Greg. 630.)

683. Rom. Vat. Gr. 1933 [xvii], $15\frac{5}{8} \times 10\frac{3}{8}$, ff. 624 (26), *chart.* St. Luke, with a Catena. (Greg. 868.)

684. Rom. Vat. Gr. 1996 [xi or xii], $10\frac{7}{8} \times 8\frac{5}{8}$, ff. 245 (25), *κεφ.*, *τίτλ.*, with a commentary. (Greg. 869.)

685. St. Saba 61 *a* [xi], Gosp., 4to. (Greg. 631.)

686. St. Saba 61 *b* [xi], Gosp., 4to. (Greg. 632.)

687. Rom. Vat. Gr. 2117 [xi], $5\frac{1}{4} \times 4\frac{3}{8}$, ff. 164 (29), *prol.*, *κεφ. t.*, *κεφ.*, *τίτλ.*, *subscr.* (later); a beautiful Evangelium. (Greg. 871.)

688. St. Saba 61 *c* [xi], Gosp., 4to. (Greg. 633.)

689. Rom. Vat. Gr. 2165 [xi], $13\frac{3}{8} \times 9\frac{7}{8}$, ff. 289 (23), 2 cols., *Carp.*,

Eus. t., κεφ. *t.*, κεφ., τίτλ., *Am.*, *Eus.*, *subscr.*, ῥήμ., στίχ., olim Columnensis 4. This was Evst. 391. (Greg. 873.)

690. Rom. Vat. Gr. 2160 [xi or xii], $8\frac{1}{4} \times 6\frac{1}{4}$, ff. 180 (26), 2 cols., *Carp., prol.*, κεφ. *t.*, κεφ., τίτλ., *Am.*, *Eus., lect., subscr.*, στίχ., *vers., pict.* 'Venit e familia principe Romanâ De Alteriis, cujus stemma argenteum in tegmine habet.' (Greg. 872.)

691. Rom. Vat. Gr. 2187 [xii or xiii], $11\frac{1}{4} \times 7\frac{3}{4}$, ff. 383 (27), olim Columnensis 26. St. John, with Commentary of Theophylact. (Greg. 874.)

692. Rom. Vat. Gr. 2247 [?], $7\frac{7}{8} \times 5\frac{7}{8}$, ff. 228 (23), *Eus. t., prol.* (John), κεφ. *t., pict.*, κεφ., τίτλ., *Am., Eus., lect., syn.*; a fine codex. Column. 86. (Greg. 875.)

693. Rom.Vat. Gr. 2275 [xvi], $13\frac{5}{8} \times 9\frac{1}{4}$, ff. 2 + 17 (40), *chart.*, fragments of SS. Matt. and John with comm. (Greg. 876.)

694. Rom. Vat. Gr. 2290 [A. D. 1197], $10\frac{1}{2} \times 8\frac{1}{4}$, ff. 218 (25), 2 cols., *Carp., Eus. t., prol.*, κεφ. *t.*, κεφ., τίτλ., *Am., Eus., vers.* A splendid codex. It has been numbered 2161. (Greg. 877.)

695. St. Saba 61 *d* [xi], Gosp., 4to. (Greg. 634.)

696. Rom. Vat. Reg. Gr. 3 [xiii, Greg. xi], $13\frac{7}{8} \times 10\frac{1}{2}$, ff. 256 (30), St. Luke and St. John, with commentary of Chrys.; begins Luke iii. 1. (Greg. 884.)

697. Rom. Vat. Reg. Gr. 5 [xv], $11\frac{5}{8} \times 8\frac{3}{4}$, ff. 439 (29), *chart.* St. Matthew, with a commentary. (Greg. 885.)

698. (Act. 268, Paul. 324, Apoc. 117.) Rom. Vat. Reg. Gr. 6 [A. D. 1454], $13\frac{1}{2} \times 9\frac{3}{4}$, ff. 336 (59), *chart.*, κεφ. *t.* The Gospels, with commentary of Nicetas of Naupactus; Acts and St. Paul, with commentary of Theophylact; Apoc., with the commentary of an anonymous writer. (Greg. 886.)

699. Rom. Vat. Reg. Gr. 9 [xi], $11\frac{3}{4} \times 9\frac{7}{8}$, ff. 197 (38). St. John, with a commentary. (Greg. 887.)

700. St. Saba 61 *e* [xi], Gosp., 4to. (Greg. 635.)

701. St. Saba 62 *a* [xii], Gosp., 4to. (Greg. 636.)

702. St. Saba 62 *b* [xii], Gosp., 4to. (Greg. 637.)

703. Rom. Vat. Ottob. 37 [xii], $13\frac{1}{2} \times 18\frac{1}{2}$, ff. 248 (46), *Eus. t.*, κεφ. *t.*, κεφ., τίτλ., *Am., Eus., lect., vers.*, with the commentary of Theophylact. Pars i et ii. Olim Altemprianus. (Greg. 878.)

704. Rom. Vat. Ottob. 100 [xvi], ff. 105, *chart.*, part of St. Luke, with commentary. (Greg. 879.)

705. Rom. Vat. Ottob. 208 [xv], $8\frac{3}{8} \times 5\frac{3}{8}$, ff. 255 (17), *chart., pict.*, κεφ., τίτλ., *Am.* A fine Evangelium, with pictures. (Greg. 880.)

706. St. Saba 62 *c* [xii], Gosp., 4to. (Greg. 638.)

707. ⎫ Rom. Vat. Ottob. 453, 454, 456 [xiii, Greg. xv], $13\frac{3}{4} \times 9\frac{1}{4}$, ff.
708. ⎬ 171 + 171 + 181 (31), *chart.* The Gospels, with Theophylact's
709. ⎭ commentary. Dr. Gregory, having examined these three, pronounces them parts of the same MS. (Greg. 881.)

710. St. Saba G2 *d* [xii], Gosp., 4to. (Greg. 639.) Dr. Gregory identifies 710 with Evan. 146.

711. St. Saba 62 *e* [xii], Gosp., 4to. (Greg. 640.)

712. St. Saba, Tower Library 45 [xi], Gosp., 4to. (Greg. 641.)

713. Rom. Vat. Pal. 32 [xi or x], $14\frac{1}{4} \times 10\frac{1}{2}$, ff. 181, 2 cols. St. John, with commentary of Chrys. (Greg. 882.)

714. Rom. Vat. Pal. 208 [xv], $8\frac{1}{8} \times 5\frac{1}{3}$, ff. 247 (24), *chart*. St. John, with Theophylact's commentary. (Greg. 883.)

715. St. Saba, Tower Library 46 [xii], Gosp., 4to. (Greg. 642.)

716. St. Saba, Tower Library 47 [xi], Gosp., 4to. (Greg. 643.)

717. Patmos, St. John 2 [xii], Gosp., scholia, 4to. (Greg. 467.)

718. Patmos, St. John 6 [x], Gosp., 4to, *syn.*, *men*. (Greg. 468.)

719[1]. Patmos, St. John 21 [xii], Gosp., fol. (Greg. 469.)

720. Cyprus, Larnaca [xii], Gosp., 4to, *syn*. (Greg. 644.) Five more were noted by Mr. Coxe, but he was unable through illness to see them. They have been examined since then by Dr. Gregory.

721. Constantinople ἁγίου τάφου 436 [xiii], $7\frac{7}{8} \times 5\frac{7}{8}$, ff. ? (22), written by several hands, *Eus. t.*, κεφ. *t.*, *Am.*, *Eus*. (See Greg. 646.)

722. Constant. ἁγ. τάφ. 520 [xiii], $10 \times 7\frac{3}{8}$, ff. ? (24), 2 cols., *Carp., Eus. t., prol., κεφ. t., pict., Am., Eus., subscr., vers., syn., men.* (*See* Greg. 647.)

723. Rom. Angelic. B. i. 5 [xii, Greg. xiv], $11\frac{1}{2} \times 8\frac{3}{4}$, ff. ? (33), κεφ. *t., subscr., στίχ., syn.* Formerly belonged to Card. Passionei. Matt. and Mark with catena. (Greg. 847.)

724. Constant. ἁγ. τάφ. 574 [xiv], $9\frac{1}{2} \times 7$, ff. ? (23), κεφ. *t., lect., subscr. Mut.* end of Mark, beg. and end of Luke, many places in John. (Greg. 648.)

725. Constant. τοῦ ἑλληνικοῦ φιλολογικοῦ συλλόγου 1 [A. D. 1303?], $11\frac{1}{2} \times 8\frac{5}{8}$, ff. 294 (44), *chart.*, 2 cols. Gospels with commentary much in a later hand. Written by a certain George. (*See* Greg. 649.)

726. Constant. τ. ἑλλ. φιλ. συλλόγ. 5 [xiii], $5\frac{1}{4} \times 7$, ff. ? (24), κεφ. *t., Am., lect., subscr., στίχ., vers., syn., men. Mut.* (*See* Greg. 650.)

727, 728, 731, 733. Chalké, Trinity Monastery, ten miles from Constantinople, seen by Dr. Millingen, and reported by Coxe, four Evang., with silver clasps, numbered by him 1, 2, 3, 4. These four MSS. (727, 728, 731, and 733) seem to be the same as those which Dr. Gregory has recorded as 'Chalcis monasterii Trinitatis 11 et 12,' and 'Chalcis scholae 8' and 27 (A. D. 1370, fol., κεφ. *t., lect., ἀναγν., syn., men.*), the latter of which with two more (*see* below, 734, 735) he saw. Dr. Millingen mentions eight; but Dr. Gregory records only six, which must be taken to be the number. *See* Prolegomena 1144–49, p. 608.

729. Rom. Barberini iv. 86 (olim 228) [x, Greg. xii], $11\frac{1}{3} \times 8\frac{1}{2}$, ff. 381 (35?), 2 cols. St. John, with Cyril's commentary. (Greg. 850.)

---

[1] For the other Evann. at Patmos, *see* No. 1160, &c.

730. Rom. Barb. iv. 77 (ol. 210) [xvii], $10\frac{3}{4} \times 8$, ff. 152 (21), *chart*. St. John, with Books v and vi of Cyril's commentary. (Greg. 849.)

732. Rom. Borgian. (Propag.) L. vi. 10 [A. D. 1300], $9\frac{1}{2} \times 6\frac{1}{2}$, ff. 165, κεφ., τίτλ., *Am., syn., men.* The Gospels, with Menologium. 'Birchius eo usus est:' but he makes no mention of it. (Greg. 852.)

734. Chalké, 'Chalcis scholae' 95 [xiii], 4to, *pict*.

735. Chalké (Act. 288, Paul. 336), 'Chalcis scholae' 133 [xiii], 4to.

736. Bought of Muller, the London bookseller, and collated by H. B. Swete, D.D., Regius Professor of Divinity, Cambridge [xi or xii, Greg. xiv], $7\frac{1}{4} \times 6$, ff. 254, in modern binding. After signature 28 seven leaves [xiv?] containing John xviii. 39, ὑμῖν ἵνα to the end are supplied. *Syn., men., prol., vers.*, κεφ. τ., κεφ., *Am.* (*Eus.* later), *lect., subscr.* like Λ, στίχ. In the margin are textual corrections, some *primâ manu*. The readings are sometimes curious. (Greg. 718.)

737. Ox. Bodl. Misc. Gr. 314, found at Rhodes in 1882, and procured through Mr. Edmund Calvert [xi], $7\frac{1}{2} \times 6$, ff. 118 (21), 2 cols., κεφ. τ., κεφ., τίτλ., *Am., Eus., lect., subscr.*, στίχ., ῥήμ. *Mut.* Matt. v. 40—xxi. 1; Luke xv. 4—xxii. 49; xxiv. 34—52; John iv. 14—ix. 11; xiii. 3—xv. 10; xvi. 21—xxi. 25 (some fresh leaves having been lately purchased). It was apparently written by an Armenian scribe (F. Madan). A later hand [xiii] supplies Luke iii. 25—iv. 11; vi. 25-42 in palimpsest, over writing not much earlier than itself. (Greg. 709.)

The following MSS. (738-774) are from the late Abbé Martin's list of MSS. at Paris (*see* 'Description Technique'), and are numbered by him as they are given here:—

738. (Act. 262, Apoc. 123.) Par. Nat. Suppl. Gr. 159 [xiii, Greg. xiv], $15\frac{3}{4} \times 11\frac{3}{8}$, ff. 406 (36), κεφ. τ., κεφ., τίτλ., *lect.* (Greg. 743.)

739. Par. Nat. Suppl. Gr. 919 [xiii, Greg. xv], $5\frac{1}{4} \times 4\frac{7}{8}$, ff. 19 (47), *Eus. t., prol., syn., men.* (remarkable), κεφ., *Am., Eus., lect.* Contains Matt. ii. 13—ix. 17. (Greg. 751.)

740. Par. Nat. Suppl. Gr. 611 [x, Greg. xi], $10\frac{1}{2} \times 7\frac{3}{4}$, ff. 396 (47), *Carp., Eus. t.*, κεφ. τ., κεφ., τίτλ., *Am., Eus., prol.* Section of adultery omitted, a leaf probably lost. (Greg. 746.)

741. Par. Nat. Suppl. Gr. 612 [A. D. 1164], $9\frac{3}{4} \times 7\frac{1}{2}$, ff. 376 (53), *Carp., Eus. t.*, κεφ. τ., τίτλ., *prol., Am., Eus., lect., pict.* Commentary. (Greg. 747.)

742. Par. Nat. Suppl. Gr. 914 [xi-xii], $11\frac{3}{4} \times 8\frac{3}{4}$, ff. 319 (20), κεφ., τίτλ., *Am., pict., subscr.* (Greg. 750.)

743. Par. Nat. Gr. 97 [xiii], $8\frac{5}{8} \times 6\frac{1}{8}$, ff. 152 (28), κεφ., τίτλ., *Am., lect., Mut.* John xx. 15-end. Has a double termination to St. Mark written by George. (Greg. 579.)

744. Par. Nat. Gr. 119 [xi, Greg. xii or xiii], $6 \times 4\frac{1}{2}$, ff. 382 (25), Greg. 388 (16), *Carp., Eus. t.*, κεφ. τ., κεφ., τίτλ., *Am., syn., men., lect.* A beautiful MS. (Greg. 580.)

745. Par. Nat. Gr. 179 [xvi, Greg. xiv], $13\frac{1}{2} \times 9\frac{7}{8}$, ff. 246 (50), 2 cols., κεφ. τ., κεφ., τίτλ. Beautiful; Gospels with Theoph. (Greg. 727.)

746. Par. Nat. Gr. 181 [xiii, Greg. xiv], $11\frac{5}{8} \times 8\frac{1}{2}$, ff. 230 (68), 2 cols., *syn.*, *pict.*, *prol.*, κεφ. t., κεφ., τίτλ., *Am.*, *lect.* Gospels with Theoph. (Greg. 728.)

747. Par. Nat. Gr. 182 [xiii], $11\frac{5}{8} \times 8\frac{1}{2}$, ff. 341 (47), 2 cols., κεφ. t., τίτλ. Gospels with Theoph. (Greg. 729.)

748. Par. Nat. Gr. 183 [xiv], $9\frac{7}{8} \times 6\frac{1}{2}$, ff. 331 (32), *chart.*, *prol.*, κεφ. t., τίτλ. *Mut.* John xvi. 4-end. Gospels with Theoph. (Greg. 730.)

749. Par. Nat. Gr. 184 [xiv], $9\frac{1}{2} \times 5\frac{3}{4}$, ff. 426 (40), *chart.*, *prol.*, κεφ. t., τίτλ., *Am.*, *pict.* Gospels with Theoph. (Greg. 731.)

750. Par. Nat. Gr. 185 [xiii or xiv], ff. 271 (38), *chart.*, *syn.*, *Eus. t.*, *prol.*, *Am.*, *lect.*, κεφ., τίτλ. Gospels with Theoph. (Greg. 732.)

751. Par. Nat. Gr. 190 [xii], $11\frac{5}{8} \times 8\frac{3}{4}$, ff. 347 (42), *prol.*, κεφ. t., *pict.* (Matt.), κεφ., τίτλ. (Greg. 733.)

752. Par. Nat. Gr. 192 [xiv or xv], $11\frac{3}{4} \times 8\frac{5}{8}$, ff. 297 (39), (269–297 *chart.*). SS. John, Matt., Luke with Theoph. (Greg. 734.)

753. Par. Nat. Gr. 196 (xiii, Greg. xv), $9\frac{1}{4} \times 6\frac{1}{8}$, ff. 164 (50), latter part a palimpsest. SS. Matt. and Luke with Theoph. *Mut.* Matt. i. 1—vii. 16 (xii. 33, and other places, Greg.) (Greg. 735.)

754. Par. Nat. Gr. 198 [xi or xii], $10\frac{7}{8} \times 7\frac{3}{4}$, ff. 235 (34), κεφ. t., κεφ., τίτλ. Gospels with Theoph. (Greg. 736.)

755. Par. Nat. Gr. 204 [xiii], $10\frac{1}{2} \times 8\frac{1}{8}$, ff. 176 (30), Matt. with Theoph. (Greg. 737.)

756. Par. Nat. Gr. 205 [A.D. 1327], $11\frac{1}{2} \times 8\frac{1}{4}$, ff. 80 (38), *chart.*, κεφ. t., κεφ., τίτλ. Matt. with Theoph. (Greg. 738.)

757. Par. Nat. Gr. 207 [xv], $13\frac{1}{2} \times 8\frac{1}{8}$, ff. 48 (39). Luke with Theoph. (Greg. 739.)

758. Par. Nat. Suppl. Gr. 903 [xii], ?, ff. 278, κεφ. t., κεφ., τίτλ., *Am.*, *lect.*, *subscr.* *Mut.* in many places. (*See* Greg. 748, who also notes that Nat. Gr. 214 is only a homily.)

759. Par. Nat. Suppl. Gr. 219 [xii or xiii], $9\frac{1}{4} \times 8\frac{1}{4}$, ff. 367 (27), τίτλ. (Matt.), *pict.* (Luke). Gospels with Theoph. (Greg. 744.)

760. Par. Nat. Suppl. Gr. 1035, frag. [viii ?] ff. 12; [xi or xii], 8×6, ff. 182 (35), *membr.* and *chart.* (*Am.*, *lect.* later). Matt. xxiii. 11–21. (*See* Greg. 753.)

761. Par. Nat. Gr. 234 [xii or xiii, Greg. xiv or xv], $9\frac{3}{4} \times 7$, ff. 441 (36), (Greg. 444 (33, &c.)), *chart.*, *syn.*, κεφ., τίτλ., *lect.* Gospels with Theoph. (Greg. 740.)

762. Par. Nat. Gr. 235 [xiv], $9\frac{3}{4} \times 6\frac{1}{2}$, ff. 362 (26–52), *chart.*, τίτλ., *lect.* Gospels with Theoph. (Greg. 741.)

763. Par. Nat. Suppl. Gr. 1076 [xi], small fol., ff. 465, *Carp.* Brought from Janina. (*See* Greg. 754.)

764. Par. Nat. Gr. 1775 [xv–xvi], $8\frac{1}{2} \times 6$, ff. 160, *chart.* St. John with Theoph. (Greg. 742.)

765. Par. Nat. Coislin. Gr. 128 [Mart. xi, xii, Greg. xiii], $12\frac{5}{8} \times 9\frac{5}{8}$, ff. 344 (40), *prol.*, κεφ. *t.*, τίτλ. Gospels with Theoph. (Greg. 1261.)

766. Par. Nat. Coisl. Gr. 129 [xiii, xiv], $12\frac{7}{8} \times 9\frac{1}{2}$, ff. 317 (43), 2 cols. Gospels with Theoph. (Greg. 1262.)

767. Par. Nat. Coisl. Gr. 198 [xiii, xiv], $9\frac{3}{4} \times 6\frac{1}{2}$, ff. 434 (26), *chart.*, κεφ. *t.*, τίτλ., *Am.*, *Eus.* Gospels with Theoph. (Greg. 1263.)

768. Par. Nat. Coisl. Gr. 203 [xii, xiii], $9\frac{3}{4} \times 7\frac{3}{4}$, ff. 435 (33), κεφ. *t.*, *pict.*, τίτλ. *Mut.* in places. Gospels with commentary. (Greg. 1265.)

769. Par. Nat. Coisl. Gr. 206 [x or xi], $11 \times 8\frac{1}{2}$, ff. 432 (25), *syn.*, κεφ. *t.*, κεφ., τίτλ., *lect.* (2 vols., Greg.). (Greg. 1266.)

770. (Paul. 478.) Par. Nat. Coisl. Gr. 207 [xiv], $10\frac{7}{8} \times 7\frac{7}{8}$, ff. 295 (36), *chart.* St. John and Rom., 2 Cor., Gal. i. 1—ii. 15 with Theoph. (Greg. 1267.)

771. Par. Nat. Suppl. Gr. 1080 [xiv], 4to, *chart.*, ff. 332. Brought from Janina. (*See* Greg. 755.)

772. Par. Nat. Suppl. Gr. 1083 [xi], 4to, ff. 179. *Mut.* at end. Written by Michaelis. (*See* Greg. 756.)

773. Par. Nat. Suppl. Gr. 904 [xii or xiii], $13 \times 9\frac{1}{2}$, ff. 199 (40), *prol.*, κεφ., τίτλ. Fragment of Gosp. with Theoph. (Greg. 749.)

774. Par. Nat. Suppl. Gr. 927 [xii or xiii], $6\frac{1}{2} \times 4\frac{1}{2}$, ff. 199 (26), (*syn.*, *men.*, *chart.*), κεφ., τίτλ., *Am.*, *pict.*, *lect.* (later). (Greg. 572.)

CHAPTER IX.

CURSIVE MANUSCRIPTS OF THE GOSPELS.

PART III.

WE have now come to Dr. Gregory's list, where Dr. Scrivener's and the Abbé Martin's have ceased, and shall follow it, except in the case of MSS. which have been already recorded, and which therefore must be replaced by other MSS. Whenever no independent information is at hand, the MS. will be simply noted, and the reader is referred to Dr. Gregory's 'Prolegomena' under the same number. Information from other sources than Dr. Gregory's book will in each case, where the Editor has discovered it, be duly given. Whenever no reference is made to Dr. Gregory's list, the numbers in both lists are the same.

The particulars added to MSS. at Athens are taken from the Catalogue by K. Alcibiades I. Sakkelion, obligingly lent me with others by Mr. J. Rendel Harris; but the press-marks of the MSS. have apparently been changed since Dr. Gregory examined them, and I have not succeeded in obtaining information upon this point. I have therefore identified the MSS. as best I could, and have inserted queries when there seemed to be doubt. The number in brackets is the present press-mark. The two measurements often differ; I have followed that of Sakkelion.

775. Athens, Nat. Sakkelion 3 (58) [xiii], $4\frac{3}{4} \times 4$, ff. 223. Belonged to John Cantacuzenus.

776. Ath. Nat. Sakkel. 5 (76) [xii], $8\frac{1}{4} \times 5\frac{5}{8}$, ff. 387, *pict.*, *prol.*

777. Ath. Nat. Sakkel. 6 (93) [xiv], $8\frac{5}{8} \times 5\frac{3}{4}$, ff. 185, *pict.*

778. Ath. Nat. Sakkel. 7 (80) [xiv], $9\frac{1}{2} \times 6\frac{3}{4}$, ff. 195, *pict.*

779. Ath. Nat. 1 (127) [xiv], $7\frac{7}{8} \times 5\frac{7}{8}$, ff. 171, *pict.*

780. Ath. Nat. 5 (121) [xi], $8\frac{1}{4} \times 6\frac{3}{8}$, ff. 241, scholia in red.

781. Ath. Nat. 14 (110 ?) [xv], $8\frac{3}{8} \times 5\frac{7}{8}$, ff. 197.

782. Ath. Nat. 16 (81 ?) [xiv], $9 \times 7\frac{1}{9}$, ff. 277.
783. Ath. Nat. 17 (71 ?) [xiv], $11\frac{3}{9} \times 8\frac{3}{8}$, ff. 211, *pict*.
784. Ath. Nat. 20 (87 ? ?) [xiv], $8\frac{5}{8} \times 5\frac{7}{8}$, ff. 161, *cotton, pict. Mut.* beg., κεφ.
785. Ath. Nat. 21 (118) [xi], $7\frac{1}{2} \times 5\frac{7}{8}$, ff. 230, *pict*.
786. Ath. Nat. 22 (125 ?) [xv], $7\frac{1}{5} \times 4\frac{3}{4}$, ff. 280.
787. Ath. Nat. 23 (108 ?) [xiv], ff. 305.
788. Ath. Nat. 26 (74 ?) [x], $8\frac{5}{8} \times 6\frac{3}{4}$, ff. 219, *pict*.
789. Ath. Nat. 27 (134 ?) [xii–xiv], $5\frac{1}{8} \times 4$, ff. 250 (1–23 and 245–50, *chart*.).
790. Ath. Nat. 39 (95 ? ?), $11 \times 7\frac{7}{9}$, ff. 163, *mut.* beg. (167 ff.) and end (many). SS. John and Luke, with commentary of Titus of Bostra.
791. Ath. Nat. 60 (77) [xiv], $8\frac{5}{8} \times 5\frac{7}{8}$, ff. 229, *pict*.
792. (Apoc. 111.) Ath. Nat. 67 M (107) [xv], $3\frac{1}{2} \times 2\frac{3}{4}$, ff. 145. Beautifully written in very small letters.
793. Ath. Nat. 71 (75) [xiv], $6\frac{3}{4} \times 5\frac{7}{8}$, ff. 255, *pict*.
794. (Act. 269, Paul. 401.) Ath. Nat. 118 (122), $8\frac{1}{4} \times 5\frac{7}{8}$, ff. 269.
795. Ath. Nat. 150 (109 ? ?) [xv], $5\frac{7}{8} \times 4$, ff. 324. (In Greg. '2' for '?': else how could *syn., men.,* &c., occur in two leaves?)
796. (Act. 321, Paul. 276.) Ath. Nat. 767 (160) [xi], $6\frac{3}{8} \times 4\frac{3}{8}$, ff. 323, *Eus. t., pict.*
797. Ath. Nat. (111 ?) [xv], $7\frac{1}{2} \times 5\frac{1}{2}$, ff. 223.
798. Ath. Nat. (137 ?) [xiv], $6\frac{3}{4} \times 4\frac{3}{4}$, ff. 113, *mut.* ff. 2 at beg., and from Mark viii. 3 to end of Gospels, *pict*.
799. Ath. Nat. 117 [xi], $7\frac{7}{8} \times 5\frac{1}{2}$, ff. 366.
800. Ath. Nat. 150 (65 ?) [xii], $10\frac{3}{4} \times 7\frac{1}{2}$.
801. (Act. 326, Paul. 313.) Ath. Nat. (130) [xv], $8\frac{1}{4} \times 5\frac{1}{2}$, ff. 324.
802. Ath. Nat. (99) [xiv], $9\frac{7}{8} \times 7\frac{1}{2}$, ff. 24. St. Luke i. 1—vi. 13.
803. Ath. Nat. (88) [xvi], $8\frac{5}{8} \times 5\frac{7}{8}$, ff. 176. Gospels except St. John.
804. Ath. τῆς Βουλῆς. 805. Ath. τῆς Βουλῆς.
806. Ath. τῆς Βουλῆς. 807. Ath. τῆς Βουλῆς.
808. (Act. 265, Paul. 403, Apoc. 150.) Ath. Dom. Mamoukac.
809. Ath. Dom. Mamoukac. 810. Ath. Dom. Οἰκονόμου 6.
811. Ath. Soc. Archaeolog. Christ. 812. Corcyra, Abp. Eustathius.
813. Corcyra, Abp. Eustathius. 814. Corcyra, Abp. Eustathius.
815. Corcyra, Comes de Gonemus. 816. Corcyra.
817. Basle, A. N. iii. 15. 818. Escurial Ψ. iii. 13.
819. Escurial Ψ. iii. 14. 820. Escurial Ω. i. 16.
821. Madrid, Reg. O. 10. 822. Madrid, Reg. O. 62.
823. (Act. 266, Paul. 404.) Berlin Reg. 8vo. 13.
824. Vienna, Imp. Gr. Theol. 19. (Greg. 719.)

825. Vienna, Imp. Gr. Theol. 79, 80. (Greg. 720.)
826. Vienna, Imp. Gr. Theol. 90. (Greg. 721.)
827. Vienna, Imp. Gr. Theol. 95. (Greg. 722.)
828. Vienna, Imp. Gr. Theol. 122. (Greg. 723.)
829. Vienna, Imp. Priv. Bibl. 7972. (Greg. 724.)
830. Milan, Ambr. A. 178 supr. (Greg. 589.)
831. Parma, Reg. 15. (Greg. 590.)
832. (Act. 143.) Florence, Laurentian Libr. vi. 5.
833. Florence, Laurent. vi. 26.   834. Flor. Laur. xi. 6.
835. Flor. Laur. xi. 8.   836. Flor. Laur. xi. 18.
837. Milan, Ambr. E. S. iv. 14. Ff. 34–66.
838. Formerly Milan, 'Hoeplii.'   839. Messina, Univ. 88.
840. Messina, Univ. 100.   841. Modena, iii. F. 13.
842. Modena, G. 9.   843. Naples, Nat. Libr. II. AA. 37.
844. Padua, Univ. 695.   845. Pistoia, Fabron. Libr. 307.

846. Athens, Nat. Theol. (150, 12) [xv], $11\frac{3}{4} \times 8\frac{1}{2}$ (Act. 209, Paul. 399, Apoc. 146), ff. 414, *syn.*, *men.*, κεφ., *prol.*, *pict.* (Greg. 757.)

847. Athens, Nat. Theol. (151, 13) [xiv], $5\frac{1}{2} \times 4$, ff. 301, κεφ. t., κεφ., τίτλ., *pict.*, &c. (Greg. 758.)

848. Ath. Nat. Theol. (152, 14) [xiii], $8\frac{5}{8} \times 5\frac{7}{8}$, ff. 295, *Carp.*, *Eus. t.*, *prol.*, κεφ. t., *prol. Theophyl.*, *pict.*, κεφ., τίτλ., &c., *vers.*, *syn.*, *men.*, ἀναγν. (Greg. 759.)

849. Ath. Nat. Theol. (153, 15) [xiv], $8\frac{1}{4} \times 6\frac{3}{8}$, ff. 283, *Eus. t.* (Greg. 760.)

850. Ath. Nat. Theol. (154, 16) [xiv], $8\frac{1}{4} \times 6$, ff. 281, *syn.*, *men.*, *Carp.*, *Eus. t.*, *prol.*, κεφ. t., κεφ. (Greg. 761.)

851. Rom. Propag. L. vi. 9.

852. Ath. Nat. Theol. (155, 17) [xiv], $9 \times 6\frac{3}{8}$, ff. 332, *syn.* (Greg. 762.)

853. Rom. Casanatensis G. ii. 9.

854. Ath. Nat. Theol. (156, 18) [xv], $9\frac{1}{2} \times 6\frac{3}{8}$, ff. 324 (4 *chart.*), *pict.* (Greg. 763.)

855. Ath. Nat. Theol. (157, 19) [xii], $11\frac{3}{8} \times 7\frac{1}{2}$, ff. 316, *mut.* at beg. and end. (Greg. 764.)

856. Ath. Nat. Theol. (158, 20) [xiv], $7\frac{1}{2} \times 5\frac{1}{2}$, ff. 229. (Greg. 765.)

857. Ath. Nat. Theol. (159, 21) [xiv], $7\frac{7}{8} \times 4\frac{3}{4}$, ff. 316 (12 *chart.*). (Greg. 766.)

858. (Act. 267, Paul. 400.) Ath. Nat. Theol. (160, 22) [xi], ff. 323, *Eus. t.*, *pict.* (Greg. 767.)

859. Ath. Nat. Theol. (161, 23) [xiv], $7\frac{1}{5} \times 5\frac{1}{2}$, ff. 222 (14 *chart.*). (Greg. 768.)

860. Rom. Vat. Gr. 774.

861. Ath. Nat. Theol. (162, 24) [xv], $9 \times 6\frac{3}{8}$, ff. 253. (Greg. 769.)

862. Ath. Nat. Theol. (203, 66) [xi], $10\frac{5}{8} \times 7\frac{7}{8}$, ff. 270, *mut.* beg. and end. (Greg. 770.)

863. Ath. Nat. Theol. (204, 67) [x], $12\frac{1}{2} \times 9$, ff. 153, *mut.* middle and end, *vers.* (Greg. 771.)

864. Rom. Vat. Gr. 1253.   865. Rom. Vat. Gr. 1472.

866. Rom. Vat. Gr. 1882, ff. 10–16 (Apoc. 115).

867. Ath. Nat. Theol. (489, 216) [xv], $10\frac{1}{4} \times 7\frac{1}{2}$, ff. 387 (21 *chart.*, comm. of Theophylact). (Greg. 772.)

868. Ath. Nat. Sakkelion 1 (56) [x], $13\frac{3}{8} \times 9\frac{7}{8}$, ff. 285, *pict.*, *mut.*, *Carp.*, *Eus. t.* (Greg. 773.)

869. Ath. Nat. Sakkel. 2 (57) [xi–xii], $10\frac{1}{4} \times 7\frac{7}{8}$, ff. (368 – 3 plain =) 365, *pict.*, *Carp.*, *Eus. t.*, *vers.* (Greg. 774.)

870. Rom. Vat. Gr. 2115, ff. 166–170.

871. Montpelier, Schol. Med. H. 446. (Greg. 577.)

872. Arras, 970. (Greg. 578.)   873. Rom. Vat. Gr. 2165.

874. Dessau. (Greg. 651.)

875. Munich, Reg. 594. (Greg. 652.)

876. Berlin, Reg. Gr. 4to, 12. (Greg. 657.)

877. Strasburg, Ed. Reuss. (Greg. 663.)

878. Petersburg, Imp. Muralt. 56 (vii). (Greg. 567.)

879. Petersburg, Imp. Muralt. 67. (Greg. 568.)

880. Petersburg, Imp. Muralt. 105. (Greg. 574.)

881. Brussels, Reg. 11,358. (Greg. 725.)

882. Brussels, Reg. 11,375. (Greg. 726.)

883. Rom. Corsin. 41 G. 16. (Greg. 591.)

884. London, Mr. White 2. (Greg. 702.)

885. Formerly London, Quaritch [1251]. (Greg. 703.)

886. Manchester, Rylands Library, formerly Quaritch [xiii], $4\frac{3}{4} \times 3\frac{1}{4}$, ff. 324 (18), 2 cols., with Latin version to St. Matthew. (Greg. 704.)

887. Hackney, Lord Amherst, formerly Quaritch [xiii], $9\frac{1}{2} \times 6\frac{3}{4}$, ff. 253 (18), κεφ. *t.*, *pict.* (Greg. 705.)

888. Venice, St. Mark 26.   889. Venice, St. Mark 30.

890. Venice, St. Mark 31.   891. Venice, St. Mark 32. (Paul. 325.)

892. Lond. Brit. Mus. Add. 33,277 [x], $6 \times 4\frac{1}{2}$, ff. 353 (20), *chart.* at end and later, *syn.*, *men.*, κεφ. *t.*, κεφ., *lect.*, *Am.*, *Eus.*, *vers.*, *subscr.* Beautifully written in minute characters, but damaged and faded. Bought from H. L. Dupuis in 1887. (Collated by J. R. Harris, Journal of Biblical Literature, ix. 1890.)

893. Venice, St. Mark i. 61.   894. Venice, St. Mark ii. 144.

895. Cheltenham, 6899. (Greg. 665.)

896. Edinburgh, Mackellar.

897. Edinburgh, Univ. David Laing 6.
898. Edinburgh, Univ. Laing, 667.
899. Massachusetts, Harvard. (Greg. 666.)
900. New Caesarea (U.S.A.), Madison, Drew 3. (Greg. 667.)
901. Tennessee (U.S.A.), Sewance, Benton 2. (Greg. 670.)
902. Tennessee, Sewance, Benton 3. (Greg. 669.)
903. Cairo, Patriarch. Alex. 421. 904. Cairo, Patriarch. Alex. 952.
905. Athos, St. Andrew A'. 906. Athos, St. Andrew E'.
907. Athos, St. Andrew H'. 908. Athos, St. Andrew Θ'.
909. Athos, Vatopedi 206. 910. Athos, Vatopedi 207.
911. Athos, Vatopedi 211. 912. Athos, Vatopedi 212.
913. Athos, Vatopedi 213. 914. Athos, Vatopedi 214.
915. Athos, Vatopedi 215. 916. Athos, Vatopedi 216.
917. Athos, Vatopedi 217. 918. Athos, Vatopedi 218.
919. Athos, Vatopedi 219 [June, 1112, Greg. 1116], 16mo. Written by one Constantine. (Greg. Constantius.)
920. Athos, Vatopedi 220. 921. Athos, Vatopedi 414.
922. Athos, Gregory 3. (Act. 270, Paul. 407, Apoc. 151.)
923. Athos, Gregory τοῦ ἡγουμένου. 924. Athos, Dionysius 4.
925. Athos, Dionysius 5. 926. Athos, Dionysius 7.
927. Athos, Dionysius 8. 928. Athos, Dionysius 9.
929. Athos, Dionysius 12. 930. Athos, Dionysius 22.
931. Athos, Dionysius 23. 932. Athos, Dionysius 24.
933. Athos, Dionysius 25. 934. Athos, Dionysius 26.
935. Athos, Dionysius 27. 936. Athos, Dionysius 28.
937. Athos, Dionysius 29. 938. Athos, Dionysius 30.
939. Athos, Dionysius 31. 940. Athos, Dionysius 32.
941. Athos, Dionysius 33. 942. Athos, Dionysius 34.
943. Athos, Dionysius 35. 944. Athos, Dionysius 36.
945. Athos, Dionysius 37. 946. Athos, Dionysius 38.
947. Athos, Dionysius 39. 948. Athos, Dionysius 40.
949. Athos, Dionysius 64. 950. Athos, Dionysius 67.
951. Athos, Dionysius 80. 952. Athos, Dionysius 310.
953. Athos, Dionysius 311. 954. Athos, Dionysius 312.
955. Athos, Dionysius 313. 956. Athos, Dionysius 314.
957. Athos, Dionysius 315. 958. Athos, Dionysius 316.
959. Athos, Dionysius 317. 960. Athos, Dionysius 318.
961. Athos, Dionysius 319. 962. Athos, Dionysius 320.
963. Athos, Dionysius 321. 964. Athos, Docheiariou 7.

965. Athos, Docheiariou 21.
966. Athos, Docheiariou 22.
967. Athos, Docheiariou 30.
968. Athos, Docheiariou 35.
969. Athos, Docheiariou 39.
970. Athos, Docheiariou 42.
971. Athos, Docheiariou 46.
972. Athos, Docheiariou 49.
973. Athos, Docheiariou 51.
974. Athos, Docheiariou 52.
975. Athos, Docheiariou 55.
976. Athos, Docheiariou 56.
977. Athos, Docheiariou 59.
978. Athos, Docheiariou 76.
979. Athos, Docheiariou 142.
980. Athos, Esphigmenou 25.
981. Athos, Esphigmenou 26.
982. Athos, Esphigmenou 27.
983. Athos, Esphigmenou 29.
984. Athos, Esphigmenou 30.
985. Athos, Esphigmenou 31.
986. Athos, Esphigmenou 186.

987. Athos, Zographou 4 [xii], 8vo, ff. 176. Repaired with paper leaves at beginning and end.

988. Athos, Zographou 14 [1674], 8vo. Written by one Theocletus.

989. Athos, Iveron 2.
990. Athos, Iveron 5.
991. Athos, Iveron 7.
992. Athos, Iveron 9.
993. Athos, Iveron 18.
994. Athos, Iveron 19.
995. Athos, Iveron 21.
996. Athos, Iveron 28. (Act. 278, Paul. 431.)
997. Athos, Iveron 29. (Act. 279, Paul. 432.)
998. Athos, Iveron 30.
999. Athos, Iveron 31. (Act. 280, Paul. 433.)
1000. Athos, Iveron 32.
1001. Athos, Iveron 33.
1002. Athos, Iveron 51.
1003. Athos, Iveron 52.
1004. Athos, Iveron 53.
1005. Athos, Iveron 55.
1006. Athos, Iveron 56.
1007. Athos, Iveron 59.
1008. Athos, Iveron 61.
1009. Athos, Iveron 63.
1010. Athos, Iveron 66.
1011. Athos, Iveron 67.
1012. Athos, Iveron 68.
1013. Athos, Iveron 69.
1014. Athos, Iveron 72.
1015. Athos, Iveron 75.
1016. Athos, Iveron 371.
1017. Athos, Iveron 548.
1018. Athos, Iveron 549.
1019. Athos, Iveron 550.
1020. Athos, Iveron 562.
1021. Athos, Iveron 599.
1022. Athos, Iveron 607.
1023. Athos, Iveron 608.
1024. Athos, Iveron 610.
1025. Athos, Iveron 636.
1026. Athos, Iveron 641.
1027. Athos, Iveron 647.
1028. Athos, Iveron 665.
1029. Athos, Iveron 671.
1030. Athos, Iveron 809.
1031. Athos, Iveron 871.
1032. Athos, Caracalla 19.
1033. Athos, Caracalla 20.

1034. Athos, Caracalla 31.
1035. Athos, Caracalla 34.
1036. Athos, Caracalla 35.
1037. Athos, Caracalla 36.
1038. Athos, Caracalla 37.
1039. Athos, Caracalla 111.
1040. Athos, Caracalla 121.
1041. Athos, Caracalla 128.
1042. Athos, Caracalla 198.
1043. Athos, Constamonitou 1. Theophylact on SS. Matt. and John?
1044. Athos, Constamonitou 61 [xvi], 8vo, *chart.*, *mut.*
1045. Athos, Constamonitou 106 [xiii], 16mo. Begins with St. Luke.
1046. Athos, Coutloumoussi 67.
1047. Athos, Coutloumoussi 68.
1048. Athos, Coutloumoussi 69.
1049. Athos, Coutloumoussi 70.
1050. Athos, Coutloumoussi 71.
1051. Athos, Coutloumoussi 72.
1052. Athos, Coutloumoussi 73.
1053. Athos, Coutloumoussi 74.
1054. Athos, Coutloumoussi 75.
1055. Athos, Coutloumoussi 76.
1056. Athos, Coutloumoussi 77.
1057. Athos, Coutloumoussi 78.
1058. Athos, Coutloumoussi 90ª. (Act. 283, Paul. 472.)
1059. Athos, Coutloumoussi 278.
1060. Athos, Coutloumoussi 281.
1061. Athos, Coutloumoussi 283.
1062. Athos, Coutloumoussi 284.
1063. Athos, Coutloumoussi 285.
1064. Athos, Coutloumoussi 286.
1065. Athos, Coutloumoussi 287.
1066. Athos, Coutloumoussi 288.
1067. Athos, Coutloumoussi 289.
1068. Athos, Coutloumoussi 290.
1069. Athos, Coutloumoussi 291.
1070. Athos, Coutloumoussi 293.
1071. Athos, Laura *.
1072. (Act. 284, Paul. 476, Apoc. 160.) Athos, Laura *.
1073. (Act. 285.) Athos, Laura *.
1074. Athos, Laura *.
1075. (Act. 286, Paul. 478, Apoc. 161.) Athos, Laura *.
1076. Athos, Laura *.
1077. Athos, Laura *.
1078. Athos, Laura *.
1079. Athos, Laura *.
1080. Athos, Laura *.

* Dr. Gregory has seen these ten MSS., but gives no press-mark.

1081. Athos, Xeropotamou 103.
1082. Athos, Xeropotamou 105.
1083. Athos, Xeropotamou 107.
1084. Athos, Xeropotamou 108.
1085. Athos, Xeropotamou 115.
1086. Athos, Xeropotamou 123.
1087. Athos, Xeropotamou 200.
1088. Athos, Xeropotamou 205.
1089. Athos, Xeropotamou 221.
1090. Athos, in Ecclesia.
1091. Athos, Panteleemon xxv.
1092. Athos, Panteleemon xxvi.
1093. Athos, Panteleemon xxviii.
1094. (Act. 287, Paul. 480, Apoc. 182.) Athos, Panteleemon xxix.
1095. Athos, Paul 4 [xiv], 8vo, *pict.*, τίτλ., *syn.*, *men.*

EVANN. 1034-1148. 279

1096. Athos, Paul 5 [xiii], 8vo. A leaf, 2 cols., of St. Matt. added at the end.

1097. Athos, Protaton 41 [x], 8vo. With histories of the Evangelists.

1098. Athos, Simopetra 25. 1099. Athos, Simopetra 26.
1100. Athos, Simopetra 29. 1101. Athos, Simopetra (34 ?).
1102. Athos, Simopetra 38. 1103. Athos, Simopetra 39.
1104. Athos, Simopetra 40. 1105. Athos, Simopetra 41.
1106. Athos, Simopetra 63. 1107. Athos, Simopetra 145.
1108. Athos, Simopetra 146. 1109. Athos, Simopetra 147.
1110. Athos, Stauroniketa 43. 1111. Athos, Stauroniketa 53.
1112. Athos, Stauroniketa 54. 1113. Athos, Stauroniketa 56.
1114. Athos, Stauroniketa 70. 1115. Athos, Stauroniketa 97.
1116. Athos, Stauroniketa 127. 1117. Athos, Philotheou 5.
1118. Athos, Philotheou 21. 1119. Athos, Philotheou 22.
1120. Athos, Philotheou 33. 1121. Athos, Philotheou 39.
1122. Athos, Philotheou 41. 1123. Athos, Philotheou 44.
1124. Athos, Philotheou 45. 1125. Athos, Philotheou 46.
1126. Athos, Philotheou 47. 1127. Athos, Philotheou 48.
1128. Athos, Philotheou 51. 1129. Athos, Philotheou 53.
1130. Athos, Philotheou 68. 1131. Athos, Philotheou 71.
1132. Athos, Philotheou 72. 1133. Athos, Philotheou 74.
1134. Athos, Philotheou 77. 1135. Athos, Philotheou 78.
1136. Athos, Philotheou 80. 1137. Athos, Philotheou 86.

1138. Athos, Chiliandari 5 [xii], 8vo, *orn.*

1139. Athos, Chiliandari 19 [xviii], 8vo, *chart.*

1140. Athos, Chiliandari 105 [xiv], 4to. Golden letters, very handsome, 11 lines, 2 cols.

1141. Berat, Archbp. 1142. Berat, Mangalemine Church.

1143. Berat, Church τοῦ εὐαγγελισμοῦ.

1144. New York, Syracuse. (Greg. 668.)

1145. Athens, Nat. Libr. 13 [xv], $5\frac{1}{8} \times 4$, ff. 299.

1146. Ath. Nat. Libr. 139 [xv], $6\frac{3}{8} \times 4\frac{3}{8}$, ff. 444. *Mut.* at beg. and end. With commentary. Two palimpsest leaves [viii].

1147. Ath. Nat. Libr. 347 [ix-x], $7\frac{7}{8} \times 5\frac{1}{8}$, ff. 131. Palimpsest. Other writing. Hymns and Prayers [A. D. 1406].

1148. Jerusalem, Patriarchal Library 25 [xi], $11\frac{3}{8} \times 9\frac{1}{2}$, ff. 273 (17), *syn.*, κεφ. t., *proll.*, στίχ., *scholia*. *Mut.* from fire and damp, Luke i. 1–25; John xxi. 17–end; ff. 127, 128 partially mutilated[1].

[1] For all these MSS. (Evann. 1148, 1149, 1261, 1262, 1263, 1265–1268, 1274–1279), see Ἱεροσολομιτικὴ Βιβλιοθήκη, κ.τ.λ., ὑπὸ Α. Παπαδοπούλου Π. Κεραμέως. Τόμος Πρῶτος. Ἐν Πετρουπόλει, 1891.

1149. (Paul. 53.) Jerus. Patr. Libr. 28 [xi], 11 × 9¼, ff. 212 (21), κεφ. t., στίχ., scholia. Brought in 1562 by Peter τοῦ Καραμανίτου.

1150. Constantinople, St. Sepulchre 227.

1151. Constantinople, St. Sepulch. 417.

1152. Constantinople, St. Sepulch. 419.

1153. Constantinople, St. Sepulch. 435.

1154. Constantinople, St. Sepulch. 439.

1155. Constantinople, St. Sepulch. 441.

1156. Lesbos, Mon. τοῦ Λείμωνος 356. Commentary of St. Chrysostom on St. John, and commentary of Theophylact on St. Matt., perhaps with St. Matt. [xiv], 12¾ × 10¼, by the hand of Michael the monk, partly on vellum (ff. 1-4, and 121-125, 2 cols.), chiefly on cotton (ff. 116, 1 col.). (Papadop. Kar. Παράρτημα τοῦ ΙΕ´ τόμου. Constantinople, 1885.)

1157. Lesb. Mon. τοῦ Λείμων. 67 [xi], 9¼ × 7⅛, ff. 395, κεφ., subscr. Latin between the lines of John i. 1-12.

1158. Lesb. Mon. τοῦ Λείμων. 97 chart. [xv], 7⅞ × 5¾, with two vellum leaves [xi].

1159. Lesb. Mon. τοῦ Λείμων. 99 [xiv, end], 9½ × 6⅜, ?, κεφ. t., pict., Luke mut., John wanting.

1160. Patmos 58.	1161. Patmos 59 [x], 4to. Seen by Coxe.	
1162. Patmos 60.	1163. Patmos 76.	1164. Patmos 80.
1165. Patmos 81.	1166. Patmos 82.	1167. Patmos 83.
1168. Patmos 84.	1169. Patmos 90.	1170. Patmos 92.
1171. Patmos 94.	1172. Patmos 95.	1173. Patmos 96.
1174. Patmos 97.	1175. Patmos 98.	1176. Patmos 100.
1177. Patmos 117.	1178. Patmos 203.	1179. Patmos 275.
1180. Patmos 333.	1181. Patmos 335.	

1182. Thessalonica, ἑλληνικοῦ γυμνασίου 6.

1183. Thess. ἑλλην. γυμνασ. 11.

1184. Thess., at the house of Κυ. Σπυρίου.

1185. Sinai, Mt. Catherine 148.	1186. Sinai, Mt. Catherine 149.
1187. Sinai, Mt. Cath. 150.	1188. Sinai, Mt. Cath. 151.
1189. Sinai, Mt. Cath. 152.	1190. Sinai, Mt. Cath. 153.
1191. Sinai, Mt. Cath. 154.	1192. Sinai, Mt. Cath. 155.
1193. Sinai, Mt. Cath. 156.	1194. Sinai, Mt. Cath. 157.
1195. Sinai, Mt. Cath. 158.	1196. Sinai, Mt. Cath. 159.
1197. Sinai, Mt. Cath. 160.	1198. Sinai, Mt. Cath. 161.
1199. Sinai, Mt. Cath. 162.	1200. Sinai, Mt. Cath. 163.
1201. Sinai, Mt. Cath. 164.	

1202. (Act. 417.)   Sinai, Mt. Cath. 165.

1203. Sinai, Mt. Cath. 166.   1204. Sinai, Mt. Cath. 167.

1205. Sinai, Mt. Cath. 168.   1206. Sinai, Mt. Cath. 169.
1207. Sinai, Mt. Cath. 170.   1208. Sinai, Mt. Cath. 171.
1209. Sinai, Mt. Cath. 172.   1210. Sinai, Mt. Cath. 173.
1211. Sinai, Mt. Cath. 174.   1212. Sinai, Mt. Cath. 175.
1213. Sinai, Mt. Cath. 176.   1214. Sinai, Mt. Cath. 177.
1215. Sinai, Mt. Cath. 178.   1216. Sinai, Mt. Cath. 179.
1217. Sinai, Mt. Cath. 180.   1218. Sinai, Mt. Cath. 181.
1219. Sinai, Mt. Cath. 182.   1220. Sinai, Mt. Cath. 183.
1221. Sinai, Mt. Cath. 184.   1222. Sinai, Mt. Cath. 185.
1223. Sinai, Mt. Cath. 186.   1224. Sinai, Mt. Cath. 187.
1225. Sinai, Mt. Cath. 188.   1226. Sinai, Mt. Cath. 189.
1227. Sinai, Mt. Cath. 190.   1228. Sinai, Mt. Cath. 191.
1229. Sinai, Mt. Cath. 192.   1230. Sinai, Mt. Cath. 193.
1231. Sinai, Mt. Cath. 194.   1232. Sinai, Mt. Cath. 195.
1233. Sinai, Mt. Cath. 196.   1234. Sinai, Mt. Cath. 197.
1235. Sinai, Mt. Cath. 198.   1236. Sinai, Mt. Cath. 199.
1237. Sinai, Mt. Cath. 200.   1238. Sinai, Mt. Cath. 201.
1239. Sinai, Mt. Cath. 203.   1240. Sinai, Mt. Cath. 259.
1241. Sinai, Mt. Cath. 260.   1242. Sinai, Mt. Cath. 261.
1243. Sinai, Mt. Cath. 262.   1244. Sinai, Mt. Cath. 263.
1245. Sinai, Mt. Cath. 264.   1246. Sinai, Mt. Cath. 265.
1247. Sinai, Mt. Cath. 266.   1248. Sinai, Mt. Cath. 267.
1249. Sinai, Mt. Cath. 268.   1250. Sinai, Mt. Cath. 269.
1251. Sinai, Mt. Cath. 270.   1252. Sinai, Mt. Cath. 302.
1253. Sinai, Mt. Cath. 303.   1254. Sinai, Mt. Cath. 304.
1255. Sinai, Mt. Cath. 305.   1256. Sinai, Mt. Cath. 306.
1257. Smyrna, Schol. Evan. Γ´. 1.   1258. Smyrn. Schol. Evan. Γ´. 2.
1259. Smyrn. Schol. Evan. Γ´. 5.
1260. Cortona, Bibl. Commun. 201.

1261. Jerusalem, Patriarch. Libr. 31 [xi], $10\frac{1}{2} \times 8$, ff. 295 (20), *Eus. t.*, *prol.*, *pict.*, κεφ. *t.* Brought from Tauronesus to Constantinople before 1683.

1262. (Act. 417, Paul. 57, Apoc. 153.) Jerus. Patr. Libr. 37 [xi], $9\frac{3}{5} \times 7$, ff. 355 (31), κεφ. *t.*, *proll.*, *pict.*, *carp.*, *glossary*, κεφ. *Mut.* end of 1 Pet., Heb.–end. Has signature of Patriarch Sophronius, A.D. 1604–5. According to another note Thomas and Georgilas and their relatives offered it in 1589.

1263. Jerus. Patr. Libr. 41 [xi], $9\frac{1}{4} \times 6\frac{1}{2}$, ff. 298 (21), of which three are plain, τίτλ., κεφ., *pict.* Fine letters.

1264. Paris, Nat. Coislin. Gr. 201.

1265. Jerus. Patr. Libr. 42 [xi], $9 \times 7\frac{1}{2}$, 248 (19), τίτλ., κεφ. (gold). *Mut.* at beginning of each Evangelist, and several leaves cut off at the end.

1266. Jerus. Patr. Libr. 46 [xii], $8\frac{1}{2} \times 6\frac{3}{8}$, ff. 278 (25), one leaf cut out after f. 80, and ff. 15 and 16 palimpsest.

1267. (Act. 329, Paul. 380.) Jerus. Patr. Libr. 47 [xi], $8\frac{5}{8} \times 6\frac{1}{4}$, ff. 216 (40), 130–137 being cotton [xiii], *vers., pict., syn.* Very beautiful. Brought from Cyprus.

1268. Jerus. Patr. Libr. 48 [xi], $8 \times 6\frac{3}{8}$, ff. 258 (7 being plain), κεφ. *t., Carp., Eus. t., orn.*

1269. Rom. Vat. Urb. 4.   1270. Cairo, Patriarch. Alex. 82.

1271. Cairo, Patriarch. Alex. 87.   1272. Athens, Nat. 111.

1273. Auckland (New Zealand), City Library.

1274. Jerus. Patr. Libr. 49 [xi, 1st quarter], $8\frac{1}{4} \times 6\frac{5}{8}$, ff. 306 (18), 8 being blank, κεφ. *t.* (gold), *Carp., Eus. t., pict., syn., men.*

1275. Jerus. Patr. Libr. 56 [xi], $7\frac{1}{4} \times 5\frac{3}{4}$, ff. 218 (23), *Eus. t.* (κανόνιον ?), κεφ. *t., pict., syn.* Came from St. Saba.

1276. Jerus. Patr. Libr. 59 [xi], $5\frac{1}{2} \times 4\frac{1}{4}$, ff. 299 (23), 12 blank, *Carp.,* κεφ. *t., pict., lect.* First page in vermilion, rest in gold. Written in Palestine.

1277. Jerus. Patr. Libr. 60 [xi], $5\frac{1}{2} \times 4\frac{3}{4}$, ff. 299 (23), 12 blank, κεφ. *t., Carp., Eus. t.* (κανόνιον), *pict.* First page in vermilion, rest in gold on purple.

1278. Jerus. Patr. Libr. 62 [May 1, 1721], ?, ff. 385, 2 cols., *chart.* In Greek and Turkish (written in Greek letters). *Prol., pict.*

1279. Jerus. Patr. Libr. 139 [xiv], $11\frac{3}{8} \times 8\frac{1}{4}$, ff. 124 (34), *chart.*

1280. Lesbos, τ. Λείμωνος μονῆς 141 [xv], $8\frac{5}{8} \times 5\frac{7}{8}$, ff. ?, *chart. Mut.* beginning and end, and in other places.

1281. Lesbos, τ. Λείμωνος μονῆς 145 [xv], $8\frac{1}{2} \times 5\frac{3}{4}$. *Chart.*

1282. Lesbos, τ. Λείμωνος μονῆς 227 [xii], $6\frac{1}{2} \times 5\frac{1}{8}$, ff. 136. *Mut.* Matt. i. 1—vii. 5; Mark i. 1–15; Luke xix. 32—John xxi. 25.

1283. Lesbos, Μανταμάδου, Ταξίαρχοι ΚΑ [xiii], $8\frac{5}{8} \times 6\frac{1}{2}$, ff. 288. Written by one Macarius.

1284. Mitylene, Libr. of Gymnasion 9 [xii–xiii], $10\frac{1}{4} \times 7\frac{1}{2}$, ff. 292 + 8 *chart.*, 2 cols., *pict.*

1285. Mityl. Libr. Gym. 41 [x], $7\frac{1}{2} \times 5\frac{3}{8}$, ff. 258. *Mut.* at beginning, &c. ff. 3 [xiii].

1286. Andros, Μονὴ ἁγία 1 [1156], size not given, ff. 342 (20), κεφ.*t., pict.*

1287. Andros, M. ἁγ. 33 [xii–xiii]. One leaf *mut.*

1288. Andros, M. ἁγ. 34 [1523], 6 ff. at end *chart.* Well written.

1289. Andros, M. ἁγ. 35. Like the last, several perished folios have been replaced by paper ones.

1290. Andros, M. ἁγ. 37 [xii]. Sumptuous binding with precious stones and silver tablets.

1291. Andros, M. ἁγ. 38. *Chart., vers.*

1292. Andros, M. ἁγ. 48 [1709]. Beautiful and perfect. Κεφ. *t., pict.*

1293. Andros, M. ἀγ. 49 [1234]. Κεφ. and other ornaments cut out. Like 34.

1294. Andros, M. ἀγ. 50 [xii–xiii]. *Mut.* at beginning and end, &c.

1295. Kosinitsa, Mon. Libr. 219 [1285].

1296. Kosinitsa, Mon. Libr. 58 [ix–x], 12 × 8, ff. 288. *Pict.*, κεφ. t., *proll.* (various), *scholia.* Written in early minuscules.

1297. (Act. 416, Paul. 377.) Kosinitsa, Mon. Libr. 216 [?], $7\frac{3}{4} \times 5\frac{3}{4}$, *pict.*

1298. Kosinitsa, Mon. Libr. 217, *Carp., Eus. t., pict.*

1299. Kosinitsa, Mon. Libr. 218, *pict.*

1300. Kosinitsa, Mon. Libr. 219.   1301. Kosinitsa, Mon. Libr. 220.

1302. Kosinitsa, Mon. Libr. 222.

1303. Kosinitsa, Mon. Libr. 223 [1471], ?, ff. 201.

1304. Kosinitsa, Mon. Libr. 198.

1305. Athos, Protaton 15 [xi], 2 cols.

1306. Athos, Prot. 44 [xiv], 2 cols., *chart.*

1307. Athos, Paul. 1 [xiv], 4to, ff. 50. Written by one Matthew. *Mut.*

1308. Athos, Chiliandari 6 [xiii], 8vo. *Mut.* at beginning and elsewhere.

1309. Athos, Constamonitou 99 [xiv]. Palimpsest over Latin Lives and Martyrdom of Saints [xii].

1310. Athos, Xenophon 1 [1181], 4to, 2 cols. Written by John, a reader from Buthrotus.

1311. Athos, Xenophon 3 [xiii], 8vo, 2 cols. *Mut.*

1312. Athos, Xenophon 58 [xvi], 8vo, *chart.*

1313. Athens, Nat. Libr. 72 [A.D. 1181], $10\frac{3}{8} \times 7\frac{7}{8}$, ff. 191.

1314. Ath. Nat. Libr. 92 [xiv], $5\frac{1}{2} \times 4$, ff. 277, *Carp., Eus. t.,* κεφ. t., with a peculiar description of the Eusebian Canons.

1315. Ath. Nat. Libr. 113 [xi], $7\frac{1}{2} \times 5\frac{1}{2}$, ff. 232.

1316. Ath. Nat. Libr. 123 [A.D. 1145], $8\frac{1}{4} \times 5\frac{7}{8}$, ff. 189, *pict.*

1317. Ath. Nat. Libr. 128 [xii], $6\frac{3}{4} \times 5\frac{7}{8}$, ff. 181.

1318. Ath. Nat. Libr. 132 [x], $6\frac{3}{8} \times 4\frac{3}{4}$, ff. 210.

1319. Ath. Nat. Libr. 135 [xv], $9 \times 7\frac{1}{2}$, ff. 150.

1320. Earl of Crawford 1 [xi], $8\frac{1}{2} \times 6\frac{1}{2}$, ff. 239 (25), *Carp., Eus. t.* (*prol.*, κεφ., τίτλ. in blue by another hand), *lect.* with ἀρχ. and τέλ. later), *Am., Eus., subscr.,* κεφ. t. Exquisitely written and ornamented. Perfect, except that κεφ. t. in Matt. is torn out. Memorandum on last leaf of the birth of Theodora [Oct. 2, 1320].

1321. Earl of Crawford 2 [xi–xii], $5\frac{1}{2} \times 4$, ff. 240 (21, 20), κεφ. t., *pict.,* κεφ., τίτλ., *Am., subscr., vers.* (Luke), *syn., men.* Beautifully written, though not equal to the last. Has suffered from age. Written by Paul a monk. The third leaf in St. Luke lost: otherwise perfect.

CHAPTER X.

CURSIVE MANUSCRIPTS OF THE ACTS AND CATHOLIC EPISTLES.

*1. (Evan. 1.)

2. (Paul. 2.) Basil. Univ. A. N. iv. 4 (formerly B. ix. 38) [xiii or xiv Burgon], 5⅞ × 3⅝, ff. 216 (27), with short Introductions to the books, once belonged to the Preaching Friars, then to Amerbach, a printer of Basle. Erasmus grounded on this copy, in some passages with some alterations of the MS., the text of his first edition (1516), and he calls it 'exemplar mirè castigatum.' His binder cut off a considerable part of the margin (Hoskier). It is Mill's B. 2 (Battier, Wetstein).

3. (Evan. 3.)

4. (Paul. 4.) Basil. A. N. iv. 5 (formerly B. x. 20) [xv], 6¼ × 4¾, ff. 287 (18), Mill's B. 3, badly written by several hands, and full of contractions: the Pauline Epistles preceding the Catholic. Erasmus made some use of this copy and of its marginal readings (e. g. Acts viii. 37; xv. 34; xxiv. 6-8) for forming his text (Battier, Wetstein).

5. (Evan. 5.)   6. (Evan. 6.)

7. (Paul. 9.) Paris, Nat. Gr. 102 [x, Greg. xi, Omont xii], 7¼ × 5⅞, ff. 390 (20), *prol.*, κεφ. τ., τίτλ., *pict.*, seems to be Stephen's ι', although ι' is cited in error Luke v. 19; John ii. 17: it nearly resembles Cod. 5 and the Latin version. In this copy, and in Paul. H, 12, 17, 20, 137, Mr. Vansittart re-collated the beginning of the Epistle to the Hebrews.

8. (Paul. 10.) Stephen's ια', now missing, cited about 400 times by that editor, in 276 of which it supports the Latin versions (Mill, N. T., Proleg. § 1171). Stephen cites ια' (apparently in error) four times in the Gospels, once in the Apocalypse (Matt. x. 8; 10; xii. 32; John ii. 17; Apoc. xiii. 4).

9. (Paul. 11.) Cambridge, Univ. Libr. Kk. 6. 4 [xi], 6¾ × 4¾, ff. 247 (22), *lect. Mut.* Acts iii. 6-17; 1 Tim. iv. 12—2 Tim. iv. 3; Heb. vii. 20—xi. 10; xi. 23-end. Bp. Marsh has fully proved that this copy, which once belonged to Stephen's friend Vatablus, Professor of Hebrew at Paris, is his ιγ'. This copy also is twice quoted by Stephen in the Gospels (Matt. xxvii. 64; John ii. 17), through mere oversight. Dr. Hort states that it is rich in detached readings in Cath. Epp., not in Acts or Paul.

10. (Paul. 12, Apoc. 2.) Par. Nat. Gr. 237, Stephen's ιε' [x], 8½ × 6¾, ff. 246 (28), *prol.*, κεφ. τ., τίτλ., κεφ., *subscr.*, στίχ., neatly written, with scholia and other matter. Le Long identified this, and about five other

of Stephen's manuscripts: its value in the Apocalypse is considerable (Wetstein, Scholz).

11. (Paul. 140.) Par. Nat. Gr. 103 [x, Greg. xi], $8\frac{1}{2} \times 6\frac{3}{4}$, ff. 333 (18), *prol.*, with scholia. *Mut.* Acts ii. 20–31.

12. (Paul. 16, Apoc. 4.) Par. Nat. Gr. 219 [xi], $12\frac{3}{8} \times 9\frac{1}{3}$, ff. 313 (40), *prol.*, κεφ. t., κεφ., τίτλ., *syn.*, *men.*, neat, with Arethas' commentary on the Apocalypse, and Œcumenius' on the other books. Like Evann. 16, 19, 317, it once belonged to the Medici: in 1518 it was given by the Greek Janus Lascar to 'Petro Masieli' of Constance, and was used by Donatus of Verona for an edition of Œcumenius (Wetstein, Scholz).

*13. (Evan. 33.)   14. (Evan. 35.)

15. Par. Nat. Coislin. 25 [xi], $12\frac{3}{8} \times 9\frac{1}{4}$, ff. 254 (36), *prol.*, κεφ. t., κεφ., τίτλ., *subscr.*, στίχ., described by Montfaucon (as were also Act. 16–18), compared with Pamphilus' revision, *prol.*, and a commentary digested by Andreas, a priest (Wetstein).

16. (Paul. 19.) Par. Nat. Coisl. 26 [xi, Greg. x], $11\frac{5}{8} \times 9$, ff. 381 (40), *prol.*, with a commentary much like that of Œcumenius, and a catena of various Fathers: also a life of St. Longinus on two leaves [ix]. It once belonged to the monastery of St. Athanasius on Athos, βιβλίον τῆς τετάρτης θέσεως (Wetstein).

17. (Paul. 21, Apoc. 19.) Par. Nat. Coisl. 205 [written by Anthony, a monk, A.D. 1079, Indict. 2], $9\frac{7}{8} \times 7$, ff. 270 (27), *prol.*, κεφ. t., κεφ., τίτλ., *lect.*, *subscr.*, στίχ., *syn.* *Mut.* 1 Cor. xvi. 17—2 Cor. i. 7; Heb. xiii. 15-25; with Apoc. i. 1—ii. 5 in a recent hand (Wetstein).

18. (Paul. 22, Apoc. 18.) Par. Nat. Coisl. 202, 2, ff. 1-26 [xi] on vellum, the rest [xiii] on cotton paper, $9\frac{5}{8} \times 7\frac{1}{8}$, ff. 302 (22), with scholia to the Acts and Catholic Epistles, Andreas' commentary to the Apocalypse, *prol.* to St. Paul's Epistles (Wetstein).

19. (Evan. 38.)

20. (Paul. 25.) Brit. Mus. Royal MS. I. B. I, once Westminster 935 [xiv], $10 \times 7\frac{3}{4}$, ff. 144 (22), *chart.*, *Euthal.*, *prol.* in Cath. and Paul. *Mut.* and in bad condition, almost illegible in parts (Wetstein). The Pauline Epistles precede the Acts and Catholic Epistles. Casley notices one leaf lost in the Hebrews (after ὡς υἱοῖς ὑμῖν πρός ch. xii. 7).

21. (Paul. 26.) Cambridge, Univ. Libr. Dd. xi. 90 [xiii], $6\frac{1}{2} \times 5\frac{1}{4}$, ff. 159 (24), *prol.*, *lect.*, στίχ. *Mut.* Acts i—xii. 2; xiv. 22—xv. 10; Rom. xv. 14-16; 24-26; xvi. 4-20; 1 Cor. i. 15—iii. 12; 2 Tim. i. 1—ii. 4; Tit. i. 9—ii. 15; Philem. ii–end of Hebrews. *Prol.* to Pauline Epistles only, copy is Mill's *Lu.*, but he forgot to name it in his Prolegomena. It was re-discovered and collated by Wetstein, and is probably Bentley's Q (Ellis, Bentleii Critica Sacra, p. xxix). John Berriman, in the manuscript notes to his own copy of his 'Critical Dissertation on 1 Tim. iii. 16' (1741), which he presented to the British Museum in 1761, tells us that this codex [then Cant. 495] was identified 'by several collations of many texts by different hands (Professor Francklin and others), and by other circumstances' to have been Professor Luke's (MS. note on p. 104).

22. (Paul. 75 in the same hand.) Brit. Mus. Add. 5115 and 5116, once Dr. Mead's (Berriman), then Askew's [xii], 7⅝ × 5¾, ff. 127 + 174 (22), κεφ. τ., κεφ., prol., syn., lect. (later). *Mut.* Acts i. 1–11: (Acts i—xx collated by Paulus for Griesbach: Bloomfield): Scholz's date [ix] is an error.

23. (Paul. 28, Apoc. 6.) Oxf. Bodl. Barocc. 3 [xi], 5 × 4, ff. 297 (21), prol. (Euth.), κεφ. τ., a beautiful little book, written at Ephesus, beginning Acts xi. 13, ending Apoc. xx. 1: the opening chapters are supplied in a late hand. Tregelles calls this 'a very obscure manuscript.' With scholia on the Epistles, and a full and unique commentary on the Apocalypse, edited by J. A. Cramer, 1840 (Mill, Caspar Wetstein, Griesbach). This copy is Bentley's χ in Trin. Coll. B. xvii. 5 (*see* Evan. 51). *Mut.* Acts iii. 10—xi. 13; xiv. 6—xvii. 19; xx. 28—xxiv. 12; 1 Pet. ii. 2–16; iii. 7–21; 2 Cor. ix. 15—xi. 9; Gal. i. 1–18; Eph. vi. 1–19; Phil. iv. 18–23; Rev. i. 10–17; ix. 12–18; xvii. 10—xviii. 8, and in other places.

*24. (Paul. 29.) Camb. Christ's Coll. F. 1. 13 [xii], 8⅓ × 6, ff. 303 (22). *Mut.* Acts i. 1–11; xviii. 20—xx. 14; James v. 14—1 Pet. i. 4, and some leaves of this fine copy are torn or decayed: there are also many changes by a later hand (Mill's Cant. 2, Scrivener's 1): unpublished collations were made by Bentley (Trin. Coll. Camb. B. xvii. 10, 11), and by Jo. Wigley for Jackson (Jesus Coll. Camb. O. Θ. 1).

25. (Paul. 31, Apoc. 7.) Brit. Mus. Harl. 5537 [Pentecost, A. D. 1087, Indict. 10], 4½ × 3½, ff. 286 (23), (with a lexicon, *chart.*), *prol.*, κεφ. τ., κεφ., some *lect.*, *subscr.*, στίχ., an important copy, from the neighbourhood of the Aegean. *Mut.* 1 John v. 14—2 John 6 (Mill, Griesbach, Bloomfield, Scrivener's 1 in Apoc.)[1].

26. (Paul. 32.) Brit. Mus. Harl. 5557 [xii], 7 × 6, ff. 293 (22), *syn.*, *men.* (*prol.*, κεφ. τ. Paul.), *lect.*, some *subscr.* and στίχ. *Mut.* Acts i. 1–11; 1 Cor. xi. 7—xv. 56. This copy and the next bear Covell's emblem '*Luceo*,' and the date Constantinople, 1675, but he got Act. 27 from Adrianople. (Mill, Paulus in Acts i–iii Bloomfield.)

27. (Paul. 33.) Brit. Mus. Harl. 5620 [xv], 8¼ × 6, ff. 134 (22), *chart.*, is of some weight: there are no chapter-divisions *primâ manu*; the writing is small and abbreviated (Mill, Griesbach, Bloomfield).

28. (Paul. 34, Apoc. 8.) Brit. Mus. Harl. 5778, is Covell's 5 or Sinai manuscript [2] [xii], 8¾ × 6½, ff. 156 (30), κεφ., τίτλ., *lect.*, *subscr.*, στίχ., in wretched condition, and often illegible. *Mut.* Acts i. 1–20; Apoc. vi. 14 —viii. 1; xxii. 19–21, perhaps elsewhere (Mill, Bloomfield for Act., Paul., Scrivener's d for Apoc.).

29. (Paul. 35.) Geneva, Libr. 20 [xi or xii], 5¾ × 4, ff. 269 (18),

---

[1] Mr. Ellis (Bentleii Critica Sacra, pp. xxviii, xxix) represents, among facts which I am better able to verify, that Act. and Epp. 25, 26, and Epp. 15, were collated by Wetstein, and his labours preserved at Trin. Coll. Cambridge (B. xvii. 10, 11). The manuscripts he indicates so ambiguously must be Paul. 25, 26, and Act. 15, since Wetstein is not known to have worked at Act. 25, 26, or Paul. 15.

[2] Covell once marked this codex 5, but afterwards gave it the name of the Sinai MS. (little anticipating worthier claimants for that appellation), reserving 5 for Harl. 5777 or Evan. 446.

brought from Greece, beautifully but carelessly written, without subscriptions; in text much like Act. 27 (readings sent to Mill, Scholz).

30. (Paul. 36, Apoc. 9.) Oxf. Bodleian Misc. Gr. 74 [xi], $10\frac{3}{4} \times 7$, ff. 333 (24), *prol.*, κεφ. *t.*, some κεφ., *subscr.*, στίχ., brought from the East by Bp. Huntington, beginning Acts xv. 19, but 3 John, Jude, the Apocalypse, and St. Paul's Epistles (which stand last) are in a somewhat earlier hand than the rest. (Mill's Hunt. 1.)

*31. (Evan. 69.) 32. (Evan. 51.)

33. (Paul. 39.) Oxf. Lincoln Coll. Gr. 15 B. 82 [xii], $7\frac{5}{8} \times 6$, ff. 206 (27), *prol.*, *pict.*, *lect.*, some τίτλ., στίχ., *syn.*, *men.*, presented in 1483 by Robert Flemmyng, Dean of Lincoln, a beautiful and interesting codex, with *pict.*, *prol.*, *lect.*, *syn.*, *men.*, and the numbers of the στίχοι noted in the subscriptions. *Mut.* 2 Pet. i. 1–15; Rom. i. 1–20 (Walton's Polyglott, Mill, Dobbin ' Cod. Montfort.,' who regards it as the manuscript from which this portion of the latter was mainly copied). The Epistle of Jude stands between James and 1 Peter. Vansittart notes its affinity in text with Act. 13.

*34. (Evan. 61.) 35. (Evan. 57.)

36. Oxf. New College, 36 (58) [xii, end], $10 \times 7\frac{3}{4}$, ff. 245 (39), *prol.*, κεφ., τίτλ., valuable text, with a catena of Fathers, enumerated by Mill (N. T., Proleg. § 1390), and edited by Cramer, Oxford, 1838 (Walton's Polyglott, Mill).

37. (Paul. 43.) Oxf. New Coll. 37 (59) [xiii], $9\frac{1}{4} \times 6\frac{3}{4}$, ff. 298 (20), *prol.*, κεφ. *t.*, τίτλ., perhaps a little later than Cod. 36, erroneously described by Walton, and after him by Wetstein, as part of Evan. 58, a much later manuscript. Heb. xiii. 21–25 is supplied in a recent hand. It is a beautiful copy, with marginal glosses (Walton's Polyglott, Mill, Dobbin).

*38. (Paul. 44.) Lugduno-Batav. 77, Voss. Gr. Q. 2 [xiii], $7\frac{1}{4} \times 5\frac{1}{4}$, ff. 215 (22), *prol.*, *lect.*, ἀναγν., *subscr.*, στίχ., *syn.*, *men.*, once belonging to Petavius, a Councillor of Paris, given by Queen Christina to Is. Vossius (Mill, Wetstein, Dermout 1825).

39. (Paul. 45, Apoc. 11.) Petavii 2, age and present locality not stated. *Mut.* Acts i. 1—xviii. 22; James i. 1—v. 17; 3 John 9—Jude 25; 1 Cor. iii. 16—x. 13 (Extracts in Mill; J. Gachon).

40. (Paul. 46, Apoc. 12.) Vat. Reg. Gr. 179 [xi], $9\frac{7}{8} \times 7\frac{1}{2}$, ff. 169 (27), *prol.*, κεφ. *t.*, κεφ., τίτλ., *lect.*, *subscr.*, στίχ., *men.*, with a mixed text and the end of Titus (from ch. iii. 3), Philemon, and the Apocalypse in a later hand. This copy, given by Christina to Alexander VIII (1689–91), is of considerable importance, and, as containing all Euthalius' labours on the Acts and the Epistles, was largely used by Laur. Zacagni for his edition of the Prologues, &c., of Euthalius (Extracts in Mill, Zacagni, Birch; Griesbach adds, ' Gagnaeus eundem sub Dionysiani nomine laudasse creditur ').

41. (Evan. 175.)

*42. (Paul. 48, Apoc. 13, Evst. 287, Apost. 56.) Frankfort on the Oder Gymnasium, once Seidel's [xi], $8\frac{1}{8} \times 5\frac{7}{8}$, ff. 302 (23), κεφ. *t.*, κεφ., *lect.*, carelessly written, with some rare readings. *Mut.* Acts ii. 3–34 (xxvii. 19–34 is in a later hand); 2 Pet. i. 1, 2; 1 John v. 11–21; Apoc. xviii. 3–13 (N. Westermann, H. Middeldorpf). One leaf of a Lectionary is added, containing Matt. xvii. 16–23; 1 Cor. ix. 2—12. This copy often agrees closely with the Complutensian text and Laud. 81 (Evan. 51) jointly.

43. (Evan. 76.)

44. (Like Evan. 82, Paul. 51, Apoc. 5) certain manuscripts cited by Laurentius Valla. Dr. Hort's Cod. 44 is B.-C. III. 37, which is our Act. 221, Paul. 265.

45. (Paul. 52, Apoc. 16.) Hamburg, City Library, Cod. Gr. 1252 [xv], $7\tfrac{7}{8} \times 5\tfrac{7}{8}$, ff. 268 (22), *chart.*, *prol.* With its companion Cod. M of St. Paul's Epistles, it was lent to Wetstein in 1717 and to Bengel, by Z. C. Uffenbach. It once belonged to Jo. Ciampini at Rome, is carelessly written, but from a good text: 'plura genuina omittens, quam aliena admiscens,' Bengel.

46. (Paul. 55.) Monacensis Reg. 375 [xi, Greg. x], $12\tfrac{1}{2} \times 9\tfrac{3}{8}$, ff. 381 (40), στίχ. (marked peculiarly in archaic fashion—J. R. Harris—e. g. 1 Cor. ΗΗΗΗΗΔΔ), is Bengel's Augustan. 6, with Œcumenius' commentary and some rare readings (Bengel, Matthaei, Scholz). All the Augsburg MSS. of the N. T. (*see* Evann. 83, 426–8, Paul. 54, 125, 126) were removed to Munich in 1806.

47. (Evan. 90.) 48. (Evan. 105.) 49. (Evan. 92.)

50. (Paul. 8.) Stephen's ζ' is unknown, though it was once in the Royal Library at Paris; that is, if Evan. 8, Reg. 49, is Stephen's ζ' in the Gospels, which Mr. Vansittart seems to have proved. Stephen seldom cites ζ', or (as Mill puts the case) 'textus ipsius ferè universus absorptus est in hac editione' (N. T., Proleg. § 1167). *See* Evan. 8.

51. (Paul. 133, Apoc. 52.) Paris, Nat. Gr. 56, once Mazarin's [xii], $10 \times 6\tfrac{3}{8}$, ff. 375 (23), *prol.*, κεφ., *lect.*, *subscr.* *Mut.* Apoc. xxii. 17–21.

52. (Paul. 50.) Cod. Rhodiensis, some of whose readings Stunica, the chief of the Complutensian editors, cites in controversy with Erasmus: it may have been his own property, and cannot now be identified. Whatever Mill states (on 1 John iii. 16), it is not now at Alcalá.

*53. (Paul. 30.) Camb. Emman. Coll. i. 4. 35 [xii], $3\tfrac{3}{4} \times 3$, ff. 214 (24), *prol.*, κεφ. t., τίτλ., κεφ., the writing being among the minutest and most elegant extant. It is Mill's Cant. 3, Scrivener's n (a facsimile is given Plate xii. No. 33), and is in bad condition, in parts almost illegible. It begins 2 Pet. ii. 4, and there is a hiatus from 1 John iii. 20 to the middle of Œcumenius' Prologue to the Romans: *mut.* also 1 Cor. xi. 7— xv. 56, and ends Heb. xi. 27. From 1 Tim. vi. 5 another and far less careful hand begins: but the manuscript exhibits throughout many abbreviations. Has some marginal notes *primâ manu.* Given to the College 'in Testimonium grati animi' by Sam. Wright, a member of the College, in 1598.

54. (Evan. 43.) Paris, Arsenal Libr. The second volume of this book

(containing the Acts and all the Epistles on 189 leaves) is judged by the present librarian to be a little more modern than the first volume. They were both 'ex dono R. P. de Berzian' (sic) to the Oratory of San Maglorian.

55. Readings of a *second* copy of St. Jude contained in Cod. 47. Tischendorf, in his eighth edition, cites this copy in Acts xvi. 6, apparently by mistake.

56. (Paul. 227.)   Oxf. Bodl. E. D. Clarke 4 [xii], 9 × 6, ff. 220 (27), *prol.* (names and miracles of Apostles, &c.), κεφ. t., κεφ., *lect., subscr., στίχ., syn.* (extracts, &c. by Dean Gaisford).

(This number was assigned by Wetstein and Griesbach to certain readings of four Medicean manuscripts (only one in the Acts), which, like those of No. 102 of the Gospels, were found by Wetstein in the margin of Rapheleng's Plantin Greek Testament (1591). Identical with Act. 84, 87–89.—Birch, Scholz.)

57. (Evan. 234.)

58. (Paul. 224.)   Oxf. Bodl. Clarke 9 [xiii], 7 × 5, ff. 181 (26), *lect. Mut.* Heb. xiii. 7–25 (Gaisford).   (58 of Wetstein is the same codex as 22; Scholz substitutes the above.)

59. (Paul. 62.)   Brit. Mus. Harl. 5588 [xiii], 10 × 6$\frac{1}{2}$, 132 (36), cotton paper, *prol.*, full *lect.*, κεφ., *subscr.*, στίχ.   On the first leaf we read 'liber hospitalis de Cusa trevirencis dioc. R^{mi}...'   See Evan. 87 (Griesbach, Bloomfield).

60. (Paul. 63, Apoc. 29.)   Brit. Mus. Harl. 5613 [May, A. D. 1407, Indict. 15], 8$\frac{1}{2}$ × 5$\frac{3}{4}$, ff. 267 (26), *prol., subscr.,* στίχ.   *Mut.* Apoc. xxii. 2–18.   (Griesbach collated fifty-five chapters of Acts and Epp., Griesbach and Scrivener's e in Apocalypse.)

*61. Brit. Mus. Add. 20,003 [April 20, A. D. 1044, Indict. 12], 7 × 6$\frac{1}{2}$, ff. 57 (23), κεφ. t. in St. James. This has been called the most important cursive copy of the Acts [but is much overrated—Ed.], was formerly called Io^{ti} (p^{scr}), discovered by Tischendorf in Egypt in 1853, and sold to the Trustees of the British Museum in 1854, was written by one John, a monk, with rubrical marks added in a later hand.   *Mut.* ch. iv. 8— vii. 17; xvii. 28—xxiii. 9; 297 verses.   Independent collations have been made by Tischendorf (Anecd. sacra et prof., pp. 7, 8, 130–46), by Tregelles, and by Scrivener (Cod. Augiensis, Introd., pp. lxviii–lxx). Its value is shown not so much by the readings in which it stands alone, as *by its agreement with the oldest uncial copies*, where their testimonies coincide.   ((Paul. 61) comprised extracts made by Griesbach from the margin of a copy of Mill's N. T. in the Bodleian (*see* Evan. 236), where certain readings are cited under the notation *Hal.*   These are now known to be taken from Evan. 440, Act. 111, Paul. 221, or Scrivener's v of the Gospels, o of the Acts and Epistles—Tischendorf, Tregelles.)

62. (Paul. 65.)   Par. Nat. Gr. 60, once Colbert's [xiv], 14 × 9$\frac{1}{2}$, ff. 135 (35), *chart., prol.,* κεφ. t., κεφ., τίτλ., *lect., subscr.,* στίχ., *syn.*, with scholia (Wetstein, Griesbach, Scholz).

63. (Paul. 68.)   Vindobon. Caesar, Nessel. 313 [xiv], 7$\frac{3}{8}$ × 5$\frac{3}{4}$, ff. 157 (26), *prol.,* κεφ. t., *lect., subscr.,* στίχ., *syn.*, scholia (Treschow, Alter, Birch).

VOL. I.   U

64. (Paul. 69.) Vind. Caes. Ness. 303 [xii], $7\frac{3}{8} \times 5\frac{3}{4}$, ff. 279 (22), *prol.*, κεφ. *t.*, *lect.*, *subscr.*, *syn.*, *men.*, carefully written by one John, brought by Ogier de Busbeck from Constantinople, like Cod. 67 and many others of this collection (Treschow, Alter, Birch).

*65. (Evan. 218.)

66. (Paul. 67, Apoc. 34.) Vind. Caes. Ness. 302 [xii, Greg. xi], $7\frac{1}{4} \times 5\frac{1}{2}$, ff. 368 (22), *prol.*, κεφ. *t.*, *pict.*, *lect.*, *subscr.*, στίχ., *vers.*, *syn.*, *men.*, scholia, and other matter: three several hands have made corrections, which Griesbach regarded as far more valuable than the text (cited by him 66**). *Mut.* Apoc. xv. 6—xvii. 3; xviii. 10—xix. 9; xx. 8—xxii. 21. It once belonged to Arsenius Archbishop of Monembasia (*see* Evan. 333, Evst. 113), then to Sebastian Tengnagel and Jo. Sambuc (A. C. Hwiid 1785 for the Acts, Treschow, Alter, Birch).

67. (Paul. 70.) Vind. Caes. Ness. 221 [written by one Leo at Constantinople, December, 1331, Indict. 14], $8\frac{3}{4} \times 7$, ff. 174 (31), *prol.*, κεφ. *t.*, *lect.*, *subscr.*, στίχ., *syn.*, *men.*, elegant but inaccurate (Treschow, Alter, Birch).

68. (Paul. 73.) Upsal. Univ. Gr. 1, $9 \times 6\frac{3}{4}$, ff. 220 (38), is in fact two separate manuscripts bound together, both of high value. The first part [xii] contains the Acts (commencing ch. viii. 14), Rom., 1 Cor. to ch. xv. 38: the second [xi] begins 1 Cor. xiii. 6, and extends through the Pauline and Catholic Epistles, which follow them. In the text of St. Paul it much resembles Paul. 17. A catena is annexed, which is an abridgement of Œcumenius, and the portion in duplicate (1 Cor. xiii. 6—xv. 38) has contradictory readings (P. F. Aurivill [Orville?], 1786). It was bought at Venice by Sparvenfeldt in 1678 (Belsheim).

69. (Paul. 74, Apoc. 30.) Guelpherbytanus xvi. 7, August., $8\frac{7}{8} \times 6\frac{1}{8}$, ff. 204 (29), *chart.*, also in two hands: the first (Acts and Epistles) [xiii], written by George a monk, the Apocalypse [xiv]. It exhibits a remarkable text, and has many marginal readings and *prol.* (Knittel, Matthaei).

All from 70 to 96 were slightly collated by Birch, and except 81, 93–6 by Scholz also.

70. (Evan. 131.) 71. (Evan. 133.)

72. (Paul. 79, Apoc. 37.) Rom. Vat. Gr. 366 [xiii, Greg. xv], $7\frac{3}{4} \times 5\frac{3}{8}$, ff. 218 (24), *chart.*, *prol.*

73. (Paul. 80.) Rom. Vat. Gr. 367 [xi], $8\frac{1}{8} \times 6\frac{3}{8}$, ff. 165 (30), an excellent manuscript used by Caryophilus (*see* Evan. 112).

74. Rom. Vat. Gr. 760 [xii], $10\frac{1}{8} \times 8\frac{1}{4}$, ff. 257 (24), contains only the Acts with a catena.

75. (Evan. 141.) 76. (Evan. 142.) 77. (Evan. 149.)

78. (Paul. 89.) Rom. Alexandrino-Vat. Gr. 29 [xii, Greg. x], $10 \times 7\frac{1}{4}$, ff. 177 (21), a good copy, but *mut.* 2 Cor. xi. 15—xii. 1; Eph. i. 9—Heb. xiii. 25. Traced to Strasburg in the possession of H. Boecler, and identified with 201 (Scr., 3rd ed.) by Dr. Gregory.

79. (Paul. 90.) Rom. Urbino-Vat. Gr. 3 [xi], $7\frac{3}{8} \times 5\frac{1}{2}$, ff. 161 (30).

80. (Paul. 91, Apoc. 42.) Rom. Pio-Vat. Gr. 50 [xii], $6\frac{5}{8} \times 5\frac{1}{3}$, ff. 327 (21).

81. Rom. Barberin. Gr. vi. 21 [xi, Greg. xiv], 13¾ × 10¾, with a commentary (Birch). Scholz could not find this copy, which has remarkable readings: it contains but one chapter of the Acts and the Catholic Epistles.

82. (Evan. 180.)

83. (Paul. 93.) Naples, Bibl. Nat. ii. Aa. 7 [x, Greg. xii], 10⅜ × 7¾, ff. 123 (37), 2 cols., written by Evagrius and compared with Pamphilus' copy at Caesarea (*see* Act. 15): στίχοι sometimes in the margin. *See* below, Act. 173.

84. (Paul. 94.) Florence, Laurent. iv. 1 [x], 12¾ × 10⅛, ff. 244 (21), has St. Chrysostom's commentary on the Acts, that of Nicetas of Heraclea on all the Epistles.

85. (Paul. 95.) Flor. Laurent. iv. 1 [xiii], 12¼ × 10, ff. 288 (31), *chart.*, contains the Acts and *Pauline* Epistles with Theophylact's commentary.

86. (Paul. 96, Apoc. 75.) Flor. Laurent. iv. 30 [xi, Greg. x], 7½ × 5¾, ff. 377 (18), with a commentary. Tregelles states that this is the same copy as Cod. 147, the press-mark 20 being put by Birch in error for 30.

87. (Paul. 97.) Flor. Laurent. iv. 29 [x], 10¼ × 7¾, ff. 294 (19), with scholia, *prol.*, and a modern interlinear Latin version in the Epistles, for the use of beginners.

88. (Paul. 98.) Flor. Laurent. iv. 31 [xi], 7 × 5½, ff. 276 (24), *prol. Mut.* in fine Titi.

89. (Paul. 99, Apoc. 45.) Flor. Laurent. iv. 32, 5 × 3½, 276 (27), written by John Tzutzuna, priest and monk, December, 1093, Indict. 1, in the reign of Alexius Comnenus, Nicolas being Patriarch of Constantinople. *Prol., syn.*, and a treatise of Dorotheus, Bishop of Tyre in Julian's reign, on the seventy disciples and twelve Apostles, which is found also in Act. 10, 179, Burdett-Coutts II. 4 (Paul. 266), in Erasmus' N. T. (1516), and partly in Stephen's of 1550. *See* Cave's 'Hist. Lit.,' vol. i. pp. 164–172.

90. (Evan. 197.)   91. (Evan. 201.)   92. (Evan. 204.)

*93. (Evan. 205.)   *94. (Evan. 206.)   *95. (Evan. 209.)

*96. (Paul. 109.) Venet. Marc. 11 [xi, Greg. xiii or xiv], 11¼ × 9½, ff. 304 (?), 3 cols., an important copy, often resembling Act. 142, from the monastery of St. Michael de Troyna in Sicily. It has both a Latin and an Arabic version. *Mut.* Acts i. 1–12; xxv. 21—xxvi. 18; Philemon. Act. 93–96 and Paul. 106–112 were collated by G. F. Rinck, 'Lucubratio Critica in Act. Apost. Epp. Cath. et Paul.' Basileae, 1830.

97. (Paul. 241.) Guelpherbyt. Biblioth. Gud. gr. 104. 2 [xii], 7¼ × 5¾, ff. 226 (27), once belonging to Langer, librarian at Wolfenbüttel, who sent a collation to Griesbach. *Mut.* Acts xvi. 39—xvii. 18: it has marginal scholia from Chrysostom and Œcumenius, prayers and dialogues subjoined. Deposited by one Theodoret in the Catechumens' library of the Laura (monastery) of St. Athanasius on Athos.

Act. 98–107 were accurately collated by Matthaei for his N. T.

*98. (Paul. 113, Apost. 77.) Dresden, Reg. A. 104 [xi], $11\frac{3}{4} \times 8\frac{5}{8}$, ff. 186 (40), 2 cols., once belonged to Jeremias the patriarch of the monastery of Stauroniketa on Athos. Matthaei professes that he chiefly followed this manuscript, which is divided into three parts: viz. a_1 Church Lessons from the Acts, so arranged that no verse is lost, with various readings and scholia in the margin: a_2 (or simply a) the text with marginal various readings and scholia: a_3 Church Lessons from the Acts and Epistles. Identified by Gregory with Act. 107.

*99. (Paul. 114.) Mosq. Synod. 5 (Mt. c) [April, A.D. 1445, Greg. 1345], folio, ff. 464, *chart.*, contains also the Life and Speeches of Gregory Naz. and much other matter, from the Iberian or Iveron monastery on Athos, carelessly written by Theognostus, Metropolitan of Perga and Attalia: *prol., syn., men., Euthal.*, and some Patristic writings.

*100. (Paul. 115.) Mosq. Synod. 334 (Mt. d) [xi], 4to, ff. ?, with a catena and scholia.

*101. (Paul. 116.) Mosq. Synod. 333 (Mt. f) [xiii], 4to, ff. 240, *chart. B., prol., syn.*, carefully written, with scholia to the Acts.

*102. [This is Cod. K of the Catholic and Pauline Epistles, cited according to Matthaei's notation. Hort's 102 is k^{scr}.]

*103. (Paul. 118.) Mosq. Synod. 193 (Mt. h) [xii], folio, ff. 236, from the Iveron monastery on Athos, is a volume of scholia, with the entire text in its margin for Acts i. 1—ix. 12; elsewhere only in fragments after the usual manner of scholia.

*104. (Evan. 241.)   *105. (Evan. 242.)

*106. (Paul. 122.) Mosq. Synod. 328 (Mt. m) [xi], 4to, ff. 228, *prol.*, κεφ. t., *lect., syn.*, carefully written, from the Vatopedi monastery on Athos, has *prol., syn.*, and the Psalms annexed.

107[1]. (Paul. 491.) Lond. Brit. Mus. Add. 22,734 [xi–xii], $11\frac{5}{8} \times 9\frac{1}{4}$, ff. 248 (13–25), *prol.*, κεφ., *subscr.*, στίχ. With comm. of Œcumenius. *Mut.* Acts iv. 15-22; xxiii. 15-30; Rom. v. 13—vi. 21; vi. 22—end of Phil.; Col. iii. 15—iv. 11; Heb. xiii. 24-25 (pt.). Bears name of Jo. Card. de Salviatis, and arms of Pius VI. Bought of Sp. P. Lampros of Athens in 1853. (Greg. 204.)

108. (Evan. 226.)   109. (Evan. 228.)

Codd. 110–181 were first added to the list by Scholz, who states that he collated entire 115, 133, 160; in the greater part 120-3, 126, 127, 131, 137, 161-3, 174; the rest slightly or not at all.

110. (Evan. 568.)   (Greg. 247.)

Erase Evan. 441, being a printed edition (see p. 239). Hort's 110 is a^{scr}, which is our 182.

*111. (Evan. 440.) This is Scrivener's o Act. and Paul.

112. Cantabrig. 2068 erase: it is the same as Cod. 9. Hort's 112 is c^{scr}, which is our 184. Instead of it Greg. inserts—

---

[1] *See* under 98.

(Paul. 179.) Modena, Este ii. G. 3 [ix or x], $13 \times 8\frac{7}{8}$, ff. ? (30), *prol.*, *Euthal.*, being part of uncial H in minuscules (*see* under H of Acts).

*113. (Evan. 18.)

Codd. 113, 114, 117, being 132, 134, 137 of St. Paul respectively, together with Act. 127 and Paul. 139, 140, 153, have been collated by J. G. Reiche, in his 'Codicum aliquot Graecorum N. T. Parisiensium nova descriptio: praemissis quibusdam de neglecti MSS. N. T. studii causâ.' Gott. 1847.

*114. (Paul. 134.) Par. Nat. Gr. 57 [xiii, Greg. xi], $11\frac{5}{8} \times 8\frac{3}{4}$, ff. 231 (24), 2 cols., *κεφ.*, *syn.*, *men.*, &c., a valuable copy, with some portions of the Septuagint version, and prayers for the service of the Greek Church.

115. (Paul. 135.) Par. Nat. Gr. 58, once Colbert's (as were 118, 121, 122, 124, 128, 129) [xiii, Greg. xi], $10\frac{1}{8} \times 7\frac{3}{4}$, ff. 174 (28), *prol.*, *κεφ. t.*, *subscr.*, *στίχ.*, begins Acts xiv. 27, ends 2 Tim.; no liturgical notes.

116. (Paul. 136, Apoc. 53.) Par. Nat. Gr. 59, once Teller's [xvi], 11×8, ff. 331 (21), *chart.*, *prol.*, and scholia to the Catholic Epistles.

*117. (Evan. 263, Paul. 137) of some value.

118. (Paul. 138, Apoc. 55.) Par. Nat. Gr. 101 [xiii], $9\frac{1}{8} \times 6\frac{1}{4}$, ff. 200 (28), *chart.*, *prol.*, *κεφ. t.*, *κεφ.*, *subscr.*, *στίχ.* *Mut.* Acts xix. 18—xxii. 17.

119. (Paul. 139, Apoc. 56.) Par. Nat. Gr. 102 A [x, but Apoc. xiii], $9\frac{1}{4} \times 6\frac{3}{4}$, ff. 229 (26, 25), *prol.*, *lect.*, *subscr.*, *στίχ.*, *ἀναγν.*, *men.* *Mut.* 2 Cor. i. 8—ii. 4. Cath. follow Paul., as in Cod. 120.

120. (Paul. 141.) Par. Nat. Gr. 103 A [xi, Greg. xiii], $9\frac{5}{8} \times 6\frac{5}{8}$, ff. 243 (22), *κεφ. t.*, *lect.*, *ἀναγν.*, *subscr.*, *στίχ.*, *prol.* beginning Acts xxi. 20 (v. 38—vi. 7; vii. 6–16; 32—x. 25 *chart.* [xiii]). *Mut.* Acts xxviii. 23—Rom. ii. 26; Phil. i. 5—1 Thess. iv. 1; v. 26—2 Thess. i. 11; 1 John ii. 11—iii. 3; 24—v. 14; 2 John; ending 3 John 11.

121. (Paul. 142.) Par. Nat. Gr. 104 [xiii], $7\frac{1}{4} \times 5$, ff. 257 (24), *chart.*, *prol.*, *κεφ. t.*, *τίτλ.*, *lect.*, *subscr.*, *στίχ.*, *syn.*, August. de Thou's, then Colbert's.

122. (Paul. 143.) Par. Nat. Gr. 105 [xi or x], $8\frac{1}{8} \times 6\frac{1}{4}$, ff. 248 (17), *prol.*, *κεφ.*, *τίτλ.*, *subscr.*, *στίχ.*, correctly written, but fragments, viz. Acts xiii. 48—xv. 22; 29—xvi. 36; xvii. 4—xviii. 26; xx. 16—xxviii. 17; 1 Pet. ii. 20—iii. 2; 1 John iii. 5; 21—v. 9; 2 John 8—3 John 10; Jude 7—Rom. iv. 16; 24—vii. 9; 18—1 Cor. i. 28; ii. 13—viii. 1; ix. 6—xiv. 2; 10—Gal. i. 10; ii. 4—Eph. i. 18; 1 Tim. i. 14—v. 5.

123. (Paul. 144.) Par. Nat. Gr. 106 A [xiv], $8\frac{5}{8} \times 6\frac{1}{8}$, ff. 276 (29), *prol.*, *κεφ. t.*, *κεφ.*, *τίτλ.*, *lect.*, *subscr.*, *στίχ.* Hymns. *Mut.* 1 Pet. i. 9—ii. 7.

124. (Paul. 149, Apoc. 57.) Par. Nat. Gr. 124 [xvi], 16mo, beautifully written by Angelus Vergecius.

125. (Paul. 150.) Par. Nat. Gr. 125 [xiv], $6\frac{5}{8} \times 7\frac{7}{8}$, ff. 394 (16), *prol.*, *lect.*, *subscr.*, *ἀναγν.*, *στίχ.*, from Constantinople.

126. (Paul. 153.) Par. Nat. Gr. 216, from Medici collection [x], $12\frac{3}{4} \times 9\frac{1}{2}$, ff. 333 (21), 2 cols., *prol.*, *κεφ. t.*, *κεφ.*, *τίτλ.*, *subscr.*, *στίχ.*, probably written at Constantinople, with catena, sometimes in uncial, occasionally, esp. in Heb., as late as [xvi].

*127. (Paul. 154.)   Par. Nat. Gr. 217 [xi], $12\frac{5}{8} \times 10\frac{1}{8}$, ff. 373 (28–33), *prol.*, κεφ. *t.*, *subscr.*, στίχ., carelessly written (Vansittart), collated by Reiche. It has a catena. Act., scholia (Cath.), Theodoret's commentary (Paul.).

128. (Paul. 155.)   Par. Nat. Gr. 218 [xi], $12\frac{1}{2} \times 10$, ff. 317 (37), with a catena.

129. (Paul. 156.)   Par. Nat. Gr. 220 [xiii, Greg. xiv], $11\frac{1}{2} \times 8\frac{1}{2}$, ff. 388 (41), 2 cols., a commentary, the text sometimes suppressed.

130. Par. Nat. Gr. 221 [xii], $11\frac{1}{8} \times 8\frac{1}{2}$, ff. 177 (14), from the East, with a catena. *Mut.* Acts xx. 38—xxii. 3; 2 Pet. i. 14—iii. 18; 1 John iv. 11—Jude 8.

131. (Paul. 158.)   Par. Nat. Gr. 223, once Boistaller's, contains Paul. with *prol.* and catena, [A. D. 1045], $11\frac{1}{2} \times 8\frac{1}{2}$, ff. 273 (23), by Theopemptus, a reader, followed by Act. and Cath. [xii].

132. (Evan. 330.)

133. (Paul. 166.)   Turin, Univ. C. vi. 19 [xiii, Greg. xii], $8 \times 5\frac{3}{4}$, ff. 295 (24), *chart.*, *pict.*, *prol.*, in a clear large hand; Dr. Hort noticed remarkable readings in the Catholic Epistles. The Epistle to the Hebrews precedes 1 Timothy, as Pasinus notes in his Catalogue.

134. (Paul. 167.)   Turin, Univ. B. v. 19 [xi, Greg. xii or xiii], $8\frac{1}{4} \times 6$, ff. 370 (19), *prol.*, *mut.* Acts i, ii. Pasinus notes that the Pauline precede the Catholic Epistles.

135. (Evan. 339.)

136. (Paul. 169.)   Turin, Univ. C. v. 1 [xii], $9\frac{1}{4} \times 7$, ff. 174 (27), *prol.*, κεφ. *t.*, *lect.*, *syn.*.. *Mut.* in Heb.

137. (Paul. 176.)   Milan, Ambros. E. 97 sup. [xi, Greg. xiii], $10\frac{1}{8} \times 7\frac{3}{8}$, ff. 276 (23), *prol.*, *lect.*, ἀναγν., *subscr.*, στίχ., bought at Corfu: so like Codd. DE^{scr} (Act. 184) and the margin of the Harkleian Syriac in the Acts, as to assist us when DE are mutilated, especially in additions: e.g. Acts xxvii. 5; xxviii. 16; 19 (*bis*). *See* Scrivener's 'Cod. Bezae,' Introd., p. lix, note.

138. (Paul. 173.)   Milan, Ambros. E. 102 sup. [xiv, Greg. xv], $9\frac{3}{4} \times 6\frac{3}{4}$, ff. 202 (19), *chart.*, once J. V. Pinelli's; it contains the Epistles only.

139. (Paul. 174.)   Milan, Ambros. H. 104 sup. [written March 20, 1434, Indict. 12, by one Athanasius], $11\frac{1}{2} \times 8\frac{5}{8}$, ff. 164 (31), 2 cols., *prol.*, *subscr.*, στίχ., *chart.*, bought at Padua, 1603.

140. (Paul. 215, Apoc. 74.)   Venice, 546 [partly xi on vellum, partly xiii *chart.*], $11\frac{1}{2} \times 9\frac{5}{8}$, ff. 268 (21), *prol.*, στίχ. The Epistles have a catena, the Apocalypse a commentary.

141. (Evan. 189.)

142. (Paul. 178.)   Modena, iii. B. 17 [xii], $7\frac{1}{8} \times 5\frac{3}{8}$, ff. ?, *prol.*, *subscr.*, στίχ., valuable, but with many errors; see however Act. 96.

143. (Evan. 832.)   Contains the Catholic Epistles, but not the Acts.

144. (Evan. 363.)   145. (Evan. 365.)   146. (Evan. 367.)

147. Ven. St. Mark ii. 61.

ACT. 127–162.   295

148. (Paul. 184.) Flor. Laurent. Convent. Soppr. 191 [written A. D. 984, Indict. 12, by Theophylact, priest and doctor of law], $13\frac{1}{2} \times 9\frac{1}{2}$, ff. 342, *prol.*, once belonged to the Benedictine Library of St. Mary.

149. (Paul. 349, Apoc. 180.) Flor. Laurent. Conv. Soppr. 150 [xiii, Greg. xii], $8\frac{7}{8} \times 5\frac{1}{4}$, ff. 144 (32), 2 cols., *subscr.*, στίχ., contains the Catholic Epistles, with a Latin version.

150. (Evan. 368.)   151. (Evan. 386.)
152. (Evan. 1202.)   153. (Evan. 444.)

154. (Paul. 187.) Rom. Vat. Gr. 1270 [xv, Greg. xiv], $8\frac{3}{4} \times 6\frac{1}{2}$, ff. 164 (36), *prol.*, κεφ. *t.*, *lect.*, contains the Acts, Catholic Epistles, Rom., 1 Cor., with a commentary.

155. (Paul. 188.) Rom. Vat. Gr. 1430 [xii], $14 \times 11\frac{1}{4}$, ff. 270 (20), *prol.*, with a commentary in another hand. It does not contain the Acts, but all the Epistles.

156. (Paul. 190.) Rom. Vat. Gr. 1650 [Jan. 1037], $13\frac{1}{2} \times 10\frac{3}{4}$, ff. 187 (43), 2 cols., *prol.*, κεφ. *t.*, κεφ., τίτλ., *lect.*, *subscr.*, στίχ., *vers.*, *Euthal.*, written for Nicolas Archbishop of Calabria by the cleric Theodore. The Pauline Epistles have a commentary : it begins Acts v. 4.

157. (Paul. 191.) Rom. Vat. Gr. 1714 [xii], $8\frac{1}{2} \times 6\frac{3}{4}$, ff. 46 (25), *prol.*, κεφ. *t.*, κεφ., τίτλ., *lect.*, ἀναγν., *subscr.*, στίχ., is a heap of disarranged fragments, containing Acts xviii. 14—xix. 9 ; xxiv. 11—xxvi. 23 ; James iii. 1—v. 20 ; 3 John with κεφ. and ὑπόθεσις to Jude ; Rom. vi. 22—viii. 32 ; xi. 31—xv. 23 ; 1 Cor. i. 1—iii. 12.

158. (Paul. 192.) Rom. Vat. Gr. 1761 [xi], $9\frac{1}{2} \times 7\frac{1}{5}$, ff. 481 (21), *prol.*, κεφ. *t.*, κεφ., τίτλ. From this copy Mai supplied the lacunae of Cod. B in the Pauline Epistles.

159. Rom. Vat. Gr. 1968, Basil. 7 [xi, Greg. x], $6\frac{1}{4} \times 4\frac{1}{4}$, ff. 84 (22), *prol.*, κεφ. *t.*, κεφ., τίτλ., *lect.*, *subscr.*, contains the Acts, James, and 1 Peter, with scholia, whose authors' names are given. *Mut.* Acts i. 1—v. 29 ; vi. 14—vii. 11.

160. (Paul. 193, Apoc. 24.) Rom. Vat. Gr. 2062 [xi, Greg. x], $10\frac{5}{8} \times 8$, ff. 287 (26), κεφ., τίτλ., *subscr.*, στίχ., with copious scholia accompanied by the authors' names : it begins Acts xxviii. 19, ends Heb. ii. 1.

161. (Paul. 198, Apoc. 69.) Rom. Vat. Ottob. Gr. 258 [xiii, Greg. xiv], $9\frac{3}{4} \times 7\frac{3}{8}$, ff. 216 (32), 2 cols., *chart.*, *prol.*, *subscr.*, with a Latin version : it begins Acts ii. 27, and the last chapters of the Apocalypse are lost. The latter part was written later [xiv].

162. (Paul. 200.) Rom. Vat. Ottob. Gr. 298 [xv, Greg. xiv], $6\frac{3}{4} \times 4\frac{3}{4}$, ff. 265 (27), 2 cols., with the Latin Vulgate version (with which Scholz states that the Greek has been in many places made to harmonize) in a parallel column, contains many transpositions of words, and unusual readings introduced by a later hand [1].

---

[1] Cod. 162 has attracted much attention from the circumstance that it is the only unsuspected witness among the Greek manuscripts for the celebrated text 1 John v. 7, 8, whose authenticity will be discussed in Vol. II. Ch. XII. A facsimile of the passage in question was traced in 1829 by Cardinal Wiseman for Bishop Burgess, and published by Horne in several editions of his 'Introduction,'

163. (Paul. 201.) Rom. Vat. Ottob. Gr. 325 [xiv], $7\frac{5}{8} \times 4\frac{7}{8}$, ff. 215 (26) *chart.*, *prol.*, *κεφ. t.* *Mut.* Acts iv. 19—v. 1.

164. (Evan. 390.)

165. Rom. Vat. Ottob. Gr. 417 [xiv, Greg. xvi], $8\frac{3}{8} \times 5\frac{3}{4}$, ff. 339 (21), *chart.*, contains the Catholic Epistles, with works of St. Ephraem and others.

166. (Paul. 204, Apoc. 22.) Rom. Vallicell. B. 86 [xii–xiv, Greg.], $7 \times 4\frac{7}{8}$, ff. 258 (26), i. e. ff. 1–103 [xii], by George, son of Elias; 104–191 [xiii], by Joachim, a monk; 192–228 [xii] also by George; 229–254 [xiv]; and four prefatory leaves, *chart.*, were added later [xvi]. *Prol.*, *κεφ.*, *τίτλ.*, *subscr.*, *στίχ.* Described with facsimile in Bianchini, Evan. Quadr., vol. ii. pt. 1, pp. 535–8.

167. (Evan. 393.)

168. (Paul. 205.) Rom. Vallicell. F. 13 [xiv], $9\frac{1}{4} \times 6\frac{3}{8}$, ff. 204 (40), *chart.*, *prol.*, *ἀναγν.*, *subscr.*, *στίχ.*

169. (Paul. 206.) Rom. Ghigian. R. v. 29 [June 12, 1394 [1]], $11\frac{1}{2} \times 8\frac{1}{2}$, ff. 248 (21), *prol.*, *κεφ.*, *lect.*, *ἀναγν.*, *syn.*, *men.*, *subscr.*, *στίχ.*, written by Joasaph at Constantinople in the monastery *τῶν ὁδηγῶν*. *See* Evangelistarium 86.

170. (Evan. 394.)

171, 172 (Paul. 209, 210) are both Collegii Romani [xvi], fol., *chart.* Dr. Gregory could not find them in 1886.

173. (Paul. 211.) Naples, Nat. Libr. ii. Aa. 8 [xi], $8\frac{3}{4} \times 6\frac{5}{8}$, ff. 245 (22), *prol.*, *κεφ. t.*, *κεφ.*, *τίτλ.*, *lect.*, *ἀναγν.*, *subscr.*, *στίχ.*, and *μαρτυρίαι* cited from Scripture and profane writers. This codex has 1 John v. 7, 8 in the margin, by a recent hand. Tregelles suggests that this is probably the same copy as Cod. 83, the readings ascribed to it being extracted from the margin of that manuscript.

174. (Paul. 212.) Naples, Nat. Libr. ii. Aa. 9 [xv], $8\frac{1}{2} \times 5\frac{5}{8}$, ff. 208 (27), *chart.*, *prol.*, *κεφ. t.*, *lect.*, *subscr.*, *στίχ.*

175. (Paul. 216.) Messina, St. Basil 104 [xii], $11\frac{5}{8} \times 8\frac{7}{8}$, ff. 241 (25), 2 cols., *prol.*, *κεφ. t.*, *lect.*, *subscr.*, *στίχ.*, *men.*

176. (Evan. 421.)

177. (Evan. 122.)

178. (Paul. 242, Apoc. 87 or m^scr.) Cheltenham, Phillipps 1461 [xi or xii, Greg. xiv and xv], $9\frac{1}{2} \times 6\frac{1}{2}$, ff. 229 (27), (Hoskier), bought at Meerman's sale in 1824 by the late Sir T. Phillipps, Bart., of Middle Hill, Worcestershire. The Pauline Epistles are written smaller than the rest, but in the same clear hand. *Lect.*, *κεφ. t.*, *prol.*, *κεφ.* (but not in the Apocalypse), flourished rubric capitals. Scrivener in 1856 fully

as also by Tregelles (Horne, vol. iv. p. 217). If the facsimile is at all faithful, this is as rudely and indistinctly written as any manuscript in existence; but the illegible scrawl between the Latin column in the post of honour on the left, and the Greek column on the right, has been ascertained by Mr. B. H. Alford (who examined the codex at Tregelles' request) to be merely a consequence of the accidental shifting of the tracing paper, too servilely copied by the engraver.

[1] Scholz says 1344, and Tischendorf corrects but few of his gross errors in these Catalogues: but A. M. 6902, which he cites from the manuscript, is A. D. 1394.

collated Apoc. (whose text is valuable), the rest slightly. It is sadly mutilated; it begins Acts iv. 24; *mut.* Acts v. 2–16; vi. 2—vii. 2; 16—viii. 10; 38—ix. 13; 26–39; x. 9–22; 43—xiii. 1; xxiii. 32—xxiv. 24; xxviii. 23—James i. 5; iii. 6—iv. 16; 2 Pet. iii. 10—1 John i. 1; iii. 13—iv. 2; Jude 16–25; Rom. xiv. 23 (xvi. 25-27 was there placed)—xv. 14; 1 Cor. iii. 15—xv. 23; 2 Cor. x. 14—xi. 19; xiii. 5–13; Eph. i. 1—ii. 14; v. 29—vi. 24; Col. i. 24-26; ii. 4-7; 2 Thess. i. 1—iii. 5; Heb. ix. 3—x. 29; Apoc. xiv. 4–14: ending Apoc. xxi. 12. The ὑποθέσεις and tables of κεφ. before each Epistle have suffered in like manner.

179. (Paul. 128, Apoc. 82.) Munich, Royal Libr. 211 [xi, Delitzsch xiii], $10\frac{5}{8} \times 8\frac{3}{8}$, ff. 227 (25), *lect., prol., ὑπογραφαί,* Dorotheus' treatise (see Act. 89), fragments of *Eus. t.*, and (in a later hand) marginal scholia to St. Paul. Belonged to Zomozcrab, the Bohemian. The text is very near that commonly received. The portion of this manuscript which contains the Apocalypse is described by Delitzsch, Handschriftliche Funde, Leipzig, 1862, pp. 45–48, with a facsimile of Apoc. viii. 12, 13.

180. (Evan. 431.) Important, but seems to have perished in 1870 at Strasburg.

181. (Evan. 400[1].)

The following codices also are described by Scrivener, Cod. Augiens., Introd. pp. lv–lxiv, and their collations given in the Appendix.

*182. a^scr (Paul. 252). Lond. Lambeth 1182 [xii, Greg. xiii], $10\frac{1}{2} \times 6\frac{7}{8}$, ff. 397 (20), *chart.*, brought (as were also 183–6) by Carlyle from a Greek island. A later hand [xiv] supplied Acts i. 1—xii. 3; xiii. 5–15; 2, 3 John, Jude. In this copy and 183 the Pauline Epistles precede the Catholic). *Lect., pict., κεφ., prol., syn., men., ἀποδημίαι παύλου, ἀντίφωνα* for Easter, and other foreign matter. The various readings are interesting, and strongly resemble those of Cod. 69 of the Acts, and Cod. 61 hardly less, especially in Acts xiii–xvii. This is Hort's Cod. 110. (Greg. 214.)

*183. b^scr (Paul. 253). Lond. Lamb. 1183 [A. D. 1358], 10 × 7, ff. 236 (27), *chart., mut.* 1 Cor. xi. 7–27; 1 Tim. iv. 1—v. 8. *Syn., prol., κεφ. t., τιτλ., mut., κεφ., lect.,* in a beautiful hand, with many later corrections. (Greg. 215.)

*184. c^scr (Paul. 254). Lond. Lamb. 1184 [xv], 4to, *chart., mut.* Acts vii. 52—viii. 25. Having been restored in 1817 (Evan. 516), its readings (which, especially in the Acts and Catholic Epistles, are very

---

[1] Here again we banish to the notes Scholz's list from Cod. 182 to Cod. 189, for the reasons stated after Evan. 449.
182. (Paul. 243.) Library of St. John's monastery at Patmos [xii], 8vo, also another [xiii] 8vo.
183. (Paul. 231.) Library of the Great Greek monastery at Jerusalem 8 [xiv], 8vo. This must be Coxe's No. 7 [x], 4to, beginning Acts xii. 6.
184. (Paul. 232, Apoc. 85.) Jerusalem 9 [xiii], 4to, with a commentary. This is evidently Coxe's No. 15, though he dates it at the end of [x].
185. (Paul. 233.) St. Saba, Greek monastery, 1 [xi], 12mo.
186. (Evan. 457.)   187. (Evan. 462.)
188. (Paul. 236.) St. Saba 15 [xii], 4to.   189. (Evan. 466.)

important) are taken from an excellent collation (Lamb. 1255, 10-14) made for Carlyle about 1804 by the Rev. W. Sanderson of Morpeth. The text much resembles that of Act. 61, and is almost identical with that of B.-C. III. 37 (Act. 221) and of Act. 137. This is Hort's Cod. 112. (Greg. 216.)

*185. d^{scr} (Paul. 255). Lond. Lamb. 1185 [xiv?], 8¾ × 5¾, ff. 209 23-5), *prol.*, κεφ. t., κεφ., *lect.*, *subscr.*, *men.*, στίχ., *chart.*, miserably mutilated and ill-written. It must be regarded as a collection of fragments in at least four different hands, pieced together by the most recent scribe. *Mut.* Acts ii. 36—iii. 8; vii. 3-59; xii. 7-25; xiv. 8-27; xviii. 20—xix. 12; xxii. 7—xxiii. 11; 1 Cor. viii. 12—ix. 18; 2 Cor. i. 1-10; Eph. iii. 2—Phil. i. 24; 2 Tim. iv. 12—Tit. i. 6; Heb. vii. 19—ix. 12. We have 1 Cor. v. 11, 12; 2 Cor. x. 8-15, written by two different persons. (Greg. 217.)

*186. e^{scr} (Paul. 321) seems to have been Lond. Lamb. 1181 [xiv], 4to of the Acts, Catholic and Pauline Epistles (as we learn from the Lambeth Catalogue, but having been returned (*see* Evan. 516), we have access only to a tolerable collation of Acts i. 1—xxvii. 12, made by the Rev. John Fenton for Carlyle (Lamb. 1255, 27-33). In its text it much resembles Cod. E. (Greg. 218.)

*187. f^{scr} (Evan. 543). (Greg. 194.)

*188. g^{scr} (Evan. 542). (Greg. 193.)

189. (Evan. 825.) (Greg. 258.) 190. (Evan. 503.)

191. (Paul. 245.) Oxf. Ch. Ch. Wake 38 [xi], 7 × 5½, ff. 306 (23), *prol.*, *Euthal.*, κεφ. t., κεφ., τίτλ., *subscr.*, *syn.*, *men.*, in small and neat characters, from St. Saba (brought to England with the other Wake manuscripts in 1731), contains a catena, and at the end the date 1312 (ἐτελειώθη τὸ παρὸν ἐν ἔτει ϛωκ΄) in a later hand. *Mut.* Acts i. 1-11.

192. (Paul. 246.) Oxf. Ch. Ch. Wake 37 [xi], 8 × 6, ff. 237 (23), κεφ., *vers.* *Mut.* Acts xii. 4—xxiii. 32. The last leaf is a palimpsest, *chart.* at end about 1490 A.D., the vellum being about 1070, *mut.* 6 leaves at beginning and 16-24.

*193. (Evan. 492.) (Greg. 199.) 194. (Evan. 451.) (Greg. 206.)

195. Modena, Este ii. A. 13 [xiii, Greg. xv], 4 × 3¼, ff. ?, *lect.*, *syn.*, *men.* (*See* Greg. 238.)

196. Modena, Este ii. C. 4 [xi or xii], 9⅝ × 8, ff. ? *Prol.* ἀποδημία and μαρτ. Paul., κεφ., τίτλ., *subscr.*, στίχ., *vers.*, *syn.* (*See* Greg. 239.)

197. (Evan. 461.) (Greg. 207.)

198. (Paul. 280.) Cheltenham, Phillipps 7681 [A.D. 1107], 12¼ × 8⅞, ff. 268 (24), 2 cols., is a copy of the Acts and all the Epistles from the Hon. F. North's collection. A grand folio in a very large hand (Hoskier). (Greg. 225.)

199. Cheltenham, Phillipps 7682 (Evan. 531). (Greg. 255.)

200. Cheltenham, Phillipps 1284 (Evan. 527). (Greg. 254.)

201. (Paul. 396, Apoc. 86.) Athens, National Library (490, 217) [xiv, Greg. xv], 10⅝ × 6¾, ff. 453 (42), *chart.*, *prol.*, κεφ. t., κεφ. *mut.* at

beginning and end, with commentary of Theophylact, and Andreas (alone) on Apocalypse. (Greg. 251. See Act. 78.)

Besides Evann. 226 and 228, entered above as Act. 108 and 109, Montana sent to Mr. Kelly a list of eight more in the Escurial (Greg. 230–237, who inserts Σ. i. 5 for 206).

202. Escurial ρ. iii. 4 [xiii].   203. Escurial τ. iii. 12 [xiii].
204. Escurial χ. iii. 3 [xii].   205. Escurial χ. iii. 10 [xii].
206. Escurial χ. iv. 2 [xiv].   207. Escurial ψ. iii. 6 [xi].
208. Escurial ψ. iii. 18 [x].   209. Escurial ω. iv. 22 [xv].

210. (Paul. 247.) Paris, St. Geneviève, A. O. 35 [xiv, Greg. xv], $7 \times 4\frac{3}{4}$, ff. 132 (24), beautifully written and illuminated, contains the Catholic and Pauline Epistles. Some name like Λασκαρις stands on fol. 1 in silver letters enclosed by a laurel-leaf. Described to Burgon by the librarian, M. Ruelle. (Greg. 415.)

The next three are at Oxford:

211. (Evan. 488.) (Greg. 200.)

212. (Paul. 250.) Oxf. Bodl. Canon. Gr. 110 [x], $7\frac{1}{2} \times 5\frac{1}{4}$, ff. 380 (18), *pict., prol.* (Euthal.), κεφ. t., κεφ., τίτλ., *subscr., στίχ.* (Paul.), a beautiful copy of the Acts and all the Epistles. For its collation, see Evan. 105. It also contains one leaf from Cyril's Homilies, and two other later. (Greg. 221.)

213. (Paul. 251.) Oxf. Bodl. Misc. Gr. 118 [xiii], $9 \times 6\frac{1}{2}$, ff. 149 (29), *syn., men., prol. Euthal.* (Paul.), κεφ. t., τίτλ., *lect., subscr. Mut.*, also contains the Acts and all the Epistles. (Greg. 222.)

214. (Evan. 846.) (Greg. 258.)

215. Parham 6 (Evan. 534). (Greg. 202.)

216. (Paul. 234.) Parham 79. 14 [1009], $10\frac{1}{4} \times 8$, ff. ?, *subscr., στίχ.*, from St. Saba; a facsimile in Parham Catalogue. This copy and the next two contain the Acts and all the Epistles. (Greg. 226.)

217. (Paul. 235.) Parham 80. 15 [xi, Greg. xii], $10\frac{5}{8} \times 8\frac{1}{2}$, ff. ?, *prol., subscr., στίχ.*, from Caracalla, with a marginal commentary. (Greg. 227.)

218. (Paul. 236.) Parham 81. 16 [xiii], $13\frac{1}{4} \times 8\frac{5}{8}$, ff. ?, *prol.*, κεφ., τίτλ., *subscr., syn., men.*, from Simopetra on Athos. (Greg. 228.)

The Baroness Burdett-Coutts has three copies of the Acts, two of the Catholic Epistles, viz.:

*219. B.-C. II. 7 (Evan. 549). (Greg. 201.)

*220. (Paul. 264.) B.-C. III. 1, Acts and all the Epistles, the Pauline preceding the Catholic [xi or xii], $11\frac{1}{2} \times 8$, ff. 375 (22), on fine vellum, with broad margins. This is one of the most superb copies extant of the latter part of the N. T., on which so much cost was seldom bestowed as on the Gospels. The illuminations before each book, the golden titles, subscriptions, and capitals, are very rich and fresh: the rubrical directions are in bright red at the top and bottom of the pages. The preliminary matter consists of *syn.* of the Apostolos, ὑπόθεσις to the

Acts, Εὐθαλίου διακόνου περὶ τῶν χρόνων τοῦ κηρύγματος τοῦ ἁγίου παύλου, κεφ. t. of the Acts, in all twenty pages. There are no other tables of κεφάλαια, but their τίτλοι and κεφ. are given throughout the manuscript. To each Epistle is prefixed the ordinary ὑπόθεσις or *prol., vers.*, and to eight of them Theodoret's also. Three leaves at the beginning of Epistles (containing portions of *prol.* and 2 Cor. i. 1–3; Eph. i. 1–4; Heb. i. 1–6) have been shamefully cut out for the sake of the illuminations. A complete menology of eighteen pages closes the volume. At the end of Jude we find in golden letters κ̅ε̅ 'ι̅ῦ̅ χ̅ε̅ υἱὲ τοῦ θῦ ἐλέησόν με τὸν πολιαμάρτητον ἀντώνϊον τάχα καὶ μοναχὸν τὸν μαλεύκην. (Greg. 223.)

*221. (Paul. 265.) B.-C. III. 37 [xii], 6 × 4, 270 (20)+6 *membran.* [xiv or later], and *chart.* [xv] (beginning and end), *men., lect., subscr.*, contains the Acts, Catholic and Pauline Epistles complete. This copy is full of instructive variations, being nearest akin to the Harkleian Syriac *cum asterisco* and to c^cr (184), then to a^scr (182), 137, 100, 66**, 69, d^scr (185) next to 27, 29, 57**. (Greg. 224.)

222. (Evan. 560.) (Greg. 257.)

*223. (Paul. 262.) Brit. Mus. Egerton 2787 [xiv], $7\frac{3}{4} \times 5\frac{3}{8}$, ff. 244 (22), *mut.* Jude 20–25, containing the Acts and all the Epistles, neatly written and bound in the original oak boards. After being offered for £60 in London from 1869 to 1875, it was bought by Dean Burgon, and, like Evan. 563, passed to his nephew, the Rev. W. F. Rose, and was obtained for the Museum in 1893. *Prol.*, κεφ. t., κεφ., τίτλ., ἀρχ. and τέλ., *subscr.*, στίχ., *syn., men.*, at the beginning, but it has been ill used, and the text corrected by an unskilful hand. Its faded ornaments were executed in lake. (Greg. 229.)

*224. (Evan. 507) w^scr. Hort's Act. 102. (Greg. 195.)

Besides the British Museum copies already described (Act. 22, 25–8, 59, 91) we must add:

*225 or j^scr. Lond. Brit. Mus. Burney 48 [xiv], $14\frac{3}{4} \times 10\frac{1}{4}$, end of St. Chrysost. vol. ii, ff. (230–244) 15, *chart., prol.*, κεφ. t., κεφ., *lect.*, τίτλ., *subscr.*, στίχ., elegantly written, contains the Catholic Epistles (except that of St. Jude), with important variations. (Greg. 219.)

226. (Evan. 576.) (Greg. 196.)   227. (Evan. 582.) (Greg. 197.)

228. (Evan. 584.) (Greg. 198.)

229. (Paul. 270.) Lond. Brit. Mus. Add. 19,388 [xiii or xiv], $7\frac{1}{4} \times 5\frac{3}{4}$, ff. 94 (21), *prol.*, κεφ., *subscr.*, τίτλ., *lect.*, very neat, bought of Simonides in 1853, contains only 2 Cor. xi. 25—1 Pet. iii. 15, for which order *see* Vol. I. p. 73. (Greg. 220.)

Act. 226–229 were also examined by Dr. Bloomfield.

230. Lond. Brit. Mus. Add. 19,392 [xi], ff. $14 \times 10\frac{1}{2}$, ff. $(2+1+2=)5$, (1) two leaves of wonderful beauty, containing James i. 1–23, the heading illuminated, κεφ. at the tops of the pages, with a commentary on three sides of the text in a very minute hand; (2) one leaf of an Evst. out of a volume which fell into the hands of General Menon, and was presented by Mr. Harris of Alexandria to the Brit. Mus., con-

taining Matt. vi. 13–18 (*see* Evst. 262) ; (3) two leaves containing Luke xxiv. 25–35 ; John i. 35–51. (Greg. 203.)

231. (Evan. 603.) (Greg. 256.)

232. (Paul. 271, Apoc. 107.) Lond. Brit. Mus. Add. 28,816 [A. D. 1111, Indict. 4], 11½ × 8½, ff. 149 (32), *prol.*, κεφ. *t.*, κεφ., *lect.* (no τίτλ.), *subscr.*, μαρτ., στίχ., a splendid copy, bought (*see* Evan. 603) of Sir Ivor Guest in 1871. A facsimile is exhibited in the Palaeographical Society's work, Plate 84. It begins with Euthalii ἔκθεσις of the chapters of the Acts. Euthalius' Prologue also precedes the Pauline Epistles, and that of Arethas (σύνοψις σχολική) the Apocalypse, with a table of his seventy-two κεφάλαια. Throughout the volume the numerals indicating the κεφάλαια of each book stand in the margin in red, and a list of the κεφ. before each. There are many marginal glosses in a very minute hand. *Mut.* 1 Cor. xvi. 15—Prol. to 2 Cor., and one leaf (Eph. v. 3—vi. 16) is supplied [xv] *chart.* There are ten leaves at the end containing foreign matter, by the same hand, and in the colophon, besides the date, we read that the monk Andreas wrote it εἰς τὸ ὄρος τοῦ π̄ρ̄σ̄ καὶ a͡γ μελετίου τῆς μυοπόλεως ἐν τῇ μονῇ τοῦ σ̄ρ̄σ̄, adding of himself (as well he might) πολλὰ γὰρ ἐκοπίασα ἐν τρισὶν ἔτεσιν κτίζων αὐτήν. The foreign matter includes an exposition of the errors condemned by the seven general councils (ff. 143–5), resembling that in Evan. 69. (Greg. 205.)

233. (Evan. 605.) (Greg. 253.) 234. (Evan. 608.) (Greg. 417.)

235. (Evan. 472.)

Belsheim enables us to add

236. (Paul. 273, Apoc. 108.) Upsal, Univ. Gr. 11 [xii], 6½ × 4¾, ff. 182 (33), containing the Acts, Epistles, and Apocalypse. (Greg. 335.)

237. (Evan. 616, Paul. 274.) (Greg. 269.)

He also found

238. Linköping, Benzel 35, once belonging to Eric Benzel [1675–1743], Archbishop of Upsal [x], 4to, ff. 244, very beautiful, *lect.* at beginning and end, contains the Acts and all the Epistles (Paul. 272), the Epistle to the Hebrews preceding 1 Tim. *Mut.* 2 Thess. iii. 7—Heb. i. 5. (Greg. 334.)

239. Rom. Vat. Gr. 652 [xiv], 11 × 7½, ff. 105, *chart.*, the Acts only for all that appears, with Theophylact's commentary, as printed in full in vol. iii (pp. 189–317, Praef. p. viii) of the Venice edition of Theophylact, 1758. *Lect.*, κεφ., τίτλοι, ἀρχ. and τέλη (Burgon). (Greg. 325.)

Fourteen copies were seen by Mr. Coxe in the East, which are numbered below. Compare Scholz's list.

240. (Paul. 282, Apoc. 109.) Paris Nat. 'Arménien 9' [xi], 11½ × 9, ff. 323 (36), 2 cols., *prol.*, κεφ. *t.*, *lect.*, *subscr.*, στίχ. Greek and Armenian. (Greg. 301.)

241. (Paul. 283.) Messina, Univ. 40 [xii, Greg. xiii], 13¾ × 10¼, ff. 224 (28), *chart.*, *prol.*, *mut.* Begins at Acts viii. 2, ends at Hebrews viii. 2. Has a commentary. (Greg. 320.)

242. (Evan. 622, Paul. 290, Apoc. 110.) Crypta Ferrata Λ'. α'. 1. (Greg. 267.)

243. (Paul. 291.) Crypta Ferrata A. β. 1 [x], 9 × 7⅛, ff. 139 (25), 2 cols., *Euth., prol., κεφ. t., κεφ., τίτλ., lect., subscr., στίχ.* John (1, 2, 3), Jude, Paul. (Heb., Tim.). *Mut.* 2 Tim. iv. 8—end. (Greg. 317.)

244. (Paul. 292.) Crypta Ferrata A. β. 3 [xi or xii], 10¼ × 6¾, ff. 172 (29), 2 cols., *prol., lect., subscr., στίχ., syn., men.* (Greg. 318.)

245. (Paul. 293.) Crypta Ferrata A. β. 6 [xi], 9 × 6¾, ff. 193 (26), *prol.* (Paul.), *lect., subscr., στίχ., men., mut.* at the end. (Greg. 319.)

246. (Paul. 294.) Rom. Vat. Gr. 1208, 11 × 7⅞, ff. 395 (19), *pict., κεφ. t., κεφ., τίτλ.* Abbate Cozza-Luzi confirms Berriman's account (pp. 98, 99) of the splendour of this codex. It is written in gold letters and is said to have belonged to Carlotta, Queen of Jerusalem, Cyprus, and Armenia, who died at Rome, A.D. 1487, and probably gave this book to pope Innocent VIII, whose arms are painted at the beginning. It contains effigies of SS. Luke, James, Peter, John, Jude, Paul. (Greg. 326.)

247. (Paul. 295.) Rom. Pal.-Vat. Gr. 38 [xi], 8¾ × 6⅜, ff. 351 (24), *prol., κεφ. t., κεφ., τίτλ., subscr., στίχ.* (Greg. 330.)

248. (Paul. 298.) Berlin, Königl. (Hamilton) 244 (625) [A.D. 1090?], 5⅞ × 4¾, ff. 330 (22), *prol., κεφ. t., subscr., στίχ., syn., men.* It contains the Acts, Cath. and St. Paul, as Dr. C. de Boor informs us. (*See* Greg. 303.)

249. (Paul. 299.) Berlin, Königl. Gr. 4to, 40 [xiii, Greg. xi], 10¾ × 5¾, ff. 222 (26), 2 cols., *prol., κεφ. t., lect., subscr., στίχ.*, same contents as the preceding. (*See* Greg. 252.)

250. (Paul. 300.) Berlin, Königl. Gr. 4to, 43 [xi, Greg. xiv], 9⅝ × 7, ff. 116 (39), *prol., κεφ., τίτλ., lect., subscr., στίχ., syn., men.*, same contents as the preceding, but commences with the Psalms. (*See* Greg. 302.)

251. (Paul. 301.) Berlin, Königl. Gr. 4to, 57 [xiv, Greg. xiii], 8⅝ × 6, ff. ?, *prol., κεφ. t., chart.*, same contents as Act. 248. (*See* Greg. 248.)

252. (Evan. 642, Paul. 302.) Berlin, Königl. Gr. 8vo, 9. (Greg. 213.)

253, 254, 255, 257, 260 were discovered on the spot by Dr. Gregory not to be Codd. Act.

253. (Paul. 248.) Cairo, Patriarch. Alex. Library 8 [xiv], 4to, *chart.*, Cath. (Greg. 240.)

254. (Paul. 275.) Cair. Patr. Alex. Libr. 59 [xi], 4to, Acts and all Epistles. (Greg. 241.)

255. (Paul. 296.) Cair. Patr. Alex. Libr. 88 [xi], fol, Acts and all Epistles, after Psalms. (Greg. 242.)

256. (Paul. 322.) Rom. Vat. Gr. 2099 [x, Greg. xi], 7¼ × 6, ff. 125 (21), *Euth., κεφ., τίτλ., lect., subscr.* Though numbered from 'Acts,' it contains only the Cath. Epp. (*See* Greg. 329.)

257. (Paul. 303.) Jerusalem, Holy Sepulchre 7 [x], 4to. Act., Cath., Paul., begins at Acts xii. 6. (Greg. 183?)

258. (Paul. 306.) Jerus. Holy Sep. 15 [x, end], 4to, with rich scholia. (Greg. 184 ?)

259. (Evan. 657.)   (Greg. 208.)

260. (Evan. 661.)   (Greg. 209.)

261. (Paul. 336.)   Rom. Casanatensis G. ii. 6 [xv or xvi], $12\tfrac{7}{8} \times 23\tfrac{1}{4}$, ff. ?, *subscr.*, *vers.*, στίχ., Catholic and Pauline Epistles with a catena. (*See* Greg. 321.)

The next three were added by the Abbé Martin.

262. (Evan. 738.)   (Greg. 259.)

263. Par. Nat. Suppl. Gr. 906 [xii–xiii], $8\tfrac{1}{8} \times 5\tfrac{3}{4}$, ff. 48 (20). *Mut.* Acts xi. 5–22; xvi. 1–16; xxii. 10—xxviii. 31; James i. 1—ii. 18; iv. 3—v. 20. *Prol.* (Greg. 249.)

264. (Paul. 337.) Paris, Nat. Coislin. 224 [xi], 10×8, ff. 379 (20), *syn.*, *Euth.*, Act., Cath., Paul. (Greg. 250.)

We now follow Dr. Gregory's order as far as is possible, and refer students to his pages where Library Catalogues and other sources of information do not supply particulars.

265. (Evan. 808.)   266. (Evan. 823.)
267. (Evan. 858.) (Greg. 261.)   268. (Evan. 698.)
269. (Evan. 794.) (Greg. 262.)   270. (Evan. 922.)
271. (Evan. 927.)   272. (Evan. 935.)
273. (Evan. 941.)   274. (Evan. 945.)
275. (Evan. 956.)   276. (Evan. 959.)
277. (Evan. 986.)   278. (Evan. 996.)
279. (Evan. 997.)   280. (Evan. 999.)
281. (Evan. 1003.)   282. (Evan. 1040.)
283. (Evan. 1058.)   284. (Evan. 1072.)
285. (Evan. 1073.)   286. (Evan. 1075.)
287. (Evan. 1094.)   288. (Evan. 1149.)
289. (Evan. 1240.)   290. (Evan. 1241.)
291. (Evan. 1242.)   292. (Evan. 1243.)
293. (Evan. 1244.)   294. (Evan. 1245.)
295. (Evan. 1246.)   296. (Evan. 1247.)
297. (Evan. 1248.)   298. (Evan. 1249.)
299. (Evan. 1250.)   300. (Evan. 1251.)

301. (Paul. 334, Apoc. 109.) St. Saba 20 [xi, beginning], 4to, Act., Cath. (Greg. 243.)

302. (Paul. 313.) St. Saba 35 [xi], 4to. (Greg. 244.)

303. (Apoc. 185.) Lesbos, τ. Λείμωνος μονῆς 132 [xv], $8\tfrac{1}{4} \times 5\tfrac{1}{4}$, *chart.*, *mut.* at beginning and end.

304. (Paul. 331.) Athens, Nat. Theol. (207, 70) [xiii], $6\tfrac{3}{8} \times 4\tfrac{3}{4}$, ff. 321. Very beautiful. Written by Cosmas.

305. (Paul. 332.) Ath. Nat. Theol. (208, 7) [xiv], $7\frac{1}{2} \times 5\frac{1}{5}$, ff. 273, with Œcumenius.

306. (Paul. 333.) Ath. Nat. Theol. (209, 72) [A. D. 1364], $8\frac{1}{4} \times 5\frac{7}{8}$, ff. 250. Written by Constantine Alexopoulos. Restored by Nicolaus in A.D. 1464.

307. (Paul. 469, Apoc. 111.) Ath. Nat. 43 (149 ?) [x], $8\frac{5}{8} \times 6\frac{3}{8}$.

308. (Paul. 420.) Ath. Nat. (45).

309. (Paul. 300, Apoc. 124.) Ath. Nat. 64 (91) [x], $9 \times 7\frac{1}{8}$, ff. 327. Apoc. ends at xviii. 22.

310. Ath. Nat. 66 (105) [x], $9\frac{7}{8} \times 7\frac{1}{2}$, ff. 293. Sixteen homilies of St. Chrysostom on the Acts. Eight leaves at the beginning are of cent. xiv.

311. (Paul. 419.) Ath. Nat. 221 (129 ?) [xiii], $5\frac{3}{8} \times 4\frac{1}{4}$, ff. 224.

312. (Paul. 421.) Ath. Nat. (119) [xii], $9\frac{7}{8} \times 5\frac{1}{2}$, ff. 356, *chart*.

313. (Paul. 422.) Ath. Nat. 89 [xii], $11\frac{3}{8} \times 8\frac{1}{4}$, ff. 220. *Mut.* Acts i. 1—vii. 35.

314. Zante.   315. (Paul. 474.) Petersburg, Imp. Porfirianus.

316. Madrid, Royal O. 78.

317. (Evan. 667.) Coxe, St. Saba 53. (Greg. 211.)

318. (Evan. 673.) Coxe, St. Saba 54. (Greg. 212.)

319. (Paul. 318.) Patmos 27 [xii], fol., Act., Cath., Paul., with marginal gloss. Coxe.

320. (Paul. 320.) Patmos 31 [ix], fol., Act., Cath., Paul. Coxe.

321. (Evan. 796.) (Greg. 263.)   322. Athos, Iveron 639.

323. (Paul. 429.) Lesb. τ. Λείμ. 55.   324. Jerusalem, Holy Cross 1.

325. (Paul. 495, Apoc. 187.) Athens, Nat. Libr. 91 [x], $9 \times 7\frac{1}{8}$, ff. 327, *orn., mus., mut.* Apoc. xviii. 22–end.

326. (Evan. 801.) (Greg. 264.)   327. Rom. Vat. Gr. 1227.

328. (Evan. 665.) (Greg. 210.)   329. (Evan. 1267.)

330. (Paul. 491.) Jerus. Patr. Libr. 462 [xiv]?, 535 pages *chart.*, ff. 60 (58 first and 2 last [xxi], κεφ. t., *syn., proll.*

331. (Paul. 145.) Contains also James, 1 Pet., 2 Pet. i. 1–3.

332. (Paul. 434.) Ven. Marc. ii. 114.

333. (Paul. 435.) Edinburgh, Mr. Mackellar.

334. (Paul. 319.) Rom. Vat. Gr. 1971 [x], $6\frac{3}{4} \times 5\frac{1}{4}$, ff. 247 (31), 2 cols., *Euth., proll.,* κεφ. t., *lect.,* ἀναγν., *subscr.,* στίχ., *men.* (See Greg. 268.)

335. (Paul. 329.) Vindob. Caes. Gr. Theol. 141. (Greg. 245.)

336. Athos, Vatopedi 41.   337. Ath. Vat. 201.

338. Ath. Vat. 203.   339. Ath. Vat. 210.

340. Ath. Vat. 259.   341. Ath. Vat. 328.

342. Ath. Vat. 380.   343. Ath. Vat. 419.

344. Ath. Dionysius 68.   345. Ath. Dion. 75.

346. Ath. Dion. 382.	347. Ath. Docheiariou 38.
348. Ath. Doch. 48.	349. Ath. Doch. 136.
350. Ath. Doch. 139.	351. Ath. Doch. 147.
352. Ath. Esphigmenou 63.	353. Ath. Esphig. 64.
354. Ath. Esphig. 65.	355. Ath. Esphig. 66.
356. Ath. Esphig. 67.	357. Ath. Esphig. 68.
358. Ath. Iveron 24.	359. Ath. Iveron 25.
360. Ath. Iveron 37.	361. Ath. Iveron 57.
362. Ath. Iveron 60.	363. Ath. Iveron 642.
364. Ath. Iveron 643.	365. Ath. Iveron 648.
366. Ath. Constamonitou 108.	367. Ath. Coutloumoussi 16.
368. Ath. Coutloum. 57.	369. Ath. Coutloum. 80.
370. Ath. Coutloum. 81.	371. Ath. Coutloum. 82.
372. Ath. Coutloum. 83.	373. Ath. Coutloum. 275.
374. Ath. Paul 2.	375. Ath. Protaton 32.
376. Ath. Simopetra 42.	377. Ath. Stauroniketa 52.
378. Ath. Philotheou 38.	379. Ath. Philoth. 76.
380. Beratinus Archiepisc.	381. Cairo, Patriarch. Alex. 942.
382. Chalcis, Mon. Trin. 16.	383. Chalcis, Schol. 9.
384. Chalcis, Schol. 26.	385. Chalcis, Schol. 33.
386. Chalcis, Schol. 96.	387. Patmos, St. John 14.
388. Patmos, St. John 15.	389. Patmos, St. John 16.
390. Patmos, St. John 263.	391. Thessalonica, Gr. Gymn. 12.
392. Thessalonica, Gr. Gymn. 15.	393. Thessalonica, Gr. Gymn. 16.
394. Sinaitic 274.	395. Sinaitic 275.
396. Sinaitic 276.	397. Sinaitic 277.
398. Sinaitic 278.	399. Sinaitic 279.
400. Sinaitic 280.	401. Sinaitic 281.
402. Sinaitic 282.	403. Sinaitic 283.
404. Sinaitic 284.	405. Sinaitic 285.
406. Sinaitic 287.	407. Sinaitic 288.
408. Sinaitic 289.	409. Sinaitic 290.
410. Sinaitic 291.	411. Sinaitic 292.
412. Sinaitic 293.	413. Sinaitic 300.
414. Sinaitic 301.	

415. (Paul. 329.) Vindob. Caes. Gr. Theol. 150. (Greg. 246.)

From Ἱεροσολυμιτικὴ Βιβλιοθήκη, by Papadopoulos Kerameus.

416. (Paul. 58, Apoc. 181.) Jerusalem, Patriarch. Libr. 38 [xi beg.], $9\frac{3}{8} \times 7\frac{1}{2}$, ff. 280 (i.e. 89+234), (syn. for July and August [xiii]), pict.,

mut. Acts i. 1–11, Life of St. Paul. Heb. at end of Paul. Written at Constantinople by Theophanes. Belonged to Matthew a monk, and to monastery of St. Saba.

417. (Paul. 64.) Jerus. Patr. Libr. 43 [xii], 8⅞ × 6, ff. 138 (28). *Prol., mut.* Acts i. 1—xii. 9. Epp. of Paul with Heb. at end follow Acts. Came from St. Saba.

From Ἔκθεσις Παλαιογραφικῶν καὶ Φιλολογικῶν Ἐρεύνων ἐν Θράκῃ καὶ Μακεδονίᾳ, by Papadopoulos Kerameus.

418. (Paul. 492.) Cosinitsa, Ἁγία Μονή, Ματθαῖος ἱερεύς 54 [A.D. 1344], Acts, Cath. Epp. Written by the aforenamed.

From Κατάλογος τῶν ἐν ταῖς Βιβλιοθήκαις τοῦ Ἁγίου Ὄρους Ἑλληνικῶν Κωδίκων ὑπὸ Σπυρίδωνος Π. Λαμπρός 1888.

419. (Paul. 493, Apoc. 185.) Athos, Monastery of St. Paul 2 [A.D. 800??], 4to, said to have been written by the Empress Mary, who had been divorced by Constantine VI, and shut up in a convent in Cilicia. At the end of the Apoc. it has the subscription, σταυρέ, φύλαττε βασίλισσαν Μαρίαν. Some leaves in the beginning and middle *chart.* [xviii].

420. (Paul. 494.) Athens, Nat. Libr. 222 [xvii], 12⅕ × 7⅞, ff. 246. After the Κατηχήσεις of Theodorus Studita, Act., Cath., Paul.

CHAPTER XI.

CURSIVE MANUSCRIPTS OF ST. PAUL'S EPISTLES.

*1. (Evan. 1.)   2. (Act. 2.)   3. (Evan. 3.)
4. (Act. 4.)   5. (Evan. 5.)   6. (Evan. 6.)

7. Basil. A. N. iii. 11, 11¼ × 8½, ff. 387 (11), *prol.*, with notes and a finely written marginal commentary, ends Heb. xii. 18. But Rom., 1, 2 Cor. are in a different hand. It is plain that Erasmus must have used this copy, cf. Rom. v. 21; vi. 19; viii. 35; xv. 31; xvi. 22; 1 Cor. xi. 15; 2 Cor. v. 4; ix. 8; 12; Gal. i. 6; iii. 27; Phil. iii. 9; Col. i. 6; iii. 17; 1 Thess. i. 7; Tit. iii. 8; Philem. 15; Heb. v. 4; vii. 5, in all which places it countenances peculiar readings of his first edition. It contained τό in Rom. iv. 4, but not καὶ πεισθέντες in Heb. xi. 13 (Wetstein, Hoskier).

8. (Act. 50.)   9. (Act. 7.)   10. (Act. 8.)
11. (Act. 9.)   12. (Act. 10.) See Act. 7.

13. Certain readings cited by J. le Fevre d'Etaples, in his commentary on St. Paul's Epistles, Paris, 1512.

14. (Evan. 90.)

15. A manuscript cited by Erasmus, belonging to Amandus of Louvain.

16. (Act. 12.)   *17. (Evan. 33.) See Act. 7.
18. (Evan. 35.)   19. (Act. 16.)

20. Par. Nat. Coislin. Gr. 27, described (as is Cod. 23) by Montfaucon [x], 13¾ × 10½, ff. 252 (39), in bad condition, with *prol.* and a catena, from Laura at Athos (Wetstein). See Act. 7.

21. (Act. 17.)   22. (Act. 18.)

23. Par. Nat. Coisl. Gr. 28 [A.D. 1056], 14¾ × 10½, ff. 272 (47), *prol.*, κεφ., τίτλ., *subscr.*, στίχ. (Wetstein, Scholz). From Laura.

24. (Evan. 105.)   25. (Act. 20.)   26. (Act. 21.)

27. Cambr. Univ. Libr. Ff. i. 30 [xii], 11¾ × 8¼, ff. 169 (varies), *prol.*, κεφ. t., κεφ., *lect.*, *subscr.*, στίχ., with Œcumenius' commentary: Rom. and 1, 2 Cor. are wanting (Wetstein, 1716). Bradshaw found that this manuscript, which came to Cambridge in 1574, is only the second part of Paul. 42, the last quire of the latter being numbered κα΄, while the first in Cod. 27 is κβ΄. Hort's Paul. 27 is k^{scr} or Paul. 260.

28. (Act. 23.)   *29. (Act. 24.)   *30. (Act. 53.)

31. (Act. 25.)   32. (Act. 26.)   33. (Act. 27.)
*34. (Act. 28.)   35. (Act. 29.)   36. (Act. 30.)
*37. (Evan. 69.) 38. (Evan. 51.)   39. (Act. 33.)
*40. (Evan. 61.) 41. (Evan. 57.)

42. Oxf. Magdalen Coll. Gr. 7 [xii], $11\frac{3}{4} \times 8\frac{1}{4}$, ff. 170 (varies), *prol.*, κεφ., *lect.*, contains Rom., 1, 2 Cor. surrounded by Œcumenius' commentary (Walton's Polyglott, Mill). First part of Paul. 27.

43. (Act. 37.)   *44. (Act. 38.)
45. (Act. 39.)   46. (Act. 40.)

47. Oxf. Bodl. Roe 16 [xi], $11\frac{3}{8} \times 8\frac{1}{2}$, ff. 255 (15), *prol.*, *subscr.*, στίχ., with a Patristic catena, in a small and beautiful hand, having a text much resembling that of Cod. A, and Cod. B still more often when the two stand alone: its history is the same as that of Evan. 49. The Epistle to the Hebrews precedes 1 Tim. (Mill, Roe 2, Tregelles for his edition of the N. T.: inspected by Vansittart.)

*48. (Act. 42.)   49. (Evan. 76.)   50. (Act. 52.)
51. (Evan. 82, Act. 44, Apoc. 5.)   52. (Act. 45.)

53 of Wetstein is now Paul. Cod. M, the portion containing the Hebrews, or Bengel's Uffenbach 2 or 1. Instead—
    (Evan. 1149.)   (Greg. 336.)

54. Monacensis Reg. Gr. 412 [xii], $11\frac{7}{8} \times 8\frac{3}{8}$, ff. 358 (24), is Bengel's August. 5 (see Act. 46), containing Rom. vii. 7—xvi. 24, with a catena from twenty Greek authors (*see* Paul. 127), stated by Bengel to resemble that in the Bodleian described by Mill (N. T., Proleg. § 1448).

55. (Act. 46.)

56. This is worthless as being a transcript of Erasmus' first edition, then just published. Instead—
    (Evan. 1262.)

*57. (Evan. 218.)

58. Rom. Vat. Gr. 1650 [1]=Act. 156, Paul. 190. Instead—
    (Act. 416.)

59. Par. Nat. Coisl. Gr. 204 [xi], $11 \times 8\frac{7}{8}$, ff. 312 (32). *Mut.* Rom., 1 Cor., 2 Cor. is in the 3rd of 3 vols. *See* Cramer's Catena. (Greg.) Wetstein and Griesbach comprise readings of two Medicean manuscripts of the Ephes. and Philipp., derived from the same source as Evan. 102, Act. 56, Apoc. 23.

60. Codices cited in the Correctorium Bibliorum Latinorum.

*61. (Act. 61.)   62. (Act. 59.)   63. (Act. 60.)

64 of Griesbach is the portion of Evan. M. Instead—
    (Act. 417.)

65. (Act. 62.)

---

[1] From the monastery of Grotta Ferrata, near Tusculum, 'Ubi degunt ab antiquo tempore monachi, ordinis S. Basilii Magni, ritum Italo-Graecum observantes,' Holmes. Praef. ad Pentateuch. on his Cod. 128, which came to the Vatican from the same place. It is the traditional Villa Luculli.

66. Lond. Brit. Mus. Harl. 5552 [xvi], 6½ × 4¼, ff. 233 (18). This number included readings extracted by Griesbach from the margin of this MS., which itself he considers but a transcript of Erasmus' first edition (Symb. Crit., p. 166).

67. (Act. 66.)   67** resembles Cod. B, yet is independent of it (Eph. iii. 9, iv. 9, &c.).   'These marginal readings must have been derived from a MS. having a text nearly akin to that of the fragmentary MS. called M, though not from M itself' (Hort, Introduction, p. 155).

68. (Act. 63.)   69. (Act. 64.)   70. (Act. 67.)

71. Vindobon. Caesar. Gr. 61 [xii, Greg. x or xi], 9½ × 6¾, ff. 170 (29), 2 cols., prol., κεφ. t., κεφ., τίτλ., lect., μαρτ., subscr., ἀναγν., στίχ. Mut. Rom. i. 1–4 ; ii. 3–8, &c.   Titus ; Philem. ; with Hebrews before 1 Tim. It includes a commentary and catechetical lectures of St. Cyril of Jerusalem (Alter, Birch, Greg.).

72. (Evan. 234.)   73. (Act. 68.)

74. (Act. 69.)

75. (Brit. Mus. Add. 5116, see Act. 22.)

*76. Leipzig, Univ. Gr. 361 [xiii], 12½ × 9½, ff. out of 327, 85 (35), prol., κεφ., contains Rom., 1 Cor., Gal., and part of Eph., with Theophylact's commentary, and other matter (Matthaei, Gregory).

Codd. 77–112 were cursorily collated by Birch, and nearly all by Scholz.

77. (Evan. 131.)   78. (Evan. 133.)
79. (Act. 72.)   80. (Act. 73[1].)

81. Rom. Vat. Gr. 761 [xii], 13¾ × 10, ff. 266, Euth., κεφ., τίτλ., subscr., στίχ., with Œcumenius' commentary.   The Epistle to the Hebrews is wanting.

82. Rom. Vat. Gr. 762 [xii], 12⅛ × 9, ff. 411, Euth., contains Rom., 1, 2 Cor., with a catena.

83. Rom. Vat. Gr. 765 [xi], 14⅕ × 11⅝, ff. 177, Euth., with a commentary.

84. Rom. Vat. Gr. 766 [xii], 14¾ × 11⅜, prol., κεφ., τίτλ., with a commentary.

85. (Apoc. 39.)   Rom. Vat. Gr. 1136 [xiii, Greg. xiv], 10 × 6¾, ff. 60 (46), contains *first* the Apocalypse (beginning ch. iii. 8) with a Latin version, then St. Paul's Epistles ending 1 Tim. vi. 5, with many unusual readings.

86. (Evan. 141.)   87. (Evan. 142.)
88. (Evan. 149.)   89. (Act. 78.)
90. (Act. 79.)   91. (Act. 80.)
92. (Evan. 180.)   93. (Act. 83.)
94. (Act. 84.)   95. (Act. 85.)

[1] Birch shows the connexion of Caryophilus with this important copy (which much resembles the Leicester manuscript, Evan. Cod. 69) from James v. 5, and especially from 3 John 5 μισθόν for πιστόν, a *lectio singularis*. In this codex, as in the others cited, Heb. stands before 1 Tim.

96. (Act. 86.) The same copy as Paul. 183 in the last edition.

97. (Act. 87.)   98. (Act. 88.)   99. (Act. 89.)

100. Flor. Laurent. x. 4 [xii], 12¼ × 9½, ff. 426 (28), with a commentary and additional scholia [xiv], from the Cistercian monastery of S. Salvator de Septimo, in the diocese of Florence.

101. Flor. Laurent. x. 6 [xi, Greg. x], 13½ × 10¼, ff. 285, *prol.*, κεφ. t., κεφ., τίτλ., *subscr.*, στίχ., with a catena supplying the authors' names.

102. Flor. Laurent. x. 7 [xi], 13 × 9⅜, ff. 270, *prol.*, κεφ., τίτλ., *subscr.*, στίχ., *syn.*, *men.*, a life of St. Paul, and catena with such names attached as Theodoret, Chrysostom, Œcumenius, Severianus, &c.

103. Flor. Laurent. x. 19 [xiii], 9¾ × 7⅜, ff. 260, *prol.*, κεφ. t., κεφ., τίτλ., *lect.*, *subscr.*, στίχ., *syn.*, *men.*, with a catena. At the end is a date, 'A.D. 1318, Ind. 1, Timotheus.'

*104. (Evan. 201 or b^scr.) Examined by Bloomfield.

105. (Evan. 204.) Dean Burgon has received a facsimile of 1 Tim. iii. 16 from the librarian at Bologna.

106. (Evan. 205.)   107. (Evan. 206.)

108. (Evan. 209.)   *109. (Act. 96.)

*110. Venet. Marc. 33 [xi], 15¾ × 12⅞, ff. 369, *prol.*, with a catena, much being taken from Œcumenius (Rink, as also 111, 112: *see* Act. 96).

*111. Ven. Marc. 34 [xi], 13⅛ × 10½, ff. 332, *prol.*, κεφ. t., κεφ., τίτλ., *vers.*, with a commentary.

*112. Ven. Marc. 35 [xi], 14½ × 11¾, ff. 159 (40), with a commentary, a fragment beginning 2 Cor. i. 20, ending Heb. x. 25; *mut.* 1 Thess. iv. 13—2 Thess. ii. 14.

Codd. 113-124 were collated by Matthaei.

*113. (Act. 98.)   *114. (Act. 99.)

*115. (Act. 100.)   *116. (Act. 101.)

*117. (Act. 102.)   *118. (Act. 103.)

*119. Mosc. Synod. 292 [x–xii], 4to, ff. 462, from the monastery of Pantocrator on Athos, contains 1, 2 Corinth., with Theophylact's commentary. (Matthaei.)

*120. (Evan. 241.)   *121. (Evan. 242.)

*122. (Act. 106.)

*123. Mosc. Syn. 99 [x or xi], fol., ff. 241, *prol.*, κεφ. t., with scholia, from St. Athanasius' monastery (Laura).

*124. Mosc. Syn. 250 (Mt. q) [xiv], 8vo, ff. 40 (i.e. 117-157), on cotton paper, from the monastery of Vatopedi on Athos, contains Rom. i-xiii, with Theophylact's commentary and other writings.

Codd. 125-230 were first catalogued by Scholz, who professes to have collated entire Paul. 177-179, in the greater part Paul. 157, the rest slightly or not at all.

125. Munich, Reg. Gr. 504 [*dated* Feb. 1, 1387, Indict. 10], 8⅝ × 5½, ff. 381 (33), *prol.*, on cotton paper, with Theophylact's commentary in black

ink, and the text (akin to it) in red. Bought by Nicetas 'primicerius sceuophylactus' for eight golden ducats of Rhodes[1]. *Mut.* Philemon.

126. Munich, Reg. Gr. 455, either a copy of, or derived from Cod. 125. [*dated* Feb. 17, Indict. 12, probably A.D. 1389], $10\frac{1}{2} \times 8\frac{1}{4}$, ff. 439 (32), *chart.*, also *mut.* Philem.; with Theophylact's commentary, and some homilies of Chrysostom. From internal reasons 125 is probably the older of the two (J. Rendel Harris).

127. Munich, Reg. Gr. 110 [xvi], $13\frac{1}{3} \times 8\frac{1}{2}$, ff. 112, *chart.*, once at the Jesuits' College, Munich, contains Rom. vii. 7—ix. 21, with a catena. It was found by Scholz to be, what indeed it professes, a mere copy of part of Cod. 54. (Greg. 54a.)

128. (Act. 179.)

129. Munich, Reg. Gr. 35 [xvi], $13\frac{5}{8} \times 8\frac{1}{2}$, ff. 488 (30), *chart.*, with catena.

130. (Evan. 43.)   131. (Evan. 330.)
*132. (Evan. 18: *see* Act. 113.)   133. (Act. 51.)
*134. (Act. 114.)   135. (Act. 115.)
136. (Act. 116.)   *137. (Evan. 263.)   *See* Act. 7.
138. (Act. 118.)   *139. (Act. 119), Reiche, as also
*140. (Act. 11.)   141. (Act. 120.)
142. (Act. 121.)   143. (Act. 122.)
144. (Act. 123.)

145. Par. Nat. Gr. 108, 109, 110, 111 [xvi, Greg. xv], $7 \times 4\frac{3}{4}$, ff. 308 (14), *prol.*, κεφ. τ., κεφ. *Mut.* Gal., Eph. (2 Cor. xiii. 1–13 later). Written by George Hermonymus. *See* Act. 331. (Gregory under Act. 331.) Once Colbert's, as were 146, 147, 148.

146, 147, 148—included under 145.

149. (Act. 124.)   150. (Act. 125.)

151. Par. Nat. Gr. 126 [xvi], $4\frac{3}{4} \times 3$, ff. 168 (18), *subscr.*, written (like 149) by Angelus Vergecius.

152. Instead of Par. Nat. Gr. 136a (omit Greg.)—
    (Evan. 657.)   (Greg. 264.)
*153. (Act. 126) Reiche.   154. (Act. 127.)
155. (Act. 128.)   156. (Act. 129.)

157. Par. Nat. Gr. 222 [xi], $12\frac{1}{2} \times 10\frac{1}{2}$, ff. 227, *pict.*, once Colbert's, brought from Constantinople in 1676, with a commentary. *Mut.* Rom. i. 1–11; 21–29; iii. 26—iv. 8; ix. 11–22; 1 Cor. xv. 22–43; Col. i. 1–16.

158. (Act. 131.)

159. (Apoc. 64.) Par. Nat. Gr. 224 [xi], $11\frac{3}{4} \times 8\frac{3}{4}$, ff. 274, *prol.*, *pict.*, κεφ. τ., κεφ., τίτλ., *subscr.*, στίχ., very elegant. The Pauline Epistles have a catena, the Apocalypse Arethas' commentary.

---

[1] The gold ducat coined for the Military Order of St. John at Rhodes (*see* Ducange) was worth 9s. 6d. English money.

160. Par. Nat. Gr. 225 [xvi], 12×8, ff. 401 (29), *chart.*, a fragment of St. Paul, with Theophylact's commentary.

161. Par. Nat. Gr. 226 [xvi], $12\frac{1}{4} \times 8\frac{1}{2}$, ff. 96 (34), *chart.*, contains the Romans, with a commentary.

162. Par. Nat. Gr 227 [xvi], $13\frac{1}{2} \times 9$, ff. 213 (31), *chart.*, once Bigot's, contains a catena on 1 Cor. xvi.

163. Par. Nat. Gr. 238 [xiii], $7\frac{3}{4} \times 5\frac{1}{4}$, ff. 391 (23), from Adrianople, contains Heb. i–viii, with a catena.

164. Par. Nat. Gr. 849 [xvi], $12\frac{7}{8} \times 9\frac{1}{8}$, ff. 261 (30), *chart.*, *prol.*, *subscr.*, once a Medicean manuscript, contains Theodoret's commentary with text.

165. Turin, Univ. C. vi. 29 [xvi], $8\frac{1}{8} \times 5\frac{5}{8}$, ff. 71 (17), *chart.*, contains from 1 Thess. to Hebrews.

166. (Act. 133.) 167. (Act. 134.)

168. Turin, Univ. C. v. 10, $8\frac{5}{8} \times 6\frac{3}{8}$, ff. 239 (29), *prol.*, *κεφ. t.*, *στίχ.*, and a commentary: it begins Rom. iii. 19.

169. (Act. 136.) 170. (Evan. 339.)

171. Milan, Ambros. B. 6 inf. [xiii], $13\frac{1}{8} \times 10\frac{1}{4}$, ff. 241, *prol.*, *κεφ. t.*, *κεφ.*, *τίτλ.*, *subscr.*, *στίχ.*, with a commentary: it ends Heb. iv. 7, and Rom. i. 1—2 Cor. v. 19 are later, on cotton paper.

172. Milan, Ambr. A. 51 sup. [xii], $8\frac{1}{8} \times 6\frac{5}{8}$, ff. 175 (35), *lect.*, *subscr.*, with an abridgement of Chrysostom's commentary: bought at Reggio in Calabria, 1606.

173. (Act. 138.) 174. (Act. 139.)

175. Milan, Ambr. F. 125 sup. [xv], $12\frac{1}{8} \times 7\frac{1}{2}$, ff. 341 (30), *chart.*, with a continuous commentary: it was brought from Thessaly.

176. (Act. 137.)

*177. Modena, Este ii. A. 14 [xv], 16mo. Lost (Greg.).

*178. (Act. 142.)

*179. Modena, Este ii. G. 3,—the minuscule part of Act. H. The Pauline Epistles with a commentary are [xii].

180. (Evan. 363.) 181. (Evan. 643.)

182. (Evan. 367.) 183. (Act. 254.)

184. (Act. 148.) 185. (Evan. 393.)

186. (Evan. 394.) 187. (Act. 154.)

188. (Act. 155.)

189. Rom. Vat. Gr. 1649 [xiii], $12\frac{7}{8} \times 10$, ff. 137 (48), 2 cols., *prol.*, with Theodoret's commentary: Heb. precedes 1 Tim.

190. (Act. 156.) 191. (Act. 157.)

192. (Act. 158.) 193. (Act. 160.)

194. (Evan. 175.)

195. Rom. Vat. Ottob. 31 [x, Greg. xi], $14\frac{5}{8} \times 10\frac{1}{4}$, ff. 181, *mut.* Rom.

and most of 1 Cor.; with a continuous commentary, and such names as Œcumenius, Theodoret, Methodius, occasionally mentioned.

196. Rom. Vat. Ottob. 61 [xv], $9\frac{3}{4} \times 6\frac{3}{4}$, ff. 198 (48), *chart.*, with a commentary: here, as in Paul. 189, the Epistle to the Hebrews precedes 1 Tim.

197. (Apoc. 78.) Rom. Vat. Ottob. 176 [xv], 8vo, *chart.*

198. (Act. 161.)   199. (Evan. 386.)

200. (Act. 162.)   201. (Act. 163.)

202. Rom. Vat. Ottob. 356 [xv], $9\frac{1}{2} \times 6\frac{5}{9}$, ff. 144 (22), *chart.*, 'olim Aug. ducis ab Altamps,' contains Rom. with a catena.

203. (Evan. 390.)   204. (Act. 166.)

205. (Act. 168.)   206. (Act. 169.)

207. Rom. Ghigian. R. v. 32 [A.D. 1394], $10 \times 6\frac{3}{8}$, ff. 279 (42), *chart.*, with a commentary.

208. Rom. Ghigian. R. viii. 55 [xi], $14\frac{3}{4} \times 10\frac{5}{8}$, ff. 168, *prol., κεφ. τ., subscr., στίχ.*, with Theodoret's commentary.

209. (Act. 171.)   210. (Act. 172.)

211. (Act. 173.)   212. (Act. 174.)

213. Rom. Barberin. iv. 85 [A.D. 1338, Greg. 1330?], $10\frac{5}{8} \times 8\frac{1}{8}$, ff. 267, *prol., κεφ., τίτλ., subscr., στίχ.*, scholia. From the reading τοῦ θεοῦ καὶ πατρὸς τοῦ χριστοῦ Col. ii. 2 (*see* below, Vol. II. Chap. XII), this must be one of the Barberini manuscripts described under Evan. 112.

214. Vindobon. Caesar. theol. 167 (166?) [xv, Greg. xiv], $9\frac{3}{8} \times 6\frac{1}{4}$, ff. 70 (40), on cotton paper, contains Rom. with a catena, 1 Cor. with Chrysostom's and Theodoret's commentaries, which influence the readings of the text.

215. (Act. 140.)   216. (Act. 175.)

217. Palermo, I. E. 11 [xii, Greg. x], $8\frac{5}{8} \times 6\frac{3}{4}$, ff. 61 (23), *prol., κεφ. τ., subscr., στίχ.*, begins 2 Cor. iv. 18; *mut.* 2 Tim. i. 8—ii. 14; ends Heb. ii. 9.

218. (Evan. 421.)   219. (Evan. 122.)

220. (Evan. 400.)   *221. (Evan. 440) is o^{scr}.

222. (Evan. 451.)   (Greg. 462.)   223. (Evan. 461.)   (Greg. 463.)

224. (Act. 58.)

Substitute for 225 (=Cod. 11)—

225. Milan, N. 272 sup. [xvi], $9\frac{3}{8} \times 6\frac{1}{8}$, *chart.*, 'S. Pauli Epistolae, cum notis marginalibus' (Burgon). (*See* Greg. 478.)

Substitute for 226 (=Cod. 27)—

226. Florence, Libreria Riccardi 85, rather modern, 8vo, 'Marsilii Ficini Florentini.'

227. (Act. 56 of Scholz.)   228. (Evan. 226.)

229. (Evan. 228.)

230. (Instead of Evan. 368) (Evan. 665)[1]. (Greg. 266.)
231. (Evan. 531.) (Greg. 305.)
232. Escurial ψ. iii. 2 [xv], Montana after Haenel, *chart.* (Greg. 472.)
233. Parham 6 (Evan. 534). (Greg. 258.)
234. (Act. 216.) (Greg. 281.)   235. (Act. 217.) (Greg. 282.)
236. (Act. 218.) (Greg. 283.)   237. (Act. 309.) (Greg. 300.)
238. (Evan. 431.)   239. (Evan. 189.)
240. (Evan. 444.) (Greg. 240.) 241. (Act. 97.)
242. (Act. 178.) (Greg. 242.)   243. (Evan. 605.) (Greg. 303.)
244. (Evan. 503.)   245. (Act. 191.)
246. (Act. 192.)   247. (Act. 210.)
248. (Instead of Act. 201=89) (Act. 253). (Greg. 284.)

Next follow three at Oxford:

249. (Evan. 488.) (Greg. 247.) 250. (Act. 212.) (Greg. 276.)
251. (Act. 213.) (Greg. 277.)

The next ten are Scrivener's, collated in the Appendix to Codex Augiensis:

*252. (Act. 182.) (Greg. 270.)   *253. (Act. 183.) (Greg. 271.)
*254. (Act. 184.) (Greg. 272.)   *255. (Act. 185.) (Greg. 273.)

*256. (Apoc. 93.) Lambeth 1186 or e^scr [xi], 4to, of which a facsimile is given in the Catalogue of Manuscripts at Lambeth, 1812. It contains the Pauline Epistles and the Apocalypse only. It begins Rom. xvi. 15 and ends Apoc. xix. 4. *Mut.* 1 Cor. iv. 19—vi. 1; x. 1-21; Heb. iii. 14—ix. 19; Apoc. xiv. 16—xv. 7. *Lect., prol.,* τίτλ., κεφ., to each Epistle, and a few marginal glosses. (Greg. 290.)

*257. (Evan. 543.) (Greg. 251.) *258. (Evan. 542.) (Greg. 249.)
*259. (Evan. 568.) *[h^scr : *see* Act. 189.] (Greg. 250.)
*260. (Evan. 507.) This is Hort's Paul. 27. (Greg. 252.)
261. Petersburg, Muralt. 8 (Evan. 476). (Greg. 131.)
262. (Act. 223.) (Greg. 248.)
263. *See* Apoc. 91. Contains Heb. ix. 14—xiii. 25 [xv]. (Greg. 293.)

The Baroness Burdett-Coutts has three copies of the Pauline Epistles:

*264. (Act. 220.) (Greg. 278.)   *265. (Act. 221.) (Greg. 279.)

*266. (Evan. 603, Apoc. 89.) Burdett-Coutts (Highgate) II. 4 [x or xi], 11½ × 8½, ff. 67, *orn., proll.,* κεφ. τ., τίτλ. (not in Apocalypse). The ten Pauline Epistles from the Ephesians onwards (that to the Hebrews preceding 1 Timothy), and the Apocalypse complete. On three leaves at the end is the (unfinished) ἐπίγραμμα of Dorotheus of Tyre described

---

[1] Here again we set Scholz's codices in a note, substituting others in their room. Scholz's run, 231. (Act. 183.) 232. (Act. 184.) 233. (Act. 185.) 234. (Evan. 457.) 235. (Evan. 462.) 236. (Act. 188.) 237. (Evan. 466.) 243. (Act. 182), two separate codices.

above, Act. 89. Citations from the Old Testament are specially marked, and the margin contains some scholia and corrections, apparently by the first hand. (Greg. 306.)

267. Brit. Mus. Add. 7142 [xiii], 11¾ × 9, ff. 198, *prol.*, Life of St. Paul, κεφ. τ., κεφ., τίτλ. (*lect.* mostly later), *subscr.*, στίχ., with commentary, partly *mut.* (Greg. 291.)

268. (Evan. 576.) (Greg. 253.)   269. (Evan. 584.) (Greg. 255.)

270. (Act. 229.) (Greg. 275.)   271. (Evan. 603.) (Greg. 306.)

272. (Act. 238.) (Greg. 436.)   273. (Act. 236.) (Greg. 437.)

274. (Act. 237.) (Greg. 319.)

275. Instead of Basil. (only a comm., Greg.)—(Act. 254.) (Greg. 285.)

276. (Act. 321.) (Greg. 312.)   277. (Evan. 492.) (Greg. 256.)

278. (Evan. 560.) (Greg. 307.)   279. (Evan. 582.) (Greg. 254.)

280. (Act. 198.) (Greg. 280.)   281. (Evan. 527.) (Greg. 304.)

282. (Act. 240, Apoc. 109.) (Greg. 259.)

283. (Act. 241.) (Greg. 426.)   284. (Act. 195), Rom. i. 1–5.

285. (Act. 196.) (Greg. 476.)

286. Milan, Ambr. E. 2 infra [xiii], 13¼ × 10¼, ff. 268 (32), *chart.* Four leaves in vellum [xii], 2 cols. The catena of Nicetas 'textus particulatim praemittit commentariis.' (*See* Greg. 393.)

287. Milan, Ambr. A. 241 inf. [xvi], 12⅞ × 8¾, ff. 104 (20), copy of the preceding. (*See* Greg. 393ᵃ.) 'Est Catena ejusdem auctoris ex initio, sed non complectitur totum opus.'

288. Milan, Ambr. D. 541 inf. [xi], 15 × 12¼, ff. 323, *prol.*, κεφ., τίτλ., *subscr.*, στίχ. Text and catena on all St. Paul's Epistles. Came from Thessaly. (*See* Greg. 392.)

289. Milan, Ambr. C. 295 inf. [xi], 14 × 11⅛, ff. 190, *proll.*, κεφ., τίτλ., *subscr.*, στίχ. With a catena. (*See* Greg. 391.)

290. (Evan. 622, Act. 242, Apoc. 110.) (Greg. 316.)

291. (Act. 243.) (Greg. 423.)   292. (Act. 244.) (Greg. 424.)

293. (Act. 245.) (Greg. 425.)   294. (Act. 246.) (Greg. 430.)

295. (Act. 247.) (Greg. 433.)

296. Already mentioned as 213 (Gregory): instead—
(Act. 255.) (Greg. 286.)

297. Rom. Barberini vi. 13 [xi, Greg. xii], 13⅝ × 10½, ff. 195 (18), with scholia, *subscr.*, στίχ., *mut.* (Cf. Greg. 396.)

298. (Act. 248.) (Greg. 261.)   299. (Act. 249.) (Greg. 302.)

300. (Act. 250.) (Greg. 260.)   301. (Act. 251.) (Greg. 298.)

302. (Evan. 642, Act. 252.) (Greg. 269.)

303. Already mentioned as 225 (Gregory): instead—
(Act. 257.) (Greg. 231.)

304. (Evan. 661.) (Greg. 265.)

305. Rom. Vat. Gr. 549 [xii], $8\frac{1}{4} \times 8\frac{1}{4}$ (?), ff. 380 (29), with Theophylact's commentary. (*See* Greg. 398.)

306. Only a commentary of St. Chrysostom, instead—
(Act. 258.) (Greg. 232.)

307. Rom. Vat. Gr. 551 [x], ff. 283, some of St. Paul's Epistles, with commentary of Chrysostom. (Greg. under 398.)

308. Rom. Vat. Gr. 552 [xi], ff. 155, Hebrews, with commentary of Chrysostom. (Greg. under 398.)

Codd. 309, 316, 318, 320, 321, 329, 331–334 are only commentaries of St. Chrysostom (Gregory). Other MSS. are inserted instead.

309. (Act. 301.) (Greg. 242.)

310. Rom. Vat. Gr. 646 [xiv, Greg. xiii], $10\frac{3}{4} \times 7$, ff. 250 ? (31), *chart.*, with commentary of Euthymius, Pars. i et ii. (Greg. 399.)

311. (Evan. 671.) (Greg. 400.)

312. Rom. Vat. Gr. 648 [A.D. 1232], ff. 338, *chart.*, written at Jerusalem by Simeon 'qui et Saba dicitur.' (Greg. 401.)

313. (Act. 239.) (Greg. denies the 'Paul.')

314. Rom. Vat. Gr. 692 [xii, Greg. xi], $13\frac{7}{8} \times 10$, ff. 93, 2 cols., *mut.* Corinthians, Galatians, Ephesians, with commentary. (Greg. 402.)

315. Rom. Vat. Gr. 1222 [xvi], $12 \times 8\frac{1}{8}$, ff. 437 (28), *prol.*, κεφ. t., *subscr.*, στίχ., Rom., Heb., 1, 2 Cor., 1, 2 Tim., Eph., with Theophylact's commentary. (Greg. 403.)

316. (Evan. 667.) (Greg. 267.)

317. (Evan. 673.) (Greg. 268.) · 318. (Act. 319.)

319. (Act. 334.) (Greg. 431.) 320. (Act. 320.)

321. (Act. 186.) (Greg. 274.)

322. (Act. 256.) (Greg. 432.)

323. Rom. Vat. Gr. 2180 [xv], $11\frac{5}{8} \times 8\frac{1}{4}$, ff. 294 (36), *chart.*, κεφ. t., *syn.*, *men.*, with commentary of Theophylact. (*See* Greg. 454.)

324. Rom. Vat. Alex. 4 [x], $12\frac{7}{8} \times 10\frac{3}{4}$, ff. 256 (28), 2 cols., Romans with commentary of Chrysostom. 'Fuit monasterii dicti.' (*See* Greg. 480.)

325. (Evan. 698, Apoc. 117.) (Greg. 317.)

326. Rom. Vat. Ottob. 74 [xv], $12\frac{3}{4} \times 9$, ff. 291 (29) ?, *chart.*, Romans, with Theodoret's commentary. (Greg. 476d.)

327. Rom. Vat. Pal. Gr. 10 [x], $13\frac{1}{2} \times 9\frac{1}{2}$, ff. 268, *proll.*, κεφ., τίτλ., *subscr.*, στίχ., with a Patristic commentary, 'Felkman adnotat.' (Greg. 406.)

328. Rom. Vat. Pal. Gr. 204 [x], $13\frac{1}{4} \times 9\frac{3}{8}$, ff. 181, with commentary of Œcumenius. (Greg. 407.)

329. (Act. 335.) (Greg. 289.)

330. Rom. Vat. Pal. Gr. 423 [xii], $11\frac{3}{4} \times 9\frac{1}{2}$, ff. 2, Coloss. and Thessalon., with commentary. (*See* Greg. 376e.)

331. (Act. 304.) (Greg. 292.) 332. (Act. 305.) (Greg. 295.)

333. (Act. 306.) (Greg. 296.) 334. (Act. 301.) (Greg. 287.)

335. A theological treatise (Greg.). Instead—
(Act. 415.) (Greg. 297.)
336. (Act. 261.) (Greg. 427.)
Instead of Cod. 337. (Greg.)
337. (Act. 264.) (Greg. 299.)
The next four MSS. are from the Abbé Martin's list.
338. Par. Nat. Suppl. Gr. 1001 [xiv], 11⅜ × 8⅜, ff. 12 (31). Fragments of Rom., 2 Tim., Col., Heb. (Greg. 376.)
339. Par. Nat. Coisl. Gr. 95 [xi], 13⅞ × 10, ff. 348 (28), *prol.*, κεφ. *t.*, κεφ., τίτλ., *subscr.*, στίχ. (Greg. 380.)
340. Par. Nat. Coisl. Gr. 217 [xiii], 11 × 8½, ff. 227 (52), *proll.*, κεφ. *t.*, κεφ., τίτλ., *subscr.*, *vers.*, στίχ. (Greg. 381.)
341. (Evan. 38.) (Martin.) (Greg. 377.)

We now follow Dr. Gregory's order, only stating the MS. where there is only his authority to rely upon, and referring students to his list for the information which he has diligently gathered, often by personal examination upon the spot.

342. (Evan. 1245.)   343. (Evan. 1246.)
344. (Evan. 1247.)   345. (Evan. 1248.)
346. (Evan. 1249.)   347. (Evan. 1250.)
348. (Evan. 1251.)   349. (Act. 149.)
350. Leyden, Univ. 66.   351. (Act. 307.)
352. (Act. 381.)   353. (Act. 382.)
354. (Act. 383.)   355. (Act. 384.)
356. (Act. 385.)   357. (Act. 386.)
358. (Act. 387.)   359. (Act. 388.)
360. (Act. 389.)   361. (Act. 390.)
362. (Act. 391.)   363. (Act. 392.)
364. (Act. 393.)   365. (Act. 394.)
366. (Act. 395.)   367. (Act. 399.)
368. (Act. 400.)   369. (Act. 403.)
370. (Act. 413.)

371. Madison, New Caesarea, America.
372. Lond. Brit. Mus. Arundel 534 [xiv], 10¾ × 7, ff. 418 (31). With Theophylact.
373. Vindobon. Caes. Gr. Theol. 157.
374. Besançon, City Libr. 200.   375. Par. Nat. Gr. 224 A.
376. Par. Nat. Suppl. Gr. 1035.
377. Escurial ψ. ii. 20. (Greg. 376c.)
378. Par. Nat. Coisl. Gr. 29.   379. Par. Nat. Coisl. Gr. 30.
380. (Evan. 1267.)   381. (Act. 330.)
382. Athens, Nat. 69 (100) [x], 10⅝ × 7½, ff. 377. *Mut.* beg. and end, with commentary of Œcumenius and others: ff. 44 at beg. [xv].

383. Ath. Nat. 100 (96) [xiii], $12\frac{1}{8} \times 8\frac{5}{8}$, ff. 319. First leaf perished.
384. Escurial χ. iv. 15.
385. Bologna, Univ. 2378.
386. Florence, Laur. vi. 8.
387. Flor. Laur. x. 9.
388. Flor. Laur. xi. 7.
389. Flor. Laur. Conv. Soppr. 21.
390. Milan, Ambr. A. 62 inf.
391. Milan, Ambr. C. (E ?) 295.
392. Milan, Ambr. D. 541 inf.
393. (Act. 309.) (Greg. 300.)
394. Naples, Nat. II. B. 23.
395. Naples, II. B. 24.
396. (Act. 418.) (Greg. 301.)
397. Rome, Casanatensis G. v. 7.
398. (Evan. 825.) (Greg. 308.)
399. (Evan. 757.) (Greg. 309.)
400. (Evan. 767.) (Greg. 310.)
401. (Evan. 794.) (Greg. 311.)
402. (Evan. 801.) (Greg. 313.)
403. (Evan. 808.) (Greg. 314.)
404. (Evan. 823.) (Greg. 315.)
405. Rom. Vat. Ottob. 17.
406. (Evan. 891.) (Greg. 318.)
407. (Evan. 922.) (Greg. 320.)
408. Venet. Marc. 36.
409. Athos, Coutloumoussi 90[b].
410. Ath. Coutloum. 129.
411. Constantinople, Holy Sepulchre 2.
412. Constant. H. Sep. 3.
413. Patmos, St. John 61.
414. Patmos, St. John 62.
415. Patmos, St. John 63.
416. Patmos, St. John 116.
417. St. Saba, Tower 41.
418. Groningen, Univ. A. C. 1.
419. (Act. 311.)
420. (Act. 308.)
421. (Act. 312.)
422. (Act. 313.)
423. (Evan. 927.) (Greg. 321.)
424. (Evan. 935.) (Greg. 322.)
425. (Evan. 941.) (Greg. 323.)
426. (Evan. 945.) (Greg. 324.)
427. (Evan. 959.) (Greg. 325.)
428. (Evan. 1267.)
429. (Act. 323.) (Apoc. 127.)
430. (Evan. 986.) (Greg. 326.)
431. (Evan. 996.) (Greg. 327.)
432. (Evan. 997.) (Greg. 328.)
433. (Evan. 999.) (Greg. 329.)
434. (Act. 332.)
435. (Act. 333.)
436. (Evan. 1003.) (Greg. 330.)
437. (Evan. 1040.) (Greg. 331.)
438. (Act. 344.)
439. (Act. 346.)
440. (Act. 347.)
441. (Act. 348.)
442. (Act. 349.)
443. (Act. 350.)
444. (Act. 351.)
445. (Act. 352.)
446. (Act. 353.)
447. (Act. 354.)
448. (Act. 355.)
449. (Act. 356.)
450. (Act. 357.)
451. (Act. 358.)
452. (Act. 359.)
453. (Act. 360.)
454. (Act. 361.)
455. (Act. 362.)
456. (Act. 366.)
457. (Act. 368.)

458. (Act. 369.) 459. (Act. 370.)
460. (Act. 371.) 461. (Act. 372.)
462. (Act. 373.) 463. (Act. 374.)
464. (Act. 375.) 465. (Act. 376.)
466. (Act. 377.) 467. (Act. 378.)
468. (Act. 379.) 469. (Act. 307.)
470. Escurial τ. iii. 17. 471. Athens, Nat. (259)?
472. (Evan. 1058.)   (Greg. 332.) 473. (Act. 205.)
474. (Act. 315.) 475. (Act. 209.)
476. (Evan. 1072.)   (Greg. 333.) 477. (Act. 232.)
478. (Evan. 1075.)   (Greg. 334.) 479. (Act. 195.)
480. (Evan. 1094.)   (Greg. 335.) 481. (Evan. 1240.)   (Greg. 337.)
482. (Evan. 1241.)   (Greg. 338.) 483. (Evan. 1242.)   (Greg. 339.)
484. (Evan. 1243.)   (Greg. 340.) 485. (Evan. 1244.)   (Greg. 341.)
486. (Act. 303.) 487. (Act. 419.)
488. (Act. 420.) 489. (Act. 325.)

490. Dublin, Trin. Coll. D. i. 28 [xiv], $8\frac{1}{2} \times 5\frac{1}{2}$, ff. 8, Rom. viii. 23 (ἑαυτούς) ... xiv. 10 κρι | ινεις. Inked over in places by another hand [xvi]. Κεφ. Collated by Dr. T. K. Abbott (*Hermathena*, xviii. 233, 1892).

491. (Act. 107.)

CHAPTER XII.

CURSIVE MANUSCRIPTS OF THE APOCALYPSE.

1. Mayhingen, Oettingen-Wallerstein [xii], $9\frac{1}{8} \times 5\frac{7}{8}$, ff. 90 (15 last *chart*.], the only one used in 1516 by Erasmus (who calls it 'exemplar vetustissimum') and long lost, contains the commentary of Andreas of Caesarea, in which the text is so completely imbedded that great care is needed to separate the one from the other. *Mut.* ch. xxii. 16–21, ending with τοῦ δαδ. This manuscript was happily re-discovered in 1861 by Professor F. Delitzsch at Mayhingen in Bavaria in the library of the Prince of Oettingen-Wallerstein, and a critical account of it published by him (illustrated by a facsimile) in the first part of his 'Handschriftliche Funde' (1861). Tregelles also, in the second part of the same work, published an independent collation of his own (with valuable 'Notes' prefixed), which he had made at Erlangen in 1862. The identity of Apoc. 1 with the recovered copy is manifest from such *monstra* as ἐβάπτισας ch. ii. 3, which is found in both; from the reading συνάγει ch. xiii. 10, and from the clauses put wrong by Erasmus, as being lost in the commentary, e.g. ch. ii. 17; iii. 5, 12, 15; vi. 11, 15. Of this copy Dr. Hort says (Introd. p. 263) that 'it is by no means an average cursive of the common sort. On the one hand it has many individualisms and readings with small and evidently unimportant attestation : on the other it has a large and good ancient element, . . . and ought certainly (with the somewhat similar 38) to stand high among secondary documents.'

2. (Act. 10, Stephen's ιε'.)

3. Codex Stephani ις', unknown; cited only 77 times throughout the Apocalypse in Stephen's edition of 1550, and that very irregularly; only once (ch. xx. 3) after ch. xvii. 8. It was not one of the copies in the King's Library, and the four citations noticed by Mill (N. T., Prol. § 1176) from Luke xxii. 30; 67; 2 Cor. xii. 11; 1 Tim. iii. 3, are probably mere errors of Stephen's press.

4. (Act. 12.)

5. Codices Laurentii Vallae (*see* Evan. 82); the readings of which Erasmus used.

Codd. 6, 26, 27, 28 were rather loosely collated for Wetstein by his kinsman Caspar Wetstein, chaplain to Frederick, Prince of Wales.

APOC. 1–34.

6. (Act. 23.) *7. (Act. 25, 1ˢᶜʳ.)
*8. (Act. 28, dˢᶜʳ.) 9. (Act. 30.)
10. (Evan. 60.) 11. (Act. 39.)
12. (Act. 40.) *13. (Act. 42.)
*14. (Evan. 69, fˢᶜʳ.) [1]

15. Fragments of ch. iii, iv, annexed to Cod. E Evan. in a later hand.

16. (Act. 45.) 17. (Evan. 35.)
18. (Act. 18.) 19. (Act. 17.)

20. (Evan. 175), a few extracts made by Bianchini: so Apoc. 24.

21, 22 of Wetstein were two unknown French codices, cited by Bentley in his specimen of Apoc. xxii, and made Wetstein's 23 (Act. 56). Scholz, discarding these three as doubtful, substitutes—

21. Rom. Vallicell. D. 20 [xiv, Greg. xv], $12\frac{7}{8} \times 8\frac{1}{2}$, ff. 93 (28), *chart.*

22. (Act. 166.) 23. (Evan. 367.) [2]
24. (Act. 160.) 25. (Evan. 149.)
*26. (Evan. 492.) 27. (Evan. 503.)

*28. Oxf. Bodl. Bar. 48 [xv], $8 \times 5\frac{1}{2}$, ff. 24 (22), *chart.*, κεφ., τίτλ., contains mixed matter by several hands, and is nˢᶜʳ of the Apocalypse, *mut.* ch. xvii. 5—xxii. 21 (ch. v. 1–5 is repeated in the volume in a different hand). This is an important copy, akin to Apocc. 7 and 96. Bentley also named it κ in his collation extant in the margin of Trin. Coll. B. xvii. 5 (*see* Evan. 51).

*29. (Act. 60, eˢᶜʳ.) 30. (Act. 69.)

*31. Lond. Brit. Mus. Harl. 5678 [xv], $11\frac{1}{4} \times 8\frac{1}{4}$, ff. 244 (24), *chart.*, *prol.*, is cˢᶜʳ, but ch. i–viii had been loosely collated for Griesbach by Paulus. Like Evan. 445 it once belonged to the Jesuits' College at Agen, and is important for its readings. Has much miscellaneous matter.

32. Dresdensis, Reg. A. 124 [xv, Griesb. x], $7\frac{3}{4} \times 4\frac{3}{4}$, ff. 16, belonged to Loescher, then to Brühl, collated by Dassdorf and Matthaei (Mt. t). The close resemblance in the text of Apocc. 29–32 is somewhat overstated by Griesbach.

*33. (Evan. 218.) 34. (Act. 66.)

---

[1] Mr. B. W. Newton superintended the publication of Tregelles' last part of his Greek New Testament under circumstances which disarm criticism, but Tregelles could hardly have meant that in the Apocalypse 'much of Cod. 14 (Leicestrensis) has been supplied by a later hand from the Codex Montfortianus, Apoc. 92' (Introductory Notice, p. 1). The original hand remains unchanged in the Leicester copy, even on the last torn leaf containing portions of Apoc. xix, but the converse supposition is very maintainable, though not quite certain, that the Apocalypse in Cod. 92 was transcribed from Cod. 14.

[2] Gregory has substituted this for Scholz's 23, which he finds does not contain Apoc. Whatever readings he cites under these three numbers, are simply copied from Wetstein (Kelly's 'Revelation,' Introd. p. xi, note). Dr. Gregory has seen all the four.

35. Vindob. Caes. Gr. Theol. 307 [xiv], $7\frac{1}{8} \times 5\frac{5}{8}$, ff. 32 (20), with Andreas' commentary: brought from Constantinople by de Busbeck (Alter). Described by Delitzsch, Handschriftliche Funde (part ii), p. 41 (1862). In text it closely resembles Cod. 87.

36. Vindob. Caes. Suppl. Gr. 93 [xiv, Greg. xiii], $6\frac{3}{8} \times 4\frac{3}{8}$, ff. 56 (36), *prol.*, *κεφ.*, *τίτλ.*, ends ch. xix. 20, with Andreas' commentary: the text is in *στίχοι* (Alter), having much in common with Codd. ℵ, 7.

37. (Act. 72.)

*38. Rom. Vat. Gr. 579 [xiii, Greg. xv], $8\frac{3}{8} \times 5\frac{1}{4}$, ff. 24 (30), on cotton paper, in the midst of foreign matter. The text (together with some marginal readings (*primâ manu*) closely resembles that of Codd. AC, and was collated by Birch, inspected by Scholz and Tregelles, and subsequently recollated by B. H. Alford at the request of Tregelles (*see* Evan. T).

39. (Paul. 85.) 40. (Evan. 141.)

41. Rom. Vat. Reg. Gr. 68 [xiv, Greg. xv], $9\frac{1}{8} \times 6$, ff. 70 (14), *chart.*, *proll.*, *κεφ. t.*, with extracts from Œcumenius and Andreas' commentary (Birch, Scholz: so Apoc. 43).

42. (Act. 80.)

43. Rom. Barberini iv. 56 [xiv], $9\frac{3}{4} \times 7$, ff. 5 (58) at end, 2 cols., contains ch. xiv. 17—xviii. 20, with a commentary, together with portions of the Septuagint.

44. (Evan. 180.) 45. (Act. 89.) 46. (Evan. 209.)

*47. (Evan. 241.) *48. (Evan. 242.)

*49. Moscow, Synod. 67 (Mt. o) [xv], fol., ff. 58, *chart.*, with Andreas' commentary, and Gregory Nazianzen's Homilies.

*50. Mosc. Synod. 206 (Mt. p) [xv], fol. *chart.*, ff. 35, like Evann. 69, 206, 233, is partly of parchment, partly paper, from the Iberian monastery on Athos; it also contains lives of the Saints.

*50^2. Also from the Iberian monastery [x], is Matthaei's r, Tischendorf's 90.

Apocc. 51–84 were added to the list by Scholz, of which he professes to have collated Cod. 51 entirely, as Reiche has done after him; 68, 69, 82 nearly entire; twenty-one others cursorily, the rest (apparently) not at all. Our 87 is Scrivener's m, collated in the Apocalypse only.

*51. (Evan. 18.) 52. (Act. 51.) 53. (Act. 116.)

54. (Evan. 263.) 55. (Act. 118.) 56. (Act. 119.)

57. (Act. 124.)

58. Par. Nat. Gr. 19, once Colbert's [xvi], $7\frac{7}{8} \times 5\frac{3}{4}$, ff. 36 (22), *chart.*, with 'Hiob et Justini cohort. ad Graec.' Scholz.

59. Par. Nat. Suppl. Gr. 99^a [xvi], $8\frac{1}{8} \times 5\frac{5}{8}$, ff. 83, *chart.*, with a commentary. Once Giles de Noailles'.

60. Rom. Vat. Gr. 656 [xiii or xiv], $6\frac{3}{4} \times 4\frac{5}{8}$, ff. 207 (17), *chart.*, with Andreas'. (*See* Gregory 79.)

61. Par. Nat. Gr. 491, once Colbert's [xiii], $9\frac{1}{2} \times 6\frac{1}{3}$, ff. 13, on cotton paper, *mut.*, with extracts from Basil, &c.

62. Par. Nat. Gr. 239 [A. D. 1422], $8\frac{5}{8} \times 5\frac{5}{8}$, ff. 119 (26), *chart.*, with Andreas' commentary.

63. Par. Nat. Gr. 241 [xvi], $8\frac{1}{4} \times 5\frac{7}{8}$, ff. 294, *chart.*, with Andreas' commentary. Once de Thou's, then Colbert's.

64. (Paul. 159.)

65. Moscow, Univ. Libr. 25 [xii], 4to, ff. 7 (once Coislin's 229), contains ch. xvi. 20—xxii. 21.

66. (Act. 419.)

67. Rom. Vat. Gr. 1743 [dated December 5, 1302], $8\frac{7}{8} \times 6\frac{1}{2}$, ff. ?, κεφ., τίτλ., with Andreas' commentary.

68. Rom. Vat. Gr. 1904, vol. 2 [xi], $11\frac{1}{4} \times 8\frac{1}{8}$, ff. 19, contains ch. vii, 17—viii. 12; xx. 1—xxii. 21, with Arethas' commentary, and much foreign matter. This fragment (as also Apoc. 72 according to Scholz, who however never cites it) agrees much with Cod. A.

69. (Act. 161.)   70. (Evan. 386.)

71. Athens, Nat. Libr. 142 [xv], $5\frac{7}{8} \times 4\frac{3}{8}$, ff. 233, with other matter.

*72. Rom. Ghigianus R. iv. 8 [xvi], $8\frac{1}{4} \times 5\frac{1}{4}$, ff. ?, *chart.*, with Andreas' commentary. Collated hastily by the late W. H. Simcox.

73. Rom. Corsin. 41. E. 37 [xv or xvi], $7\frac{5}{8} \times 4\frac{7}{8}$, ff. 97 (30), κεφ., τίτλ. (*See* Gregory.)

74. (Act. 140.)   75. (Act. 86.)

76. (Act. 421.)

77. Florence, Laur. vii. 9 [xv, Greg. xvi], $8\frac{3}{8} \times 5\frac{1}{2}$, ff. 363 (25), *chart.*, with Arethas' commentary.

78. (Paul. 197.)

*79. Munich, Reg. Gr. 248 [xvi], $9\frac{1}{4} \times 6\frac{1}{4}$, ff. 84 (28), *chart.*, *prol.*, κεφ., τίτλ.; once Sirlet's, the Apostolic chief notary (*see* Evan. 373 and Evst. 132), with Andreas' commentary, whose text it follows. That excellent and modest scholar Fred. Sylburg collated it for his edition of Andreas, 1596, one of the last labours of his diligent life. An excellent copy.

80. Monac. Reg. Gr. 544 (Bengel's Augustan. 7) [xii Sylburg, xiv Scholz, who adds that it once belonged to the Emperor Manuel Palaeologus, A. D. 1400], $8 \times 5\frac{3}{4}$, ff. 169 (20), *prol.*, κεφ., τίτλ., on cotton paper, with Andreas' commentary.

81. Monac. Reg. Gr. 23 [xvi], $14 \times 9\frac{1}{4}$, ff. 83 (30), *chart.*, κεφ., τίτλ., with works of Gregory Nyssen, and Andreas' commentary, used by Theod. Peltanus for his edition of Andreas, Ingoldstadt, 1547. Peltanus' marginal notes from this copy were seen by Scholz.

82. (Act. 179.)

83. (Evan. 339): much like Apoc. B.

84. (Evan. 368.)[1]

85. Escurial ψ. iii. 17 [xii], 'con commentarios Cl. Pablo' (Haenel and Montana).

86. (Act. 251.)   (Greg. 122.)

*87. (Act. 178), m^scr. *See* Apoc. 35.

88. (Evan. 205.)

*89. (Paul. 266.)   B.-C. II. 4.   (Greg. 108.)

*90. Dresd. Reg. A. 95 [x Griesb., Scholz xv], $12\frac{1}{4} \times 9$, ff. 16 (30), 2 cols. This is 50^2 Scholz (Mt. r).

*91. (Paul. 263.)   Rom. Vat. Gr. 1209 [xv], $10\frac{3}{4} \times 10\frac{5}{8}$, ff. ?. Mico's collation of the modern supplement to the great Cod. B, made for Bentley, and published in Ford's 'Appendix' to the Codex Alexandrinus, 1799. The whole supplement from Heb. ix. 14 ριεῖ τὴν συνείδησιν including the Apocalypse (but not the Pastoral Epistles) is printed at full length in Vercellone and Cozza's edition of Cod. Vaticanus (1868).

92. (Evan. 61.) Published by Dr. Barrett, 1801, in his Appendix to Evan. Z, but suspected to be a later addition. See Apoc. 14, note.

Wm. Kelly, 'The Revelation of John edited in Greek with a new English Version,' 1860, thus numbers Scrivener's collations of six copies not included in the foregoing catalogue—

*93. (Paul. 256 or e^scr), a^scr.   *94. (Evan. 201), b^scr.

*95. Parham 82. 17, g^scr [xii], $10\frac{1}{4} \times 7\frac{3}{4}$, brought by the late Lord de la Zouche in 1837 from Caracalla on Athos: it contains an epitome of the commentary of Arethas, in a cramped hand much less distinct than the text, which ends at ch. xx. 11. There are no divisions into chapters. This 'special treasure,' as Tregelles calls it, was regarded by him and Alford as one of the best cursive manuscripts of the Apocalypse: Dr. Hort judges it inferior to none. It agrees with Cod. A alone or nearly so in ch. xviii. 8, 10, (19), 23; xix. 14: compare also its readings in ch. xix. 6 (bis), 12.

*96. Parham 67 (?). 2, h^scr [xiv], $11\frac{1}{4} \times 7\frac{3}{8}$, ff. 22 (28), κεφ., on glazed paper, very neat, also from Caracalla, complete and in excellent preservation, with very short scholia here and there. These two manuscripts were collated by Scrivener in 1855, under the hospitable roof of their owner.

*97. (Evan. 584.) Brit. Mus. Add. 17,469, j^scr [xiv], collated only in Apoc.

*98. (Evan. 488.) Oxf. Bodl. Can. 34, k^scr [dated in the Apocalypse July 18, 1516]. The Pauline Epistles [dated Oct. 11, 1515] precede the Acts. Collated only in Apoc.

99. (Act. 83 ?)   (*See* Greg.) Cited, like the next, by Tischendorf.

---

[1] After this again we withdraw Scholz's copies, as virtually included in Coxe's, putting others in their room. They are 85. (Act. 184.)   86. (Evan. 462), thrice cited ineunte libro (Tischendorf). 86^2 of Scholz, being 89 of Tischendorf (Evan. 466).

100. Naples, Nat. II. Aa. 10 ? [xiv or xv], $10\frac{1}{4} \times 7\frac{3}{8}$. (*See* Greg.)

101. (Evan. 206.)   102. (Evan. 451.)   (Greg. 103.)

103. Petersburg, Muralt. 129 [xv], 4to, ff. 25 (35), *chart., prol.*

104. (Evan. 531.)   (Greg. 107.)   105. (Act. 301.)   (Greg. 104.)

106. (Evan. 605.)   107. (Act. 232.)   (Greg. 181.)

108. (Act. 236.)   109[1]. (Act. 240.)   (Greg. 102.)

110. (Evan. 622.)   (Greg. 113.)   111. (Act. 307.)   (Greg. 105.)

112. Dresden, Reg. 187 [xvi], 8×6, ff. 21 (26). With Andreas. (*See* Greg. 182.)

113. Messina, Univ. 99 [xiii], $10\frac{5}{8} \times 8\frac{3}{8}$, ff. 138 (24), 2 cols., with commentary. (*See* Greg. 146.)

114. Rom. Vat. Gr. 542 [A.D. 1331], $11 \times 8\frac{1}{4}$, ff. 105 (29). With Andreas and Homm. of Chrysostom. (*See* Greg. 153.)

115. (Evan. 866.)   (Greg. 114.)

116. Rom. Vat. Gr. 1976 [xvii, Greg. xvi], $8\frac{3}{8} \times 5\frac{5}{8}$, ff. 114 (20), *chart.*, κεφ., τίτλ., with commentary of Andreas. (*See* Greg. 157.)

117. (Evan. 698, Paul. 324.)   (Greg. 115.)

118. Rom. Vat. Ottob. Gr. 283 [A.D. 1574, a Jo. Euripioto], $8\frac{3}{8} \times 5\frac{7}{8}$, ff. 123 (22), *chart.*, κεφ., Andreas. (Greg. 160.)

119. Rom. Vat. Pal. Gr. 346 [xv], $14\frac{3}{8} \times 10$, ff. 86 (30), *prol.*, κεφ. t., κεφ., τίτλ., Andreas. (*See* Greg. 161.)

120. Rom. Angelic. A. 4. 1 [A.D. 1447], $8\frac{1}{2} \times 5\frac{1}{2}$, ff. 86 (29), *chart.*, κεφ., τίτλ., Andreas. (*See* Greg. 149.)

121. Rom. Angelic. B. 5. 15 [xv], $8\frac{1}{8} \times 5\frac{3}{4}$, ff. ?, *chart.*, much liturgical information. (*See* Greg. 150.)

122. Rom. Ghig. R. V. 33 [xiv], $10 \times 7\frac{1}{4}$, ff. 28 (32), much theological writing, collated by W. H. Simcox, ff. 347, *chart.* Andreas and Œcumenius. (*See* Greg. 151.)

123. (Evan. 738.)   124. (Act. 309.)

125. (Act. 207.)   126. (Act. 208.)

127. (Act. 323.)   128. (Act. 332.)

129. (Act. 238.)   130. (Act. 359.)

131. (Act. 362.)   132. (Act. 374.)

133. (Act. 384.)   134. (Act. 386.)

135. (Act. 399.)   136. Vindob. Caes. Gr. Theol. 69.

137. Vind. Caes. Theol. 163.   138. Vind. Caes. Gr. Theol. 220.

139. Par. Nat. Gr. 240.   140. Par. Nat. Coisl. Gr. 256.

141. Athens, bibl. τῆς Βουλῆς.   142. (Paul. 202.)

143. Escurial χ. iii. 6.   144. Madrid. O. 19 (7).

---

[1] We cannot identify 109, Bentley's R (Regis Galliae, 1872): cf. Ellis, Bentleii Critica Sacra, Intr. p. xxix.

145. Florence, Laur. vii. 29.
146. (Evan. 757.) (Greg. 110.)
147. Modena, Este iii. E. 1.
148. Modena, Este iii. F. 12.
149. (Evan. 792.) (Greg. 111.)
150. (Evan. 808.) (Greg. 112.)
151. (Evan. 922.) (Greg. 116.)
152. Rom. Vat. Gr. 370.
153. (Evan. 1262.)
154. Rom. Vat. Gr. 1190.
155. Rom. Vat. Gr. 1426. (Act. 264.) (Greg. 121.)
156. (Act. 159.)
157. (Evan. 986.) (Greg. 117.)
158. Rom. Vat. Gr. 2129. (Cf. Evst. 389.)
159. Rom. Vat. Ottob. Gr. 154.
160. (Evan. 1072.) (Greg. 118.)
161. (Evan. 1075.) (Greg. 119.)
162. Venice, Mark i. 40.
163. Ven. Mark ii. 54.
164. Athos, Anna 11.
165. Athos, Vatopedi 90.
166. Athos, Vatop. 90 (2).
167. Athos, Dionysius 163. (Cf. Evst. 642.)
168. Athos, Docheiariou 81.
169. Athos, Iveron 34.
170. Athos, Iveron 379.
171. Athos, Iveron 546.
172. Athos, Iveron 594.
173. Athos, Iveron 605.
174. Athos, Iveron 644.
175. Athos, Iveron 661.
176. Athos, Constamonitou 29.
177. Athos, Constam. 107.
178. Patmos, St. John 12.
179. Patmos, St. John 64.
180. (Act. 149.)
181. (Act. 417.)
182. (Evan. 1094.) (Greg. 120.)
183. Thessalonica, Ἑλληνικὸν Γυμνάσιον 10. (Cf. Apost. 163.)
184. (Act. 422.)

CHAPTER XIII.

EVANGELISTARIES, OR MANUSCRIPT SERVICE-BOOKS OF THE GOSPELS.

HOWEVER grievously the great mass of cursive manuscripts of the New Testament has been neglected by Biblical critics, the Lectionaries of the Greek Church, partly for causes previously stated, have received even less attention at their hands. Yet no sound reason can be alleged for regarding the testimony of these Service-books as of slighter value than that of other witnesses of the same date and character. The necessary changes interpolated in the text at the commencement and sometimes at the end of lessons are so simple and obvious that the least experienced student can make allowance for them[1]: and if the same passage is often given in a different form when repeated in the same Lectionary, although the fact ought to be recorded and borne in mind, this occasional inconsistency must no more militate against the reception of the general evidence of the copy that exhibits it, than it excludes from our roll of critical authorities the works of Origen and other Fathers, in which the selfsame variation is even more the rule than the exception. Dividing, therefore, the Lectionaries that have been hitherto catalogued (which form indeed but a small portion of those known to exist in Eastern monasteries and Western libraries) into Evangelistaria, or Evangeliaria, containing extracts from the Gospels, and Praxapostoli or Apostoli comprising extracts from the Acts and Epistles; we purpose to mark with an asterisk the few that have been really collated, including them in the same list with the majority which have been examined superficially, or not at all. Uncial copies (some as late as the eleventh

---

[1] In the sixth lesson for the Holy Passions the prefatory clause to Mark xv. 16 is founded on an obvious misconception: Τῷ καιρῷ ἐκείνῳ οἱ στρατιῶται ἀπήγαγον τὸν ἰῦ εἰς τὴν αὐλὴν τοῦ καϊάφα, ὅ ἐστι πραιτώριον. We remember no similar instance of error.

century) will be distinguished by †. The uncial codices of the Gospels amount to one hundred and six, those of the Acts and Epistles only to seven or eight, but probably to more in either case, since all is not known about some of the Codd. recorded here. Lectionaries are usually (yet see below, Evst. 111, 142, 178, 244, 249, 255, 256, 262, 266, 268, 275, Apost. 52, 69) written with two columns on a page, like the Codex Alexandrinus, FGI (1–6, 7) LMN^{b}PQRTUXΘ^{d}Λ, 8, 184, 207, 360, 418, 422, 463, 509 of the Gospels, and Cod. M of St. Paul's Epistles.

†1. Par. Nat. Gr. 278 [x ? Omont xiv], $11\frac{7}{8} \times 9\frac{1}{2}$, Unc., ff. 265, 2 cols., *mut.* (Wetstein, Scholz).

†2. Par. Nat. Gr. 280 [ix, Greg. x], $11\frac{1}{4} \times 8\frac{1}{2}$, Unc., ff. 257 (18), 2 cols., *mus., mut.* (Wetstein, Scholz).

†3. Oxf. Lincoln Coll. Gr. ii. 15 [x, Greg. xi], $11\frac{1}{4} \times 9$, Unc., ff. 282 (19), *mus. rubr., men.*, with coloured and gilt illuminations and capitals, and red crosses for stops: three leaves are lost near the end (Mill).

4. Cambr. Univ. Libr. Dd. 8. 49, or Moore 2 [xi], $10\frac{3}{4} \times 8\frac{1}{2}$, ff. 199 (24), 2 cols., *mus. rubr.* (Mill).

†5. Oxf. Bodl. Barocc. 202 [x], 12×9, Unc., ff. 150 (19), 2 cols., *mus. rubr.*, ends at Matt. xxiii. 4, being the middle of the Lesson for Tuesday in Holy Week (Burgon). *Mut.* initio (Mill, Wetstein). This is Bentley's *a* in Trin. Coll. B. xvii. 5 marg. (*see* Evan. 51).

*†6. (Apost. 1.) Leyden, Univ. Scaliger's 243 [xi ?], $7\frac{5}{8} \times 5\frac{1}{4}$, Unc., ff. 278 (18), 2 cols., *chart.*, with an Arabic version, contains the Praxapostolos, Psalms, and but a few Lessons from the Gospels (Wetstein, Dermout).

7. Par. Nat. Gr. 301 [written by George, a priest, A.D. 1205]. $12 \times 9\frac{1}{4}$, ff. 316 (23), 2 cols.   (Evst. 7–12, 14–17, were slightly collated by Wetstein, Scholz.)

8. Par. Nat. Gr. 312 [xiv], $13\frac{1}{2} \times 11$, ff. 309 (29), 2 cols., written by Cosmas, a monk.

9. Par. Nat. Gr. 307 [xiii], $11\frac{3}{4} \times 9\frac{1}{2}$, ff. 260 (24), 2 cols., *mus.*

10. Par. Nat. Gr. 287 [xi, Greg. xiii], $12\frac{2}{3} \times 9\frac{5}{8}$, ff. 142 (23), 2 cols., *mut.*

11. Par. Nat. Gr. 309 [xiii], $11\frac{3}{4} \times 9$, ff. 142, 2 cols., *mus., mut.*

12. Par. Nat. Gr. 310 [xiii], 12×9, ff. 366 (24), 2 cols., *mus., mut.*

†13. Par. Nat. Coisl. Gr. 31 [x, Greg. xi], $14\frac{1}{2} \times 10\frac{1}{4}$, Unc., ff. 283 (18), 2 cols., *mus. aur., pict.*, most beautifully written, the first seven pages in gold, the next fifteen in vermilion, the rest in black ink, described by Montfaucon (Scholz). Wetstein's 13 (Colbert. 1241 or Reg. 1982) contains no Evangelistarium.

14. Par. Nat. Gr. 315 [xv, Greg. xvi], $10\frac{5}{8} \times 7\frac{1}{2}$, ff. 348 (22), 2 cols., *chart.* Wrongly set down as Evan. 322.

15. Par. Nat. Gr. 302 [xiii], $10 \times 7\frac{1}{2}$, ff. 310 (22), 2 cols., *mut.*

16. Par. Nat. Gr. 297 [xii], 10⅜ × 8½, ff. 199 (19), 2 cols., much *mut.*

†17. Par. Nat. Gr. 279 [xii, Greg. ix], 10¼ × 7¾, Unc., ff. 199 (19), 2 cols., *mut.* (Tischendorf seems to have confounded 13 and 17 in his N. T., Proleg. p. ccxvi, 7th edition.)

18. Oxf. Bodl. Laud. Gr. 32 [xii], 11½ × 9½, ff. 276 (22), 2 cols., much *mut.*, beginning John iv. 53. Codd. 18–22 were partially examined by Griesbach after Mill.

19. Oxf. Bodl. Misc. Gr. 10 [xiii], 12¼ × 8¾, ff. 332 (24), 2 cols., *mus. rubr., mut.*, given in 1661 by Parthenius, Patriarch of Constantinople, to Heneage Finch, Earl of Winchelsea, our Ambassador there. This and Cod. 18 are said by Mill to be much like Stephen's ϛ', Evan. 7.

20. Oxf. Bodl. Laud. Gr. 34 [written by Onesimus, April, 1047, Indiction 15], 11½ × 9½, ff. 177 (22), 2 cols., *orn., mus. rubr., mut.*[1]

21. Oxf. Bodl. Seld. B. 56 [xiv], 9¼ × 7¼, ff. 59 (28), 2 cols., a fragment containing Lessons in Lent till Easter, coarsely written.

22. Oxf. Bodl. Seld. B. 54 [xiv], 10¼ × 8, ff. 63 (25), 2 cols., *men.*, a fragment, with Patristic homilies [xi].

†23. Unc., Mead's, then Askew's, then D'Eon's, by whom it was sent to France. Wetstein merely saw it. Not now known.

†24. Munich, Reg. Gr. 383 [x], 12½ × 9½, ff. 265 (21), 2 cols., Unc., *men.*, the Lessons for Saturdays and Sundays (σαββατοκυριακαί: see Evst. 110, 157, 186, 221, 227, 283, 289), *mut.* (Bengel, Scholz). Is this Cod. Radzivil, with slightly sloping uncials [viii], of which Silvestre gives a facsimile (Paléogr. Univ., ii. 61)?

25. Lond. Brit. Mus. Harl. 5650 [xii], 9¼ × 6, ff. 267 (22), a palimpsest, whose later writing is by Nicephorus the reader. The older writing, now illegible, was partly uncial, *mut.*

25ᵇ represents a few Lessons in the same codex by a later, yet contemporary hand (Bloomfield).

Evst. 25–30 were very partially collated by Griesbach.

†26. (Apost. 28.) Oxf. Bodl. Seld. supra (1) 2 [xiii], 8 × 5¾, ff. 180, *mut.*, a palimpsest, but the earlier uncial writing is illegible, and the codex in a wretched state, the work of several hands.

†27. Oxf. Bodl. 3391, Seld. supra (2) 3, a palimpsest [ix uncial, xiv later writing], 9 × 6¾, ff. 150 (89–95 cursive), 2 cols., *mut.*, in large ill-formed characters.

Evst. 26, 27 were collated by Mangey, 1749, but his papers appear to be lost.

28. Oxf. Bodl. Misc. Gr. 11 [xiii], 9¾ × 7½, ff. 203 (21), 2 cols., *orn., mut.* at end and on June 14, in two careless hands.

---

[1] Laud. Gr. 36, which in the Bodleian Catalogue is described as an Evangelistarium, is a collection of Church Lessons from the Septuagint read in Lent and the Holy Week, such as we described above. It has red musical notes, and seems *once* to have borne the date A.D. 1028. It is Dean Holmes' No. 61 (Praef. ad Pentateuch).

29. Oxf. Bodl. Misc. Gr. 12 [xii or xiii], 10 × 8, ff. 156 (23), 2 cols., *mus.*, *mut.* Elegantly written, but much worn.

30. (Apost. 265.) Oxf. Bodl. Cromw. 11 [the whole written in 1225 by Michael, a χωρικὸς καλλιγράφος], 8 × 6, ff. 208. After Liturgies of Chrys., Basil, Praesanctified, εὐαγγέλια ἀναστάσιμα, Evst. (p. 290) and Apost. (p. 149), i.e. lections from Epistles and Gospels for great feasts.

31. Norimberg. [xii], 4to, ff. 281 (Doederlein). Its readings are stated by Michaelis to resemble those of Codd. D (e.g. Luke xxii. 4), L, 1, 69.

*32. Gotha, Ducal Libr. MS. 78 [xii, Greg. xi], $13\frac{1}{2} \times 9\frac{7}{8}$, ff. 273 (20), 2 cols., carelessly written, but with important readings: see Luke xxii. 17, &c., Vol. II. Chap. XII. Edited by Matthaei, 1791.

†33. Card. Alex. Albani [xi], 4to, Unc., a menology edited by Steph. Ant. Morcelli, Rome, 1788.

†34. Munich, Reg. Gr. 329 [x, Greg. ix], 11 × 8, 3 vols., ff. 430 (18), 2 cols., Unc., in massive uncials, from Mannheim, the last three out of four volumes, the menology suiting the custom of a monastery on Athos (Rink, Scholz). Burgon refers to Hardt's Catalogue, iii. 314 seq.

Evst. 35–39 were inspected or collated by Birch, 40–43 by Moldenhawer.

†35. Rom. Vat. Gr. 351 [x], $13\frac{1}{4} \times 9\frac{7}{8}$, ff. 151 (11), Unc., contains only the Lessons for holidays.

*†36. Rom. Vat. Gr. 1067 [ix], $13\frac{3}{8} \times 10$, ff. 368 (21), 2 cols., Unc., a valuable copy, completely collated.

37. (Apost. 7.) Rom. Propaganda, Borgian. L. xvi. 6 [xi, Greg. xii], $10\frac{3}{4} \times 8\frac{1}{2}$, ff. 160 (24), 2 cols., contains only thirteen Lessons from the Gospels.

For the next two see 117, 118. Hort's $38 = x^{scr}$, $39 = y^{scr}$. (*See* Hort, pp. 77 note, and 296–7.) Instead—

38. Lond. Brit. Mus. 25,881 [xv, Greg. xiv], ff. 4 at end (24), 2 cols., Matt. xviii. 12–18; iv. 25—v. 30; xviii. 18–20. (Greg. 328a.)

39. Lond. Brit. Mus. 34,059 [xii], $10 \times 8\frac{1}{4}$, ff. 238 (21), 2 cols., ends with ἀναγνώσματα and τὰ διάφορα. Bought of A. Carlenizza of Pola, in 1891.

†40. Escurial I [x], 4to, Unc., *mus.*, kept with the reliques there as an autograph of St. Chrysostom. It was given by Queen Maria of Hungary (who obtained it from Jo. Diassorin) to Philip II. Moldenhawer collated fifteen Lessons. The text is of the common type, but in the oblong shape of the letters, false breathings and accents, the red musical notes, &c., it resembles Evst. 1, though its date is somewhat lower. Omitted by Montana.

†41. Escurial χ. iii. 12 [x, or xi with Montana], 4to, ff. 204, Unc., *mus.*, very elegant: the menology (as also that of Evst. 43) suited to the use of a Byzantine Church.

†42. Escurial χ. iii. 13 [ix, or xi with Montana], 4to, ff. 227, Unc., *mut.* at the beginning. Two hands appear, the earlier leaning a little to the right.

43. Escurial χ. iii. 16 [xi, or xii with Montana], 4to, *mut.* at the beginning, in large cursive letters; with full *men.*

44. (Apost. 8.)   Havniens. Reg. 1324 [xv, Greg. xii], 10½ × 7½, ff. 195, 2 cols., *mut.*, and much in a still later hand. Its history resembles that of Evann. 234-5 (Heusler).

†45. Vindobon. Caesar. Jurid. 5 [x], 11⅝ × 7⅞, Unc., 2 cols., six leaves from the binding of a law-book: the letters resemble the Tübingen fragment, Griesbach's R (*see* p. 139) or Wetstein's 98 (Alter).

†46. Vind. Caesar. Suppl. Gr. 12 [ix], 6½ × 5½, ff. 182 (9), Unc., on purple vellum with gold and silver letters. There is a Latin version (Bianchini, Treschow, Alter). Silvestre has a facsimile, Paléogr. Univ., No. 69.

*†47. Moscow, S. Synod. 43 [viii], fol., ff. 246, 2 cols., 'a barbaro scriptus est, sed ex praestantissimo exemplari,' Matthaei (B), whose codices extend down to 57.

*48. Mosc. Syn. 44 (Mt. c) [by Peter, a monk, A.D. 1056], fol., ff. 250, 2 cols., from the Iberian monastery at Athos. In 1312 it belonged to Nicephorus, Metropolitan of Crete.

*49. Mosc. Typograph. Syn. 11 (Mt. f) [x and xi], fol., ff. 437, 2 cols., *pict.* Superior in text to Cod. 48, but much in a later hand.

*†50. Mosc. Typ. Syn. 12 (Mt. H) [viii ?], fol., ff. 231, Unc. A very valuable copy, whose date Matthaei seems to have placed unreasonably high. [Greg. xiv.]

*51. Mosc. Typ. Syn. 9 (Mt. t) [xvi], 4to, ff. 42, *chart.*

*52. (Apost. 16.)   Mosc. Syn. 266 (Mt. ξ) [xiv], 4to, ff. 229, contains a Euchology and ἀποστολοευαγγέλια, as also do 53, 54, 55.

*53. (Apost. 17.)   Mosc. Syn. 267 (Mt. χ) [xiv or xv], 4to, ff. 333, *chart.*, from the monastery of Simenus on Athos.

*54. (Apost. 18.)   Mosc. Syn. 268 (Mt. ψ) [written A.D. 1470, by Dometius, a monk], 4to, ff. 344, *chart.*, from the Vatopedion monastery on Athos.

*55. (Apost. 19.)   Mosc. Typ. Syn. 47 (Mt. ω) [the Apost. copied at Venice, 1602], 4to, ff. 586, *chart.*, wretchedly written.

*56. (Apost. 20.)   Mosc. Typ. Syn. 9 (Mt. 16) [xv or xvi], 16mo, ff. 42, *chart.*, fragments of little value.

*57. Dresdensis Reg. A. 151 (Mt. 19) [xv], 8½ × 6½, ff. 408 (20), *chart.*, came from Italy, and, like Apoc. 32, once belonged to Loescher, then to the Count de Brühl. It is a Euchology, or Greek Service Book (Suicer, Thesaur. Ecclesiast., i. p. 1287), described in Matthaei, Appendix to St. John's Gospel, p. 378.

Evst. 58-157 were added to the list by Scholz, who professes to have collated entire 60; in the greater part 81, 86.

58. Par. Nat. Suppl. Gr. 50 [xv], 11 × 8¼, ff. 49 (11), *chart.*, brought from some church in Greece.

59. Instead of what was really Evan. 289—

Lond. Egerton 2163 [xii–xiii], $12\frac{1}{8} \times 8$, ff. 207 (26, 25), handsome, titles in gold, initials in gold and colours, *mus. rubr.*, *pict.*, *mut.* (Greg. 339.)

*60. (Apost. 12.) Par. Nat. Gr. 375, once Colbert's, formerly De Thou's [A.D. 1022], $9\frac{1}{4} \times 6\frac{3}{4}$, ff. 195 (28); it contains many valuable readings (akin to those of Codd. ADE), but numerous errors. Written by Helias, a priest and monk, 'in castro de Colonia,' for the use of the French monastery of St. Denys.

†61. (Evan. 747.) Par. Nat. Gr. 182 [x], 4to, a fragment.

62. Instead of what was really Evan. 303—

Lond. Brit. Mus. Add. 29,713 [late xi, Greg. xiv], 13×10, ff. 296 (25), very handsome, illuminated head-pieces and initial letters, some in gold. (Greg. 332.)

†63. Par. Nat. Gr. 277 [ix], $11\frac{1}{4} \times 8\frac{1}{4}$, ff. 158 (22), 2 cols., Unc., *mut.* at the beginning and end.

†64. Par. Nat. Gr. 281 [ix], $10\frac{7}{8} \times 8$, ff. 210 (22), 2 cols., Unc., from Constantinople; many leaves are torn.

†65. Par. Nat. Gr. 282 [ix], $11\frac{3}{4} \times 9\frac{1}{4}$, ff. 213 (20), 2 cols., Unc., a palimpsest, with a Church-service in later writing [xiii].

†66. Par. Nat. Gr. 283 [ix], $11\frac{1}{4} \times 8\frac{1}{4}$, ff. 275 (19), 2 cols., Unc., also a palimpsest, with the older writing of course misplaced; the later (*mut.* in fine) a Church-service [xiii].

†67. Par. Nat. Gr. 284 [xi, Greg. xii], $11\frac{1}{2} \times 9\frac{1}{8}$, ff. 270 (18), 2 cols., Unc., *mus.*, *pict.*, 'optimae notae.'

68. Par. Nat. Gr. 285, once Colbert's [xi, Greg. xii], $12\frac{3}{4} \times 9\frac{3}{8}$, ff. 357 (23), 2 cols., *mut.*, initio et fine.

69. Par. Nat. Gr. 286 [xi, Greg. xii], $12 \times 9\frac{1}{8}$, ff. 257 (25), 2 cols., *mut.*, in fine.

70. Par. Nat. Gr. 288 [xi, Greg. xii], $13\frac{1}{2} \times 10\frac{1}{2}$, ff. 313 (25), 2 cols., brought from the East in 1669. A few leaves at the beginning and end later, *chart.*

71. Par. Nat. Gr. 289, once Colbert's [July, A.D. 1066], $12\frac{3}{8} \times 8\frac{7}{8}$, ff. 159 (26), 2 cols., *mut.* Written by John, a priest, for George, a monk, partly on vellum, partly on cotton paper.

72. Par. Nat. Gr. 290 [A.D. 1257], $9\frac{7}{8} \times 7\frac{5}{8}$, ff. 190, 2 cols. Written by Nicolas. To this codex is appended—

†72^{b}, three uncial leaves [ix], *mus.*, containing John v. 1–11; vi. 61–69; vii. 1–15.

73. Par. Nat. Gr. 291 [xii], $10\frac{3}{4} \times 8\frac{3}{8}$, ff. 34 (25), 2 cols., *mus.*, *mut.*

74. Par. Nat. Gr. 292, once Mazarin's [xii], $9\frac{5}{8} \times 8$, ff. 274 (18), 2 cols.

75. Par. Nat. Gr. 293, from the East [xii], $11 \times 8\frac{7}{8}$, ff. 250 (29), 2 cols.

76. Par. Nat. Gr. 295, once Colbert's [xii], $12\frac{7}{8} \times 9\frac{1}{8}$, ff. 182 (28), 2 cols., *mus.*, *mut.*

77. Par. Nat. Gr. 296 [xii], $10\frac{7}{8} \times 8\frac{1}{2}$, ff. 258 (20), 2 cols., from Constantinople.

78. Par. Nat. Gr. 298, once Colbert's [xii], $10 \times 7\frac{1}{2}$, ff. 95 (28), 2 cols., *mus.*, *mut.* Some hiatus are supplied later on cotton paper.

79. Par. Nat. Gr. 299 [xii, Greg. xiv], $12\frac{1}{2} \times 9\frac{7}{8}$, ff. 120 (26), 2 cols., *mut.* initio et fine.

80. Par. Nat. Gr. 300 [xii], $10\frac{1}{2} \times 8\frac{1}{4}$, ff. 128, 2 cols.

81. Par. Nat. Gr. 305 [xiii, Greg. xiv], $11\frac{5}{8} \times 9\frac{1}{4}$, ff. 197 (22), 2 cols., *mut.*, perhaps written in Egypt. Some passages supplied [xv] on cotton paper.

82. (Apost. 31.) Par. Nat. Gr. 276 [xv, Greg. xiv], $9\frac{3}{4} \times 6\frac{1}{2}$, ff. 150 (27), *mut.*, *chart.*, with Lessons from the Prophets.

83. (Apost. 21.) Par. Nat. Gr. 294 [xi, Greg. xii], $11 \times 8\frac{1}{2}$, ff. 245 (26), 2 cols.

84. (Apost. 9.) Par. Nat. Suppl. Gr. 32 a [xii, Greg. xiii], $12\frac{5}{8} \times 8\frac{5}{8}$, ff. 212 (66), 2 cols., and

85. (Apost. 10.) Par. Nat. Suppl. Gr. 33 [xii], $11\frac{5}{8} \times 8\frac{7}{8}$, ff. 248, 2 cols., have Lessons from the Old and New Testament.

86. Par. Nat. Gr. 311 [July, 1336, Indict. 4], $13\frac{5}{8} \times 10$, ff. 382 (20), 2 cols. Written by Charito, given by the monk Ignatius to the monastery τῶν ὁδηγῶν or Θεοτόκου at Constantinople (*see* Act. 169): afterwards it was Boistaller's, and is described by Montfaucon. John vii. 53—viii. 11 is at the end, obelized, and not appointed for any day, since the names of Pelagia or Theodora are not in the menology of this copy.

87. Par. Nat. Gr. 313 [xiv], $10 \times 7\frac{3}{4}$, ff. 121, 2 cols., once Colbert's (as were 88–91; 99–101).

88. Par. Nat. Gr. 314 [xiv], $12\frac{3}{4} \times 7\frac{1}{8}$, ff. 190, 2 cols. Many verses are omitted, and the arrangement of the Lessons is a little unusual.

89. Par. Nat. Gr. 316 [xiv], $10\frac{1}{8} \times 6\frac{3}{4}$, ff. 208 (25), on cotton paper, *mut.* in fine.

90. Par. Nat. Gr. 317 [A.D. 1533, Indict. 6], $11\frac{3}{8} \times 7\frac{7}{8}$, ff. 223 (25), 2 cols., *mus. rubr.*, *chart.* Written by Stephen, a reader.

91. Par. Nat. Gr. 318 [xi, Greg. xiv], $10\frac{1}{2} \times 7\frac{3}{4}$, ff. 322, 2 cols., a subscription, &c., written in Cyprus by the monk Leontius, 1553 (Montfauc., Palaeogr. Graec., p. 89).

92. (Apost. 35.) Par. Nat. Gr. 324 [xiii, Greg. xiv], $8\frac{5}{8} \times 5\frac{3}{4}$, ff. 212 (21), on cotton paper, with fragments of the Liturgies of SS. Basil, Chrysostom, and the Praesanctified.

93. (Apost. 36.) Par. Nat. Gr. 326 [xiv, Greg. xvi], $8\frac{1}{8} \times 5\frac{3}{8}$, ff. 144, *chart.*, with the Liturgies of SS. Chrysostom and Basil.

94. (Apost. 29.) Par. Nat. Gr. 330 [xiii, Greg. xii], $7\frac{1}{8} \times 5\frac{3}{8}$, ff. 176,

mut., with a Euchology and part of a Church-service in a later hand [xv].

95. Par. Nat. Gr. 374 [xiv], 9¼ × 7, ff. 114 (32), 2 cols., from Constantinople.

96. (Apost. 262.) Par. Nat. Suppl. Gr. 115 [xii, Greg. xvi], 8½ × 5¾, ff. 171 (25), *chart.*, *mut.*, initio et fine.

97. (Evan. 324, Apost. 32.) Par. Nat. Gr. 376, only the *εὐαγγέλια τῶν πάθων* (*see* Evan. 324).

98. Par. Nat. Gr. 377 [xiii, Greg. xv], 9 × 6⅞, ff. 196 (21). Once Mazarin's; portions are palimpsest, and the older writing seems to belong to an Evangelistarium.

99. Par. Nat. Gr. 380 [xv, Greg. xvi], 8¼ × 5⅞, ff. 243 (22), *chart.* Wrongly set down as Evan. 327.

100. Par. Nat. Gr. 381 [A.D. 1550], 8¼ × 5⅞, ff. 306 (20), *chart.* Written at Iconium by Michael Maurice. Wrongly set down as Evan. 328.

101. Par. Nat. Gr. 303 [xiii, Greg. xiv], 11⅛ × 7¾, ff. 279 (25), 2 cols., grandly written. Wrongly set down as Evan. 321.

102. Milan, Ambros. S. 62 sup. [Sept. A.D. 1370], 11 × 8½, ff. 120 (35), *chart.* Written by Stephen, a priest (but with two leaves of parchment at the beginning, two at the end), bought at Taranto, 1606, with 'commentarii incerti auctoris in omnia Evangelia quae per annum in Ecclesia Graeca leguntur,' according to Burgon.

103. Milan, Ambr. D. 67 sup. [xiii], 11⅝ × 8, ff. 138 (31), 2 cols., *pict.*; bought 1606, 'Corneliani in Salentinis.' *See* Apost. 46.

104. (Apost. 47.) Milan, Ambr. D. 72 sup. [xii], 11½ × 8¾, ff. 128 (23), 2 cols., *mut.* initio et fine: brought from Calabria, 1607.

105. Milan, Ambr. M. 81 sup. [xiii], 10 × 7⅛, ff. 157 (20), 2 cols., carefully written, but the first 19 leaves [xvi] *chart.*

106. Milan, Ambr. C. 91 sup. [xiii], 11¾ × 9⅛, ff. 355 (20), 2 cols., *mut.*, splendidly written in a large cursive hand. 'Corcyrae emptus.'

107. Venice, St. Mark 548 [xi, Greg. xii], 12 × 9⅛, ff. 265 (20), 2 cols., *pict.*

108. Ven. St. Mark 549 [xi], 12⅜ × 9½, ff. 292 (23), 2 cols., *mus. rubr.*, a grand and gorgeous fol., *mut.* in fine.

109. Ven. St. Mark 550 [xi, Greg. xiv], 11⅛ × 8, ff. 206 (28), 2 cols., *mut.* (Burgon), *pict.*, *chart.*

110. Ven. St. Mark 551 [xi, Greg. xiii], 13¾ × 10¼, ff. 278 (22), 2 cols., *mut.*, a glorious codex, containing only the *σαββατοκυριακαί* (*see* Evst. 24): the last few leaves are ancient, although supplied on paper.

†111. Modena, Este ii. C. 6 [x], 9¾ × 6¼, ff. ?, Unc., *mus. rubr.*, small thick folio in one column on a page. Montfaucon assigns it to the eighth century, and Burgon admits that he might have done so too, but that it contains in the menology (Dec. 16) the name of Queen Theophano, who died A.D. 892.

112. (Apost. 41.) Flor. Laurent. Conv. Soppr. 24 [xi], $7\frac{3}{8} \times 5\frac{3}{8}$, ff. 145 (22), *mut.* initio.

113. Flor. Laur. vi. 2 [ff. 1–213, xii; the rest written by one George, xiv], $14\frac{1}{2} \times 11\frac{3}{8}$, ff. 341 (19), 2 cols. Prefixed are verses of Arsenius, Archbishop of Monembasia (*see* Evan. 333), addressed to Clement VII (1523–34).

114. Flor. Laur. vi. 7 [xii, Greg. xiv], $13\frac{3}{8} \times 10\frac{1}{4}$, ff. 180 (18), 2 cols., magnificently illuminated.

†115. Flor. Laur. vi. 21 [xi, Greg. x], $9\frac{1}{2} \times 7\frac{3}{4}$, ff. 261 (20), 2 cols., Unc., *mus. rubr.*, elegantly written.

†116. Flor. Laur. vi. 31 [x], 12×9, ff. 226 (20), 2 cols., Unc., *mus. rubr.*, elegant.

117. Flor. Laur. 244 [xii], $13\frac{1}{8} \times 10\frac{3}{4}$, ff. 119 (10), 2 cols., most beautifully written in golden cursive letters, *pict.*, once kept among the choicest κειμήλια of the Grand Ducal Palace. *See* above, Evst. 38, 39.

†118. Flor. Laur. 243, kept in a chest for special preservation [xi, Greg. xiv], $15 \times 11\frac{1}{4}$, ff. 368 (20), 2 cols., most elegant. Evst. 113–18 were described by Canon Angelo Bandini, 1787.

119. Rom. Vat. Gr. 1155 [xiii], $13\frac{3}{4} \times 10\frac{3}{8}$, ff. 268 (25), 2 cols.

120. Rom. Vat. Gr. 1256 [xiii], $14 \times 10\frac{3}{4}$, ff. 344 (20), 2 cols.

121. Rom. Vat. Gr. 1156 [xiii, Greg. xi], $14\frac{3}{8} \times 10$, ff. 419 (22), very splendid.

122. Rom. Vat. Gr. 1168 [August, 1175], $10\frac{1}{2} \times 7\frac{3}{8}$, ff. 194 (24), 2 cols., *mus. rubr.*, written by the monk Germanus for the monk Theodoret.

†123. Rom. Vat. Gr. 1522 [x], $11\frac{1}{4} \times 8\frac{3}{4}$, ff. 197 (11), 2 cols., Unc., *vers., pict.*, very correctly written, without points.

124. Rom. Vat. Gr. 1988 [xii], $7\frac{3}{4} \times 5\frac{7}{8}$, ff. 162 (24), 2 cols., *mut.* initio et fine.

125. Rom. Vat. Gr. 2017 [xi or xii], $8\frac{5}{8} \times 6\frac{1}{2}$, ff. 123 (23), 2 cols., *mut.*, with a subscription dated 1346, and a memorandum of the death (Oct. 12, 1345) and burial of one Constantia.

126. Rom. Vat. Gr. 2041 [xii], $12\frac{1}{8} \times 8\frac{7}{8}$, ff. 337 (23), 2 cols., written by one George; διὰ συνδρομῆς γεωργίου, whatever συνδρομή may mean.

†127. Rom. Vat. Gr. 2063 [ix], $10\frac{5}{8} \times 7\frac{1}{4}$, ff. 178 (20), 2 cols., *mus. rubr.*, Unc., *mut.* initio et fine. The first two leaves of the Festival Lessons [xiv]. Two not contemporaneous hands have been engaged upon this copy.

128. Rom. Vat. Gr. 2133 [xiv], $11\frac{1}{2} \times 8\frac{7}{8}$, ff. 393 (13).

129. Rom. Vat. Regin. Gr. 12 [xiii, Greg. xii], $10\frac{1}{4} \times 8\frac{1}{2}$, ff. 339 (24), 2 cols. Ff. 1–40 appear to have been written in France, and have an unusual text: ff. 41–220 [xiii] are by another hand: the other 71 leaves to the end [xv].

†130. Rom. Vat. Ottob. 2 [ix], $13\frac{1}{4} \times 9\frac{3}{8}$, ff. 343 (20), 2 vols., 2 cols., Unc., very beautiful.

131. Rom. Vat. Ottob. 175 [xiv], $9\frac{1}{2} \times 7\frac{1}{8}$, ff. 70 (12), a fragment.

132. Rom. Vat. Ottob. 326 [xv, Greg. xiv], $6\frac{3}{4} \times 5\frac{1}{4}$, ff. ?, in silver letters. Procured at Rome, Sept. 11, 1590, 'a Francisco et Accida' of Messina, and given to Cardinal Sirlet (*see* Evan. 373, Apoc. 79).

133. (Apost. 39.) Rom. Vat. Ottob. 416 [xiv], $8\frac{1}{2} \times 5\frac{1}{4}$, ff. 296 (29), 1 and 2 cols., *chart.*

134. Rom. Barberin. vi. 4 [xiii], $13\frac{1}{4} \times 11\frac{1}{4}$, ff. 343 (21), 2 cols., the first eight and last three leaves being paper.

†135. Rom. Barb. iv. 54, a palimpsest [vi Scholz, Greg. viii], $9\frac{7}{8} \times 7$, ff. 165 (23), is Tischendorf's barb^{ev}, and by him referred to the middle of the seventh century, which is a somewhat earlier date than has hitherto been assigned to Lectionaries. He has given specimens of its readings in 'Monum. sacr. ined.,' vol. i. pp. 207-210 (Matt. xxiv. 34—xxv. 16; John xix. 11-25).

136. Rom. Barb. iv. 54 [xii], the later writing of the palimpsest Evst. 135.

137. Rom. Vallicell. D. 63, once Peter Polidore's [xii], $9\frac{1}{4} \times 7\frac{1}{4}$, ff. 105 (20), 2 cols., *mut.* initio.

138. Naples, I. B. 14 [xv], $10\frac{1}{2} \times 8\frac{1}{4}$, ff. 255 (22), 2 cols., *chart.*, given by Christopher Palaeologus, May 7, 1584, to the Church of SS. Peter and Paul at Naples.

†139. Venice, St. Mark 12 [x], $12\frac{1}{2} \times 9\frac{1}{2}$, ff. 219 (17), 2 cols., *mut.* initio, with many erasures.

140. Instead of one which has no existence—
(Apost. 242.) Cairo, Patriarch. Alex. 18 [xv], 4to, *chart.*, Συναγωγὴ λέξεων ἐκ παλαιᾶς καὶ νέας (Coxe). (Greg. 759.)

141. Ven. St. Mark i. 9 [xi], $11\frac{3}{4} \times 9\frac{3}{4}$, ff. 268 (15), 2 cols., 'Monasterii Divae Catharinae Sinaitarum quod extat Zacynthi.'

142. Ven. St. Mark i. 23 [xiv], $6\frac{1}{2} \times 4\frac{3}{4}$, ff. 45 (15), *mut.*, only 45 pages, with one column on a page.

143. Instead of Evan. 468—
Jerusalem, Holy Sepulchre 12 [xi end], fol. (Coxe). (Greg. 158.)

†144. Biblio. Malatestianae of Cesena xxvii. 4, now at Rome [xii], fol., *mus. rubr.*, Unc., very splendid.

145. Bibl. Cesen. Malatest. xxix. 2 [xii], fol.

146. Cambr. Univ. Libr. Dd. viii. 23 [xi], $15\frac{1}{2} \times 11\frac{1}{2}$, ff. 212 (29), 2 cols., *syn., men., mut.* at end, neatly written for a church at Constantinople.

Evst. 147, 148 are in *Latin*, and 149 is Evan. 567. Instead—

147. St. Saba 17 [xii], 4to (Coxe). (Greg. 165.)

148. St. Saba 23 [xii], fol. (Coxe). (Greg. 168.)

149. St. Saba 24 [xi], fol. (Coxe). (Greg. 169.)

*†150. Lond. Brit. Mus. Harl. 5598 [May 27, A.D. 995, Indict. 8], $13\frac{1}{4} \times 10\frac{1}{2}$, ff. 374 (21), 2 cols., Unc., *mus. rubr., orn.*, written by

Constantine, a priest, is Scrivener's H (Cod. Augiensis, Introd. pp. xlvii ·l), for an alphabet formed from it *see* our Plate iii. No. 7. It was brought from Constantinople by Dr. John Covell, in 1677 (Evan. 65), and by him shown to Mill (N. T., Proleg. § 1426); from Covell it seems to have been purchased (together with his other copies) by Harley, Earl of Oxford. It is a most splendid specimen of the uncial class of Evangelistaria, and its text presents many instructive variations. At the end are several Lessons for special occasions, which are not often met with. Collated also by (Bloomfield), and facsimiles given by the Palaeographical Society, Plates 26, 27.

151. Lond. Brit. Mus. Harl. 5785 [xii], $12\frac{1}{2} \times 9\frac{1}{2}$, ff. 359 (18), 2 cols., *mus. rubr., orn.*, a splendid copy, in large, bold, cursive letters. At the end is a note, written at Rome in 1699, by L. A. Zacagni, certifying that the volume was then more than 700 years old. The date assigned above is more likely (Bloomfield).

†152. Lond. Brit. Mus. Harl. 5787 [x], $12\frac{1}{4} \times 9$, ff. 224 (24), 2 cols., Unc., *orn.*, the uncials leaning to the right, a fine copy, with small uncial notes, well meriting collation. Called 'Codex Prusensis' [Prusa, near mount Olympus: Scholz's 171] in a MS. note of H. Wanley. It begins John xx. 20, and is *mut.* in some other parts. For a facsimile page see the new 'Catalogue of Ancient MSS. in the British Museum' (1881), Plate 17.

153. Meerman 117 [xi], see Evan. 436?, bought at Meerman's sale by Payne, the bookseller, for £200. Its present owner is unknown. (Compare Evan. 562.)

154. Munich, Reg. Gr. 326 [xiii], $12\frac{3}{8} \times 9\frac{7}{8}$, ff. 49 (21), 2 cols., a fine fol., written very small and neatly, containing the Lessons from the season of Lent to the month of December in the menology, once at Mannheim. It seems adapted to the Constantinopolitan use.

†155. Vindobon. Caes. Gr. Theol. 209 [x], $8\frac{1}{2} \times 6\frac{1}{2}$, ff. 143 (27), *mus. rubr., pict.*, Unc., a palimpsest, over which is written a commentary on St. Matthew [xiv].

156. Rom. Vallicell. D. 4. 1 [xi], fol., ff. 380, 2 cols., described by Bianchini, Evan. Quadr., vol. ii. pt. i. p. 537; now missing. It must have been a superb specimen of ancient art: about thirty of its pictures are enumerated.

157. Oxf. Bodl., Clarke 8 [A.D. 1253], $8 \times 6\frac{3}{4}$, ff. 198 (23), 2 cols., 2 gatherings destroyed, and one leaf torn out. Written by Demetrius Brizopoulos, σαββατοκυριακαί (*see* Evst. 24)[1]. (Greg.)

---

[1] As with the MSS. of the Gospels, and for the reasons assigned above, we remove to the foot of the page, and do not reckon in our numbering, the twenty-one copies seen by Scholz in Eastern Libraries.
158. Library of the Great Greek Monastery at Jerusalem, No. 10 [xiv], fol.
159. 'Biblioth. monasterii virginum τῆς μεγάλης παναγίας a S. Melana erect.' [xiii], fol., very neat (' non sec. viii ut monachi putant,' Scholz).
160. (Apost. 33.) St. Saba 4, written there by one Antony [xiv], 8vo.
161. St. Saba 5 [xv], 8vo, *chart.* 162. St. Saba 6 [xv], 16mo, *chart.*
163. St. Saba 13 [xiii], 4to, *chart.*, adapted (as also those that follow) to the use of Palestine. 164. St. Saba [xiv], 4to.

To Dean Burgon's care and industry we owe Codd. 158–178; 181–187.

158. Par. Suppl. Gr. 27 [xi, Greg. xii], $13 \times 10\frac{7}{8}$, ff. 207 (24), 2 cols., *mus. rubr., pict.*, beautifully illuminated: 'Present de Mr. Desalleurs, ambassadeur pour le roy en 1753, remis par ordre de Mr. le Cte. d'Argenson le 7 Juillet, 1753.' (Greg. 261.)

159. Par. Suppl. Gr. 242 [xv, Greg. xvii], $16\frac{1}{4} \times 10\frac{3}{4}$, ff. 265 (27), 2 cols., *chart.*, peculiarly bound, with oriental pictures. (Greg. 262.)

160. Bologna, Univ. 3638 [xiv], $11\frac{3}{8} \times 9\frac{3}{4}$, ff. 233 (27), 2 cols., written by one Anthimus. This is No. xviii in Talman's and J. S. Assemani's manuscript Catalogue, No. 25 in Mezzofanti's Index. (Greg. 281.)

161. Parma, Reg. 14 [xiv], $11\frac{3}{8} \times 9\frac{3}{4}$, ?, 2 cols., *mus. rubr., mut.* Contains the Gospel for St. Pelagia's day. (Greg. 282.)

162. Siena, Univ. X. iv. 1 [xi or xii], $14\frac{3}{8} \times 11\frac{3}{8}$, ff. 313 (23), 2 cols., *mus. rubr., pict.*, one of the most splendid Service-books in the world, the first five columns in gold, the covers enriched with sumptuous silver enamels and graceful scroll-work. Bought at Venice in 1359 by Andrea di Grazia for the Hospital of S. Maria della Scala, of P. di Ciunta Torregiani, a Florentine merchant, who a little before had bought it at Constantinople of the agent of the Emperor John Cantacuzenus [1341–55]. (Greg. 283.)

163. Milan, †Ambr. Q. 79 sup. [x], $11\frac{7}{8} \times 8\frac{1}{4}$, a single uncial page of a Lectionary. (Greg. 284.)

164. Milan, Ambr. E. S. v. 14 [xii], $10\frac{1}{2} \times 8\frac{1}{2}$, ff. 37 (22), 2 cols., two separate fragments, one being fol., in two columns, roughly written. (Greg. 285ª.)

165. Milan, Ambr. ol. E. S. v. 13, now bound up with 164 [xiv], at f. 67, $11\frac{1}{4} \times 8\frac{1}{2}$, f. 1, 2 cols. (*See* Greg. 285.)

166. (Apost. 181.) Milan, Ambr. D. 108 sup. [xiii], $11\frac{3}{8} \times 8\frac{1}{2}$, ff. 204 (29), 2 cols. (*See* Greg. 287.)

167. Milan, Ambr. A. 150 sup. [xiii], $11\frac{7}{8} \times 9\frac{1}{2}$, ff. 124 (24), 2 cols., *mut.* (ff. 1–9, 104–123, *chart.*). (*See* Greg. 288.)

168. Milan, Ambr. C. 160 inf. [xiv], $12\frac{3}{4} \times 10$, ff. 156 (27), 2 cols. *mut.* (*See* Greg. 289.)

169. Milan, Ambr. P. 274 sup. [xiv or xv], $10\frac{3}{8} \times 7\frac{1}{2}$, ff. 198 (23), *mut.* in disorder. (*See* Greg. 290.)

165. St. Saba 17 [xv], 4to, *chart.* 166. St. Saba 21 [xiii], fol.
167. St. Saba 22 [xiv], fol. 168. St. Saba 23 [xiii], fol.
169. St. Saba 24 [xiii], fol. 170. St. Saba 25 [xiii], fol.
171. (Apost. 52.) St. Saba (unnumbered) [written July, 1059, in the monastery of Θεοτόκος, by Sergius, a monk of Olympus in Bithynia], 8vo.
†172. Library of St. John's monastery at Patmos ['iv' Scholz, obviously a misprint], fol. †173. Patmos [ix], 4to. †174. Patm. [x], 4to.
†175. Patm. [x], 4to. 176. Patm. [xii], 4to. 177. Patm. [xiii], 4to.
178. Patm. [xiv], 4to, in the same Library, but not numbered.
Some of these MSS. have been removed to Europe since Scholz made his reckoning, e. g. Parham No. 20 (Evst. 236).

Besides examining the eight Evangelistaria at St. Mark's, Venice, described in the preceding catalogue (Evst. 107–10; 139–42), Burgon found, exclusive of Evst. 175, eight more: viz.

170. Venice, St. Mark i. 4 [A.D. 1381], $8\frac{1}{2} \times 5\frac{7}{8}$, ff. 209 (22), *chart.*, rather barbarously written by the priest John. (*See* Greg. 264.)

†171. Ven. St. Mark i. 45 [x], $13\frac{3}{8} \times 10\frac{1}{2}$, ff. 78 (20), 2 cols., Unc., *mut.* initio. (Greg. 265.)

172. Ven. St. Mark i. 46 [xii?], $10\frac{1}{4} \times 8$, ff. 50 (22), 2 cols., *mus. rubr., mut.* coarse. (*See* Greg. 266.)

173. Ven. St. Mark. i. 47 [A.D. 1046 [1]], $13\frac{1}{3} \times 10\frac{3}{8}$, ff. 350 (24), 2 cols., a grand cursive folio, sumptuously adorned. (*See* Greg. 267.)

174. Ven. St. Mark i. 48 [xii], $10\frac{3}{8} \times 8\frac{1}{4}$, ff. 281 (20), 2 cols., *mus. rubr.*, with unusual contents. (*See* Greg. 268.)

*†175. ven[ev]. Ven. St. Mark i. 49 [vii or viii], $9\frac{1}{4} \times 8$, Unc., three nearly illegible palimpsest leaves (edited by Tischendorf in 'Monum. sacr. ined.,' vol. i. pp. 199, &c.), (*see* Evst. 135), containing Matt. viii. 32—ix. 1; 9–13; John ii. 15–22; iii. 22–26; vi. 16–26; or twenty-seven verses.

176. Ven. St. Mark i. 50 [xiv or xv], $11\frac{3}{8} \times 7\frac{7}{8}$, ff. 403 (22), 2 cols., *chart.* (*See* Greg. 270.)

177. Ven. St. Mark i. 51 [xv, Greg. xvii], $8 \times 5\frac{1}{2}$, *chart.*, eleven poor leaves. (Greg. 271.)

178. Ven. St. Mark i. 52 [xvi], $10\frac{1}{4} \times 7\frac{1}{2}$, ff. 276 (26), *mus. rubr., chart.*, from Corfu. (*See* Greg. 272.)

*†179. (Apost. 55.) Trèves, Cath. Libr. 143. F [x or xi], $10\frac{1}{4} \times 7\frac{3}{4}$, ff. 202 (24), Unc., called St. Simeon's, and brought by him from Syria in the eleventh century, consists chiefly of Lessons from the Old Testament. It contains many itacisms and some unusual readings. Edited in 1834 by B. M. Steininger in his 'Codex S. Simeonis exhibens lect. eccl. gr. DCCC ann. vetustate insigne.' (Greg. 179.)

†180. Vindob. Caes. 209 [ix, Greg. x], $8\frac{1}{2} \times 6\frac{1}{4}$, ff. 143 (27), Unc. and Minusc., *mus. rubr., pict.*, a palimpsest, with many itacisms (Scholz, Endlicher). Readings are given by Scholz (N. T., vol. ii. pp. lv–lxiii). (Greg. 155.)

In the Treasury of the Church of St. Mark at Venice Burgon found, besides those just named, three others, nearly ruined by the damp of the place where they are kept.

181. Ven. St. Mark, Thesaur. i. 53 [xiii, Greg. xii], $11\frac{3}{4} \times 8\frac{5}{8}$, ff. ?, 2 cols., splendidly illuminated and bound in silver and enamel. Substitute this for Wake 12 (= Evan. 492), inserted in error as Evst. 181.

[1] At the end in small gold uncials the following very curious colophon was deciphered by Dean Burgon and the learned sub-librarian Signor Veludo jointly: Μηνὶ μαίω Ἰνδ. ΙΔ. ἔτους ϛφνδ΄. προσηνέχθη παρὰ βασιλείου μοναχοῦ πρεσβυτέρου καὶ ἡγουμένου τῆς σεβασμίας μονῆς τῆς κοιμήσεως τῆς θκοῦ εἰς τὴν αὐτὴν μονὴν βιβλία τέσσαρα· τὸ αὐτὸ εὐαγγέλιον, ἀπόστολος, προφητεία, καὶ ἀναγνωστικόν, ὁ βίος τοῦ ἁγίου. καὶ ἐστύχηται δίδωσθαι ὑπὲρ τῆς αὐτῆς προσενέξαιως ἐνὶ ἑκάστω χρόνω ἀπὸ τοῦ δοχείου τῆς αὐτῆς μονῆς ὑπὲρ μνήμης αὐτ νόμισμα ἐν ἥμισον, μέχ[ρι γὰρ τού]του τὰ τῶν χριστια-ῶν [συ]νίσταται· περιφυλάττεται δὲ καὶ ἡ ἁγία μονὴ αὕτη· ἐν γὰρ τῶ τυπικῶ τῆς μονῆς περὶ τοῦ κατίδους (sic) τῶν αὐτῆς βιβλίων, καὶ περὶ τῆς διανομῆς τοῦ ἑνὸς ἡμίσου νομίσμα-τος σαφέστερον διερμηνεύει.

340   LECTIONARIES.

182. Ven. St. Mark, Thes. i. 54 [xii, Greg. xiii], $10\frac{7}{8} \times 8\frac{3}{4}$, ff. ?, 2 cols., once a fine codex, now tied up in a parcel by itself. (Greg. 276.)

183. Ven. St. Mark, Thes. i. 55 [A.D. 1439], $13 \times 10\frac{1}{2}$, ff. ?, 2 cols., *chart.*, written by Sophronius at Ferrara, poor enough inside, but kept in a glass case for the sake of its gorgeous silver cover, which came from St. Sophia's at Constantinople. (Greg. 277.)

The next three are bound in red velvet, and in excellent preservation.

184. Ven. S. Giorgio di Greco A' [xiv, Greg. xii], $12\frac{1}{4} \times 10\frac{1}{4}$, ff. 413 (21), 2 cols., is very splendidly illuminated, and was once used for the *Greek* service of this church. (Greg. 279.)

185. Ven. S. Giorgio di Greco Γ' [xiv], $9\frac{5}{8} \times 7\frac{1}{4}$, ff. 240 (28). Professes to be written by Νικολαος ὁ Μαλωτα, πρωτέκδικος τῆς ἁγιωτάτης μητροπόλεως Λακεδαίμονι. It seems to have been brought hither A.D. 1422. (Greg. 280.)

186. Ven. S. Giorgio di Greco B' [xiii], $11\frac{1}{2} \times 8\frac{1}{2}$, ff. 223 (21), 2 cols., is the largest, but contains only σαββατοκυριακαί (*see* Evst. 24). (Greg. 278.)

187. Flor. Laurent. S. Marci 706 [xi or xii], $9\frac{1}{4} \times 7\frac{7}{8}$, ff. 181 (21), 2 cols., *mus. rubr.*, cursive, much used. (Greg. 291.)

188. Rom. Vat. Pii II. Gr. 33 [x or xi], $8\frac{1}{4} \times 6$, ff. 158 (26), 2 cols., a fine specimen. (Greg. 570.)

†189. carp[ev]. Carpentras, Bibl. Urb. 11 [ix, Greg. x], $14 \times 10\frac{5}{8}$, ff. 277 (24), 2 cols., Unc., *mus. rubr.*, examined by Tischendorf in 1843. Extracts are given in his 'Anecd. sacr. et prof.,' pp. 151, &c.

†190. tisch[ev]. Leipzig, Univ. Libr. Tisch. V [viii or ix], $10\frac{3}{4} \times 8\frac{1}{2}$, ff. 89 (20), 2 cols., *mus. rubr.*, a palimpsest, described 'Anecd. sacr. et prof.,' pp. 29, &c. (Greg. 293.)

†191. (Apost. 178.) Petrop[ev]. Petrop. Caes. Muralt. 44 [ix], 4to, ff. 69, ill written, but with a remarkable text; the date being tolerably fixed by Arabic matter decidedly more modern, written 401 and 425 of the Hegira (i.e. about A.D. 1011 and 1035) respecting the birth and baptism of the two Holy infants. There are but ten Lessons from St. Matthew, and nineteen from other parts of the New Testament, enumerated by Tischendorf in 'Notitia. Cod. Sinaitici,' p. 54. This copy contains the two leaves on cotton paper, with writing by the first hand, mentioned above, p. 23, note 2 (Greg. 249.)

†192. (Apost. 73.) Petrop[ev].². Petrop. Caes. Muralt. 90 [xii], 8vo. ff. 93 (21), a fragment. Tischendorf, Notitia Cod. Sinaitici, p. 63. (Greg 256.)

193. Besançon, Bibl. Urb. 44 [?], $11\frac{5}{8} \times 7\frac{5}{8}$, ff. 210 (22), 2 cols., *mus. rubr.* (letter from M. Castan, the Librarian, to Burgon). (Greg. 263.)

†194. 1p[e]. Petrop. Caes. Muralt. iv. 13 [ix], fol., ff. 2 (21), 2 cols., Unc Matt. viii. 10–13; xxvii. 1–9; Mark vi. 14–18; Luke iv. 33–36 (Greg. 246.)

195. 3p[e]. Petrop. Caes. Muralt. (56) vii. 179 [x], fol., ff. 251 (26),

cols., and (Apost. 54) Praxapostolos (Petrop. viii. 80), 'cum Codice G [Angelico] consentiens exc. Act. xxvii. 29; xxviii. 2.' (Greg. 251.)

196. 6pe. Petrop. Caes. Muralt. (71) x. 180 [dated Salernum, 1022], 4to, ff. 170 (20), 2 cols., *mut.* throughout. (Greg. 253.)

197. 9pe. Petrop. Caes. Muralt. xi. 3. 181 [xiii], 4to, ff. 3 (20), 2 cols., fragments: Matt. xxviii. 12–18; Luke iv. 16–22; John x. 9–14; xix. 6, 9–11; 14–19, 20; 25–28: 30–35. (Greg. 258.)

198. 10pe. Panticapaeense [of Kertch?], Palaeologi, collated at Odessa, and the collation sent to Muralt. (Greg. 260.)

199. Fragments of two leaves [ix, Greg. xiii], $11\frac{1}{4} \times 7\frac{1}{4}$, ff. 176 (34), bound up in Evan. 68. (Evan. 68.)

200. The cursive Lessons which overlie the uncial fragment of St. Luke (Ξ). (Greg. 299.)

†201. Oxf. Bodl. Barocc. 197 [x], $11\frac{3}{4} \times 7\frac{1}{4}$, ff. 5 (2), 2 cols., *mus. rubr.*, uncial palimpsest leaves, used for binding. (Greg. 205.)

†202. Oxf. Bodl. Canonici Gr. 85 [ix], $13 \times 9\frac{1}{4}$, ff. 259 (18), 2 cols., *mus. rubr.*, passages and directions in later cursive hand, much *mut.* The uncials lean a little to the left. (Greg. 194.)

†203. Oxf. Bodl. Can. Gr. 92 [x], $15\frac{3}{4} \times 12$, ff. 483 (14), 2 cols., *mus. rubr.*, large folio, very splendid, with gilt initial letters. (Greg. 195.)

204. Oxf. Bodl. Can. Gr. 119 [xv], $11\frac{1}{2} \times 7\frac{1}{8}$, ff. 155 (26), *chart.*, belonging in 1626 to Nicolas, a priest. (Greg. 196.)

205. Oxf. Bodl. Can. Gr. 126, $9\frac{1}{2} \times 8$, ff. 8 (20), *chart.* (Greg. 197.)

206. Oxf. Bodl. Clarke 45 [xii], $11\frac{1}{2} \times 9$, ff. 276 (24), 2 cols., *mus. rubr., orn.* bound up in disorder (Burgon), splendid but spoiled by damp. (Greg. 198.)

207. Oxf. Bodl. Clarke 46 [xiii], 11×9, ff. 252 (21), 2 cols., *mut.* initio et fine. 'A fine ruin, miserably cropped by the modern binder: the writing is very dissimilar in parts' (Burgon). (Greg. 199.)

208. Oxf. Bodl. Clarke 47 [xii], $10\frac{1}{2} \times 8\frac{1}{2}$, ff. 292 (23), 2 cols., *mus. rubr.*, much like Evst. 206. (Greg. 200.)

209. Oxf. Bodl. Clarke 48 [xiii], $10\frac{1}{2} \times 7\frac{3}{4}$, ff. 187 (27), 2 cols., carelessly and ill written: *mut.* initio. (Greg. 201.)

210. Oxf. Bodl. Cromw. 27 [xi], $11\frac{1}{2} \times 8\frac{3}{4}$, ff. 315 (22), 2 cols., *men.*, from Athos 1727, once Irene's. (Greg. 202.)

211. Oxf. Bodl. Misc. Gr. 119 [A.D. 1067], 11×8, ff. 300 (22), *mus. rubr.*, containing two parts, (1) Evst., (2) *Men.* The first two leaves and the last two were evidently written and inserted later in place of two damaged leaves, and bear the date A.D. 1067, probably copied from the vanished leaf. (MS. note in Bodl. Cat. by Mr. E. B. Nicholson.)

† This Evst. was formerly preceded by one uncial palimpsest leaf, containing parts of Rom. xiv, Heb. i. 1–11, which are now bound up in a separate volume. The whole volume was bought of Payne and Foss, London, in 1820. (Greg. 203.)

212. Oxf. Bodl. Misc. 140 [xi], 9 × 7, ff. 305 (10), *mus. rubr.*, not in regular order, but in order of holy days, a very beautiful copy, one volume only out of a set of four. (Greg. 204.)

†213. Oxf. Christ Church, Wake 13, 12 × 9, ff. 261, contains three uncial leaves [ix], Matt. xxv. 31–36; vi. 1–18 (dox^y. in Lord's Prayer), the rest cursive [xi], *mus. rubr., orn.*, in a very large, bold, peculiar hand. Two palimpsest leaves at the end cursive in later [xv], John xx. 19—xxi. 25. (Greg. 206.)

214. Ch. Ch. Wake 14 [xii], $11\frac{1}{2} \times 9$, ff. 243 (20), 2 cols., *mus. rubr.*, miniatures on pp. 108, 174, 182, ends at Matt. xxviii. 4. Has one leaf *chart.*, and two leaves at the beginning and end from the Old Testament, 1 Kings xvii. 12, &c. (Greg. 207.)

215. Ch. Ch. Wake 15 [A.D. 1068], $9\frac{1}{2} \times 7\frac{3}{4}$, ff. 217, 2 cols., *mus. rubr.*, and 2 ff. of Old Testament (first and last) being earlier. Written by Leontius of St. Clement's (Bryennios). (Greg. 208.)

216. Ch. Ch. Wake 16 [xiii], $9\frac{1}{2} \times 7\frac{1}{2}$, ff. 217 (21), 2 cols., *mus. rubr., mut.* initio et fine. (Greg. 209.)

217. Ch. Ch. Wake 17 [xiii or xiv], $9\frac{1}{2} \times 7$, ff. 227 (21), 2 cols., 15 ff. (213–227) by a later hand, *mut.* in fine. (Greg. 210.)

218. Ch. Ch. Wake 18 [palimpsest xiv over xi], $12\frac{1}{4} \times 8\frac{1}{4}$, ff. 218 (29), 2 cols., *orn., men.*, ill written. The first leaf contains the history of St. Varus and six martyrs. (Greg. 211.) This is Walker's E: his H is

219. Ch. Ch. Wake 19 [xi], $11 \times 8\frac{1}{2}$, ff. 248 (20), 2 cols., *orn., mus. rubr.* Of this codex the ninth leaf is wanting. (Greg. 212.)

220. Ch. Ch. Wake 23 [xi], $11\frac{3}{4} \times 9\frac{1}{2}$, ff. 256 (25), 2 cols., *mus. rubr., men.*, an elegant copy. The last page has Mark xvi. 9–20. (Greg. 213.)

*221. Camb. Trin. Coll. O. iv. 22 [xii], $12\frac{1}{3} \times 9$, ff. 249 (18), 2 cols., *mus. rubr., orn.*, once Dean Gale's (*see* Evan. 66), in a bold hand, with illuminations and red musical notes. There are daily Lessons from Easter to Pentecost, but afterwards only σαββατοκυριακαί (*see* Evst. 24), with full Saints' Day Lessons. (*See* Scrivener, Critica Sacra, p. xiv.) (Greg. 186.)

*222 or z^{scr}. Camb. Christ's Coll. F. 1. 8 [xi], $11\frac{3}{4} \times 9$, ff. 436 (30), *orn., syn.*, is much fuller than most Lectionaries, and contains many minute variations[1]: it exhibits a subscription dated 1261, Indict. 4, much later than the codex, and a note stating that Francis Tayler, Preacher at Christ's Church, Canterbury [the Cathedral], gave it to the College in 1654. There are also four Lessons from the prophets, and four from St. Paul (Apost. 53). A facsimile is given, Cod. Augiens. Introd., p. li. This is Hort's 59. (Greg. 185.)

The next four were collated by Dr. Bloomfield for his 'Critical Annotations on the Sacred Text.'

---

[1] Thus 222, with only two other Evangelistaria (6, 13) and Evan. 59 by the first hand, supports Cod. ℵ and Eusebius in the significant omission of υἱοῦ Βαραχίου, Matt. xxiii. 35.

(36)

ΓΟΝΤΟϹ ἘΓΈΝΕΤΟ ΝΕ
ΦΕΛΗ ΚΑΙ ἘΠΕϹΚΙΑϹΕΝ
ΑΥΤΟΥϹ ἘΦΟΒΉΘΗϹΑ

Α Ζ Φ Ξ Ρ Ω

(37)

μεμνημῶν ορϐ
ωτηρκλιρημκ
τοδαμοριομοξε
ληλυθῶϲ :-

(40)

(38)

τ. τοιϲ ηλαφιεϲμένον ἰδου οἱ
ἐν ἱματιϲμῶ ἐνδόξω και τρυ
φῆ ὑπάρχοντεϲ ἐν τοιϲ βαϲιλει
οιϲ εἰϲιν ἃ λλα τι ἐξεληλυθα

223. Lond. Lambeth Archiepiscopal Library 1187 [xiii], $10\frac{1}{4} \times 7\frac{3}{8}$, ff. 177 (26), 2 cols., *mus. rubr.* (Greg. 229.)

224. Lond. Lamb. 1188 [xiii], $11\frac{1}{4} \times 8\frac{1}{2}$, ff. 318 (22–4), 2 cols., *mus. rubr.*, judged by Bloomfield to be the fullest and most accurate here, or at the British Museum. (Greg. 230.)

225. Lond. Lamb. 1189 [xiii], $8\frac{3}{4} \times 7\frac{1}{4}$, ff. 160 (27), 4 cotton (later), τίτλ. (Greg. 231.)

226. Lond. Lamb. 1193, $9\frac{1}{4} \times 6\frac{7}{8}$, ff. 153 (26), *mus. rubr., mut.* at the end. Bloomfield assigns this to [ix], but Archdeacon Todd, in his (undated) 'Account of Greek Manuscripts,' &c., at Lambeth, sets it down as [xiii]. (Greg. 232.)

227. Lond. Sion College A. 32. 1, Ev. 1 (2) [xii], $10\frac{1}{4} \times 8\frac{1}{2}$, ff. 246 (19), 2 cols., *mus. rubr., orn.*, 194 leaves of σαββατοκυριακαί, a noble copy, one leaf (149) being much mutilated, one leaf in later writing [xvi], and perhaps one leaf lost at the end: otherwise complete, with fair illuminations and red musical notes. (Greg. 234.) For its history *see* Evan. 518, as also that of

228. Lond. Sion Coll. A. 32. 1, Ev. 1 (2) [xiv], $10\frac{1}{4} \times 7\frac{5}{8}$, ff. 142 (23–25), 2 cols., *mus. rubr., mut.* beginning and end. It begins at the Lesson for the third day of the second week (John iii. 19) and ends at Mark vi. 19, in the Lesson for Aug. 29. Two leaves are on paper, not much later than the rest. There is a Lesson for Aug. 1, not very common, τῶν ἁγίων μακκαβαίων, Matt. x. 16, &c. (Greg. 235.)

229. Lond. Sion Coll. A. 32. 1, Ev. 1 (4) [xiv, Greg. xiii], $10 \times 9\frac{1}{8}$, ff. 217 (19, 20), 2 cols., *mus. rubr., mut.* at end, is complete up to the Lesson for July 20 (Elijah), Luke iv. 22, broken off at οὐδεὶς αὐτῶν ver. 27. On the fly-leaf we read Τὸ παρὸν θύον καὶ ἱερὸν εὐαγγέλιον ὑπάρχι κτῆμα τοῦ θήου καὶ ἁγίου ναοῦ τοῦ ἁγίου ἀποστώλου καὶ εὐαγγελιστοῦ μάρκου καὶ εἰ τῆς ἀποξένοι αὐτὸ ἐκ τοῦ ναοῦ ἔχαιτο τῷ ἐπιτίμῳ[-ίῳ ?] τῶν ἁγ. π̄ρων, with the date of $a_\prime\chi\iota\theta$ (1619). (Greg. 236.)

230. Glasgow, Hunterian Museum V. 5. 10 [A.D. 1259], $10\frac{1}{2} \times 7\frac{7}{8}$, ff. 112, 2 cols., *mut.* Belonged to Caesar de Missy. (*See* Greg. 239.)

231. Glasg. Hunt. Mus. V. 3. 3 [xii or xiii], $10\frac{1}{4} \times 8\frac{1}{4}$, ff. 251, 2 cols. From the monastery of Πρόδρομος, given by Nicetas. (*See* Greg. 240.)

232. (Apost. 44.) Glasg. Hunt. Mus. V. 4. 3, perhaps [A.D. 1199], $10\frac{3}{4} \times 8\frac{1}{4}$, ff. 176 (26), 2 cols.. Belonged once, like the two last, to De Missy. (*See* Greg. 241.)

The next two were collated by Scrivener—

*†233. P2ˢᶜʳ. Parham 66. 1 [ix], $10\frac{1}{2} \times 7\frac{3}{8}$, three folio leaves from the monastery of Docheiariou on Athos, containing the thirty-three verses, Matt. i. 1–11; 11–22; vii. 7, 8; Mark ix. 41; xi. 22–26; Luke ix. 1–4. (Greg. 182.)

*†234. Pˢᶜʳ. (or paˢᶜʳ.) Parham 83. 18 [June, A.D. 980], $12\frac{1}{4} \times 8\frac{5}{8}$, ff. 222 (22), 2 cols., belonged to the late Lord de la Zouche, who brought it from Caracalla on Athos in 1837, beautifully written at Ciscissa, in Cappadocia Prima; a note dated 1049 is subjoined by a reviser, who

perhaps made the numerous changes in the text, and added two Lessons in cursive letters. *See* Plate xiii, No. 36. Also 'Cod. Augiens.,' Introd., pp. l–lv. (Greg. 181.)

235. Parham 84. 19 [xi], $14\frac{1}{2} \times 11\frac{1}{2}$, ff. 188 (25), 'the right royal codex,' partly written in gold, perhaps by the Emperor Alexius Comnenus (1081–1118). (Greg. 233.)

236. Parham 85. 20 [xii], $13\frac{3}{8} \times 9\frac{7}{8}$, *mus. rubr.*, brought from St. Saba in 1834, must be on Scholz's list. (Greg. 344.)

237. Ashburnham 205 [xii], $10\frac{3}{4} \times 7\frac{1}{4}$, ff. 127, *mus.*, *mut.*, roughly executed and apparently made up of several copies: seen by Coxe and Burgon. (Greg. 237.) Loose in the book is

†238. Ashburnham 208* [xiii], $10\frac{3}{4} \times 8\frac{1}{2}$, ff. 9, Unc., palimpsest, the fragment of a menology for November and December. These were purchased by the late Earl of Ashburnham at the sale of the library of 'Athenian Aberdeen,' who brought them from Greece. (Greg. 237ª.)

239. Burdett-Coutts I. 2. A fragment of 173 leaves [xiii], $10\frac{3}{4} \times 8\frac{1}{5}$, one being on paper [xv] and 30 leaves palimpsest; having under the Church Lessons, in leaning uncials of two columns [viii or ix], fragments of legends relating to Saints in the menology, including the Apocryphal ἀποδημία of Barnabas. *Pict.*, capitals in red ink. (Greg. 214.)

240. B.-C. I. 8 [xiii], $9\frac{3}{4} \times 7\frac{3}{4}$, is also a palimpsest, with uncial writing in two columns (almost illegible) under the later Church Lessons on the last leaf and the third, fourth, fifth, and seventh leaves from the end: *mut.* at the thirteenth Sunday of St. Matthew, and ends in the tenth εὐαγγέλιον ἀναστασιμόν John xxi. 3 (ἀνέβησαν). (Greg. 215.)

241. B.-C. I. 23 [xiii], $9\frac{1}{4} \times 7\frac{1}{2}$, a poor copy, with illuminations, the last leaf only being lost. (Greg. 217.)

242. B.-C. I. 24 [xiv], $12\frac{1}{2} \times 10\frac{1}{5}$, *chart.*, complete, but the first leaf in a later hand. (Greg. 218.)

243. B.-C. II. 5 [xi or xii], $11 \times 8\frac{3}{8}$, a fine copy, with headings, &c., in gold, and red musical or tone notes. Begins John i. 17, thence complete to the Lesson εἰς ἐπινίκια βασιλέων. At the end are nine later leaves. (Greg. 219.)

244. B.-C. II. 16 [xiii], $8\frac{3}{4} \times 6\frac{1}{2}$, a palimpsest, with only one column on a page. Ends Luke ii. 59. (Greg. 220.)

245. B.-C. II. 30 [xiv], $11\frac{3}{8} \times 7\frac{1}{2}$, on glazed paper, complete. Titles and capitals in red. *Syn.* on a leaf of the binding. (Greg. 221.)

246. B.-C. III. 21 [xiii], *pict.*, *mut.*, with illuminations. Ends in the Lesson for Aug. 29, Mark vi. 22. (Greg. 222.)

247. B.-C. III. 34 [xiii], $10\frac{1}{4} \times 7\frac{3}{4}$, neat and complete. A colophon states the scribe to be Romanus, a priest. (Greg. 224.)

248. B.-C. III. 43 [April 28, 1437, Ind. 15], $11\frac{1}{2} \times 8\frac{3}{8}$, ff. 206, *chart.* (Greg. 225.)

[B.-C. III. 44 is Evst. 289, described below, Apost. 78.]

249. B.-C. III. 46 [xiv], $8\frac{7}{8} \times 7\frac{1}{4}$, ff. 220, *mut.* in the beginning of the Saints' Day Lessons: fifteen leaves are palimpsest, over writing full two centuries earlier, containing in double columns Lessons of the Septuagint from Genesis, Proverbs, and Isaiah. The other 205 leaves have only one column on a page. (Greg. 226.)

250. B.-C. III. 52 [xiii, Greg. xiv], $9\frac{1}{4} \times 7\frac{5}{8}$, *chart.*, is but a fragment. (Greg. 227.)

The following are Euchologies (*see* Evst. 57), and are repeated among the Lectionaries of the Apostolos:

251. (Apost. 64.) B.-C. I. 10 [xii or xiii], $7\frac{3}{8} \times 4\frac{3}{8}$, ff. 60 (17), *orn.*, wherein to the ordinary contents of a Euchology, and the Liturgies of SS. Chrysostom, Basil, and Presanctified, are annexed Church Lessons in a cramped and apparently later hand. (*See* Scrivener, Critica Sacra.) (Greg. 216.)

252. (Apost. 66.) B.-C. III. 29 [xiv or xv], $8\frac{1}{2} \times 6$, ff. 172, *men.* Liturgies as in last, and other matter, on coarse paper, Lessons both from the Gospels and Epistles. (*See* Scrivener, Critica Sacra.) (Greg. 223.)

253. (Apost. 67.) B.-C. III. 42 [xiv], 6×4, ff. 310 (22), on stout glazed paper, with the Liturgies as in Evst. 251, and much matter in various hands, has fifteen Lessons from the Gospels, Acts, and Epistles, and three from Isaiah, lxvi–lxviii. (*See* Scrivener, Critica Sacra.) (Greg. 315.)

253². (Apost. 68.) B.-C. III. 53 [xv], $8\frac{1}{2} \times 5\frac{3}{4}$, ff. 177 (26), 2 cols., *chart.*, *men.*, *mut.*, rudely written with capitals in red. (Greg. 228.)

254. Coniston, John Ruskin [xiii or xiv, Greg. xi or xii], $12\frac{3}{4} \times 10\frac{1}{4}$, ff. 144 (21), 2 cols., *mus. rubr.*, *mut.*, but well repaired. (Greg. 238.)

255. London, Brit. Mus. Egerton 2786 [xiii], $8\frac{4}{8} \times 6$, ff. 157 (20–27), a palimpsest, *mut.* at the beginning (thirty-two leaves) and end, rather rudely written in single columns, on coarse parchment, with vermilion ornamentation. It abounds in uncouth *itacisms*. After Mr. Woodhouse's death it belonged to Alderman Bragge from 1869 to 1876, then to Dean Burgon, then to Rev. W. F. Rose. Bought in 1893. (Greg. 346.)

256. Lond. Brit. Mus. Arundel 536 [xiii], 9×6, ff. 217 (25), besides 3 at beginning, *chart.*, *mus. rubr.*, with Lections from the Epistles. (Greg. 187.)

*†257. Lond. Brit. Mus. Arundel 547, is x^{scr} [ix], $11\frac{1}{2} \times 9$, ff. 329 (22), 2 cols., Unc., *mus. rubr.*, *pict.*, *mut.* at the end, but followed by a leaf in a rather later hand, containing John viii. 12–19; 21–23. *See* our facsimile, Plate vi. No. 16. A collation by Bentley is preserved at Trinity College (B. xvii. 8). This is Hort's Cod. 38. (Greg. 183.)

258. (Apost. 53.) Lond. Brit. Mus. Harl. 5561 [xiv], $7\frac{1}{4} \times 5\frac{1}{2}$, ff. 276 (194 vell. + 82 [xv] *chart.*), is a Euchology (*see* Evst. 57), containing many short Lessons from the Gospels, Acts, and Epistles. (Greg. 340.)

259. Lond. Brit. Mus. Burney 22, is y^{scr} [A.D. 1319], $11\frac{1}{2} \times 8\frac{1}{2}$, ff. 248 (27), 2 cols. (*see* facsimile, Plate xiii, No. 37), remarkable for its wide departures from the received text, and for that reason often cited by Tischendorf and Alford on the Gospels. See also Westcott, in Smith's

Dictionary of the Bible, 'New Testament.' Part of the first leaf (John i. 11-13) is on paper and later: Evst. 257, 259 are described in Scrivener's 'Collations of the Holy Gospels,' Introd. pp. lix–lxiii. Like Evst. 23 it was once D'Eon's. This is Hort's Cod. 39. (Greg. 184.)

260. Lond. Brit. Mus. Add. 5153 [A.D. 1032], $10\frac{1}{2} \times 7\frac{1}{2}$, 2 vols., ff. 141 and 133 (20), 2 cols., *chart.*, *mus. rubr.*, first five ff. vol. i. *mut.* and damaged. (Greg. 188.)

261. Lond. Brit. Mus. Add. 11,840 [xii], $11 \times 8\frac{1}{2}$, ff. 236 (22), 2 cols., *mus. rubr.*, *mut.*, from Bp. Butler's collection, a very fine specimen. (Greg. 189.)

262. Lond. Brit. Mus. Add. 17,370 [xi], $12\frac{3}{4} \times 9\frac{1}{4}$, three leaves: one in double columns (Matt. vi. 14-21), two in single columns [xiii?] Luke xxiv. 25-35; John i. 35-51. Sir F. Madden's note on the first fragment is 'Presented by Mr. Harris of Alexandria, June 28, 1848. A leaf of a Greek Lectionary taken [*by the Arabs* deleted] out of a volume which afterwards fell into the hands of Gen. Menou.' *See* Act. 230. (Greg. 190.)

263. Lond. Brit. Mus. Add. 18,212 [xii], $11 \times 8\frac{1}{4}$, ff. 297 (21), 2 cols., *mus. rubr.*, much *mut.* at the end, and an older leaf from the Old Testament prefixed (Bloomfield). (Greg. 191.)

264. Lond. Brit. Mus. Add. 19,460 [xiii], $9\frac{1}{4} \times 7\frac{1}{4}$, ff. 104 (31), 2 cols., *mut.* at the beginning and end, in coarse and very unusual black writing (Bloomfield). (Greg. 192.)

265. Lond. Brit. Mus. Add. 19,737 [xiii], $12\frac{3}{4} \times 10$, ff. 279 (23), 2 cols., *mus. rubr.*, bought at Sotheby's, 1854. *Mut.* at the end, with illuminations, and frequent and beautiful gilt letters. (Greg. 318.)

266. Lond. Brit. Mus. Add. 19,993 [A.D. 1335], $9\frac{3}{4} \times 7$, ff. 281 (23), in a bold hand and peculiar style. At the beginning is an Advertisement, signed G. Alefson, which ends literally thus: 'Je l'ai acheté seulement pour le sauver des mains barbares qui allait le destruire intierement au prix de sch. 15 a Chypre, A.D. 1851.' (Bloomfield.) (Greg. 193.)

267. Lond. Brit. Mus. Add. 21,260 [xiii], 12×10, ff. 360 (20), 2 cols., *mus. rubr.*, *orn.*, purchased of Messrs. Boone in 1856. *Mut.* at the end. The first forty leaves of this splendid copy are injured by damp. (Greg. 319.)

268. Lond. Brit. Mus. Add. 21,261 [xiii], $8\frac{1}{2} \times 5\frac{3}{4}$, ff. 196 (19), written by various hands. Purchased of Mr. H. Stevens, 1856. (Greg. 320.)

269. Lond. Brit. Mus. Add. 22,735 [xiii], $12\frac{1}{2} \times 9\frac{1}{2}$, ff. 304 (*sic*), (23), 2 cols., *mus. rubr.*, a fine, complete and interesting codex, bought (like Evann. 596, 597) of Sp. P. Lampros of Athens in 1859: as were also Evst. 270, 271, 272. Seven leaves of Patristic matter are bound up with it at the end. (Greg. 321.)

270. Lond. Brit. Mus. Add. 22,742 [xiii], $11\frac{1}{2} \times 8\frac{3}{4}$, ff. 79 (24), 2 cols., *mus. rubr.* (later), rather old and much mutilated throughout. (Greg. 322.)

271. Lond. Brit. Mus. Add. 22,743 [xii ?], 14½ × 9½, ff. 213 (18), 2 cols., *caps.* and *mus. rubr.* in dull brown ink, somewhat roughly executed, apparently written with a reed pen. *Mut.* The last leaf is a fragment of Chrysostom, Hom. xlv, on Genesis. (Greg. 323.)

Evst. 265, 269, 271 sometimes agree with each other in departing from the ordinary week-day Church Lessons, and suggest, as Dean Burgon observes, some local fashion which is well worth investigating for textual purposes. The student will have noticed, in our Table of Lessons appended to Chap. III, how often two other codices, Apost. 64, or B.-C. III. 24 and Evst. 253, or B.-C. III. 42, depart from the common use of Church Lesson books, but only for the middle days of the week: not, it would seem, for Saturdays and Sundays.

272. Lond. Brit. Mus. Add. 22,744 [xiii], 11 × 8¼, ff. 189 (23), 2 cols., a beautiful copy, *mut.* at the beginning (to Sat. of third week), the end, and elsewhere, with red musical notes. *See* Evst. 269. (Greg. 324.)

273. Lond. Brit. Mus. Add. 24,374 [xiii], 11½ × 9, ff. 90 (18), 2 cols., *mus. rubr., mut.* (Greg. 325.)

274. Lond. Brit. Mus. Add. 24,377 [xiv and xii], 12 × 8¾, ff. 350 (21), 2 cols., *mus. rubr.*, the first and some other leaves being lost; fol. 180, which is later, has palimpsest cursive writing under it. (Greg. 326.)

275. Lond. Brit. Mus. Add. 24,378 [xiii], 13 × 8¾, ff. 270, 2 cols., part of a Menaeum, in a small hand, written in a single column: imperfect and damaged in places. (Greg. 927.)

276. Lond. Brit. Mus. Add. 24,379 [xiv], 14¼ × 11, ff. 178 (28), 2 cols., much *mut.* throughout, with liturgical headings and some crosses in red for stops. (Greg. 327.)

277. Lond. Brit. Mus. Add. 24,380 [xiv], 11 × 9, ff. 126, 2 cols., *mus. rubr., mut.* at beginning (to sixth day of seventh week) and end. (Greg. 328.)

Evst. 273-277 were purchased of H. Stanhope Freeman in 1862, as was also Evan. 600.

278. Lond. Brit. Mus. Add. 27,860 [xi or xii], 8 × 5½, ff. 115 (28), 2 cols., belonged to Sir F. Gage. (Greg. 329.)

279. Lond. Brit. Mus. Add. 28,817 [June 9, 1185], 11 × 8¾, ff. 306 (21), 2 cols. *Mut.* throughout, clear, in fine condition and peculiar style. (Greg. 330.) Like Evan. 603, bought in 1871 of Sir Ivor B. Guest, as was

280. Lond. Brit. Mus. Add. 28,818 [July, 1272], 9¾ × 7, ff. 118 (27), 2 cols., *chart.*, begins John xvii. 20. The subscription states that it was written διὰ χειρὸς ἐμοῦ τοῦ ἁμαρτωλοῦ τολμῶ εἰπεῖν τοῦ ἱερέως τοῦ μεταξάρη. (Greg. 331.)

*281. Lond. Brit. Mus. Add. 31,208 [xiii], 12¼ × 9½, ff. 272 (21), 2 cols., *mus. rubr.*, bought of a dealer at Constantinople, cruelly mutilated (eighty-four leaves being missing), but once very fine. Collated by the Rev. W. F. Rose, who found it much to resemble Evst. 259 (y^{scr}).

Burgon gives a French version of an Armenian note, dated 908 of the Armenian era, or A.D. 1460, of no special interest. (Greg. 333.)

282. Lond. Brit. Mus. Add. 31,919 [A.D. 1431], 12¾ × 10, ff. 108, formerly Blenheim 3. D. 13, the uncial eighth century palimpsest of the Gospels we have designated as Y, contains Lessons from the Gospels, written by Ignatius, Metropolitan of Selymbria in Thrace, being the February portion of a Menaeum. (Greg. 334.)

283. Lond. Brit. Mus. Add. 31,920 [xi], 9¼ × 8, ff. 226 (21), 2 cols., formerly Blenheim 3. C. 14, containing only σαββατοκυριακαί (see Evst. 24), singularly unadorned, but very interesting and genuine. (Greg. 335.)

284. Lond. Brit. Mus. Add. 31,921 [xiii], 10 × 8, ff. 178 (24), 2 cols., *mus. rubr.*, *mut.*, formerly Blenheim 3. C. 13, with Church Lessons for every day of the week. Several pages in a recent hand stand at the beginning: the first hand commences Matt. vi. 31. (Greg. 336.)

285. Lond. Brit. Mus. Add. 31,949 [xiii], 11 × 8½, ff. 103 (27), 2 cols., much dilapidated and *mut.*, was a gift to the Museum. (Greg. 337.)

†286. Sinai, St. Catharine's, Golden Evst. [ix–xi], 11¼ × 8½ × 3½, ff. abt. 200 (16), 2 cols., *pict.*, 'written in large and beautiful golden uncials,' divided into 'verses' like the modern, has breathings and accents. For specimen of writing, &c., see Burgon, Aug. 9, 1882. It was seen in 1862 by Burgon, in 1864 by the Rev. E. M. Young, and Mr. Jo. Dury Geden (*Athenaeum*, Nov. 12 and 19, 1864). It is said to be deteriorated by the promiscuous handling of strangers, although E. A. Sophocles tells us that local tradition absurdly assigns it to the Emperor Theodosius [d. 395] as the actual scribe; unless, as Mr. Geden suggests, Theodosius III (A.D. 716) be meant. The volume opens with the Gospels for the first five days of Easter week, which are followed by about sixty-five more from other parts of the yearly services. (Greg. 300.)

*287. (Act. 42, Apost. 56) contains only Matt. xvii. 16–23. (Greg. 923.)

288. Oxf. Bodl. Misc. Gr. 307 [xii], 12 × 9½, ff. 335 (22), 2 cols., *pict.*, *mus. rubr.*, *men.*, very beautiful. Mr. Madan of the Bodleian transcribed a note on the last leaf, showing that it once belonged to the Palaeologi. (Greg. 341.)

289. Oxf. Bodl. Misc. Gr. 308, from Constantinople [xii or xiii], 11½ × 9¼, ff. 217 (21), 2 cols., *mus. rubr.*, *men.* Initial letters of Byzantine character, σαββατοκυριακαί (see Evst. 24), has lost a very few lines at the end. (Greg. 342.)

290. (Apost. 78.) (Greg. 476.)

291. Camb. Univ. Libr. Add. 679. 1 [xii], 10 × 8¼, ff. 170 (18), being a companion book to Apost. 79, containing only the week-day Lessons, except that two sets belong to Saturday and Sunday. Begins Matt. vii. 10, being on the sixth day of the first week of that Evangelist. *Mut.* elsewhere, but the end complete with a colophon, and fragments of two additional leaves. Initial capitals in red. (Greg. 305.)

292. (Apost. 80.) Camb. Univ. Libr. Add. 1836 [xiii], $6\frac{1}{2} \times 5\frac{1}{4}$, ff. (185 – 54 =) 131 (17), *mus. rubr.* Sunday and two Saturday Lessons only for Epistles and Gospels. *Mut.* first fifty and four other leaves. Begins second Sunday in St. Matthew (iv. 23). *Men.* full, followed by two Epistles and Gospels as *ἀκολουθία εἰς ὁσίους*. Additional Lessons in another hand are inserted about the season of Epiphany. (Greg. 306.)

293. Camb. Univ. Libr. Add. 1839 [xii or xiii], $10 \times 7\frac{1}{2}$, ff. (192 – 88 =) 104 (17), 2 cols.: *σαββατοκυριακαί* only (*see* Evst. 24). *Mut.* first seventy-seven and ten other leaves. Begins sixth Sunday of St. Luke (viii. 39). *Men.* ending Dec. 26. (Greg. 307.)

294. Camb. Univ. Libr. Add. 1840 [xi or xii], $11\frac{1}{2} \times 8\frac{1}{2}$, ff. 112 (31), 2 cols., *mus. rubr.* From the eleventh Sunday of St. Luke downwards the week-day Lessons are omitted. *Men.* followed by Gospels for several occasions. The arrangement of the week-day Lessons in the Gospels of St. Matthew, St. Mark, and St. Luke differs much from that usually found, though fundamentally akin to it. *Mut.* at the end and many other leaves. (Greg. 308.)

†295. Camb. Univ. Libr. Add. 1879. 2 [x], $11\frac{3}{4} \times 7\frac{7}{8}$, ff. 8 (22), 2 cols., Unc., *orn.*, *mus. rubr.* *Σαββατοκυριακαί* from eleventh Sunday in St. Luke (xiv. 20) to Sunday of the Publican (xviii. 14). Evst. 295–7 are from Tischendorf's collection. (Greg. 309.)

296. Camb. Univ. Libr. Add. 1879. 12 [xi or xii], $9\frac{1}{2} \times 6\frac{1}{4}$, ff. 4 (25), 2 cols., *mus.*, containing from sixth Saturday in Lent (John xi. 41) to Liturgy for Palm Sunday (John xii. 11). and part of Matins (from Matt. xxi. 36) and Vespers (to Matt. xxiv. 26) for Monday in Holy Week. (Greg. 310.)

297. Camb. Univ. Libr. Add. 1879. 13 [xii], $10 \times 8\frac{1}{2}$, ff. 4, *mut.*, 2 cols., Greek and Arabic, being only the upper part of four leaves of *σαββατοκυριακαί* in fifth and sixth Sundays of St. Luke (ch. xvi. 24 f.; 28–30; viii. 16–18; 21; 27; 29 f.; 32–34; 38 f.). (Greg. 311.)

298. Oxf. Keble Coll. [xiii], $9\frac{3}{4} \times 6\frac{3}{4}$, ff. 151 (25), 2 cols., some *mus. rubr.*, *syn.*, *men.*, *orn.*, presented in 1882 by Mr. Greville Chester, beginning with the Lesson for the second day of the fifth week after Easter, and ending with the Lesson for St. Helena's day, May 21. (Greg. 343.)

†299. Par. Nat. Gr. 975. B [x], $12\frac{1}{2} \times 9\frac{1}{2}$, ff. 55 (22), 2 cols., *mus. rubr.*, Unc., palimpsest, frag. of St. Luke, *men.* ff. 33, 34, 39, 40 [ix], Chrys. and Zosimus. (*See* Greg. 363.)

300. Messina, Univ. 65 [xii], $13\frac{3}{4} \times 10\frac{1}{2}$, ff. 318 (25), 2 cols., *mus. rubr.* (Greg. 513.)

†301. Mess. Univ. 66 [ix], $13\frac{7}{8} \times 9\frac{5}{8}$, ff. 256 (28), 2 cols., Unc., *mus. rubr.*, *mut.* (Greg. 514.)

302. Mess. Univ. 75 [xiii], $12\frac{1}{4} \times 9\frac{1}{2}$, ff. 136 (22), 2 cols., *mus. rubr.*, *mut.* at beginning and end. (Greg. 516.)

303. Mess. Univ. 96 [xii], $10\frac{1}{2} \times 7\frac{7}{8}$, ff. 298 (24), 2 cols., *mus. rubr.* (Greg. 519.)

304. Mess. Univ. 98 [A.D. 1148], $10\frac{5}{8} \times 8\frac{1}{2}$, ff. 275 (24), 2 cols. (Greg. 520.)

305. Mess. Univ. 73 [xii], $12\frac{7}{8} \times 9\frac{7}{8}$, ff. 223 (28), 2 cols., written at Messina by Nilus the monk in the monastery of St. Salvador: he records (at p. 26ᵇ) the earthquake which happened Sept. 26, 1173, Codex Graeco-Siculus. (Greg. 515.)

306. Mess. Univ. 58 [xiv, Greg. xv or xvi], $11\frac{1}{2} \times 8\frac{1}{2}$, ff. 236 (17), *chart.*, written by three different calligraphers. (Greg. 512.)

307. Mess. Univ. 94 [xii], $10\frac{1}{2} \times 7\frac{3}{4}$, ff. 184 (21), 2 cols., *mus. rubr.*, *mut.* at beginning, breaking off at Sept. 24 in the menology. (Greg. 517.)

308. Mess. Univ. 111 [xii], $9\frac{1}{2} \times 8$, ff. 119 (23), 2 cols., *mut.* at beginning and end. (Greg. 521.)

309. Mess. Univ. 112 [xii], $9\frac{1}{2} \times 7\frac{1}{2}$, ff. 146 (21), 2 cols., *mus. rubr.*, *mut.* at beginning and end. (Greg. 522.)

310. Mess. Univ. 170 [xii], $8\frac{5}{8} \times 6\frac{1}{4}$, ff. 187 (20), 2 cols., *mut.* at beginning and end. (Greg. 524.)

311. Mess. Univ. 95 [xiii], $11\frac{1}{4} \times 8\frac{1}{8}$, ff. 186 (23), 2 cols., *mus. rubr.*, *mut.* from pp. 42–75. (Greg. 518.)

312. (Apost. 112.) Mess. Univ. 150 [xii or xiii], $6\frac{1}{2} \times 5\frac{1}{4}$, ff. 60 (22). A fragment. (*See* Greg. 523.)

313. Crypta Ferrata, A. a. 7 [xii], $9\frac{5}{8} \times 7\frac{7}{8}$, ff. 45 (25), 2 cols., *mus. nigr.*, σαββατοκυριακαί mutilated. (Greg. 463.)

314. Crypt. Ferr. A. a. 9 [xii], $13\frac{3}{4} \times 9\frac{7}{8}$, ff. 292 (25), 2 cols., *mus. rubr.*, *mut.*, a beautiful codex, and very full in its Lections. (Greg. 464.)

315. Crypt. Ferr. A. a. 10 [xi], $12\frac{7}{8} \times 10\frac{1}{4}$, ff. 246 (22), 2 cols., *mus. rubr.*, much foreign matter, a very beautiful codex. (Greg. 465.)

316. Crypt. Ferr. A. a. 11 [xv], $6\frac{1}{4} \times 4\frac{7}{8}$, ff. 181 (14), *mut.* σαββατοκυρ. (Greg. 466.)

317. Crypt. Ferr. A. a. 12 [xiv, Greg. x or xi], $6\frac{3}{8} \times 4\frac{3}{4}$, ff. 97 (22), *mut.* (Greg. 467.)

318. Crypt. Ferr. A. a. 13 [xv], $6\frac{3}{8} \times 4\frac{7}{8}$, ff. 62 (18), partly palimpsest, *mut.* (Greg. 468.)

319. Crypt. Ferr. A. a. 14 [xii], $9\frac{1}{2} \times 6\frac{3}{4}$, ff. 73 (23), 2 cols., *mut.* at beginning and end. (*See* Greg. 469.)

320. Crypt. Ferr. A. a. 15 [xi], $7\frac{1}{8} \times 5\frac{7}{8}$, ff. 69 (23). Closely resembles Evst. 33. (Greg. 470.)

321. Crypt. Ferr. A. a. 16 [xi], $7\frac{7}{8} \times 5\frac{3}{8}$, ff. 55 (26), 2 cols., a fragment from St. John. (Greg. 471.)

322. (Apost. 90.) Crypt. Ferr. A. β. 2 [xi], $5\frac{7}{8} \times 4$, ff. 259 (ff. 159–213), with many excerpts from Fathers. (Greg. 478.)

323. (Apost. 90.) Crypt. Ferr. A. δ. 2 [x], $5\frac{7}{8} \times 4\frac{3}{8}$, ff. 155, much from Old Testament, *mut.* (Greg. 473.)

†324. Par. Nat. Suppl. Gr. 805, ff. 1–7 [ix], $11\frac{1}{2} \times 8\frac{1}{8}$, ff. 7 (19), Unc., palimpsest, *mus. rubr.*, fragm. (*See* Greg. 370.)

325. (Apost. 92.) Crypt. Ferr. A. δ. 4 [xiii], $9\frac{7}{8} \times 7\frac{1}{4}$, ff. 257. Written by 'Johannes Rossanensis.' Contains Lections from Old and New Testaments. (Greg. 475.)

326. St. Saba 25 [xi], fol. Coxe. (Greg. 170.)

327. St. Saba 26 [xi], fol. Coxe.

328. St. Saba 40 [xii], fol. In Greek and Arabic. Coxe.

329. St. Saba 44 [xii], 4to. Coxe.

330. Crypt. Ferr. A. δ. 11 [three fragments]:—
    (1) [xi], $9\frac{3}{4} \times 7\frac{1}{2}$, ff. 2 (22), 2 cols.;
    (2) [xii], $6\frac{1}{4} \times 4\frac{5}{8}$, ff. 2 (23);
    (3) [xiii], $8\frac{5}{8} \times 6\frac{3}{4}$, ff. 4 (22), 2 cols., *mus. rubr.* (*See* Greg. 472.)

331. Crypt. Ferr. A. δ. 16 [x], $9\frac{1}{2} \times 7\frac{1}{8}$, ff. 234 (25), 2 cols., palimpsest. (Greg. 480.)

†332. Crypt. Ferr. A. δ. 17 [x], $7\frac{7}{8} \times 5\frac{7}{8}$, ff. 25 (27), Unc., palimpsest, fragm. (Greg. 481.)

†333. Crypt. Ferr. A. δ. 19 [x], $7\frac{1}{2} \times 5\frac{1}{8}$, ff. 39 (24), 2 cols., Unc., palimpsest, *mut.* (Greg. 482.)

334. (Apost. 95.) Crypt. Ferr. A. δ. 20 [xii, Greg. x or xi], $9 \times 6\frac{3}{4}$, ff. 21 (22), 2 cols., *mut.* (Greg. 483.)

335. Crypt. Ferr. A. δ. 21 [x], 13×9, ff. 97 (31), palimpsest, *mut.* (Greg. 484.)

336. Crypt. Ferr. A. δ. 22 [x or xi], $6\frac{3}{4} \times 5\frac{1}{4}$, ff. 113, 2 cols., palimpsest, *mut.* (Greg. 485.)

†337. (Apost. 96.) Crypt. Ferr. A. δ. 24 [four fragments]:—
    (1) Also called z'. a'. 2 [xiii], $9\frac{3}{4} \times 6\frac{3}{4}$, ff. 2 (28), 2 cols.;
    (2) Also B'. a'. 23 [viii or ix], $7\frac{7}{8} \times 5\frac{1}{3}$, palimpsest, Unc., ff. 2 (27), 2 cols.;
    (3) Also z'. a'. 24 (R paul.);
    (4) Also Γ. B'. 3 [xi], $7\frac{3}{8} \times 5\frac{1}{2}$. *See* also 340. (Greg. 486^{a-d}.)

338. Crypt. Ferr. Γ. a. 18 [xvii], $10\frac{1}{4} \times 7\frac{7}{8}$, ff. 170, Evangelia ἑωθινά. (Greg. 487.)

339. (Apost. 97.) Crypt. Ferr. Γ. β. 2 [xi], $6\frac{3}{4} \times 5\frac{1}{5}$, ff. 151, a Euchology, contains only a few Lections. (Greg. 488.)

340. (Apost. 98.) Crypt. Ferr. Γ. β. 3 [xiv], $7\frac{3}{8} \times 5\frac{1}{2}$, ff. 201 (19), Euchology. Contains only a few Lessons. (Greg. 486^{d2}.)

341. (Apost. 99.) Crypt. Ferr. Γ. β. 6 [xiii or xiv], $7\frac{1}{8} \times 4\frac{3}{4}$, ff. 101 (21). Contains only a few Lections. (Greg. 489.)

342. Crypt. Ferr. Γ. β. 7 [ix or x], $6\frac{3}{4} \times 5\frac{1}{2}$, ff. 173 (17), Euchology. Contains only a few Lections. (Greg. 490.)

343. Crypt. Ferr. Γ. β. 8 [Greg. xiii], ff. 8 palimpsest at end of ff. 145 [xii]. (*See* Greg. 491.)

344. (Apost. 100.) Crypt. Ferr. Γ. β. 9 [xvi], $4\frac{1}{4} \times 3\frac{1}{8}$, ff. 95, Euchology. Contains only a few Lections. (Greg. 492.)

345. Crypt. Ferr. Γ. β. 11 [xii], $5\frac{1}{2} \times 4\frac{3}{4}$, ff. 20, Euchology. Contains only a few Lections. (Greg. 493.)

346. (Apost. 101.) Crypt. Ferr. Γ. β. 12 [xiv], $5\frac{7}{8} \times 4\frac{3}{4}$, ff. 98, Euchology. Contains only a few Lections. (Greg. 494.)

347. (Apost. 102.) Crypt. Ferr. Γ. β. 13 [xiii], $9 \times 6\frac{1}{4}$, ff. 118 (18), Euchology. Written by 'Johannes Rossanensis.' (Greg. 495.)

348. Crypt. Ferr. Γ. β. 14 [xiii], $7\frac{1}{2} \times 5\frac{1}{2}$, ff. 54 (23). Euchologium with a few Lections. (Greg. 496.)

349. (Apost. 103.) Crypt. Ferr. Γ. β. 15 [xi–xiii], $7\frac{1}{8} \times 5\frac{1}{8}$, ff. 41 (22), Euchology. Contains only a few Lections. (*See* Greg. 497.)

350. (Apost. 104.) Crypt. Ferr. Γ. β. 17 [A.D. 1565], $8\frac{1}{4} \times 5\frac{7}{8}$, ff. 269 (21), *chart.* The Saturday and Sunday Lessons begin at fol. 121. (*See* Greg. 498.)

351. (Apost. 105.) Crypt. Ferr. Γ. β. 18 [xiv], St. Saba 55 [xii], 4to. Coxe. Contains very few Lections.

352. (Apost. 106.) Crypt. Ferr. Γ. β. 19 [xvi], $11\frac{3}{8} \times 8\frac{1}{4}$, ff. 145 (28), *chart.* The Apostolo-Evangeliarium begins at fol. 16. (*See* Greg. 500.)

353. (Apost. 107.) Crypt. Ferr. Γ. β. 23 [A.D. 1641]. $12\frac{1}{2} \times 8\frac{5}{8}$, ff. 75. It is a Euchologium with a few Lections. (*See* Greg. 501.)

354. (Apost. 108.) Crypt. Ferr. Γ. β. 24 [xvi], $12\frac{1}{2} \times 9$, ff. 302 (28), *chart.* Liturgical information. (*See* Greg. 502.)

355. Crypt. Ferr. Γ. β. 35 [xiii], $7\frac{1}{8} \times 5\frac{7}{8}$, ff. 83 (21), liturgical. Contains only a few Lections. (*See* Greg. 503.)

356. (Apost. 109.) Crypt. Ferr. Γ. β. 38 [xvii], $11\frac{3}{4} \times 8\frac{5}{8}$, ff. 91. Contains only a few Lections. (*See* Greg. 504.)

357. (Apost. 110.) Crypt. Ferr. Γ. β. 13 [xvi], $10\frac{1}{4} \times 7\frac{1}{2}$, ff. 344, *chart.*, liturgical. (Greg. 505.)

358. (Apost. 111.) Crypt. Ferr. Δ. β. 22 [xviii], $15\frac{5}{8} \times 10\frac{5}{8}$, ff. 77 (27), *chart.* Contains only a few Lections. (Greg. 506.)

359. Crypt. Ferr. Δ. γ. 26 [xiv], $4\frac{1}{4} \times 3\frac{1}{8}$, ff. 115 (19). The Evangelia [*ἑωθινά*]. (Greg. 507.)

360. Crypt. Ferr. Δ. δ. 6 [xviii], $16 \times 10\frac{5}{8}$, ff. ?, palimpsest. Fragments. (*See* Greg. 508.)

361. St. Saba, Tower Library 12 [xi], 4to. Coxe.

362. Syracuse 'Seminario' 3 [A.D. 1125], $8\frac{3}{8} \times 5\frac{1}{2}$, ff. 255 (25), 2 cols. (Greg. 574.)

363. Lond. Lambeth 1194 [xiii, Greg. xi], $7\frac{1}{2} \times 5\frac{1}{2}$, ff. 218 (17), fifty-one Lessons from Gospels—forty-eight from Acts and Epistles, *mus. rubr.*, *mut.* Menaeum ending in June. (Greg. 477.)

364. St. Saba, Tower 16 [xii], 4to, with Lections from Old Testament. Coxe.

365. St. Saba, Tower 52 [xi], 4to, *mus.* Coxe.

366. Par. Nat. Suppl. Gr. 74 [xiv or xv, Greg. xii], $7\frac{3}{4} \times 5\frac{3}{8}$, ff. 72, 2 cols., *mus. rubr.* Formerly Huet's, who gave it to the Jesuits. Contains the Evangelia ἑωθινά. It is rather a Euchologium, and is of little value. (Greg. 366.)

†367. Par. Nat. Suppl. Gr. 567 [xv], 13×10, ff. 173 (14), 2 cols., Unc., apparently modern. Given by the same to the library. Saturday and Sunday Lections. (Greg. 367.)

368. Berlin, Reg. Gr. 'Hamilton 245' [x, Greg. xii], $12\frac{7}{8} \times 9\frac{3}{8}$, ff. 378 (21), 2 cols., *pict.* A magnificent specimen. (Greg. 381.)

369. Berlin, Reg. Gr. 'Hamilton 246' [xiii], $13\frac{1}{3} \times 10\frac{1}{8}$, ff. ?, 2 cols. At the beginning of the volume is a fragment of a more ancient Evangelium, not extending beyond the Eusebian tables of Canons, superbly illuminated. (Greg. 382.)

370. Berlin, Reg. Gr. 51 fol. [xiii, Greg. xii], $12\frac{5}{8} \times 9\frac{1}{2}$, ff. 214 (26), 2 cols. (*See* Greg. 375.)

371. Berlin, Reg. Gr. 52 fol. [xii], $11\frac{1}{2} \times 9$, *mus. rubr.* (Greg. 376.)

372. Berlin, Reg. Gr. 53 fol. [xii, Greg. xi], $11\frac{3}{4} \times 8\frac{3}{4}$, ff. 248 (21), 2 cols., *mus. rubr.* (*See* Greg. 377.)

373. Berlin, Reg. Gr. 4to, 46 [xiii, Greg. xii], $10\frac{3}{4} \times 8$, ff. 46, 2 cols., *mus. rubr.*, ends with the Saturday of Pentecost. (Greg. 378.)

374. Berlin, Reg. Gr. 4to, 61 [xiii], $11\frac{1}{2} \times 8\frac{1}{2}$, *mus. rubr.*, begins with the Saturday after Pentecost, and contains the Menologium. (Greg. 379.)

375. Berlin, Reg. Gr. 4to, 64 [xii, xiii], $10\frac{1}{2} \times 8\frac{1}{8}$, *mut.* at the commencement. (Greg. 380.)

376. Rom. Vat. Gr. 352 [xi, Greg. xiii or xvi], $12\frac{1}{2} \times 9\frac{3}{8}$, ff. 244 (23), 2 cols., with Menology. (Greg. 540.)

†377. Rom. Vat. Gr. 353 [x], $11\frac{5}{8} \times 8\frac{1}{8}$, ff. 237 (20), 2 cols., Unc. Gospel Lections. (Greg. 541.)

†378. Rom. Vat. Gr. 355 [x], $13 \times 10\frac{1}{8}$, ff. 315 (19), 2 cols., Unc. (Greg. 542.)

†379. Rom. Vat. Gr. 357 [x], $15\frac{3}{8} \times 12\frac{3}{4}$, ff. 322 (15), 2 cols., *mus. rubr.* (Greg. 543.)

380. Rom. Vat. Gr. 362 [x, Greg. xi], $7\frac{3}{4} \times 5\frac{7}{8}$, ff. 200 (23). (Greg. 544.)

381. Rom. Vat. Gr. 540 [x], fol., ff. 4 (20), 2 cols., *mus. rubr.*, a fragment prefixed to St. Chrysostom on St. John. (*See* Greg. 545.)

382. Rom. Vat. Gr. 781 [xii, Greg. x or xi], $9\frac{7}{8} \times 7\frac{1}{2}$, ff. 152 (27), 2 cols., 'fuit Blasii praep. Cryptae Ferratae.' (Greg. 546.)

383. Rom. Vat. Gr. 1534 [xiii or xiv], $13\frac{1}{4} \times 10\frac{1}{2}$, ff. 223 (25), 2 cols. (Greg. 549.)

384. Rom. Vat. Gr. 1601 [xiii, Greg. xii], $9\frac{3}{8} \times 7\frac{1}{4}$, ff. 193 (22), 2 cols. (Greg. 550.)

385. Rom. Vat. Gr. 1813 [xiii], $7\frac{1}{8} \times 5\frac{1}{4}$, ff. out of 266 – 3 (19). Evangelia ἐωθινά. (Greg. 552.)

386. Rom. Vat. Gr. 1886 [xiii], $10 \times 7\frac{3}{8}$, ff. 110 (29), 2 cols. (Greg. 553.)

387. (Apost. 118.) Rom. Vat. Gr. 2012 [xv], ff. 211. Contains only a few Gospel Lections. (Greg. 556.)

388. Rom. Vat. Gr. 2100 [xiv], $7 \times 5\frac{1}{4}$, ff. 79 (19), with a commentary. (Greg. 560.)

389. Rom. Vat. Gr. 2129 [xv, Greg. xiv], *chart.*, ff. 5 out of 701. Lections during Lent. (Greg. 561.)

†390. Rom. Vat. Gr. 2144 [viii], $8\frac{1}{4} \times 5\frac{5}{8}$, ff. 193 (22), 2 cols., Unc. Brought from Constantinople. (Greg. 563.)

†391. Patmos 4 [xi], 4to, Unc. Coxe. (Greg. ?)

392. Rom. Vat. Gr. 2167 [xiii], $12\frac{1}{4} \times 9$, ff. 361 (21), 2 cols., *pict.* Olim 'Columnensis.' (Greg. 564.)

†393. Rom. Vat. Gr. 2251 [viii ?], $8\frac{1}{4} \times 5\frac{1}{2}$, ff. 4 (22), 2 cols., Unc. Olim 'Columnensis.' At the beginning and end of a larger MS. (Greg. 565.)

394. Rom. Vat. Alex. Gr. 44 [xvii], $8\frac{1}{4} \times 5\frac{7}{8}$, ff. 355 (20), *chart.*, by different hands, with a commentary. (Greg. 571.)

395. (Apost. 121.) Rom. Vat. Alex. Gr. 59 [xii], $11 \times 7\frac{3}{4}$, ff. 137 (47). Gospels and Epistles for Holy Week. Lections from Old and New Test. (Greg. 573.)

†396. Rom. Vat. Ottob. Gr. 444 A, B [ix], $10 \times 7\frac{3}{8}$, ff. 2 (22), 2 cols., Unc., with fragments of Gospels. (Greg. 566.)

†397. Rom. Vat. Palat. Gr. 1. A [ix or x], $10\frac{1}{4} \times 7\frac{5}{8}$, ff. 2 (23), 2 cols. Unc. A mere fragment. (Greg. 567.)

398. Rom. Vat. Palat. Gr. 221 [xiii, Greg. xv], $9\frac{5}{8} \times 4\frac{1}{4}$ (?), ff. 397 (32) *chart.*, with the commentary of Xiphilinus. (Greg. 568.)

399. Rom. Vat. Palat. Gr. 239 [xv, Greg. xvi], $8\frac{3}{4} \times 5\frac{3}{4}$, ff. 122 (?) (23), *chart.*, with a commentary. (Greg. 569.)

†400. Patmos 10 [xi], 4to, Unc. Coxe. (Greg. ?)

†401. Patmos 22 [xi], fol., Unc. Coxe. (Greg. ?)

†402. Patmos 81 [viii], 4to, Unc. Coxe. (Greg. ?)

403. Rom. Barberini iv. 43 [xii, Greg. xiii or xiv], $9\frac{1}{2} \times 7\frac{1}{4}$, ff. 22 (23), 2 cols., *mus. rubr.*, *pict.*, beautifully illuminated. (Greg. 535.)

404. Rom. Barb. iv. 30 [xii], 9×7, ff. 223 (22), 2 cols. (Greg. 534.)

405. Rom. Barb. iv. 53 [xiii, Greg. xi or xii], $9\frac{3}{4} \times 7\frac{1}{2}$, ff. 161 (22) 2 cols., *mus. rubr.*, *mut.*, *chart.* (Greg. 536.)

406. Rom. Barb. iv. 13 [xii], ff. 143. Contains only a few Lection (Greg. 531.)

407. Rom. Barb. iv. 25 [xiv, Greg. xi or xii], $9 \times 5\frac{3}{4}$, ff. 159. Contains only certain Lections. (Greg. 532.)

408. (Apost. 218.) Rom. Barb. iv. 1 [xiv–xvi], ff. 323, *chart.* Contains only a few Lections. (Greg. 530.)

409. Rom. Barb. iii. 22 [xv], ff. 254, *chart.* Contains only a few Lections. (Greg. 528.)

410. (Apost. 124.) Rom. Barb. iii. 129 [xiv], ff. 189. (Greg. 529.)

411. Rom. Barb. vi. 18 [xii], $12\frac{3}{8} \times 10\frac{3}{8}$, *mut.*, but beautifully illuminated with Menology. (Greg. 537.)

412. Milos [xii], fol., a fragment. Coxe. (Greg. 804.)

413. Constantinople, Patriarch of Jerusalem 10 [xii], 4to, a palimpsest written over a geometrical treatise [xi]. Coxe.

†414. Rom. Ghig. R. vii. 52 [ix, Greg. x or xi], $11\frac{3}{4} \times 9\frac{3}{8}$, ff. 227 (12), 2 cols., *mus. rubr.*, 'cod. nobilissimus, charact. uncialibus: habet titulum *Hebdomadae magnae Officium Graecorum:* e CP. advectus est ad Conventum Collis Paradisi, et hinc ad Bibliothecam Chisianam.' (Greg. 538.)

415. (Apost. 256.) Par. Nat. 13 [xii–xiii, Greg. xi or xii], $15\frac{5}{8} \times 11\frac{3}{4}$, ff. 478 (68), 2 cols. See Martin, p. 165. (Greg. 935.)

416. Par. Nat. Suppl. Gr. 24 [xiii], $13 \times 9\frac{3}{4}$, ff. 339 (22), 2 cols., *mus. rubr.* See Martin, p. 165. (Greg. 364.)

417. Par. Nat. Suppl. Gr. 29 [xii], $9\frac{3}{4} \times 7\frac{5}{8}$, ff. 198 (20), 2 cols., *mus. rubr.*, *mut.* See Martin, p. 165. (Greg. 365.)

418. Par. Nat. Suppl. Gr. 179, 180 [xiii], $9\frac{1}{4} \times 5\frac{7}{8}$, f. 1 (26). See Martin, p. 166. (Greg. 928.)

419. Par. Nat. Suppl. Gr. 1096 [xiii–xiv], $7\frac{1}{4} \times 5\frac{1}{4}$, ff. 33 (26), *men.* (Greg. 374.)

420. Auckland, City Library. (Greg. 474.)

†421. Par. Nat. Suppl. Gr. 686 [xi, Greg. ix], $11\frac{3}{4} \times 9$, ff. 2 (21), 2 cols., *mus. rubr.* Martin, p. 167. (Greg. 368.)

422. Par. Nat. Suppl. Gr. 687 [xii], $13\frac{1}{2} \times 10\frac{1}{8}$, ff. 2 (20), 2 cols., *mus. rubr.* Martin, p. 167. (Greg. 499.)

423. Par. Nat. Suppl. Gr. 758 [xii], $11 \times 8\frac{5}{8}$, ff. 111 (28), 2 cols., *orn.*, *mus. rubr.* Martin, p. 167. (Greg. 369.)

424. Par. Nat. Suppl. Gr. 834 [xiii], $11\frac{1}{8} \times 9$, ff. 90 (27), 2 cols., *mus. rubr.* Martin, p. 168. (Greg. 371.)

425. Par. Nat. Suppl. Gr. 905 [A.D. 1055 ?], $11\frac{7}{8} \times 9\frac{3}{4}$, ff. 254 (20), 2 cols., *pict.*, *men.* Martin, p. 168. (Greg. 372.)

426. Par. Nat. Gr. 235 [xii], $12\frac{3}{4} \times 10$, ff. 235 (24), 2 cols., *mus. rubr.*, *men.*, greatly *mut.* Martin, p. 168. (Greg. 361.)

†427. Par. Nat. Gr. 228, Greg. 928 [ix], $11\frac{1}{2} \times 8\frac{1}{2}$, ff. 240 (20), 2 cols., palimpsest with menaeum [xii–xiii] written over, 2 ff. at beginning, and 1 after p. 48, *chart.* and later, *Am.*, Unc. Martin, p. 169. (Greg. 362.)

428. (Apost. 257.) Par. Nat. Gr. 263 [xiii], $15 \times 10\frac{7}{8}$, ff. 200 (62),

2 cols., *mut.* at end. Came from Mon. of Panteleemon at Athos. Martin, p. 170. (Greg. 936.)

For the rest, *see* Gregory, pp. 744, &c. The press-marks in the Athenian MSS. have been changed since Dr. Gregory examined them. I have had great difficulty in identifying them, and am in doubt as to many where a (?) is inserted. The figures in brackets are the present press-marks. Dr. Gregory's are given first.

429. Athens, Nat. Libr. 12 (66?) [xi], $11\frac{3}{4} \times 9\frac{1}{2}$, ff. 196.

430. Ath. Nat. 13 (70?) [A.D. 1350], $12\frac{1}{2} \times 9$, ff. 199, *pict.*

431. Ath. Nat. 13 (146?) [xv], $11 \times 9\frac{1}{2}$, ff. 174, *chart.*

432. Ath. Nat. 15 (64?), $13\frac{3}{8} \times 9\frac{1}{2}$, ff. 287, *mut.* at end.

433. Ath. Nat. 17 (82) [xii], $9 \times 7\frac{1}{8}$, ff. 139, *mut.* at end.

434. Ath. Nat. 18 (68?) [xii], 11×9, ff. 220, *pict., mut.* at end.

435. Ath. Nat. 19 (79) [xiv], $8\frac{5}{8} \times 7\frac{1}{4}$, ff. 191.

436. Ath. Nat. 19 (73) [A.D. 1545], $12\frac{1}{2} \times 8\frac{1}{4}$, ff. 314 (? 251+63 later).

437. Ath. Nat. 24 (67?) [x], 11×9, ff. 260, *mus.*

438. Ath. Nat. 25 (112?) [xv], $7\frac{1}{2} \times 5\frac{1}{2}$, ff. 119.

439. (Apost. 193.) Ath. Nat. 66 (670?) [xii], $8\frac{1}{4} \times 5\frac{7}{8}$, ff. 132, Euchology followed by Apostoloeuaggelia.

440. (Apost. 194.) Ath. Nat. 112 (126) [A.D. 1504], $8\frac{1}{4} \times 5\frac{7}{8}$, ff. 276.

441. Ath. Nat. (69) [xii], $11\frac{3}{8} \times 8\frac{5}{8}$, ff. 200, the last three blank.

442. Ath. Nat. (63?) [x end], $11\frac{3}{4} \times 9\frac{1}{2}$, ff. 294.

443. (Apost. 195.) Ath. Nat. 86. I cannot find this, which is a menaeum, or the two next.

†444ª. Ath. Nat. ?   444ᵇ. Ath. Nat. ?

445. Ath. Nat. (84?) [xiv], $11\frac{3}{8} \times 8\frac{5}{8}$, ff. 148.

446. (Apost. 196.) Ath. Nat. (661?) [xv], $7\frac{7}{8} \times 6\frac{3}{8}$, ff. 138. Liturgical matter followed by Apostoloeuaggelia.

447. Ath. Nat. (85?) [xiv], $11 \times 7\frac{7}{8}$, ff. 102.

448. Ath. Nat. 124 [xii], $10\frac{5}{8} \times 8\frac{5}{8}$, ff. 174, *mus.*

449. Ath. Nat. (62?) [xii], $11\frac{3}{4} \times 9$, ff. 329, *mus.*

450. Ath. τῆς Βουλῆς.   451. Ath. M. Bournias.

452ª. Ath. M. Bournias.   452ᵇ. Ath. M. Bournias.

453. Ath. M. Varouccas.

454. Dublin, Trin. Coll. A. i. 8, fol. 1.

455. Toledo, Conv. Canon. arm. 31, no. 31.

456. Corcyra, Abp. Eustathius.   457. Corcyra, Abp. Eustathius.

458. Corcyra, Abp. Eustathius.   459. Corcyra, M. Eleutherius.

460. Corcyra, M. Eleutherius.   461. Corcyra, M. Eleutherius.

462. Corcyra, M. Arist. St. Varouccas.

463. Andover, Mass. U. S. A., Theol. Seminary 1 [xv or xiv], $8\frac{1}{4} \times 6$, ff. 194 (24), (26 (?) *chart.*), part palimpsest. Hoskier. (Greg. 180.)

464. Athos, Simopetra 148. (Greg. 479.)

†465. Moscow, Syn. 313 (ol. 300). (Greg. 242.)

†466. Petersburg, Caes. Muralt. 21 (69). (Greg. 243.)

†467. Petersburg, Caes. Mur. 35. (Greg. 244.)

†468. Petersburg, Caes. Mur. 36. (Greg. 245a.)

†469. Petersburg, Caes. Mur. 37. (Greg. 245b.)

470. Petersburg, Caes. Mur. 40. (Greg. 247.)

471. Petersburg, Caes. Mur. 43. (Greg. 248.)

472. Petersburg, Caes. Mur. 55. (Greg. 250.)

473. Petersburg, Caes. Mur. 69. (Greg. 252.)

474. Petersburg, Caes. Mur. 80. (Greg. 254.)

475. Petersburg, Caes. Mur. 84. (Greg. 255.)

476. Petersburg, Caes. Mur. 37a. (Greg. 257.)

477. Petersburg, Caes. Mur. 112. (Greg. 259.)

478. Venice, St. Mark ii. 17. (Greg. 273.)

479. Venice, St. Mark ii. 143. (Greg. 274.)

480. Milan, Ambr. E. 101 sup. (Greg. 286.)

481. Tubingen, Univ. 2. (Greg. 294.)

482. Bandur. *ev.* Formerly Montfaucon's. (Greg. 295.)

483. Cambridge, Mass. U. S. A., Harvard Univ. 1h (Dr. 69) [ix], $12\frac{1}{4} \times 8\frac{5}{8}$, ff. 6 (19), 2 cols. *See* Hoskier, MS. 604, App. ii. (Greg. 296.)

484. Camb. Mass. U. S. A., Harv. Univ. 2h [xii], $10\frac{3}{4} \times 8$, ff. 230 (23), 2 cols., *men.* (ff. 171–230), accompanied by an Apost. Hoskier. (Greg. 297.)

485. Camb. Mass. U. S. A., Harv. Univ. 3h (A. R. G. 1. 3) [xiii], $12\frac{1}{2} \times 9\frac{1}{2}$, ff. 202 (25), 2 cols., twelve leaves or parts of leaves later, *mut., mus. rubr., men.* Hoskier. (Greg. 298.)

486. Madison, New Caesarea, Theol. Seminary, Drew MS. 2. (Greg. 301.)

487. Sewickley, Pennsylvania, Mr. R. A. Benton. (Greg. 302a.)

488. Cambridge, Clare College [xiv], $8\frac{1}{4} \times 6$, ff. 163 (21), *mut.* at end. Brought from Constantinople, and presented by Mr. J. Rendel Harris, Fellow of the College.

489. Sewickley, Pennsylvania, Mr. R. A. Benton. (Greg. 302b.)

490. Sewanee, Tennessee, Mr. A. A. Benton. (Greg. 302c.)

491. Princetown, New Caesarea, Theol. Seminary. (Greg. 303.)

492. Woolwich (?), Mr. Ch. C. G. Bate. (Greg. 304.)

493. Sinaiticus (Λ. 1, *see* under Evan. Λ). (Greg. 312.)

494. Lond. Highgate, Burdett-Coutts II. 5. (Greg. 313.)

495. Lond. Highgate, B.-C. II. 14. (Greg. 314.)

†496. Lond. Brit. Mus. Add. 14,637 [vii], $11\frac{3}{8} \times 7\frac{1}{8}$, ff. 23, 2 cols., Unc., fragments. Palimpsest [x] in Syriac. (Greg. 316.)

†497. Lond. Brit. Mus. Add. 14,638 [viii, Greg. ix], $6\frac{1}{2} \times 4\frac{7}{8}$, ff. (26−8=) 18 (20). Fragments. Palimpsest under Syriac. (Greg. 317.)

498. (Apost. 288.) Jerus. Patr. Libr. 105 [A.D. 1762, May 11], $12\frac{3}{4} \times 9$, ff. 228, pict., vers. Written by Athanasius, ἱερεὺς Σαρασίτος. (Kerameus.)

†499. London, Brit. Mus. Burney 408 [x], $8 \times 6\frac{1}{2}$, ff. 163 (22), 2 cols. Palimpsest, hardly legible, Unc., latter part, as Greg. has discovered, in early minuscules. Bought in 1872. (Greg. 338.)

500. Wisbech, Peckover 70. (Greg. 345.)

501. Vindob. Caes. Gr. Theol. 160. (Greg. 347.)

502. Vindob. Archduke Rainer (1). (Greg. 348.)

503. Vindob. Archd. Rainer (2). (Greg. 349.)

504. Montpelier, School of Medicine H. 405. (Greg. 350.)

505. Late Henri Bordier. (Greg. 351.)

506. Paris, late Emman. Miller 4. (Greg. 352.)

†507. Paris, late Emman. Miller 5. (Greg. 353.)

†508. Paris, late Emman. Miller 6. (Greg. 354.)

†509. Paris, late Emman. Miller 7. (Greg. 355.)

510. Florence, Laurent. Gaddianus 124.

511. Flor. Riccardi 69, ff. 111.

†512. Paris, late Emman. Miller 8. (Greg. 356.)

†513. Paris, late Emman. Miller 9. (Greg. 357.)

†514. Paris, late Emman. Miller 10. (Greg. 358.)

†515. Paris, late Emman. Miller 11. (Greg. 359.)

†516. Paris, late Emman. Miller 12. (Greg. 360.)

†517. Par. Nat. Suppl. Gr. 1081. (Greg. 373.)

518. (Apost. 259.) Athens, Nat. Theol. 25 (163) [xii], $12\frac{3}{4} \times 9\frac{7}{8}$, ff. 327, mut. at beg. Beautiful and decorated, mus. rubr., pict., vers. (Greg. 383.)

519. Ath. Nat. Theol. 26 (164) [xii], $13\frac{3}{4} \times 10\frac{1}{4}$, ff. 291, mus. (Greg. 384.)

520. Ath. Nat. Theol. 27 (165) [xiv], $11\frac{3}{4} \times 9$, ff. 162, mus. (Greg. 385.)

521. Ath. Nat. Theol. 28 (166) [xiv], $12\frac{7}{8} \times 8\frac{5}{8}$, ff. 236, mut. at beg. mus. (Greg. 386.)

522. Ath. Nat. Theol. 29 (167) [xiv], $12\frac{1}{8} \times 9$, ff. 243, mus. (Greg. 387.)

523. Ath. Nat. Theol. 30 (168) [xv], $12\frac{1}{2} \times 8\frac{1}{4}$, ff. 217, presented to the Church of Christ τοῦ Μανιτρί in A.D. 1527. (Greg. 388.)

524. Ath. Nat. Theol. 31 (169) [xiv], $12\frac{1}{2} \times 9$, ff. 212, mus. (Greg. 389.)

525. Messina, Univ. 175.

526. Pistoia, Fabronianus.

527. Rom. Angelicus D. ii. 27.

528. Athens, Nat. Theol. 32 (170) [xiv], $12\frac{1}{8} \times 8\frac{5}{8}$, ff. 144. (Greg. 390.)

529. Ath. Nat. Theol. 33 (171) [xvi], $12\frac{1}{4} \times 8\frac{5}{8}$, ff. 355. (Greg. 391.)

530. Ath. Nat. Theol. 34 (172) [xiv], $12\frac{1}{8} \times 9\frac{7}{8}$, ff. 212, *mut.* at beg. and end, *mus.* (Greg. 392.)

531. Ath. Nat. Theol. 35 (173) [xiv], $11\frac{3}{4} \times 9$, ff. 248, *mut.* at beg and end, *vers.*, written by one Michael. (Greg. 393.)

532. Ath. Nat. Theol. 36 (174) [xiv], $11\frac{3}{4} \times 9\frac{1}{2}$, ff. 305, *mut.* at end, *vers.* Very much ornamented; very beautiful and valuable. (Greg. 394.)

533. Rom. Barb. iv. 28.

534. Ath. Nat. Theol. 37 (175) [xiv], $11\frac{3}{4} \times 8\frac{5}{8}$, ff. 180—last 18 *chart.* (Greg. 395.)

535. Ath. Nat. 38 (176) [A. D. 1328], $11\frac{3}{4} \times 8\frac{1}{4}$, ff. 222. Written by Hilarion of Beroea. (Greg. 396.)

536. Ath. Nat. 39 ? (Greg. 397.)

537. Ath. Nat. 40 (177) [xiv], $11 \times 8\frac{1}{4}$, ff. 79, *mut.* at beg. Matt. and Luke. Palimpsest. Under-writing [viii]. Written by Joseph. (Greg. 398a, b.)

†538. Ath. Nat. 41 (178) [A. D. 1311], $11 \times 8\frac{1}{4}$, ff. 266. Written by Leon. (Greg. 399a, b.)

539. Rom. Vat. Gr. 350.

540. Athos, Dionysius 23. (Greg. 400.)

541. Athens, Nat. Theol. 42 (179) [A. D. 1311], $11 \times 8\frac{1}{4}$, ff. 266, *mus.* Written by Leon. (Greg. 401.)

542. Ath. Nat. Theol. 43 (180) [A. D. 1089], $10\frac{5}{8} \times 8\frac{1}{4}$, ff. 204, *mus.* Written by Andreas. (Greg. 402.)

543. Ath. Nat. Theol. 44 (181) [xiv], $9\frac{7}{8} \times 7\frac{1}{2}$, ff. 257, *mus.* (Greg. 403.)

544. Ath. Nat. Theol. 45 (182) [xii], 11×9, ff. 156, *mut.* at beg. and end, *mus.* (Greg. 404.)

545. Rom. Vallicell. C. 7.

546. Ath. Nat. Theol. 46 (183) [xiv], $10\frac{5}{8} \times 8\frac{5}{8}$, ff. 151. (Greg. 405.)

547. Rom. Vat. Gr. 1217.

548. (Apost. 229.) Rom. Vat. Gr. 1228.

549. Ath. Nat. Theol. 47 (184) [xv], $11\frac{3}{4} \times 8\frac{5}{8}$, ff. 242. (Greg. 406.)

550. Ath. Nat. Theol. 48 (185) [xii], $11 \times 8\frac{1}{4}$, ff. 260, *mus.* (Greg. 407.)

551. Rom. Vat. Gr. 1625.

552. Ath. Nat. Theol. 49 (186) [xii], $11\frac{3}{8} \times 9$, ff. 167, *mus.* (Greg. 408.)

553. Ath. Nat. Theol. 50 (187) [xii], $11\frac{3}{8} \times 8\frac{1}{4}$, ff. 270, *mut.* at beg., *mus.* Written by George. (Greg. 409.)

554. (Apost. 221.) Rom. Vat. Gr. 1973.

555. (Apost. 222.) Rom. Vat. Gr. 1978.

556. Ath. Nat. Theol. 51 (188) [xi], $8\frac{1}{4} \times 5\frac{7}{8}$, ff. 302, *mus.* (Greg. 410.)

557. (Apost. 224.) Rom. Vat. Gr. 2051.

558. (Apost. 225.) Rom. Vat. Gr. 2052.

559. Rom. Vat. Gr. 2061.

560. Ath. Nat. Theol. 52 (189) [xv], $8\frac{1}{4} \times 5\frac{7}{8}$, ff. 156, *mus.* (Greg. 411.)

561. Ath. Nat. Theol. 53 (190) [xii], $9\frac{7}{8} \times 8\frac{1}{4}$, ff. 255, *mus.* (Greg. 412.)

562. Rom. Vat. Gr. 2138.

563. Ath. Nat. Theol. 54 (191) [xii], $11\frac{3}{8} \times 9$, ff. 158, *mut.* at beg. and end, *mus.* (Greg. 413.)

564. Ath. Nat. Theol. 55 (192) [xv], $6\frac{3}{4} \times 5\frac{1}{8}$, ff. 239. Palimpsest, *mut.* at beg. and end. (Greg. 414.)

†565. Ath. Nat. Theol. 56 (193) [xv], $9 \times 6\frac{3}{4}$, ff. 215, much *chart.* The two last leaves are palimpsest [ix], Unc. (Greg. 415.)

566. Ath. Nat. Theol. 57 (194) [xv], $11 \times 8\frac{1}{4}$, ff. 395, *pict.* Note of date, about A. D. 1450, at end. (Greg. 416.)

567. Ath. Nat. Theol. 58 (195) [A. D. 1536], $10\frac{5}{8} \times 8\frac{1}{4}$, ff. 396, *chart.* Beautifully written by John. (Greg. 417.)

568. Ath. Nat. Theol. 59 (196) [xv], $10\frac{1}{4} \times 8\frac{1}{4}$, ff. 206, *chart.*, *mut.* at end. (Greg. 418.)

569. Ath. Nat. Theol. 60 (197) [xv], $7\frac{7}{8} \times 5\frac{1}{8}$, ff. 341, *chart.* (Greg. 419.)

570. Ath. Nat. Theol. 61 (198) [xv], $9 \times 6\frac{3}{4}$, ff. 342, *chart.* (Greg. 420.)

571. (Apost. 188.) Ath. Nat. Theol. 62 (199) [xiv], $9\frac{1}{2} \times 7\frac{1}{8}$, ff. 292, *mus.* (Greg. 421.)

572. (Apost. 189.) Ath. Nat. Theol. 63 (200) [xv], $11 \times 8\frac{1}{4}$, ff. 340, *mut.* at beg. and end, and in other places. Michael of Damascus was the diorthote, or possessor. (Greg. 422.)

573. (Apost. 190.) Ath. Nat. Theol. 64 (201) [A. D. 1732], $8\frac{1}{4} \times 5\frac{7}{8}$, ff. 32. Written by Nicephorus. (Greg. 423.)

574. Ath. Nat. Theol. 65 (202) [xii], $11\frac{5}{8} \times 8\frac{5}{8}$, ff. 68. Separate fragments (four, Greg.), *mus.* (Greg. 424.)

575. (Apost. 113.) Syracuse, Seminary 4.

576. Venice, St. Lazarus 1631.

577. Athos, Dionysius 378.

578. Edinburgh, Univ. Laing 9.

579. Athos, St. Andrew Γ'.

580. Athos, St. Andrew Λ'.

581. Athos, St. Andrew ς'.

582. Athos, St. Andrew Z.

583. Athos, Vatopedi 48.

584. Athos, Vatopedi 192.

585. Athos, Vatopedi 193.

586. Athos, Vatopedi 194.

587. Athos, Vatopedi 195.

588. Athos, Vatopedi 196.

589. Athos, Vatopedi 197.

590. Athos, Vatopedi 198.

591. Athos, Vatopedi 200.

592. Athos, Vatopedi 202.

593. Athos, Vatopedi 204.

594. Athos, Vatopedi 205.

595. Athos, Vatopedi 208.

596. Athos, Vatopedi 209.
598. Athos, Vatopedi 221.
600. Athos, Vatopedi 224.
602. Athos, Vatopedi (226).
604. Athos, Vatopedi 228.
606. Athos, Vatopedi 230.
608. Athos, Vatopedi 232.
610. Athos, Vatopedi 234.
612. Athos, Vatopedi 236.
614. Athos, Vatopedi 238.
616. Athos, Vatopedi 240.
618. Athos, Vatopedi 242.
620. Athos, Vatopedi 253.
622. Athos, Vatopedi 255.
624. Athos, Vatopedi 257.
626. Athos, Vatopedi 291.
628. Athos, Dionysius 2.
630. Athos, Dionysius 6.
632. Athos, Dionysius 13.
634. Athos, Dionysius 15.
636. Athos, Dionysius 17.
638. Athos, Dionysius 19.
640. Athos, Dionysius 21.
642. Athos, Dionysius 163.
644. Athos, Dionysius 303.
646. Athos, Dionysius 305.
648. Athos, Dionysius 307.
650. Athos, Dionysius 309.
652. Athos, Docheiariou 10.
654. Athos, Docheiariou 14.
656. Athos, Docheiariou 19.
658. Athos, Docheiariou 24.
660. Athos, Docheiariou 58.
662. Athos, Esphigmenou 19.
664. Athos, Esphigmenou 21.
666. Athos, Esphigmenou 23.
668. Athos, Esphigmenou 27.
670. Athos, Esphigmenou 35.
672. Athos, Iveron 1.

597. Athos, Vatopedi 220.
599. Athos, Vatopedi 223.
601. Athos, Vatopedi (225).
603. Athos, Vatopedi (227).
605. Athos, Vatopedi 229.
607. Athos, Vatopedi 231.
609. Athos, Vatopedi 233.
611. Athos, Vatopedi 235.
613. Athos, Vatopedi 237.
615. Athos, Vatopedi 239.
617. Athos, Vatopedi 241.
619. Athos, Vatopedi 243.
621. Athos, Vatopedi 254.
623. Athos, Vatopedi 256.
625. Athos, Vatopedi 271.
627. Athos, Dionysius 1.
629. Athos, Dionysius 3.
631. Athos, Dionysius 11.
633. Athos, Dionysius 14.
635. Athos, Dionysius 16.
637. Athos, Dionysius 18.
639. Athos, Dionysius 20.
641. Athos, Dionysius 85.
643. Athos, Dionysius 302.
645. Athos, Dionysius 304.
647. Athos, Dionysius 306.
649. Athos, Dionysius 308.
651. Athos, Docheiariou 1.
653. Athos, Docheiariou 13.
655. Athos, Docheiariou 15.
657. Athos, Docheiariou 23.
659. Athos, Docheiariou 36.
661. Athos, Docheiariou 137.
663. Athos, Esphigmenou 20.
665. Athos, Esphigmenou 22.
667. Athos, Esphigmenou 24.
669. Athos, Esphigmenou 28.
671. Athos, Esphigmenou 60.
673. Athos, Iveron 3.

674. Athos, Iveron 4.
675. Athos, Iveron 6.
676. Athos, Iveron 20.
677. Athos, Iveron 23.
678. Athos, Iveron 35.
679. Athos, Iveron 36.
680. (Apost. 229.) Athos, Iveron 39.
681. Athos, Iveron 635.
682. Athos, Iveron 637.
683. Athos, Iveron 638.
684. Athos, Iveron 639.
685. Athos, Iveron 640.
686. Athos, Iveron 825.
687. Athos, Iveron 826.
688. Athos, Caracalla 3.
689. Athos, Caracalla 11.
690. Athos, Caracalla 15.
691. Athos, Caracalla 16.
692. Athos, Caracalla 17.
693. Athos, Constamonitou 6.
694. Athos, Constamonitou 98.
695. Athos, Constamonitou 100 [xii], 2 cols., *men.* Omitted by Gregory, who has erroneously inserted the Evan. 99 instead (*see* Spyridon P. Lampros).
696. Athos, Coutloumoussi 60.
697. Athos, Coutloumoussi 61.
698. Athos, Coutloumoussi 62.
699. Athos, Coutloumoussi 63.
700. Athos, Coutloumoussi 64.
701. Athos, Coutloumoussi 65.
702. Athos, Coutloumoussi 66.
703. Athos, Coutloumoussi 86.
†704. Athos, Coutloumoussi 90.
705. Athos, Coutloumoussi 279.
706. Athos, Coutloumoussi 280.
707. (Apost. 233.) Athos, Coutloumoussi 282.
708. Athos, Coutloumoussi 292.
709. (Apost. 234.) Athos, Coutloumoussi 356.
710. Athos, Xenophon 1.
711. Athos, Xenophon 58.
712. Athos, Xenophon 59.
713. Athos, Xenophon 68. (Greg. 71.)
714. Athos, Xeropotamou 110.
715. Athos, Xeropotamou 112.
716. Athos, Xeropotamou 118.
717. Athos, Xeropotamou 122.
718. Athos, Xeropotamou 125.
719. Athos, Xeropotamou 126.
720. Athos, Xeropotamou 234.
721. Athos, Xeropotamou 247.
722. Athos, Panteleemon L.
723. Athos, Panteleemon IV. vi. 4.
724. Athos, Panteleemon IX. v. 3.
725. Athos, Panteleemon XXVII. vi. 2.
726. Athos, Panteleemon XXVII. vi. 3.
727. Athos, Panteleemon XXVIII. i. 1.
728. Athos, Paul 1.
729. Athos, Protaton 11.
730. Athos, Protaton 14.
731. Athos, Protaton 15.
732. Athos, Protaton 44.
733. Athos, Protaton 56.
734. Athos, Simopetra 17.
735. Athos, Simopetra 19.

736. Athos, Simopetra 20. 737. Athos, Simopetra 21.
738. Athos, Simopetra 24. 739. Athos, Simopetra 27.
740. Athos, Simopetra 28.
741. (Apost. 237.) Athos, Simopetra 30.
742. Athos, Simopetra 33.
743. (Apost. 238.) Athos, Simopetra 70.
744. Athos, Stauroniketa 1. 745. Athos, Stauroniketa 27.
746. Athos, Stauroniketa 42. 747. Athos, Stauroniketa 102.
748. Athos, Philotheou 1. 749. Athos, Philotheou 2.
750. Athos, Philotheou 3.
751. (Apost. 239.) Athos, Philotheou 6.
752. Athos, Philotheou 18. 753. Athos, Philotheou 25.
754. Athos, Philotheou 61.
755. (Apost. 240.) Athos, Philotheou 213.
756. Athos, Chiliandari 6. 757. Athos, Chiliandari 15.
758. Beratinus, in a Church.
759. Athens, Nat. Sakkelion 4. (Greg. 425.)
760. Cairo, Patr. Alex. 927. 761. Cairo, Patr. Alex. 929.
762. Cairo, Patr. Alex. 943. 763. Cairo, Patr. Alex. 944.
764. Cairo, Patr. Alex. 945. 765. Cairo, Patr. Alex. 946.
766. Cairo, Patr. Alex. 948. 767. Cairo, Patr. Alex. 950.
768. Cairo, Patr. Alex. 951. 769. Cairo, Patr. Alex. 953.
770. Chalcis, Mon. Trinity 1. 771. Chalcis, Mon. Trinity 2.
772. Chalcis, Mon. Trinity 3. 773. Chalcis, Mon. Trinity 4.
774. Chalcis, Mon. Trinity 5. 775. Chalcis, Mon. Trinity 6.
776. Chalcis, Mon. Trinity 7. 777. Chalcis, Mon. Trinity 8.
778. Chalcis, Mon. Trinity 9. 779. Chalcis, Mon. Trinity 10.
780. Chalcis, School 1. 781. Chalcis, School 2.
782. Chalcis, School 3. 783. Chalcis, School 4.
784. Chalcis, School 5. 785. Chalcis, School 6.
786. Chalcis, School 7. 787. Chalcis, School 12.
788. Chalcis, School 74 (75?). 789. Chalcis, School 84.
790. Constantinople, St. George's Church.
791. Constantinople, St. George's. 792. Constantinople, ἁγίου τάφου.
793. Constantinople, ἁγίου τάφου.
794. Constantinople, ἁγίου τάφου 426.
795. Constantinople, ἁγίου τάφου 432.
796. Constantinople, τ. ἑλληνικοῦ φιλολογικοῦ συλλόγου.
797. (Apost. 243.) Jerusalem, Coll. St. Cross 6.

798. Lesbos, τ. Λείμωνος μονῆς 1 [ix or x], $11\frac{3}{4} \times 9\frac{1}{2}$, ff. 79 (20), 2 cols., περικοπαί from the Evangelists John, Matt., Luke, Mark, κατὰ παννύχια, men. (Kerameus.)

799. Lesbos, τ. Λείμωνος μονῆς 37 [x–xi], $11\frac{3}{4} \times 9\frac{1}{4}$, ff. 288, 2 cols., mus. (Kerameus.)

800. Lesbos, τ. Λείμ. μον. 38 [xi], $11\frac{3}{4} \times 9\frac{1}{2}$, ff. 208, 2 cols., mus. (Kerameus.)

801. Lesbos, τ. Λείμ. μον. 40 [xiv], $12\frac{1}{8} \times 8\frac{1}{4}$, chart. (Kerameus.)

802. Lesbos, τ. Λείμ. μον. 41 [xii–xiii], $12\frac{1}{2} \times 9$, ff. 221, 2 cols., orn. (Kerameus.)

803. Lesbos, τ. Λείμ. μον. 66 [xii–xiii], $9\frac{5}{8} \times 6\frac{3}{4}$, ff. 428, the last chart. written on in A.D. 1558. Mus. (Kerameus.)

804. (Apost. 191.) Athens, Nat. 3 (685) [xv], $6\frac{3}{5} \times 4\frac{3}{4}$, ff. 187, mut. at beg. Apostoloeuaggelia for the Feasts of the whole year after Liturgical matter. (Greg. 426.)

805. Patmos 68.
806. Patmos 69.
807. Patmos 70.
808. Patmos 71.
809. Patmos 72.
810. Patmos 73.
811. Patmos 74.
812. Patmos 75.
813. Patmos 77.
814. Patmos 78.
815. Patmos 79.
816. Patmos 85.
817. Patmos 86.
818. Patmos 87.
819. Patmos 88.
820. Patmos 89.
821. Patmos 91.
822. Patmos 93.
823. Patmos 99.
824. Patmos 101.
825. Patmos 330.
826. Patmos 331.
827. Patmos 332.

828. (Apost. 192.) Athens, Nat. ς? (Greg. 427.)

829. Athens, Nat. 10? (Greg. 428.)

830. Thessalonica, Ἑλλην. γυμνασίου Α΄.

831. Thess. Ἑλλην. γυμνασίου Β΄.
832. Thess. Ἑλλην. γυμνασίου Γ΄.
833. Thess. Ἑλλην. γυμνασίου Δ΄.
834. Thess. Ἑλλην. γυμνασίου Ε΄.
835. Thess. Ἑλλην. γυμνασίου Ζ΄.
836. Thess. Ἑλλην. γυμνασίου Θ΄.
837. Thess. Ἑλλην. γυμνασίου ΙΔ΄.
838. Thess. Μ. Σπύριος.
839. Sinai 205.
840. Sinai 206.
841. Sinai 207.
842. Sinai 208.
843. Sinai 209.
†844. Sinai 210.
†845. Sinai 211.
846. Sinai 212.
†847. Sinai 213.
†848. Sinai 214.
†849. Sinai 215.
850. Sinai 216.

851. Sinai 217. 852. Sinai 218.
853. Sinai 219. 854. Sinai 220.
855. Sinai 221. 856. Sinai 222.
857. Sinai 223. 858. Sinai 224.
859. Sinai 225. 860. Sinai 226.
861. Sinai 227. 862. Sinai 228.
863. Sinai 229. 864. Sinai 230.
865. Sinai 231. 866. Sinai 232.
867. Sinai 233. 868. Sinai 234.
869. Sinai 235. 870. Sinai 236.
871. Sinai 237. 872. Sinai 238.
873. Sinai 239. 874. Sinai 240.
875. Sinai 241. 876. Sinai 242.
877. Sinai 243. 878. Sinai 244.
879. Sinai 245. 880. Sinai 246.
881. Sinai 247. 882. Sinai 248.
883. Sinai 249. 884. Sinai 250.
885. Sinai 251. 886. Sinai 252.
887. Sinai 253. 888. Sinai 254.
889. Sinai 255. 890. Sinai 256.
891. Sinai 257. 892. Sinai 258.
893. Sinai 271. 894. (Apost. 260.) Sinai 272.
895. (Apost. 261.) Sinai 273. 896. Sinai 550.
897. Sinai 659. 898. Sinai 720.
899. Sinai 738. 900. (Apost. 247.) Sinai 748.
901. Sinai 754. 902. Sinai 756.
903. Sinai 775. 904. Sinai 796.
905. Sinai 797. 906. Sinai 800.
907. Sinai 929. 908. (Apost. 248.) Sinai 943.
909. Sinai 957. 910. Sinai 960.
911. (Apost. 249.) Sinai 961. 912. Sinai 962.
913. Sinai 965. 914. Sinai 968.
915. (Apost. 258.) Sinai 972. 916. (Apost. 251.) Sinai 973.
917. (Apost. 252.) Sinai 977. 918. Sinai 981.
919. Sinai 982. 920. Sinai 986.
921. Sinai 1042.
922. Oxf. Bodl. Clarke 9. (*See* Act. 58.)
923. Jerusalem, Patriarchal Library 33 [end of x or beg. of xi], $10\frac{1}{4} \times 8\frac{1}{4}$, ff. 335 (221—252=32) [xiii], *mus. rubr., syn., orn.* (Papadopoulos Kerameus.)

924. (Apost. 253.) Rom. Vat. Reg. 54.

925. Venice, St. Mark 188.

926. Lond. Brit. Mus. Add. 10,068 [?], 9 × 7, ff. 124, 2 cols., palimpsest, illegible and will not repay investigation.

927. Jerus. Patr. Libr. 161 [xvii], $11\frac{1}{3} \times 8\frac{1}{3}$, *chart.*, collections of bits of Evst. (Kerameus.)

928. Jerus. Patr. Libr. 526 [A. D. 1502], $12\frac{3}{3} \times 8\frac{3}{3}$, ff. 108, 2 cols., *syn.*, with many directions. (Kerameus.)

929. New York, Seminary of Theol. Univ.

930. Lond. Brit. Mus. Add. 19,459 [xii, Greg. xiii], $11\frac{1}{2} \times 9\frac{1}{4}$, ff. 230 (24–8), 2 cols. (ff. 22 inserted later), *mus. rubr.*, *mut.* beg. and end, &c.

931. (Apost. 126.) Venice, St. Mark ii. 130.

932. Jerus. Patr. Libr. 530, *chart.*, Turkish in Greek letters. (Kerameus.)

933. Petersburg, Caes. Muralt. 64 (ix. 1).

934. St. Saba 55 [xii], 4to. Coxe.

935. Quaritch 8 [about A. D. 1200], ff. 346 (26), 2 cols., *mut.*, letters in red, green, blue, yellow, bound in red morocco case. (Catalogue, Dec. 1893.)

936. Lesb. τ. Λείμ. μον. 100. Ἀποστολοευαγγέλια in the midst of the four Liturgies and other matter. (Kerameus.)

937. Lesb. τ. Λείμ. μον. 146 [A. D. 1562–66], $7\frac{7}{3} \times 5\frac{3}{4}$. Begins with St. Matt. (Kerameus.)

938. Lesb. ἐν μονῇ Ἁγίου Ἰωάννου τοῦ Θεολόγου 11 [xii], $9\frac{1}{4} \times 7$, ff. 157 (2, 5, and 6 being chart., one is of the eleventh century). (Kerameus.)

939. Lesb. Ἁγ. Ἰωάνν. 12, $8\frac{7}{3} \times 7\frac{1}{3}$, ff. 110. (Kerameus.)

940. Lesb. Benjamin Library at Potamos ΛΛ [A. D. 1565], $12\frac{1}{3} \times 8\frac{1}{4}$, ff. 378. (Kerameus.)

941. Athos, Constamonitou 98 [xiv], 2 cols., *mus.*, *men.* (Sp. P. Lampros.)

942. Athos, Constam. 100.

†943. Athens, Nat. Libr. 60 [ix], $13\frac{3}{8} \times 5\frac{7}{8}$?, ff. 87, Unc., *mus.*

944. Ath. Nat. Libr. 78 [x], $13\frac{3}{4} \times 10\frac{1}{4}$, ff. 143. Palimpsest under fifteenth century writing. *Mus.*

945. Ath. Nat. Libr. 83 [xv], $11 \times 7\frac{7}{8}$, ff. 324, *chart.*, *mut.* at end.

946. Ath. Nat. Libr. 97 [xii], $12\frac{1}{2} \times 8\frac{5}{8}$, ff. 136, *mut.* at beg. and end, *mus.*

947. (Apost. 227.) Ath. Nat. Libr. 126 [A. D. 1504], $8\frac{1}{4} \times 5\frac{7}{8}$, ff. 276, written by Euthymius.

948. Ath. Nat. Libr. 143 [A. D. 1522], $7\frac{1}{2} \times 5\frac{7}{8}$, ff. 242. A few leaves wanting at beginning.

949. Ath. Nat. Libr. 147 [xii beg.], $9\frac{7}{8} \times 6\frac{3}{4}$, ff. 255—first eight injured. *Mus.*

950. Ath. Nat. Libr. 148 [xv end], $7\frac{1}{2} \times 5\frac{7}{8}$, ff. 104, *mut.* at beg. and end.

The following thirteen MSS. in the National Library at Athens contain portions of Apostoloeuaggelia:—

951. (Apost. 277.) 668, $7\frac{1}{2} \times 5\frac{1}{2}$, ff. 282.
952. (Apost. 278.) 685, $5\frac{7}{8} \times 4\frac{3}{4}$, ff. 187.
953. (Apost. 279.) 700, $5\frac{7}{8} \times 4$, ff. 326.
954. (Apost. 280.) 707, $6\frac{1}{4} \times 4\frac{3}{4}$, ff. 131.
955. (Apost. 281.) 750, $8\frac{5}{8} \times 6\frac{1}{4}$, ff. 117.
956. (Apost. 282.) 757, $8\frac{1}{4} \times 5\frac{1}{2}$, ff. 120.
957. (Apost. 283.) 759, $8\frac{1}{4} \times 6\frac{1}{4}$, ff. 129.
958. (Apost. 284.) 760, $7\frac{7}{8} \times 5\frac{1}{2}$, ff. 262.
959. (Apost. 285.) 766, $8\frac{1}{4} \times 5\frac{7}{8}$, ff. 134.
960. (Apost. 286.) 769, $5\frac{1}{2} \times 4$, ff. 175.
961. (Apost. 287.) 784, $5\frac{7}{8} \times 4\frac{3}{8}$, ff. 36.
962. (Apost. 288.) 786, $5\frac{1}{8} \times 4$, ff. 48.
963. (Apost. 289.) 795, $7\frac{1}{2} \times 5\frac{1}{2}$, ff. 495 [1].

[1] †Evan. T^d and T^e and Λ (1) should also properly be classed as Lectionaries. Apost. 15, and perhaps Apost. 24, also contains Lessons from the Gospels. The two copies of the Gospels, Lowes formerly Askew, membr. 4to, mentioned by Scholz (N. T., vol. i. p. cxix , and stated by Marsh on Michaelis, vol. ii. p. 662, to have been bought at Askew's sale by Mr. Lowes, the bookseller, are shown by the sale catalogue to have Evangelistaria. They have not yet been traced. (Ed. 3.)

CHAPTER XIV.

LECTIONARIES CONTAINING THE APOSTOLOS OR PRAXAPOSTOLOS.

*†1. (Evst. 6.)

2. Lond. Brit. Mus. Cotton. Vesp. B. xviii [xi], 11 × 8¼, ff. 230 (16), 2 cols., *mus. rubr.*, *mut.* initio et fine (Casley)[1]. In a fine bold hand. The Museum Catalogue is wrong in stating that it contains Lessons from the Gospels. They exactly correspond with those in our list, five of the Saints' Day Lessons being from the Catholic Epistles.

3. Readings sent to Mill (N. T., Proleg. § 1470) by John Batteley, D.D., as taken from a codex, now missing, in Trinity Hall, Cambridge. The extracts were from 1 Peter and John. Griesbach's Paul. 3 is Bodl. 5 (Evst. 19), cited by Mill only at Hebr. x. 22, 23.

4. (Evst. 112.)

*5. Gottingen, Univ. MS. Theol. 54 [xv], 10¾ × 7¼, ff. 50 (28), 2 cols., formerly of the monastery Constamonitou on Athos, afterwards De Missy's (Matthaei's v). (Paul. 5 of Griesbach = Evst. 30.)

6. (Evan. 117, ff. 183–202.)   7. (Evst. 37.)
8. (Evst. 44.)   9. (Evst. 84.)
10. (Evst. 85.)

11. Par. Nat. Suppl. Gr. 104 [xii, Greg. xiii], 9¾ × 7½, ff. 139 (24), well written in some monastery of Palestine: with marginal notes in Arabic.

*12. (Evst. 60.)

*13. Moscow, Synod. 4 (Mt. b) [x], fol., ff. 313, 2 cols., important: once belonged to the Iveron monastery; renovated by Joakim, a monk, A. D. 1525. Cited by Tregelles as Frag. Mosq.

*14. Mosc. Synod. 291 (Mt. c) [xii], 4to, ff. 276, well written, from the monastery Esphigmenou on Athos.

*15. Mosc. Typogr. Syn. 31 (Mt. tz) [A. D. 1116], fol., ff. 200, a few Lections from 1 John at the end of Lections from Old Testament.

*16. (Evst. 52.)   *17. (Evst. 53.)
*18. (Evst. 54.)   *19. (Evst. 55.)
*20. (Evst. 56.)

---

[1] In 1721. *See* Monk's 'Life of Bentley,' vol. ii. p. 149. This is Bentley's O, John Walker's collation of which is preserved at Trin. Coll. (B. xvii. 34). Ellis, Bentleii Critica Sacra, Introd. pp. xxix, xxx.

Apost. 21-48 comprise Scholz's additions to the list, of which he describes none as collated entire or in the greater part. He seems, however, to have collated Cod. 12 entire.

21. (Evst. 83.)

22. Par. Nat. Gr. 304 [xiii, Greg. xiv], $13\frac{5}{8} \times 10\frac{3}{4}$, ff. 302 (22), 2 cols., brought from Constantinople: *mut.* in fine.

23. Par. Nat. Gr. 306 [xii], $13 \times 10\frac{1}{8}$, ff. 187 (28), 2 cols., *mut.* initio et fine.

24. Par. Nat. Gr. 308 [xiii], ff. 201, *mut.*, contains six Lections from 1 John and 1 Pet., more from the Old Testament.

25. Par. Nat. Gr. 319 [xi, Greg. xii], $12\frac{1}{4} \times 8\frac{1}{2}$, ff. 274 (22), ill written, with a Latin version over some portions of the text. Once Colbert's.

26. Par. Nat. Gr. 320 [xii], $9\frac{1}{3} \times 7\frac{3}{4}$, ff. 208 (21), 2 cols., *mus. rubr., mut.*

27. Par. Nat. Gr. 321, once Colbert's [xiii, Greg. xiv], $11\frac{3}{8} \times 8$, ff. 237 (23), *mut.*, and illegible in parts.

28. (Evst. 26.)   29. (Evst. 94.)

30. Par. Nat. Gr. 373 [xiii, Greg. xiv], $8\frac{3}{8} \times 6\frac{3}{4}$, ff. 118 (21), *mut.* initio et fine: with some cotton-paper leaves at the end.

31. (Evst. 82.)   32. (Evan. 324, Evst. 97.)

33. Par. Nat. Gr. 382 [xiii, Greg. x], $9\frac{1}{2} \times 7\frac{1}{8}$, 271 (22), 2 cols., *mus. rubr.* Once Colbert's.

34. Par. Nat. Gr. 383, once Colbert's [xv, Greg. xvi], $8\frac{3}{8} \times 5\frac{1}{4}$, ff. 206 (31), *chart.* In readings it is much with Apost. 12.

35. (Evst. 92.)   36. (Evst. 93.)

37. Ath. Nat. Libr. 103 [xv], $9 \times 6\frac{1}{4}$, ff. 199.

38. Rom. Vat. Gr. 1528 [xv], $8\frac{1}{4} \times 6$, ff. 235 (26), *chart.*, written by the monk Eucholius.

39. (Evst. 133.)

40. Rom. Barberini 18 [x], 4to, a palimpsest (probably uncial, though not so stated by Scholz), correctly written, but mostly become illegible. The later writing [xiv] contains Lessons from the Old Testament, with a few from the Catholic Epistles at the end.

41. Rom. Barb., unnumbered [xi], 4to, *mut.* ff. 1-114.

42. Rom. Vallicell. C. 46 [xvi], $8\frac{1}{2} \times 6\frac{1}{4}$, ff. 115 (24), *chart.*, with other matter.

†43. (Evan. 561.) The palimpsest [viii or ix], written over the Gospels and table of Lessons, and containing Rom. xv. 30-33; 1 Cor. iv. 9-13; xv. 42-5; 2 Cor. ix. 6, 7.

44. (Evst. 232.)

45. Glasgow, Hunt. Mus. V. 3. 4 [A. D. 1199], $11 \times 7\frac{7}{8}$, ff. 239 (22), 2 cols., *mus. rubr.* Written by order of Luke of Antioch. Belonged to Caesar de Missy.

46. Milan, Ambr. C. 63 sup. [xiv], $9\frac{1}{4} \times 5\frac{3}{8}$, ff. 153 (27), *mut.*, bought (like Evst. 103) in 1606, 'Corneliani in Iapygiâ.'

47. (Evst. 104.)   48. (Evst. 222.)[1]   (Greg. 59.)

49. Rom. Vat. Gr. 2068 [xi], $9\frac{3}{4} \times 7\frac{1}{2}$, ff. 232 (24), 2 cols., *pict.*, *mut.* at end, formerly Basil 107, described with a facsimile by Bianchini, Evan. Quadr., vol. ii. pt. 1, p. 523 and Plate iv: ἐκλογάδιον τοῦ ἀποστόλου. (Greg. 120.)

50. Modena, Este Libr. ii. D. 3 [xv], $11\frac{3}{8} \times 7\frac{7}{8}$, *chart.*, seen by Burgon. (Greg. 89.)

51. Besançon, Public Libr. 41 [xii], $9\frac{1}{4} \times 6\frac{3}{4}$, ff. 141 (21), 2 cols. (M. Castan: *see* Evst. 193.)   (Greg. 86.)

52. Lond. Brit. Mus. 32,051 [xi, xii, Greg. xiii], $10\frac{1}{2} \times 7\frac{3}{4}$, ff. 192 (29), 2 cols., *mut.* at end, *mus. rubr.*, got from Heraclea by Archd. Payne for the Duke of Marlborough, A.D. 1738. Formerly Blenheim 3. C. 12. (Greg. 65.)

53. (Evst. 258.)   (Greg. 186.)   54. (Evst. 195.)   (Greg. 73.)

*55. (Evst. 179.)   (Greg. 55.)

*56. (Act. 42, Evst. 287) contains only 1 Cor. ix. 2–12.   (Greg. 56.)

57. Lond. Lamb. 1190 [xiii, Greg. xi], 10×7, ff. 130 (25), 2 cols., neatly written, with many letters gilded, *mut.* at the beginning and end, and uninjured. Archdeacon Todd in the Lambeth Catalogue, p. 50, mistakes this for a copy of the Acts and all the Epistles. Bloomfield examined Apost. 57, 59–62. (Greg. 60.)

58. Oxf., Ch. Ch. Wake 33 [A.D. 1172], $11 \times 8\frac{1}{4}$, ff. 266, *mus.*, *men.*, the ink having quite gone in parts. (Greg. 58.)

59. Lambeth 1191 [xiii], $8 \times 6\frac{1}{2}$, ff. 75 (19), much injured, *mut.* at the beginning and end.   (Greg. 61.)

60. Lamb. 1194 [xiii], $8\frac{3}{8} \times 7\frac{5}{8}$, ff. 109 (17), *chart.*, *mut.* at the end, the writing very neat, the letters often gilded. (Greg. 62.)

61. Lamb. 1195 [xiii, Greg. xv], $10\frac{3}{4} \times 7\frac{1}{4}$, ff. 75 (17), *chart.*, *mut.* at the beginning. (Greg. 63.)

62. Lamb. 1196 [xiii, Greg. xii], $10\frac{3}{4} \times 8$, ff. 219 (23), 2 cols., *mut.* at the end. (Greg. 64.)

63. Instead of this, which is Act. 315 (Greg.)—
Oxford, Lincoln Coll. 4 [xii], 8×6, ff. 107 (?), *mus. rubr.*, *mut.* beginning and end.

*64. B.-C. I. 10 (Evst. 251).   (Greg. 66.)

*65. B.-C. III. 24 [xii or xiii], 4to.   (Greg. 68.)

*66. B.-C. III. 29 (Evst. 252).   (Greg. 67.)

*67. B.-C. III. 42 (Evst. 253).   (Greg. 184.)

---

[1] As in our preceding lists, we remove to this foot-note Scholz's six copies seen at St. Saba, and occupy their numbers by other manuscripts. They are Apost. 49. St. Saba 16 [xiv], 4to, *chart.*   50. St. Saba 18 [xv], 8vo.   51. St. Saba 26 [xiv], fol.   52. (Evst. 171.)   53. (Evst. 160.)   54. St. Saba (unnumbered) [xiii], 4to.

*68. B.-C. III. 53 (Evst. 253²). (Greg. 263.)

69. Brit. Mus. Add. 29,714 [A. D. 1306], 10¾ × 8½, ff. 178 (28), written by one Ignatius; *syn.*, was bought of Nicolas Parassoh in 1874. (Greg. 81.)

70. Bentley's Q=Apost. 52. (*See* Ellis, Bentleii Crit. Sacr. xxx; Berriman, Crit. Dissertation on 1 Tim. iii. 16, p. 105.) Instead— Cambridge, Mass. U.S.A., Harvard Univ. 2 (A. R. g. 3. 10) [xii], 11½ × 8½, ff. 281 (23), 2 cols., *orn.* (f. 202 *mut.*), *men.*, apparently by the same hand as Evst. 484, but more beautiful. Hoskier, App. II, pp. 3, 4. (Greg. 75.)

*†71. Leipzig, Univ. Libr. Tisch. vi. f. [ix or x], 9¾ × 7, Unc., f. 1 (24), 2 cols., containing Heb. i. 3-12, published in 'Anecd. sacr. et profan.,' p. 73, &c. (Greg. 80.)

*†72. Petrop. Caes. Muralt. 38, 49 [ix], 8vo, one leaf of a double palimpsest, now at St. Petersburg, the oldest writing containing Acts xiii. 10; 2 Cor. xi. 21-23, cited by Tischendorf (N. T., Proleg., p. ccxxvi, 7th edition). (Greg. 70.)

†73. (Evst. 192.) (Greg. 180.)

†74. Oxf. Bodl. Arch. Seld. 9 supr., palimpsest, containing under the Christmas sermons of Proclus, Patriarch of Constantinople, almost illegible Lessons from the Septuagint, with one or two from the Epistles of SS. Peter and John. (Greg. 84.)

75. Lond. Brit. Mus. Add. 11,841 [xii or xiii, Greg. xi], 8 × 5½, ff. 86 (22), 2 cols., *mut.* Amidst Old Test. Lections are (1) ff. 52–54, 1 John iii. 21–24, 26; iv. 9–19; 20–25; v; (2) f. 78 (which should precede f. 74) is a Lesson for June 28 ($\overline{\kappa\eta}$) τῶν ἁγίων ἀποστόλων πέτρου καὶ παύλου, ἀνάγνωσμα γ, containing 1 Pet. i. 3–19; ii. 11–24 (ζήσομεν). (Greg. 79.)

76. Oxf. Bodl. Misc. Gr. 319 [xiii], 11 × 8, ff. 14 (22), 2 cols., *mus. rubr.*, four leaves being biblical, written by Symeon a reader, ἁγιοσυμεωνίτης: the date, if once extant in the red letters of the colophon, being now rubbed away. There are nine ἀναγνώσματα. The book is either a Euchology or a Typicum, more probably the former. The first Lesson is 2 Tim. iii. 2-9. The remainder are numbered as Lessons for the δεκαήμερον, or Twelve days from Christmas to Epiphany: they run thus, α' Rom. v. 18–21 : β' viii. 3–9 : γ' ix. 29–33 : δ' 2 Cor. v. 15–21 : ε' Gal. iii. 28—iv. 5 : ϛ' Col. i. 18–22 : ζ' Phil. iii. 3–9 : η' Rom. viii. 8–14. Found in a drawer by Mr. E. B. Nicholson, Bodley's Librarian. (Greg. 83.)

77. (Act. 98, portions marked as a_1 and a_3.) (Greg. 82.)

78. (Evst. 290.) Lond. B.-C. III. 44 [xiv], 4to, *chart.*, of 339 surviving leaves, is a *Typicum* in two separate hands, and contains twenty-nine Lessons: viz. eleven from the Old Testament, six from the Apocrypha, two from the Gospels (Matt. xi. 27-30; Mark viii. 34—ix. 1), ten from St. Paul's Epistles. (Greg. 78.)

79. Camb. Univ. Libr. Add. 679. 2 [xii or xiii], 10 × 8¼, ff. 102 (18), being the companion volume to Evst. 291, contains week-day Epistles

from St. Paul. The first quire is in a different hand. *Mut.* six leaves. Ends sixth day of thirty-third week (2 Thess. ii. 1). (Greg. 77.)

80. (Evst. 292.) (Greg. 183.)

81. =Apost. 52. Instead—
Milan, Ambros. C. 16 inf. [xiii], $9 \times 7\frac{1}{4}$, ff. 29 (34), 2 cols. (Greg. 112.)

Scholz says of Evst. 161, and to the same effect Coxe of Evst. Cairo 18, 'continet lect. et pericop.;' which may possibly mean that these copies should be reckoned for the Apostolos also.

82. Messina, Univ. 93 [xii or xiii], $9\frac{7}{8} \times 7\frac{3}{4}$, ff. 331 (22), 2 cols., perfect. (*See* Greg. 113.)

83. Crypta Ferrata, A. β. 4 [x], $5\frac{7}{8} \times 4\frac{3}{4}$, ff. 139 (19), *mut.*, Praxapostolos. (*See* Greg. 103.)

84. Crypta Ferrata, A. β. 5 [xi], $7\frac{1}{2} \times 6\frac{1}{4}$, ff. 245 (20), 2 cols., *mus. rubr.*, a most beautiful codex. (*See* Greg. 104.)

85. Crypta Ferrata, A. β. 7 [xi], $5\frac{7}{8} \times 4\frac{3}{4}$, ff. 64 (27), *mut.*, Praxapostolos. (*See* Greg. 105.)

86. Crypta Ferrata, A. β. 8 [xii or xiii, Greg. xiv], $6\frac{1}{4} \times 4\frac{3}{4}$, ff. 27 (16), carelessly written, and injured by damp, fragments, Praxapostolos. (*See* Greg. 106.)

87. Crypta Ferrata, A. β. 9 [xii], $5\frac{7}{8} \times 4\frac{1}{4}$, ff. 104 (22), Praxapostolos. (*See* Greg. 107.)

88. Crypta Ferrata, A. β. 10 [xiii], $6\frac{1}{4} \times 5\frac{1}{4}$, ff. 16 (22), *mut.*, fragmentary, with unusual Saints' days. (*See* Greg. 108.)

89. Crypta Ferrata, A. β. 11 [xi], $11\frac{3}{8} \times 8\frac{5}{8}$, ff. 191 (25), 2 cols., *mus. rubr., mut.* (*See* Greg. 109.)

90. (Evst. 322.) Crypta Ferrata. (Greg. 102.)

91. (Evst. 323.) Crypta Ferrata. (Greg. 197.)

92. (Evst. 325.) Crypta Ferrata. (Greg. 198.)

93. (Evst. 327.) Crypta Ferrata. (Greg. 172.)

94. (Evst. 328.) Crypta Ferrata. (Greg. 173.)

95. (Evst. 334.) Crypta Ferrata. (Greg. 201.)

96. (Evst. 337.) Crypta Ferrata. (Greg. 200.)

97. (Evst. 339.) Crypta Ferrata. (Greg. 201.)

98. Venice, St. Mark ii. 115 [xi or xii], $12\frac{1}{2} \times 9\frac{1}{4}$, ff. 277 (21–23), 2 cols., *mus. rubr.* (*See* Greg. 124.)

99. (Evst. 341.) Crypta Ferrata. (Greg. 202.)

100. (Evst. 344.) Crypta Ferrata. (Greg. 203.)

101. (Evst. 346.) Crypta Ferrata. (Greg. 204.)

102. (Evst. 347.) Crypta Ferrata. (Greg. 205.)

103. (Evst. 349.) Crypta Ferrata. (Greg. 206.)

104. (Evst. 350.) Crypta Ferrata. (Greg. 207.)

105. (Evst. 351.)   Crypta Ferrata.   (Greg. 169.)
106. (Evst. 352.)   Crypta Ferrata.   (Greg. 208.)
107. (Evst. 353.)   Crypta Ferrata.   (Greg. 209.)
108. (Evst. 354.)   Crypta Ferrata.   (Greg. 210.)
109. (Evst. 356.)   Crypta Ferrata.   (Greg. 211.)
110. (Evst. 357.)   Crypta Ferrata.   (Greg. 212.)
111. (Evst. 358.)   Crypta Ferrata.   (Greg. 213.)
112. (Evst. 312.)   Messina, fragm.   (Greg. 214.)

113. (Evst. 575.)   Syracuse, Seminario 4, *chart.*, ff. 219, *mut.*, given by the Card. Landolina. (Greg. 228.)

114. Venice, St. Mark ii. 128 [xiv], $8\frac{1}{2} \times 6$, ff. 361 (19), *mut.* (See Greg. 125.)

115. (Evst. 931.)   Ven. St. Mark ii. 130. (Greg. 126.)

116. Rom. Vat. Gr. 368 [xiii], $10 \times 7\frac{3}{4}$, ff. 136 (26), 2 cols., Old Test. Lections at end. (Greg. 118.)

117. (Evst. 381) Vat.   (Greg. 264.)

118. (Evst. 387) Vat.   (Greg. 223.)

119. Rom. Vat. Gr. 2116 [xiii], $7\frac{1}{2} \times 5\frac{1}{4}$, ff. 111 (21), *mut.* (See Greg. 121.)

120. Rom. Vat. Alex. Gr. 11 [xiv, Greg. xii], $11 \times 7\frac{7}{8}$, ff. 169 (24), *mut.* (Greg. 123.)

121. (Evst. 395.)   Rom. Vat. Alex. 59. (Greg. 227.)

122. Rom. Vat. Alex. Gr. 70 [A. D. 1544], $7\frac{7}{4} \times 5\frac{1}{4}$, ff. 18, 'in fronte pronunciatio Graeca Latinis literis descripta.' (Greg. 255.)

123. Rom. Vat. Pal. 241 [xv], $8\frac{5}{8} \times 7\frac{3}{4}$, ff. 149 (21), *chart.* (Greg. 122.)

124. (Evst. 410.)   Rom. Barb.   (Greg. 216.)

125. Rom. Barb. iv. 11 [A. D. 1566], $8\frac{3}{4} \times 6\frac{1}{4}$, ff. 158 (19), *chart., mut.* (Greg. 114.)

126. Rom. Barb. iv. 60 [xi, Greg. xii], $9\frac{7}{8} \times 7\frac{3}{4}$, ff. 322 (22), *mus. rubr.*, a fine codex with *menologium.* (Greg. 115.)

127. Rom. Barb. iv. 84 [xiii, Greg. xii], $11 \times 7\frac{3}{4}$, ff. 189 (24), 2 cols., with *men., mut.* (Greg. 116.)

128. (Evst. 415.)   Martin.   (Greg. 256.)

129. (Evst. 96.)   Martin.   (Greg. 262.)

130. Par. Nat Suppl. Gr. 800 [xiv], $8\frac{5}{8} \times 5\frac{7}{8}$, ff. 115 (23), *chart., mut.* at end. Martin, p. 174. (Greg. 88.)

131. Athos, Docheiariou 20.   132. Athos, Docheiariou 27.
133. Athos, Docheiariou 141.   134. Athos, Docheiariou 146.
135. Athos, Iveron 831.   136. Athos, Caracalla 10.
137. Athos, Caracalla 156.

138. Athos, Constamonitou 21 [xvii], 8vo, *chart., mut.*
139. Athos, Constamonitou 22 [xiv], 8vo, cotton.
140. Athos, Constamonitou 23 [xv], 8vo, *chart.* (Σπ. Λαμπρός.)
141. Athos, Coutloumoussi 277. 142. Athos, Coutloumoussi 344.
143. Athos, Coutloumoussi 355. 144. Athos, Protaton 54.
145. Athos, Simopetra 6. 146. Athos, Simopetra 10.
147. (Evst. 479.) Athos, Simopetra 148.
148. Athos, Simopetra 149. 149. Athos, Simopetra 150.
150. Athos, Simopetra 151. 151. Athos, Stauroniketa 129.
152. Athos, Philotheou 17. 153. Beratinus, Abp.
154. Chalcis, Mon. Holy Trinity 13.
155. Chalcis, Mon. Holy Trin. 14.
156. Chalcis, Mon. Holy Trin. 15.
157. Chalcis, School 59. 158. Chalcis, School 74.
159. Chalcis, School 88. 160. Patmos 11.
161. Patmos 12. 162. Thessalonica, Ἑλλην. Γυμν. 8.
163. Thess. Ἑλλην. Γυμν. 10. 164. Thess. Ἑλλην. Γυμν. 13.
165. Sinai 296. 166. Sinai 297.
167. Sinai 298. 168. Sinai 299.
169. Athos, Dionysius 386. (Greg. 127.)
170. (Evst. 642.)
171. Petersburg, Caes. Muralt. 38. (Greg. 70^a.)
172. Petersburg, Caes. Muralt. 49. (Greg. 70^b.)
173. Petersburg, Caes. Muralt. 40^a. (Greg. 71.)
174. Sinai 294. 175. (Evst. 261.)
176. (Evst. 240.) 177. (Evst. 232.)
178. (Evst. 191.) (Greg. twice, 69 and 178.)
179. (Evst. 472.)
180. Athos, Dionysius 387. (Greg. 128.)
181. (Evst. 166.) 182. (Evst. 169.)
183. Petersburg, Caes. Muralt. 45^a. (Greg. 72.)
184. Athos, Dionysius 392. (Greg. 129.)
185. (Evst. 275.) 186. Docheiariou 17. (Greg. 130.)
187. (Evst. 420.) 188. (Evst. 571.)
189. (Evst. 572.) 190. (Evst. 573.)
191. (Evst. 804.) 192. (Evst. 828.)
193. (Evst. 439.) 194. (Evst. 440.)
195. (Evst. 443.) 196. (Evst. 446.)
197. Petersburg, Caes. Mur. 110. (Greg. 74.)

198. New York, Astor's Library. (Greg. 76.)
199. (Evst. 290.)
200. Vienna, Caes. Gr. Theol. 308. (Greg. 85.)
201. Par. Nat. Gr. 922, fol. A. (Greg. 87a.)
202. Par. Nat. Suppl. Gr. 804, ff. 88 and 89. (Greg. 87b.)
†203. Wisbech, Peckover, Unc., palimpsest. (Greg. 90.)
204. Athens, Nat. 68 (203) [xiii], $10\frac{5}{8} \times 8\frac{3}{8}$, ff. 218, *mus.* (Greg. 91.)
205. Athens, Nat. 69 (206), [xv], $8\frac{5}{8} \times 5\frac{7}{8}$, ff. 347, *mut.* (Greg. 92.)
206. (Evst. 393.) Athens, Nat. (35) ? (Greg. 93.)
207. (Evst. 422.) Athens, Nat. (63). (Greg. 94).
208. (Evst. 423.) Athens, Nat. (64) *sic.* (Greg. 95.)
209. Ath. Nat. 95 (115) [A. D. 1576], $8\frac{1}{2} \times 5\frac{7}{8}$, ff. 192, *mut.* at beg. (Greg. 96.)
210. Athens, Nat. ? (Greg. 97 ?)
211. Athens, Nat. ? (116 ?) [xv], $8\frac{5}{8} \times 5\frac{7}{8}$, ff. 141. (Greg. 98.)
212. Athens, Nat. ? (114) [xvii], $8\frac{1}{4} \times 6\frac{1}{4}$, ff. 190. (Greg. 99.)
213. Sinai 295. (Greg. 117.)
214. Escurial X. iv. 9. (Greg. 100.)
215. (Evst. 410.) 216. Escurial Ψ. iii. 9. (Greg. 101.)
217. (Evst. 408.) 218. (Evst. 407.)
219. (Evst. 533.) 220. (Evst. 548.)
221. (Evst. 554.) 222. (Evst. 555.)
223. Florence, Laurent. St. Mark 704. (Greg. 111.)
224. (Evst. 557.) 225. (Evst. 558.)
226. (Evst. 572.)
227. Lesbos, τ. Λείμωνος μονῆς 55, Act., Paul., Cath., Apoc., *syn., men., proll., mus. rubr.* (Kerameus.)
228. Lesb. τ. Λείμ. μον. 137 [xv], $8\frac{1}{8} \times 4\frac{7}{8}$, *chart.* (Kerameus.)
229. (Evst. 680.) 230. (Evst. 686.)
231. (Evst. 687.) 232. (Evst. 693.)
233. (Evst. 707.) 234. (Evst. 709.)
235. (Evst. 712.) 236. (Evst. 721.)
237. (Evst. 741.) 238. (Evst. 743.)
239. (Evst. 751.) 240. (Evst. 755.)
241. (Evst. 757.) 242. (Evst. 759.)
243. (Evst. 797.) 244. (Evst. 829.)
245. (Evst. 837.) 246. (Evst. 893.)
247. (Evst. 900.) 248. (Evst. 908.)
249. (Evst. 911.) 250. (Evst. 915.)

251. (Evst. 916.) 252. (Evst. 917.)
253. (Evst. 924.) 254. (Evst. 929.)
255. Andros, Μονή 'Αγία 2, ff. 140. Injured, but well written. ('Αντ. Μηλιαράκης.)
256. Andros, Μονή 'Αγία 3, *chart.*, moth-eaten. ('Αντώνιος Μηλιαράκης.)
257. (Evst. 428.) 258. (Evst. 272.)
259. (Evst. 518.) 260. (Evst. 894.)
261. (Evst. 895.)
262. Athos, Protaton 32, 4to, amidst other matter, κεφ. t., *syn.*, *men.* (Σπ. Λαμπρός.)
263. Crypta Ferrata, Α'. δ'. 24. (Greg. 110.)
264. (Evst. 952.) 265. (Evst. 30.)
266. Athos, Gregory 60 [xvi], 16mo, *chart.*, *mut.*
267. Kosinitsa, 'Αγία Μονή, 'Ιωάννης ὁ Περευτέσης (?) 198 [A. D. 1503], written by the aforenamed.
268. Kos. 'Αγ. Μον., Νίκολλος 55 [xi], written by the aforenamed.
269. Kos. 'Αγ. Μον., Συμέων Λουτζέρες 195 [A. D. 1505], written by the aforenamed.
270. Ath. Nat. Libr. 101 [xiv], 9 x 7⅛, ff. 169, *mut.* at beginning and end.
271. Ath. Nat. Libr. 102 [xvii], 8⅜ x 6¼, ff. 229.
272. Ath. Nat. Libr. 106 [xiv–xv], 9½ x 7⅛, ff. 243, *mut.* at beginning and end.
273. Ath. Nat. Libr. 133 [xiv], 8⅜ x 5½, ff. 348, *pict.*
274. Ath. Nat. Libr. 144 [xv], 8¼ x 5⅞, ff. 76, *mut.* at beginning and end.

275. (Evst. 956.) 276. (Evst. 957.)
277. (Evst. 958.) 278. (Evst. 959.)
279. (Evst. 960.) 280. (Evst. 961.)
281. (Evst. 962.) 282. (Evst. 963.)
283. (Evst. 964.) 284. (Evst. 965.)
285. (Evst. 966.) 286. (Evst. 967.)
287. (Evst. 968.) 288. (Evst. 498.)

ADDITIONAL UNCIALS.

𝈺. At Kosinitsa, Ἁγία Μονή 124 [x], 10⅜ × 7, ff. 339, Evan., Act., Cath., Apoc., Paul. (*sic*). Written by Sabbas, a monk, in tenth century, with marginal writing [xiii].

𝈻. At Kosinitsa, Ἁγ. Μον. 375 [ix–x], 7¼ × 13, ff. 301 (16, 19, or 21). The two first gatherings are mice-eaten. Τίτλοι in vermilion, ἀναγνώσματα, κεφ. τ., *subscr.*, Evan. *Mut.* Matt. i. 1—ix. 1.

𝈼. *a.* Athos, Protaton 13 [vi], 4to, ff. 2, appended to Homilies of Chrysostom, and containing fragments of the Evangelists.

b. Athos, Protaton 14 [vi], ff. 3, with fragments of St. John appended at beginning and end to Lives of Saints.

c. Athos, Protaton 20 [vi], 2 cols.

d. Athos, Protaton 56 [vi], ff. 10, 2 cols., at beginning and end of a hortatory discourse [xiv], containing fragments of the Evangelists.

TOTAL NUMBER OF GREEK MANUSCRIPTS AS RECKONED IN THE SIX CLASSES

UNCIALS:—

Evangelia	71	
Acts and Catholic Epistles	19	
St. Paul's Epistles	27	
Apocalypse	7	
Total		124

CURSIVES:—

Evangelia	1321	
Acts and Catholic Epistles	420	
St. Paul's Epistles	491	
Apocalypse	184	
Evangelistaria	963	
Apostolos	288	
Total		3667
Grand Total		3791

APPENDIX A.

CHIEF AUTHORITIES.

The chief authorities used in corrections and additions in this Edition have been as follows:—

1. MS. Notes and other remains of Dr. Scrivener, such as 'Adversaria Critica Sacra,' just being published.

2. My own examination of the MSS. in London, Oxford, and Cambridge, with obliging help as to those in the British Museum from Mr. G. F. Warner, of the MSS. Department.

3. Burgon's Letters to the *Guardian*, 1873-74, 1882, and 1884.

4. As to Parisian MSS., the Abbé Martin's 'Description technique des MSS. Grecs relatifs au N. Test., conservés dans les Bibliothèques de Paris,' Paris, 1884. And Omont's 'Facsimilés des MSS. Grecs datés de la Bibliothèque Nationale du ix et du xiv.'

5. Κατάλογος τῶν Χειρογράφων τῆς Ἐθνικῆς Βιβλιοθήκης τῆς Ἑλλαδος ὑπὸ Ἰωάννου Σακκελίωνος καὶ Ἀλκιβιάδου Ἰ. Σακκελίωνος. Ἐν Ἀθήναις, 1892.

6. Ἱεροσολυμιτικὴ Βιβλιοθήκη, ἤτοι Κατάλογος τῶν ἐν ταῖς Βιβλιοθήκαις τοῦ ἁγιωτάτου ἀποστολικοῦ τε καὶ καθολικοῦ ὀρθοδόξου πατριαρχικοῦ θρόνου τῶν Ἱεροσολύμων καὶ πάσης Παλαιστίνης ἀποκειμένων Ἑλληνίκων Κωδίκων, κ.τ.λ.: ὑπὸ Παπαδοπούλου Κεραμέως, κ.τ.λ. Ἐν Πετροπόλει, 1891.

7. Ἐν Κωνσταντινουπόλει Ἑλληνικὸς Φιλολογικὸς Σύλλογος. Μαυρογορδάτειος Βιβλιοθήκη. Παραρτήματα τοῦ ΙΕ Τόμου (1884), τοῦ ΙϚ Τόμου (1885), τοῦ ΙΖ Τόμου (1886), τοῦ ΙΗ Τόμου (1888). Ἐν Κωνσταντινουπόλει.

8. Ὑπομνήματα Περιγραφικὰ τὸν Κυκλάδων Νήσων κατὰ μέρος ὑπὸ Ἀντωνίου Μηλιαράκη. Ἄνδρος, Κέως, ὑπὸ Ἀ. Παπαδυπούλου τοῦ Κεραμέως. Ἐν Ἀθήναις, 1880.

9. Ἔκθεσις Παλαιογραφικῶν καὶ Φιλολογικῶν Ἐρευνῶν ἐν Θράκῃ καὶ Μακεδονίᾳ: ὑπὸ Α. Παπαδοπούλου Κεραμέως. Ἐν Κωνσταντινουπόλει, 1886.

10. Κατάλογος τῶν ἐν ταῖς Βιβλιοθήκαις τοῦ Ἁγίου Ὄρους Ἑλληνικῶν Κωδίκων: ὑπὸ Σπυρίδωνος Π. Λάμπρου.

11. Catalogus Codicum Bibliotheca Imperialis Publicae Gr. et Lat. Edvardus de Muralto. Petropoli, 1840.

12. And especially the learned Prolegomena to Tischendorf, 8th edition, drawn up and issued by Dr. C. R. Gregory, who has with the greatest diligence examined a vast number of MSS. on the spot. I have had a difficult task in steering between my duty to the learned public *in*

the short time allowed me for the preparation of this edition, and the desire of Dr. Gregory that I should not take more of the information supplied in his work than I could help. What I have chiefly done has been to insert his measurements, where I could obtain no others, translating them into inches, and some other particulars upon such MSS. as had been already described in the third edition. In the case of the newly-discovered MSS., which have been first recorded by Dr. Gregory, I have only mentioned them, with a general reference to Dr. Gregory's book, except where information from other sources has come to hand. I have the pleasure of paying a tribute in the case of MSS. which I have examined upon his track to the great skill and accuracy of his examinations.

APPENDIX B.

ON FACSIMILES.

Since the application of photography in its more perfect forms to manuscripts for the purpose of representing their character accurately to scholars who have no opportunity of examining the manuscripts for themselves, the older facsimiles have in greater measure lost their value. It seems, therefore, hardly worth while to refer to the collections of facsimiles made by Montfaucon, or Bianchini, or Silvestre, or Westwood, other representations when they are to be had being so much more faithful and instructive.

The following are some of the most valuable of recent collections:—

1. Palaeographical Society, Facsimiles of MSS. and Inscriptions, ed. E. A. Bond, E. M. Thompson, and G. F. Warner, first series, 3 vols., London, 1873–1883 ; second series, 1884, &c., in progress, fol.

This collection contains the following Gr. Test. MSS.:—

Series I.

B, Plate 104.	ℵ, Plate 105.
A, Plate 106.	D, 14, 15.
D, Clarom. 63, 64.	E, Laudianus, 80.
Evst., Parham, 83.	Brit. Mus. Harl. 5598, 26, 27.
Brit. Mus. Add. 17,470, 202.	Rom. Vat. Gr. 1208, 131.
Brit. Mus. Add. 28,816, 843.	Brit. Mus. Add. 28,818, 204.
Brit. Mus. Add. 22,506, 205.	Brit. Mus. Add. 19,993, 206.
Camb. Trin. Coll. B. 17. 1, 127.	Δ, Sangallensis, semi-uncial, 179.
Codex Argenteus (Gothic), 118.	

Series II.

Oxf. Bodl. Misc. Gr. 313, 7. Rom. Vat. Gr. 2138, 87.

2. A considerable selection from the large assemblage of MSS. at Paris has been issued in facsimile by M. Omont, in his three volumes, pub-

lished in 1887, 1890, and 1892 respectively, viz. Facsimilés des Manuscrits Grecs des xv et xiv siècles, reproduits en photolithographie d'après les originaux de la Bibliothèque Nationale, Paris, 4to.

Facsimilés des Manuscrits Grecs datés de la Bibliothèque Nationale du ixe au xive siècle, Paris, fol.

Facsimilés des plus anciens Manuscrits Grecs en onciale et en minuscule de la Bibliothèque Nationale du ive au xiie siècle, Paris, fol.

3. For Spain, Martin (A.), Facsimilés des Manuscrits d'Espagne, gravés d'après les photographies de Charles Graux, 2 vols., Paris, 1891, 8vo and atlas.

4. Wattenbach (W.) and Velsen (A. von), Exempla Codicum Graecorum literis minusculis scriptorum, Heidelberg, 1878, fol.

APPENDIX C.

ON DATING BY INDICTION.

SOME account of the old way of dating Greek MSS. by indiction has been already given (p. 42, n. 2), but it may be convenient to our readers to have a fuller description to refer to. Such a description may be found in Mr. Maunde Thompson's admirable Manual on Greek and Latin Palaeography, pp. 322-3, which, by the kind permission of the author, is reproduced here.

'Mediaeval Greek MSS. are dated sometimes by the year of the indiction, sometimes by the year of the world according to the era of Constantinople, sometimes by both indiction and year of the world.

The Indiction was a cycle of fifteen years, which are severally styled, Indiction 1, Indiction 2, &c., up to Indiction 15, when the series begins afresh. The introduction of this system is attributed to Constantine the Great. From the circumstance of the commencement of the indiction being reckoned variously from different days, four kinds of indictions have been recognized, viz. :—

i. The Indiction of Constantinople, calculated from the 1st of September, A.D. 312.

ii. The Imperial or Caesarian Indiction (commonly used in England and France), beginning on the 24th of September, A.D. 312.

iii. The Roman or Pontifical Indiction (commonly used in dating papal bulls from the ninth to the fourteenth century), beginning on the 1st of January (or the 25th of December, when that day was reckoned as the first day of the year), A.D. 313.

iv. The Indiction used in the register of the parliament of Paris, beginning in October.

APPENDIX D. 381

The Greeks made use of the Indiction of Constantinople[1].
To find the indiction of a year of the Christian era, add 3 to the year (because A. D. 1 = Indiction 4), and divide the sum by 15: if nothing remains, the indiction will be 15; if there is a remainder, it will be the number of the indiction. But it must not be forgotten that the Indiction of Constantinople begins on the first of September, and consequently that the last four months of a year of the Christian era belong to the next indiction year.

The year of the Creation of the World was calculated, according to the era of Constantinople, to be B.C. 5508. The first day of the year was the 1st of September.

To reduce the Mundane era of Constantinople to the Christian era, deduct 5508 from the former for the months of January to August; and 5509 for September to December.

A chronological table, showing the corresponding years of the Mundane era, the Christian era, and the Indiction, from A. D. 800 to A. D. 1599, will be found in Gardthausen's "Griechische Palaeographie," pp. 450-459.'

Mr. Thompson also refers to an article by Mr. Kenyon in *The Classical Review*, March, 1893, p. 110, where the Egyptian puzzle is noticed, to one by Wilcken in 'Hermes,' xxviii. p. 230, and one by Viereck in 'Philologus,' lii. p. 219, and generally to the interesting and valuable Introduction to the British Museum upon Greek Papyri.

APPENDIX D.

ON THE 'PHMATA.

THE following ingenious and probably sound explanation of what has been long a *crux* to Textual Critics, comes from a Lecture by Mr. Rendel Harris, 'On the Origin of the Ferrar Group,' delivered at Mansfield College, Oxford, on Nov. 6, 1893, and since published (C. J. Clay and Sons), and courteously sent to the editor by the accomplished author. The explanation is given in Mr. Harris' own words (pp. 7-10): but the whole of his pamphlet should be consulted by those who are interested in this study.

'In Scrivener's Introduction to the New Testament (ed. 3, p. 65) we are told that "besides the division of the text into στίχοι or lines, we find in the Gospels alone another division into ῥήματα or ῥήσεις, 'sentences,' differing but little from the στίχοι in number. Of these last the precise

---

[1] An independent mode of reckoning the commencement of the indiction was followed in Egypt under the later Roman Empire. The indiction there began normally in the latter half of the month Pauni, which corresponds to about the middle of June; but the actual day of commencement appears to have been variable and to have depended upon the exact period of the rising of the Nile.— 'Catalogue of Greek Papyri in the British Museum,' pp. 197, 198.

numbers vary in different copies, though not considerably, &c." And on p. 66 we find the following statistical statement:

> Matthew has 2522 ῥήματα
> Mark   „ 1675   „
> Luke   „ 3803   „
> John   „ 1938   „

These figures are derived from MSS. of the Gospels, in which we frequently find the attestation given both of the ῥήματα and the στίχοι: e. g. Cod. Ev. 173 gives for

> Matthew ,βφκϑ´ ῥήματα,
> ,βφξ´ στίχοι,

while the corresponding figures for Mark and Luke are

> Mark ,αχοε´ } and Luke ,γωγ´ }
>   ,αχδ´ }   βψν´ }

No explanation, as far as I know, has ever been given of these curiously numbered ῥήματα. The word is, certainly, a peculiar one to use, if short sentences are intended, such as are commonly known by the terms "cola and commata."

It has occurred to me that perhaps the explanation might lie in the fact that ῥῆμα was here a literal translation of the Syriac word ܦܬܓܡܐ. Let us then see whether ܦܬܓܡܐ is the proper word to describe a verse, either a fixed verse, like a hexameter, or a sense-line. A reference to Payne Smith's Lexicon will show that it may be used in either of these senses, for example, we are told that it is not only used generally of the verses of Scripture, but that it may stand for "*comma, membrum versus, sentential brevior quam versus*, στίχος, Schol. ad Hex. Job. ix. 33; ܣܟܘ ܦܬܓܡܐ, Tit. ib. Ps. ix; ܚܠܦ ܦܬܓܡܐ, ib. Ex. xxx. 22 marg.: insunt in Geneseos libro ܩ ܦܬܓܡܐ ᴍᴍᴍᴍᴅɪx, coloph. ad Gen., it. C.S.B. 2 et sic ad fin. cuiusque libri; in libris poeticis sententia est hemistichio minor, e.g. in Ps. i. insunt versus sex sed ܚܡܫ; in Ps. ii. versus duodecim, sed ܫܬ ܠܐ."

It seems, therefore, to be used in Syriac much in the same way as στίχος in Greek.

Now there is in one of the Syriac MSS. on Mount Sinai (Cod. Sin. Syr.) a table of the Canonical books of the Old and New Testaments with their measured verses. We will give some extracts from this table; but first, notice that the Gospels are numbered as follows:

> Matthew has 2522 ܦܬܓܡܐ
> Mark   „ 1675   „
> Luke   „ 3083   „
> John   „ 1737   „

and the whole of the four Evangelists 9218, which differs slightly from the total formed by addition, which, as the figures stand, is 9017.

On comparing the table with the numbers given by Scrivener from Greek MSS., viz.

APPENDIX D. 383

> Matt.= 2522 ῥήματα
> Mark = 1675 ,,
> Luke = 3803 ,,
> John = 1938 ,,

we see at a glance that we are dealing with the same system; Luke should evidently have 3083, the Greek number being evidently an excessive one; and if we assume that John should be 1938 the total amounts exactly to the 9218 given for the four Gospels.

This is very curious, and since the ῥήματα are now proved to be rightly equated to ܩ̈ܦܐܠ, and this latter word is a proper word to describe a verse or στίχος, the ῥήματα appear to be a translation of a Syriac table.

Perhaps we may get some further idea about the character of the verses in question by turning to the Sinai list, which is not confined to the Gospels, but ranges through the whole of the Old and New Testaments.

The Stichometry in question follows the list of the names of the seventy disciples, which list is here assigned to Irenaeus, bishop of Lugdunum. After which we have

ܘܗܕܐ ܣܘܡܚܠܐ ܘܚܠܝܣܐ ܕܩܕܡܐ
ܡܪܝܩܐ: ܘܐܝܬ ܒܗ ܩܠܝ̈ܥܐ ܐܠܦ
ܚܡܫ ܡܐܐ ܫܬܥܣܪ: ܕܐܘܛܐ
ܩܠܝ̈ܥܐ ܐܘܚܐ ܐܠܦܝ̈ܐ ܘܫܒܥܡܐܐ
ܘܫܡܢܐܝܢ:

i.e. Genesis has 4516 verses
followed by

Exodus 3378 ,,
Leviticus 2684 ,,
Numbers 3481 ,,
Deuteronomy 2982 ,,
Total for the Law 17041 ,,
Joshua 1953 ,,
Judges 2088 ,,
&c.

When we come to the New Testament, it seems at first sight as if the verses which are there reckoned cannot be the Greek equivalent hexameters: for we are told that Philemon contains 53 verses, and the Epistle to Titus 116, numbers which are in excess of the Euthalian reckoning, 38 and 97 verses respectively, and similarly in other cases. The suggestion arises that the lines here reckoned are sense lines, and this is therefore the meaning to be attached to the ῥήματα of the MSS. But upon this point we must not speak too hastily.

The interest of the Sinai stichometry is not limited to this single point: its list of New Testament books is peculiar in order and contents. There seem to be no Catholic Epistles, and amongst the Pauline Epistles, Galatians stands first; note also the curious order Hebrews, Colossians, Ephesians, Philippians.

* I do not think there can be the slightest doubt that our explanation of the origin of the ῥήματα is correct * * * *.'

APPENDIX E.

TABLE OF DIFFERENCES BETWEEN THE FOURTH EDITION OF DR. SCRIVENER'S PLAIN INTRODUCTION AND DR. GREGORY'S PROLEGOMENA.

I. *Evangelia.*

Greg.	Scriv.	Greg.	Scriv.	Greg.	Scriv.	Greg.	Scriv.	Greg.	Scriv.
450	Scholz	490	.. 574	519	.. 505	548	.. 535	577	.. 871
451	.. 481	491	.. 576	520	.. 506	549	.. 536	578	.. 872
		492	.. 577	521	.. 562	550	.. 537	579	.. 743
452		493	.. 578	522	.. 488	551	.. 538	580	.. 744
|	} Scholz	494	.. 325	523	.. 489	552	.. 539	581	.. 450
466		495	.. 581	524	.. 490	553	.. 540	582	.. 451
467	.. 717	496	.. 582	525	.. 491	554	.. 541	583	.. 452
468	.. 718	497	.. 583	526	.. 610	555	.. 609	584	.. 453
469	.. 719	498	.. 584	527	.. 482	556	.. 526	585	.. 454
470	.. 509	499	.. 586	528	.. 483	557	.. 524	586	.. 455
471	.. 510	500	.. 587	529	.. 484	558	.. 525	587	.. 456
472	.. 511	501	.. 588	530	.. 485	559	.. 518	588	.. 457
473	.. 512	502	.. 589	531	.. 327	560	.. 520	589	.. 830
474	.. 513	503	.. 590	532	.. 545	561	.. 521	590	.. 831
475	.. 515	504	.. 585	533	.. 546	562	.. 522	591	.. 883
476	.. 566	505	.. 567	534	.. 547	563	.. 519	592	.. 461
477	.. 508	506	.. 492	535	.. 548	564	.. 478	593	.. 462
478	.. 575	507	.. 493	536	.. 549	565	.. 473	594	.. 470
479	.. 542	508	.. 494	537	.. 550	566	.. 479	595	.. 468
480	.. 568	509	.. 495	538	.. 552	567	.. 878	596	.. 465
481	.. 569	510	.. 496	539	.. 551	568	.. 879	597	.. 464
482	.. 570	511	.. 497	540	.. 553	569	.. 475	598	.. 466
483	.. 543	512	.. 498	541	.. 554	570	.. 479	599	.. 467
484	.. 571	513	.. 499	542	.. 555	571	.. 474	600	.. 463
485	.. 572	514	.. 500	543	.. 556	572	.. 480	601	.. 643
486	.. 517	515	.. 501	544	.. 557	573	.. 328	602	.. 644
487	.. 516	516	.. 502	545	.. 558	574	.. 880	603	.. 645
488	.. 514	517	.. 503	546	.. 559	575	.. 477	604	.. 646
489	.. 507	518	.. 504	547	.. 534	576	.. 580	605	.. 647

APPENDIX E.

Greg.	Scriv.	Greg.	Scriv.	Greg.	Scriv.	Greg.	Scriv.	Greg.	Scriv.
606	.. 648	655	.. 635	704	.. 886	753	.. 760	859	.. 672
607	.. 649	656	.. 642	705	.. 887	754	.. 763		
608	.. 650	657	.. 876	706	.. 486	755	.. 771	861	.. 674
609	.. 634	658	.. 636	707	.. 606	756	.. 772	862	.. 675
610	.. 652	659	.. 637	708	.. 607	757	.. 846	863	.. 676
611	.. 653	660	.. 638	709	.. 737	758	.. 847		
612	.. 654	661	.. 639	710	.. 81	759	.. 848	867	.. 680
613	.. 655	662	.. 632	711	.. 617	760	.. 849	868	.. 683
614	.. 656	663	.. 877	712	.. 560	761	.. 850	869	.. 684
615	.. 657	664	.. 605	713	.. 561	762	.. 851	870	..
616	.. 658	665	.. 895	714	.. 563	763	.. 854	871	.. 687
617	.. 659	666	.. 899	715	.. 564	764	.. 855	872	.. 690
618	.. 660	667	.. 900	716	.. 565	765	.. 856	873	.. 689
619	.. 661	668	..1144	717	.. 606	766	.. 857	874	.. 691
620	.. 662	669	.. 902	718	.. 736	767	.. 858	875	.. 692
621	.. 663	670	.. 901	719	.. 824	768	.. 859	876	.. 693
622	.. 664	671	. 544	720	.. 825	769	.. 861	877	.. 694
623	.. 665	672	.. 618	721	.. 826	770	.. 862	878	.. 703
624	.. 667	673	.. 619	722	.. 827	771	.. 863	879	.. 704
625	.. 673	674	.. 620	723	.. 828	772	.. 867	880	.. 705
626	.. 674	675	.. 621	724	.. 829	773	.. 868	881	.. 708
627	.. 678	676	.. 527	725	.. 881	774	.. 869	882	.. 713
628	.. 679	677	.. 528	726	.. 882			883	.. 714
629	.. 681	678	.. 529	727	.. 745			884	.. 696
630	.. 682	679	.. 530	728	.. 746	824	.. 622	885	.. 697
631	.. 685	680	.. 531	729	.. 747	825	.. 623	886	.. 698
632	.. 686	681	.. 532	730	.. 748	826	.. 624	887	.. 699
633	.. 688	682	.. 533	731	.. 749	827	.. 625		
634	.. 695	683	..1145	732	.. 750	828	.. 626		
635	.. 700	684	..1146	733	.. 751	829	.. 627	899	.. 613
636	.. 701	685	..1147	734	.. 752	830	.. 628	900	.. 614
637	.. 702	686	.. 573	735	.. 753	831	.. 629	901	.. 615
638	.. 706	687	.. 579	736	.. 754			902	.. 616
639	.. 710	688	.. 592	737	.. 755	839	.. 630		
640	.. 711	689	.. 593	738	.. 756	840	.. 631	1144	.. 727
641	.. 712	690	.. 594	739	.. 757			1145	.. 728
642	.. 715	691	.. 595	740	.. 761	847	.. 723	1146	.. 731
643	.. 716	692	.. 596	741	.. 762	848	.. 611	1147	.. 733
644	.. 720	693	.. 597	742	.. 764	849	.. 730	1148	.. 734
645	.. 591	694	.. 598	743	.. 738	850	.. 729	1149	.. 735
646	.. 721	695	.. 599	744	.. 759	851	..		
647	.. 722	696	.. 600	745	.. 633	852	.. 732	1261	.. 765
648	.. 724	697	.. 601	746	.. 740			1262	.. 766
649	.. 725	698	.. 602	747	.. 741			1263	.. 767
650	.. 726	699	.. 603	748	.. 758	854	.. 666		
651	.. 874	700	.. 604	749	.. 773	855	.. 668	1265	.. 768
652	.. 875	701	.. 523	750	.. 742	856	.. 669	1266	.. 769
653	.. 640	702	.. 884	751	.. 739	857	.. 670	1267	.. 770
654	.. 641	703	.. 885	752	.. 774	858	.. 671	1268	.. 110

II. Acts and Catholic Epistles.

Greg.	Scriv.	Greg.	Scriv.	Greg.	Scriv.	Greg.	Scriv.	Greg.	Scriv.
182	Scholz	204	.. 107	226	.. 216	248	.. 251	301	.. 240
183	.. 257	205	.. 232	227	.. 217	249	.. 263	302	.. 250
184	.. 258	206	.. 194	228	.. 218	250	.. 264	303	.. 248
185	}	207	.. 197	229	.. 223	251	.. 201		
186		208	.. 259	230	.. 202	252	.. 249	317	.. 243
187		209	.. 260	231	.. 203	253	.. 233	318	.. 244
188	} Scholz	210	.. 328	232	.. 204	254	.. 200	319	.. 245
189		211	.. 317	233	.. 205	255	.. 199	320	.. 241
190		212	.. 318	234	.. 206	256	.. 231	321	.. 261
191		213	.. 252	235	.. 207	257	.. 222		
192	}	214	.. 182	236	.. 208	258	.. 289	325	.. 239
193	.. 188	215	.. 183	237	.. 209	259	.. 260	326	.. 246
194	.. 187	216	.. 184	238	.. 195	260	.. 209		
195	.. 224	217	.. 185	239	.. 196	261	.. 267	328	.. 319
196	.. 226	218	.. 186	240	.. 253	262	.. 269	329	.. 256
197	.. 227	219	.. 225	241	.. 254	263	.. 321	330	.. 247
198	.. 228	220	.. 229	242	.. 255	264	.. 326	334	.. 238
199	.. 193	221	.. 212	243	.. 301			335	.. 236
200	.. 211	222	.. 213	244	.. 302	267	.. 242		
201	.. 219	223	.. 220	245	.. 335	268	.. 334	415	.. 210
202	.. 215	224	.. 221	246	.. 415	269	.. 237	416	.. 147
203	.. 230	225	.. 198	247	.. 110				

III. Paul.

Greg.	Scriv.	Greg.	Scriv.	Greg.	Scriv.	Greg.	Scriv.	Greg.	Scriv.
131	.. 261	248	.. 262	266	.. 230	284	.. 248	302	.. 299
231	.. 303?	249	.. 258	267	.. 316	285	.. 275	303	.. 243
232	.. 306?	250	.. 259	268	.. 317	286	.. 296	304	.. 281
233	}	251	.. 257	269	.. 302	287	.. 334	305	.. 231
234		252	.. 260	270	.. 252	288	.. 316	306	.. 266
235		253	.. 268	271	.. 253	289	.. 329	307	.. 278
236	} Scholz	254	.. 279	272	.. 254	290	.. 256	308	.. 398
237		255	.. 269	273	.. 255	291	.. 267	309	.. 399
238		256	.. 277	274	.. 321	292	.. 331	310	.. 400
239	}	257	.. 249	275	.. 270	293	.. 263	311	.. 401
240	.. 240	258	.. 233	276	.. 250	294	.. 226	312	.. 276
241	Scholz	259	.. 282	277	.. 251	295	.. 332	313	.. 402
242	.. 242	260	.. 300	278	.. 264	296	.. 333	314	.. 403
243	Scholz	261	.. 298	279	.. 265	297	.. 335	315	.. 404
244	.. 244	262	.. 222	280	.. 280	298	.. 301	316	.. 290
245	.. 245	263	.. 223	281	.. 234	299	.. 337	317	.. 325
246	.. 246	264	.. 152	282	.. 235	300	.. 237	318	.. 406
247	.. 247	265	.. 304	283	.. 236	301	.. 396	319	.. 274

APPENDIX E. 387

Greg.	Scriv.	Greg.	Scriv.	Greg.	Scriv.	Greg.	Scriv.	Greg.	Scriv.
320	.. 407	333	.. 476	376e	.. 330	401	.. 312	426	.. 283
321	.. 423	334	.. 478	377	.. 341	402	.. 314	427	.. 336
322	.. 424	335	.. 480			403	.. 315	430	.. 294
323	.. 435	336	.. 53			404	.. 323	431	.. 319
324	.. 426	337	.. 481	380	.. 339			432	.. 322
325	.. 427	338	.. 482	381	.. 340			433	.. 295
326	.. 430	339	.. 487	392	.. 288	406	.. 327	436	.. 272
327	.. 431	340	.. 484	393	.. 286	407	.. 328	437	.. 273
328	.. 432	341	.. 485	393a	.. 287			472	.. 232
329	.. 433			396	.. 297			476	.. 285
330	.. 436			398	.. 305	423	.. 291	476a	.. 326
331	.. 437	376	.. 338	399	.. 310	424	.. 292	478	.. 225
332	.. 472	376c	.. 377	400	.. 311	425	.. 293	480	.. 324

IV. *Apocalypse.*

Greg.	Scriv.	Greg.	Scriv.	Greg.	Scriv.	Greg.	Scriv.	Greg.	Scriv.
101	.. 103	109	.. 101	117	.. 157			158	..
102	.. 109	110	.. 146	118	.. 160	149	.. 120	159	..
103	.. 102	111	.. 149	119	.. 161	150	.. 121	160	.. 118
104	.. 105	112	.. 150	120	.. 182	151	.. 122	161	.. 119
105	.. 111	113	.. 110	121	.. 153				
		114	.. 115	122	.. 86	153	.. 114	181	.. 107
107	.. 104	115	.. 117					182	.. 112
108	.. 89	116	.. 151	146	.. 113	157	.. 116		

V. *Evangelistaries.*

Greg.	Scriv.	Greg.	Scriv.	Greg.	Scriv.	Greg.	Scriv.	Greg.	Scriv.
155	.. 180	174	..	191	.. 263	208	.. 215	225	.. 248
158	..	175	..	192	.. 264	209	.. 216	226	.. 249
159	..	176	..	193	.. 266	210	.. 217	227	.. 250
160	..	177	..	194	.. 202	211	.. 218	228	.. 253²
161	..	178	..	195	.. 203	212	.. 219	229	.. 223
162	..	179	.. 179	196	.. 204	213	.. 220	230	.. 224
163	..	180	.. 463	197	.. 205	214	.. 239	231	.. 225
164	..	181	.. 234	198	.. 206	215	.. 240	232	.. 226
165	..	182	.. 233	199	.. 207	216	.. 251	233	.. 235
166	..	183	.. 257	200	.. 208	217	.. 241	234	.. 227
167	..	184	.. 259	201	.. 209	218	.. 242	235	.. 228
168	..	185	.. 222	202	.. 210	219	.. 243	236	.. 229
169	..	186	.. 221	203	.. 211	220	.. 244	237	.. 237
170	.. 326	187	.. 256	204	.. 212	221	.. 245	237a	.. 238
171	..	188	.. 260	205	.. 201	222	.. 246	238	.. 254
172	..	189	.. 261	206	.. 213	223	.. 252	239	.. 230
173	..	190	.. 262	207	.. 214	224	.. 247	240	.. 231

Greg.	Scriv.	Greg.	Scriv.	Greg.	Scriv.	Greg.	Scriv.	Greg.	Scriv.
241	.. 232	289	.. 168	336	.. 284	385	.. 520	467	.. 317
242	.. 465	290	.. 169	337	.. 285	386	.. 521	468	.. 318
243	.. 466	291	.. 187	338	.. 499	387	.. 522	469	.. 319
244	.. 467	292	.. 189	339	.. 59	388	.. 523	470	.. 320
245[a]	.. 468	293	.. 190	340	.. 258	389	.. 524	471	.. 321
245[b]	.. 469	294	.. 481	341	.. 288	390	.. 528	472	.. 330
246	.. 194	295	.. 482	342	.. 289	391	.. 529	472[c]	.. 330
247	.. 470	296	.. 483	343	.. 298	392	.. 530	473	.. 323
248	.. 471	297	.. 484	344	.. 236	393	.. 531	474	.. 420
249	.. 191	298	.. 485	345	.. 500	394	.. 532	475	.. 325
250	.. 472	299	.. 200	346	.. 255	395	.. 534	476	.. 290
251	.. 195	300	.. 286	347	.. 501	396	.. 535	477	.. 363
252	.. 473	301	.. 486	348	.. 502	397	.. 536	478	.. 322
253	.. 196	302[a]	.. 487	349	.. 503	398[ab]	.. 537	480	.. 331
254	.. 474	302[b]	.. 489	350	.. 504	399[ab]	.. 538	481	.. 332
255	.. 475	303	.. 491	351	.. 505	400	.. 540	482	.. 333
256	.. 192	304	.. 492	352	.. 506	401	.. 541	484	.. 334
257	.. 476	305	.. 291	353	.. 507	402	.. 542	485	.. 336
258	.. 197	306	.. 292	354	.. 508	403	.. 543	486[a]	.. 337
259	.. 477	307	.. 293	355	.. 509	404	.. 544	486[d]	.. 340
260	.. 198	308	.. 294	356	.. 512	405	.. 546	487	.. 338
261	.. 158	309	.. 295	357	.. 513	406	.. 549	488	.. 339
262	.. 159	310	.. 296	358	.. 514	407	.. 550	489	.. 341
263	.. 193	311	.. 297	359	.. 515	408	.. 552	490	.. 342
264	.. 170	312	.. 493	360	.. 516	409	.. 553	491	.. 343
265	.. 171	313	.. 494	361	.. 426	410	.. 556	492	.. 344
266	.. 172	314	.. 495	362	.. 427	411	.. 560	493	.. 345
267	.. 173	315	.. 253	363	.. 299	412	.. 561	494	.. 346
268	.. 174	316	.. 496	364	.. 416	413	.. 563	495	.. 347
269	.. 175	317	.. 497	365	.. 417	414	.. 564	496	.. 348
270	.. 176	318	.. 265	366	.. 366	415	.. 565	497	.. 349
271	.. 177	319	.. 267	367	.. 367	416	.. 566	498	.. 350
272	.. 178	320	.. 268	368	.. 421	417	.. 567	499	.. 422
273	.. 478	321	.. 269	369	.. 423	418	.. 568	500	.. 352
274	.. 479	322	.. 270	370	.. 324	419	.. 569	501	.. 353
275	.. 181	323	.. 271	371	.. 424	420	.. 570	502	.. 354
276	.. 182	324	.. 272	372	.. 425	421	.. 571	503	.. 355
277	... 183	325	.. 273	373	.. 517	422	.. 572	504	.. 356
278	.. 186	326	.. 274	374	.. 419	423	.. 573	505	.. 357
279	.. 184	327	.. 276	375	.. 370	424	.. 574	506	.. 358
280	.. 185	328	.. 277	376	.. 371	425	.. 759	508	.. 359
281	.. 160	328[a]	.. 38	377	.. 372	426	.. 804	509	.. 360
282	.. 161	329	.. 278	378	.. 373	427	.. 828		
283	.. 162	330	.. 279	379	.. 374	428	.. 829	512	.. 306
284	.. 163	331	.. 280	380	.. 375			513	.. 300
285	164, 5	332	.. 62	381	.. 368	463	.. 313	514	.. 301
286	.. 480	333	.. 281	382	.. 369	464	.. 314	515	.. 305
287	.. 166	334	.. 282	383	.. 518	465	.. 315	516	.. 302
288	.. 167	335	.. 283	384	.. 519	466	.. 316	517	.. 307

APPENDIX E.   389

Greg.	Scriv.	Greg.	Scriv.	Greg.	Scriv.	Greg.	Scriv.	Greg.	Scriv.
518	.. 311	532	.. 407	545	.. 381	560	.. 388	572	.. 572
519	.. 303	534	.. 404	546	.. 382	561	. 389	573	.. 395
520	.. 304	535	.. 403	547	.. 547	562	.. 562	574	.. 362
521	.. 308	536	.. 405	548	.. 548	563	.. 390	804	.. 412
522	.. 309	537	.. 411	549	.. 383	564	.. 392	923	.. 288
523	.. 312	538	.. 414	550	.. 384	565	.. 393		
524	.. 310	539	..	551	..	566	.. 396	927	.. 275
		540	.. 376	552	.. 385	567	.. 397	928	.. 418
528	.. 409	541	.. 377	553	.. 386	568	.. 398	935	.. 415
529	.. 410	542	.. 378			569	.. 399	936	.. 428
530	.. 408	543	.. 379	556	.. 387	570	.. 188		
531	.. 406	544	.. 380			571	.. 394		

VI. *Apostolos.*

Greg.	Scriv.	Greg.	Scriv.	Greg.	Scriv.	Greg.	Scriv.	Greg.	Scriv.
49	⎫	75	.. 70	100	.. 214	126	.. 115	202	.. 99
50	⎪	76	.. 198	101	.. 216	127	.. 169	203	.. 100
51	⎬ Scholz	77	.. 79	102	.. 90	128	.. 180	204	.. 101
52	⎪	78	.. 78	103	.. 83	129	.. 184	205	.. 102
53	⎪	79	.. 75	104	.. 84	130	.. 186	206	.. 103
54	⎭	80	.. 71	105	.. 85			207	.. 104
55	.. 55	81	.. 69	106	.. 86			208	.. 106
56	.. 56	82	.. 77	107	.. 87	169	.. 105	209	.. 107
58	.. 58	83	.. 76	108	.. 88	170	.. 170	210	.. 108
59	.. 48	84	.. 74	109	.. 89	171	.. 70a	211	.. 109
60	.. 57	85	.. 200	110	.. 263	172	.. 93	212	.. 110
61	.. 59	86	.. 51	111	.. 223	173	.. 94	213	.. 111
62	.. 60	87a	.. 201	112	.. 81			214	.. 112
63	.. 61	87b	.. 202	113	.. 82	180	.. 73	215	.. 215
64	.. 62	88	.. 130	114	.. 125			216	.. 124
65	.. 52	89	.. 50	115	.. 126	183	.. 80		
66	.. 64	90	.. 203	116	.. 127	184	.. 67	227	.. 121
67	.. 66	91	.. 204	117	.. 213	185	.. 185	228	.. 113
68	.. 65	92	.. 205	118	.. 116	186	.. 53		
69	.. 178	93	.. 206					255	.. 122
70	.. 72	94	.. 207	120	.. 49			256	.. 128
70b	.. 172	95	.. 208	121	.. 119	197	.. 91		
71	.. 173	96	.. 209	122	.. 123	198	.. 92		
72	.. 183	97	.. 210	123	.. 120	199	.. 199	262	.. 129
73	.. 54	98	.. 211	124	.. 98	200	.. 96	263	.. 68
74	.. 197	99	.. 212	125	.. 114	201	.. 97	264	.. 117

INDEX I.

OF GREEK MANUSCRIPTS.

Index of Greek Manuscripts of the New Testament, arranged according to the countries where they are and the owners to whom they belong.

(N.B.—The Reference is always made to the MSS., which are described in their proper places.)

BRITISH EMPIRE.
ENGLAND.

		Total MSS.
Amherst, Lord.........Evan. 887...		1
Ashburnham, Earl of		3
204......................Evan. 544		
205.........................Evst. 237		
205*.........................Evst. 238		
Braithwaite, J. B.		3
1..........................Evan. 327		
2..........................Evan. 328		
3..........................Evan. 236		
(British and Foreign Bible Soc., London)...Evan. ⊟ & Evst. 200		2
Burdett-Coutts, Baroness		19
B.-C. I. 1 ....Evan. 612		
II. 16, 18 ....Evann. 551–2		
III. 4, 5, 9, 10........Evann. 555–8		
III. 21 ....Evst. 246		
III. 24 ....Apost. 65		
III. 29 ....Evst. 252		
III. 34 ....Evst. 247		
III. 37 ....Act. 221		
III. 41 ....Evan. 559		
III. 42 ....Evst. 253		
III. 43, 46, 52, 53 ......Evst. 248, 249, 250, 253²		
III. 44 ....Apost. 78		
(Cambridge)—		
UNIVERSITY LIBRARY		25
Dd. 8. 23 ....Evst. 146		
Dd. 8. 49 ....Evst. 4		
Dd. 9. 69 ....Evan. 60		
Dd. 11. 90............Act. 21		
Ff. 1. 30 ....Paul. 27		
Hh. 6. 12 ....Evan. 609		

		Total MSS.
Kk. v. 35 ....Evan. 62		
Kk. 6. 4..................Act. 9		
Ll. 2. 13 ....Evan. 70		
Mm. 6. 9 ....Evan. 440		
Nn. 2. 36 ....Evan. 443		
Nn. 2. 41 (Bezae)......Evan. D		
Add. 679. 1 ....Evst. 291		
679. 2 ....Apost. 79		
720 ....Evan. 618		
1836..............Evst. 292		
1837..............Evan. 619		
1839..............Evst. 293		
1840..............Evst. 294		
1875..............Evan. Tᵒ		
1879. 2..........Evst. 295		
1879. 11 ....Evan. 620		
1879. 12 ....Evst. 296		
1879. 13 ....Evst. 297		
1879. 24 ....Evan. 621		
CHRIST'S COLLEGE		2
F. i. 8 ....Evst. 222		
F. i. 13 ....Act. 24		
CLARE COLLEGE ...Evst. 488 ...		1
EMMANUEL COLLEGE		1
I. 4. 35 ....Act. 53		
GONVILLE AND CAIUS COLLEGE...		1
403........................Evan. 59		
TRINITY COLLEGE		6
B. viii. 5 ....Evan. Wᵈ		
B. x. 16..............Evan. 507		
B. x. 17..............Evan. 508		
B. xvii. 1 (Augiens.)...Paul. F		
O. iv. 22..............Evst. 221		
O. viii. 3 ....Evan. 66		

392   INDEX I.

	Total MSS.
(Cheltenham)—	
FENWICK, Middle Hill	10
1284 ....Evan. 527	
1461 ....Act. 178	
2387 ....Evan. 528	
3886 ....Evan. 529	
3887 ....Evan. 530	
7681 ....Act. 198	
7682 ....Evan. 531	
7712 ....Evan. 532	
7757 ....Evan. 533	
13975 ....Evan. 526	
Coniston, Ruskin ....Evst. 254 ...	1
Crawford, Earl of ...Evann. 1320, 1321 ...	2
Herries, Lord ....Evan. 580...	1
(Holkham)—	
EARL OF LEICESTER	2
3............Evan. 524	
4............Evan. 525	
(Lambeth Palace)	25
Cod. 528 ....Evan. 71	
1175 ....Evan. 509	
1176 ....Evan. 510	
1177 ....Evan. 511	
1178 ....Evan. 512	
1179 ....Evan. 513	
1180 ....Evan. 514	
1181?(or 1255)...Act. 186	
1182 ....Act. 182	
1183 ....Act. 183	
1184 ....Act. 184	
1185 ....Act. 185	
1186 ....Paul. 256	
1187, 1188, 1189 Evst. 223–5	
1190, 1191 ......Apost. 59, 60	
1192 ....Evan. 515	
1193 ....Evst. 226	
1194 ....Evst. 363	
1195, 1196 ......Apost. 61–2	
1255 or C. 4 ...Evan. 516	
1350 ....Evan. 517	
(Leicester)............Evan. 69 ...	1
(London)—	
BRITISH MUSEUM	136
Codex Alexandrinus	
Arundel 524............Evan. 566	
534............Paul. 372	
536............Evst. 256	
547............Evst. 257	
Burney 18............Evan. 568	
19............Evan. 569	
20............Evan. 570	
21............Evan. 571	
22............Evst. 259	

	Total MSS.
Burney 23............Evan. 572	
48............Act. 225	
408............Evst. 499	
Cotton, Vesp. B. xviii. Apost. 2	
Titus C. xv ...Evan. N	
Egerton 2163............Evst. 59	
2610............Evan. 604	
2783............Evan. 563	
2784............Evan. 565	
2785............Evan. 564	
2786............Evst. 255	
2787............Act. 223	
Harleian 1810 ....Evan. 113	
5537 ....Act. 25	
5538 ....Evan. 567	
5540 ....Evan. 114	
5552 ....Paul. 66	
5557 ....Act. 26	
5559 ....Evan. 115	
5561 ....Evst. 258	
5567 ....Evan. 116	
5588 ....Act. 59	
5598 ....Evst. 150	
5613 ....{ Paul. M / Act. 60 }	
5620 ....Act. 27	
5647 ....Evan. 72	
5650 ....Evst. 25, 25[b]	
5678 ....Apoc. 31	
5684 ....Evan. G	
5731 ....Evan. 117	
5736 ....Evan. 445	
5776 ....Evan. 65	
5777 ....Evan. 446	
5778 ....Act. 28	
5784 ....Evan. 447	
5785 ....Evst. 151	
5787 ....Evst. 152	
5790 ....Evan. 448	
5796 ....Evan. 444	
Royal MS. I. B. I. ...Act. 20	
Additional Manuscripts—	
4949..................Evan. 44	
4950, 4951 ....Evan. 449	
5107..................Evan. 439	
5111, 5112 ....Evan. 438	
5115, 5116 ....Act. 22	
5117..................Evan. 109	
5153..................Evst. 260	
5468..................Evan. 573	
7141..................Evan. 574	
7142..................Paul. 267	
10068................Evst. 926	
11300................Evan. 575	
11836................Evan. 576	
11837................Evan. 201	
11838................Evan. 577	
11839................Evan. 578	
11840................Evst. 261	
11841................Apost. 75	
11859–60............Evan. 608	
11868................Evan. 579	

OF GREEK MANUSCRIPTS. 393

Add. MSS. (cont.)—   Total MSS.
14637, 14638 ....Evst. 496-7
14744...................Evan. 202
15581...................Evan. 580
16183...................Evan. 581
16184...................Evan. 582
16943...................Evan. 583
17136...................Evan. N^b
17211...................Evan. R
17370...................Evst. 262
17469...................Evan. 584
17470...................Evan. 585
17741...................Evan. 586
17982...................Evan. 587
18211...................Evan. 588
18212...................Evst. 263
19386...................Evan. 110
19387...................Evan. 589
19388...................Act. 229
19389...................Evan. 590
19392...................Act. 230
19459...................Evst. 930
19460...................Evst. 264
19737...................Evst. 265
19993...................Evst. 266
20003...................Act. 61
21260...................Evst. 267
21261...................Evst. 268
22506...................Evan. 591
22734...................Act. 107
22735...................Evst. 269
22736...................Evan. 592
22737...................Evan. 593
22738...................Evan. 594
22739...................Evan. 595
22740...................Evan. 596
22741...................Evan. 597
22742...................Evst. 270
22743...................Evst. 271
22744...................Evst. 272
24112...................Evan. 598
24373...................Evan. 599
24374...................Evst. 273
24376...................Evan. 600
24377...................Evst. 274
24378...................Evst. 275
24379...................Evst. 276
24380...................Evst. 277
25881...................Evst. 38
26103...................Evan. 601
27860...................Evst. 278
27861...................Evan. 602
28815...................Evan. 603
28816...................Act. 232
28817...................Evst. 279
28818...................Evst. 280
29713...................Evst. 62
29714...................Apost. 69
31208...................Evst. 281
31919...................Evst. 282
                  Evan. Υ
31920...................Evst. 283
31921...................Evst. 284

Add. MSS. (cont.)—   Total MSS.
31949...................Evst. 285
32051...................Apost. 52
32277...................Evan. 892
32341...................Evan. 325
34059...................Evst. 39
34107...................Evan. 321
34108...................Evan. 322

Butler ....Evan. 632 ... 1

Highgate, Burdett-Coutts...... 20
I. 2....................Evst. 239
I. 3, 4, 7 ....Evann. 545-7
I. 8 ....Evst. 240
I. 9 ....Evan. 548
I. 10 ....Evst. 251
I. 23, 24 ....Evst. 241-2
II. 4 ....Evan. 603
II. 5 ....Evst. 243
II. 5 (?), II. 14 ....Evst. 494-5
II. 7, 13 ....Evann. 549-50
II. 23 ....Evst. 244
II. 26¹, 26² ....Evann. 553-4
II. 30 ....Evst. 245
III. 1 ....Act. 220

Sion College 4
A. 32. 1 (1) ....Evst. 227
A. 32. 1 (2) ....Evst. 228
A. 32. 1 (3) ....Evan. 518
A. 32. 1 (4) ....Evst. 229

(Manchester)....................... 1
Rylands Libr. ....Evan. 886

(Oxford)—

    BODLEIAN 78

Barocc. 3 ....Act. 23
        29 ....Evan. 46
        31 ....Evan. 45
        48 ....Apoc. 28
        59 ....Evan. 610
      197 ....Evst. 201
      202 ....Evst. 5
Canon. Gr. 33........Evan. 288
        34........Evan. 488
        36........Evan. 489
        85........Evst. 202
        92........Evst. 203
     110........Act. 212
     112........Evan. 490
     119........Evst. 204
     122........Evan. 491
     126........Evst. 205
E. D. Clarke 4........Act. 56
       5........Evan. 98
       6........Evan. 107
       7........Evan. 111
       8........Evst. 157
       9........Act. 58
      10........Evan. 112
      45........Evst. 206

394 INDEX I.

	Total MSS.
E. D. Clarke 46........Evst. 207	
47........Evst. 208	
48........Evst. 209	
Cromwell 11............Evst. 30	
15............Evan. 482	
16............Evan. 483	
27............Evst. 210	
Laud 3................Evan. 52	
31................Evan. 51	
32................Evst. 18	
33................Evan. 50	
34................Evst. 20	
35................Act. E	
Misc. Gr. 1............Evan. 48	
5............Evan. O^b	
8............Evan. 96	
9............Evan. 47	
10............Evst. 19	
11............Evst. 28	
12............Evst. 29	
13............Evan. 118	
17............Evan. 484	
74............Act. 30	
76............Evan. 67	
118............Act. 213	
119............Evst. 211	
136............Evan. 105	
140............Evst. 212	
141............Evan. 485	
293............Evan. 486	
305............Evan. 606	
306............Evan. 607	
307............Evst. 288	
308............Evst. 289	
310............Evan. Λ	
313............Evan. Γ	
314............Evan. 737	
319............Apost. 76	
323............Evan. 81	
MS. Bibl. Gr. d. 1......Evan. 562	
e. 1......Evan. 82	
Roe 1 ....Evan. 49	
16 ....Paul. 47	
Selden supra (1) 2 ...Evst. 26	
(2) 3 ...Evst. 27	
(6) 5 ...Evan. 55	
(28) 53...Evan. 53	
(29) 54...Evan. 54	
B. 54 (47) ......Evst. 22	
B. 56 (49) ......Evst. 21	
Arch. 9 ....Apost. 74	
MS. Gr. Lit. c. 1 ......T^f	
MS. Clar. Pr. b. 2......T^{wold}	
Christ Church	29
Wake 13 ....Evan. W^e	
12 ....Evan. 492	
13 ....Evst. 213	
14 ....Evst. 214	
15 ....Evst. 215	
16 ....Evst. 216	
17 ....Evst. 217	
18 ....Evst. 218	

	Total MSS.
Wake 19 ....Evst. 219	
20 ....Evan. 74	
21 ....Evan. 493	
22 ....Evan. 494	
23 ....Evst. 220	
24 ....Evan. 495	
25 ....Evan. 496	
26 ....Evan. 73	
27 ....Evan. 497	
28 ....Evan. 498	
29 ....Evan. 499	
30 ....Evan. 500	
31 ....Evan. 501	
32 ....Evan. 502	
33 ....Apost. 58	
34 ....Evan. 503	
36 ....Evan. 504	
37 ....Evan. W^f & Act. 192	
38 ....Act. 191	
39 ....Evan. 505	
40 ....Evan. 506	
Keble College ...Evst. 298 ...	1
Lincoln College	6
4 ....Evst. 63	
15 ....Evst. 3	
16 ....Evan. 95	
17 ....Evan. 68 & Evst. 199	
18 ....Evan. 56	
82 ....Act. 33	
Magdalen College................	2
7 ....Paul. 42	
9 ....Evan. 57	
New College........................	3
58 ....Act. 36	
59 ....Act. 37	
68 ....Evan. 58	
(Parham Park, Sussex)............	17
Lord de la Zouche.	
66. 1...............Evst. 233	
67. 2...............Apoc. 96	
71. 6...............Evan. 534	
72. 7...............Evan. 535	
73. 8...............Evan. 536	
74. 9...............Evan. 537	
75. 10...............Evan. 538	
76. 11...............Evan. 539	
77. 12...............Evan. 540	
78. 13...............Evan. 541	
79. 14...............Act. 216	
80. 15...............Act. 217	
81. 16...............Act. 218	
82. 17...............Apoc. 95	
83. 18...............Evst. 234	
84. 19...............Evst. 235	
85. 20...............Evst. 236	

OF GREEK MANUSCRIPTS. 395

	Total MSS.
Quaritch i ....Evan. 469 ...	4
ii ....Evan. 471	
viii..........Evst. 935	
Formerly ...Evan. 885	
Ruskin, John ....Evst. 254 ...	1
Swete, H. B., Dr.......Evan. 736 ...	2
Evan. 737	
White, Mr. ....Evan. 523 ...	1
Winchelsea, Earl of Evan. 106 ...	1
(Wisbech)—	
PECKOVER	5
1...................Evan. 560	
2...................Evan. 561	
...................Apost. 43	
70 ....Evst. 500	
...................Apost. 203	
Woolwich ?, Bate......Evst. 492 ...	1
Wordsworth, Bp. ...Evan. 542 ...	1

IRELAND.
(Dublin)—

	Total MSS.
TRINITY COLLEGE	3
Evan. Z	
D. i. 28 ....Paul. 490	
A. i. 2, fol. 1......Evst. 454	

SCOTLAND.

Bute ....Evan. 64 ...	1
(Edinburgh)	5
Libr. A. c. 25 ....Evan. 519	
Mackellar ....Evan. 896	
Act. 333	
Univ. D. Laing 6, 667 Evann. 897-8	
Univ. Laing ....Evst. 578	
(Glasgow)—	
HUNTER MUSEUM	7
V. 3. 3...............Evst. 231	
V. 3. 4...............Apost. 45	
V. 4. 3...............Evst. 232	
V. 5. 10 ....Evst. 230	
V. 7. 2...............Evan. 520	
Q. 7. 10 ....Evan. 521	
S. 8. 141...........Evan. 522	
Duke of Hamilton's collection.	

NEW ZEALAND.

Auckland ....Evan. 1273	2
Evst. 420	

FOREIGN COUNTRIES.
BELGIUM.

	Total MSS.
Brussels	2
Reg. 11358, 11375 ...Evann. 881-2	

DENMARK.

Copenhagen	3
Havniensis 1322 ......Evan. 234	
1323 ......Evan. 235	
1324 ......Evst. 44	

EGYPT.

Cairo	2
Cod. P. Kerameus......Evan. T^s	
Patr. Alex. 2, 15, 16,	
17, 68 ....Evann. 643-7	
421, 952 ....Evann. 903-4	
82, 87 ....Evann. 1270-1	
8, 59, 88 ....Act. 253-5	
942 ....Act. 381	
18 ....Evst. 140	
927, 929, 943,	
944, 945, 946,	
948, 950, 951,	
953 ....Evst. 760-9	
Μετοικία of St. Cath. 7 Evan. 648	

FRANCE.

Arras 970 ....Evan. 872 ...	1
Besançon 41 ....Apost. 51 ...	2
44 ....Evst. 193	
Bordier, Henri ......Evst. 505 ...	1
Carpentras 11 ....Evst. 189...	1
Dessau................Evan. 874...	2
200 ....Paul. 374	
Montpelier,Sch.M.446Evan. 871...	2
405 Evst. 504	
Paris—	
NATIONAL LIBRARY 298	
Nat. Gr. RI 9 C	
13..............Evst. 415	
14..............Evan. 33	
19..............Apoc. 58	
47..............Evan. 18	
48..............Evan. M	
49..............Evan. 8	
50..............Evan. 13	
51..............Evan. 260	
52..............Evan. 261	
53..............Evan. 262	
54..............Evan. 16	
55..............Evan. 17	
56..............Act. 51	
57..............Act. 114	

396 INDEX I.

Nat. Gr. (cont.)—

		Total MSS.
58	Act. 115	
59	Act. 116	
60	Act. 62	
61	Evan. 263	
62	Evan. L	
63	Evan. K	
64	Evan. 15	
65	Evan. 264	
66	Evan. 265	
67	Evan. 266	
68	Evan. 21	
69	Evan. 267	
70	Evan. 14	
71	Evan. 7	
72	Evan. 22	
73	Evan. 268	
74	Evan. 269	
75	Evan. 270	
76	Evan. 272	
77	Evan. 23	
78	Evan. 26	
79	Evan. 273	
80	Evan. 275	
81	Evan. 276	
81 a	Evan. 277	
82	Evan. 278	
83	Evan. 9	
84	Evan. 4	
85	Evan. 119	
86	Evan. 279	
87	Evan. 280	
88	Evan. 281	
89	Evan. 29	
90	Evan. 282	
91	Evan. 10	
92	Evan. 283	
93	Evan. 284	
94	Evan. 31	
95	Evan. 285	
96	Evan. 286	
97	Evan. 743	
98	Evan. 287	
99	Evan. 288	
100	Evan. 30	
100 a	Evan. 289	
101	Act. 118	
102	Act. 7	
102 a	Act. 119	
103	Act. 11	
103 a	Act. 120	
104	Act. 121	
105	Act. 122	
106	Evan. 5	
106 a	Act. 123	
107	Paul. D	
108	Paul. 145	
109	Paul. 146	
110	Paul. 147	
111	Paul. 148	
112	Evan. 106	
113	Evan. 291	
114	Evan. 292	

Nat. Gr. (cont.)—

		Total MSS.
115	Evan. 27	
116	Evan. 32	
117	Evan. 293	
118	Evan. 294	
119	Evan. 744	
120	Evan. 295	
121, 122	Evan. 11	
123	Evan. 296	
124	Act. 124	
125	Act. 125	
126	Paul. 151	
177	Evan. 299	
178	Evan. 24	
179	Evan. 745	
181	Evan. 746	
182	Evan. 747 and Evst. 61	
183	Evan. 748	
184	Evan. 749	
185	Evan. 750	
186	Evan. 300	
187	Evan. 301	
188	Evan. 20	
189	Evan. 19	
190	Evan. 751	
191	Evan. 25	
192	Evan. 752	
193	Evan. 302	
194	Evan. 304	
194 a	Evan. 303	
195	Evan. 305	
196?	Evan. 103	
196	Evan. 753	
197	Evan. 306	
198	Evan. 754	
199	Evan. 307	
200	Evan. 308	
201	Evan. 309	
202	Evan. 310	
203	Evan. 311	
204	Evan. 755	
205	Evan. 756	
206	Evan. 312	
207	Evan. 757	
208	Evan. 313	
209	Evan. 314	
210	Evan. 315	
211	Evan. 316	
212	Evan. 317	
213	Evan. 318	
216	Act. 126	
217	Act. 127	
218	Act. 128	
219	Act. 12	
220	Act. 129	
221	Act. 130	
222	Paul. 157	
223	Act. 131	
224	Paul. 159	
224 a	Paul. 375	
225	Paul. 160	
226	Paul. 161	

OF GREEK MANUSCRIPTS. 397

Nat. Gr. (cont.)—	Total MSS.
227............Paul. 162	
228, 263........Evst. 427-8	
230............Evan. 12	
231............Evan. 319	
232............Evan. 320	
234............Evan. 761	
235............Evan. 762 and Evst. 426	
237............Act. 10	
238.,...........Paul. 163	
239............Apoc. 62	
240............Apoc. 139	
241............Apoc. 63	
276............Evst. 82	
277............Evst. 63	
278............Evst. 1	
279............Evst. 17	
280............Evst. 2	
281............Evst. 64	
282............Evst. 65	
283............Evst. 66	
284............Evst. 67	
285............Evst. 68	
286............Evst. 69	
287............Evst. 10	
288............Evst. 70	
289............Evst. 71	
290............Evst. 72, 72[b]	
291............Evst. 73	
292............Evst. 74	
293............Evst. 75	
294............Evst. 83	
295............Evst. 76	
296............Evst. 77	
297............Evst. 16	
298............Evst. 78	
299............Evst. 79	
300............Evst. 80	
301............Evst. 7	
302............Evst. 15	
303............Evst. 101	
304............Apost. 22	
305............Evst. 81	
306............Apost. 23	
307............Evst. 9	
308............Apost. 24	
309............Evst. 11	
310............Evst. 12	
311............Evst. 86	
312............Evst. 8	
313............Evst. 87	
314............Evst. 88 and Evan. W[a]	
315............Evst. 14	
316............Evst. 89	
317............Evst. 90	
318............Evst. 91	
319............Apost. 25	
320............Apost. 26	
321............Apost. 27	
324............Evst. 92	
326............Evst. 93	

Nat. Gr. (cont.)—	Total MSS.
330............Evst. 94	
373............Apost. 30	
374............Evst. 95	
375............Evst. 60	
376............Evan. 324	
377............Evst. 98	
378............Evan. 326	
379............Evan. 28	
380............Evst. 99	
381............Evst. 100	
382............Apost. 33	
383............Apost. 34	
491............Apoc. 61	
849............Paul. 164	
922, fol. A......Apost. 201	
975............Evst. 299	
1775...........Evan. 764	

Nat. Suppl. Gr.

24, 29 ....Evst. 416-7	
27............Evst. 158	
32............Evst. 84	
33............Evst. 85	
50............Evst. 58	
74............Evst. 366	
75............Evan. 271	
79............Evan. 274	
99............Apoc. 59	
104............Apost. 11	
108............Evan. 290	
115............Evst. 96	
118............Evan. 323	
140............Evan. 297	
159............Evan. 738	
175............Evan. 298	
185............Evan. 120	
219............Evan. 759	
227............Evan. 633	
242............Evst. 159	
567............Evst. 367	
611, 612........Evann. 740-1	
686, 687, 758...Evst. 421-3	
800............Apost. 130	
804............Apost. 202	
805............Evst. 324	
834............Evst. 424	
903............Evan. 758	
904.....……...Evan. 773	
905............Evst. 425	
906............Act. 263	
911............Evan. 634	
914............Evan. 742	
919............Evan. 739	
1001...........Paul. 338	
1035...........Evan. 760	
1076...........Evan. 763	
1080...........Evan. 771	
1081...........Evst. 517	
1083...........Evan. 772	
1096...........Evst. 419	

Nat. Coisl. 1 ....Evan. F[a]

19 ....Evan. 329	
20 ....Evan. 36	

	Total MSS.
Nat. Coisl. (cont.)—	
21 ....Evan. 37	
22 ....Evan. 40	
23 ....Evan. 39	
24 ....Evan. 41	
25 ....Act. 15	
26 ....Act. 16	
27 ....Paul. 20	
28 ....Paul. 23	
31 ....Evst. 13	
95 ....Paul. 339	
128 ....Evan. 765	
129 ....Evan. 766	
195 ....Evan. 34	
196 ....Evan. 330	
197 ....Evan. 331	
198 ....Evan. 767	
199 ....Evan. 35	
200 ....Evan. 38	
201 ....Evan. 1264	
202 ....Paul. H	
202, 2 ....Act. 18	
203 ....Evan. 768	
204 ....Paul. 59	
205 ....Act. 17	
206 ....Evan. 769	
207 ....Evan. 770	
217 ....Paul. 340	
224 ....Act. 264	
95, 217 ......Paul. 339–40	
29, 30, 95, 217 Paul. 378–81	
ARSENAL OF PARIS	1
(Gr.) 4 ....Evan. 43	
LOUVRE, EGYPT. MUS. Paul. T ...	1
MILLER, EMMAN., 4, 5	9
6, 7..............Evst. 506–9	
8, 9, 10, 11, 12 ......Evst. 512–16	
PAR. BIBL. ARM. 8409 Evan. 43 ...	1
PAR. NAT. ARMÉN. 9...Act. 240 ...	1
ROYAL INSTITUTE AT PARIS 3 ....Evan. 288...	1
ST.GENEVIÈVE A.O. 34 Evan. 121... A. O. 35...........Act. 210	2
Poictiers................Evan. 472...	1

GERMANY.

	Total MSS.
Berlin	24
Kön. Gr. 4to, 39, 47, 55, 66, 67; 8vo, 3, 4, 9..........Evann. 635–42	
13 ....Evan. 823	
12 ....Evan. 876	
51, 52, 53; 4to, 46, 61, 64..........Evst. 370–5	
4to, 40, 43, 57; 8vo, 9..............Act. 249–52	
Hamilton 244 ....Act. 248	
245, 246 ....Evst. 368–9	
12mo, 10 ....Evan. 400	

	Total MSS.
Dresden	10
Boerner...............Paul. G	
Reg. A. 95 ....Apoc. 90	
100 ....Evan. 254	
104 ....Act. 98	
123 ....Evan. 258	
124 ....Apoc. 32	
145 ....Evan. 252	
172 ....Evan. 241	
187 ....Apoc. 112	
151 ....Evst. 57	
Frankfort-on-Oder Act. 42 ...	1
Giessen ....Evan. 97 ...	1
Gottingen ....Evan. 89 ...	2
Gottingen 2 ....Apost. 5	
Groningen	1
Univ. A. C. 1..........Paul. 418	
Hamburg	3
Wolf. B ....Evan. H	
City Libr. ....Paul. M or 53	
City Libr. 1252........Act. 45	
Leipzig......................................	6
Matt. 18 ....Evan. 99	
Matt. s. ....Paul. 76	
Tischendorf i. ....Evan. Θ^a	
Tischendorf iv. ....Evan. 478	
Tischendorf v. ....Evst. 190	
Tischendorf vi. ....Apost. 71	
Munich—	
UNIV. LIBR. $\frac{1}{18}$......Evan. X ...	1
ROYAL LIBRARY....................	27
23................Apoc. 81	
35................Paul. 129	
36................Evan. 423	
37................Evan. 425	
83................Evan. 424	
99................Evan. 432	
110................Paul. 127	
208................Evan. 429	
210................Evan. 422	
211................Act. 179	
248................Apoc. 79	
326................Evst. 154	
329................Evst. 34	
375................Act. 46	
381................Evan. 428	
383................Evst. 24	
412................Paul. 54	
437................Evan. 430	
455................Paul. 126	
465................Evan. 427	
473................Evan. 426	
504................Paul. 125	
518................Evan. 83	
544................Apoc. 80	
568................Evan. 84	
569................Evan. 85	
594................Evan. 875	

	Total MSS.
Nüremburg ....Evst. 31 ...	1
Oettingen-Wallerstein, Prince of ....Apoc. 1 ...	1
Pesth....................................	2
Eubeswald..............Evan. 100	
Jancovich ....Evan. 78	
Posen....................................	1
Lycaei Aug. ....Evan. 86	
Saxe-Gotha............................	1
Ducal, MS. 78 ....Evst. 32	
[Strasburg	3
From Molsheim (destroyed)..............Evan. 431]	
Ed. Reuss...............Evan. 877	
Trèves	2
Cuzan....................Evan. 87	
Cath. Libr. 143........Evst. 179	
Tubingen ....Evst. R ...	2
2 ....Evst. 481	

Vienna—

IMPERIAL LIBRARY	44
Vind. Caes. Ness.	
1 ....Evan. 218	
2 ....Evan. N	
15 ....Evst. 45	
28 ....Evan. 76	
29 ....Evan. 77	
30 ....Evan. 123	
31 ....Evan. 124	
32 ....Evan. 219	
33 ....Evan. 220	
34 ....Act. 66	
35 ....Act. 63	
36 ....Act. 64	
37 ....Act. 67	
38 ....Evan. 221	
39 ....Evan. 222	
40 ....Evan. 223	
41 ....Evst. 155	
42 ....Evan. 434	
46 ....Paul. 214	
248 ....Apoc. 35	
Vind. Caes. Suppl. Gr.	
4 ....Evan. 108	
5 ....Evan. 3	
6 ....Evan. 125	
7 ....Evst. 46	
8 ....Evan. 224	
9 ....Evan. 225	
10 ....Paul. 71	
26 ....Apoc. 36	
Imp. Priv. Libr. 7972 Evan. 829	
Imp. Gr. Theol. 19,	
79–80, 90, 95, 122 Evann. 824–8	
141 ....Act. 335	
150 ....Act. 415	
157 ....Paul. 373	

Imp. Gr. Theol. (cont.)—	Total MSS.
69, 163, 220......Apoc. 136–8	
Rainer 1, Rainer	
2 ....Evst. 502–3	
209 ....Evst. 180	
308 ....Apost. 200	
Wolfenbüttel ....Evan. O^a ...	6
Carolin. A, B..........Evann. P, Q	
xvi. 7 ....Act. 69	
xvi. 16 ....Evan. 126	
Gud. gr. 104. 2........Act. 97	
Zittau ....Evan. 605 ...	1

GREECE.

Athens	185
Nat. 3 ....Evst. 804	
5 ....Evst. 828	
10 ? ....Evst. 829	
Nat. Sakkel. 58, 76, 93,	
80, 127, 121, 110, 81,	
71, 87, 118, 125, 108,	
74, 134, 95, 77, 107,	
75, 122, 109. 160,	
111, 137, 117, 65,	
130, 99, 88............Evann. 775–803	
150 (12), 151 (13),	
152 (14), 153 (15),	
154 (16) ....Evann. 846–50	
155 (17)..................Evan. 852	
156 (18), 157 (19),	
158 (20), 159 (21),	
160 (22), 161 (23)...Evann. 854–9	
162 (24), 203 (16)...Evann. 862–3	
489 (216), 56, 57 ...Evann. 867–9	
13, 139, 347 ....Evann. 1145–7	
111 ....Evan. 1272	
72, 92, 113, 123, 128,	
132, 135..............Evann. 1313–9	
207 (70), 208 (71),	
209 (72), 43 (149 ?),	
45, 64 (91), 66 (105),	
221 (129), 119, 89 Act. 304–13	
(490, 217) ....Act. 201	
69 (100), 100 (96)...Paul. 382–3	
259......................Paul. 471	
Nat. Libr. 163, 164,	
165, 166, 167, 168,	
169..................Evst. 518–24	
170, 171, 172, 173,	
174..................Evst. 528–32	
175, 176, ?, 177, 178 Evst. 534–8	
179, 180, 181, 182...Evst. 541–4	
183 ....Evst. 546	
184, 185..............Evst. 549–50	
186, 187..............Evst. 552–3	
188 ....Evst. 556	
189, 190..............Evst. 560–1	

INDEX I.

Nat. Libr. (*cont.*)— Total MSS.
191, 192, 193, 194,
195, 196, 197, 198,
199, 200, 201, 202...Evst. 563-74
66 ?, 70 ?, 146 ?, 64 ?,
82, 68 ?, 79, 73, 67 ?,
112 ?, 670 ?, 126, 69,
63 ?, 86, ?, ?, 84 ?,
661 ?, 85 ?, 124, 62 ? Evst. 429-49
4......................Evst. 759
60, 78, 83, 97, 126,
143, 147, 148, 668,
685, 700, 707, 750,
757, 759, 760, 766,
769, 784, 786, 795...Evst. 943-63
203, 206............Apost. 204-5
115, and 3 others...Apost. 209-12
101, 102, 106, 133,
144....................Apost. 270-4
103....................Apost. 37
Τῆς Βουλῆς............Evann. 804-7
Evst. 450
Apoc. 141
Mamoukae............Evann. 808-9
Οἰκονόμου 6............Evan. 810
Soc. Archaeol. Christ. Evan. 811
M. Bournias ....Evst. 451-2[b]
M. Varouccas..........Evst. 453
Evst. 462

Corfu.. 11
Corfu ....Evann. 812-16
Abp. Eustathius ......Evst. 466-8
M. Eleutherius ....Evst. 459-61

Zante ....Act. 314 ... 1

HOLLAND.

Leyden 66 ....Paul. 350 ... 6
74 ....Evan. 79
77 ....Act. 38
74 A ....Evan. 122
Gronovii 131 ....Evan. 435
Scaligeri 243 ....Evst. 6

Utrecht ....Evan. F ... 1

ITALY.

Bologna—
Royal Library................... 2
Bibl. Univ. 2775 ......Evan. 204
3638 ......Evst. 160

Cortona 301 ....Evan. 1260 1

Ferrara—
Municipal Library............... 2
119, N. A. 4 ....Evan. 450
187, N. A. 7 ....Evan. 451

Florence— Total MSS.
Grand Ducal Library........ 55
Laurent. iv. 1 ....Act. 84
iv. 5 ....Act. 85
iv. 20 ....Act. 86
iv. 29 ....Act. 87
iv. 30 ....Act. 147
iv. 31 ....Act. 88
iv. 32 ....Act. 89
vi. 2 ....Evst. 113
vi. 5 ....Evan. 832
vi. 7 ....Evst. 114
vi. 11 ....Evan. 182
vi. 13 ....Evan. 363
vi. 14 ....Evan. 183
vi. 15 ....Evan. 184
vi. 16 ....Evan. 185
vi. 18 ....Evan. 186
vi. 21 ....Evst. 115
vi. 23 ....Evan. 187
vi. 24 ....Evan. 364
vi. 25 ....Evan. 188
vi. 26 ....Evan. 833
vi. 27 ....Evan. 189
vi. 28 ....Evan. 190
vi. 29 ....Evan. 191
vi. 30 ....Evan. 192
vi. 31 ....Evst. 116
vi. 32 ....Evan. 193
vi. 33 ....Evan. 194
vi. 34 ....Evan. 195
vi. 36 ....Evan. 365
vii. 9 ....Apoc. 77
vii. 29 ....Apoc. 145
viii. 12 ....Evan. 196
viii. 14 ....Evan. 197
x. 4 ....Paul. 100
x. 6 ....Paul. 101
x. 7 ....Paul. 102
x. 19 ....Paul. 103
xi. 6 ....Evan. 834
xi. 8 ....Evan. 835
xi. 18 ....Evan. 836
Aedil. 221 ....Evan. 198
Med. Pal. 243 ....Evst. 118
244 ....Evst. 117
Laurent. Conv. Soppr.
24 ....Apost. 4
53 ....Evan. 367
150 ....Act. 149
159 ....Evan. 200
160 ....Evan. 199
171 ....Evan. 366
176 ....Evan. 362
191 ....Act. 148
Laurent. Gaddianus
124 ....Evst. 510
Laurent. St. Mark
704 ....Apost. 223
706 ....Evst. 187

OF GREEK MANUSCRIPTS.   401

	Total MSS.
LIBRERIA RICCARDI	5
5 ....Evan. 370	
69 ....Evst. 511	
84 ....Evan. 368	
85 ....Paul. 226	
90 ....Evan. 369	
Messina	21
Univ. Libr. 18 ....Evan. 420	
40................Act. 241	
88, 100..........Evann. 630–1	
93 ....Apost. 82	
99............Apoc. 113	
65, 66, 75, 96, 98, 73, 58, 94, 111, 112, 170, 95,	
150 ....Evst. 300–12	
175 ....Evst. 525	
St. Basil 104 ....Act. 175	
Milan—	
AMBROSIAN LIBRARY	46
A. 51 sup. or 15........Paul. 172	
A. 62 inf. ....Paul. 390	
A. 152 sup...........Evst. 167	
A. 241 inf...........Paul. 287	
B. 6 inf. ....Paul. 171	
B. 56 ....Evan. 348	
B. 62 ....Evan. 350	
B. 70 sup. ....Evan. 351	
B. 93 ....Evan. 352	
C. 16 ....Evst. 81	
C. 63 sup. .. ..Apost. 46	
C. 91 sup. ....Evst. 106	
C. 160 sup............Evst. 168	
C. 295 inf. ....Paul. 289	
D. 67 sup. ....Evst. 103	
D. 72 sup. ....Evst. 104	
D. 108 sup............Evst. 166	
D. 161 inf. ....Evan. 458	
D. 282 inf............Evan. 459	
D. 298 inf............Evan. 460	
D. 541 inf............Paul. 288	
E. 2 inf. ....Paul. 286	
E. 63 sup. ....Evan. 457	
E. 97 sup............Act. 137	
E. 101 sup............Evst. 480	
E. 102 sup............Act. 138	
E. 295............Paul. 391	
F. 61 sup. ....Evan. 349	
F. 125 sup............Paul. 175	
G. 16 sup. ....Evan. 344	
H. 13 sup. ....Evan. 343	
H. 104 sup............Act. 139	
L. 79 sup. ....Evst. 163	
M. 48 sup............Evan. 456	
M. 81 sup. ....Evst. 105	
M. 93............Evan. 353	
N. 272 sup............Paul. 225	
P. 274 sup............Evst. 169	
S. 23 sup. ....Evan. 346	
S. 62 sup. ....Evst. 102	

	Total MSS.
Z. 34 sup. ....Evan. 461	
E. S. iii. 13............Evst. 165	
E. S. iv. 14............Evst. 164, and Evan. 837	
17 ....Evan. 345	
35 ....Evan. 347	
Formerly Hoeplii ......Evan. 838	
Modena	16
Este ii. A. 1 ....Evan. 454	
ii. A. 5 ....Evan. 455	
ii. A. 9 ....Evan. 358	
ii. A. 13............Act. 195	
ii. A. 14............Paul. 177	
iii. B. 17............Act. 142	
ii. C. 4 ....Act. 196	
ii. C. 6............Evst. 111	
ii. D. 3 ....Apost. 50	
ii. G. 3 ....Act. H Also Act. 112	
iii. B. 16 ....Evan. 359	
iii. B. 17 ....Act. 142	
iii. F. 13 ....Evan. 839	
G. 9 ....Evan. 842	
iii. E. 1 ....Apoc. 147	
iii. F. 12 ....Apoc. 148	
Naples	12
I. B. 14 ....Evst. 138	
II. AA. 3............Evan. 401	
4............Evan. 403	
5............Evan. 402	
7............Act. 83	
8............Act. 173	
9............Act. 174	
37............Evan. 843	
II. B. 23, 24 ....Paul. 394–5	
II. C. 15 ....Evan. R or W[b]	
Scotti ....Evan. 404	
Padua, Univ. 695 ......Evan. 844...	1
Palermo, I. E. 11 ......Paul. 217...	1
Parma	6
Reg. 5 ....Evan. 452	
14 ....Evst. 161	
15 ....Evan. 831	
95 ....Evan. 453	
1821 ....Evan. 361	
2319 ....Evan. 360	
Pistoia, Fabr. Libr. 307 Evan. 845... Evst. 526	2
Rome—	
VATICAN	213
Vat. Gr. 54 ....Evst. 924	
163 ....Evan. 177	
165 ....Paul. 58	
349 ....Evan. 127	
350 ....Evst. 539	
351 ....Evst. 35	
352, 353 ......Evst. 376 7	
354 ....Evan. S	

VOL. I.   D d

Vat. Gr. (cont.)—	Total MSS.
355 ....Evst. 378	
356 ....Evan. 128	
357 ....Evst. 379	
358 ....Evan. 129	
359 ....Evan. 130	
360 ....Evan. 131	
361 ....Evan. 132	
362 ....Evst. 380	
363 ....Evan. 133	
364 ....Evan. 134	
365 ....Evan. 135	
366 ....Act. 72	
367 ....Act. 73	
368 ....Apost. 116	
370 ....Apoc. 152	
540 ....Evst. 381	
542 ....Apoc. 114	
549 ....Paul. 305	
551 ....Paul. 307	
552 ....Paul. 308	
579 ....Apoc. 38	
643, 644, 645 Evann. 668–70	
646 ....Paul. 310	
647 ....Evan. 671	
648 ....Paul. 312	
652 ....Act. 239	
665 ....Evan. 136	
692 ....Paul. 314	
756 ....Evan. 137	
757 ....Evan. 138	
758 ....Evan. 139	
760 ....Act. 74	
761 ....Paul. 81	
762 ....Paul. 82	
765 ....Paul. 83	
766 ....Paul. 84	
774 ....Evan. 860	
781 ....Evst. 382	
1067 ....Evst. 36	
1090 ....Evan. 674	
1136 ....Paul. 85	
1155 ....Evst. 119	
1156[1] ....Evst. 120	
1157 ....Evst. 121	
1158 ....Evan. 140	
1159 ....Evan. 371	
1160 ....Evan. 141	
1161 ....Evan. 372	
1168 ....Evst. 122	
1190 ....Apoc. 154	
1191 ....Evan. 675	
1208 ....Act. 246	
1209 ....B	
1210 ....Evan. 142	
1217 ....Evst. 547	
1221 ....Evan. 676	
1222 ....Paul. 315	
1228 ....Evst. 548	

[1] So Scholz's index, and we may suppose correctly, but in his Catalogue of Evangelistaria he numbers it 1256.

Vat. Gr. (cont.)—	Total MSS.
1229 ....Evan. 143	
1253 ....Evan. 864	
1254 ....Evan. 144	
1270 ....Act. 154	
1423 ....Evan. 373	
1426 ....Act. 264	
1430 ....Act. 155	
1445 ....Evan. 374	
1472 ....Evan. 865	
1522 ....Evst. 123	
1528 ....Apost. 38	
1533 ....Evan. 375	
1534 ....Evst. 383	
1539 ....Evan. 376	
1548 ....Evan. 145	
1618 ....Evan. 377	
1625 ....Evst. 551	
1641 ....Evst. 384	
1649 ....Paul. 189	
1650 ....Act. 156	
1658 ....Evan. 378	
1670 ....Paul. M	
1714 ....Act. 157	
1743 ....Apoc. 67	
1761 ....Act. 158	
1769 ....Evan. 379	
1813 ....Evst. 385	
1882 ....Evan. 866	
1886 ....Evst. 386	
1895 ....Evan. 680	
1904 ....Apoc. 68	
1933 ....Evan. 683	
1968 ....Act. 159	
1971 ....Act. 334	
1976 ....Apoc. 116	
1973, 1978 ...Evst. 554–5	
1983 ....Evan. 173	
1988 ....Evst. 124	
1996 ....Evan. 684	
2002 ....Evan. 174	
2012 ....Evst. 387	
2017 ....Evst. 125	
2041 ....Evst. 126	
2051, 2052 ...Evst. 557–8	
2061 ....Act. ℶ, Paul. ℶ, and Evst. 559	
2062 ....Act. 160	
2063 ....Evst. 127	
2066 ....Apoc. B	
2068 ....Apost. 49	
2070 ....Evan. 382	
2080 ....Evan. 175	
2099 ....Act. 256	
2100 ....Evst. 388	
2113 ....Evan. 176	
2115 ....Evan. 870	
2116 ....Apost. 119	
2117 ....Evan. 687	
2129 ....Apoc. 158 and Evst. 389	
2133 ....Evst. 128	
2138 ....Evst. 562	

Vat. Gr. (cont.)—	Total MSS.
2139 ....Evan. 380	
2144 ....Evst. 390	
2160 ....Evan. 690	
2165 ....Evan. 689	
2167 ....Evst. 392	
2180 ....Paul. 323	
2187 ....Evan. 691	
2247 ....Evan. 692	
2251 ....Evst. 393	
2275 ....Evan. 693	
2290 ....Evan. 694	
3785 ....Evan. N	

Vat. Alex. Gr.

3 ....Evan. 696	
4 ....Paul. 324	
5 ....Evan. 697	
9 ....Evan. 699	
11 ....Apost. 120	
12 ....Evst. 129	
28 ....Evan. 154	
29 ....Act. 78	
33 ....Evst. 188	
44, 59 ....Evst. 394–5	
68 ....Apoc. 41	
70 ....Apost. 122	
79 ....Evan. 155	
179 ....Act. 40	
189 ....Evan. 156	

Vat. Ottob. Gr.

2 ....Evst. 130	
17 ....Paul. 405	
31 ....Paul. 195	
37 ....Evan. 703	
61 ....Paul. 196	
66 ....Evan. 386	
74 ....Paul. 326	
100 ....Evan. 704	
154 ....Apoc. 159	
175 ....Evst. 131	
176 ....Paul. 197	
204 ....Evan. 387	
208 ....Evan. 705	
212 ....Evan. 388	
258 ....Act. 161	
283 ....Apoc. 118	
297 ....Evan. 389	
298 ....Act. 162	
325 ....Act. 163	
326 ....Evst. 132	
356 ....Paul. 202	
381 ....Evan. 390	
416 ....Evst. 133	
417 ....Act. 165	
432 ....Evan. 391	
444 ....Evst. 396	
453, 454, 456 ......Evann. 707–9	

Vat. Palat. Gr.

5 ....Evan. 146	
10 ....Paul. 327	
20 ....Evan. 381	
32 ....Evan. 713	
38 ....Act. 247	

Vat. Palat. Gr. (cont.)—	Total MSS.
89 ....Evan. 147	
136 ....Evan. 148	
171 ....Evan. 149	
189 ....Evan. 150	
204 ....Paul. 328	
208 ....Evan. 714	
220 ....Evan. 151	
227 ....Evan. 152	
229 ....Evan. 153	
1. A, 221, 239......Evst. 397–9	
241 ....Apost. 123	
346 ....Apoc. 119	
423 ....Paul. 330	

Pio-Vat. Gr. 50 ....Act. 80
55 ....Evan. 158

Vat. Urb. 2 ....Evan. 157
3 ....Act. 79
4 ....Evan. 1269

ROM. ANGELICA...............	8
A. 1. 5 ....Evan. 178	
A. 2. 15 ....Act. L	
A. 4. 1 ....Apoc. 120	
A. 4. 11 ....Evan. 179	
B. 1. 5 ....Evan. 723	
B. 5. 15 ....Apoc. 121	
D. ii. 27 ....Evst. 527	
D. 3. 8 ....Evan. 611	

ROM. BARBERINI	34
iii. 6 ....Evan. 167	
iii. 17 ....Evan. 161	
iii. 38 ....Evan. 164	
iii. 45 ....Apost. 40	
iii. 131 ....Evan. 166	
iv. 11, iv. 60, iv. 84...Apost. 125–7	
iv. 27 ....Evan. 160	
iv. 28 ....Evst. 533	
iv. 31 ....Evan. 162	
iv. 43, iv. 30, iv. 53, iv. 13, iv. 25, iv. 1, iii. 22, iii. 129, vi. 18 ....Evst. 403–11	
iv. 54 ....Evst. 135–6	
iv. 56 ....Apoc. 43	
iv. 64 ....Evan. 159	
iv. 85 ....Paul. 213	
iv. 86, 77 ....Evann. 729–30	
v. 16 ....Evan. 163	
v. 17 ....Evann. Y & 392	
v. 37 ....Evan. 165	
vi. 4 ....Evst. 134	
vi. 9 ....Evan. 168	
vi. 13 ....Paul. 297	
vi. 21 ....Act. 81	
No mark............Apost. 41	

ROM. PROPAGANDA	6
? ....Evann. T & T^d	
L. vi. 6 ....Evst. 37	
9 ....Evan. 851	
10 ....Evan. 732	
19 ....Evan. 180	

INDEX I.

	Total MSS.
ROM. CASANATENSIS	4
G. ii. 6 ....Act. 261	
G. ii. 9 ....Evan. 853	
G. iv. 1 ....Evan. 395	
G. v. 7 ....Paul. 397	
COLLEGII ROMANI	5
Evann. 383-5	
Act. 171-2.	
ROM. CORSINI	2
41 G. 16 ....Evan. 883	
41 E. 37 ....Apoc. 73	
ROM. CRYPTA FERRATA	64
A. α. 1-6............Evann. 622-7	
A. α. 8, 17 ....Evann. 628-9	
A'. α'. 1, A. β. 1, A. β.	
3, A. β. 6 ....Act. 242-5	
A. α. 7, A. α. 9, A. α. 10, A. α. 11, A. α. 12, A. α. 13, A. α. 14, A. α. 15, A. α. 16, A. β. 2. A. δ. 2............Evst. 313-23	
A. δ. 4 ....Evst. 325	
A. δ. 11, A. δ. 16, A. δ. 17, A. δ. 19, A. δ. 20, A. δ. 21, A. δ. 22, A. δ. 24 (q. v.), Γ. α. 18, Γ. β. 2, Γ. β. 3, Γ. β. 6, Γ. β. 7, Γ. β. 8, Γ. β. 9. Γ. β. 11, Γ. β. 12, Γ. β. 13, Γ. β. 14, Γ. β. 15, Γ. β. 17, Γ. β. 18, Γ. β. 19, Γ. β. 23, Γ. β. 24, Γ. β. 35, Γ. β. 38, Γ. β. 13, Δ. β. 22, Δ. γ. 26, Δ. δ. 6 ....Evst. 330-60	
A. β. 4, A. β. 5, A. β. 7, A. β. 8, A. β. 9, A. β. 10, A. β. 11 ....Apost. 83-9	
A. δ. 24 ....Apost. 263	
Fragment ....Paul. R, Evst.	
ROM. GHIGIAN.	7
R. iv. 6 ....Evan. 396	
R. iv. 8 ....Apoc. 72	
R. v. 29 ....Act. 169	
R. v. 32 ....Paul. 207	
R. v. 33 ....Apoc. 122	
R. vii. 52 ....Evst. 414	
R. viii. 55 ....Paul. 208	
ROM. MALATESTIAN.	2
xxvii. 4 ....Evst. 144	
xxix. 2 ....Evst. 145	
ROM. VALLICELL.	14
B. 86 ....Act. 166	
B. 133 ....Evan. 169	
C. 4 ....Evan. 397	
C. 7 ....Evst. 545	

	Total MSS.
C. 46 ....Apost. 42	
C. 61 ....Evan. 170	
C. 73 ....Evan. 171	
D. 20 ....Apoc. 21	
[(missing) D. 4. 1 ....Evst. 156]	
D. 63 ....Evst. 137	
E. 22 ....Evan. 393	
E. 40 ....Evan. 617	
F. 13 ....Act. 168	
F. 17 ....Evan. 394	
Rossano ....Evan. Σ ...	1
Siena	1
Univ. X. iv. 1 ....Evst. 162	
Syracuse ....Evan. 421...	5
............Evan. 1144	
Seminario ...Evst. 362	
............Evst. 486	
............Apost. 113	
Turin	18
Univ. B. i. 9 ....Evan. 333	
B. ii. 17 ....Evan. 336	
B. iii. 2 ....Evan. 335	
B. iii. 8 ....Evan. 334	
B. iii. 25 ....Evan. 337	
B. v. 4 ....Evan. 342	
B. v. 8 ....Evan. 339	
B. v. 19 ....Act. 134	
B. vii. 6 ....Evan. 340	
B. vii. 14 ....Evan. 341	
B. vii. 33 ....Evan. 338	
C. ii. 4 ....Evan. 332	
C. ii. 5 ....Evan. 398	
C. ii. 14 ....Evan. 399	
C. v. 1 ....Act. 136	
C. v. 10 ....Paul. 168	
C. vi. 19 ....Act. 133	
C. vi. 29 ....Paul. 165	
Venice	89
St. Lazarus 1531 ......Evan. 470	
1631 ......Evst. 576	
Ven. Marc. i. 40 ......Apoc. 162	
i. 57 ......Evan. 465	
i. 58 ......Evan. 462	
i. 59 ......Evan. 464	
ii. 7 ......Evan. 463	
ii. 54 ......Apoc. 163	
ii. 61 ......Act. 147	
ii. 114 ......Act. 332	
ii. 17 } ...Evst. 478-9	
ii. 143 }	
ii. 188 ......Evst. 498	
ii. 130 ......Evst. 931	
ii. 115 ......Apost. 198	
ii. 128 ......Apost. 114	
S. Marc. 5 ....Evan. 205	
6 ....Evan. 206	
8 ....Evan. 207	
9 ....Evan. 208	
10 ....Evan. 209	

OF GREEK MANUSCRIPTS. 405

S. Marc. (cont.)—	Total MSS.
11	Act. 96
12	Evst. 139
26	Evan. 888
27	Evan. 210
28	Evan. 357
29	Evan. 354
30, 31, 32	Evann. 889–91
33	Paul. 110
34	Paul. 111
35	Paul. 112
36	Paul. 408
61, 144	Evann. 893–4
494	Evan. 466
495	Evan. 467
539	Evan. 211
540	Evan. 212
541	Evan. 355
542	Evan. 213
543	Evan. 214
544	Evan. 215
545	Evan. 356
546	Act. 140
548	Evst. 107
549	Evst. 108
550	Evst. 109
551	Evst. 110
Nanian. 1. 8	Evan. U
1. 9	Evst. 141
1. 10	Evan. 405
1. 11	Evan. 406
1. 12	Evan. 407
1. 14	Evan. 408
1. 15	Evan. 409
1. 17	Evan. 410
1. 18	Evan. 411
1. 19	Evan. 412
1. 20	Evan. 413
1. 21	Evan. 414
1. 22	Evan. 415
1. 23	Evst. 142
1. 24	Evan. 416
1. 25	Evan. 417
1. 28	Evan. 418
1. 34	Evan. 463
1. 45	Evst. 171
1. 46	Evst. 172
1. 47	Evst. 173
1. 48	Evst. 174
1. 49	Evst. 175
1. 50	Evst. 176
1. 51	Evst. 177
1. 52	Evst. 178
Ven. Mark Gr.	
1. 3	Evan. 217
1. 4	Evst. 170
1. 56	Evan. 468
1. 57	Evan. 465
1. 58	Evan. 462
1. 59	Evan. 464
1. 60	Evan. 419

	Total MSS.
TREASURY OF ST. MARK'S CHURCH.	
Ven. Thesaur. 1. 53	Evst. 181
1. 54	Evst. 182
1. 55	Evst. 183
CHURCH OF S. GIORGIO DI GRECO.	
A'	Evst. 184
Γ'	Evst. 185
B'	Evst. 186
Verona	1
Psalter	Evan. O^c

PALESTINE.

Jerusalem	42
Holy Cross 1	Act. 324
6	Evst. 797
46	Evan. 663
Holy Sepulc. 2, 5, 6, 14, 17, 31, 32, 33, 40, 41, 43, 44, 45, 46	Evann. 649–62
7, 15	Act. 257–8
12	Evst. 143
Patr. Libr. 28	Evan. 1149
31, 37, 41	Evann. 1261–3
42, 46, 47, 48	Evann. 1265–8
38, 43	Act. 416–7
49, 56, 59, 60, 62, 139	Evann. 1274–9
33	Evst. 923
105	Evst. 925
161, 526	Evst. 927–8
462	Act. 330
530	Evst. 932
St. Saba 27, 52	Evann. 34 664–5
54	Evan. 673
56, 57, 58	Evann. 677–9
59, 60	Evann. 681–2
61 a and b	Evann. 685–6
61 c	Evan. 688
61 d	Evan. 695
61 e, 62 a, 62 b	Evann. 700–2
62 c	Evan. 706
62 d, 62 e	Evann. 710–1
Tower Libr. 12	Evst. 361
16, 52	Evst. 364–5
17, 23, 24	Evst. 147–9
20, 35	Act. 301–2
25, 26, 40, 44	Evst. 326–9
41	Paul. 417
45	Evan. 712
46, 47	Evann. 715–6

	Total MSS.
Sinai	184

148, 149, 150, 151, 152,
153, 154, 155, 156,
157, 158, 159, 160,
161, 162, 163, 164,
165, 166, 167, 168,
169, 170, 171, 172,
173, 174, 175, 176,
177, 178, 179, 180,
181, 182, 183, 184,
185, 186, 187, 188,
189, 190, 191, 192,
193, 194, 195, 196,
197, 198, 199, 200,
201, 203, 259, 260,
261, 262, 263, 264,
265, 266, 267, 268,
269, 270, 302, 303,
304, 305, 306 ......Evann.
                  1185–1256
274, 275, 276, 277, 278,
279, 280, 281, 282,
283, 284, 285, 287,
288, 289, 290, 291,
292, 293, 300, 301 Act. 394–
                             414
Golden......... . ...Evst. 286
Sinaiticus, Λ. 1 ....Evst. 493
205, 206, 207, 208, 209,
210, 211, 212, 213,
214, 215, 216, 217,
218, 219, 220, 221,
222, 223, 224, 225,
226, 227, 228, 229,
230, 231, 232, 233,
234, 235, 236, 237,
238, 239, 240, 241,
242, 243, 244, 245,
246, 247, 248, 249,
250, 251, 252, 253,
254, 255, 256, 257,
258, 271, 272, 273,
550, 659, 720, 738,
748, 754, 756, 775,
796, 797, 800, 929,
943, 957, 960, 961,
962, 965, 968, 972,
973, 977, 981, 982,
986, 1042...............Evst. 839–
                             921
296, 297, 298, 299 ...Apost. 165–8
294 ....Apost. 174
295 ....Apost. 213

RUSSIA.

	Total MSS.
Moscow	45

Syn. 4 ....Apost. 13
    5 ....Act. 99
   42 ....Evan. 237
   43 ....Evst. 47

Syn. 44 ....Evst. 48
   45 ....Evan. 259
   47 ....Evan. 239
   48 ....Evan. 238
   49 ....Evan. 240
   61 ....Paul. N^c or O
   67 ....Apoc. 49
   94 ....Evan. 249
   98 ....Act. K and 102
   99 ....Paul. 123
  120 ....Evan. O and
                            257
139 ....Evan. 255
193 ....Act. 103
206 ....Apoc. 50
250 ....Paul. 124
261 ....Evan. 246
264 ....Evan. 248
265 ....Evan. 245
266 ....Evst. 52
267 ....Evst. 53
268 ....Evst. 54
291 ....Apost. 14
292 ....Paul. 119
313 ....Evst. 465
328 ....Act. 106
333 ....Act. 101
334 ....Act. 100
373 ....Evan. 247
380 ....Evan. 242
cista ....Evan. V and
                            250
Fragments ......Paul. O^b
Typ. Syn. 1 ....Evan. 244
        3 ....Evan. 256
        9 ....Evst. 51 and
                            56
   11 ....Evst. 49
   12 ....Evst. 50
   13 ....Evan. 243
   31 ....Apost. 15
   47 ....Evst. 55
University 25............Apoc. 65
Tabul. Imp. ....Evan. 251

	Total MSS.
St. Petersburg	59

Petropolitanus Sinaiticus...Cod. ℵ
                        Evan. O^f
                        Evan. Π
Porphyrianus............Act. P and
                        Apost. 63
Sangermanensis........Paul. E
Tischendorf. II ....Evan. I
Porphyry, Bp. ....Evan. T^b, T^c
                        Act. 315
                        Paul. N
                        Paul. O^a
Evann. Θ^b, Θ^c, Θ^d, Θ^e, Θ^f, Θ^g, Θ^h
  21, 35, 36, 37, 40,
  43, 55, 69, 80, 84,
  37^a, 112............Evst. 466–77
                        Act. G

OF GREEK MANUSCRIPTS.

Porphyry, Bp. (cont.)— **Total MSS.**
  St. Paul (Q) papyrus
  St. Paul (palimpsest)
Olim Coislin..............Evan. 437
Petropol. (Kiow) ......Evan. 481
  98 ....Evan. 474
  iv. 13 ....Evst. 194
  vi. 470 .....Evan. 473
  vii. 179 .....Evst. 195
  viii. 80 ......Apost. 54
  ix. 3. 471 ...Evan. 475
  x. 180.........Evst. 196
  xi. 3. 181 ...Evst. 197
Muralt. 10P° ....Evst. 198
  38...............Apost. 72
  38, 49, 40ᵃ ...Apost. 171-3
  44..............Evst. 191
  45ᵃ ....Apost. 183
  56, 67, 105 ......Evann. 878-80
  64...............Evst. 933
  90...............Evst. 192
  97...............Evan. 479
  99...............Evan. 480
  105 ....Evan. 476
  110 ....Apost. 197
  118 ....Evan. 477
  129 ....Apoc. 103

SPAIN.

Escurial i................Evst. 40 ... 29
  P. iii. 4 ......Act. 202
  T. iii. 12......Act. 203
  T. iii. 17......Paul. 470
  Υ. ii. 8 .....Evan. 233
  Φ. iii. 5 .....Evan. 230
  Φ. iii. 6 .....Evan. 231
  Φ. iii. 7 .....Evan. 232
  X. iii. 3 .....Act. 204
  X. iii. 6 .....Apoc. 143
  X. iii. 10......Act. 205
  X. iii. 12......Evst. 41
  X. iii. 13......Evst. 42
  X. iii. 15......Evan. 227
  X. iii. 16......Evst. 43
  X. iv. 2 ......Act. 206
  X. iv. 9 ......Apost. 214
  X. iv. 12......Evan. 228
  X. iv. 15......Paul. 384
  X. iv. 17......Evan. 226
  X. iv. 21......Evan. 229
  Ψ. iii. 2 ......Paul. 232
  Ψ. iii. 6 ......Act. 207
  Ψ. iii. 13, 14 Evann. 818-9
  Ψ. iii. 17......Apoc. 85
  Ψ. iii. 18......Act. 208
  Ω. i. 16.........Evan. 820
  Ω. iv. 22......Act. 209
Madrid, Reg. O. 10, 62 Evann. 821-2 4
  O. 78 ....Act. 316
  O. 19 (7)........Apoc. 144
Toledo ....Evst. 455... 1

SWEDEN.

Linköping 1
  Benzel 35 ....Act. 238
Upsal 6
  Univ. Gr. 1 ....Act. 68
  4 ....Evan. 613
  9 ....Evan. 614
  11 ....Act. 236
  12 ....Evan. 616
  13 ....Evan. 615

SWITZERLAND.

Basle, A. N. iii. 11 ......Paul. 7 ... 9
  A. N. iii. 12 ......Evan. E and Apoc. 15
  A. N. iii. 15 ......Evan. 817
  A. N. iv. 1 ....Evan. 2
  A. N. iv. 2 ....Evan. 1
  A. N. iv. 4 ....Act. 2
  A. N. iv. 5 ....Act. 4
  O. ii. 23 ....Evan. 94
  O. ii. 27 ....Evan. 92
Geneva 19................Evan. 75 ... 2
  20................Act. 29
St. Gall ....Evan. Δ ... 3
  17................Evan. Oᵉ
    Evan. Wᶜ
Zurich ....Evan. Oᵈ ... 1

TURKEY.

ORIENTAL MONASTERIES.

Albania 7
  Beratinus..............Evan. Φ
  Berat, Abp.............Evann. 1141
    Act. 380
    Apost. 153
  In churches............Evann. 1142-43
    Evst. 758
Andros 1, 33, 34, 35, 37, ... 11
  38, 48, 49, 50 ....Evann. 1286-94
  2, 3 ....Apost. 255-6
Chalcis 37
  Mon. Trin. 1, 2, 3, 4 ...Evann. 727, -28, -31, -32
  Schol. 95, 133...........Evann. 734-5
  Trin. 16; Schol. 9, 26, 33, 96 ....Act. 382-6
  Trin. 1, 2, 3, 4, 5, 6, 7, 8, 9, 10; Schol. 1, 2, 3, 4, 5, 6, 7, 12, 74, 84 ....Evst. 770-89
  Trin. 13, 14, 15; School 59, 74, 88............Apost. 154-9

INDEX I.

Constantinople .... Total MSS. 21

Ἁγ.τάφ. 436, 520 ...... Evann. 721-2
574 .... Evan. 724
'Ελλ. φιλ. συλλ. 1, 5 ...Evann. 725-6
Patriarch of Jerusalem's
  Library 10 .... Evst. 413
St. George 1, 2; ἁγ. τάφ.
  1, 2, 426, 432; 'Ελλ.
  φιλ. συλλ. .... Evst. 790-6
St. Sepulchre 227, 417,
  419, 435, 439, 441 ...Evann.
                              1150-5
2, 3 .... Paul. 411-12

Kosinitsa 124, 275 ...... ב, ו, p. 377...15
  219, 58, 216, 217, 218,
  219, 220, 222, 223,
  198 .... Evann. 1295-
                              1304
  3 MSS. .... Apost. 267-9

Lesbos 23
Mon. 356, 67, 97, 99 ...Evann.
                              1156-9
141, 145, 227, Ταξιάρχοι Evann.
                              1280-3
132 .... Act. 303
55 .... Act. 323
Τ. Λείμωνος 1, 37, 38, 40,
  41, 66 .... Evst. 798-803
100, 146 .... Evst. 936-7
55, 137 .... Apost. 227-8
'Ιωάννου 11, 12 ...... Evst. 938-9
Benjamin Library at
  Potamos .... Evst. 940

Milos .... Evst. 412... 1

Mitylene 9, 41 .... Evann. ... 2
                              1284-5

Patmos 66
St. John 2, 6, 21 ..... Evann. 717-9
58, 59, 60, 76, 80, 81,
  82, 83, 84, 90, 92, 94,
  95, 96, 97, 98, 100,
  117, 203, 275, 333,
  335 .... Evann.
                              1160-81
27, 31 .... Act. 319-20
14, 15, 16, 263 ...... Act. 387-90
61, 62, 63, 116 ...... Paul. 413-6
12, 64 .... Apoc. 178-9
4 .... Evst. 391
10, 22, 81 .... Evst. 400-2
68, 69, 70, 71, 72, 73, 74,
  75, 77, 78, 79, 85, 86,
  87, 88, 89, 91, 93, 99,
  101, 330, 331, 332 ...Evst. 805-27
11, 12 .... Apost. 160-1

Smyrna Γ' 1, 2, 5 ...... Evann. ... 3
                              1257-9

Thessalonica .... Total MSS. 19
'Ελλην. Γυμνασίου
  6, 11 .... Evann.
                              1182-3
A, B, Γ, Δ, E, Z, Θ, IΔ Evst. 830-7
12, 15, 16 .... Act. 391-3
10 .... Apoc. 183
8, 10, 13 .... Apost. 162-4
M. Σπύριος 1 .... Evan. 1184
  2 .... Evst. 838

Athos 519
Anna 11 .... Apoc. 164
Caracalla 19, 20, 31, 34,
  35, 36, 37, 111,
  121, 128, 198 ...... Evann. 1032-
                              42
3, 11, 15, 16, 17 .... Evst. 688-92
10, 156 .... Apost. 136-7
Constamonitou 1, 61,
  106 .... Evann. 1043-5
99 .... Evan. 1309
108 .... Act. 366
29, 107 .... Apoc. 176-7
6, 98, 100 .... Evst. 693-5
98, 100 .... Evst. 941-2
21, 22, 23 .... Apost. 138-40
Chiliandari 5, 19, 105 ...Evann.
                              1138-40
6 .... Evan. 1308
6, 15 .... Evst. 756-7
Coutloumoussi 67, 68,
  69, 70, 71, 72, 73, 74,
  75, 76, 77, 78, 90ᵃ,
  278, 281, 283, 284,
  285, 286, 287, 288,
  289, 290, 291, 293 ...Evann. 1046-
                              70
16, 57, 80, 81, 82, 83,
  275 .... Act. 367-73
90ᵇ, 129 .... Paul. 409-10
60, 61, 62, 63, 64, 65,
  66, 86, 90, 279, 280,
  282, 292, 356 ...... Evst. 696-709
277, 344, 355 ...... Apost. 141-3
Dionysius .... Evan. Ω
4, 5, 7, 8, 9, 12, 22,
  23, 24, 25, 26, 27, 28,
  29, 30, 31, 32, 33, 34,
  35, 36, 37, 38, 39, 40,
  64, 67, 80, 310, 311,
  312, 313, 314, 315,
  316, 317, 318, 319,
  320, 321 .... Evann. 924-
                              63
68, 75, 382 .... Act. 344-6
163 .... Apoc. 167
1, 2, 3, 6, 11, 13, 14,
  15, 16, 17, 18, 19, 20,
  21, 85, 163, 302, 303,
  304, 305, 306, 307,
  308, 309 .... Evst. 627-50
23 .... Evst. 540

OF GREEK MANUSCRIPTS. 409

Dionysius (*cont.*)—   Total MSS.
378 ....Evst. 577
386 ....Apost. 169
387 ....Apost. 180
392 ....Apost. 184
Docheiariou 7, 21, 22,
   30, 35, 39, 42, 46,
   49, 51, 52, 55, 56,
   59, 76, 142 ....Evann. 964-79
   38, 48, 136, 139, 147 Act. 347-51
   81 ....Apoc. 168
   1, 10, 13, 14, 15, 19,
   23, 24, 36, 58, 137...Evst. 651-61
   20, 27, 141, 146 .....Apost. 131-4
Esphignenou 25, 26, 27,
   29, 30, 31, 186......Evann. 980-6
   63, 64, 65, 66, 67, 68 Act. 352-7
   19, 20, 21, 22, 23, 24,
   27, 28, 35, 60 ......Evst. 662-71
Gregory 3, and τ. ἡγου-
   μένου ....Evann. 922-3
   In Ecclesia.........Evan. 1090
Iveron 2, 5, 7, 9, 18, 19,
   21, 28, 29, 30, 31, 32,
   33, 51, 52, 53, 55, 56,
   59, 61, 63, 66, 67, 68,
   69, 72, 75, 371, 548,
   549, 550, 562, 599,
   607, 608, 610, 636,
   641, 647, 665, 671,
   809, 871 ....Evann. 989-
                           1031
639 ....Act. 322
24, 25, 37, 57, 60, 642,
   643, 648 ....Act. 358-65
34, 379, 546, 594, 605,
   644, 661 ....Apoc. 169-75
1, 3, 4, 6, 20, 23, 35,
   36, 39, 635, 637,
   638, 639, 640, 825,
   826 ....Evst. 672-87
831 ....Apost. 135
Laura ....Evan. Ψ
             Evann. 1071-
                          80
             Act. S
             Paul. S
Panteleemon 25, 26, 28,
   29 ....Evann. 1091-4
L, IV. vi. 4, IX. v.
   3, XXVII. vi. 2,
   XXVII. vi. 3,
   XXVIII. i. 1 ......Evst. 722-7
Paul 4, 5...............Evann.
                         1095-6
1 ....Evan. 1307
2 ....Act. 374
1 ....Evst. 728
Philotheou 5, 21, 22,
   33, 39, 41, 44, 45, 46,
   47, 48, 51, 53, 68, 71,
   72, 74, 77, 78, 80, 86, Evann.
                         1117-37

Philotheou (*cont.*)—   Total MSS.
38, 76 ....Act. 378-9
1, 2, 3, 6, 18, 25, 61,
   213 ....Evst. 748-55
17......................Apost. 152
Protaton 41.............Evan. 1097
15, 44 ....Evann.
                        1305-6
32.......................Act. 375
11, 14, 15, 44, 56 ...Evst. 729-33
54......................Apost. 144
32......................Apost. 262
Simopetra 25, 26, 29,
   34, 38, 39, 40, 41,
   63, 145, 146, 147...Evann.
                      1098-1109
42......................Act. 376
148.....................Evst. 464
17, 19, 20, 21, 24, 27,
   28, 30, 33, 70 ......Evst. 734-43
6, 10, 148, 149, 150,
   151 ....Apost.
                       145-50
St. Andrew...............Evan. ℶ
A', E', H', Θ' ....Evann. 905-8
Γ', Λ', ς, Z ....Evst. 579-82
Stauroniketa 43, 53, 54,
   56, 70, 97, 127......Evann.
                      1110-6
52......................Act. 377
1, 27, 42, 102 ....Evst. 744-7
129 ....Apost. 151
Vatopedi 206, 207, 211,
   212, 213, 214, 215,
   216, 217, 218, 219,
   220, 414 ....Evann. 909-
                         21
41, 201, 203, 210, 259,
   328, 380, 419 ......Act. 336-43
90, 90 (2)..............Apoc. 165-6
48, 192, 193, 194, 195,
   196, 197, 198, 200,
   202, 204, 205, 208,
   209, 220, 221, 223,
   224, 225, 226, 227,
   228, 229, 230, 231,
   232, 233, 234, 235,
   236, 237, 238, 239,
   240, 241, 242, 243,
   253, 254, 255, 256,
   257, 271, 291 ....Evst. 583-
                         626
Xenophon 1, 3, 58......Evann.
                        1310-2
1, 58, 59, 68 ....Evst. 710-13
Xeropotamou 103, 105,
   107, 108, 115, 123,
   200, 205, 221 ......Evann. 1081-
                        89
110, 112, 118, 122,
   125, 126, 234, 247 Evst. 714-21
Zographou 4, 14........Evann. 987-8

410   INDEX I.

UNITED STATES.	Total MSS.
Massachusetts—	
CAMBRIDGE, HARVARD	5
Greg. 466 ....Evan. 899	
1^h, 2^h, 3^h.................Evst. 483-5	
K. 1,....................Apost. 74	
ANDOVER............Evst. 463...	1
New Caesarea—	
MADISON..........................	3
Drew 3...............Evan. 900	
?...................Paul. 371	
2...................Evst. 486	
PRINCETOWN ....Evst. 491...	1
New York	2
Seminary, Theol. Univ. Evst. 929	
Astor's Library ....Apost. 198	
Pennsylvania	2
SEWICKLEY ....Evst. 487, 489	
Tennessee—	
SEWANEE............................	3
Benton 2, 3 ....Evann. 901-2	
Evst. 490	

	Total MSS.
Manuscripts whose present location is unknown	30
Evst. Banduri...Evst. 482 (*see* Evan. O)	
Evan. T^s	
Evan. 42	
Evan. 88, 91, 93	
Evan. 101 (Uffenbach 3)	
Evan. 102	
Evan. 104 (Vigner)	
Evan. 181 (Xavier)	
Evan. 216	
Evan. 253	
Evan. 436	
Evan. 543 (Theodori)	
Act. 8	
Act. 39	
Act. 44	
Act. 50	
Act. 52	
Act. 55, i. e. Evan. 90	
Act. 171	
Act. 172	
Paul. 13	
Paul. 15	
Paul. 60	
Apoc. 3	
Apoc. 5	
Evst. 23	
Evst. 33	
Evst. 153	
Evst. 156	
Apost. 3 (Batteley)	

TOTAL NUMBER OF GREEK MSS., ARRANGED ACCORDING TO COUNTRIES.

British Empire	438	Brought forward 1788	
Belgium (2), Denmark (3), Holland (7), Sweden (7)	19	Palestine	260
		Russia	104
Egypt	26	Spain	34
France	324	Switzerland	15
Germany	140	Turkey (Oriental Monasteries)	724
Greece	197	United States	17
Italy.....................................	644	Places unknown	30
Carried forward 1788		Total...................	2972

INDEX II.

OF WRITERS, PAST OWNERS, AND COLLATORS OF MSS.

E (Evan.), A (Acts and Cath. Epp.), P (Paul), Apoc. (Apocalypse), Evst. (Evangelistarium), Apost. (Apostolos).

Abbott, T. K. ....Z (E)
    490 (E)
Aberdeen, Earl of ...544 (E)
Accida...................132 (Evst.)
Accidas, F. ....376 (E)
Adrianople ....163 (P)
Ædilium, Lib..........198 (E)
Agen......................445 (E), 31 (Apoc.)
Ailli, H. ....331 (E)
Aldi ....131 (E)
Alefson, G. ....266 (Evst.)
Alex. II ....N, p. 91
Alex. II, Comnenus...86 (E), 235 (Evst.)
Alex. VIII, Pope ...40 (A)
Alexius ....241, 388 (E)
Alexopoulos, Const....306 (A)
Alford, B. H. ....T (E)
    38 (Apoc.)
Alford, Dean ....B, p. 114
Altamps, Duke of ...202 (P)
Altemprianus ....703 (E)
Alter.....................N (E)
    3, 77, 124, 218–225 (E)
Alypius, C. ....248 (E)
Amerbach ....2 (A)
Andreas, monk ......232 (A)
———, scribe ....180 (E), 542 (Evst.)
Andriani, A. ....391 (E)
Angelus, J. ....386 (E)
Anthimus...............160 (Evst.)
Antonius ....220 (A)
    445 (E)
Antony, priest ......343 (E)
    p. 337 note
Archipelago, Gk. ...509 (E)
Arendt ....431 (E)
Argenson ....158 (Evst.)
Argyropolus ....229 (E)
Arrivabene ....448 (E)

Arsenius, Abp. ......333 (E), 66 (A)
    675 (E)
———, Provost ....310 (E)
Arundel, Earl of ......566 (E)
Arundell, F. V. J. ...588 (E)
Askew, Ant............444 (E)
    22 (A)
    23 (Apoc.)
Athanasius, Convent of St. ....36, 39 (E)
———, Monastery of St. 254, 330 (E)
    16, 97 (A)
    123 (P)
———, Gk. monk ......116 (E)
———, priest ....498 (Evst.)
———, scribe ....139 (A)
'Athenian Aberdeen' 238 (Evst.)
Audley, Bp. ....56 (E)
Augia, Dives..........F (P)
Aymont ....D (P)
Azzolini, Card. ....154–156 (E)

Banduri, A. ....O (E)
Barrett ....61 (E)
Bartholomew ....164 (E)
Bartolocci ....B, p. 110
Basilian Monks' Lib. 173–177 (E)
Batiffol, P. ....Φ (E)
Batteley.................3 (Apost.)
Battier, J...............E (E)
Begtrup.................33 (E)
Bengel, J................E (E), 2 (E)
Bennet, G..............516 (E)
Bentley, R. ....A, p. 103 n
    B, p. 110
    D (E)
    G, H (E)
    113, 117, 507, 508 (E)
    24 (A)

Bentley, R. ....F (P)
  28 (Apoc.)
  257 (Evst.)
———, T.................B, p. 110
Benzel, E. ....238 (A)
Benzelstierna ....400 (E)
Benzil ....400 (E)
Berzi, P. de ....43 (E)
Berziau, de ....54 (A)
Bessarion, Card. .....B, p. 105
  205-215, 217 (E)
Bey, Dr. H. B.........N, p. 91
Beza, Theodore........D (E, A)
Bianchini ....L (A)
Bigot ....162 (P)
Birch ....B, p. 110
  S, T (E), L (A)
  124, 127, 131, 157,
  209, 218-225 (E)
  70-96 (A)
  77-112 (P)
  38 (Apoc.)
  35-39 (Evst.)
Björnsthal..............615, 616 (E), 236
  (A)
Blasius ....293 (E)
  382 (Evst.)
Blenheim, Sunderland
  Lib. ....Y (E)
  523 (E)
  282-284 (Evst.)
  52 (Apost.)
Bloomfield, S. T. ......573-590 (E)
  22 (A), 104 (P)
  150, 223-6 (Evst.)
Bodet, W................70 (E)
Boecler, H. ....78 (A)
Boener, C. F. ....G (P)
  78 (E)
Bohn ....562 (E)
Boistaller 263, 301, 306, 314
  (E), 131 (A), 86
  (Evst.)
Boivin ....C, p. 122
Bonvisi family ....452 (E)
Boone...................267 (Evst.)
Boreel, J. ....F (E)
Borrell ....588 (E)
Bourbon, Card. ....17 (E)
Bragge, Alderman ...255 (Evst.)
Braun...................405 (E)
Brixius ....228 (E)
Brizopoulos ....157 (Evst.)
Brühl...................32 (Apoc.)
  57 (Evst.)
Brunswick, Duke of...P, Q (E)
Brussels, Dom. Lib. ...3 (E)
Brynkley ....69 (E)
Bulkeley ....63, 64 (E)
Bunckle.................70 (E)
Burdett-Coutts.........545-553 (E)
Burgon, Dean ....B, p. 114
  X (E)

Burgon, Dean 2, 346, 464, 562-
  565 (E)
  223 (A)
  35 (Apoc.)
  255 (Evst.)
Burney, Ch. ....514, 568 (E)
Busbeck, O. de 123, 218, 221, 222,
  434 (E)
  64 (A), 67 (A)
Butler, S., Bp. 201, 576-579, 608
  (E)
  261 (Evst.)
Bynaeus ....80 (E)

Caesarea ....H (P)
—— Philippi ....575 (E)
Calistus ....286 (E)
Calvert, E. ....737 (E)
Camerarius ....88 (E)
Camps, de, F. ....M (E)
Cannabetes, N. ....18 (E)
Canonici...............216, 488-491 (E)
Cantacuzenus ....775 (E),162 (Evst.)
Caracalla ....534 (E), 234
  (Evst.), 95, 96
  (Apoc.)
  217 (A), 537, 538
  (E)
Carlenizza.............39 (Evst.)
Carlotta, Q. ....246 (A)
Carlyle, J. D. ....509 (E)
  182 (A)
Carpzov, S. B. & J. G. 78 (E)
Cassan ....517 (E)
Catharine, St., Sinai, see Sinai
Cellérier..............75 (E)
Ceriani ....346 (E)
Cerularius.............437 (E)
Chalké,Trinity Monas-
  tery ....513 (E)
Chambellan ....287 (E)
Charito ....86 (Evst.)
Chark, W. ....61, 69 (E)
Charles I, king .....A. pp. 97, 98
Chester, Rev. G. J....325 (E)
———, Greville ....T³ (E), 298 (Evst.)
Chiesley, Sir J. ....519 (E)
Chisiana, Lib. ....414 (Evst.)
Christina, Q...........154-156 (E), 38,
  40 (A)
Chrysographus.........347 (E)
Chrysostom, Monas-
  tery of St. ......408 (E)
Ciampini ....45 (A)
Cisissa ....234 (Evst.)
Claromontanus.........D (P)
Clement................61 (E)
Clermont, Jesuit Coll.
  at ....436 (E)
Coislin, Bp. ....H (P)
  34-41, 437 (E), 69
  (Apoc.)

OF WRITERS, PAST OWNERS, AND COLLATORS. 413

Colbert ....267, 273, 279, 281–283, 286–288, 291, 294, 296, 310, 315, 318, 319 (E) 62, 115, 121 (A) 145–148, 157 (P) 58, 61, 63 (Apoc.) 60, 68, 71, 76, 78, 87–91, 99–101 (Evst.) 25, 27, 33, 34 (Apost.)
Columnensis ....689 (E), 392, 393 (Evst.)
Comuto, Prince........Ξ (E)
Conant ....573 (E)
Constamoniton, Mon. 5 (Apost.)
Constantine, Emp. ...118 n 2
——, monk ....174, 577, 919 (E)
——, priest ....150 (Evst.)
Constantinople........509, 606, 607, 1261 (E) 125 (A), 157 (P) 64, 77, 95, 281, 289, 390 (Evst.) 22 (Apost.)
Corbinelli ....200 (E)
Corcyra ....623 (E), 106 (Evst.)
Cordatus ....73 (E)
Corfu, Univ. of.........583 (E)
Cornelianus ....103 (Evst.), 46 (Apost.)
Corsendonck, Convent at ....3 (A, P)
Corvenus ....77, 78 (E)
Cosmas, monk ....590 (E), 304 (A), 8 (Evst.)
—— Oricell. ....368 (E)
—— Vanaretus ......590 (E)
Covell, Dr. ....65 (E), 26, 27 (A), 150 (Evst.)
Cowper, B. H. ....A, p. 104
Coxe ....105, 591 (E), 212 (A)
Cozza..................B, p. 117
Croze, La ....G, H (E)
Crusius ....430 (E)
Cure ....D, p. 114
Cureton, Canon........R (E)
Curzon, R. (Lord de la Zouche)............534–541 (E) 95 (Apoc.) 234 (Evst.)
Cusa, de Hosp. ......59 (A)
Cuza, N. de ....87, 129 (E)
Cyprus, Q. of..........140 (E)
Cyril Lucar ....A, pp. 97, 98

Damarius ....228 (E)
Damascenus ....488 (E)
Dandolo ....233 (E)

Daniel, Bp. of Proconnesus ....65 (E)
Dassdorf ....32 (Apoc.)
Denys, St. ....60 (Evst.)
D'Eon ....23 (Apoc.), 259 (Evst.)
Dermout ....122, 435 (E), 6 (Evst.)
De Rossi ....360, 361 (E)
Desalleurs ....158 (Evst.)
Diassorin ....40 (Evst.)
Dickinson, J. ....D, p. 126
Didot ....80 (E)
Dionysius, Monast. of O (E), K (A), 240 (E)
——, monk ....255 (E)
Dizomaeus..........288 (E)
Dobbin, Dr. ....58, 61 (E)
Docheiariou ....233 (Evst.)
Dodwell............64 (E)
Dometius ....54 (Evst.)
Dupuis ....321, 322, 892 (E)
Dupuy, C., J., and P. D (P)

Engelbreth ....209 (E)
Ephesus, Abp. of ...71 (E)
Eschenbach, von ...105 (E)
Escurial ....569 (E)
Esphigmenou, Monast. 14 (Apost.)
Eucholius ....38 (Apost.)
Eugenia ....165 (E)
Euphemius ....634, 651 (E)
Euthymius ....947 (Evst.)
Evagrius ....83 (A)

Faber...............90 (E)
Fasch, A. ....92, 94 (E)
Fenton, Jo. ....186 (A)
Finch...............19 (Evst.)
Fleck...............L (A)
Flemyng, Dean.....33 (A)
Florence, Grand Ducal Palace at ....117 (Evst.)
——, St. Maria, Lib. at 199, 200 (E)
——, St. Mark, at......201–203 (E)
Forerunner, Monast. of 261 (E), 231 (Evst.)
Foss ....211 (Evst.)
Franciscus ....132 (Evst.)
Francius ....G (P)
Francklin, Prof. ...21 (A)
Freeman, H. S. ...599 (E), 273–277 (Evst.)
Fresne, Du ....260, 309 (E)
Friars, Grey (Camb.) 591 (E)
——, Minor (Oxf.) ...59 (E)
——, Preaching ....2 (A)
Froy, F. ....61 (E)

Gabriel (Met. of Philadelphia)............333 (E)
——, monk ....491 (E)
Gage, F. ....278 (Evst.)

INDEX II.

Gage, T. .... 602 (E)
Gale, T. .... 66 (E), 221 (Evst.)
Gehl .... 89 (E)
George, monk .... 69 (A), 71 (Evst.)
——, scribe .... 725, 743 (E), 166 (A), 113, 126, 553 (Evst.)
——, son of Elias...... 166 (A)
Georgilas .... 1262 (E)
Georgios .... 78 (E)
Georgirenus .... 279 (E)
Gerbert .... Δ (E)
Germain, St., des Prés E (P), 437 (E)
Germanus .... 122 (Evst.)
Giorgi .... T (E)
Gleichgross .... 86 (E)
Goad, T. .... 64 (E)
Gonzaga .... 448 (E)
Googe .... 62 (E)
Graeirus .... 80 (E)
Grazia, di .... 162 (Evst.)
Gregory, monk .... 438 (E)
Griesbach .... L (E), M (P)
  33, 118, 236, 440 (E)
  60 (A)
  18–22, 25–30 (Evst.)
  5 (Apost.)
Gross .... V (E)
Grotta Ferrata .... M of Gregory (A)
Guest, J. .... 232 (A)
——, J. B. .... 603 (E), 232 (A), 279, 280 (Evst.)
Guildford, Lord........ 529, 531 (E)

Hacket, Bp. .... p. 89 note
Hackwell .... 96 (E)
Hagen, J. van der...... 80 (E)
Hamilton .... 632 (E), 368, 369 (Evst.)
Hammond, Dr. .... 57 (E)
Hantin .... 62² (E)
Harley, Earl of Oxford D (P), 150 (Evst.)
Harnack .... Σ (E)
Harris (of Alex.) ...... 230 (A), 262 (Evst.)
——, J. R. .... 892 (E), 488 (Evst.)
Hatcher .... 59 (E)
Hayne .... 69 (E)
Heimbach .... 209 (E)
Helias, priest .... 60 (Evst.)
Henry IV, king .... 269 (E)
Heraclea, Ch. of ...... 523 (E), 52 (Apost.)
Heringa .... F (E)
Hermonymus .... 30, 62², 70, 287, 288 (E)
  145 (P)
Herries, Lord .... 580 (E)
Hext, Capt. J. .... 617 (E)
Hieracis Deiparae, Monast. .... 281 (E)
Hilarion .... 535 (Evst.)
Hincklemann .... 90 (E)
Hoffmann .... 124 (E)

Hort, Dr. .... T° (E)
Hoskier .... 75, 604 (E)
Huet .... 366 (Evst.)
Hug .... B, p. 105
Huish .... A, p. 103
Huntingdon, Earl of... 64 (E)
Huntington, Bp. .... 67 (E), 30 (A)

Iberian Monastery ...243, 259 (E)
  99, 103 (A)
  50, 50² (Apoc.)
  48 (Evst.)
  13 (Apost.)
Ignatius (Metrop.) ...282 (Evst.)
——, monk .... 86 (Evst.)
——, scribe .... 69 (Apost.)
Innocent VIII .... 246 (A)
Irene .... 210 (Evst.)
Iveron, see Iberian

Jackson................ 69, 106, 573 (E)
James, monk .... 507 (E)
Janina .... 763, 771 (E), 266 (P), 89 (Apoc.)
Jeremias, Patr. .... 98 (A)
Jerusalem, Lib. .... 416 (A)
Joachim, monk......... 166 (A), 13 (Apost.)
Joasaph............... 410, 561 (E), 169 (A)
John .... 374 (E), 267 (Apost.)
——, monk .... 560 (E), 61 (A)
——, priest .... 245, 429 (E), 71, 170 (Evst.)
——, reader .... 592, 1311 (E)
—— Rossan .... 325, 347 (Evst.)
——, scribe .... 180 (E), 64 (A), 567 (Evst.)
Johnson, T. .... 72 (E)
Jones, J. .... 64 (E)
Joseph, monk .... 422 (E), 537 (Evst.)
Junius, P. .... G (P)
Justinas, St. .... 200 (E)
Justinian, Aug. .... 285 (E)

Knobelsdorf, W. E. de 433 (E)
Kuster .... C, p. 122

Lambeth, Lib. .... 514, 516 (E), 186 (A)
Lammens .... 527 (E)
Lampros, Sp. P. .... 269–272 (E), 592, 596, 597 (E)
  107 (A), 418 (A), 269 (Evst.)
Landolina .... 113 (Apost.)
Landolini .... 421 (E)
Langer .... 97 (A)
Larroque .... 27–33 (E)
Lascar, J. .... 12 (A)
Lascaris............... 210 (A)
Laud, Abp. .... E (A)

OF WRITERS, PAST OWNERS, AND COLLATORS. 415

Laura, Monast. ......S (A), 20, 23 (P)
Leo (of Calabria)......124 (E)
——, scribe ....164,589 (E),67 (A)
Leon ....538, 541 (Evst.)
Leontius ....186, 430 (E), 91, 215 (Evst.)
Lesoeuf ....80 (E)
Loescher ....32 (Apoc.), 57 (Evst.)
Louis, St. ....38 (E)
Louis XIV ....M (E), 279 (E)
Lucas, P. ....264 (E)
Lucas...................289 (E)
Lucca, Lib. ....452 (E)
Luke, monk ....230 (E)
——, Prof. ....21 (A)
Lyons, Jesuits' Pub. Lib. ....298 (E)
——, Monast. of St. Iren. ....D, p. 125

Macarius ....1283 (E)
Macdonald ....581, 582 (E)
Maglorian, San, Oratory of ....54 (A)
Mai, Card. ....B, p. 112
Maius ....97 (E)
Mangey, Th. ....483, 492, 496, 498, 503 (E)
26, 27 (Evst.)
Manuel ....162, 293 (E)
Mare, P. de la ....265 (E)
Maria, Jo................285 (E)
——, Q. ....40 (Evst.)
——, St. ....367 (E)
Marini ....N (E)
Marsh, Abp. ....118 (E)
Mary, St., Ben. Lib. ...148 (A)
—— Deipara, St.,Convent ....R (E)
——, empress ....419 (A)
——, St., of Patirium ℈ (A, P)
Masieli, P. ....12 (A)
Matthaei ....V (E), K (A)
89,237-259,605(E)
98-107 (A)
76, 113-124 (P)
32 (Apoc.)
47 (Evst.)
5 (Apost.)
Matthew, monk ......416, 418 (A)
——, scribe ....1307 (E)
Maura ....459, 460 (E)
Maurice................100 (Evst.)
Mauron ....341 (E)
Maurus ....427 (E)
Maximilian ....p. 213 note
146 (E)
Mazarin, Card. ....103, 278, 302, 305, 308, 311, 313, 324 (E)
51(A),74,98(Evst.)
Mead, Dr. ....22 (A), 23 (Apoc.)

Medici ....16, 19, 121, 196, C (E), 317 (E)
12,126 (A),164(P)
Meerman ....122, 436, 562 (E), 178 (A), 153 (Evst.)
Meletius ....248, 281 (E)
Mendham..............562 (E)
Menon ....230 (A),262(Evst.)
Merlin ....601 (E)
Michael................30 (Apoc.), 531 (Evst.)
——, St., Monast. ...253 (E)
——, monk ....S (E)
1156 (E)
—— priest ....394 (E)
Michaelis ....772 (E)
Mico ....B, p. 110
91 (Apoc.)
Middeldorpf ....42 (A)
Mieg ....F (P)
Mill ....D, p. 126
K (E), E (P), 51, 59, 69 (E), 18-22 (Evst.)
Missy, Caesar de .....44, 449, 520, 521, 543 (E), 230,231 (Evst.)
5, 45 (Apost.)
Moira, John, Earl of...64 (E)
Moldenhawer ....226-233 (E), 35-40 (Evst.)
Molsheim, Jes. Coll. ...431 (E)
Montagnana, P. de ...217 (E)
Montfaucon ....O (E), 482 (Evst.)
Montfort, Dr. ....61 (E)
Moore, Bp. ....60, 62², 70 (E)
Morrian................288 (E)
Mould ....116, 444 (E)
Müller, Prof. ....E (E)
Muller ....736 (E)
Munich, Jes. Coll. ...127 (P)
Münter................U (E)
Muralt ....B, p. 110
473-477 (E)

Nanianus ....U (E)
Nani family ....405-418 (E)
Naples, Conv. of St. Jo. de Carbon....108 (E)
Napoleon I ....B, p. 105
Nathanael, N. ....228 (E)
Neophytus............591 (E)
Nepho ....439 (E)
Nicephorus ....276 (E), 25, 48, 573 (Evst.)
Nicetas ....126 (P),231(Evst.)
Nicholas, St., Monast. 40 (E)
Nicolas ....291 (E), 72 (Evst.)
——, Abp. ....156 (A)
——, Card. ....87 (E)
——, monk ....97 (E)
——, priest ....204 (Evst.)

416 INDEX II.

Nicolas, scribe ....268 (Apost.)
Nicolaus ....306(A),185(Evst.)
Nilus.....................305 (Evst.)
Noailles, G. de ....59 (Apoc.)
Norfolk, Duke of.....566 (E)
North, Hon. F. ....471, 531, 532, 583 (E), 198 (A)

Ὁδηγῶν, τῶν, Monast. 86 (Evst.)
Odessa ....198 (Evst.)
Onesimus ....20 (Evst.)

Pachonius ....241 (E)
Padua ....139 (A)
——, St.John in Virid., Monast. ....217 (E)
Palaeologus, Chr.......138, 288 (Evst.)
——, Emp. ....80 (Apoc.)
Palatine, Elector's Lib. p. 213 note 146 (E)
Panagiotes, M. ......274 (E)
Pannonius..............100 (E)
Panteleemon, Monast. 428 (Evst.)
Pantocrator, Monast. 74, 482, 493, 495, 507, 508 (E), 119 (P), 211 (Evst.)
Pappelbaum ....400 (E)
Paradisi, Collis........414 (Evst.)
Parassoh ....69 (Apost.)
Paris, City Lib. ......288 (E)
——, Nat. Lib. ......272 (E)
——, Sorbonne ....290 (E)
Parodus of Smyrna ...Π (E)
Parrhasius..............108 (E)
Parsons, D. ....617 (E)
Parthenius, Patr. ...19 (Evst.)
Passionei, Card. ......L (A) 611 (E), 723 (E)
Patmos ....466 (E), 588 (E)
Patriarchal Chamber A, p. 98
Paul, Abp. ....165 (E)
——, priest ....26 (E)
Paulus ....22 (A), 32 (Apoc.)
Payne....................436, 562 (E)
——, E. ....518, 529 (E), 153, 227–229 (Evst.)
——, T. (Archd.) .....523(E),52(Apost.)
Peckover, J. ....560, 561 (E)
Perron, Card. ....91 (E)
Petavius ....38 (A)
Peter, monk ....48 (Evst.)
Peter τοῦ Καραμανίτου1149 (E)
Petra, Monast.........87 (E)
Philip, monk..........414 (E)
Phillipps, Sir T. ......526–533 (E), 178 (A)
Philotheus..............235 (E)
Philotheou, Monast. ...237, 240, 247 (E)
Phlebaris ....489 (E)
Pickering ....543 (E)
Picus ....488 (E)
Pinelli ....348 (E), 138 (A)

Pithaeus ....42 (E)
Pius II ....158 (E)
Polidore................137 (Evst.)
Porphyry ....ℵ, p. 91
Q (P)
Pressburg, Lib. of the Lycaeum ....86 (E)
Prusa, SS. Cosm. and Damian.,Monast. 405 (E)
Puttick ....598 (E)

Quaritch ....560, 561, 885–887 (E)
Quirini ....B, p. 187

R., A. F. ....207 (E)
Ragusio, J. de ....E (E)
Reggio ....172 (P)
Reiche, J. G. ....113, 114, 117, 127 (A) 139, 140, 153 (P), 54 (Apoc.)
Rettig ....Δ (E)
Ῥενδίνη, Monast. ...322 (E)
Rhodes ....737 (E), 125 (P)
Rhosen ....205 (E)
Rhosus ....448 (E)
Rich, C. J. ....574 (E)
Ridolphi, Card. ......C, p. 121
Rinck....................209 (E), 96 (A)
Rink ....110–112 (P)
Rivet....................155 (E)
Rocchi ....B, p. 118
Rodd, H. ....585 (E)
——, T. ....272, 584 (E)
Roe, Sir T. ....49 (E)
Romana De Alteriis..690 (E)
Romanus, priest ....247 (Evst.)
Rome, Barberini Lib. 159 (E)
Rose, W. F. ....20, 22, 300, 346, 563, 564, 565 (E), 223 (A) 255, 281 (Evst.)
Rostgaard ....234, 235 (E)
Roth ....I (E)
Royal Society ....566 (E)
Rulotta ....B, p. 110
Rutgersius............155 (E)

Saba, St., Conv. ....I (E), Iᵃ (A P), Iᶠ (A)
——, Monast. ....310, 535, 539–541, 1275 (E) 191, 216, 416, 417 (A), 236 (Evst.)
Sakkelion ....N (E)
Salernium ....196 (Evst.)
Salvador, St. ....204 (E)
Salvator, S., de Sept., Conv. of............195 (E), 100 (P)
Salviati, Card. de ....107 (A)
Sambuc ....66 (A)

OF WRITERS, PAST OWNERS, AND COLLATORS.

Sanderson, W. ....184 (A)
Sanguntinianus.........288 (E)
Scala, S. Maria della 162 (Evst.)
Schoenleben ....105 (E)
Scholz ....B, p. 110
    W^a, K, M, X, Y (E)
    H, L (A)
    6, 20, 33-41, 75, 138-144, 146-157, 159, 160, 162, 164-171, 173-175, 177-180, 201, 260, 262, 270, 271, 277, 284, 285, 298-301, 324, 346, 352, 365, 382, 428 (E)
    70-80, 82-92, 115, 120-123, 126, 127, 131, 133, 137, 160-163, 174 (A)
    77-112 P (nearly), 157, 177-179 (P)
    51, 68, 69, 82 (Apoc.)
    7, 60, 81, 86 (Evst.)
    12 (Apost.)
Scio ....390 (E)
Scrivener ....N^c, W^d (E), G (P)
    59, 66, 69, 71, 201, 299, 300, 440, 492, 503, 507-517, 545-559, 566 (E)
    61, 178, 182-188 (A)
    252-261 (P)
    87, 93-98 (Apoc.)
    221, 233, 234 (Evst.)
Scultet, A. ....96 (E)
Seguier ....34-41 (E)
Seidel, A. E. ....G, H (E), 42 (A)
Sepulveda ....B, p. 109
Sergius ....B, p. 118
Simcox, W. H. ....624 (E), 72 (Apoc.)
Simenus, Monast. ...53 (Evst.)
Simeon ....312 (P), 179 (Evst.)
Simon.................K (E)
Simonides, Const. ...110, 589 (E), 229 (A)
Simopetra ....218 (A)
Sinai, St. Cath., Mon. N, p. 90; 141, 413, 577, 581, 582 (E)
Sirlet, Card. ....373 (E), 79 (Apoc.), 132 (Evst.)
Smalbroke, S. ....484 (E)
Smyrna ....444 (E)
Sophonius ....1262 (E)
Sophronius ....183 (Evst.)
Sotheby...............265 (Evst.)
Sparvenfeldt..........613 (E), 68 (A)
Statius, A. ....69, 171 (E)

Steininger ....179 (Evst.)
Stella, P. ....284 (E)
Stephen, priest ......102 (Evst.)
——, R. ....D, p. 122
    L (E)
——, reader ....90 (Evst.)
Stevens ....268 (Evst.)
Stierzienbecher, A. F. 614 (E)
Stosch ....D (P), p. 175
Strangford............526 (E)
Strasburg ....180 (A)
Stunica ....52 (A)
Suchtelen ....542 (E)
Sussex, Duke of ......543 (E)
Swete, H. B. ....736 (E)
Sylburg, F. ....79 (Apoc.)
Symeon ....76, 269 (Apost.)
Synesius ....585 (E)
Syria ....515 (E)

Taurinus, St., Monast. 91 (E)
Tauronesus ....1261 (E)
Tayler, F. ....222 (Evst.)
Teller of Rheims ....119, 284, 285, 304 (E)
Tengnagel, S. ....66 (A)
Teudatus ....493 (E)
Thecla ....A, p. 98
Theocletus ....988 (E)
Theodora ....388, 473 (E)
Theodore, Abp. ....E (A)
    74, 233, 412, 543, 571 (E)
    156 (A)
Theodoret............97 (A), 122 (Evst.)
Theodosius ....413 (E)
Theognostus..........99 (A)
Theopemptus ....131 (A)
Theophanes ....416 (A)
Theophilus ....570 (E)
Theophylact, priest ..148 (A)
Thessaly ....175, 288 (P)
Thévenot ....272 (E)
Thomas ....1262 (E)
Thorpe ....528 (E)
Thou, de, Aug. ......121 (A), 63 (Apoc.), 60 (Evst.)
Tiffin, W. ....69 (E)
Timotheus............103 (P)
Tischendorf ....N, p. 90
    B, p. 115
    Γ, Θ^a, Θ^{bd}, Θ^e, Λ (E)
    O^a (P)
    C, p. 122
    E, F^a, G, H, I, K, L, P, Q, R, S, T^a, T^c, U, X, Ξ, Π (E)
    E, H, L (A), D, F, R (P)
    620, 621 (E), 61 (A), 175, 295-297 (Evst.), 72 (Apost.)

VOL. I.   E e

INDEX II.

Titoff .... 476 (E)
Torregiani .... 162 (Evst.)
Traheron, P. .... 71 (E)
Tregelles .... E, G, H, K, M, R
  U, X, Γ, Δ, Λ, Ξ (E)
  H, L, P (A), D, F, M (P)
  1, 33, 69, 241 (E), 61 (A), 1 (Apoc.)
Treschow .... N (E), 77, 124 (E)
Trithemius, Jo. .... 96 (E)
Troyna, St. Michael de 96 (A)
Twycross .... 63 (E)
Tzutzuna .... 89 (A)

Ubaldi .... B, p. 118
Uffenbach .... M (P)
  45 (A)
Urbino, Ducal Lib. ... 157 (E)
Uspensky, P. .... 481 (E)
Ussher, Abp. .... D, p. 126
  61, 63, 64 (E)

Vatablus .... 9 (A)
Vatopedi Monast. ... 245 (E), 106 (A),
  124 (P)
  54 (Evst.)
Velitrant Museum ... 180 (E)
Venice .... 613 (E)
—, St. Michael's ... 419, 468 (E)
Vercellone .... B, p. 117
Vergecius .... 296 (E), 124 (A), 149, 151 (P)
Verschoyle, Bp. ..... 64 (E)
Victor, St., on the Walls .... 120 (E)
Voscius, Gerard ..... X (E)
—, Is. .... 38 (A)

Wagstaff .... 517 (E)

Wake, Abp. .... 73, 74 (E). See Index I, Christ Church, Oxford
Walker, F. .... 422, 423, 495 (E)
  191 (A), 218, 219 (Apoc.)
—, J. .... 3, 73, 74 (E), 2 (Apost.)
Walton .... 64 (E)
Wanley .... 484 (E)
Ward .... 81 (E)
Wepfer .... F (P)
Werner .... B, p. 109
Westermann .... 42 (A)
Westminster .... 20 (A)
Wetstein, C. .... 492, 503 (E), 6, 26–28 (Apoc.)
—, F. .... C, p. 122
  E, F, F^a, L, M, N (E)
  D, E, F (P)
  1, 2, 33, 41, 90, 92, 94 (E)
  15, 21 (A), 25, 26 (P), 6, 7 (Evst.)
Wheeler .... 68 (E)
Wiedmann .... 405 (E)
Wigley .... 24 (A)
Williams .... 562 (E)
Winchelsea, Earl of ... 106 (E)
Woide .... T^s or T^{wol} (E)
Wolff .... G, H (E), M (P), 90 (E)
Woodhouse .... 563–5 (E), 223 (A), 255 (Evst.)
Wordsworth, Bp. Chr. 542 (E)
Wright .... R (E)
  53 (A)

Xenophon (Athos) ... 536 (E)

Zacagni .... 151 (Evst.)
Zittau, Senate of ... 605 (E)
Zomozerab .... 179 (A)

END OF VOL. I.

www.ingramcontent.com/pod-product-compliance
Lightning Source LLC
Chambersburg PA
CBHW022109300426
44117CB00007B/640